Kin

D0987862

N15 TEACHER COPY

COLLINS · LONGMAN

STUDENT ATLAS

First published 1996

© Collins-Longman Atlases 1996

The maps in this atlas are licensed to Collins-Longman Atlases and are
derived from databases © HarperCollins Publishers

HarperCollins Publishers, P O Box, Glasgow G4 0NB

Addison Wesley Longman, Edinburgh Gate, Harlow, Essex CM20 2JE

Printed in the U.K.

2 CONTENTS

4 Symbols
5 Projections
6 Latitude and Longitude
7 Scale

UNITED KINGDOM
8-9 Counties
10-11 SOUTHEAST ENGLAND
12-13 WALES and
SOUTHWEST ENGLAND
14-15 NORTHERN ENGLAND
16-17 NORTHERN IRELAND and
SOUTHERN SCOTLAND
18-19 NORTHERN SCOTLAND
20 IRELAND

21 Climate
22 Relief
23 Rock Types
24-25 Population : Migration
26-27 Economic Activity
28 Energy
29 Tourism
30-31 Transport
32-33 Greater Manchester
satellite image

EUROPE
34-35 Relief : Countries :
European Union
36 Climate
37 Population
38 Economic Activity
39 Tourism
40-41 Rhine-Schelde Estuary
satellite image : Europoort
42 NETHERLANDS, BELGIUM
and LUXEMBOURG
43 SCANDINAVIA and
the BALTIC STATES
44 FRANCE
45 FRANCE Population :
Economic Activity : Trade
46 SPAIN and PORTUGAL
47 SPAIN Population :
Economic Activity : Trade
48 GERMANY
49 GERMANY Population :
Economic Activity : Trade
50 ITALY
51 ITALY Population :
Economic Activity : Trade
52-53 MEDITERRANEAN BASIN
54-55 CENTRAL EUROPE
56-57 SOUTHEAST EUROPE
58-59 RUSSIAN FEDERATION

NORTH AMERICA
60 Relief : Countries
61 Climate
62-63 CANADA
64-65 USA
66-67 USA Population :
Economic Activity : Trade
68-69 USA San Francisco Bay
satellite image
70-71 MEXICO and the CARIBBEAN

SOUTH AMERICA
72 Relief : Countries
73 Climate
74-75 SOUTH AMERICA
76-77 BRAZIL : Sao Paulo
78-79 BRAZIL Population :
Economic Activity : Trade
80-81 BRAZIL Rondonia
satellite image

AFRICA
82 Relief : Countries
83 Climate
84-85 NORTHERN AFRICA
86 SOUTHERN AFRICA
87 KENYA
88-89 KENYA Population :
Economic Activity : Tourism :
Nairobi : Trade

ASIA
90-91 Relief : Countries :
Middle East Oil
92 Climate
93 Monsoon
94-95 MIDDLE EAST
96-97 PAKISTAN, INDIA and
BANGLADESH : Calcutta
98-99 INDIA Population :
Economic Activity : Trade
100 BANGLADESH Population :
Economic Activity : Trade
101 Ganges Delta satellite image
102-103 CHINA
104-105 SOUTHEAST ASIA
106 JAPAN
107 JAPAN Population :
Economic Activity : Trade

WORLD
113 Time Zones :
International Organizations
114-115 Countries
116-117 Relief
118-119 Climatic Regions : Ocean
Currents : Tropical Storms
120-121 Natural Vegetation
122-123 Tectonics
124-125 Population Distribution :
Density : Structure :
Metropolitan Areas
126 Birth Rates : Death Rates
127 Urban Population :
Population Change
128 Literacy : Life Expectancy
129 GNP : Car Ownership
130-131 Environment Issues
132 Energy Production :
Energy Consumption
133 Fuel Production :
Ore Production
134-135 Tourism

136-143 **STATISTICS**

144-168 **INDEX**
168 Acknowledgements

OCEANIA
108-109 PACIFIC OCEAN
110-111 AUSTRALIA & NEW ZEALAND
111 AUSTRALIA & NEW ZEALAND
Climate

POLAR REGIONS
112 THE ARCTIC OCEAN and
ANTARCTICA

SYMBOLS

Maps use special signs or symbols to represent location and to give information of interest.

Map symbols can be points, lines or areas and vary in size, shape and colour. This allows a great range of different symbols to be created. These have to be carefully selected to make maps easy to understand. Usually the same symbols are used to represent features on maps of the same type and scale within an atlas.

An important part of any map is the key which explains what the symbols represent. Each map in this atlas has its own key. Shown below are typical examples of the keys found on each reference map in the atlas. The first is found on all of the British Isles 1:1 200 000 series of maps. The second is found on the smaller scale maps of the rest of the world.

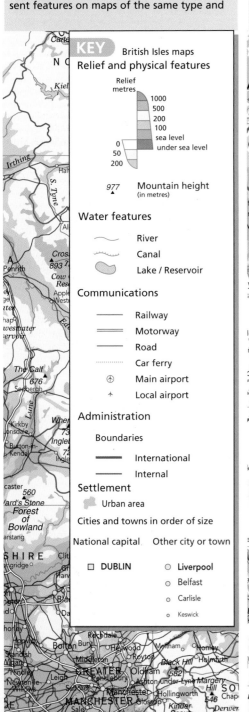

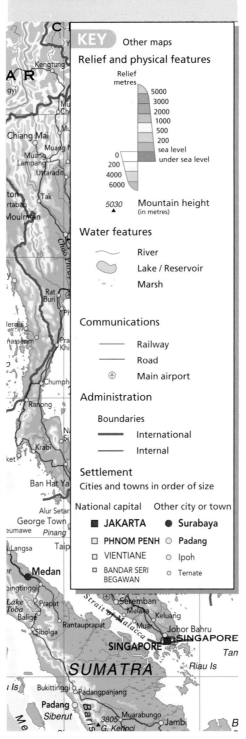

TYPE STYLES

Various type styles are used to show the difference between features on the maps in this atlas. Physical features are shown in italic and a distinction is made between land and water features.

Mountain Peaks are shown in small italics.
eg. *Ben Nevis* *Mt Kenya* *Fuji-san*

Large mountain ranges are shown in bold italic capitals.
eg. ***HIMALAYA   ALPS***
ROCKY MOUNTAINS

Rivers are also shown in small italics but in a different typeface from mountain peaks.
eg. *Thames Euphrates Rhine Amazon*

Oceans are shown in large bold italic capitals.
eg. ***ATLANTIC OCEAN***
PACIFIC OCEAN
INDIAN OCEAN

When a feature covers a large area the type is letterspaced and sometimes curved to follow the shape of the feature.
eg. *S A H A R A*
B E A U F O R T   S E A

Settlements are shown in upright type. Country capitals are shown in capitals.
eg. **LONDON**
PARIS
TOKYO
MOSCOW

The size and weight of the type increases with the population of a settlement.
eg. Westbury
Chippenham
Bristol
Birminghman

Administrative names are shown in capitals.
eg. EAST SUSSEX
RONDONIA
KERELA
CALIFORNIA

Country names are shown in large bold capitals.
eg. **CHINA**
KENYA
MEXICO

An atlas map of the world shows the whole world on a flat surface of the page. yet in reality the earth is actually a sphere. This means that a system has to be used to turn the round surface of the earth into a flat map of the world, or part of the world. This cannot be done without some distortion - on a map some parts of the world have been stretched, other parts have been compressed.

A system for turning the globe into a flat map is called a **projection**.

There are many different projections, each of which distort different things to achieve a flat map. Correct area, correct shape, correct distances or correct directions can be achieved by a projection; but by achieving any one of these things the others have to be distorted. When choosing the projection to use for a particular map it is important to think which of these things is the most important to have correct.

The projections below illustrate the main types of projections, and include some of those used in this atlas.

Cylindrical projection

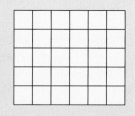

Cylindrical projections are constructed by projecting the surface of the globe on to a cylinder just touching the globe.

Conic projection

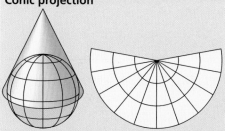

Conic projections are constructed by projecting part of the globe on to a cone which just touches a circle on the globe.

Azimuthal projection

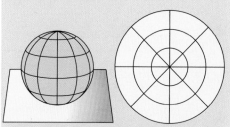

Azimuthal projections are constructed by projecting part of a globe on to a plane which touches the globe only at one point

Examples of projections

Mercator
Southeast Asia pp104-105

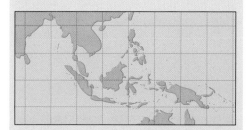

Mercator is a cylindrical projection. It is a useful projection for areas 15° N or S of the equator where distortion of shape is minimal. The projection is useful for navigation as directions can be plotted as straight lines.

Albers Equal Area Conic
Europe pp 34-35

Conic projections are best suited for areas between 30° and 60° N and S with longer east-west extent than north-south. Such an area would be Europe. Meridians are straight and equally spaced.

Lambert Azimuthal Equal Area
Australia p 110

Lambert's projection is useful for areas which have similar east-west, north-south dimensions such as Australia.

Eckert IV
World pp 114-115

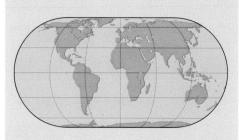

Eckert IV is an equal area projection. Equal area projections are useful for world thematic maps where it is important to show the correct relative sizes of continental areas. Ecker IV has a straight central meridian but all others are curved which help suggest the spherical nature of the earth.

Chamberlin Trimetric
Canada pp 62-63

Chamberlin trimetric is an equidistant projection. It shows correct distances from approximately three points. It is used for areas with a greater north-south than east-west extent, such as North America.

Polar stereographic
Antarctica p 112

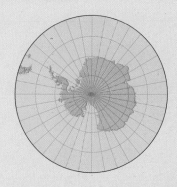

This projection shows no angular or shape distortion over small areas. All points on the map are in constant relative position and distance from the centre.

LATITUDE

Lines of latitude are imaginary lines which run in an east-west direction around the world. They are also called **parallels** of latitude because they run parallel to each other. Latitude is measured in **degrees** (°).

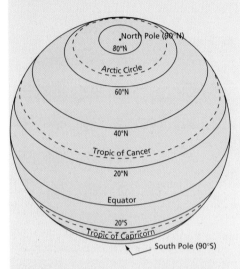

The most important line of latitude is the **Equator** (0°). The North Pole is 90° North (90°N) and the South Pole is 90° South (90°S). All other lines of latitude are given a number between 0° and 90°, either North (N) or South (S) of the Equator. Some other important lines of latitude are the Tropic of Cancer (23$\frac{1}{2}$°N), Tropic of Capricorn (23$\frac{1}{2}$°S), Arctic Circle (66$\frac{1}{2}$°N) and Antarctic Circle (66$\frac{1}{2}$°S).

The Equator can also be used as a line to divide the Earth into two halves. The northern half, north of the Equator, is the **Northern Hemisphere**. The southern half, south of the Equator, is the **Southern Hemisphere**.

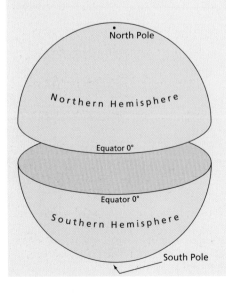

LONGITUDE

Lines of longitude are imaginary lines which run in a north-south direction, from the North Pole to the South Pole. These lines are also called **meridians** of longitude. They are also measured in **degrees** (°).

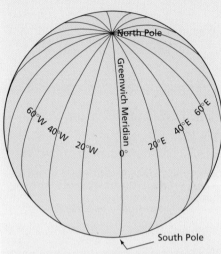

The most important line of longitude is the prime meridian (0°). This line runs through the Greenwich Observatory in London and is therefore known as the Greenwich Meridian. Exactly opposite the Greenwich Meridian on the other side of the world is the 180° line of longitude known as the International Date Line. All the other lines of longitude are given a number between 0° and 180°, either East (E) or West (W) of the Greenwich Meridian.

The Greenwich Meridian (0°) and the International Date Line (180°) can also be used to divide the world into two halves. The half to the west of the Greenwich Meridian is the Western Hemisphere. The half to the east of the Greenwich Meridian is the Eastern Hemisphere.

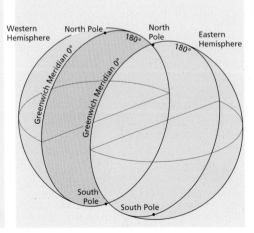

FINDING PLACES USING LATITUDE AND LONGITUDE

When lines of latitude and longitude are drawn on a map they form a grid pattern, very much like a pattern of squares.

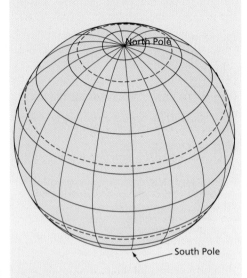

By stating the **latitude** and then the **longitude** of a place, it becomes much easier to find. On the map (below) Point A is very easy to find because it is exactly latitude 58° North of the Equator and longitude 4° West of the Greenwich Meridian (58°N,4°W).

To be even more accurate in locating a place, each degree of latitude and longitude can also be divided into smaller units called **minutes** ('). There are 60 minutes in each degree. On the map (below) Halkirk is one half (or 30/60ths) of the way past latitude 3°N, and two-thirds (or 40/60ths) of the way past longitude 3°W. Its latitude is therefore 58 degrees 30 minutes North and its longitude is 3 degrees 30 minutes West. This can be shortened to 58°30'N, 3°30'W.

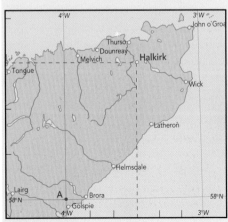

SCALE

To draw a map of any part of the world, the area must be reduced in size, or scaled down so that it will fit on to a page. The scale of a map tells us by how much the area has been reduced in size.

The scale of a map can also be used to work out distance and area. The scale of a map will show the relationship between distances on the map and distances on the ground.

Scale can be shown on a map in a number of ways:

(a) **in words**

e.g. 'one cm. to one km.' (one cm. on the map represents one km. on the ground). 'one cm. to one m.' (one cm. on the map represents one m. on the ground).

(b) **in numbers**

e.g. '1 : 100 000' or '1/100 000' (one cm. on the map represents 100 000 cm., or one km., on the ground).

'1 : 25 000' or '1/25 000' (one cm. on the map represents 25 000 cm, or 250 m., on the ground).

'1 : 100' or '1/100' (one cm. on the map represents 100 cm, or one m., on the ground).

(c) **as a line scale**

e.g.

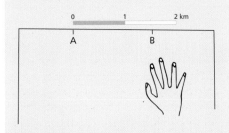

MEASURING DISTANCE ON A MAP

When a map does not have distances printed on it, we can use the scale of the map to work out how far it is from one place to another. The easiest scale to use is a line scale. You must find out how far the places are apart on the map and then see what this distance represents on the line scale. To measure the straight line distance between two points:

a) Place a piece of paper between the two points on the map,

(b) Mark off the distance between the two points along the edge of the paper,

(c) Place the paper along the line scale,

(d) Read off the distance on the scale.

Step 1

Line up the paper and mark off the distance from A to B.

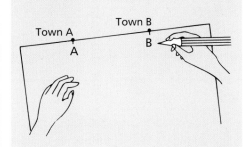

Step 2

Compare this distance with the line scale at the bottom of the map. The distance between A and B is 1.5 km on the line scale.

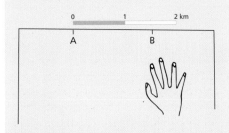

To measure the distance between two points where there are bends or curves:

(a) Place a sheet of paper on the map and mark off the start point on the edge of the paper,

(b) Now move the paper so that its edge follows the bends and curves on the map (Hint: Use the tip of your pencil to pin the edge of the paper to the curve as you pivot the paper around the curve),

(c) Mark off the end point on your sheet of paper,

(d) Place the paper along the line scale,

(e) Read off the distance on the scale.

Using a sheet of paper around a curve : Mark off the start point then twist the paper to follow the curve.

You can use the tip of your pencil to pin the paper to the curve. This stops the paper jumping off course.

MAP SCALE AND MAP INFORMATION

The scale of a map also determines how much information can be shown on it. As the area shown on a map becomes larger and larger, the amount of detail and the accuracy of the map becomes less and less.

The scale of this map is 1:5 000 000

The scale of this map is 1:10 000 000

The scale of this map is 1:20 000 000

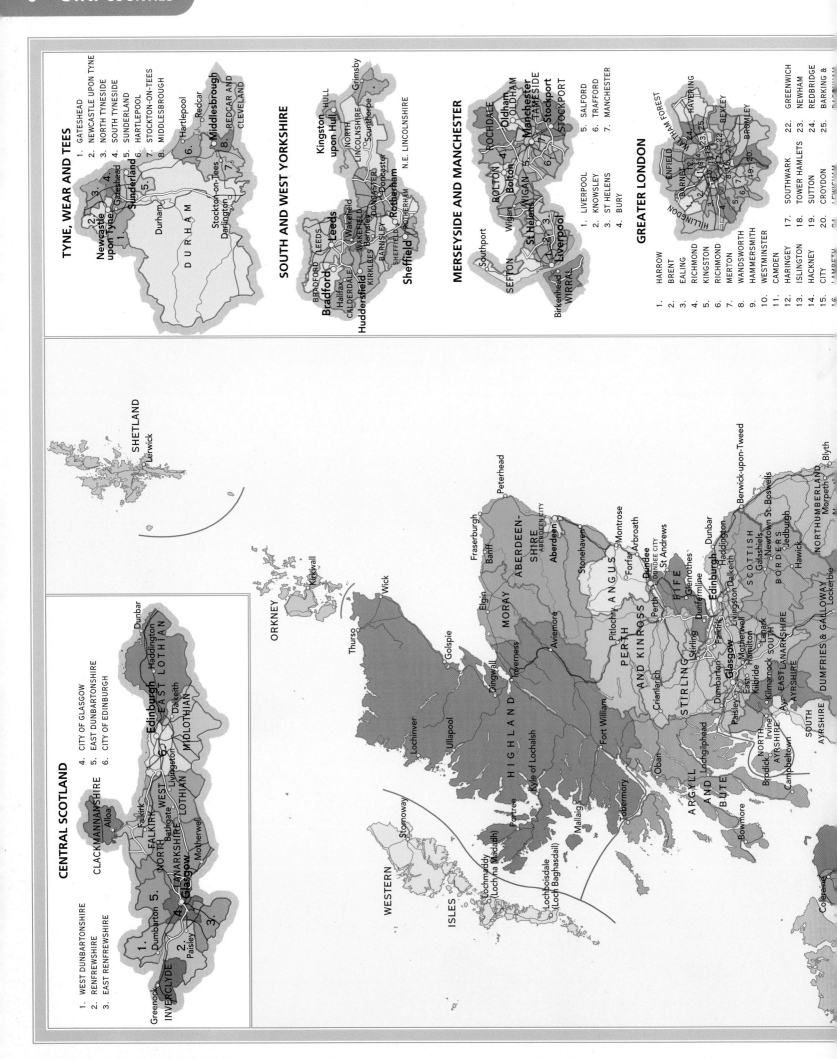

TYNE, WEAR AND TEES

1. GATESHEAD
2. NEWCASTLE UPON TYNE
3. NORTH TYNESIDE
4. SOUTH TYNESIDE
5. SUNDERLAND
6. HARTLEPOOL
7. STOCKTON-ON-TEES
8. MIDDLESBROUGH

Newcastle upon Tyne
Gateshead
Sunderland
Durham
DURHAM
Stockton-on-Tees
Darlington
Hartlepool
Redcar
Middlesbrough
REDCAR AND CLEVELAND

SOUTH AND WEST YORKSHIRE

Kingston upon Hull
HULL
Grimsby
NORTH LINCOLNSHIRE
Scunthorpe
N.E. LINCOLNSHIRE
Leeds
LEEDS
Wakefield
Bradford
BRADFORD
CALDERDALE
Halifax
Huddersfield
KIRKLEES
Barnsley
DONCASTER
Doncaster
Rotherham
ROTHERHAM
Sheffield

MERSEYSIDE AND MANCHESTER

1. LIVERPOOL
2. KNOWSLEY
3. ST HELENS
4. BURY
5. SALFORD
6. TRAFFORD
7. MANCHESTER

ROCHDALE
Oldham
OLDHAM
Manchester
TAMESIDE
Stockport
STOCKPORT
BOLTON
Bolton
WIGAN
Wigan
St Helens
Liverpool
Southport
SEFTON
Birkenhead
WIRRAL

GREATER LONDON

WALTHAM FOREST
HAVERING
ENFIELD
BARNET
HILLINGDON
BEXLEY
BROMLEY

1. HARROW
2. BRENT
3. EALING
4. RICHMOND
5. KINGSTON
6. RICHMOND
7. MERTON
8. WANDSWORTH
9. HAMMERSMITH
10. WESTMINSTER
11. CAMDEN
12. HARINGEY
13. ISLINGTON
14. HACKNEY
15. CITY
16. LAMBETH
17. SOUTHWARK
18. TOWER HAMLETS
19. SUTTON
20. CROYDON
21. LEWISHAM
22. GREENWICH
23. NEWHAM
24. REDBRIDGE
25. BARKING & DAGENHAM

CENTRAL SCOTLAND

1. WEST DUNBARTONSHIRE
2. RENFREWSHIRE
3. EAST RENFREWSHIRE
4. CITY OF GLASGOW
5. EAST DUNBARTONSHIRE
6. CITY OF EDINBURGH

Dunbar
Haddington
Edinburgh
EAST LOTHIAN
Dalkeith
MIDLOTHIAN
WEST LOTHIAN
Bathgate
Livingston
CLACKMANNANSHIRE
Alloa
Falkirk
FALKIRK
NORTH LANARKSHIRE
Motherwell
Glasgow
Paisley
Greenock
INVERCLYDE
Dumbarton

SHETLAND
Lerwick

ORKNEY
Kirkwall

WESTERN ISLES
Stornoway
Lochmaddy (Loch na Madadh)
Lochboisdale (Loch Baghasdail)

Thurso
Wick
Golspie
Dingwall
Inverness
Ullapool
Lochinver
Aviemore
Elgin
MORAY
Fraserburgh
Peterhead
Banff
ABERDEENSHIRE
Aberdeen
ABERDEEN CITY
Stonehaven
ANGUS
Forfar
Montrose
Arbroath
Dundee
DUNDEE CITY
St Andrews
FIFE
Glenrothes
Perth
PERTH AND KINROSS
Pitlochry
Dunfermline
Edinburgh
Dunbar
HIGHLAND
Fort William
Kyle of Lochalsh
Mallaig
Portree
Tobermory
Oban
Lochgilphead
Crianlarich
STIRLING
Stirling
Falkirk
Dumbarton
Glasgow
Motherwell
Hamilton
East Kilbride
SOUTH LANARKSHIRE
Lanark
Livingston
Dalkeith
Haddington
Berwick-upon-Tweed
SCOTTISH BORDERS
Galashiels
Newtown St. Boswells
Jedburgh
Hawick
ARGYLL AND BUTE
Brodick
Campbeltown
Bowmore
Kilmarnock
NORTH AYRSHIRE
Irvine
Ayr
EAST AYRSHIRE
SOUTH AYRSHIRE
DUMFRIES & GALLOWAY
Lockerbie
NORTHUMBERLAND
Morpeth
Blyth
Paisley
Renfrew
Newton St. Boswells

WEST MIDLANDS

1. WOLVERHAMPTON
2. DUDLEY
3. SANDWELL
4. WALSALL
5. BIRMINGHAM
6. SOLIHULL
7. COVENTRY

Wolverhampton · Birmingham · Solihull · Coventry

SOUTH WALES AND AVON

Abergavenny · Monmouth · Torfaen · Cwmbran · Newport · Blaenau Gwent · Merthyr Tydfil · Rhondda · Cynon · Taff · Caerphilly · Pontypridd · Bristol · Bath · South Gloucestershire · Chipping Sodbury · Bath & N.E. Somerset · N.W. Somerset · Cardiff · Vale of Glamorgan · Barry · Bridgend · Neath Port Talbot · Swansea · Weston-super-Mare

CHANNEL ISLANDS (U.K.)

ALDERNEY · GUERNSEY · St. Peter Port · JERSEY · St. Helier

ISLE OF MAN (U.K.) · Douglas

TYRONE · Omagh · ARMAGH · Armagh · DOWN · Downpatrick · Newry · FERMANAGH · Enniskillen · Belfast · Bangor · Newtownabbey · Newtownards

NORTHUMBERLAND · DURHAM · Hartlepool · Middlesbrough · Darlington · Northallerton · NORTH YORKSHIRE · Whitby · Scarborough · Ripon · Harrogate · Skipton · York · THE EAST RIDING OF YORKSHIRE · Kingston upon Hull · Bridlington · Grimsby · Scunthorpe · Doncaster · Skegness · Boston · LINCOLNSHIRE · Lincoln · Grantham

CUMBRIA · Workington · Penrith · Kendal · Barrow-in-Furness · Morecambe · Lancaster · LANCASHIRE · Blackpool · Preston · Blackburn · Bolton · Wigan · Bradford · Leeds · Huddersfield · Halifax · WEST YORKSHIRE · Barnsley · Rotherham · Sheffield · SOUTH YORKSHIRE · Chesterfield · Mansfield · NOTTINGHAMSHIRE · Nottingham · DERBYSHIRE · Derby

Southport · Birkenhead · St Helens · Liverpool · MERSEYSIDE · Manchester · Stockport · GREATER MANCHESTER · Oldham · Macclesfield · CHESHIRE · Chester · Crewe · Stoke-on-Trent · STAFFORDSHIRE · Stafford · Telford · Wolverhampton · Birmingham · Coventry · WARWICKSHIRE · Warwick · LEICESTERSHIRE · Leicester · Loughborough · Kettering · Northampton · NORTHAMPTONSHIRE

ANGLESEY · Holyhead · Bangor · Llandudno · CAERNARFON AND MERIONETHSHIRE · ABERCONWY AND COLWYN · DENBIGHSHIRE · FLINTSHIRE · WREXHAM · Wrexham · Caernarfon · Pwllheli · Dolgellau · Machynlleth · Welshpool · Newtown · SHROPSHIRE · Shrewsbury · Aberystwyth · CARDIGANSHIRE · POWYS · Llandrindod Wells · HEREFORD AND WORCESTER · Hereford · Worcester · Gloucester · GLOUCESTERSHIRE · Cheltenham

PEMBROKESHIRE · Fishguard · Haverfordwest · Pembroke · CARMARTHENSHIRE · Carmarthen · Llanelli · Swansea · Neath · Bridgend · Barry · Cardiff · Newport · Brecon · Abergavenny · Weston-super-Mare · Bristol · Bath · Trowbridge · WILTSHIRE · Swindon · Newport · Bridgwater · SOMERSET · Taunton · Yeovil · Salisbury

Barnstaple · DEVON · Exeter · Torquay · Plymouth · CORNWALL · Newquay · St Austell · Truro · Penzance · ISLES OF SCILLY

NORFOLK · King's Lynn · Norwich · Great Yarmouth · Lowestoft · SUFFOLK · Bury St Edmunds · Ipswich · Felixstowe · Harwich · CAMBRIDGESHIRE · Peterborough · Cambridge · ESSEX · Colchester · Chelmsford · Southend-on-Sea · Basildon · HERTFORDSHIRE · Hertford · Harlow · BEDFORDSHIRE · Bedford · Luton · BUCKINGHAMSHIRE · Milton Keynes · Aylesbury · OXFORDSHIRE · Oxford · BERKSHIRE · Reading · Slough · Maidenhead · Watford · London · Croydon · Reigate · SURREY · Guildford · Woking · Gravesend · Gillingham · KENT · Maidstone · Royal Tunbridge Wells · Ashford · Canterbury · Ramsgate · Dover · Folkestone · Hastings · EAST SUSSEX · Lewes · Eastbourne · Brighton · WEST SUSSEX · Chichester · Crawley · HAMPSHIRE · Basingstoke · Winchester · Southampton · Portsmouth · ISLE OF WIGHT · Newport · DORSET · Bournemouth · Poole · Weymouth

SCALE 1 : 3 000 000

0 · 25 · 50 · 75 · 100 km

Conic projection

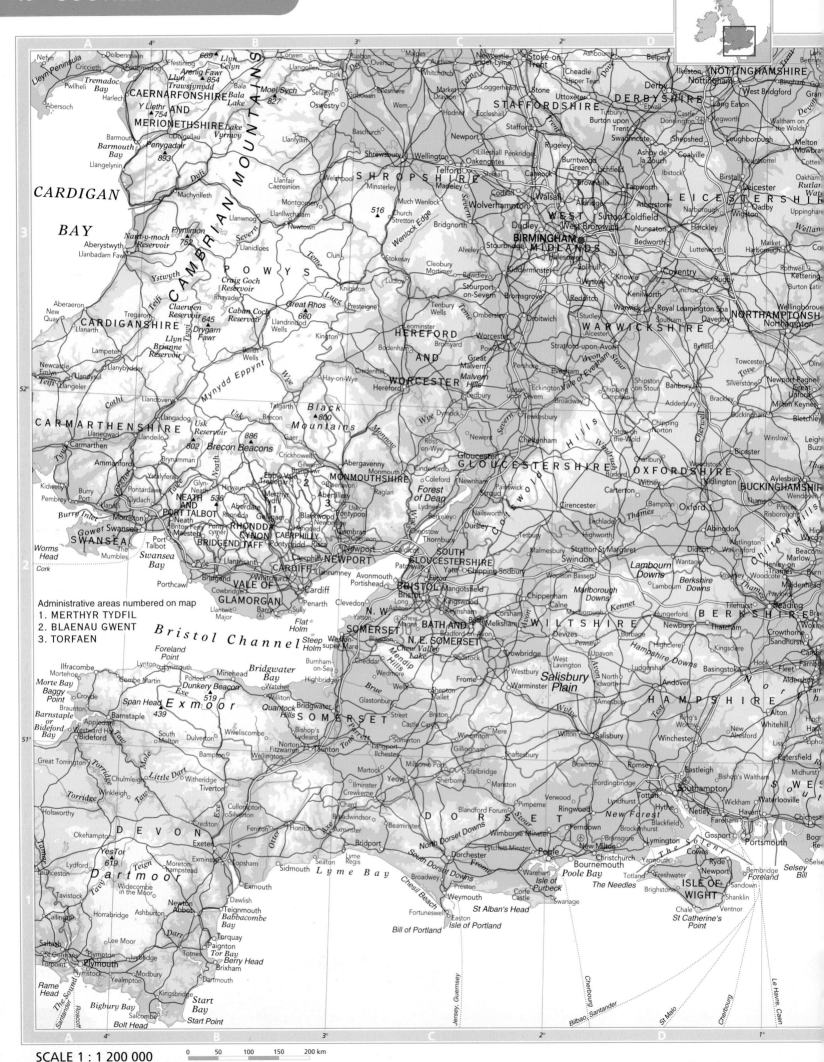

Administrative areas numbered on map
1. MERTHYR TYDFIL
2. BLAENAU GWENT
3. TORFAEN

SCALE 1 : 1 200 000

0   50   100   150   200 km

KEY

Relief and physical features

Relief
metres
1000
500
200
100
0
sea level
50
200
under sea level

893 ▲ Mountain height
(in metres)

Water features

~~~ River

~~~ Canal

Lake / Reservoir

Communications

Railway

Motorway

Road

Car ferry

⊕ Main airport

✈ Local airport

Administration

Boundaries

International

Internal

Settlement

Urban area

Cities and towns in order of size

National capital   Other city or town

■ LONDON   ● Birmingham

     ○ Reading

     ○ Oxford

     ○ Colchester

     ○ Wantage

Conic projection

SCALE 1 : 1 200 000

0   10   20   30   40 km

Seas and Bays: IRISH SEA · CARDIGAN BAY · St George's Channel · Caernarfon Bay · Liverpool Bay · Dublin Bay

Countries/Regions labelled: WEST YORKSHIRE · LANCASHIRE · GREATER MANCHESTER · MERSEYSIDE · CHESHIRE · FLINTSHIRE · DENBIGHSHIRE · WREXHAM · SHROPSHIRE · STAFFORDSHIRE · WEST MIDLANDS · HEREFORD AND WORCESTER · GLOUCESTERSHIRE · MONMOUTHSHIRE · POWYS · ABERCONWY AND COLWYN · CAERNARFONSHIRE AND MERIONETHSHIRE · CARDIGANSHIRE · CARMARTHENSHIRE · PEMBROKESHIRE · NEATH AND PORT TALBOT · RHONDDA · CAERPHILLY · ANGLESEY · MEATH · DUBLIN · WICKLOW · WEXFORD

Mountains: CAMBRIAN MOUNTAINS · Black Mountains · Brecon Beacons · Malvern Hills · Wicklow Mts · WICKLOW MTS

Towns (selection): Birmingham · West Bromwich · Dudley · Wolverhampton · Walsall · Stoke-on-Trent · Manchester · Stockport · Liverpool · Blackpool · Preston · Blackburn · Bolton · Bury · Oldham · Rochdale · Southport · Crewe · Chester · Wrexham · Shrewsbury · Telford · Worcester · Hereford · Leominster · Ludlow · Bridgnorth · Gloucester · Cheltenham · Monmouth · Abergavenny · Llandudno · Bangor · Caernarfon · Holyhead · Aberystwyth · Machynlleth · Dolgellau · Barmouth · Harlech · Pwllheli · Fishguard · Newport · Tenby · Pembroke · Milford Haven · Haverfordwest · Carmarthen · Llandeilo · Lampeter · Cardigan · New Quay · Aberaeron · Brecon · Neath · Swansea · Douglas · Dublin · Dún Laoghaire · Bray · Wexford · Wicklow · Belfast

Headlands/Points: Carmel Head · Great Ormes Head · Point of Ayr · Strumble Head · St David's Head · St Ann's Head · Carnsore Point · Cahore Point · Mizen Head · Wicklow Head · Kilmichael Point · Greenore Point · Dunany Point · Clogher Head

Islands: Anglesey · Holy Island · Bardsey · Ramsey I. · Skomer I. · Skokholm I. · Caldey Island · Lambay Island · Ireland's Eye

Spot heights: Pendle Hill 557 · Black Hill 582 · Kinder Scout 636 · 590 · Snowdon 1085 · Carnedd Llywelyn 1064 · Aran Fawddwy 905 · Cadair Idris 893 · Moel Sych 827 · Aran Benllyn 885 · Plynlimon 752 · Great Rhos 660 · 886 · 802 · 800 · 516 · Mullaghcleevaun 850 · Tonelagee 819 · Djouce Mountain 806 · 281

Rivers: Severn · Dee · Wye · Usk · Teme · Teifi · Towy · Conwy · Dovey · Trent

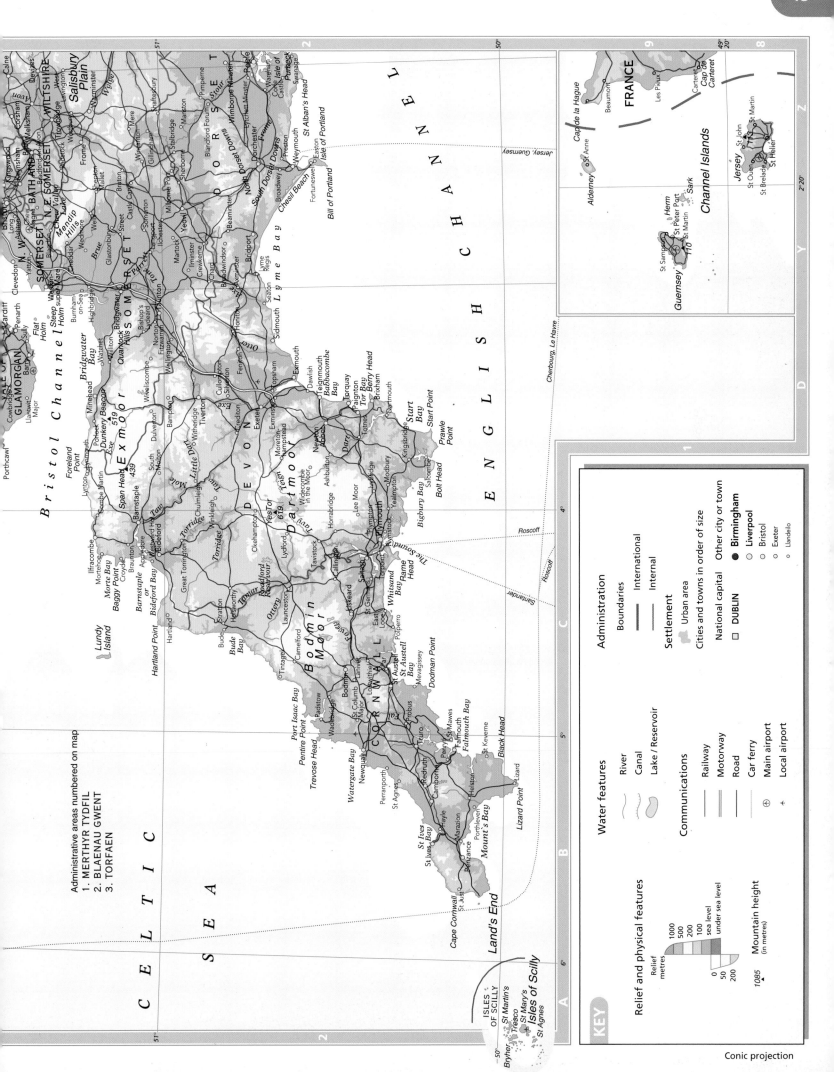

KEY

Relief and physical features

Relief metres

| 1000 |
| 500 |
| 200 |
| 100 |
| sea level |
| under sea level |

Mountain height
(in metres)

1085

0
50
200

Water features

~~~ River

〰 Canal

Lake / Reservoir

Communications

Railway

Motorway

Road

········· Car ferry

⊕ Main airport

✈ Local airport

Administration

Boundaries

International

Internal

Settlement

Urban area

Cities and towns in order of size

National capital   Other city or town

□ DUBLIN   ● Birmingham

                    ○ Liverpool

                    ○ Bristol

                    ○ Exeter

                    ○ Llandeilo

Administrative areas numbered on map
1. MERTHYR TYDFIL
2. BLAENAU GWENT
3. TORFAEN

Conic projection

CELTIC SEA

Isles of Scilly

Land's End

ENGLISH CHANNEL

Bristol Channel

FRANCE

Channel Islands

Jersey, Guernsey

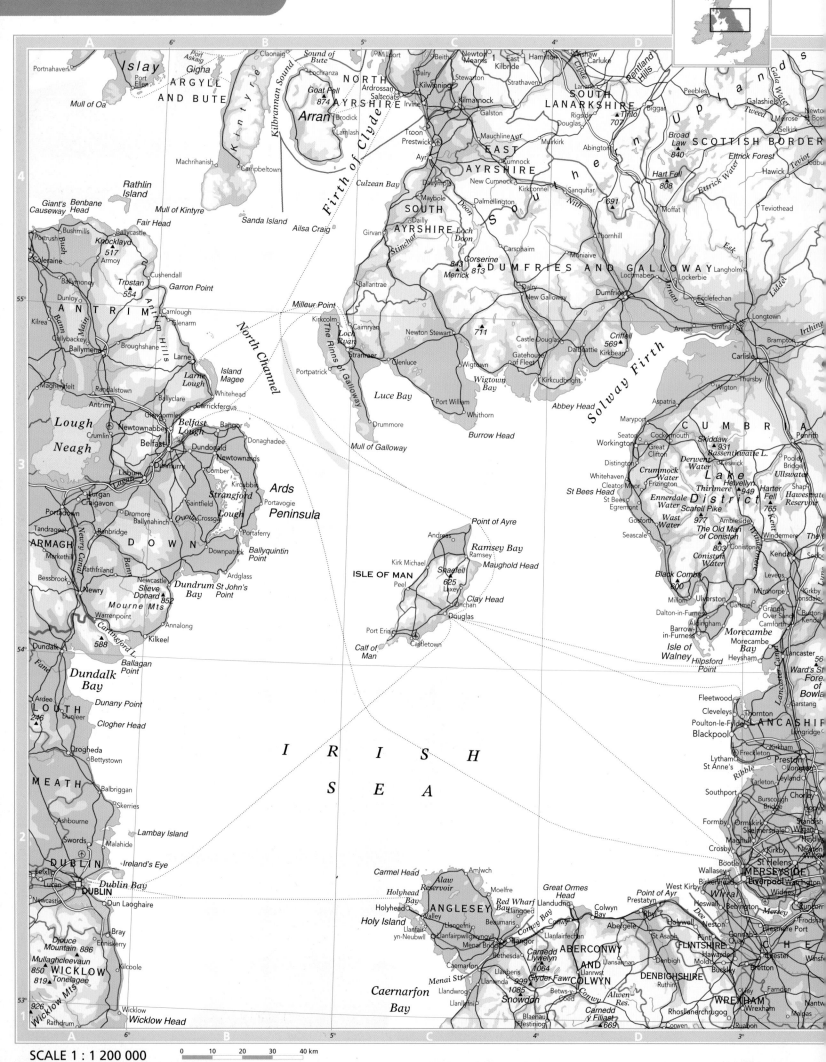

SCALE 1 : 1 200 000

0   10   20   30   40 km

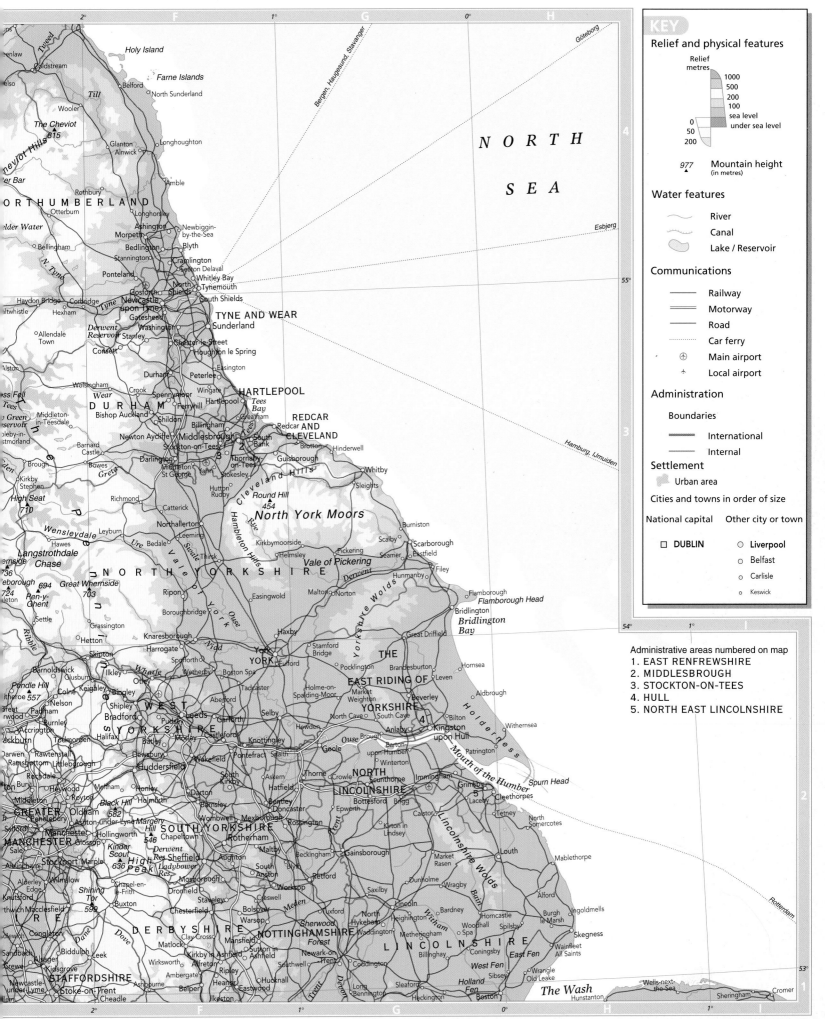

KEY

Relief and physical features

Relief
metres
1000
500
200
100
sea level
0
50
200
under sea level

▲ 977   Mountain height
(in metres)

Water features

River

Canal

Lake / Reservoir

Communications

Railway

Motorway

Road

Car ferry

⊕   Main airport

✈   Local airport

Administration

Boundaries

International

Internal

Settlement

Urban area

Cities and towns in order of size

National capital   Other city or town

☐ DUBLIN   ◉ Liverpool

                    ◯ Belfast

                    ◯ Carlisle

                    ◦ Keswick

Administrative areas numbered on map
1. EAST RENFREWSHIRE
2. MIDDLESBROUGH
3. STOCKTON-ON-TEES
4. HULL
5. NORTH EAST LINCOLNSHIRE

Conic projection

Administrative areas numbered on map
1. WEST DUNBARTONSHIRE
2. CITY OF GLASGOW
3. CLACKMANNANSHIRE
4. MIDDLESBROUGH
5. STOCKTON-ON-TEES
6. EAST RENFREWSHIRE
7. EAST DUNBARTONSHIRE
8. NORTH LANARKSHIRE

ATLANTIC OCEAN

HIGHLAND

Coll
Tiree
Staffa
Ulva
Iona
Fionnphort
Mull
Ben More 966
Loch Frisa
Loch Scridain
Ross of Mull
Tobermory
Morvern
Loch Arienas
Lochaline
Sound of Mull
Craignure
Loch Sunart
Loch Leven
Glen Coe
Kinlochleven
888
1150
Bidean nam Bian
Meall a'Bhuiridh 1108
Rannoch Moor
Ben Alder
L. Rannoch
Schiehallion
Lyon
Loch Laidon
Ben Lawers 1214
Killin
L. Earn

Firth of Lorn
Oban
Ben Cruachan 1126
Loch Etive
Orchy
Dalmally
Ben Lui 1130
Crianlarich
Ben More
Dochart 1174
Loch Tay
ARGYLL AND BUTE
Argyll
Loch Awe
Kilmelford
Luing
Scarba
Inveraray
Loch Fyne
Loch Katrine
The Trossachs
Ben Lomond 974
Loch Lubnaig
Loch Venachar
Call
STIRLING
Loch Long
Loch Lomond
Aberfoyle
Forth
Drymen

Colonsay
Scalasaig
Oronsay
Jura
Beinn an Oir 785
Sound of Jura
Tarbert
Ardrishaig
Lochgilphead
Loch Eck
Helensburgh
Alexandria
Garelochhead
Dunoon
Port Glasgow
INVERCLYDE
Greenock
Wemyss Bay
Dumbarton
Kirkintilloch
Clydebank
RENFREWSHIRE
Glasgow
Johnstone
Paisley
East Kilbride
Newton Mearns
Barrhead
Beith

Islay
Port Askaig
Portnahaven
Port Ellen
Mull of Oa
Gigha
Kintyre
Kilbrannan Sound
Claonaig
Lochranza
Sound of Bute
Bute
Rothesay
Great Cumbrae
Millport
Largs
Dalry
Kilwinning
Stewarton
Kilmarnock
Galston

NORTH AYRSHIRE
Goat Fell 874
Arran
Brodick
Lamlash
Ardrossan
Saltcoats
Irvine
Troon
Prestwick
Ayr
EAST AYRSHIRE
Mauchline
Cumnock
New Cumnock

Machrihanish
Campbeltown
Sanda Island
Mull of Kintyre
Ailsa Craig
Firth of Clyde
Culzean Bay
Girvan
SOUTH AYRSHIRE
Maybole
Dailly
Dalmellington
Loch Doon
Ballantrae
Merrick 843
Corserine 813
711
New Galloway
Milleur Point
North Channel
Kirkcolm
Cairnryan
The Rinns of Galloway
Stranraer
Glenluce
Newton Stewart
Wigtown
Gatehouse of Fleet
Luce Bay
Portpatrick
Port William
Wigtown Bay
Drummore
Whithorn
Burrow Head
Mull of Galloway

Inishtrahull
Inishtrahull Sd
Malin Head
Glengad Head
Fanad Head
Dunaff Head
Lough Swilly
Sheep Haven
Muckish Mountain 670
Errigal 752
Inishowen
Carndonagh
Slieve Snaght 615
Moville
Buncrana
Scalp 484
Inishowen Head
Magilligan Point
Portstewart
Portrush
Giant's Causeway
Bushmills
Benbane Head
Rathlin Island
Ballycastle
Fair Head
Knocklayd 517
Armoy
Trostan 554
Cushendall
Garron Point
Glenarm
Carnlough

DONEGAL
Letterkenny
Cronamuck Mountain 346
Cark Mountain 367
598
Aghla Mountain
Raphoe
Deele
Lifford
Strabane
Sion Mills
Blue Stack 676
L. Eske
Ballybofey
Stranorlar
Derg
Castlederg
Donegal
Lough Derg
Finn
Mourne
Strule
Newtownstewart
Omagh
TYRONE
Sawel Mt 683
Sperrin Mts
Draperstown
Magherafelt
Maghera
Moneymore
Cookstown
Dungannon
Fintona

LONDONDERRY
Londonderry
Eglinton
Limavady
Lough Foyle
Coleraine
Roe
Garvagh
Dungiven
Ballymoney
Kilrea
Dunloy
ANTRIM
Bann
Main
Ballymena
Ballybackey
Broughshane
Larne
Larne Lough
Island Magee
Whitehead
Carrickfergus
Antrim Hills
Glenarm

Bann
Randalstown
Antrim
Lough Neagh
Crumlin
Newtownabbey
Glengormley
Belfast Lough
Belfast
Bangor
Dundonald
Newtownards
Comber
Strangford Lough
Ards Peninsula
Portavogie
Portaferry
Ballyquintin Point

Dungannon
Dunmurry
Lisburn
Lagan
Lurgan
Craigavon
Portadown
Dromore
Ballynahinch
Saintfield
Crossgar
Downpatrick
Ardglass
Dundrum Bay
St John's Point

Blackwater
Tandragee
ARMAGH
Armagh
Markethill
Keady
Newry Canal
Banbridge
Bann
Rathfriland
Bessbrook
Newry
Warrenpoint
Newcastle
Slieve Donard 852
Mourne Mts
Annalong
Kilkeel
DOWN

FERMANAGH
Enniskillen
Lower Lough Erne
Lough Melvin
Tullybrack 376
Slieve Beagh 372
Lisnaskea
Monaghan
MONAGHAN
Clones
Ballybay
Castleblayney
Crossmaglen
Carlingford L. 588
Dundalk
Dundalk B. Point
Ballagan

Erne
Upper Lough Erne
Ulster Canal
Lisbellaw
Cuilcagh 667
Lough Allen
Slieve Anierin 586
LEITRIM
Carrick-on-Shannon
Lough Oughter
Cavan
CAVAN
Annalee
Carrickmacross
Fane
Ballyquintin

ISLE OF MAN
Point of Ayre
Andreas
Ramsey Bay
Ramsey
Kirk Michael
Maughold Head
Peel
Snaefell 625
Laxey
Clay Head
Onchan
Douglas
Port Erin
Castletown
Calf of Man

0 10 20 30 40 km

KEY

Relief and physical features

Relief metres
1000
500
200
100
0
sea level
50 under sea level
200

1214 Mountain height
(in metres)

Water features

River
Canal
Lake / Reservoir

Communications

Railway
Motorway
Road
Car ferry
Main airport
Local airport

Administration

Boundaries
International
Internal

Settlement

Urban area

Cities and towns in order of size

○ Glasgow
○ Londonderry
○ Lancaster
○ Peebles

Conic projection

KEY

Relief and physical features

Relief
metres
1000
500
200
100
sea level
0
50
200
under sea level

1344 ▲ Mountain height
(in metres)

Water features

～ River
～ Canal
Lake / Reservoir

Communications

── Railway
── Road
······ Car ferry
⊕ Main airport
✈ Local airport

Administration

Boundaries
── Internal

Settlement

Cities and towns in order of size

○ Aberdeen
○ Inverness
○ Kirkwall

Cape Wrath
Kyle of Durness
Durn

Butt of Lewis
Port of Ness

Kinlochbervie
Loch Inchard
L. Laxford
Foinaven
915

Muirneag
248
Tolsta Head

Handa Island
Scourie
Loch More

Flannan Isles

West Loch Roag
Great Bernera
Broad Bay
Stornoway
Eye Peninsula

LEWIS

Callanish

Point of Stoer

Lochinver
Loch Assynt
Canisp
846
Ben More Assynt
998

Mealasta Island

Scarp

Loch Langavat
Kebock Head

Rubha Coigeach

Cul Mor
849

Summer Isles

The Minch

WESTERN ISLES

Tirga Mor
679
Clisham
799

Loch Lurgainn

Loch Broom
Ullapool

St Kilda

Greenstone Point

Gruinard Bay
L. Ewe
An Teallach
1062
Fionn Loch
Beinn Dearg
1084

Outer Hebrides

Tarbert
Scalpay
E. L. Tarbert

Harris

Loch Langavat

Rodel

Shiant Islands
Rubha Reidh

Gair Loch
Gairloch
Loch Maree

Sgurr Mor
1110

WESTER ROSS HIGHLAND

Pabbay
Berneray
Boreray

Sound of Harris

Rubha Hunish

L. Torridon
Loch Fannich

Torridon
Shieldaig

Monach Islands

Sd of Monach

North Uist

Lochmaddy

Little Minch

L. Dunvegan

Loch Snizort
Uig

Rona
Sound of Raasay

Orrin

Benbecula
Balinvanich

The Storr
719

Portree
Raasay

Inner Sound

Loch Monar

Skye

Carn Eighe
1183

A'Chralaig
1120

South Uist

L. Bracadale

Cuillin Hills
993
Sgurr Alasdair

Blaven
928

Scalpay

Kyle of Lochalsh

ATLANTIC

Lochboisdale

Soay
L. Eishort

Cuillin Sound

Loch Cluanie
L. Loyne
Glen Moriston
Loch Garry
Glen Garry

A'Chralaig

Sd of Barra
Eriskay

Canna

Ardvasar

Sd of Sleat

L. Hourn
Ladhar Bheinn
1020

Loch Quoich

L. Lochy

OCEAN

Barra
Castlebay

Vatersay

Rum

Mallaig
L. Nevis
Loch Morar

Loch Arkaig

L. Oich

Sandray

Eigg

Arisaig

Pabbay

Mingulay

Muck

Sound of Arisaig

Eilean Shona

Loch Shiel

Fort William
1344
Stob Choire Claurigh
1177

Berneray

Point of Ardnamurchan

Coll

Loch Sunart

Sgurr Dhomhnuill
888

Ben Nevis

Loch Treig
Kinlochleven

Loch Linnhe
Loch Leven

Bidean nam Bian ▲ 1150
Glen Coe

SCALE 1 : 1 200 000

0 10 20 30 40 km

Conic projection

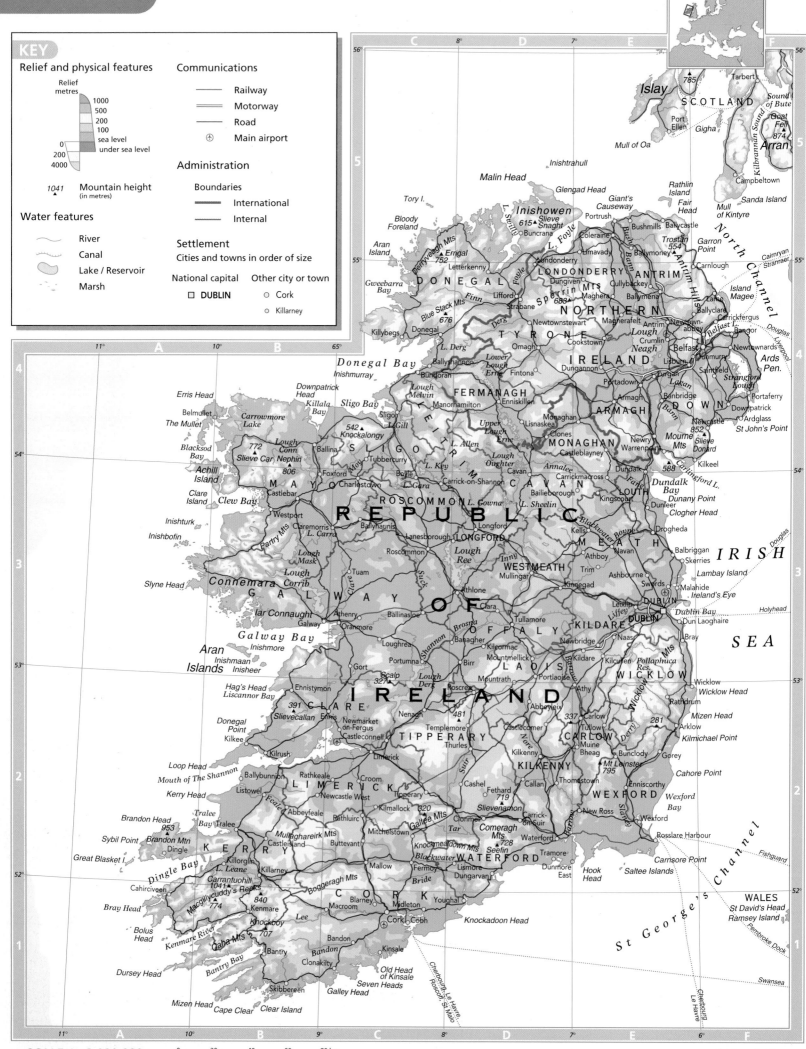

KEY

Relief and physical features

Relief metres
1000
500
200
100
0 — sea level
200 — under sea level
4000

1041 ▲ Mountain height (in metres)

Water features

River
Canal
Lake / Reservoir
Marsh

Communications

Railway
Motorway
Road
⊕ Main airport

Administration

Boundaries
— International
— Internal

Settlement

Cities and towns in order of size

National capital
□ DUBLIN

Other city or town
○ Cork
○ Killarney

SCALE 1 : 2 000 000

0   20   40   60   80 km

Conic projection

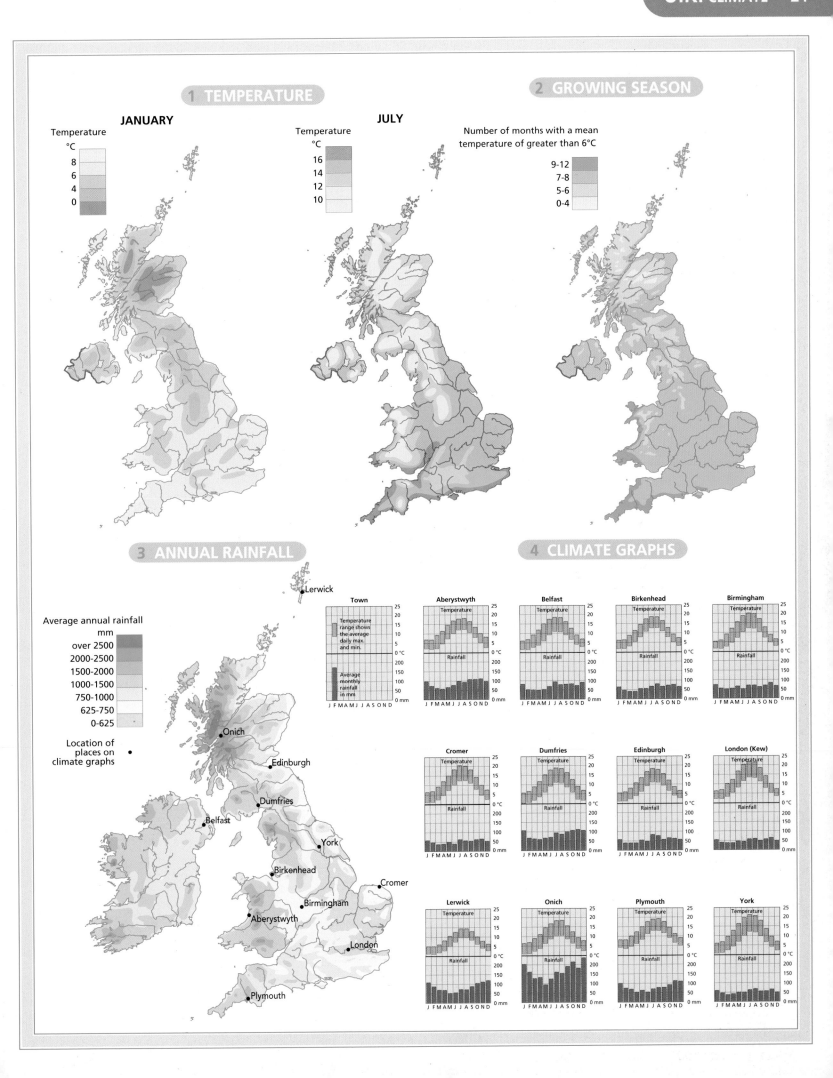

1 TEMPERATURE

JANUARY

Temperature
°C
8
6
4
0

JULY

Temperature
°C
16
14
12
10

2 GROWING SEASON

Number of months with a mean
temperature of greater than 6°C

9-12
7-8
5-6
0-4

3 ANNUAL RAINFALL

Average annual rainfall
mm
over 2500
2000-2500
1500-2000
1000-1500
750-1000
625-750
0-625

● Location of
places on
climate graphs

Lerwick

Onich

Edinburgh

Dumfries

Belfast

York

Birkenhead

Cromer

Birmingham

Aberystwyth

London

Plymouth

4 CLIMATE GRAPHS

Town

Temperature
range shows
the average
daily max.
and min.

Average
monthly
rainfall
in mm

Temperature
25
20
15
10
5
0 °C

Rainfall
200
150
100
50
0 mm

J F M A M J J A S O N D

Aberystwyth — Temperature / Rainfall

Belfast — Temperature / Rainfall

Birkenhead — Temperature / Rainfall

Birmingham — Temperature / Rainfall

Cromer — Temperature / Rainfall

Dumfries — Temperature / Rainfall

Edinburgh — Temperature / Rainfall

London (Kew) — Temperature / Rainfall

Lerwick — Temperature / Rainfall

Onich — Temperature / Rainfall

Plymouth — Temperature / Rainfall

York — Temperature / Rainfall

SCALE 1 : 4 000 000

0   50   100   150 km

Conic projection

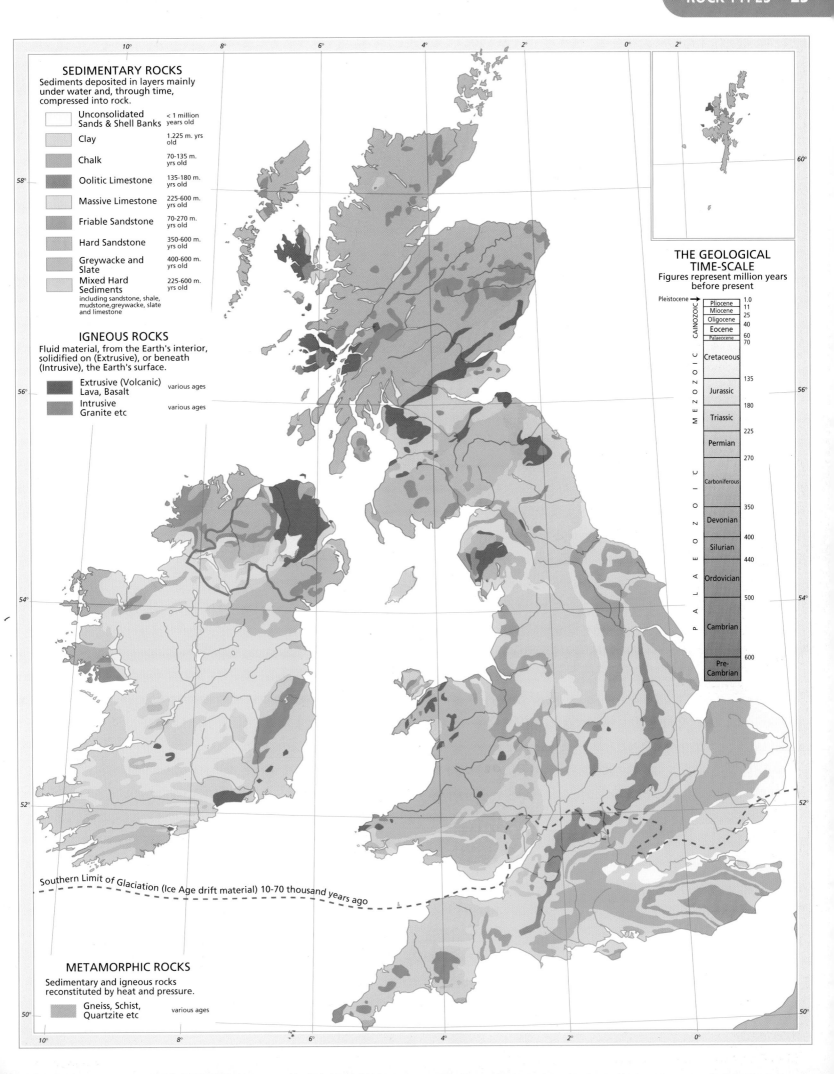

SEDIMENTARY ROCKS

Sediments deposited in layers mainly under water and, through time, compressed into rock.

	Unconsolidated Sands & Shell Banks	< 1 million years old
	Clay	1.225 m. yrs old
	Chalk	70-135 m. yrs old
	Oolitic Limestone	135-180 m. yrs old
	Massive Limestone	225-600 m. yrs old
	Friable Sandstone	70-270 m. yrs old
	Hard Sandstone	350-600 m. yrs old
	Greywacke and Slate	400-600 m. yrs old
	Mixed Hard Sediments	225-600 m. yrs old

including sandstone, shale, mudstone, greywacke, slate and limestone

IGNEOUS ROCKS

Fluid material, from the Earth's interior, solidified on (Extrusive), or beneath (Intrusive), the Earth's surface.

	Extrusive (Volcanic) Lava, Basalt	various ages
	Intrusive Granite etc	various ages

METAMORPHIC ROCKS

Sedimentary and igneous rocks reconstituted by heat and pressure.

	Gneiss, Schist, Quartzite etc	various ages

Southern Limit of Glaciation (Ice Age drift material) 10-70 thousand years ago

THE GEOLOGICAL TIME-SCALE

Figures represent million years before present

Pleistocene →

CAINOZOIC	Pliocene	1.0
	Miocene	11
	Oligocene	25
	Eocene	40
	Palaeocene	60 / 70
MEZOZOIC	Cretaceous	
		135
	Jurassic	
		180
	Triassic	
		225
	Permian	
		270
PALAEOZOIC	Carboniferous	
		350
	Devonian	
		400
	Silurian	
		440
	Ordovician	
		500
	Cambrian	
		600
	Pre-Cambrian	

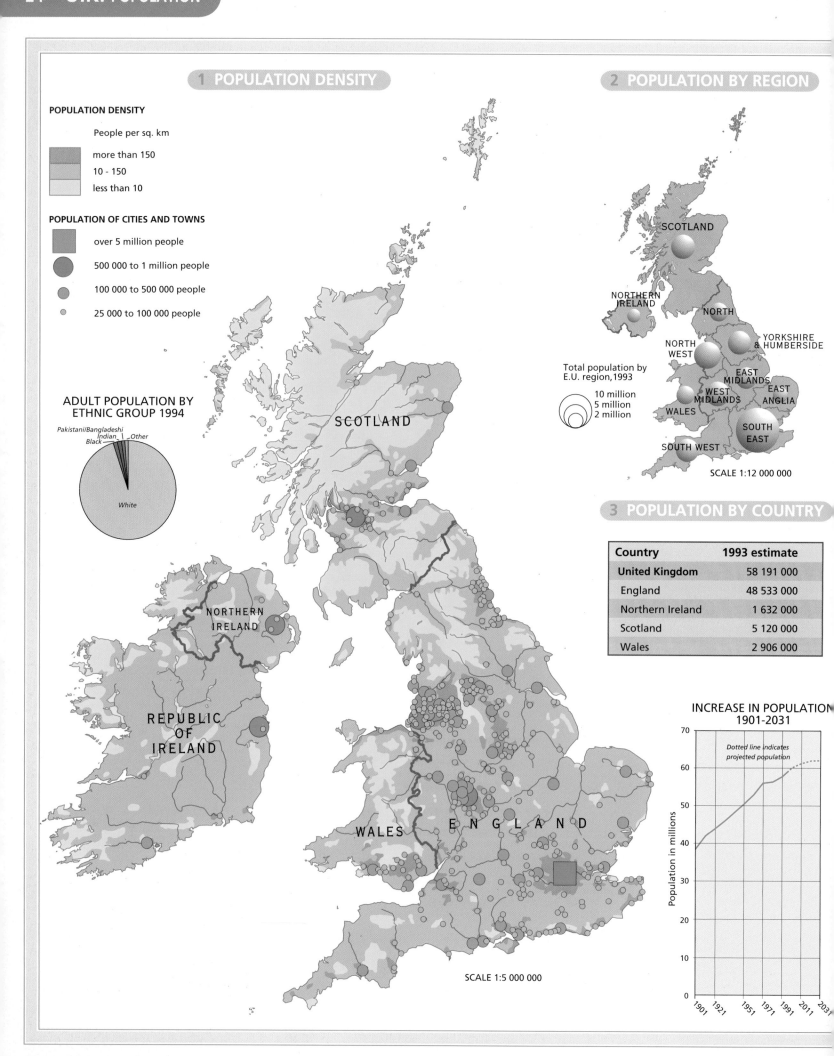

1 POPULATION DENSITY

POPULATION DENSITY

People per sq. km

more than 150

10 - 150

less than 10

POPULATION OF CITIES AND TOWNS

over 5 million people

500 000 to 1 million people

100 000 to 500 000 people

25 000 to 100 000 people

ADULT POPULATION BY ETHNIC GROUP 1994

Pakistani/Bangladeshi
Indian
Black
Other

White

SCOTLAND

NORTHERN
IRELAND

REPUBLIC
OF
IRELAND

WALES   E N G L A N D

SCALE 1:5 000 000

2 POPULATION BY REGION

SCOTLAND

NORTHERN
IRELAND

NORTH

YORKSHIRE
& HUMBERSIDE

NORTH
WEST

EAST
MIDLANDS

WEST
MIDLANDS   EAST
ANGLIA

WALES

SOUTH
EAST

SOUTH WEST

Total population by
E.U. region, 1993

10 million
5 million
2 million

SCALE 1:12 000 000

3 POPULATION BY COUNTRY

Country	1993 estimate
United Kingdom	58 191 000
England	48 533 000
Northern Ireland	1 632 000
Scotland	5 120 000
Wales	2 906 000

INCREASE IN POPULATION 1901-2031

Dotted line indicates projected population

70

60

50

40

30

20

10

0

Population in millions

1901 1921 1951 1971 1991 2011 2031

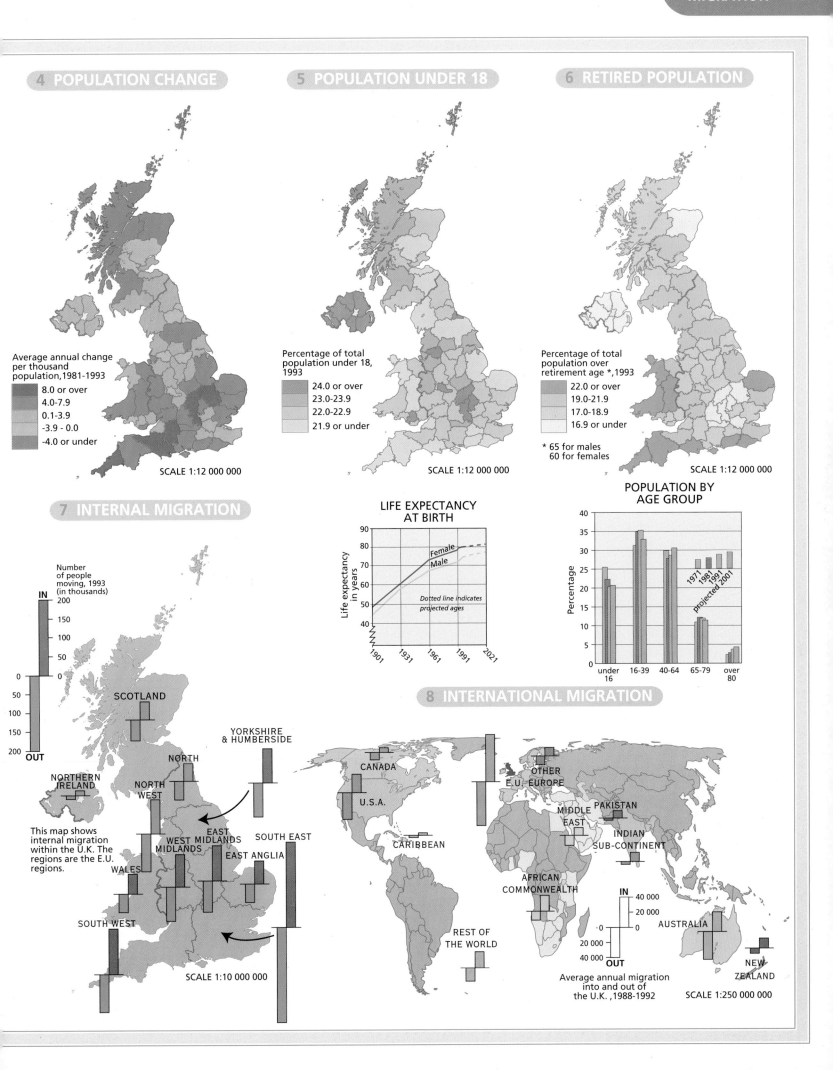

4 POPULATION CHANGE

Average annual change
per thousand
population,1981-1993

- 8.0 or over
- 4.0-7.9
- 0.1-3.9
- -3.9 - 0.0
- -4.0 or under

SCALE 1:12 000 000

5 POPULATION UNDER 18

Percentage of total
population under 18,
1993

- 24.0 or over
- 23.0-23.9
- 22.0-22.9
- 21.9 or under

SCALE 1:12 000 000

6 RETIRED POPULATION

Percentage of total
population over
retirement age *,1993

- 22.0 or over
- 19.0-21.9
- 17.0-18.9
- 16.9 or under

* 65 for males
60 for females

SCALE 1:12 000 000

7 INTERNAL MIGRATION

Number
of people
moving, 1993
(in thousands)

IN
200
150
100
50
0
50
100
150
200
OUT

SCOTLAND

YORKSHIRE
& HUMBERSIDE

NORTH

NORTHERN
IRELAND

NORTH
WEST

EAST
MIDLANDS

WEST MIDLANDS

SOUTH EAST

EAST ANGLIA

WALES

This map shows
internal migration
within the U.K. The
regions are the E.U.
regions.

SOUTH WEST

SCALE 1:10 000 000

**LIFE EXPECTANCY
AT BIRTH**

Female
Male

Dotted line indicates
projected ages

Life expectancy
in years

90
80
70
60
50
40

1901 1931 1961 1991 2021

**POPULATION BY
AGE GROUP**

Percentage

40
35
30
25
20
15
10
5
0

under 16   16-39   40-64   65-79   over 80

1971 1981 1991 projected 2001

8 INTERNATIONAL MIGRATION

CANADA

U.S.A.

CARIBBEAN

OTHER
E.U. EUROPE

MIDDLE
EAST

PAKISTAN

INDIAN
SUB-CONTINENT

AFRICAN
COMMONWEALTH

REST OF
THE WORLD

IN
40 000
20 000
0
20 000
40 000
OUT

AUSTRALIA

NEW
ZEALAND

Average annual migration
into and out of
the U.K. ,1988-1992

SCALE 1:250 000 000

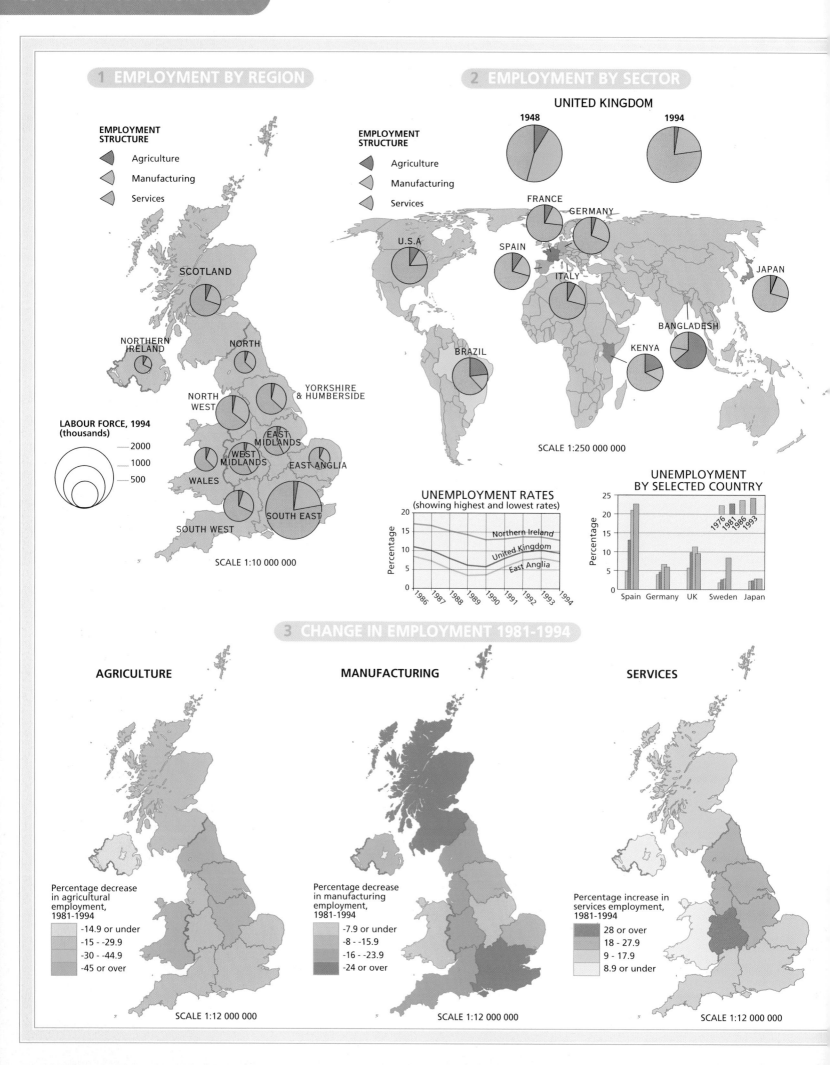

1 EMPLOYMENT BY REGION

EMPLOYMENT STRUCTURE
- Agriculture
- Manufacturing
- Services

LABOUR FORCE, 1994 (thousands)
- 2000
- 1000
- 500

SCOTLAND

NORTHERN IRELAND

NORTH

NORTH WEST

YORKSHIRE & HUMBERSIDE

EAST MIDLANDS

WEST MIDLANDS

EAST ANGLIA

WALES

SOUTH EAST

SOUTH WEST

SCALE 1:10 000 000

2 EMPLOYMENT BY SECTOR

UNITED KINGDOM

1948   1994

EMPLOYMENT STRUCTURE
- Agriculture
- Manufacturing
- Services

FRANCE

GERMANY

U.S.A

SPAIN

ITALY

JAPAN

BRAZIL

KENYA

BANGLADESH

SCALE 1:250 000 000

UNEMPLOYMENT RATES
(showing highest and lowest rates)

Northern Ireland

United Kingdom

East Anglia

Percentage

1986 1987 1988 1989 1990 1991 1992 1993 1994

UNEMPLOYMENT BY SELECTED COUNTRY

Percentage

1976 1981 1986 1993

Spain Germany UK Sweden Japan

3 CHANGE IN EMPLOYMENT 1981-1994

AGRICULTURE

Percentage decrease in agricultural employment, 1981-1994
- -14.9 or under
- -15 - -29.9
- -30 - -44.9
- -45 or over

SCALE 1:12 000 000

MANUFACTURING

Percentage decrease in manufacturing employment, 1981-1994
- -7.9 or under
- -8 - -15.9
- -16 - -23.9
- -24 or over

SCALE 1:12 000 000

SERVICES

Percentage increase in services employment, 1981-1994
- 28 or over
- 18 - 27.9
- 9 - 17.9
- 8.9 or under

SCALE 1:12 000 000

4 LAND USE

CHANGE IN AGRICULTURAL LAND USE 1961-1991

5 MANUFACTURING INDUSTRY

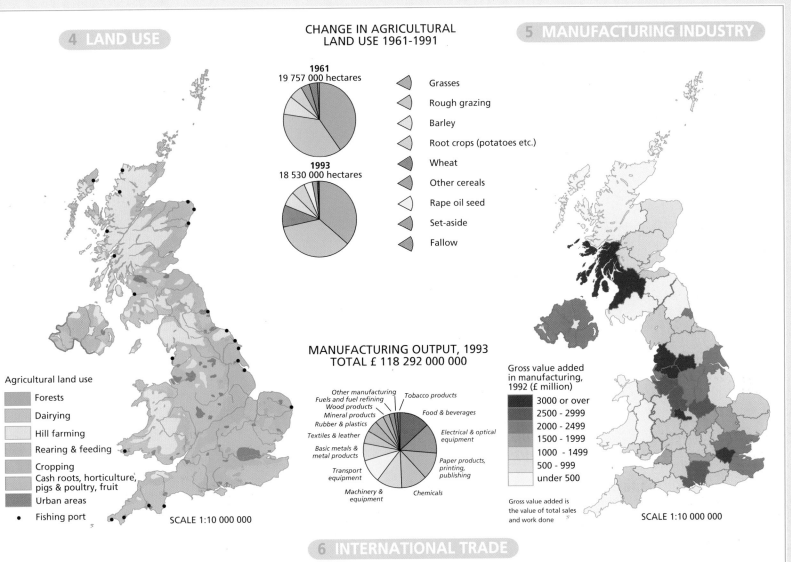

1961
19 757 000 hectares

1993
18 530 000 hectares

- Grasses
- Rough grazing
- Barley
- Root crops (potatoes etc.)
- Wheat
- Other cereals
- Rape oil seed
- Set-aside
- Fallow

MANUFACTURING OUTPUT, 1993
TOTAL £ 118 292 000 000

Other manufacturing
Fuels and fuel refining
Wood products
Mineral products
Rubber & plastics
Textiles & leather
Basic metals & metal products
Transport equipment
Machinery & equipment
Tobacco products
Food & beverages
Electrical & optical equipment
Paper products, printing, publishing
Chemicals

Agricultural land use

- Forests
- Dairying
- Hill farming
- Rearing & feeding
- Cropping
- Cash roots, horticulture, pigs & poultry, fruit
- Urban areas
- • Fishing port

SCALE 1:10 000 000

Gross value added in manufacturing, 1992 (£ million)

- 3000 or over
- 2500 - 2999
- 2000 - 2499
- 1500 - 1999
- 1000 - 1499
- 500 - 999
- under 500

Gross value added is the value of total sales and work done

SCALE 1:10 000 000

6 INTERNATIONAL TRADE

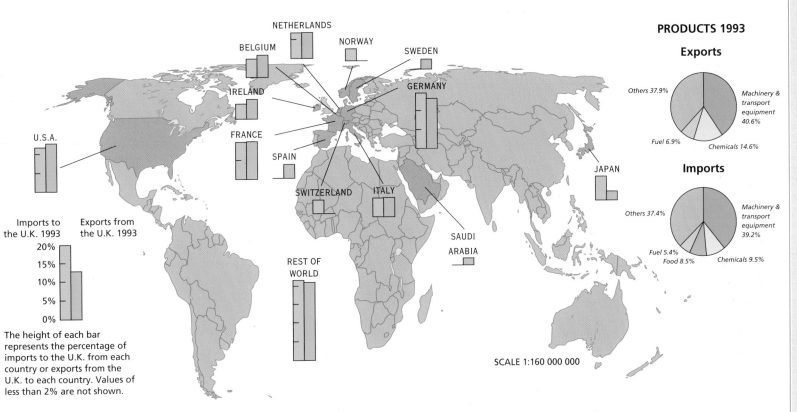

NETHERLANDS
BELGIUM
NORWAY
SWEDEN
IRELAND
GERMANY
FRANCE
SPAIN
SWITZERLAND
ITALY
U.S.A.
JAPAN
SAUDI ARABIA
REST OF WORLD

Imports to the U.K. 1993 — Exports from the U.K. 1993

- 20%
- 15%
- 10%
- 5%
- 0%

The height of each bar represents the percentage of imports to the U.K. from each country or exports from the U.K. to each country. Values of less than 2% are not shown.

SCALE 1:160 000 000

PRODUCTS 1993

Exports

Others 37.9%
Machinery & transport equipment 40.6%
Fuel 6.9%
Chemicals 14.6%

Imports

Others 37.4%
Machinery & transport equipment 39.2%
Fuel 5.4%
Food 8.5%
Chemicals 9.5%

1 ENERGY SOURCES

Coalfield (not all producing)
Oilfield
Gasfield
Oil pipeline
Gas pipeline
Oil pipeline terminal
Gas pipeline terminal
Oil refinery

Magnus
Murchison
Thistle
Tern
Statfjord
Cormorant
Brent
Hutton
Minian
Heather
Alwyn
Lyell
Dunbar
Clair
Emerald
Sullom Voe

Frigg
Bruce
Ness
Beryl

Gryphon
Brae
Central Brae
Miller
Flotta
Claymore
Piper
Donan
Scott
Balmoral
Tartan
Maureen
Buchan
Moira
Forties
Everest
Beatrice
Montrose
Nigg Bay
Lomond
St. Fergus
Kittiwake
Cruden
Gannet
Bay

NORTH SEA

Joanne
Ekofisk
Fulmar
Auk
Clyde
Angus

Imported oil

Finnart
Dalmeny
Central
Grangemouth
Scotland

Northumberland
Forbes
and Durham
Esmond
North Tees
Gordon
Teesside
Murdoch
Rough
Ravenspurn
Barrow
West
Morecambe
Sole
Ann
Killingholme
Barque
Viking
Imported oil
Easington
Amethyst
Indefatigable
Tranmere
Lancashire
Immingham
Valiant
Sean
Stanlow
Yorkshire,
Theddlethorpe
Vulcan
Thames
Notts &
Hewett
Scram
Derbys
Bacton
Leman
Midlands
Bank

Imported oil
Milford Haven
South Wales
Shellhaven
Coryton
Pembroke
Angle Bay
Llandarcy
Canvey
Severn
Kent
Fawley

OIL AND NATURAL GAS RESERVES, 1994

Middle East | Africa | Western Europe
North America | Eastern Europe | U.K.
South America | Asia and Australasia

WORLD OIL RESERVES

Percentage

Iran
Abu Dhabi
Kuwait
Iraq
Saudi Arabia

WORLD NATURAL GAS RESERVES

Percentage

Russian Federation
Iran

2 ENERGY PRODUCTION

POWER STATIONS

Pumped storage hydroelectric
Coal powered (1000MW and over)
Gas powered (1000MW and over)
Oil powered (1000 MW and over)
Nuclear

PRIMARY ENERGY CONSUMPTION, 1993

Hydro-electricity 1%
Nuclear power 9.8%
Oil 36.1%
Coal 24.9%
Natural gas 28.2%

Dounreay
Peterhead
Foyers
Cruachan
Longannet
Hunterston B
Cockenzie
Torness
Chapelcross
Ballylumford
Hartlepool
Calder Hall
Wilton
(Sellafield)
Heysham I
Heysham II
Eggborough
Ferrybridge
Drax
Wylfa
Fiddler's
West Burton
Ferry
Cottam
Dinorwig
High Marnham
Ffestiniog
Ratcliffe-on-Soar
Sizewell A
Oldbury
W. Thurrock
Bradwell
Aberthaw B
Didcot
Grain
Hinkley
Hinkley
Kingsnorth
Point A
Point B
Dungeness B
Dungeness A

UK PRODUCTION OF OIL, COAL AND NATURAL GAS

Million tonnes oil equivalent
Oil — Coal — Natural gas

120
100
80
60
40
20
0
1973 1975 1980 1985 1990 1994

Conic projection

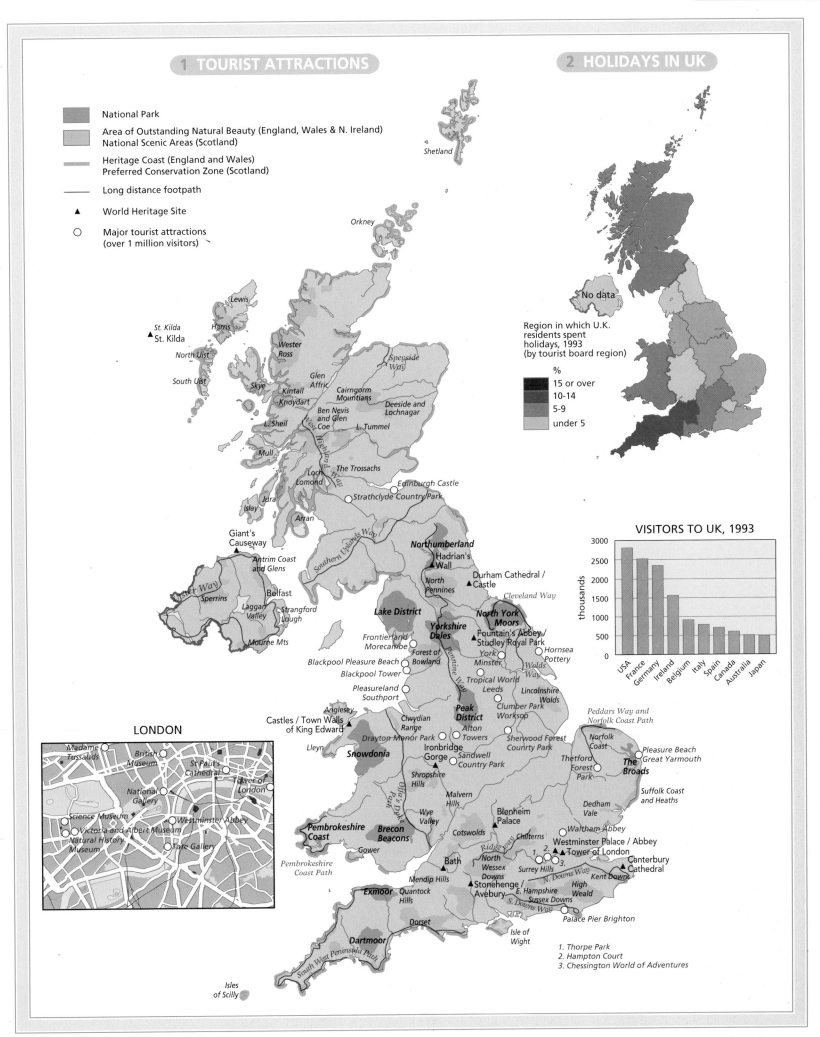

1 TOURIST ATTRACTIONS

- National Park
- Area of Outstanding Natural Beauty (England, Wales & N. Ireland) National Scenic Areas (Scotland)
- Heritage Coast (England and Wales) Preferred Conservation Zone (Scotland)
- Long distance footpath
- ▲ World Heritage Site
- ○ Major tourist attractions (over 1 million visitors)

Shetland

Orkney

Lewis

St. Kilda
▲ St. Kilda

Harris

North Uist

Wester Ross

South Uist

Glen Affric

Speyside Way

Skye

Kintail
Knoydart

Cairngorm Mountians

Ben Nevis and Glen Coe

Deeside and Lochnagar

L. Sheil

L. Tummel

West Highland Way

Mull

Jura

Islay

The Trossachs

Loch Lomond

Arran

○ Edinburgh Castle
○ Strathclyde Country Park

Southern Uplands Way

Giant's Causeway ▲

Antrim Coast and Glens

Ulster Way

Sperrins

Belfast

Laggan Valley

Strangford Lough

Mourne Mts

Northumberland

▲ Hadrian's Wall

North Pennines

Durham Cathedral / ▲ Castle

Cleveland Way

Lake District

Yorkshire Dales

North York Moors

○ Frontierland Morecambe

Forest of Bowland

Pennine Way

▲ Fountain's Abbey / Studley Royal Park

○ York Minster

○ Hornsea Pottery

○ Blackpool Pleasure Beach
○ Blackpool Tower

○ Tropical World

○ Leeds

Wolds Way

Lincolnshire Wolds

○ Pleasureland Southport

Peak District

Clumber Park
Worksop

Anglesey

Castles / Town Walls of King Edward ▲

Clwydian Range

○ Alton Towers

Lleyn

○ Drayton Manor Park

Sherwood Forest County Park

Snowdonia

Ironbridge Gorge ▲

○ Sandwell Country Park

Shropshire Hills

Norfolk Coast

Thetford Forest Park

Peddars Way and Norfolk Coast Path

○ Pleasure Beach Great Yarmouth

The Broads

Malvern Hills

Pembrokeshire Coast

Brecon Beacons

Wye Valley

Offa's Dyke Path

Blenheim Palace ▲

Cotswolds

Dedham Vale

Suffolk Coast and Heaths

Gower

Chilterns

Ridge Way

Waltham Abbey ○

1. 2.

○ Westminster Palace / Abbey
○ ▲ Tower of London

3.

Canterbury Cathedral ▲

Pembrokeshire Coast Path

Bath ○

North Wessex Downs

Surrey Hills

N. Downs Way

Kent Downs

Mendip Hills

▲ Stonehenge / Avebury

E. Hampshire

High Weald

Exmoor

Quantock Hills

Sussex Downs

S. Downs Way

Dorset

Isle of Wight

○ Palace Pier Brighton

Dartmoor

South West Peninsula Path

Isles of Scilly

1. Thorpe Park
2. Hampton Court
3. Chessington World of Adventures

LONDON

- Madame Tussauds
- British Museum
- St Paul's Cathedral
- Tower of London
- National Gallery
- Science Museum
- Victoria and Albert Museum
- Natural History Museum
- Westminster Abbey
- Tate Gallery

2 HOLIDAYS IN UK

No data

Region in which U.K. residents spent holidays, 1993 (by tourist board region)

%
- 15 or over
- 10-14
- 5-9
- under 5

VISITORS TO UK, 1993

thousands

3000
2500
2000
1500
1000
500
0

USA
France
Germany
Ireland
Belgium
Italy
Spain
Canada
Australia
Japan

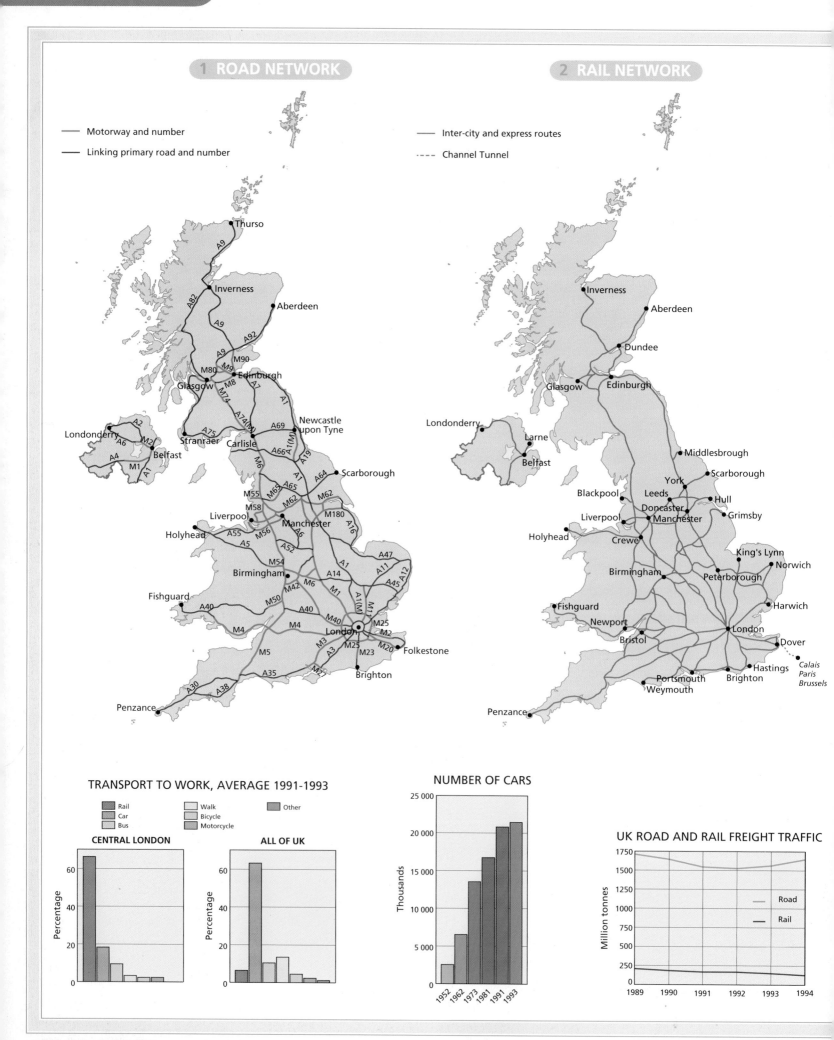

1 ROAD NETWORK

Motorway and number

Linking primary road and number

2 RAIL NETWORK

Inter-city and express routes

Channel Tunnel

TRANSPORT TO WORK, AVERAGE 1991-1993

Rail
Car
Bus
Walk
Bicycle
Motorcycle
Other

CENTRAL LONDON

ALL OF UK

NUMBER OF CARS

UK ROAD AND RAIL FREIGHT TRAFFIC

Road
Rail

SCALE 1 : 8 000 000

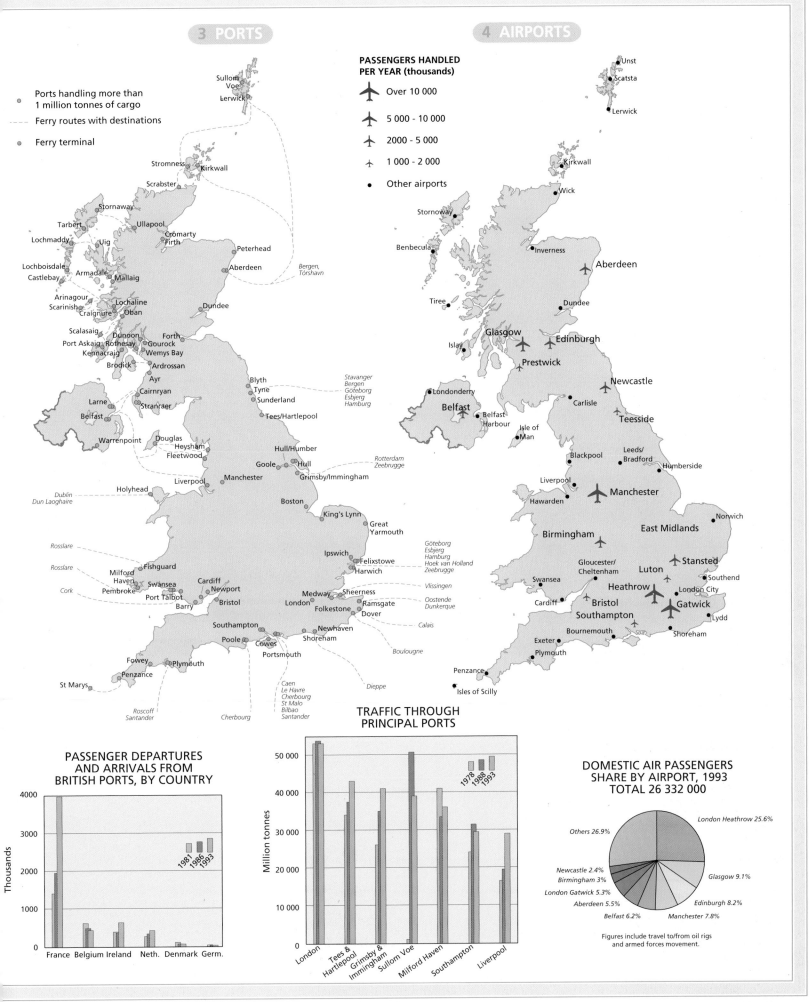

3 PORTS

4 AIRPORTS

Ports handling more than
1 million tonnes of cargo

Ferry routes with destinations

Ferry terminal

**PASSENGERS HANDLED
PER YEAR (thousands)**

Over 10 000

5 000 - 10 000

2000 - 5 000

1 000 - 2 000

Other airports

PASSENGER DEPARTURES
AND ARRIVALS FROM
BRITISH PORTS, BY COUNTRY

1981
1986
1993

Thousands

4000
3000
2000
1000
0

France   Belgium Ireland   Neth.   Denmark Germ.

TRAFFIC THROUGH
PRINCIPAL PORTS

1978
1988
1993

Million tonnes

50 000
40 000
30 000
20 000
10 000
0

London   Tees & Hartlepool   Grimsby & Immingham   Sullom Voe   Milford Haven   Southampton   Liverpool

DOMESTIC AIR PASSENGERS
SHARE BY AIRPORT, 1993
TOTAL 26 332 000

London Heathrow 25.6%
Others 26.9%
Newcastle 2.4%
Birmingham 3%
London Gatwick 5.3%
Aberdeen 5.5%
Belfast 6.2%
Manchester 7.8%
Edinburgh 8.2%
Glasgow 9.1%

Figures include travel to/from oil rigs
and armed forces movement.

Conic projection

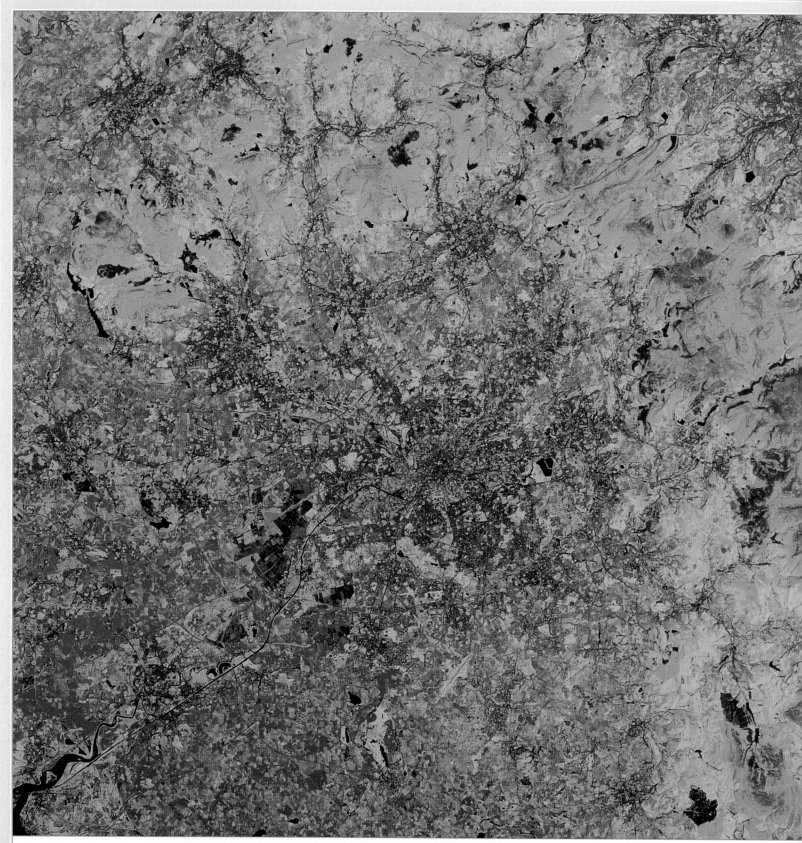

Highland

The blue/green colour corresponds to grassland over 300 metres above sea level on the map opposite. In the higher areas of the Pennines the colour becomes greener as grassland changes to moorland, for example around Shining Tor.

Lowland and arable land

The areas around Manchester appear as shades of orange and red. The cultivated areas near the river Mersey are redder.

Built up area

These areas are dark blue on the satellite image. The largest area is the Manchester urban sprawl. In the top left of the image the built up areas of Blackburn and Accrington stand out from the surrounding farmland.

Woodland

Some areas of woodland can be seen on the lower slopes of Shining Tor. There is also a small area near Alderley Edge.

Reservoir

The small distinctive shape of these can be seen in the Pennines area. Examples are Watergrove Reservoir near Whitworth and Errwood Reservoir south of Whaley Bridge.

Canal

The straight line of the Manchester Ship Canal can be seen running alongside the winding course of the river Mersey.

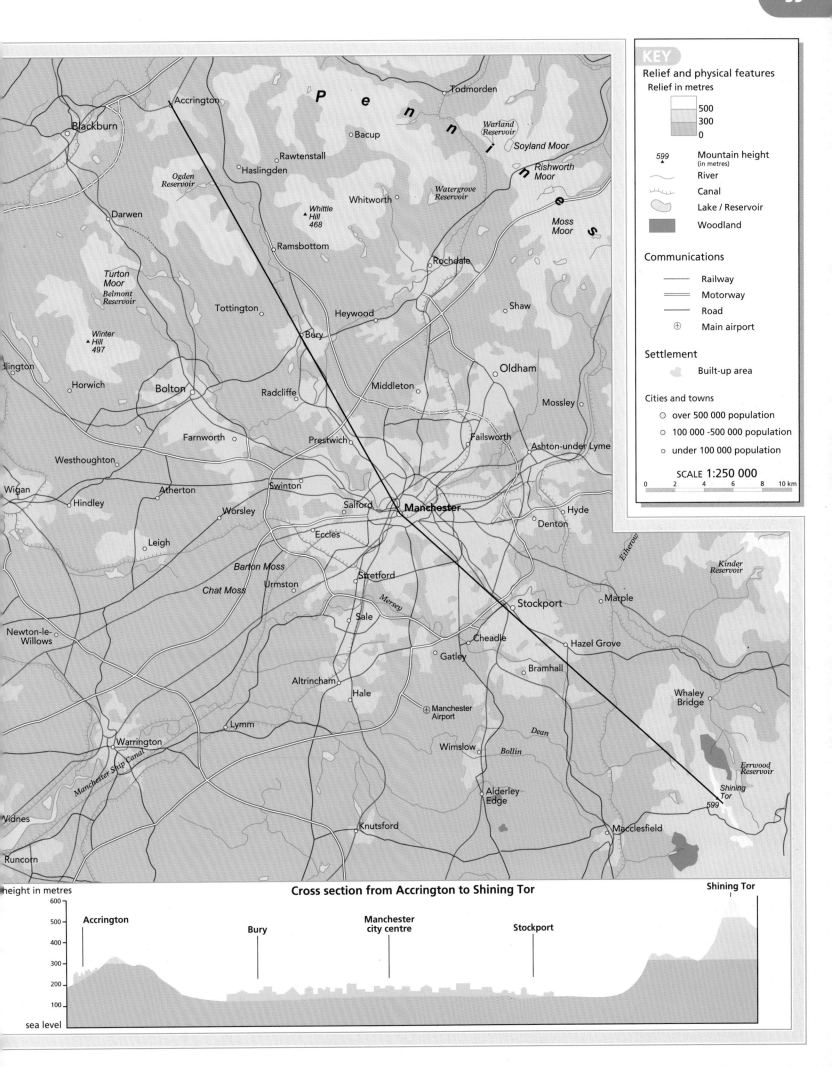

Relief and physical features
Relief in metres

	500
	300
	0

599 ▲ Mountain height (in metres)

River

Canal

Lake / Reservoir

Woodland

Communications

————— Railway

═══════ Motorway

————— Road

⊕ Main airport

Settlement

Built-up area

Cities and towns

○ over 500 000 population

○ 100 000 -500 000 population

○ under 100 000 population

SCALE 1:250 000

0 2 4 6 8 10 km

Cross section from Accrington to Shining Tor

Accrington — Bury — Manchester city centre — Stockport — Shining Tor

height in metres: 600, 500, 400, 300, 200, 100, sea level

Relief

Relief metres
5000
3000
2000
1000
500
200
sea level
0
200
4000
6000
under sea level

Ice cap

0 200 400 600 800 km

Faxaflói

Arctic Circle

Húnaflói

Vestmannaeyjar *Fontur*

Snaefell
1833

Vatnajökull

Iceland

Jan Mayen

A T L A N T I C   O C E A N

Norwegian Sea

North Cape
Sørøya
marijärvi

Lofoten Vesterålen
Vestfjorden

Scandinavia Lappland
Lule
Kemi
Ume
Indals

Gulf of Bothnia

Åland

Gulf Of Finland
Hiiumaa
Saaremaa
Gulf of
Riga
Lake
Peipus

Faeroes

Shetland

Orkney
Outer Hebrides

Ben Nevis
1344

British
Isles

North
Sea

Vänern
Mälaren
Vättern
Gotland
Öland
Bornholm
Baltic Sea

Skagerrak
Kattegat
Sjaelland
Fyn

Malin Head
Donegal Bay
Galway Bay
Shannon
Ireland
Cape Clear
St George's Channel

Snowdon
1085
Great
Britain
Pennines
Irish Sea

The Wash

NORTH EUROP
Pripet
Marshes

Weser Elbe Vistula Bug
Frisian Is
Ijsselmeer
Maas
Elbe Oder Warta
Vistula
Ore Mts
Sudeten Mts
Dniester

Land's End
Isles of
Scilly

English Channel
Channel Islands

Strait of Dover

Seine
Marne
Ardennes
Moselle
Rhine
Taunus
Bohemian Forest

Brittany

B a y   o f
B i s c a y

Gulf of
Gascony

Loire
Vienne
Seine
Allier
Saône
Jura
L. Geneva
Mont Blanc
4808
Matterhorn
4478

Rhine
Danube
Bodensee
Inn
Vosges
A L P S

Danube
Gross Glockner
3798

Carpathian Mts

Balaton
Tisza
Hungarian Plain

Mt Dore
1885
Gironde
Massif
Central

Rhône
Po

Dinaric Alps
Sava

Mures
Transylvanian Alps
Danube

C. Finisterre
Cantabrian Mts
Douro
Duero
Pyrenees
Pico de
Aneto
3404
Ebro
Gulf
of Lions

Gulf of
Genoa
Ligurian
Sea
Côte d'Azur
Corsica

Apennines

A d r i a t i c   S e a

Morava
Balkan Mts
Rhodope Mts

Tagus

C. St. Vicente
Sierra Morena
Guadalquivir
Sierra Nevada

Gulf of
Valencia
Balearic Is
Menorca
Ibiza
Mallorca
Sardinia

Strait of Bonifacio

Vesuvius
1281

Tyrrhenian
Sea

G. of
Taranto

Pindus Mts
Aegean
Evvoia
Sea

Strait of Gibraltar

M E D I T E R R A N E A N

Sicily
Strómboli
Mt Etna
3340
C. Passero

Corfu
Ionian
Sea
Zakynthos
Naxos
Dodeca

High Atlas
Toubkal
4167
Hauts Plateaux
Saharan Atlas

Crete

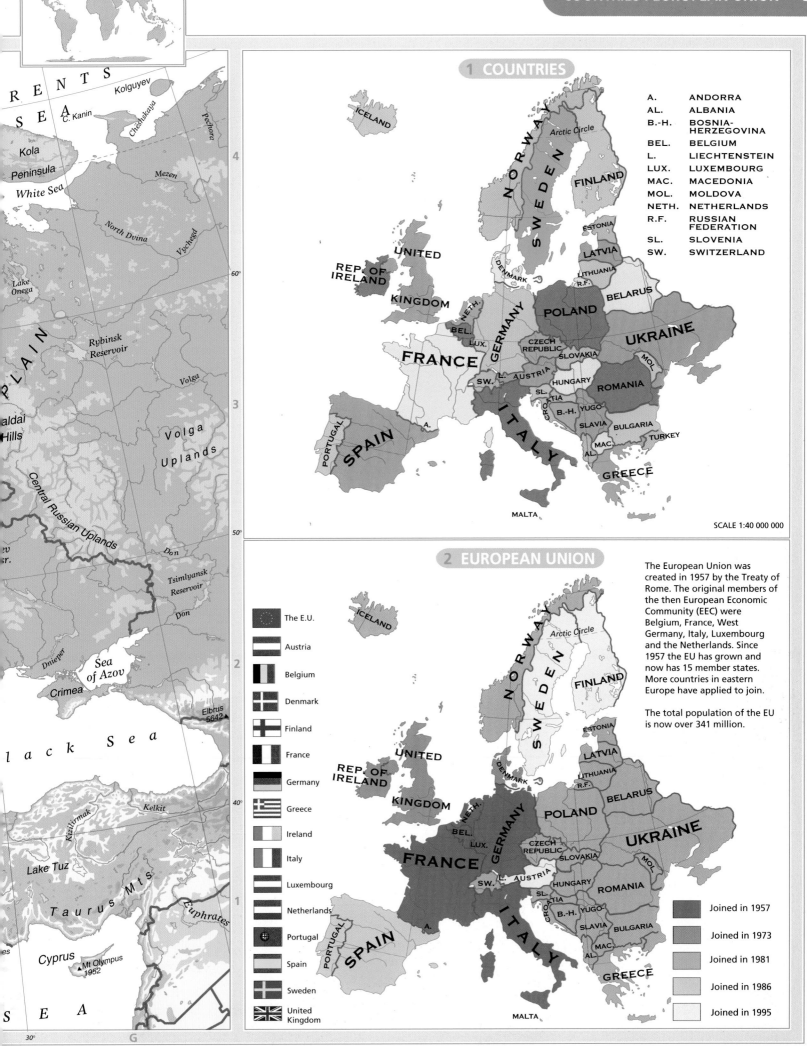

1 COUNTRIES

A.	ANDORRA
AL.	ALBANIA
B.-H.	BOSNIA-HERZEGOVINA
BEL.	BELGIUM
L.	LIECHTENSTEIN
LUX.	LUXEMBOURG
MAC.	MACEDONIA
MOL.	MOLDOVA
NETH.	NETHERLANDS
R.F.	RUSSIAN FEDERATION
SL.	SLOVENIA
SW.	SWITZERLAND

SCALE 1:40 000 000

2 EUROPEAN UNION

The European Union was created in 1957 by the Treaty of Rome. The original members of the then European Economic Community (EEC) were Belgium, France, West Germany, Italy, Luxembourg and the Netherlands. Since 1957 the EU has grown and now has 15 member states. More countries in eastern Europe have applied to join.

The total population of the EU is now over 341 million.

The E.U.
Austria
Belgium
Denmark
Finland
France
Germany
Greece
Ireland
Italy
Luxembourg
Netherlands
Portugal
Spain
Sweden
United Kingdom

Joined in 1957
Joined in 1973
Joined in 1981
Joined in 1986
Joined in 1995

Albers Equal Area Conic projection

Conic projection

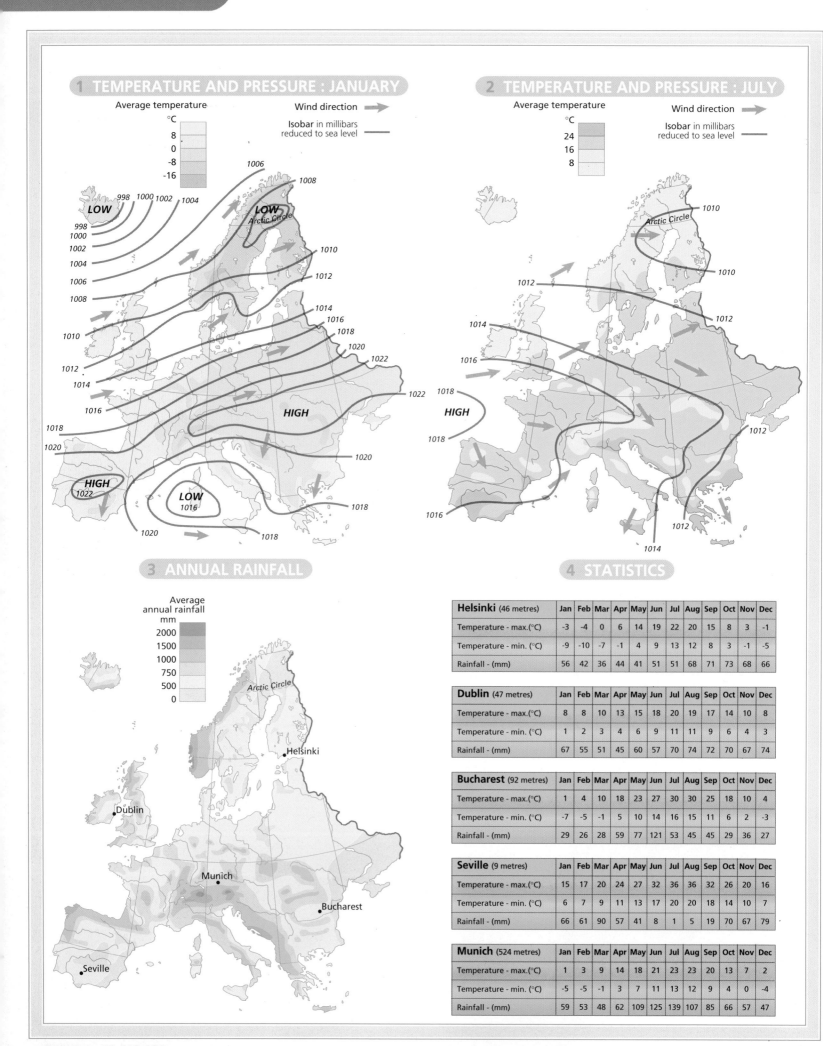

1 TEMPERATURE AND PRESSURE : JANUARY

Average temperature

°C
8
0
-8
-16

Wind direction ➡

Isobar in millibars
reduced to sea level ─────

2 TEMPERATURE AND PRESSURE : JULY

Average temperature

°C
24
16
8

Wind direction ➡

Isobar in millibars
reduced to sea level ─────

3 ANNUAL RAINFALL

Average
annual rainfall
mm
2000
1500
1000
750
500
0

4 STATISTICS

Helsinki (46 metres)	Jan	Feb	Mar	Apr	May	Jun	Jul	Aug	Sep	Oct	Nov	Dec
Temperature - max.(°C)	-3	-4	0	6	14	19	22	20	15	8	3	-1
Temperature - min. (°C)	-9	-10	-7	-1	4	9	13	12	8	3	-1	-5
Rainfall - (mm)	56	42	36	44	41	51	51	68	71	73	68	66

Dublin (47 metres)	Jan	Feb	Mar	Apr	May	Jun	Jul	Aug	Sep	Oct	Nov	Dec
Temperature - max.(°C)	8	8	10	13	15	18	20	19	17	14	10	8
Temperature - min. (°C)	1	2	3	4	6	9	11	11	9	6	4	3
Rainfall - (mm)	67	55	51	45	60	57	70	74	72	70	67	74

Bucharest (92 metres)	Jan	Feb	Mar	Apr	May	Jun	Jul	Aug	Sep	Oct	Nov	Dec
Temperature - max.(°C)	1	4	10	18	23	27	30	30	25	18	10	4
Temperature - min. (°C)	-7	-5	-1	5	10	14	16	15	11	6	2	-3
Rainfall - (mm)	29	26	28	59	77	121	53	45	45	29	36	27

Seville (9 metres)	Jan	Feb	Mar	Apr	May	Jun	Jul	Aug	Sep	Oct	Nov	Dec
Temperature - max.(°C)	15	17	20	24	27	32	36	36	32	26	20	16
Temperature - min. (°C)	6	7	9	11	13	17	20	20	18	14	10	7
Rainfall - (mm)	66	61	90	57	41	8	1	5	19	70	67	79

Munich (524 metres)	Jan	Feb	Mar	Apr	May	Jun	Jul	Aug	Sep	Oct	Nov	Dec
Temperature - max.(°C)	1	3	9	14	18	21	23	23	20	13	7	2
Temperature - min. (°C)	-5	-5	-1	3	7	11	13	12	9	4	0	-4
Rainfall - (mm)	59	53	48	62	109	125	139	107	85	66	57	47

SCALE 1 : 40 000 000

Conic projection

1 POPULATION DENSITY

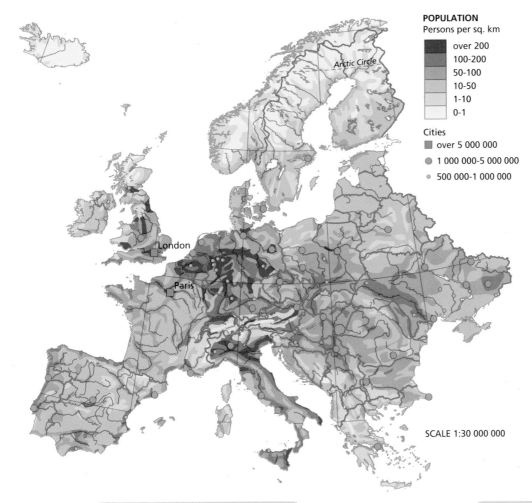

POPULATION
Persons per sq. km

- over 200
- 100-200
- 50-100
- 10-50
- 1-10
- 0-1

Cities

- over 5 000 000
- 1 000 000-5 000 000
- 500 000-1 000 000

London

Paris

Arctic Circle

SCALE 1:30 000 000

2 POPULATION TABLE

Country	% Change 1990-1995	Life expectancy (years) 1990-1995
Albania	0.9	72
Austria	0.67	76
Belarus	-0.14	70
Belgium	0.32	76
Bosnia-Herzegovina	-4.39	72
Bulgaria	-0.5	71
Croatia	-0.1	71
Czech Republic	-0.02	71
Denmark	0.16	75
Estonia	-0.58	69
Finland	0.48	76
France	0.44	77
Germany	0.55	76
Greece	0.41	78
Hungary	-0.49	69
Iceland	1.06	78
Italy	0.06	77
Latvia	-0.87	69
Lithuania	-0.06	70
Luxembourg	1.26	76
Macedonia	1.11	
Malta	0.67	76
Moldova	0.32	68
Netherlands	0.72	77
Norway	0.45	77
Poland	0.14	71
Portugal	0.09	75
Republic of Ireland	0.28	75
Romania	-0.32	70
Slovakia	0.36	71
Slovenia	0.29	73
Spain	0.18	78
Sweden	0.51	78
Switzerland	1.05	78
Ukraine	-0.1	69
United Kingdom	0.29	76
Yugoslavia	1.32	72

3 POPULATION UNDER 15

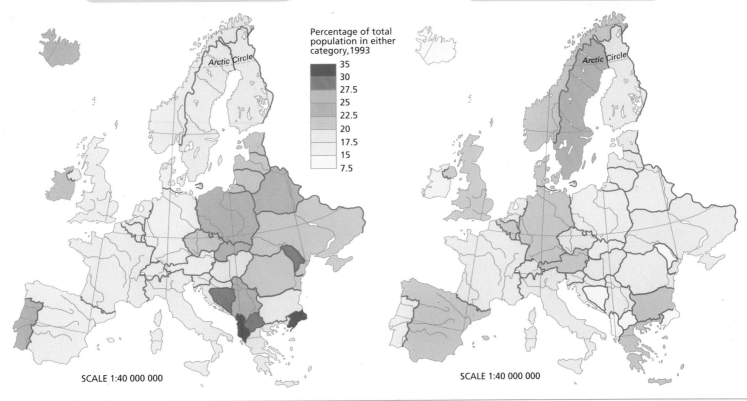

Arctic Circle

Percentage of total population in either category, 1993

- 35
- 30
- 27.5
- 25
- 22.5
- 20
- 17.5
- 15
- 7.5

SCALE 1:40 000 000

4 POPULATION OVER 60

Arctic Circle

SCALE 1:40 000 000

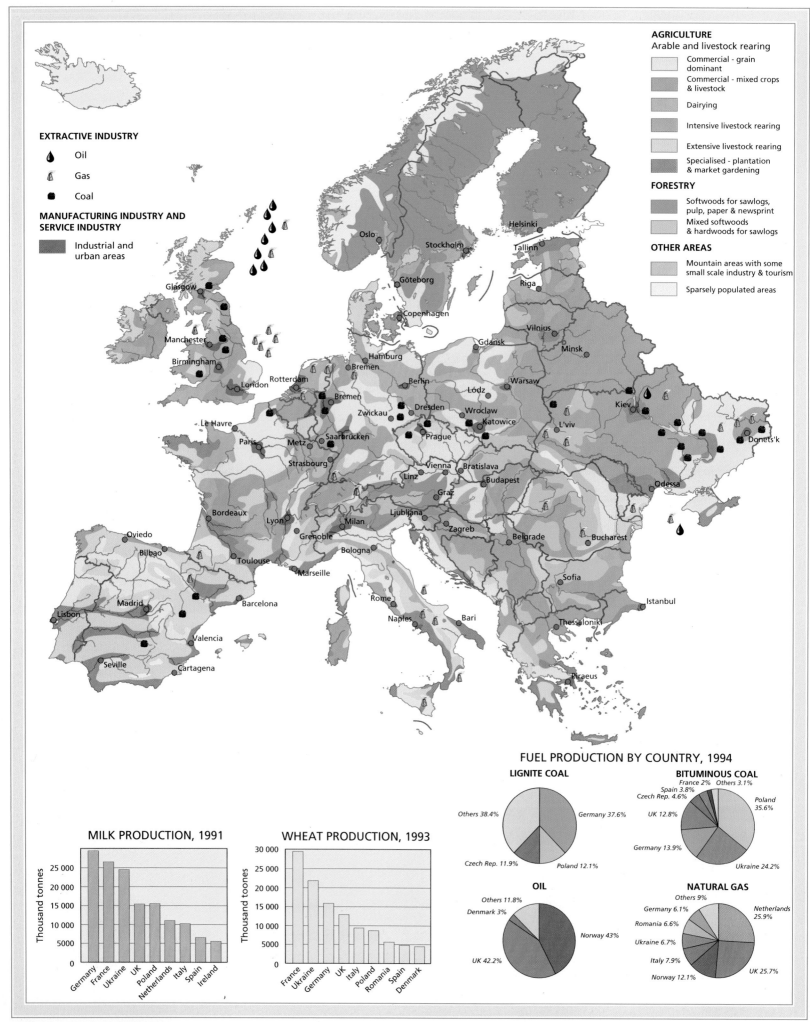

EXTRACTIVE INDUSTRY

- Oil
- Gas
- Coal

MANUFACTURING INDUSTRY AND SERVICE INDUSTRY

Industrial and urban areas

AGRICULTURE
Arable and livestock rearing

- Commercial - grain dominant
- Commercial - mixed crops & livestock
- Dairying
- Intensive livestock rearing
- Extensive livestock rearing
- Specialised - plantation & market gardening

FORESTRY

- Softwoods for sawlogs, pulp, paper & newsprint
- Mixed softwoods & hardwoods for sawlogs

OTHER AREAS

- Mountain areas with some small scale industry & tourism
- Sparsely populated areas

FUEL PRODUCTION BY COUNTRY, 1994

LIGNITE COAL
- Others 38.4%
- Germany 37.6%
- Czech Rep. 11.9%
- Poland 12.1%

BITUMINOUS COAL
- France 2%
- Others 3.1%
- Spain 3.8%
- Czech Rep. 4.6%
- UK 12.8%
- Poland 35.6%
- Germany 13.9%
- Ukraine 24.2%

OIL
- Others 11.8%
- Denmark 3%
- Norway 43%
- UK 42.2%

NATURAL GAS
- Others 9%
- Germany 6.1%
- Netherlands 25.9%
- Romania 6.6%
- Ukraine 6.7%
- Italy 7.9%
- Norway 12.1%
- UK 25.7%

MILK PRODUCTION, 1991

Thousand tonnes

Germany, France, Ukraine, UK, Poland, Netherlands, Italy, Spain, Ireland

WHEAT PRODUCTION, 1993

Thousand toones

France, Ukraine, Germany, UK, Italy, Poland, Romania, Spain, Denmark

SCALE 1 : 20 000 000

Albers equal area conic projection

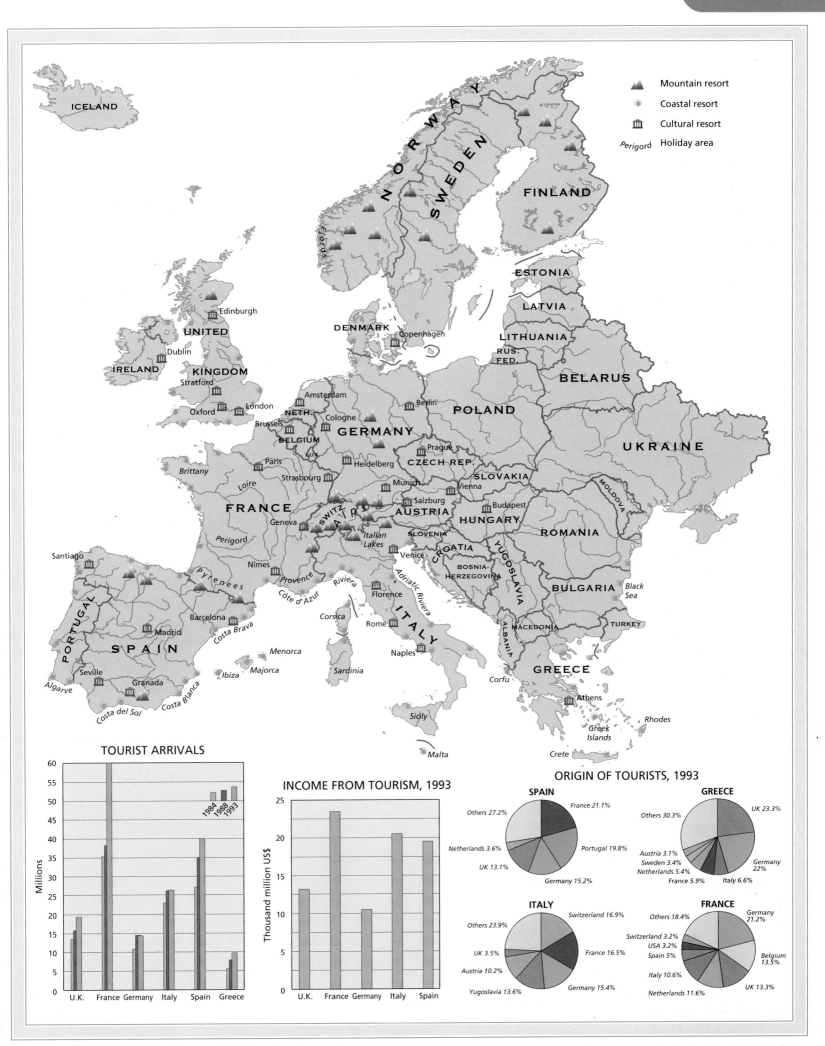

ICELAND

NORWAY
SWEDEN
FINLAND

ESTONIA
LATVIA
LITHUANIA
RUS. FED.
BELARUS

DENMARK
Copenhagen

UNITED
KINGDOM
Edinburgh
Dublin
IRELAND
Stratford
Oxford
London

Amsterdam
NETH.
Cologne
Brussels
BELGIUM
LUX.
Paris
Strasbourg

Berlin
POLAND

GERMANY
Prague
CZECH REP.
Heidelberg

Munich
Salzburg
SWITZ. ALPS
Geneva
Italian Lakes
SLOVENIA

Vienna
AUSTRIA
Budapest
HUNGARY

SLOVAKIA
MOLDOVA

UKRAINE

Brittany
Loire
FRANCE
Perigord
Nimes
Provence
Côte d'Azur
Riviera

CROATIA
YUGOSLAVIA
BOSNIA-
HERZEGOVINA

ROMANIA

BULGARIA
Black Sea

Santiago
PORTUGAL
Pyrenees
Barcelona
Madrid
SPAIN
Seville
Granada
Algarve
Costa del Sol
Costa Blanca

Menorca
Majorca
Ibiza
Corsica
Sardinia

Adriatic Riviera
Venice
Florence
ITALY
Rome
Naples

Corfu
GREECE
Athens
Rhodes
Greek Islands
Crete

MACEDONIA
ALBANIA
TURKEY

Sicily
Malta

Legend
▲ Mountain resort
● Coastal resort
🏛 Cultural resort
Perigord Holiday area

TOURIST ARRIVALS

Millions — 0 to 60

1984 1988 1993

U.K. France Germany Italy Spain Greece

INCOME FROM TOURISM, 1993

Thousand million US$ — 0 to 25

U.K. France Germany Italy Spain

ORIGIN OF TOURISTS, 1993

SPAIN
France 21.1%
Portugal 19.8%
Germany 15.2%
UK 13.1%
Netherlands 3.6%
Others 27.2%

GREECE
UK 23.3%
Germany 22%
Italy 6.6%
France 5.9%
Netherlands 5.4%
Sweden 3.4%
Austria 3.1%
Others 30.3%

ITALY
Switzerland 16.9%
France 16.5%
Germany 15.4%
Yugoslavia 13.6%
Austria 10.2%
UK 3.5%
Others 23.9%

FRANCE
Germany 21.2%
Belgium 13.5%
UK 13.3%
Netherlands 11.6%
Italy 10.6%
Spain 5%
USA 3.2%
Switzerland 3.2%
Others 18.4%

SCALE 1 : 20 000 000

Albers equal area conic projection

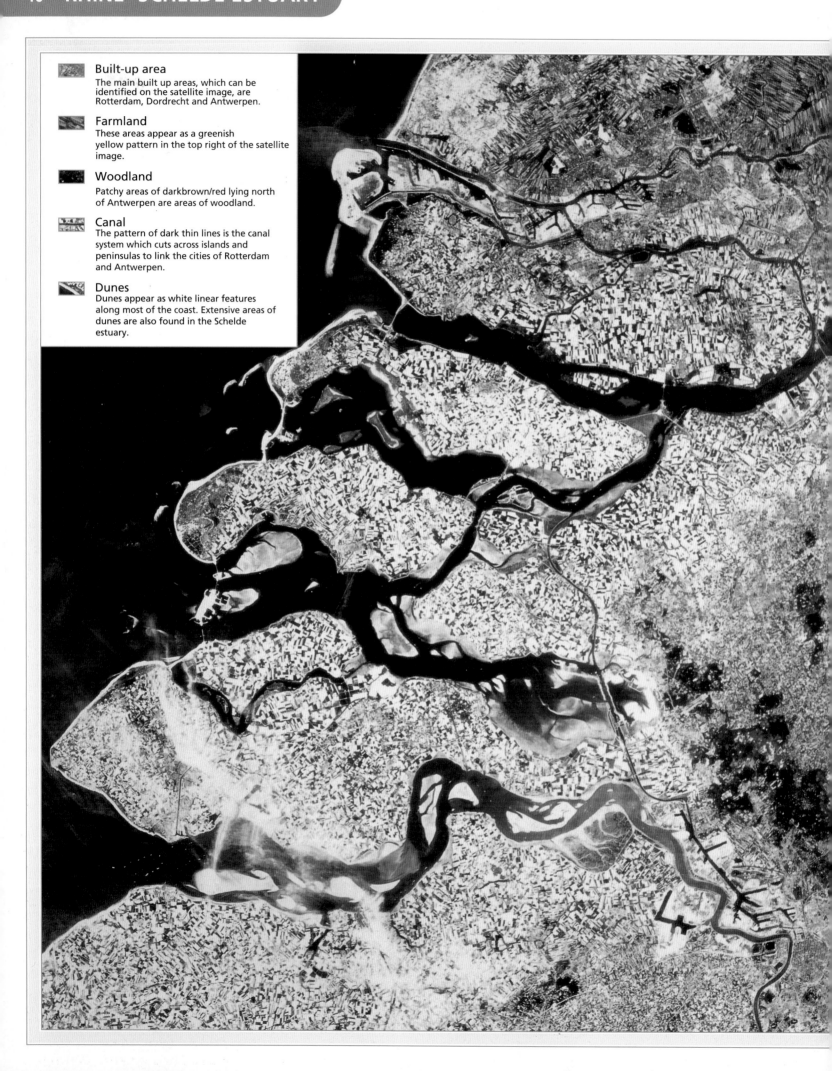

Built-up area
The main built up areas, which can be identified on the satellite image, are Rotterdam, Dordrecht and Antwerpen.

Farmland
These areas appear as a greenish yellow pattern in the top right of the satellite image.

Woodland
Patchy areas of darkbrown/red lying north of Antwerpen are areas of woodland.

Canal
The pattern of dark thin lines is the canal system which cuts across islands and peninsulas to link the cities of Rotterdam and Antwerpen.

Dunes
Dunes appear as white linear features along most of the coast. Extensive areas of dunes are also found in the Schelde estuary.

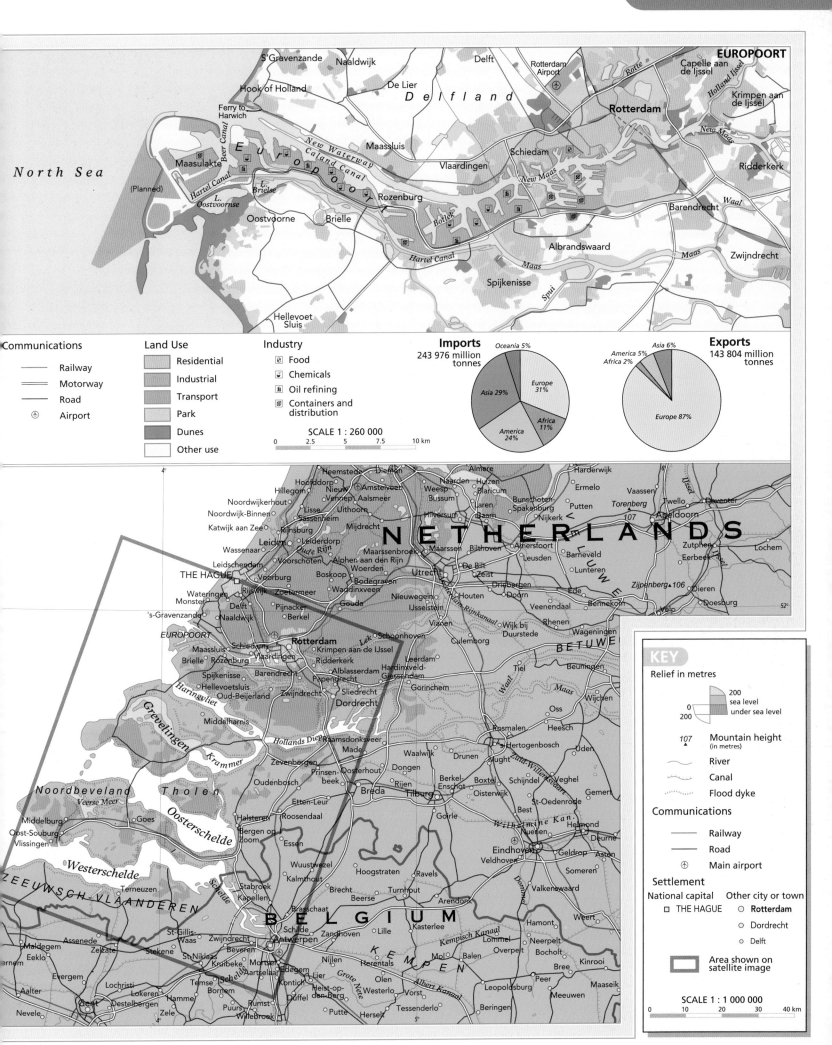

EUROPOORT

North Sea

S'Gravenzande
Naaldwijk
Delft
Rotterdam Airport
Capelle aan de Ijssel
Holland Ijssel
Hook of Holland
De Lier
Delfland
Rotterdam
Krimpen aan de Ijssel
Ferry to Harwich
Beer Canal
New Waterway
Caland Canal
Maassluis
New Maas
Schiedam
New Maas
Ridderkerk
Maasvlakte
Europoort
Vlaardingen
L. Brielse
Hartel Canal
Rozenburg
Botlek
New Maas
Barendrecht
Waal
(Planned)
L. Oostvoorne
Oostvoorne
Brielle
Maas
Albrandswaard
Zwijndrecht
Hartel Canal
Maas
Spijkenisse
Spui
Hellevoet Sluis

Communications

— Railway
═══ Motorway
— Road
✈ Airport

Land Use

Residential
Industrial
Transport
Park
Dunes
Other use

Industry

⊡ Food
⊡ Chemicals
⊡ Oil refining
⊡ Containers and distribution

SCALE 1 : 260 000

0   2.5   5   7.5   10 km

Imports
243 976 million tonnes

Oceania 5%
Europe 31%
Asia 29%
Africa 11%
America 24%

Exports
143 804 million tonnes

America 5%
Africa 2%
Asia 6%
Europe 87%

4°

Heemstede   Diemen   Almere   Harderwijk
Hoofddorp   Naarden   Huizen   Ermelo   Vaassen
Hillegom   Nieuw   Amstelveen   Weesp   Blaricum   Bunschoten-Spakenburg   Putten   *Torenberg*   Twello   Deventer
Noordwijkerhout   Lisse   Vennep   Aalsmeer   Bussum   Laren   Nijkerk   107   Apeldoorn
Noordwijk-Binnen   Sassenheim   Uithoorn   Hilversum   Baarn   Amersfoort   *VELUWE*   Zutphen   Lochem
Katwijk aan Zee   Rijnsburg   Mijdrecht   Maarssenbroek   Maarssen   Bilthoven   Barneveld   Lunteren   Eerbeek
Leiden   Leiderdorp   *Oude Rijn*   Alphen aan den Rijn   De Bilt   Leusden   Ede   *Zijpenberg▲106*   Dieren
Wassenaar   Voorschoten   Woerden   Utrecht   Zeist   Driebergen   Doorn   Bennekom   Velp   Doesburg
Leidschendam   Voorburg   Boskoop   Waddinxveen   Nieuwegein   Houten   Veenendaal   Rhenen   Wageningen
THE HAGUE   Rijswijk   Zoetermeer   Gouda   IJsselstein   Wijk bij Duurstede   *BETUWE*
Wateringen   Delft   Pijnacker   Berkel   Vianen   Culemborg   Tiel   Beuningen
Monster   Naaldwijk   Schoonhoven   *Lek*   Leerdam
's-Gravenzande   *EUROPOORT*   **Rotterdam**   Krimpen aan de IJssel   Hardinxveld-Giessendam   *Waal*   Wijchen
Maassluis   Schiedam   Ridderkerk   Gorinchem   Oss
Brielle   Rozenburg   Vlaardingen   Alblasserdam   Papendrecht   Rosmalen   Heesch
Spijkenisse   Barendrecht   Sliedrecht   Dordrecht   Hertogenbosch   Uden
Haringvliet   Hellevoetsluis   Oud-Beijerland   Zwijndrecht   Drunen   Vught
Grevelingen   Middelharnis   *Hollands Diep*   Raamsdonksveer   Waalwijk   Dongen   Berkel-Enschot   Boxtel   Schijndel   Veghel
Krammer   Made   Oosterhout   Rijen   Oisterwijk   St-Oedenrode   Gemert
Noordbeveland   *Veerse Meer*   Zevenbergen   Prinsenbeek   Tilburg   Best   Helmond
Tholen   Oudenbosch   Etten-Leur   Breda   Goirle   *Wilhelmina Kan.*   Nuenen   Deurne
Middelburg   Goes   Halsteren   Roosendaal   Geldrop   Asten
Oost-Souburg   *Oosterschelde*   Bergen op Zoom   Essen   Eindhoven   Someren
Vlissingen   Wuustwezel   Hoogstraten   Ravels   Veldhoven   Weert
Westerschelde   Kalmthout   Turnhout   Arendonk   Valkenswaard
ZEEUWSCH-VLAANDEREN   Terneuzen   Brecht   Beerse   *KEMPEN*   Hamont
Stabroek   Kapellen   Wuustwezel   *Kempisch Kanaal*   Lommel   Neerpelt   Bocholt
St-Gillis-Waas   Zwijndrecht   Schilde   Zandhoven   Lille   Mol   Overpelt
Assenede   Zelzate   Stekene   St-Niklaas   Brasschaat   Balen   Maaseik
Maldegem   Eeklo   **Antwerpen**   **BELGIUM**   Kasterlee   Leopoldsburg   Peer   Kinrooi
Evergem   Lochristi   Kruibeke   Mortsel   Nijlen   Herentals   Olen   Westerlo   Vorst   Meeuwen
Aalter   Lokeren   Temse   Bornem   Aartselaar   Edegem   Lier   Heist-op-den-Berg   Grote Nete   *Albert Kanaal*
Nevele   Hamme   Puurs   Rumst   Kontich   Duffel   Herselt   Tessenderlo   Beringen
Destelbergen   Zele   Willebroek   Putte   *Schelde*

KEY

Relief in metres

200
0   sea level
200   under sea level

107   Mountain height (in metres)

River
Canal
Flood dyke

Communications

— Railway
— Road
✈ Main airport

Settlement

National capital   Other city or town
□ THE HAGUE   ⊚ **Rotterdam**
⊚ Dordrecht
⊙ Delft

▭ Area shown on satellite image

SCALE 1 : 1 000 000

0   10   20   30   40 km

Lambert Azimuthal Equal Area projection

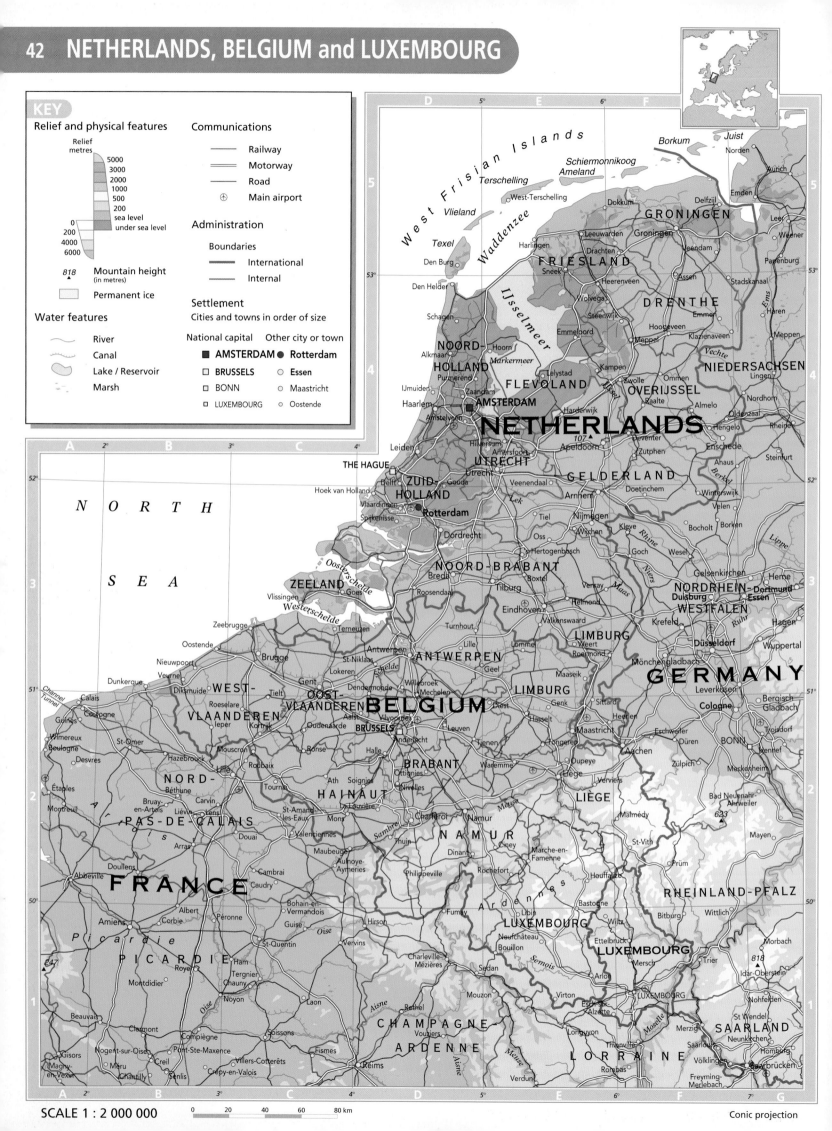

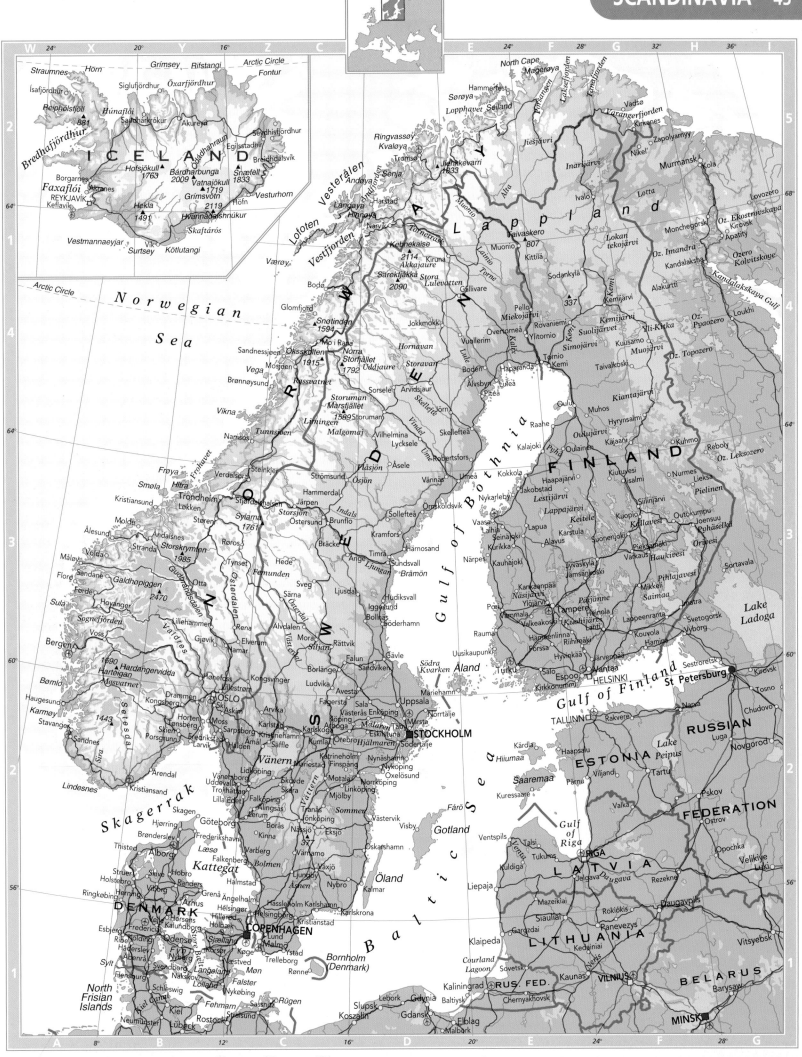

ICELAND

Straumnes · Horn · Grimsey · Rifstangi · Arctic Circle · Fontur
Ísafjördhur · Siglufjördhur · Öxarfjördhur
Reiphólsfjöll · Húnaflói · Saudhárkrókur · Akureyri · Seydhisfjördhur
881 · Egilsstadhir
Borgarnes · Hofsjökull · Bárdharbunga · Snæfell · Breidhdalsvík
Faxaflói · 1763 · 2009 · Vatnajökull · 1833
REYKJAVIK · Akranes · Óládhahraun · 1719
Keflavik · Hekla · Grimsvötn · Höfn
1491 · 2119 · Vesturhorn
Hvannadalshnúkur
Vestmannaeyjar · Surtsey · Vík · Skaftáros
Kötlutangi

Norwegian Sea

Arctic Circle

ICELAND

SCALE 1 : 7 500 000

Conic projection

KEY

Relief and physical features

Relief
metres
5000
3000
2000
1000
500
200
sea level
under sea level
200
4000
6000

4808 ▲ Mountain height
(in metres)

Permanent ice

Water features

～ River
～ Intermittent river
～ Canal
Lake / Reservoir
Marsh

Communications

— Railway
= Motorway
— Road
⊕ Main airport

Administration

Boundaries
—— International

Settlement

Cities and towns in order of size

National capital
■ PARIS
□ BERNE
□ ANDORRA
LA VELLA

Other city or town
● Lyon
○ Stuttgart
○ St-Etienne
○ Roscoff

SCALE 1 : 5 000 000

0   50   100   150   200 km

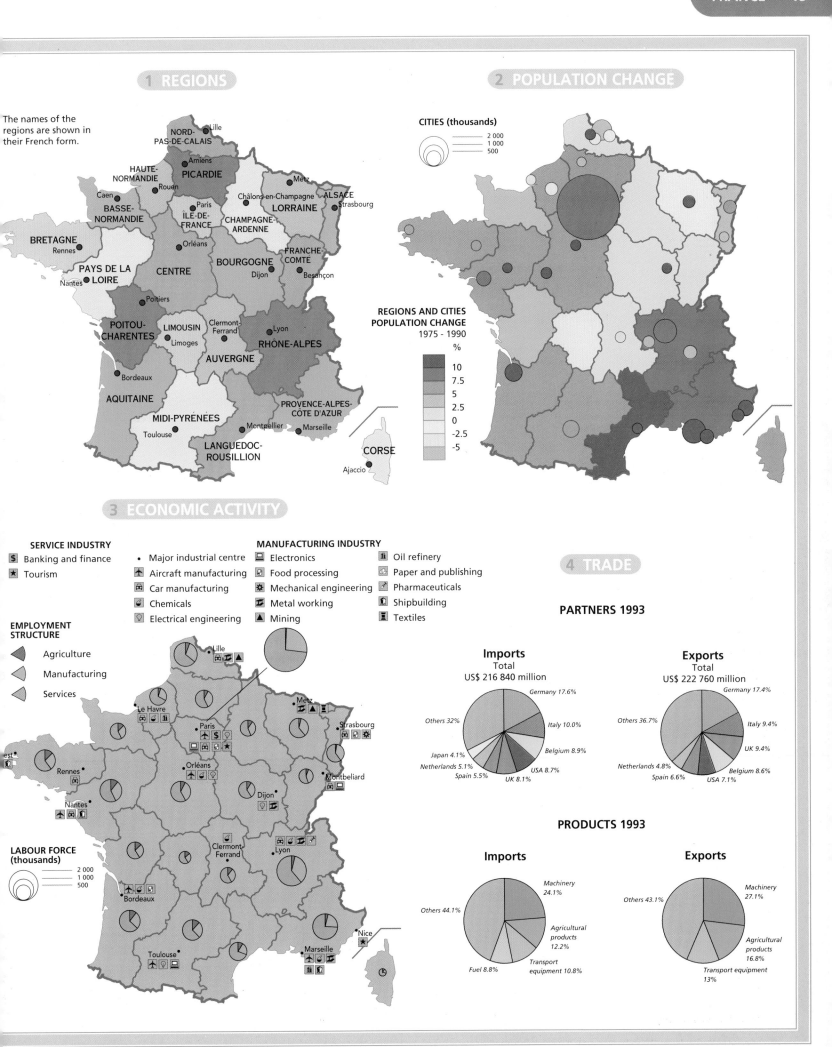

1 REGIONS

The names of the regions are shown in their French form.

NORD-PAS-DE-CALAIS • Lille
• Amiens
PICARDIE
HAUTE-NORMANDIE
• Rouen
• Caen
BASSE-NORMANDIE
• Metz
Châlons-en-Champagne
ALSACE
LORRAINE
• Strasbourg
ÎLE-DE-FRANCE
• Paris
CHAMPAGNE-ARDENNE
BRETAGNE
• Rennes
• Orléans
CENTRE
BOURGOGNE
• Dijon
FRANCHE-COMTÉ
• Besançon
PAYS DE LA LOIRE
• Nantes
• Poitiers
POITOU-CHARENTES
LIMOUSIN
• Limoges
Clermont-Ferrand
• Lyon
RHÔNE-ALPES
AUVERGNE
• Bordeaux
AQUITAINE
MIDI-PYRÉNÉES
• Toulouse
• Montpellier
PROVENCE-ALPES-CÔTE D'AZUR
• Marseille
LANGUEDOC-ROUSILLION
CORSE
• Ajaccio

2 POPULATION CHANGE

CITIES (thousands)

2 000
1 000
500

REGIONS AND CITIES POPULATION CHANGE
1975 - 1990
%

10
7.5
5
2.5
0
-2.5
-5

3 ECONOMIC ACTIVITY

SERVICE INDUSTRY
$ Banking and finance
★ Tourism

MANUFACTURING INDUSTRY
• Major industrial centre
✈ Aircraft manufacturing
🚗 Car manufacturing
🗲 Chemicals
💡 Electrical engineering

▭ Electronics
🍴 Food processing
✳ Mechanical engineering
🗲 Metal working
▲ Mining

Ⅱ Oil refinery
Paper and publishing
Pharmaceuticals
Shipbuilding
Ⅲ Textiles

EMPLOYMENT STRUCTURE
Agriculture
Manufacturing
Services

Lille
Metz
Le Havre
Paris
Strasbourg
Orléans
Montbeliard
Rennes
Nantes
Dijon
Clermont-Ferrand
Lyon
LABOUR FORCE (thousands)

2 000
1 000
500

Bordeaux
Toulouse
Marseille
Nice

4 TRADE

PARTNERS 1993

Imports
Total
US$ 216 840 million

Germany 17.6%
Italy 10.0%
Belgium 8.9%
USA 8.7%
UK 8.1%
Spain 5.5%
Netherlands 5.1%
Japan 4.1%
Others 32%

Exports
Total
US$ 222 760 million

Germany 17.4%
Italy 9.4%
UK 9.4%
Belgium 8.6%
USA 7.1%
Spain 6.6%
Netherlands 4.8%
Others 36.7%

PRODUCTS 1993

Imports

Machinery 24.1%
Agricultural products 12.2%
Transport equipment 10.8%
Fuel 8.8%
Others 44.1%

Exports

Machinery 27.1%
Agricultural products 16.8%
Transport equipment 13%
Others 43.1%

SCALE 1 : 10 000 000

0   100   200   300 km

KEY

Relief and physical features

Relief metres
5000
3000
2000
1000
500
200
sea level
0
200 under sea level
4000
6000

▲ 3482 Mountain height (in metres)

Water features

~ River
··· Intermittent river
~ Canal
◠ Lake / Reservoir
Marsh

Communications

— Railway
≡ Motorway
— Road
⊕ Main airport

Administration

Boundaries
═══ International

Settlement

Cities and towns in order of size

National capital
■ MADRID
□ ANDORRA LA VELLA

Other city or town
● Barcelona
○ Malaga
○ Pamplona
○ Benidorm

SCALE 1 : 5 000 000

0 50 100 150 200 km

Lambert Conformal Conic projection

France inset

FRANCE
Central
Massif
Limousin
Auvergne
Poitiers
Montluçon
Guéret
Bellac
Limoges
Vichy
Clermont-Ferrand
St-Étienne
Périgueux
Tulle
Brive-la-Gaillarde
Figeac
Cahors
Rodez
Mende ▲1699
Villeneuve
Agen
Montauban
Albi
Toulouse
Castres
Montpellier
Béziers
Narbonne
Carcassonne
Perpignan
Gulf of Lions

Main map

Spain
A Coruña, Ferrol, Cervo, Luarca, Avilés, Gijón, Oviedo, Llanes, Santander, Santoña
Gulf of Gascony
Capbreton, Bayonne, Biarritz, San Sebastián, Donostia, Irún
Betanzos, Lugo, CANTABRIAN MTS, Picos de Europa ▲2648, Bilbao, Gexto
Cape Finisterre, Santiago, Sarria, Monforte, León, Espigüete 2450, Reinosa, Aguilar de Campóo, Miranda de Ebro, Vitoria-Gasteiz
Vilagarcía, 2117, 2081
PYRENEES, Pamplona, Oloron, Lourdes, Mont Valier 2838, Pic d'Estats 3141, ANDORRA LA VELLA
Pontevedra, Ourense, Monforte, Astorga, Osorno, Burgos, Logroño, Huesca, Pic de Vignemale, Pico de Aneto 3404, Sa de Guara
Vigo, Tui, Verín, 1415, Bragança, Benavente, Zamora, Palencia, Sa de la Demanda 2262, Soria, Tudela, Monzón, Figueres, Girona, Costa Brava
Viana do Castelo, Braga, Mirandela, Macedo de Cavaleiros, Valladolid, Pisuerga, Duero, Aranda de Duero, Zaragoza, Lleida, Manresa, Vic, Sabadell, Mataró
Oporto, Douro, Vila Real, Lamego, Tordesillas, Medina del Campo, Duero, Calatayud, Jalón, Alcañiz, Reus, Tarragona, Barcelona, Hospitalet de Llobregat, Costa Brava
Aveiro, Viseu, Guarda, Ciudad-Rodrigo, Salamanca, Segovia, Sierra de Guadarrama 2480, Sigüenza, Calamocha, 1201, Gulf of St Jordi
Figueira da Foz, Coimbra, Sa da Estrela 1993, Béjar, Peñaranda de Bracamonte, Ávila, Guadalajara, Serranía de Cuenca 1920, Tortosa
Covilhã, 1205, MADRID, Alcalá de Henares, Arganda del Rey, Cuenca, Castelló de la Plana, Mallorca 1445
Plasencia, Sierra de Gredos, Almanzor, Fuenlabrada, Aranjuez, Tarancón, 2020, Sagunto, Palma de Mallorca
Pombal, Tiétar 2592, Alberche, Talavera de la Reina, Toledo, Júcar, Utiel, Valencia, Gulf of Valencia, Ibiza
Cáceres, Sá de Guadalupe 1601, Montes de Toledo, Alcázar de San Juan, Villarrobledo, Albacete, Cullera, Gandía, C. de la Nao
Navalmoral de la Mata, 1410, Cijara L., Ciudad Real, Manzanares, Almansa, Alcoy, Benidorm, Balearic Islands, Formentera
Portalegre, Valencia de Alcántara, Badajoz, Mérida, Don Benito, Jabalón, Valdepeñas, La Mancha, Hellín, Villena, Elda, Alicante, Costa Blanca
Amadora, LISBON, Elvas, Zafra, Llerena, Pozoblanco, 1300, Sierra de Segura 1897, Elche, Alicante
C. da Roca, Setúbal, Évora, Ardila, Guadiana, SIERRA MORENA, Andújar, Linares, Úbeda, La Sagra 2382, Murcia, Torrevieja
Bay of Setúbal, Sines, Beja, 1104, Cortegana, Córdoba, Guadalquivir, Jaén, Baza, Lorca, Cartagena, C. de Palos
Grândola, Sierra de Aracena, Écija, Puente Genil, Lucena, Alcalá la Real, Guadix, Huércal-Overa, Águilas, MEDITERRANEAN SEA
Almodôvar, Algarve, La Palma del Condado, Seville, Utrera, Osuna, Genil, Loja, Granada, Sierra Nevada, Mulhacén 3482, Almería, C. de Gata
Portimão, Lagos, Huelva, Las Marismas, Morón de la Frontera, Antequera, Vélez-Málaga, Motril
Cape St Vincent, Faro, Tavira, Sanlúcar de Barrameda, Jeréz de la Frontera, Ronda, Almuñecar
Gulf of Cádiz, Cádiz, El Puerto de Santa María, San Fernando, Marbella, Costa del Sol
C. Trafalgar, Algeciras, Gibraltar (UK), La Línea de la Concepción
Strait of Gibraltar, Pta Almina, Ceuta (Sp.), Tangier, C. Negro, I. de Alboran (Sp.)
Tetouan, MOROCCO, Chaouen, Asilah, Larache, Al Hoceima, Melilla (Sp.)

Menorca inset

Menorca
Ciutadella de Menorca
Mahón

Canary Islands inset

La Palma, Sta Cruz de la Palma, 2426, Los Llanos de Aridane, Los Canarios, La Gomera 1487, San Sebastián de la Gomera, El Hierro 1500, Frontera, Valverde, CANARY ISLANDS, San Cristóbal de la Laguna, Puerto de la Cruz, Pico del Teide 3718, Sta Cruz de Tenerife, Tenerife, Gáldar, Las Palmas de Gran Canaria, Pico de las Nieves 1949, Gran Canaria, Ingenio, Tuineje 807, Fuerteventura 724, Corralejo, Lanzarote, Teguise, Arrecife, Graciosa, Haria

1 REGIONS

The names of the regions are shown in their Spanish form.

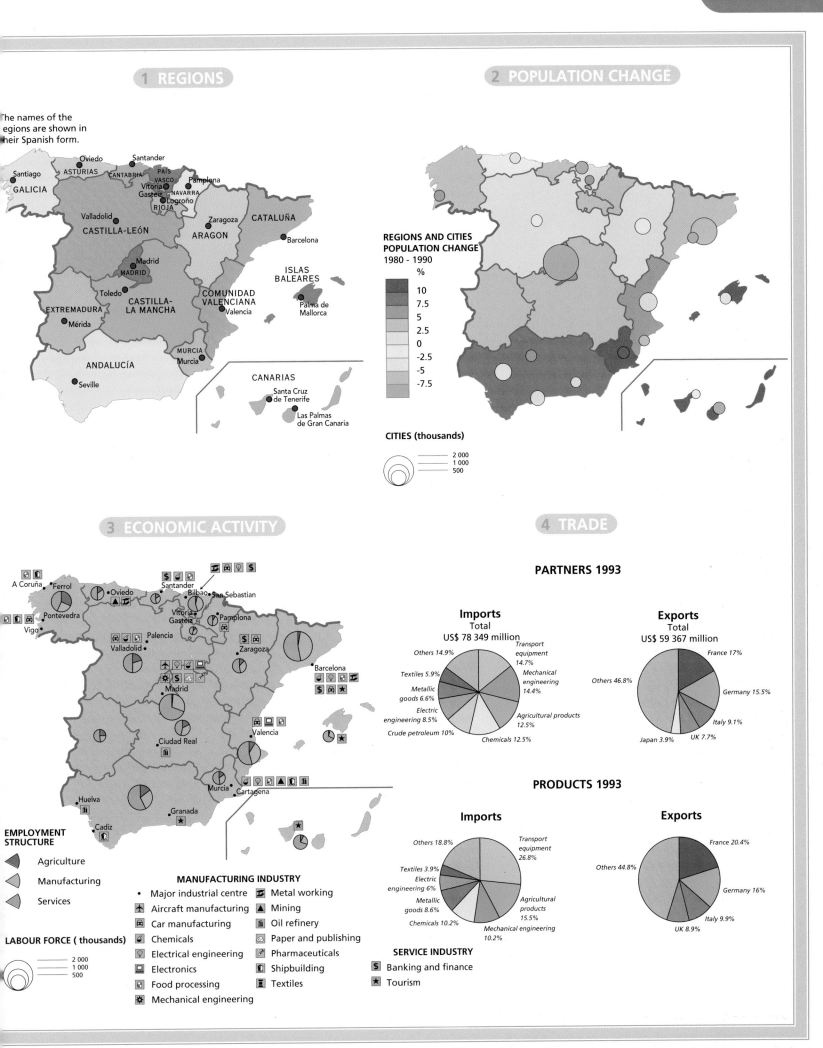

Santiago
GALICIA
Oviedo
ASTURIAS
CANTABRIA
Santander
PAÍS VASCO
Vitoria Gasteiz
Pamplona
NAVARRA
Logroño
RIOJA
Valladolid
CASTILLA-LEÓN
Zaragoza
ARAGON
CATALUÑA
Barcelona
Madrid
MADRID
Toledo
CASTILLA-LA MANCHA
COMUNIDAD VALENCIANA
Valencia
ISLAS BALEARES
Palma de Mallorca
EXTREMADURA
Mérida
MURCIA
Murcia
ANDALUCÍA
Seville

CANARIAS
Santa Cruz de Tenerife
Las Palmas de Gran Canaria

2 POPULATION CHANGE

REGIONS AND CITIES POPULATION CHANGE
1980 - 1990
%
10
7.5
5
2.5
0
-2.5
-5
-7.5

CITIES (thousands)
2 000
1 000
500

3 ECONOMIC ACTIVITY

A Coruña
Ferrol
Santander
Bilbao
San Sebastian
Oviedo
Pontevedra
Vitoria Gasteiz
Pamplona
Vigo
Palencia
Valladolid
Zaragoza
Barcelona
Madrid
Ciudad Real
Valencia
Huelva
Murcia
Cartagena
Granada
Cadiz

EMPLOYMENT STRUCTURE
Agriculture
Manufacturing
Services

LABOUR FORCE (thousands)
2 000
1 000
500

MANUFACTURING INDUSTRY
• Major industrial centre
✈ Aircraft manufacturing
🚗 Car manufacturing
Chemicals
Electrical engineering
Electronics
Food processing
☼ Mechanical engineering
⇄ Metal working
▲ Mining
Oil refinery
Paper and publishing
Pharmaceuticals
Shipbuilding
Textiles

SERVICE INDUSTRY
$ Banking and finance
★ Tourism

4 TRADE

PARTNERS 1993

Imports
Total
US$ 78 349 million

Others 14.9%
Transport equipment 14.7%
Textiles 5.9%
Mechanical engineering 14.4%
Metallic goods 6.6%
Electric engineering 8.5%
Agricultural products 12.5%
Crude petroleum 10%
Chemicals 12.5%

Exports
Total
US$ 59 367 million

France 17%
Others 46.8%
Germany 15.5%
Italy 9.1%
Japan 3.9%
UK 7.7%

PRODUCTS 1993

Imports

Others 18.8%
Transport equipment 26.8%
Textiles 3.9%
Electric engineering 6%
Metallic goods 8.6%
Agricultural products 15.5%
Chemicals 10.2%
Mechanical engineering 10.2%

Exports

France 20.4%
Others 44.8%
Germany 16%
Italy 9.9%
UK 8.9%

SCALE 1 : 12 000 000
0   100   200   300 km

KEY

Relief and physical features

Relief metres

5000	
3000	
2000	
1000	
500	
200	
0	sea level
	under sea level
200	
4000	
6000	

1142 ▲ Mountain height (in metres)

Permanent ice

Water features

~~~ River

~~~ Intermittent river

Canal

Lake / Reservoir

Marsh

Communications

——— Railway

——— Motorway

——— Road

⊕ Main airport

Administration

Boundaries

——— International

Settlement

Cities and towns in order of size

National capital

■ BERLIN
□ ZAGREB
□ BONN
□ LUXEMBOURG

Other city or town

● Munich
○ Dortmund
○ Ulm
○ Tuttlingen

SCALE 1 : 4 500 000

0   50   100   150   200 km

Lambert Conformal Conic projection

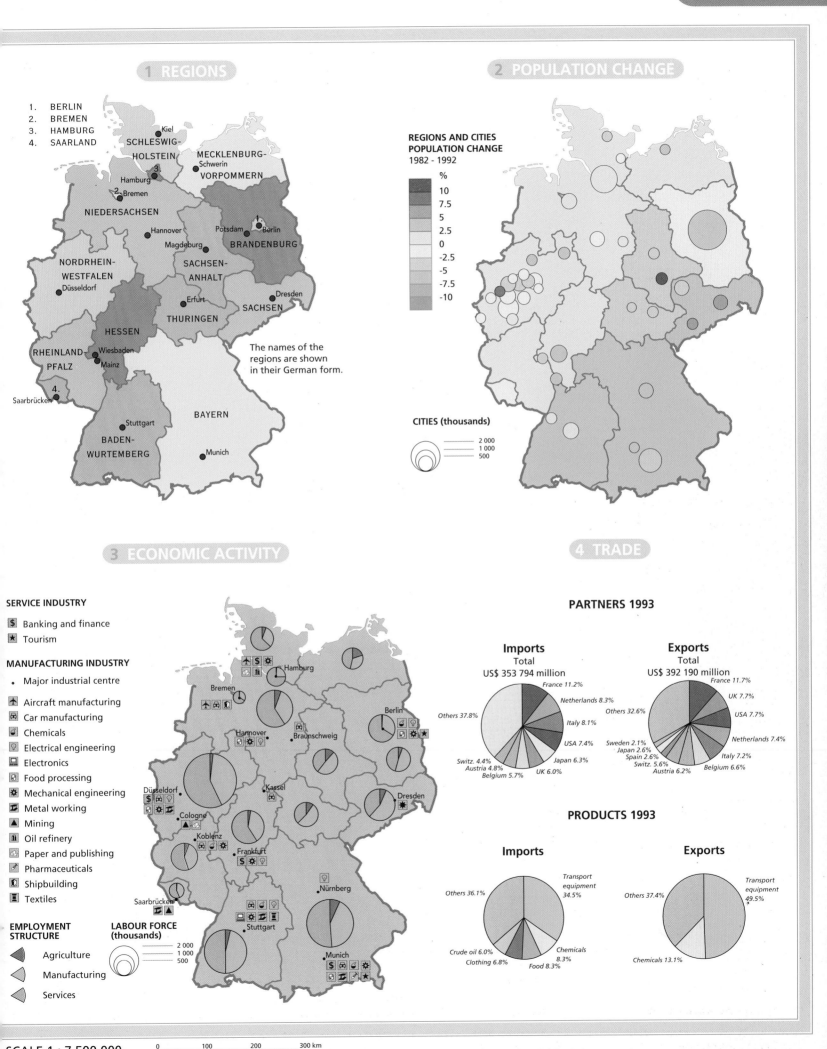

1 REGIONS

1. BERLIN
2. BREMEN
3. HAMBURG
4. SAARLAND

Kiel

SCHLESWIG-HOLSTEIN

MECKLENBURG-VORPOMMERN

Schwerin

Hamburg

Bremen

NIEDERSACHSEN

Hannover

Potsdam

Berlin

Magdeburg

BRANDENBURG

NORDRHEIN-WESTFALEN

SACHSEN-ANHALT

Düsseldorf

Erfurt

Dresden

THURINGEN

SACHSEN

HESSEN

Wiesbaden

RHEINLAND-PFALZ

Mainz

4.

Saarbrücken

Stuttgart

BAYERN

BADEN-WURTEMBERG

Munich

The names of the regions are shown in their German form.

2 POPULATION CHANGE

REGIONS AND CITIES
POPULATION CHANGE
1982 - 1992

%
10
7.5
5
2.5
0
-2.5
-5
-7.5
-10

CITIES (thousands)

2 000
1 000
500

3 ECONOMIC ACTIVITY

SERVICE INDUSTRY
$ Banking and finance
★ Tourism

MANUFACTURING INDUSTRY
• Major industrial centre

Aircraft manufacturing
Car manufacturing
Chemicals
Electrical engineering
Electronics
Food processing
Mechanical engineering
Metal working
Mining
Oil refinery
Paper and publishing
Pharmaceuticals
Shipbuilding
Textiles

EMPLOYMENT STRUCTURE

Agriculture
Manufacturing
Services

LABOUR FORCE
(thousands)

2 000
1 000
500

Hamburg
Bremen
Hannover
Braunschweig
Berlin
Düsseldorf
Kassel
Dresden
Cologne
Koblenz
Frankfurt
Saarbrücken
Nürnberg
Stuttgart
Munich

4 TRADE

PARTNERS 1993

Imports
Total
US$ 353 794 million

France 11.2%
Netherlands 8.3%
Others 37.8%
Italy 8.1%
USA 7.4%
Switz. 4.4%
Austria 4.8%
Belgium 5.7%
UK 6.0%
Japan 6.3%

Exports
Total
US$ 392 190 million

France 11.7%
UK 7.7%
USA 7.7%
Others 32.6%
Netherlands 7.4%
Sweden 2.1%
Japan 2.6%
Spain 2.6%
Switz. 5.6%
Italy 7.2%
Austria 6.2%
Belgium 6.6%

PRODUCTS 1993

Imports

Others 36.1%
Transport equipment 34.5%
Crude oil 6.0%
Clothing 6.8%
Food 8.3%
Chemicals 8.3%

Exports

Others 37.4%
Transport equipment 49.5%
Chemicals 13.1%

SCALE 1 : 7 500 000

0   100   200   300 km

Administration

Boundaries
International

Settlement
Cities and towns in order of size

National capital   Other city or town

■ ROME   ● Milan

□ SARAJEVO   ○ Genoa

□ SAN MARINO   ○ Venice

                  ○ Ragusa

KEY

Relief and physical features

Relief
metres

5000
3000
2000
1000
500
200
sea level
0
under sea level
200
4000
6000

4634 Mountain height
▲   (in metres)

Permanent ice

Water features

〰 River

〰 Canal

⬭ Lake / Reservoir

Communications

══ Railway

═══ Motorway

═══ Road

⊕ Main airport

SCALE 1 : 5 000 000

0   50   100   150   200 km

Lambert Conformal Conic projection

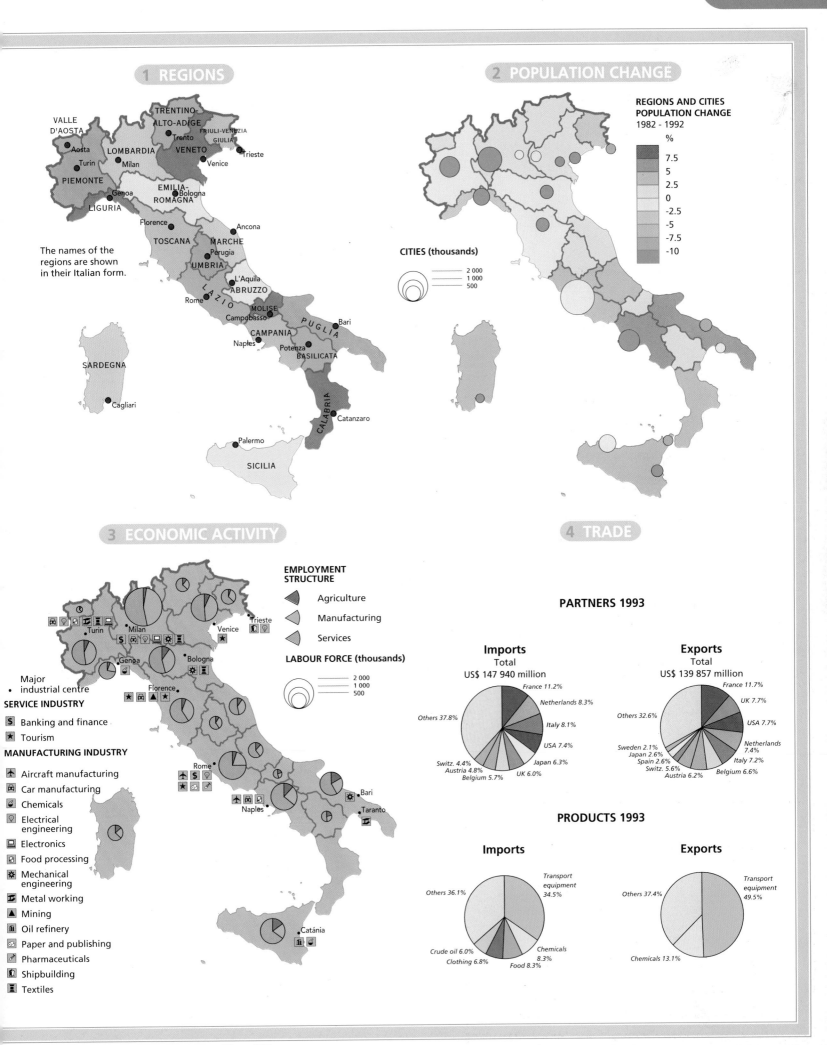

1 REGIONS

VALLE D'AOSTA
Aosta
Turin
PIEMONTE
LOMBARDIA
Milan
TRENTINO-ALTO-ADIGE
Trento
VENETO
Venice
FRIULI-VENEZIA GIULIA
Trieste
Genoa
LIGURIA
EMILIA-ROMAGNA
Bologna
Florence
TOSCANA
Ancona
MARCHE
Perugia
UMBRIA
L'Aquila
ABRUZZO
Rome
LAZIO
MOLISE
Campobasso
PUGLIA
Bari
CAMPANIA
Naples
Potenza
BASILICATA
SARDEGNA
Cagliari
CALABRIA
Catanzaro
Palermo
SICILIA

The names of the regions are shown in their Italian form.

2 POPULATION CHANGE

REGIONS AND CITIES
POPULATION CHANGE
1982 - 1992
%

| 7.5 |
| 5 |
| 2.5 |
| 0 |
| -2.5 |
| -5 |
| -7.5 |
| -10 |

CITIES (thousands)

2 000
1 000
500

3 ECONOMIC ACTIVITY

EMPLOYMENT
STRUCTURE

Agriculture
Manufacturing
Services

LABOUR FORCE (thousands)

2 000
1 000
500

Turin
Milan
Venice
Trieste
Genoa
Bologna
Florence
Rome
Naples
Bari
Taranto
Catánia

• Major industrial centre

SERVICE INDUSTRY
$ Banking and finance
★ Tourism

MANUFACTURING INDUSTRY
✈ Aircraft manufacturing
🚗 Car manufacturing
Chemicals
Electrical engineering
Electronics
Food processing
Mechanical engineering
Metal working
▲ Mining
Oil refinery
Paper and publishing
Pharmaceuticals
Shipbuilding
Textiles

4 TRADE

PARTNERS 1993

Imports
Total
US$ 147 940 million

Others 37.8%
France 11.2%
Netherlands 8.3%
Italy 8.1%
USA 7.4%
Japan 6.3%
UK 6.0%
Belgium 5.7%
Austria 4.8%
Switz. 4.4%

Exports
Total
US$ 139 857 million

Others 32.6%
France 11.7%
UK 7.7%
USA 7.7%
Netherlands 7.4%
Italy 7.2%
Belgium 6.6%
Austria 6.2%
Switz. 5.6%
Spain 2.6%
Japan 2.6%
Sweden 2.1%

PRODUCTS 1993

Imports

Others 36.1%
Transport equipment 34.5%
Chemicals 8.3%
Food 8.3%
Clothing 6.8%
Crude oil 6.0%

Exports

Others 37.4%
Transport equipment 49.5%
Chemicals 13.1%

SCALE 1 : 10 500 000

0   100   200   300 km

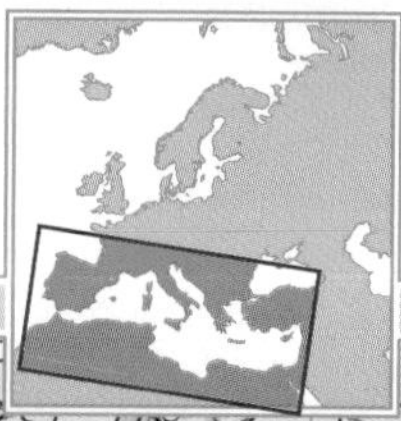

KEY

Relief and physical features

Relief
metres
5000
3000
2000
1000
500
200
0 sea level
200 under sea level
4000
6000

▲ 4808 Mountain height (in metres)

Water features

~ River
Intermittent river
Canal
Lake / Reservoir
Intermittent lake
Marsh

Communications

Railway
Road
⊕ Main airport

Administration

Boundaries
International
Disputed

Settlement

Cities and towns in order of size

National capital
■ ALGIERS
□ ATHENS
□ TIRANA
□ VALLETTA

Other city or town
● Naples
○ Valencia
○ Nice
○ Faro

SCALE 1 : 10 000 000

0   100   200   300   400 km

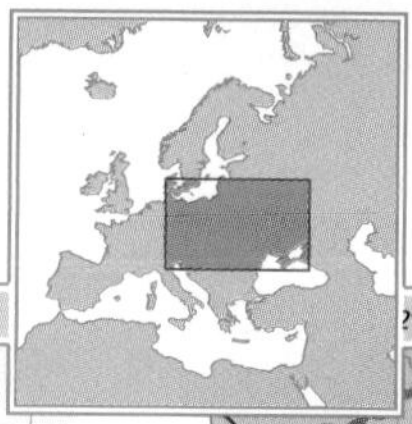

KEY

Relief and physical features

Relief
metres
5000
3000
2000
1000
500
200
0
sea level
200
under sea level
4000
6000

▲ 3798 Mountain height
(in metres)

Permanent ice

Water features

~ River
~ Canal
Lake / Reservoir
Marsh

Communications

Railway
Motorway
Road
⊕ Main airport

Administration

Boundaries
International

Settlement

Cities and towns in order of size

National capital | Other city or town
■ WARSAW | ● Kharkhiv
□ CHIŞINĂU | ○ Krakow
□ BRATISLAVA | ○ Brno
□ VADUZ | ○ Chelm

SCALE 1 : 5 000 000

0 50 100 150 200 km

Baltic Sea

SWEDEN
DENMARK
Kiel Bay
Bornholm
Gulf of Gdańsk
RUSSIAN FED
Kaliningrad
LIT

GERMANY
BERLIN
Potsdam
Poznań
POLAND
WARSAW
Łódź
Wrocław
Silesian Plateau
Kraków
Carpathian Mts

CZECH REPUBLIC
PRAGUE
Ore Mts
Sudeten Mts
Bohemian Forest

SLOVAKIA
BRATISLAVA

AUSTRIA
VIENNA
SWITZERLAND
VADUZ
ALPS
Dolomites
Gr. Glockner 3798

ITALY
Milan

SLOVENIA
LJUBLJANA
Gulf of Venice

HUNGARY
BUDAPEST

CROATIA
ZAGREB

BOSNIA-HERZEGOVINA

YUGOSLAVIA

Conic projection

KEY

Relief and physical features

Relief
metres
5000
3000
2000
1000
500
200
sea level
0
200
4000
6000
under sea level

▲ 3971   Mountain height
(in metres)

Water features

~~~~~   River

- - - -   Intermittent river

~~~~~   Canal

Lake / Reservoir

Intermittent lake

Marsh

Communications

———   Railway

═══   Motorway

———   Road

⊕   Main airport

Administration

Boundaries

———   International

———   Internal

Settlement

Cities and towns in order of size

National capital   Other city or town

■ ATHENS   ● İstanbul

□ SKOPJE   ○ Konya

□ NICOSIA   ○ Thessaloniki

○ Dubrovnik

SCALE 1 : 5 000 000

0   50   100   150   200 km

MOLDOVA

UKRAINE

Sea of Azov

RUSSIAN FEDERATION

Crimea

Mouths of the Danube

Caucasus

GEORGIA

B L A C K   S E A

TURKEY

Anatolia

Pontine Mountains

Taurus Mountains

ANKARA

of Marmara

CYPRUS

SYRIA

LEBANON

M E D I T E R R A N E A N   S E A

Rhodes

Conic projection

KEY

Relief and physical features

Relief metres

5000
3000
2000
1000
500
200
sea level
0
200
4000
6000

▲ 4750 Mountain height (in metres)

Permanent ice

Water features

~ River

Intermittent river

Lake / Reservoir

Intermittent lake

Marsh

Communications

— Railway

— Road

⊕ Main airport

Administration

Boundaries

International

Internal

Settlement

Cities and towns in order of size

National capital | Other city or town
■ MOSCOW | ● Ufa
□ RIGA | ○ Penza
□ TALLINN | ○ Archangel
□ ULAN BATOR | ○ Kotlas

SCALE 1 : 20 000 000

0   200   400   600   800 km

ICELAND

NORWEGIAN SEA

Arctic Circle

Jan Mayen (Nor.)

Faeroes (Den.)
Torshavn

NORWAY
SWEDEN
FINLAND

Bergen
Trondheim
Tromsø
North Cape

Svalbard (Norway)
Spitsbergen
Nordaustlandet
Bear Island

ARCTIC

BARENTS SEA

Franz Josef Land

Novaya Zemlya

Kara Sea

Yenisey Gulf

Gulf of Bothnia

STOCKHOLM
Uppsala
Turku

Baltic Sea

HELSINKI
G. of Finland
TALLINN
ESTONIA
RIGA
LATVIA
LITHUANIA
VILNIUS
BELARUS
MINSK

St Petersburg
Pskov
Novgorod
Tver
Smolensk
Bryansk
Orel
Kursk
Belgorod

Murmansk
Kola Pen.
C. Kanin
White Sea
Archangel
Onega
Kolguyev
Kanin Pen.
Mezen
Pechora G.
Baydaratskaya B.
Yamal Pen.
Gydanskiy Peninsula
Novyy Port

Cherepovets
Rybinsk Reservoir
Yaroslavl
Vologda
Kotlas
Sharya
Sykytyvkar
Kotlas
Ukhta Pechora
Pechora
Narodnaya 1894
Vorkuta
Salekhard

MOSCOW
Sergiyev
Tula
Ryazan'
Vladimir
Ivanovo
Kostroma
Nizhniy Novgorod
Cheboksary
Kazan
Izhevsk
Perm
Solikamsk
Berezniki
Kama
Vyatka
Ob
Khanty Mansiysk
Serov
Nizhniy Tagil
Ob
Noyabr'sk
Urengoy

RUSSIAN

West Siberian Plain

Surgut
Nizhnevartovsk

Penza
Saransk
Simbirsk
Samara
Syzran
Kuznetsk
Saratov
Tambov
Voronezh
Lipetsk

Tol'yatti
Naberezhnye Chelny
Ufa
Sterlitamak
Salavat
Chelyabinsk
Miass
Zlatoust
Yekaterinburg
Kamensk Ural'skiy
Tyumen
Tobol'sk
Kurgan
Petropavlovsk
Omsk
Tatarsk
Tomsk
Anzhero-Sudzhensk
Kemerovo
Novosibirsk
Leninsk Kuznetsk
Novokuznetsk
Barnaul
Biysk
Rubtsovsk

Orenburg
Magnitogorsk
Orsk
Aktyubinsk
Ural'sk
Kamyshin
Volgograd
Volzhskiy
Astrakhan'
Elista

Caspian Depression

URAL

KAZAKHSTAN

Kustanay
Rudnyy
Ishim
Kokshetau
Akmola
Karasuk
Pavlodar
Semipalatinsk
Temirtau
Karaganda
Lake Tengiz
Zhezkazgan
Ust-Kamenogorsk
Ayaguz
Kzyl-Orda
Balkhash
L. Balkhash
Aktogay
Zaysan
Lake Zaysan

Inset map (lower left)

ROMANIA
BUCHAREST
BULGARIA
Ruse
Varna
Burgas
Istanbul
Sakarya
TURKEY
ANKARA
Kayseri
Aleppo
SYRIA
IRAQ
Mosul
Ar Raqqah

MOLDOVA
Odessa
UKRAINE
Kharkiv
Dnipropetrovs'k
Donets'k
Zaporizhzhya
Mykolayiv
Kherson
Simferopol'
Sevastopol'
Crimea
Sea of Azov
Mariupol'
Kerch
Rostov-na-Donu
Krasnodar
Novorossiysk
Sochi
Stavropol Highlands
Sukhumi
Batumi
GEORGIA
TBILISI
CAUCASUS
Mt Elbrus 5642
Groznyy
Makhachkala
ARMENIA
YEREVAN
AZERBAIJAN
Mt Ararat 5165
BAKU
Sumqayit
Tabriz
IRAN
Lake Urmia
Lake Van

BLACK SEA

CASPIAN SEA

Neftekumsk
Ust Urt Plateau
Fort Shevchenko
Atyrau
Aktau
Aral Sea
UZBEKISTAN
Kungrad
Nukus
TURKMENISTAN
Kara Bogaz Gol Bay
Krasnovodsk

CHINA

Conic Equidistant projection

PACIFIC OCEAN

ATLANTIC OCEAN

Relief

Relief metres	
5000	
3000	
2000	
1000	
500	
200	
sea level	0
under sea level	200
	4000
	6000

Ice cap

BERING SEA
GULF OF ALASKA
BEAUFORT SEA
Greenland
BAFFIN BAY
Labrador Sea
HUDSON BAY
CANADIAN SHIELD
ROCKY MOUNTAINS
GREAT PLAINS
GULF OF MEXICO
CARIBBEAN SEA
Greater Antilles
Lesser Antilles

Wrangel I.
St Lawrence I.
Nunivak I.
Bristol Bay
Alaska Pan.
Kodiak I.
Pt Barrow
Brooks Range
Yukon
Alaska Range
▲ Mt McKinley 6194
▲ Mt Logan 6050
Alexander Archipelago
Queen Charlotte Islands
Coast Mountains
Vancouver Island
Cascade Ra.
Sierra Nevada
▲ Mt Whitney 4418
Great Basin
Great Salt L.
Snake
Yellowstone
▲ Gannett Pk 4202
Columbia
Fraser
Peace
Mackenzie Mts
Great Bear L.
Great Slave L.
Lake Athabasca
Churchill
Nelson
Lake Winnipeg
Severn
Banks Island
Victoria Island
Parry Islands
Queen Elizabeth Islands
Ellesmere Island
Baffin Island
Foxe Basin
Southampton I.
Hudson Strait
Belcher Is
Labrador
Newfoundland
Davis Strait
Denmark Strait
Cape Farewell
Arctic Circle
Iceland
Faeroes
Gulf of St Lawrence
Cape Breton I.
C. Sable
C. Cod
Lake Superior
L. Huron
L. Michigan
L. Erie
L. Ontario
St Lawrence
Appalachian Mts
Chesapeake B.
C. Hatteras
Bermuda
C. Fear
C. Canaveral
Tropic of Cancer
Ohio
Missouri
Mississippi
Arkansas
Red
Ozark Plateau
Edwards Plateau
Colorado
Grand Canyon
Colorado Plateau
Rio Grande
Guadalupe I.
Lower California
Gulf of California
C. San Lucas
Sierra Madre Occidental
Sierra Madre Oriental
Altiplano Mexicano
▲ Popocatépetl 5452
Campeche Bay
Sierra Madre del Sur
Yucatán
Yucatán Channel
Str. of Florida
Bahamas
Cuba
Hispaniola
Jamaica
Puerto Rico
Curaçao
G. of Honduras
Sierra Madre
L. Nicaragua
G. of Darién
Isthmus of Panama
Clipperton I.
I. de Coco
I. de Malpelo
Galapagos Islands
G. of Guayaquil
Orinoco
Cordillera Occidental
Cordillera Central
▲ Cotopaxi 5887
▲ Chimborazo 6272
Equator

Inset map:

GREENLAND
U.S.A.
CANADA
UNITED STATES OF AMERICA
MEXICO
BAHAMAS
CUBA
D.R.
H.
J.
B.
G.
N.
E.S.
HO.
C.R.
P.

B. BELIZE
C.R. COSTA RICA
D.R. DOMINICAN REPUBLIC
E.S. EL SALVADOR
G. GUATEMALA
H. HAITI
HO. HONDURAS
J. JAMAICA
N. NICARAGUA
P. PANAMA

SCALE 1 : 110 000 000

SCALE 1 : 37 000 000

Chamberlin Trimetric projection

1 TEMPERATURE AND PRESSURE : JANUARY

Arctic Circle

1014 1016
1012 1014 1018
1010 1018
1008
1006

1010
1012
1014
1016
1018

1020
HIGH

1018
1018

Tropic of Cancer
1018
1016

1006
1008
1010
1012
1014
1016
1018
1016

Average temperature °C

24
16
8
0
-8
-16
-24
-32

Wind direction

Isobar in millibars reduced to sea level

2 TEMPERATURE AND PRESSURE : JULY

1010
1012
1010
1008
1014

Arctic Circle

LOW
1006

1012
1014

1008
LOW
1014

HIGH
1016

1012 Tropic of Cancer
1010

LOW
1012
1010
1016
1014

Average temperature °C

32
24
16
8
0
-8

Wind direction

Isobar in millibars reduced to sea level

3 ANNUAL RAINFALL

Arctic Circle

Saskatoon
Vancouver
Detroit
Charleston
Tropic of Cancer
Acapulco

Average annual rainfall mm

3000
2000
1000
500
250
0

4 STATISTICS

Saskatoon (515 metres)	Jan	Feb	Mar	Apr	May	Jun	Jul	Aug	Sep	Oct	Nov	Dec
Temperature - max.(°C)	-13	-11	-3	9	18	22	25	24	17	11	-1	-9
Temperature - min. (°C)	-24	-22	-14	-3	3	9	11	9	3	-3	-11	-19
Rainfall - (mm)	23	13	18	18	36	66	61	48	38	23	13	15

Vancouver (14 metres)	Jan	Feb	Mar	Apr	May	Jun	Jul	Aug	Sep	Oct	Nov	Dec
Temperature - max.(°C)	5	7	10	14	18	21	23	23	18	14	9	6
Temperature - min. (°C)	0	1	3	4	8	11	12	12	9	7	4	2
Rainfall - (mm)	218	147	127	84	71	64	31	43	91	147	211	224

Charleston (3 metres)	Jan	Feb	Mar	Apr	May	Jun	Jul	Aug	Sep	Oct	Nov	Dec
Temperature - max.(°C)	14	15	19	23	27	30	31	31	28	24	19	15
Temperature - min. (°C)	6	7	10	14	19	23	24	24	22	16	11	7
Rainfall - (mm)	74	84	86	71	81	119	185	168	130	81	58	71

Acapulco (3 metres)	Jan	Feb	Mar	Apr	May	Jun	Jul	Aug	Sep	Oct	Nov	Dec
Temperature - max.(°C)	31	31	31	32	32	33	32	33	32	32	32	31
Temperature - min. (°C)	22	22	22	23	25	25	25	25	24	24	23	22
Rainfall - (mm)	6	1	0	1	36	281	256	252	349	159	28	8

Detroit (189 metres)	Jan	Feb	Mar	Apr	May	Jun	Jul	Aug	Sep	Oct	Nov	Dec
Temperature - max.(°C)	-1	0	6	13	19	25	28	27	23	16	8	2
Temperature - min. (°C)	-7	-8	-3	3	9	14	17	17	13	7	1	-4
Rainfall - (mm)	53	53	64	64	84	91	84	69	71	61	61	58

SCALE 1 : 82 000 000

Bonne projection

SCALE 1 : 17 000 000

Chamberlin trimetric projection

Vancouver I.
Nanaimo
Vancouver
Cape Flattery
Victoria
Port Angeles
Mt Baker 3285
Bellingham
Glacier Peak 3213
BRITISH COLUMBIA
Mt Assiniboine 3619
Banff
Calgary
Drumheller
SASKATCHEWAN
Saskatoon
CANADA
Melville
Yorkton
Lake Winnipeg
Dauphin
Kelowna
Penticton
Nelson
Cranbrook
ALBERTA
Medicine Hat
Lethbridge
Swift Current
Moose Jaw
Regina
Broadview
Weyburn
Estevan
MANITOBA
Brandon
Portage la Prairie
Winnipeg
Okanogan
Franklin D. Roosevelt L.
Sandpoint
Kalispell
Flathead Lake
Shelby
Havre
Milk
Glasgow
Williston
Minot
Rugby
Devils Lake
Grafton
Gran Fork
Seattle
Tacoma
WASHINGTON
Spokane
Mt Rainier 4392
Mt St Helens 2950
Astoria
Ellensburg
Yakima
Kennewick
Columbia
Great Falls
Fort Peck Res.
Missouri
MONTANA
Helena
Butte
Bozeman
Billings
Yellowstone
Miles City
Glendive
NORTH DAKOTA
Dickinson
Bismarck
Valley City
Jamestown
Fargo
Moorhead
Portland
Salem
Mt Hood 3427
Eugene
OREGON
Bend
Baker
Snake
Blue Mts
Bitterroot Range
Salmon
Big Hole
Dillon
Salmon River Mountains
ROCKY
Mobridge
Aberdeen
Lake Oahe
Watertown
SOUTH DAKOTA
Huron
Worth
C. Blanco
Grants Pass
Roseburg
Harney Basin
IDAHO
Boise
Idaho Falls
Pocatello
Sheridan
Cloud Peak 4016
Bighorn Mts
Buffalo
Gillette
Pierre
Rapid City
Mitchell
Sioux Falls
Crescent City
Klamath Falls
Lakeview
Goose Lake
Mt Shasta 4317
Redding
Red Bluff
Twin Falls
Burley
Gannett Pk 4202
WYOMING
Worland
Casper
North Platte
Eureka
Ukiah
Pt Arena
Santa Rosa
Chico
Yuba City
Reno
Carson City
Hawthorne
Pyramid L.
NEVADA
Great Salt Lake
Elko
Ogden
Rock Springs
Green
Seminoe Res.
Pathfinder Res.
Rawlins
Laramie
Cheyenne
N. Platte
Alliance
Scottsbluff
NEBRASKA
Omaha
Sacramento
Stockton
Merced
Oakland
San Francisco
San Jose
Salinas
Sierra Nevada
White Mt Peak 4342
Wheeler Peak 3981
Great Basin
UTAH
Salt Lake City
Provo
Kings Peak 4123
Uinta Mts
Green
Grand Junction
Fort Collins
Greeley
Boulder
Longmont
Denver
Aurora
Sterling
McCook
Grand Island
Kearney
Council
San Luis Obispo
Santa Maria
Santa Barbara
Pt Conception
Fresno
Bakersfield
Kern
Mt Whitney 4418
Death Valley
Delano Peak 3710
Caliente
Cedar City
Lake Powell
Colorado
Mt Peale 3877
San Juan
Montrose
Canon City
Colorado Springs
Pueblo
COLORADO
Sangre de Cristo Ra.
Lamar
Arkansas
La Junta
Great Bend
KANSAS
Dodge City
Salina
Junction City
Emporia
Las Vegas
Grand Canyon
Grand Canyon
Colorado Plateau
Wheeler Peak 4011
San Juan Mts
Trinidad
Raton
Liberal
Alva
Wichita
Ark. City
Oxnard
Los Angeles
Pasadena
Santa Ana
Long Beach
San Bernardino
Barstow
Needles
Lake Mead
Humphreys Peak 3951
Flagstaff
Prescott
Holbrook
Gallup
Santa Fe
Albuquerque
Tucumcari
Canadian
Borger
Pampa
OKLAHOMA
Oklahoma City
San Diego
Tijuana
Salton Sea
Brawley
Mexicali
Yuma
Gila
ARIZONA
Glendale
Phoenix
NEW MEXICO
Belen
Clovis
Amarillo
Lubbock
Wichita Falls
Lake Texoma
Gainesville
Ensenada
Cerro de la Encantada 3096
San Felipe
Pto Peñasco
Tucson
Silver City
Lordsburg
Las Cruces
Rio Grande
El Paso
Ciudad Juárez
Pecos
Sacramento Mts
Big Spring
Sweetwater
Abilene
Fort Worth
Dallas
C. S. Quintín
BAJA CALIFORNIA NORTE
Nogales
Magdalena
Ojinaga
Rio Grande
Pecos
Midland
Odessa
Colorado
TEXAS
Wac
Temple
Guadalupe (Mexico)
Tiburón
Angel de la Guarda
SONORA
Hermosillo
Conchos
CHIHUAHUA
Chihuahua
Alpine
Emory Peak 2380
Edwards Plateau
Austin
San Antonio
Del Rio
Sebastian Vizcaino Bay
Pta Eugenia
Cedros
BAJA CALIFORNIA
Sta Rosalia
Guaymas
Ciudad Obregón
Ciudad Delicias
Ciudad Camargo
Serranías del Burro
Piedras Negras
Eagle Pass
Victoria
Beeville
Corp Christi
BAJA CALIFORNIA SUR
B. Magdalena
San Jose
Los Mochis
SINALOA
Culiacán
La Paz
Gómez Palacio
Torreón
Hidalgo del Parra
DURANGO
Saltillo
COAHUILA
Monclova
Sabinas
Laredo
Nuevo Laredo
Kingsville
Falcon Lake
Padre Island
Tropic of Cancer
Gulf of California
Lower California
Sierra Madre Occidental
MEXICO
ZACATECAS
Monterrey
NUEVO LEÓN
Monterreros
Reynosa
Matam
TAMAULIPAS
PACIFIC OCEAN

SCALE 1 : 12 000 000

0   150   300   450   600 km

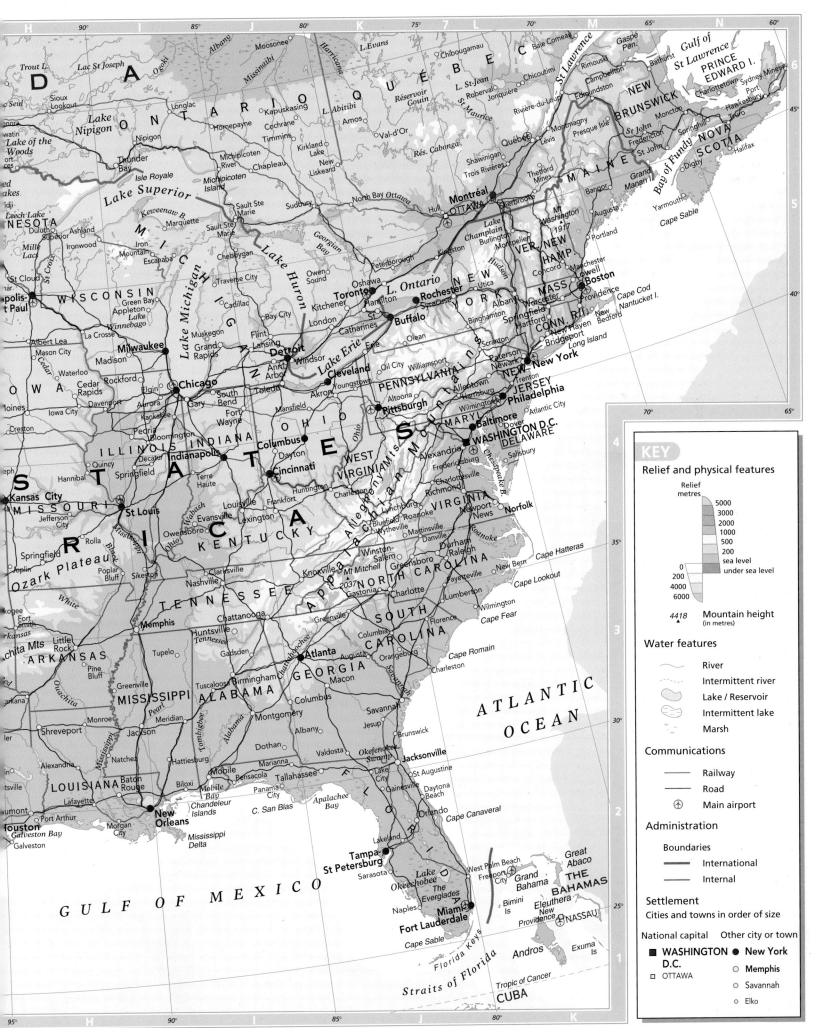

KEY

Relief and physical features

Relief metres
5000
3000
2000
1000
500
200
sea level
0
under sea level
200
4000
6000

▲ 4418   Mountain height
(in metres)

Water features

〜 River

⌇ Intermittent river

◯ Lake / Reservoir

⬭ Intermittent lake

⌇ Marsh

Communications

—— Railway

—— Road

⊕ Main airport

Administration

Boundaries

—— International

—— Internal

Settlement

Cities and towns in order of size

National capital   Other city or town

■ **WASHINGTON D.C.**   ● **New York**

□ OTTAWA   ○ Memphis

○ Savannah

○ Elko

Lambert conformal conic projection

1 POPULATION DENSITY

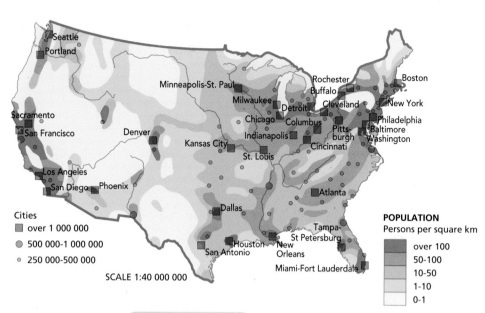

Cities
- ■ over 1 000 000
- ● 500 000-1 000 000
- • 250 000-500 000

SCALE 1:40 000 000

POPULATION
Persons per square km
- over 100
- 50-100
- 10-50
- 1-10
- 0-1

2 MAIN CITIES

City	1970 census	1990 census	% change
New York	7 771 730	7 322 564	-6
Los Angeles	2 782 400	3 485 398	25
Chicago	3 325 263	2 783 726	-16
Houston	1 213 064	1 630 553	34
Philadelphia	1 926 529	1 585 570	-18
San Diego	675 688	1 110 549	64
Detroit	1 492 914	1 027 974	-31
Dallas	836 121	1 006 877	20
Phoenix	580 275	983 403	69
San Antonio	650 188	935 933	44

3 POPULATION CHANGE

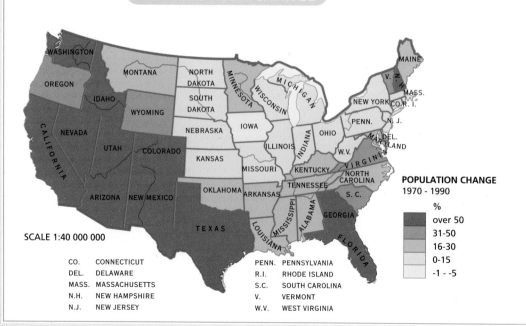

SCALE 1:40 000 000

POPULATION CHANGE
1970 - 1990
%
- over 50
- 31-50
- 16-30
- 0-15
- -1 - -5

CO.	CONNECTICUT	PENN.	PENNSYLVANIA
DEL.	DELAWARE	R.I.	RHODE ISLAND
MASS.	MASSACHUSETTS	S.C.	SOUTH CAROLINA
N.H.	NEW HAMPSHIRE	V.	VERMONT
N.J.	NEW JERSEY	W.V.	WEST VIRGINIA

4 STATE COMPARISONS

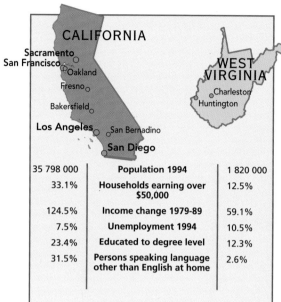

CALIFORNIA		WEST VIRGINIA
35 798 000	**Population 1994**	1 820 000
33.1%	**Households earning over $50,000**	12.5%
124.5%	**Income change 1979-89**	59.1%
7.5%	**Unemployment 1994**	10.5%
23.4%	**Educated to degree level**	12.3%
31.5%	**Persons speaking language other than English at home**	2.6%

5 POPULATION GROWTH

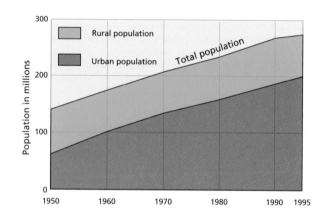

- Rural population
- Urban population
- Total population

6 IMMIGRATION

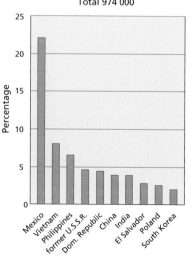

IMMIGRATION INTO U.S.A
BY COUNTRY 1992
Total 974 000

(Mexico, Vietnam, Philippines, former U.S.S.R., Dom. Republic, China, India, El Salvador, Poland, South Korea)

7 ECONOMIC ACTIVITY

• Major industrial centre

SERVICE INDUSTRY

$ Banking and finance

★ Tourism

MANUFACTURING INDUSTRY

✈ Aircraft manufacturing

🚗 Car manufacturing

🧪 Chemicals

💡 Electrical engineering

🍴 Food processing

✸ Mechanical engineering

🔧 Metal working

🛢 Oil refinery

📖 Paper and publishing

🚢 Shipbuilding

▤ Textiles

SCALE 1:40 000 000

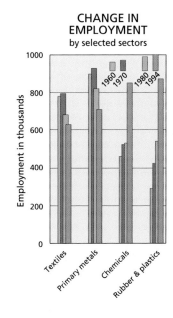

CHANGE IN EMPLOYMENT
by selected sectors

(bar chart: Employment in thousands, years 1960, 1970, 1980, 1994; sectors: Textiles, Primary metals, Chemicals, Rubber & plastics)

8 TRADE

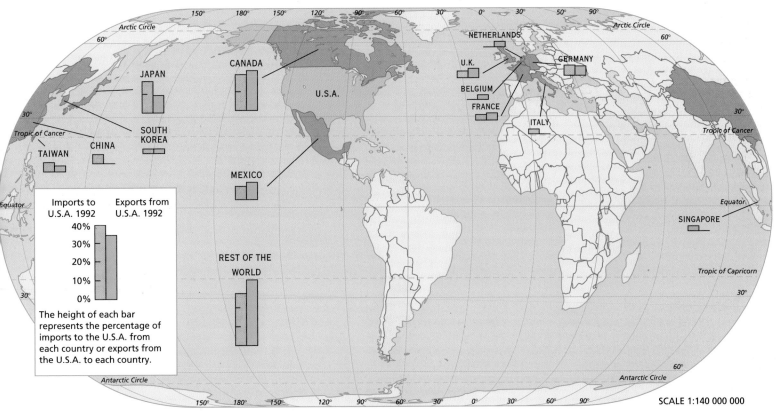

Imports to U.S.A. 1992   Exports from U.S.A. 1992

40%
30%
20%
10%
0%

The height of each bar represents the percentage of imports to the U.S.A. from each country or exports from the U.S.A. to each country.

SCALE 1:140 000 000

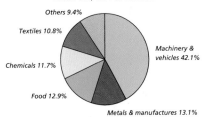

Exports 1960
Total: US$ 20 717 million

Others 9.4%
Textiles 10.8%
Chemicals 11.7%
Food 12.9%
Machinery & vehicles 42.1%
Metals & manufactures 13.1%

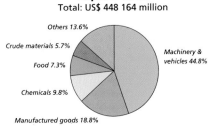

Exports 1992
Total: US$ 448 164 million

Others 13.6%
Crude materials 5.7%
Food 7.3%
Chemicals 9.8%
Machinery & vehicles 44.8%
Manufactured goods 18.8%

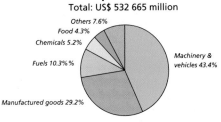

Imports 1992
Total: US$ 532 665 million

Others 7.6%
Food 4.3%
Chemicals 5.2%
Fuels 10.3% %
Machinery & vehicles 43.4%
Manufactured goods 29.2%

Built-up area

The built up area shown as blue/green on the satellite image surrounds San Francisco Bay and extends south to San Jose. Three bridges link the main built up areas across San Francisco Bay.

Woodland

Areas of dense woodland cover much of the Santa Cruz Mountains to the west of the San Andreas Fault Zone. Other areas of woodland are found on the ridges to the east of San Francisco Bay.

Marsh / Salt Marsh

Areas of dark green on the satellite image represent marshland in the Coyote Creek area and salt marshes between the San Mateo and Dumbarton Bridges.

Reservoir / lake

Lakes and reservoirs stand out from the surrounding land. Good examples are the Upper San Leandro Reservoir east of Piedmont and the San Andreas Lake which lies along the fault line.

Airport

A grey blue colour shows San Francisco International Airport as a flat rectangular strip of land jutting out into the bay.

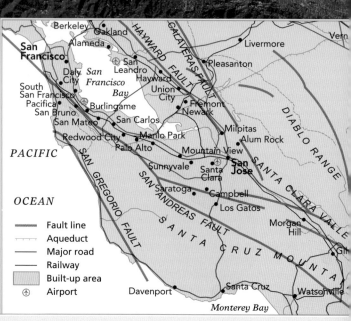

Fault line	
Aqueduct	
Major road	
Railway	
Built-up area	
⊕	Airport

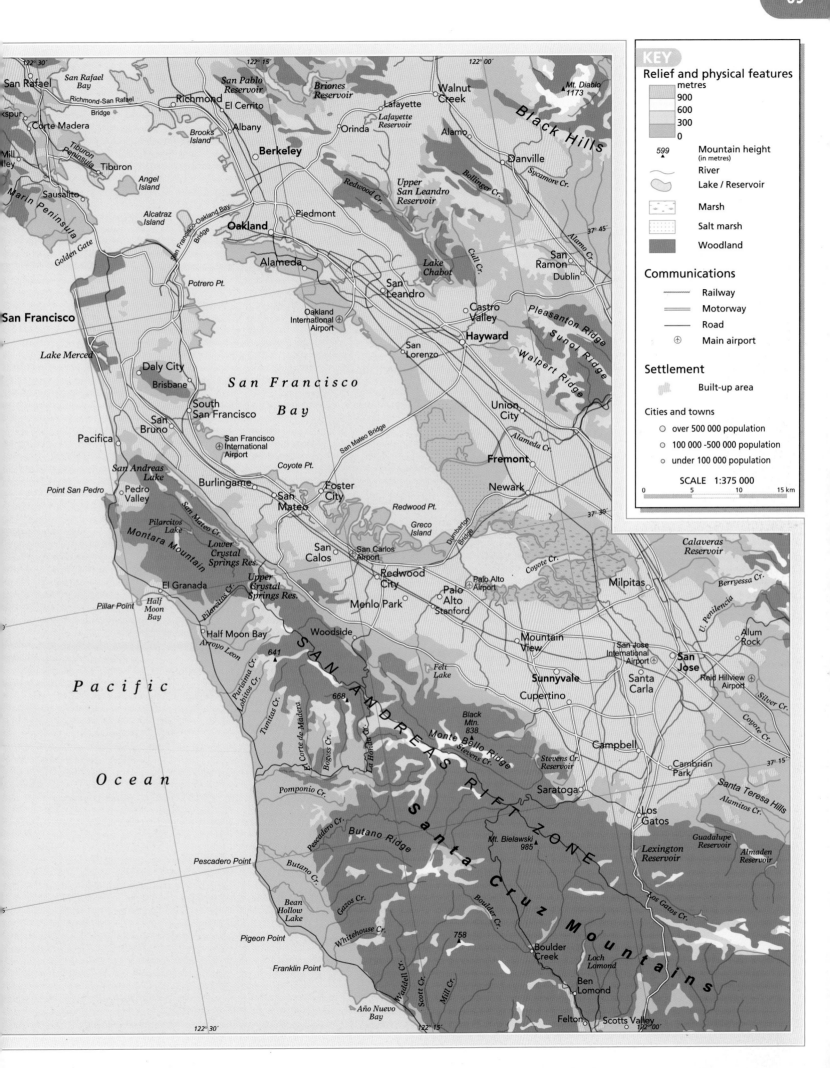

KEY

Relief and physical features

metres
900
600
300
0

599 ▲ Mountain height (in metres)

~ River

Lake / Reservoir

Marsh

Salt marsh

Woodland

Communications

───── Railway

═════ Motorway

───── Road

⊕ Main airport

Settlement

Built-up area

Cities and towns

○ over 500 000 population

○ 100 000 -500 000 population

○ under 100 000 population

SCALE 1:375 000

0   5   10   15 km

San Rafael
San Rafael Bay
Richmond-San Rafael Bridge
Richmond
El Cerrito
Albany
Brooks Island
Berkeley
Corte Madera
Tiburon Peninsula
Tiburon
Angel Island
Sausalito
Marin Peninsula
Alcatraz Island
Golden Gate
Oakland
Piedmont
Alameda
San Pablo Reservoir
Briones Reservoir
Lafayette
Orinda
Lafayette Reservoir
Walnut Creek
Alamo
Danville
Sycamore Cr.
Bollinger Cr.
Mt. Diablo 1173 ▲
Black Hills
Redwood Cr.
Upper San Leandro Reservoir
Cull Cr.
Alamo Cr.
San Ramon
Dublin
San Francisco Oakland Bay Bridge
Potrero Pt.
San Leandro
Lake Chabot
San Francisco
Oakland International Airport
Castro Valley
Hayward
Lake Merced
Daly City
Brisbane
San Bruno
South San Francisco
San Francisco Bay
San Lorenzo
Pleasanton Ridge
Sunol Ridge
Walpert Ridge
Pacifica
San Francisco International Airport
Coyote Pt.
San Mateo Bridge
Union City
Alameda Cr.
San Andreas Lake
Point San Pedro
Pedro Valley
Burlingame
San Mateo
Foster City
Fremont
Newark
Pilarcitos Lake
Montara Mountain
San Mateo Cr.
Lower Crystal Springs Res.
Redwood Pt.
Greco Island
Dumbarton Bridge
El Granada
Upper Crystal Springs Res.
San Calos
San Carlos Airport
Redwood City
Palo Alto Airport
Coyote Cr.
Calaveras Reservoir
Pilarcitos Cr.
Menlo Park
Palo Alto
Stanford
Milpitas
Berryessa Cr.
Pillar Point
Half Moon Bay
Woodside
Mountain View
San Jose International Airport
Alum Rock
Half Moon Bay
Arroyo Leon
Purisima Cr.
Lobitos Cr.
641 ▲
Felt Lake
Sunnyvale
Santa Carla
San Jose
Reid Hillview Airport
U. Penilencia
Pacific Ocean
El Corte de Madera
Bogess Cr.
Tunitas Cr.
La Honda
668 ▲
SAN ANDREAS RIFT ZONE
Monte Bello Ridge
Stevens Cr.
Black Mtn. 838
Cupertino
Campbell
Silver Cr.
Coyote Cr.
Stevens Cr. Reservoir
Cambrian Park
37° 15'
Pomponio Cr.
Santa Cruz Mountains
Saratoga
Los Gatos
Santa Teresa Hills
Alamitos Cr.
Pescadero Point
Pescadero Cr.
Butano Ridge
Mt. Bielawski 985 ▲
Lexington Reservoir
Guadalupe Reservoir
Almaden Reservoir
Butano Cr.
Los Gatos Cr.
Bean Hollow Lake
Gazos Cr.
758 ▲
Boulder Cr.
Boulder Creek
Loch Lomond
Pigeon Point
Whitehouse Cr.
Ben Lomond
Franklin Point
Waddell Cr.
Scott Cr.
Mill Cr.
Año Nuevo Bay
Felton
Scotts Valley

122° 30'   122° 15'   122° 00'
37° 45'
37° 30'

UNITED STATES OF AMERICA

MEXICO

PACIFIC OCEAN

GULF OF MEXICO

Relief and physical features

Baja California Norte, Baja California Sur, Sonora, Chihuahua, Coahuila, Nuevo León, Tamaulipas, Durango, Sinaloa, Zacatecas, San Luis Potosí, Nayarit, Jalisco, Aguascalientes, Guanajuato, Querétaro, Hidalgo, Michoacán, Morelos, Guerrero, Oaxaca, Puebla, Veracruz, Tabasco, Chiapas, Campeche, Yucatán, Quintana Roo

Sierra Madre Occidental, Sierra Madre Oriental, Sierra Madre del Sur

Gulf of California (Lower California), Gulf of Tehuantepec, Campeche Bay

San Diego, Tijuana, Ensenada, Mexicali, Phoenix, Tucson, Nogales, Hermosillo, Ciudad Obregón, Los Mochis, La Paz, Mazatlán, Culiacán, Durango, Torreón, Gómez Palacio, Ciudad Juárez, El Paso, Chihuahua, Ciudad Delicias, Ciudad Camargo, Hidalgo del Parral, Monclova, Saltillo, Monterrey, Nuevo Laredo, Laredo, Reynosa, Matamoros, Ciudad Victoria, Ciudad Madero, Tampico, San Luis Potosí, Aguascalientes, León, Guanajuato, Irapuato, Celaya, Querétaro, Guadalajara, Colima, Morelia, Uruapán, Toluca, MEXICO CITY, Cuernavaca, Puebla, Tlaxcala, Pachuca, Poza Rica, Jalapa, Veracruz, Córdoba, Orizaba, Coatzacoalcos, Minatitlán, Villahermosa, Acapulco, Chilpancingo, Oaxaca, Cd Ixtepec, Juchitán, Tuxtla Gutiérrez, Tapachula, Mérida, Campeche, Cancún, Cozumel

GUATEMALA, GUATEMALA CITY, Quezaltenango, BELIZE, BELMOPAN, EL SALVADOR, SAN SALVADOR, Santa Ana, HONDURAS, TEGUCIGALPA

Tropic of Cancer

Revillagigedo Is (Mexico), I. San Benedicto, I. Socorro, I. Marías

KEY

Relief and physical features

Relief metres
5000
3000
2000
1000
500
200
sea level
under sea level
200
4000
6000

5775 ▲ Mountain height (in metres)

Water features

River
Intermittent river
Lake / Reservoir
Intermittent lake
Marsh

Communications

Railway
Road
⊕ Main airport

Administration

Boundaries
International
Internal

Settlement
Cities and towns in order of size

National capital | Other city or town
■ MEXICO CITY | ● Puebla
□ MANAGUA | ◎ Leon
□ SAN JOSÉ | ○ Acapulco
□ CASTRIES | ○ Guanajuato

Mexican States numbered on map
1. AGUASCALIENTES
2. DISTRITO FEDERAL
3. TLAXCALA

SCALE 1 : 13 000 000

0   200   400   600   800 km

ATLANTIC
OCEAN

North Carolina
Knoxville · Mt Mitchell 2037
Chattanooga · NORTH CAROLINA · Raleigh
Greenville · Charlotte · Fayetteville · New Bern · Cape Hatteras
Atlanta · SOUTH · Columbia · Florence · Lumberton · Cape Lookout
GEORGIA · CAROLINA · Orangeburg · Cape Fear
Augusta · Savannah · Charleston · Cape Romain
Macon
Columbus
Albany · Jesup · Brunswick
Valdosta · Okefenokee Swamp · Jacksonville
Tallahassee · Lake City · St Augustine
Apalachee Bay · Gainesville · Daytona Beach
F L O R I D A · Orlando · Cape Canaveral
Tampa- · Lakeland
St Petersburg · Lake Okeechobee · West Palm Beach
Naples · The Everglades · Miami- · Fort Lauderdale
Cape Sable

Grand Bahama
Freeport City
Great Abaco
Bimini Is
Eleuthera
New Providence · NASSAU
Andros · Cat I.
San Salvador
Exuma Is · Exuma Sd · Rum Cay
Great Exuma · Long I.
THE BAHAMAS · Crooked I. Pass. · Crooked I.
Florida Keys · Straits of Florida
Acklins I.
Mayaguana
Turks and Caicos Islands (UK)
Little Inagua · Cockburn Town Turks Is
Great Inagua

Bermuda (UK) · Hamilton

HAVANA · Matanzas
Pinar del Rio · Arch. de Sabana · Arch. de Camagüey
Santa Clara
G. of Batabanó · Cienfuegos · C U B A · Ciego de Ávila · Victoria de · Holguín
Arch. de los Canarreos · Camagüey · las Tunas
Isle of Pines
Jardines de · Bayamo
la Riena · Sa Maestra · Guantánamo · Windward Passage
Little Cayman · 2005 Turquino · Santiago · Port-de-Paix
Cayman · C. Cruz · de Cuba · Cap · Santiago
Grand Cayman · Brac · Haïtien
Cayman Is (UK) · Gonaïves · HAITI · Pico Duarte 3175
Montego Bay · Jérémie · PORT-AU- · 2680
JAMAICA · KINGSTON · PRINCE · La Selle · La Romana
Les Cayes · Jacmel · DOMINICAN REPUBLIC
H i s p a n i o l a
C. Beata
Beata I.

G R E A T E R   A N T I L L E S

Swan Is (Honduras)

SAN JUAN · Virgin Is (UK) · Leeward Islands
Anegada (UK)
St John · Anguilla (UK)
Mayagüez · (USA) · Saint Martin (Fr.)
Ponce · Sint · St Barthélémy (Fr.)
PUERTO RICO · Mona · Maarten · Barbuda
(USA) · St Croix · (Neth.) · ANTIGUA & BARBUDA
(USA) · ST JOHN'S
ST KITTS- · Antigua
NEVIS
Montserrat · Guadeloupe (Fr.)
(UK) · Pointe- · Marie Galante (Fr.)
à-Pitre
DOMINICA
ROSEAU · Windward Is
Martinique · Fort-de-
(Fr.) · France
CASTRIES · BARBADOS
ST LUCIA
Kingstown · BRIDGETOWN
ST VINCENT & · The Grenadines
THE GRENADINES
GRENADA
ST GEORGE'S · Tobago

C A R I B B E A N   S E A

L e s s e r   A n t i l l e s

Caratasca Lagoon
Coco
RAS · I.de Providencia (Colombia)
Cayos Miskito
Isabella · Rio Grande
Perlas Pt · I.de San Andrés (Colombia)
Mosquitos Coast · Is del Maíz (Nic.)
NICARAGUA
Nicaragua · S. Juan

Aruba (Neth.) · Netherlands Antilles
Gallinas Pt · Los · Bonaire
Guajira · Taques · Curaçao
Pen. · Los Roques (Ven.) · Orchila (Ven.)
Ríohacha · Coro · Blanquilla (Ven.)
Maicao · G. of · La Tortuga · Los Testigos
Santa Marta · Venezuela · Los · Margarita · Tobago
Barranquilla · Cristóbal Colón · Maracaibo · Teques · Maiquetía · Cumaná · Paria Pen.
Cartagena · 5775 · Cabimas · Barquisimeto · Valencia · Los · C. Cadera
Valledupar · CARACAS · Maracay · Teques · Barcelona · Güiria
TRINIDAD & TOBAGO
PORT OF SPAIN
Trinidad
Maturín
Orinoco Delta

COSTA
RICA · SAN JOSÉ
Chirripó · Gulf of
3820 · Mosquitos · Colón · Gulf of Darién
Panama Canal · PANAMA CITY · Gulf of Morrosquillo · Sincelejo
Baru · Coronado · 3475 · Montería
Bay · Osa Pen. · David · P A N A M A · Gulf of Panamá
Gulf of Chiriquí · Azuero Pen. · Mala Pt
Nicoya · I. Coiba · Mariato Pt
Gulf of Cupica · Bucaramanga
C O L O M B I A · Cúcuta · San Cristóbal
Medellín · Bello
Quibdó · Tunja

L. Maracaibo
Valera · Cord. de Mérida
Acarigua · Guanare
Mérida · Barinas
San Fernando de Apure
V E N E Z U E L A
Ciudad Bolívar · Ciudad Guayana
Orinoco
Zaraza · Guanipa · Tigre
Meta · Cord. Oriental
Sierra Nevada del Cocuy · 5493
Meta
Cerro Yaví · 2283
La Gran Sabana
Mt Roraima · 2810
GUYANA

Lambert Azimuthal Equal Area projection

Map labels

A B C D E F

9 90° 80° 70° 60°

Yucatan Channel
Cuba
Bahamas
Yucatán
Greater Antilles
Hispaniola
Jamaica
Puerto Rico
Leeward Is
G. of Honduras
Sierra Madre
L. Nicaragua
CARIBBEAN SEA
Lesser Antilles
Windward Is
Curaçao
Trinidad

ATLANTIC
OCEAN

Isthmus of Panama
G. of Darien
Cordillera Central
Llanos
Orinoco
Mt Roraima 2810
Guiana Highlands
Essequibo

Meta
I. de Coco
I. de Malpelo
Japurá
Cotopaxi 5897
Chimborazo 6310
Marañón
Amazon Delta
Equator

Galapagos Islands
G. of Guayaquil
Amazon
Juruá
Purús
Madeira
Negro
Amazon
Tapajós
Xingu
Fernando de Noronha
C. de São Roque

Pta Negra
Selvas
A N D E S
Huascarán 6768

PACIFIC
OCEAN

Atacama Desert
L. Titicaca
L. Poopó
Planalto do Mato Grosso
Brazilian
Highlands
São Francisco
Araguaia
Tocantins
Parnaíba

Ojos del Salado 6908
Gran Chaco
Paraguay
Paraná
Agulhas Negras 2797
Trindade
Martin Vaz Is
Tropic of Capricorn

Aconcagua 6960
Paraná
Uruguay
Pampas
Rio de la Plata

SOUTH
ATLANTIC
OCEAN

Golfo de San Matías
Isla de Chiloé
Patagonia

Bahía Grande
Str. of Magellan
Tierra del Fuego
Cape Horn
Falkland Islands
South Georgia
South Sandwich Is

Inset map

VENEZUELA
GUYANA
SURINAME
FR. GUIANA
COLOMBIA
Equator
ECUADOR
PERU
BRAZIL
BOLIVIA
PARAGUAY
Tropic of Capricorn
CHILE
ARGENTINA
URUGUAY

SCALE 1 : 80 000 000

Relief legend

Relief
Relief metres
5000
3000
2000
1000
500
200
0
sea level
200
under sea level
3000
5000

Lambert Azimuthal Equal Area projection

1 TEMPERATURE AND PRESSURE : JANUARY

1014
1014
1012
1012
Equator
LOW
1010
1012
1012
1014
Tropic of Capricorn
1014
1012
1014
1012
1012

Average temperature °C
24
16
8

Wind direction
Isobar in millibars reduced to sea level

1010
1010
1010
1008
1008
1006
1006
1004
1004

2 TEMPERATURE AND PRESSURE : JULY

1010
1010
LOW
1012
1014
1014
Equator
1012
1016
1016
1018
1020

Average temperature °C
24
16
8
0

Wind direction
Isobar in millibars reduced to sea level

1018
1018
1020
1018
1016
1016
1014
1014
1012
1012
1010
1010

3 ANNUAL RAINFALL

Quito
Equator
Belem
Iguatu

Tropic of Capricorn

Average annual rainfall mm
3000
2000
1000
500
250
0

Santiago

Punta Arenas

4 STATISTICS

Quito (2879 metres)	Jan	Feb	Mar	Apr	May	Jun	Jul	Aug	Sep	Oct	Nov	Dec
Temperature - max.(°C)	22	22	22	21	21	22	22	23	23	22	22	22
Temperature - min. (°C)	8	8	8	8	8	7	7	7	7	8	7	8
Rainfall - (mm)	99	112	142	175	137	43	20	31	69	112	97	79

Belem (13 metres)	Jan	Feb	Mar	Apr	May	Jun	Jul	Aug	Sep	Oct	Nov	Dec
Temperature - max.(°C)	31	30	31	31	31	31	31	31	32	32	32	32
Temperature - min. (°C)	22	22	23	23	23	22	22	22	22	22	22	22
Rainfall - (mm)	318	358	358	320	259	170	150	112	89	84	66	155

Iguatu (209 metres)	Jan	Feb	Mar	Apr	May	Jun	Jul	Aug	Sep	Oct	Nov	Dec
Temperature - max.(°C)	34	33	32	31	31	31	32	32	35	36	36	36
Temperature - min. (°C)	23	23	23	23	22	22	21	21	22	23	23	23
Rainfall - (mm)	89	173	185	160	61	61	36	5	18	18	10	33

Santiago (520 metres)	Jan	Feb	Mar	Apr	May	Jun	Jul	Aug	Sep	Oct	Nov	Dec
Temperature - max.(°C)	29	29	27	23	18	14	15	17	19	22	26	28
Temperature - min. (°C)	12	11	9	7	5	3	3	4	6	7	9	11
Rainfall - (mm)	3	3	5	13	64	84	76	56	31	15	8	5

Punta Arenas (8 metres)	Jan	Feb	Mar	Apr	May	Jun	Jul	Aug	Sep	Oct	Nov	Dec
Temperature - max.(°C)	14	14	12	10	7	5	4	6	8	11	12	14
Temperature - min. (°C)	7	7	5	4	2	1	-1	1	2	3	4	6
Rainfall - (mm)	38	23	33	36	33	41	28	31	23	28	18	36

SCALE 1 : 68 000 000

Lambert Azimuthal Equal Area projection

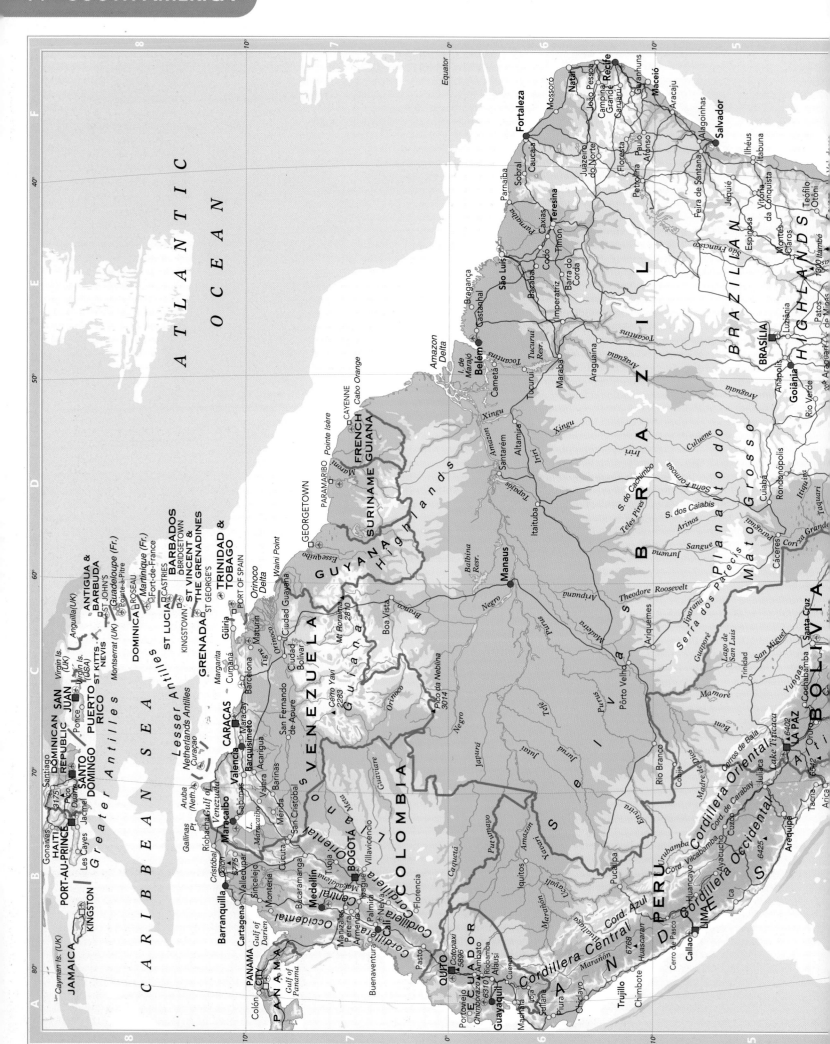

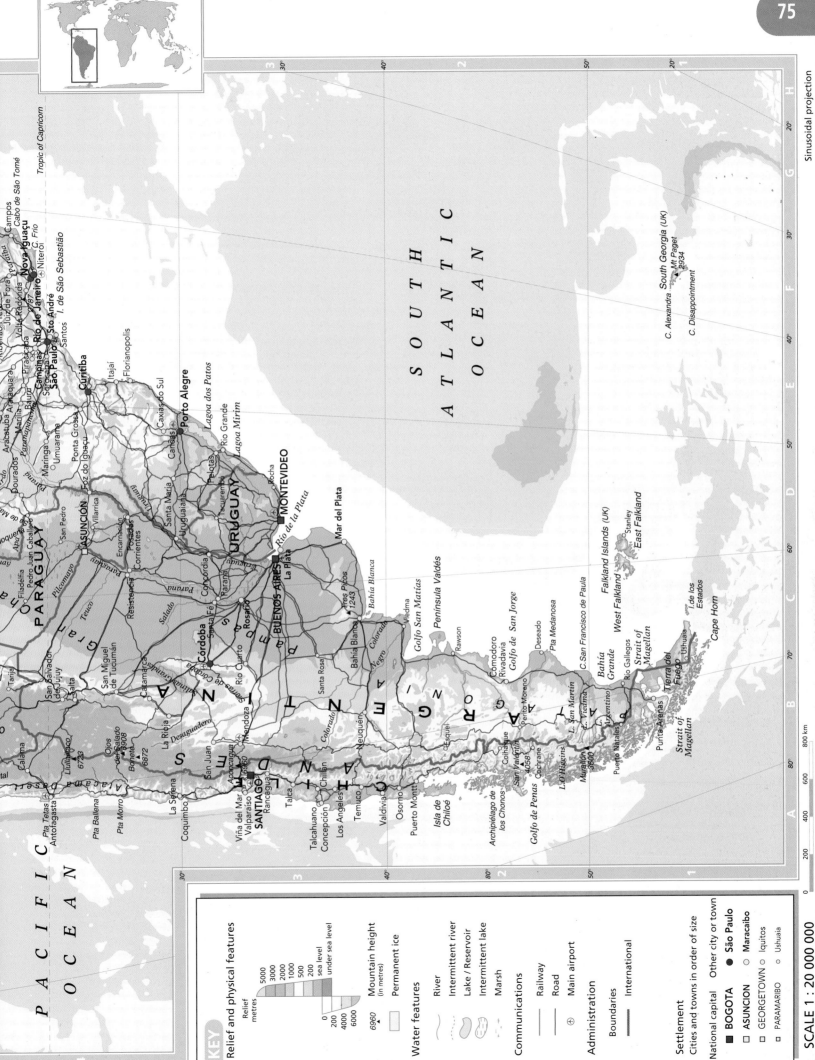

Sinusoidal projection

P A C I F I C

O C E A N

Tropic of Capricorn

Cachoeiro de Itapemirim
Campos
Cabo de São Tomé
C. Frio
Niterói
Nova Iguaçu
787
Rio de Janeiro
Sto André
I. de São Sebastião

Ribeirão Preto
Juiz de Fora
Volta Redonda
Portilha
Santos
Piracicaba
Sorocaba
Campinas
São Paulo
Bauru
Marília
Araraquara
Araçatuba

S O U T H

A T L A N T I C

O C E A N

Maringá
Dourados
Parananaíba
Paraná
Umuarama
Ponta Grossa
Itajaí
Curitiba
Florianópolis

Foz do Iguaçu
Caxias do Sul
Canoas
Porto Alegre
Lagoa dos Patos
Rio Grande
Pelotas
Lagoa Mirim

Ivaí
Uruguai
Villarrica
ASUNCIÓN
San Pedro
Encarnación
Pedro Juan Caballero
Paraná
Paraguay
Santa Maria
Uruguaiana
Concórdia
Bagé
Rocha
MONTEVIDEO

P A R A G U A Y
Filadélfia
Apa
G r a n
Pilcomayo
Teuco
Concepción
Resistencia
Corrientes
Santa Fé
Paraná
URUGUAY
Rio de la Plata
Mar del Plata

Tarija
Salta
San Salvador de Jujuy
San Miguel de Tucumán
Santiago del Estero
Salado
Córdoba
Sierras de Córdoba
Rosario
Río Cuarto
BUENOS AIRES
La Plata
Tres Picos 1243
Bahía Blanca
Calama
Antofagasta
Pta Tetas
Pta Ballena
Pta Morro
Catamarca
La Rioja
Desaguadero
San Juan
Mendoza
San Luis
Santa Rosa
Bahía Blanca
Colorado
Negro
Bahía Blanca
Viedma
Golfo San Matías
Península Valdés

C H A C O

Ojos del Salado 6908
Bonete
6872
Aconcagua 6960
SANTIAGO
Rancagua
Talca
Chillán
Neuquén
Río Negro

A N D E S

La Serena
Coquimbo
Viña del Mar
Valparaíso
San Antonio
Concepción
Talcahuano
Los Ángeles
Temuco
Valdivia
Osorno
Puerto Montt
Isla de Chiloé
Archipiélago de los Chonos
Golfo de Penas

C H I L E
A R G E N T I N A
P A T A G O N I A

Colorado
Viedma
Rawson
Comodoro Rivadavia
Golfo de San Jorge
Deseado
Pta Medanosa
C. San Francisco de Paula

Falkland Islands (UK)
Stanley
East Falkland
West Falkland

Esquel
Coihaique
San Valentín 4058
Cochrane
Perito Moreno
L. Buenos Aires
L. San Martín
O'Higgins
Murallón 3600
L. Viedma
L. Argentino
Puerto Natales
Río Gallegos
Punta Arenas
Strait of Magellan

Bahía Grande
Ushuaia
Tierra del Fuego
I. de los Estados
Cape Horn

C. Alexandra
South Georgia (UK)
Mt Paget 2934
C. Disappointment

Atacama Desert
Llullaillaco 6723

200 400 600 800 km
0   200   400

SCALE 1 : 20 000 000

KEY

Relief and physical features

Relief metres
5000
3000
2000
1000
500
200
sea level
under sea level

0
200
4000
6000

6960 ▲ **Mountain height** (in metres)

Permanent ice

Water features

~~~ River

- - - Intermittent river

Lake / Reservoir

Intermittent lake

Marsh

Communications

—— Railway

—— Road

⊕ Main airport

Administration

Boundaries

—— International

Settlement

National capital   Other city or town

■ **BOGOTA**   ● **São Paulo**

□ **ASUNCION**   ○ **Maracaibo**

▫ GEORGETOWN   ○ Iquitos

▫ PARAMARIBO   ○ Ushuaia

Cities and towns in order of size

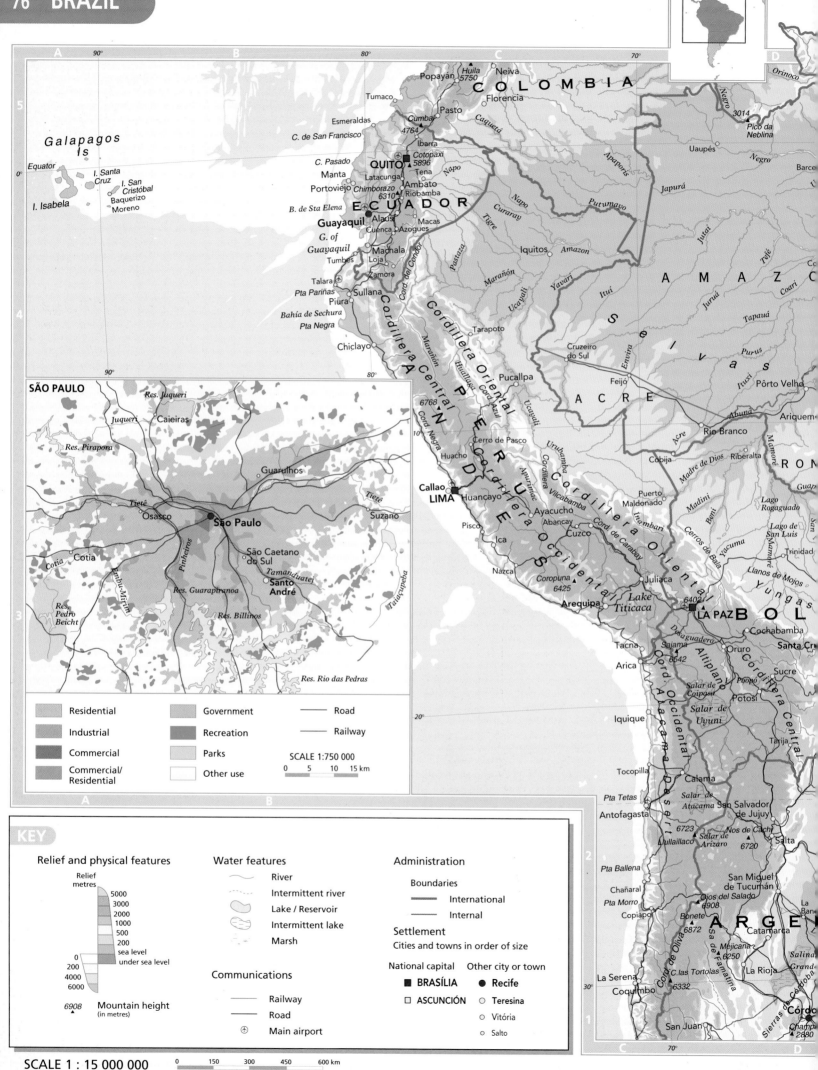

Galapagos Is

Equator

I. Santa Cruz
I. San Cristóbal
Baquerizo Moreno
I. Isabela

COLOMBIA

Popayán · Huila 5750 · Neiva
Tumaco · Pasto · Florencia
Esmeraldas
C. de San Francisco · Cumbal 4764 · Ibarra
C. Pasado
QUITO · Cotopaxi 5896
Manta · Latacunga · Tena
Portoviejo · Chimborazo 6310 · Ambato · Riobamba
B. de Sta Elena · Alausí
ECUADOR · Macas
Guayaquil · Cuenca · Azogues
G. of Guayaquil · Machala
Tumbes · Loja
Talara · Zamora
Pta Pariñas · Sullana
Piura
Bahía de Sechura
Pta Negra
Chiclayo

Orinoco
Pico da Neblina
Uaupés
Negro
Barce

Iquitos · Amazon
Napo
Curaray
Tigre
Marañón
Ucayali
Yavari
Juruá
Tefé
Coari

SELVAS

AMAZO

Cruzeiro do Sul
Feijó
ACRE
Pôrto Velho
Abuna
Ariquem
Rio Branco
Cobija
Riberalta
RON
Guap

Tarapoto
Pucallpa
6768
Cerro de Pasco
Huacho
Callao
LIMA · Huancayo
Pisco
Ica
Nazca
Coropuna 6425
Arequipa

Urubamba
Cordillera Vilcabamba
Ayacucho
Abancay
Cuzco
Cord. de Carabay

Puerto Maldonado
Madini
Beni
Llanos de Mojos
Lago Rogaguado
Lago de San Luis
Trinidad
San

PERU

Lake Titicaca
6402 · **LA PAZ** **BOL**
Cochabamba
Santa Cr

Tacna
Arica
6542 Sajama
Oruro
Poopó
Sucre
Potosí
Tarija

Altiplano
Salar de Coipasa
Salar de Uyuni

Iquique
Tocopilla
Pta Tetas
Antofagasta
Pta Ballena
Chañaral
Pta Morro
Copiapó
La Serena
Coquimbo

6723 Llullaillaco
Salar de Arizaro 6720
San Salvador de Jujuy
San Miguel de Tucumán
Nos de Cachi 6720
Salta
Ojos del Salado 6908
Bonete 6872
6250 Mejicana
6332 C. las Tortolas
ARGE
Catamarca
La Rioja
La Ban
La
Salina Grand

San Juan
Córdo
2880 Champa

SÃO PAULO

Res. Juqueri
Juqueri · Caieiras
Res. Pirapora
Res. Juqueri
Guarulhos
Tietê
Osasco
São Paulo
Cotia
Cotia
Pinheiros
São Caetano do Sul
Tamanduatei
Embu-Mirim
Res. Guarapiranoa
Santo André
Res. Pedro Beicht
Res. Billinos
Tietê
Suzano
Taiaçupeba
Res. Rio das Pedras

Residential	Government	Road
Industrial	Recreation	Railway
Commercial	Parks	
Commercial/Residential	Other use	

SCALE 1:750 000
0 5 10 15 km

SCALE 1 : 15 000 000
0 150 300 450 600 km

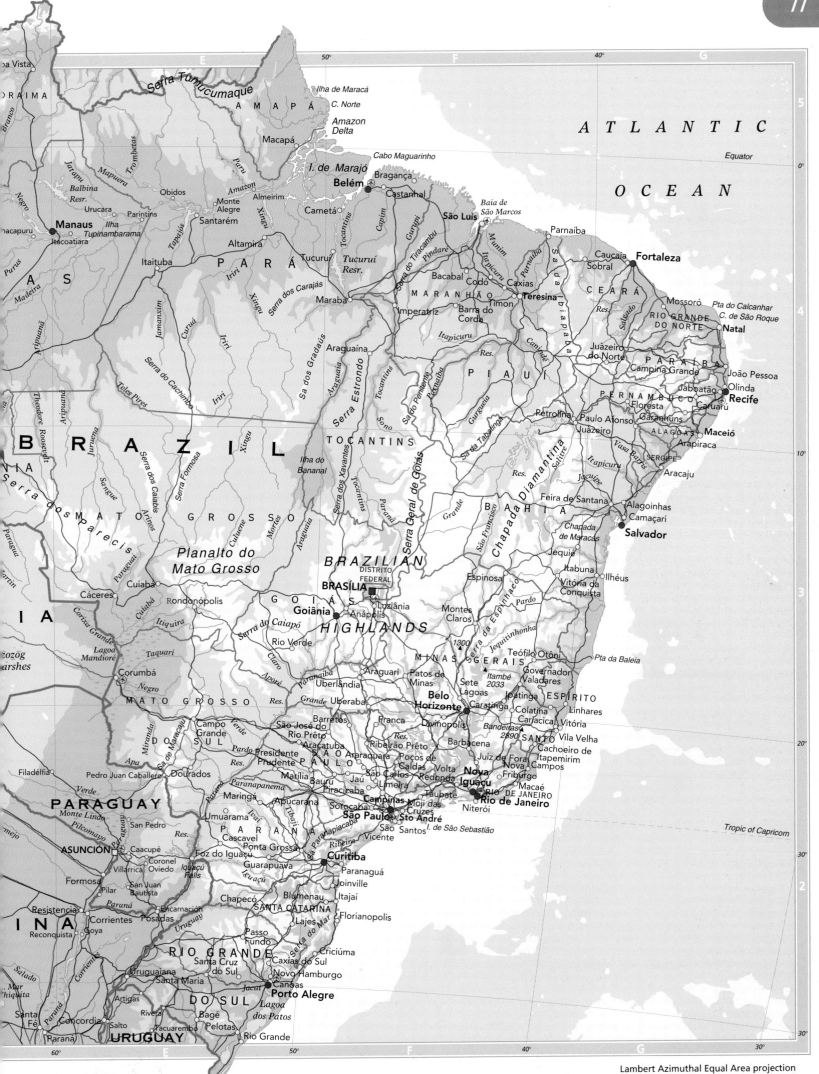

Lambert Azimuthal Equal Area projection

1 POPULATION DENSITY

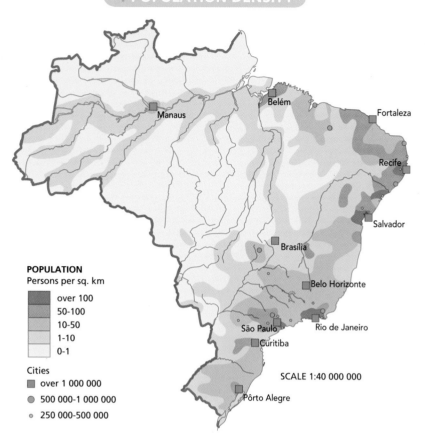

POPULATION
Persons per sq. km

- over 100
- 50-100
- 10-50
- 1-10
- 0-1

Cities

- over 1 000 000
- 500 000-1 000 000
- 250 000-500 000

SCALE 1:40 000 000

3 MAIN CITIES

City	1970 census	1991 census	% change
São Paulo	5 924 615	15 199 423	157
Rio de Janeiro	4 251 918	9 600 528	126
Belo Horizonte	1 235 030	3 461 905	180
Pôrto Alegre	885 545	3 015 960	240
Recife	1 060 701	2 859 469	169
Salvador	1 007 195	2 472 131	145
Fortaleza	857 980	2 294 524	167
Curitiba	609 026	1 975 624	224
Brasília	537 492	1 596 274	197
Belém	633 374	1 334 460	110

4 POPULATION GROWTH

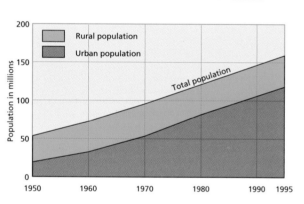

Rural population
Urban population
Total population

Population in millions

2 POPULATION CHANGE

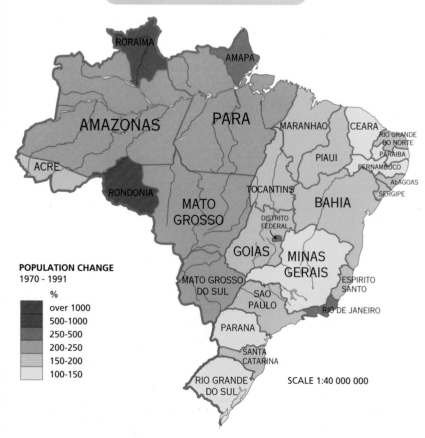

POPULATION CHANGE
1970 - 1991

%

- over 1000
- 500-1000
- 250-500
- 200-250
- 150-200
- 100-150

SCALE 1:40 000 000

5 MIGRATION

People are moving from the poorer areas of the northeast to the potentially rich areas of the undeveloped Amazon rainforest.

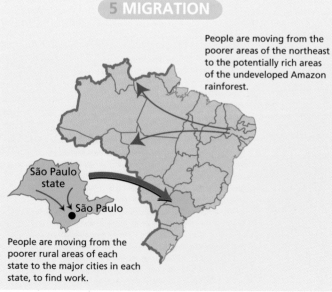

São Paulo state

São Paulo

People are moving from the poorer rural areas of each state to the major cities in each state, to find work.

6 URBAN AND RURAL CONTRASTS

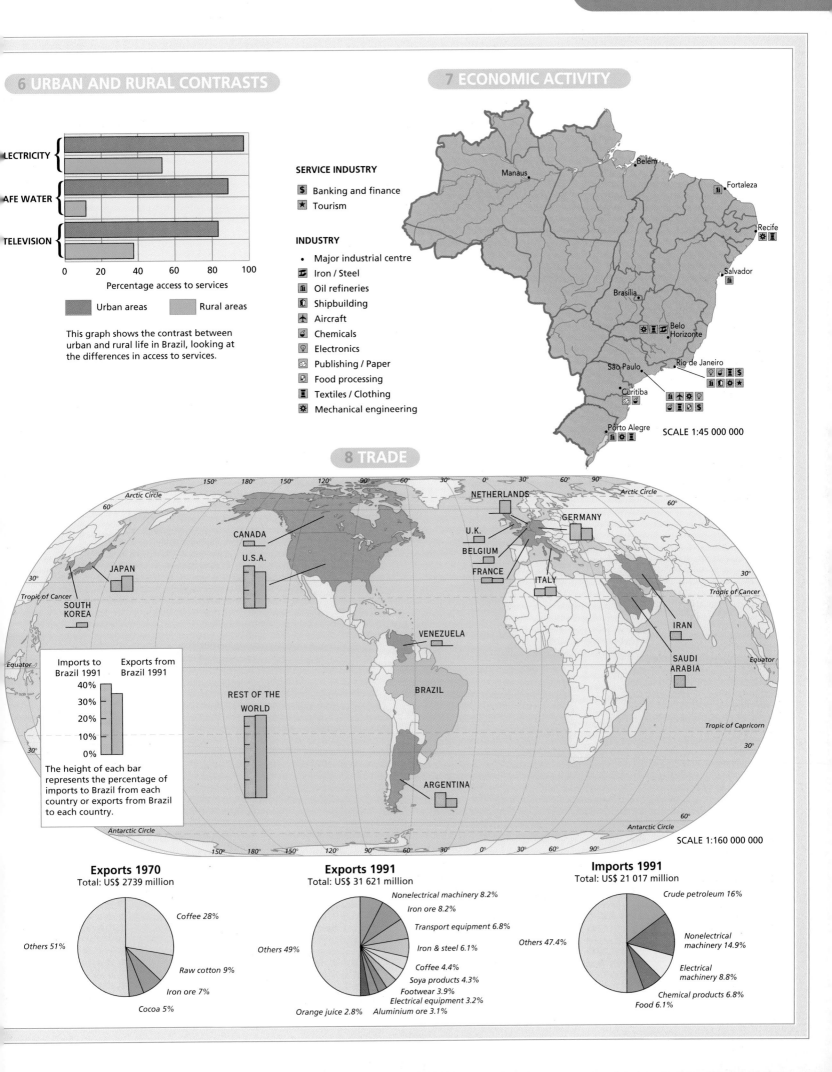

ELECTRICITY

SAFE WATER

TELEVISION

0 20 40 60 80 100
Percentage access to services

Urban areas   Rural areas

This graph shows the contrast between urban and rural life in Brazil, looking at the differences in access to services.

7 ECONOMIC ACTIVITY

SERVICE INDUSTRY

$ Banking and finance
★ Tourism

INDUSTRY

• Major industrial centre
◨ Iron / Steel
▥ Oil refineries
▣ Shipbuilding
✈ Aircraft
▧ Chemicals
▨ Electronics
▤ Publishing / Paper
▦ Food processing
▤ Textiles / Clothing
✳ Mechanical engineering

Manaus
Belém
Fortaleza
Recife
Salvador
Brasília
Belo Horizonte
São Paulo
Rio de Janeiro
Curitiba
Porto Alegre

SCALE 1:45 000 000

8 TRADE

Arctic Circle
NETHERLANDS
CANADA
U.K.
GERMANY
U.S.A.
BELGIUM
JAPAN
FRANCE
SOUTH KOREA
ITALY
IRAN
Tropic of Cancer
VENEZUELA
SAUDI ARABIA
Equator
REST OF THE WORLD
BRAZIL
Tropic of Capricorn
ARGENTINA
Antarctic Circle

Imports to Brazil 1991   Exports from Brazil 1991

40%
30%
20%
10%
0%

The height of each bar represents the percentage of imports to Brazil from each country or exports from Brazil to each country.

SCALE 1:160 000 000

Exports 1970
Total: US$ 2739 million

Coffee 28%
Others 51%
Raw cotton 9%
Iron ore 7%
Cocoa 5%

Exports 1991
Total: US$ 31 621 million

Nonelectrical machinery 8.2%
Iron ore 8.2%
Transport equipment 6.8%
Iron & steel 6.1%
Coffee 4.4%
Soya products 4.3%
Footwear 3.9%
Electrical equipment 3.2%
Aluminium ore 3.1%
Orange juice 2.8%
Others 49%

Imports 1991
Total: US$ 21 017 million

Crude petroleum 16%
Nonelectrical machinery 14.9%
Electrical machinery 8.8%
Chemical products 6.8%
Food 6.1%
Others 47.4%

Forest
Dense forest covers much of this area and the courses of the many tributaries of the river Guaporé can be followed cutting through the forest areas.

Marshy Savanna
An area of marshy savanna lies between the forest and the river Guaporé. Similar areas can also be seen south of the river around Laguna Bella Vista.

Deforested Areas
Large rectangular areas of pale blue on the satellite image are areas of deforestation, probably from commercial logging. In the bottom right of the image the pale blue line patterns are systematic deforestation due to the practice of slash and burn farming.

Highland
The highland of the Serra dos Parecis can be seen at the top right of the image.

Lakes
Several small dark blue/black outlines of lakes can be seen along the course of the river Guaporé. Laguna Bella Vista stands out clearly as a much larger feature.

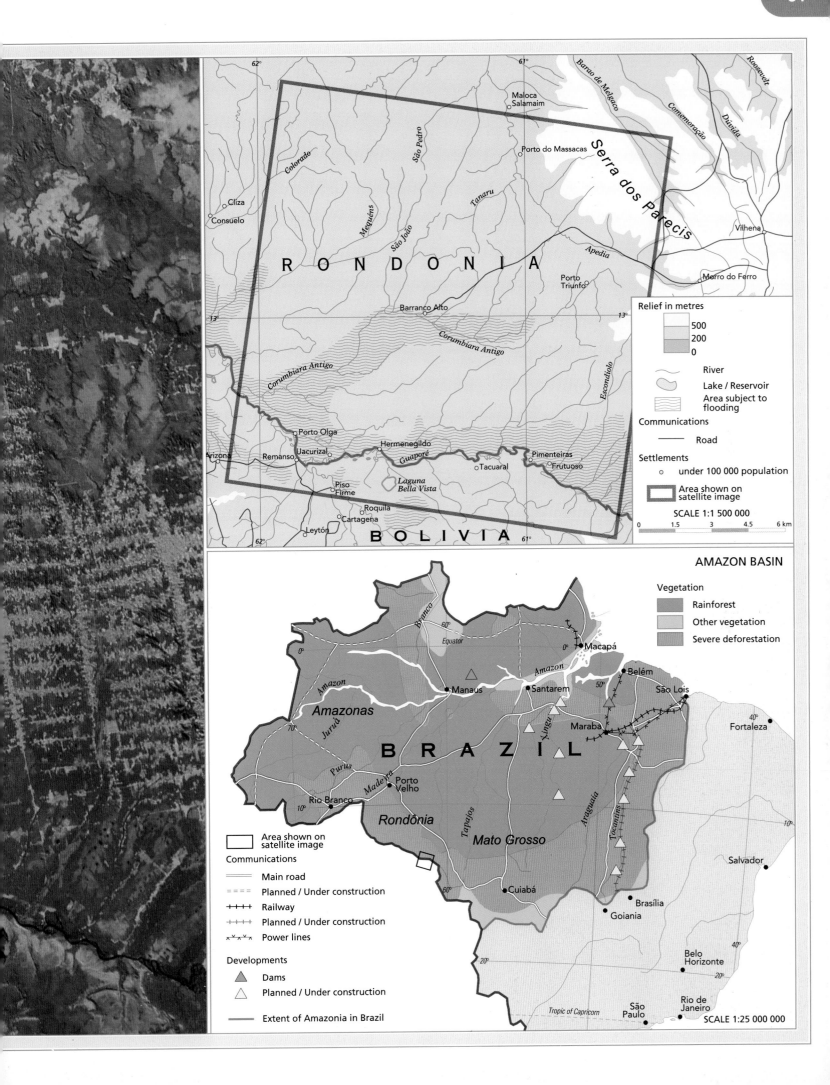

Relief in metres

- 500
- 200
- 0

~ River

Lake / Reservoir

Area subject to flooding

Communications

— Road

Settlements

○ under 100 000 population

☐ Area shown on satellite image

SCALE 1:1 500 000

0   1.5   3   4.5   6 km

Maloca Salamaim
Porto do Massacas

Serra dos Parecis

Colorado

Cliza

Consuelo

São Pedro

Tanaru

Vilhena

Meguéns

São João

R O N D O N I A

Apedia

Porto Triunfo

Morro do Ferro

Barranco Alto

13°

Corumbiara Antigo

Corumbiara Antigo

Corumbiara Antigo

Escondiolo

Porto Olga

Hermenegildo

Pimenteiras

Arizona

Remanso

Uacurizal

Guaporé

Tacuaral

Frutuoso

Laguna Bella Vista

Piso Firme

Roquila

Cartagena

Leytón

B O L I V I A

62°

61°

Barão de Melgaço

Comemoração

Dúvida

Roosevelt

AMAZON BASIN

Vegetation

- Rainforest
- Other vegetation
- Severe deforestation

Branco

Equator

Macapá

Amazon

Belém

Manaus

Santarem

São Lois

Amazonas

Amazon

Juruá

Xingu

Marabá

Fortaleza

B R A Z I L

Purus

Madeira

Porto Velho

Araguaia

Tocantins

Rio Branco

Rondônia

Tapajós

Mato Grosso

Salvador

☐ Area shown on satellite image

Communications

═══ Main road

═══ Planned / Under construction

+++++ Railway

+++++ Planned / Under construction

ʌᵛʌᵛʌ Power lines

Cuiabá

Brasília

Goiania

Developments

▲ Dams

△ Planned / Under construction

— Extent of Amazonia in Brazil

Belo Horizonte

Tropic of Capricorn

São Paulo

Rio de Janeiro

SCALE 1:25 000 000

A 20° B 10° C 0° D 10° E 20° F 30° G 40° H

Bay of Biscay
Alps
Danube
Black Sea
Caucasus Mts
Caspian Sea
C. Finisterre
Azores
Douro
Ebro
Pyrenees
Corsica
Apennines
Adriatic Sea
L. Van
40°
Tagus
Sierra Nevada
Balearic Is
Majorca
Sardinia
Taurus Mts
L. Urmia
Elburz Mts
C. St Vincent
Mediterranean Sea
Sicily
Crete
Cyprus
Tigris
Dasht-e Kavir
Madeira
Atlas Mountains
G. of Gabès
Zagros Mts
30°
Canary Is
Toubkal 4167
Gulf of Sirte
Suez Canal
Sinai
An Nafud
The Gulf
Tenerife
Qattara Depression
Nile
Hijaz Asir
Red Sea
Tropic of Cancer
S A H A R A
El Djouf
Mt Tahat 2918
Hoggar
Libyan Desert
L. Nasser
Rub'al Khali
20°
Sénégal
Djado Plateau
Tibesti
Nubian Desert
Gambia
Aïr
Mt Gréboun 1800
Emi Koussi 3415
Athara
Ras Dashen 4620
Fouta Djallon
Niger
L. Tana
Gulf of Aden
10°
Bani
White Volta
Black Volta
L. Volta
Jos Plateau
L. Chad
Chari
Logone
Benue
Darfur
J. Gimbala 3070
Blue Nile
Gezira
White Nile
Ethiopian Highlands
Shabeelle
Cape Palmas
Bight of Benin
Adamawa Highlands
Mt Cameroun 4100
Sangha
Sudd
Akobo
L. Turkana
Jubba
Gulf of Guinea
Bioco
Ubangi
Zaïre
Uele
Aruwimi
L. Albert
Mt Stanley 5119
Mt Kenya 5199
Equator
0°
Príncipe
São Tomé
Zaïre Basin
Kasai
Luataba
L. Edward
Lake Victoria
Kilimanjaro 5895
Pemba
ATLANTIC OCEAN
Zaïre
Kwilu
Chaine des Mitumba
Great Rift Valley
Masai Steppe
Zanzibar
INDIAN OCEAN
Mafia
Ascension I.
Cuanza
Lake Tanganyika
L. Mweru
Rufiji
Aldabra Is
10°
Muchinga Mts
L. Nyasa
Comoro Islands
Bié Plateau
Zambezi
Cunene
Cubango
L. Kariba
Zambezi
Madagascar
Namib Desert
Etosha Pan
Victoria Falls
Matabele Upland
Save
Mozambique Channel
20°
Okavango Delta
Kalahari Desert
Limpopo
Tropic of Capricorn
Orange
Vaal
Thabana Ntlenyana 3482
Drakensberg
30°
Great Karoo
Cape of Good Hope
C. Agulhas

Relief

Relief metres
5000
3000
2000
1000
500
200
0 sea level
under sea level
200
3000
5000

Inset map — countries:
MOROCCO, TUNISIA, WESTERN SAHARA, ALGERIA, LIBYA, EGYPT, MAURITANIA, MALI, NIGER, CHAD, SUDAN, ERITREA, SENEGAL, G., G.-B., GUINEA, BURKINA, B, NIGERIA, CENTRAL AFRICAN REPUBLIC, ETHIOPIA, SIERRA LEONE, CÔTE D'IVOIRE, GHANA, CAMEROON, UGANDA, KENYA, SOMALIA, LIBERIA, EQ. GUINEA, GABON, CONGO, ZAÏRE, R., BU., TANZANIA, ANGOLA, ZAMBIA, M., MALAWI, NAMIBIA, ZIMBABWE, MOZAMBIQUE, MADAGASCAR, BOTSWANA, SWAZILAND, SOUTH AFRICA, LESOTHO

B. BENIN
BU. BURUNDI
D. DJIBOUTI
G. GAMBIA
G.-B. GUINEA-BISSAU
M. MALAWI
R. RWANDA
T. TOGO

SCALE 1 : 115 000 000

SCALE 1 : 37 000 000

Lambert Azimuthal Equal Area projection

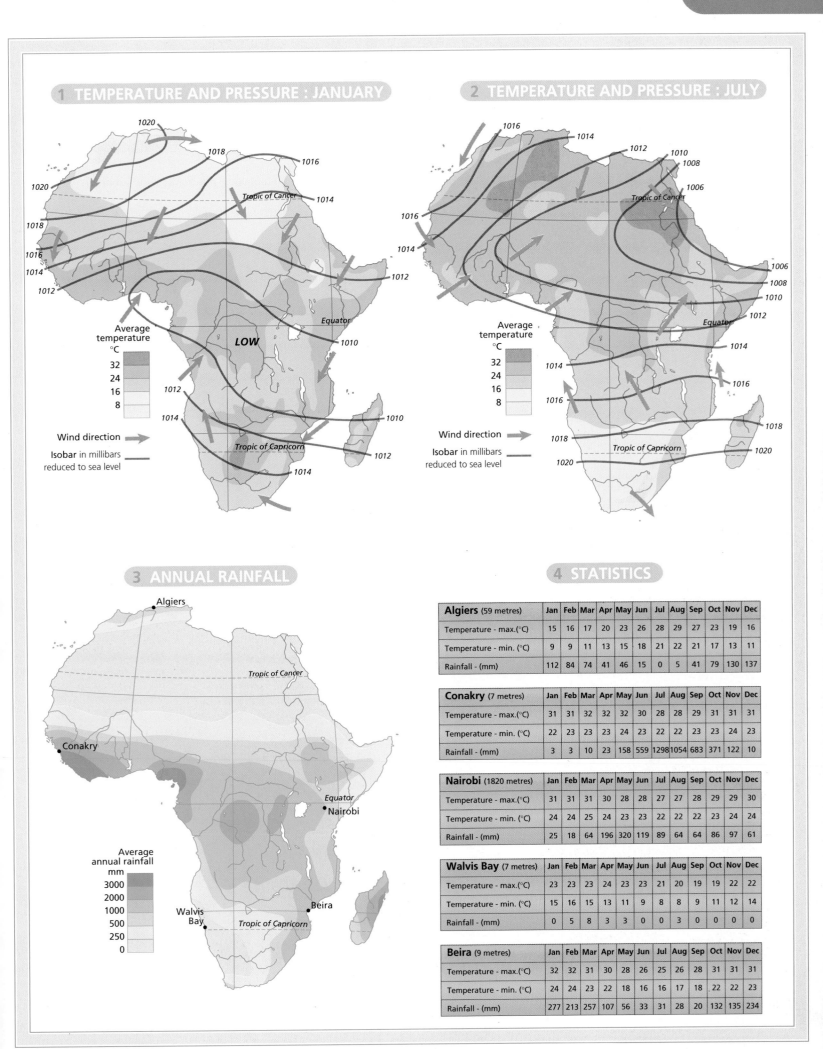

1 TEMPERATURE AND PRESSURE : JANUARY

1020
1018
1016
Tropic of Cancer
1014
1020
1018
1016
1014
1012

Average temperature
°C
32
24
16
8

LOW

1012
1014
1012
1010
1014

Wind direction
Isobar in millibars reduced to sea level

2 TEMPERATURE AND PRESSURE : JULY

1016
1014
1012
1010
1008
Tropic of Cancer
1006
1016
1014
1006
1008
1010
1012
Equator
1014

Average temperature
°C
32
24
16
8

1014
1016
1018
Tropic of Capricorn
1016
1018
1020
1020

Wind direction
Isobar in millibars reduced to sea level

3 ANNUAL RAINFALL

Algiers

Tropic of Cancer

Conakry

Equator
Nairobi

Average annual rainfall
mm
3000
2000
1000
500
250
0

Walvis Bay
Beira
Tropic of Capricorn

4 STATISTICS

Algiers (59 metres)	Jan	Feb	Mar	Apr	May	Jun	Jul	Aug	Sep	Oct	Nov	Dec
Temperature - max.(°C)	15	16	17	20	23	26	28	29	27	23	19	16
Temperature - min. (°C)	9	9	11	13	15	18	21	22	21	17	13	11
Rainfall - (mm)	112	84	74	41	46	15	0	5	41	79	130	137

Conakry (7 metres)	Jan	Feb	Mar	Apr	May	Jun	Jul	Aug	Sep	Oct	Nov	Dec
Temperature - max.(°C)	31	31	32	32	32	30	28	28	29	31	31	31
Temperature - min. (°C)	22	23	23	23	24	23	22	22	23	23	24	23
Rainfall - (mm)	3	3	10	23	158	559	1298	1054	683	371	122	10

Nairobi (1820 metres)	Jan	Feb	Mar	Apr	May	Jun	Jul	Aug	Sep	Oct	Nov	Dec
Temperature - max.(°C)	31	31	31	30	28	28	27	28	29	29	29	30
Temperature - min. (°C)	24	24	25	24	23	23	22	22	22	23	24	24
Rainfall - (mm)	25	18	64	196	320	119	89	64	64	86	97	61

Walvis Bay (7 metres)	Jan	Feb	Mar	Apr	May	Jun	Jul	Aug	Sep	Oct	Nov	Dec
Temperature - max.(°C)	23	23	23	24	23	23	21	20	19	19	22	22
Temperature - min. (°C)	15	16	15	13	11	9	8	8	9	11	12	14
Rainfall - (mm)	0	5	8	3	3	0	0	3	0	0	0	0

Beira (9 metres)	Jan	Feb	Mar	Apr	May	Jun	Jul	Aug	Sep	Oct	Nov	Dec
Temperature - max.(°C)	32	32	31	30	28	26	25	26	28	31	31	31
Temperature - min. (°C)	24	24	23	22	18	16	16	17	18	22	22	23
Rainfall - (mm)	277	213	257	107	56	33	31	28	20	132	135	234

SCALE 1 : 77 000 000

Lambert Azimuthal Equal Area projection

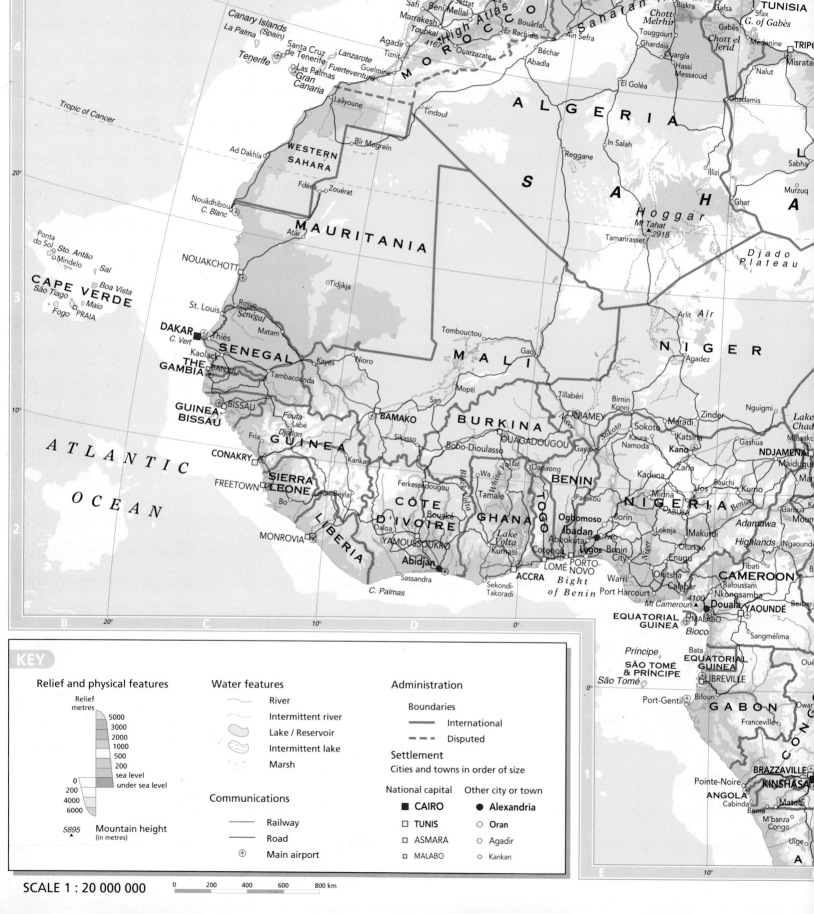

KEY

Relief and physical features

Relief
metres
5000
3000
2000
1000
500
200
sea level
under sea level
0
200
4000
6000

5895 ▲ Mountain height
(in metres)

Water features

〰 River

Intermittent river

Lake / Reservoir

Intermittent lake

Marsh

Communications

—— Railway

—— Road

⊕ Main airport

Administration

Boundaries

—— International

--- Disputed

Settlement

Cities and towns in order of size

National capital

■ CAIRO   ● Alexandria

□ TUNIS   ○ Oran

□ ASMARA   ○ Agadir

□ MALABO   ○ Kankan

Other city or town

SCALE 1 : 20 000 000

0   200   400   600   800 km

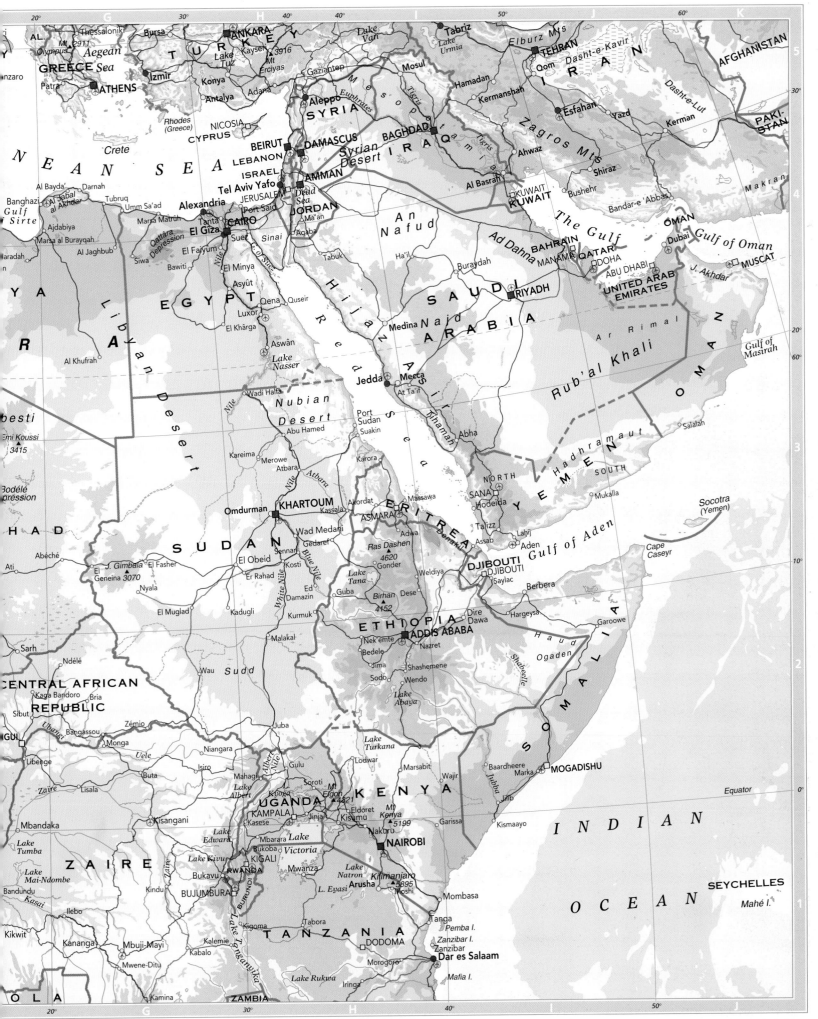

Millers Stereographic projection

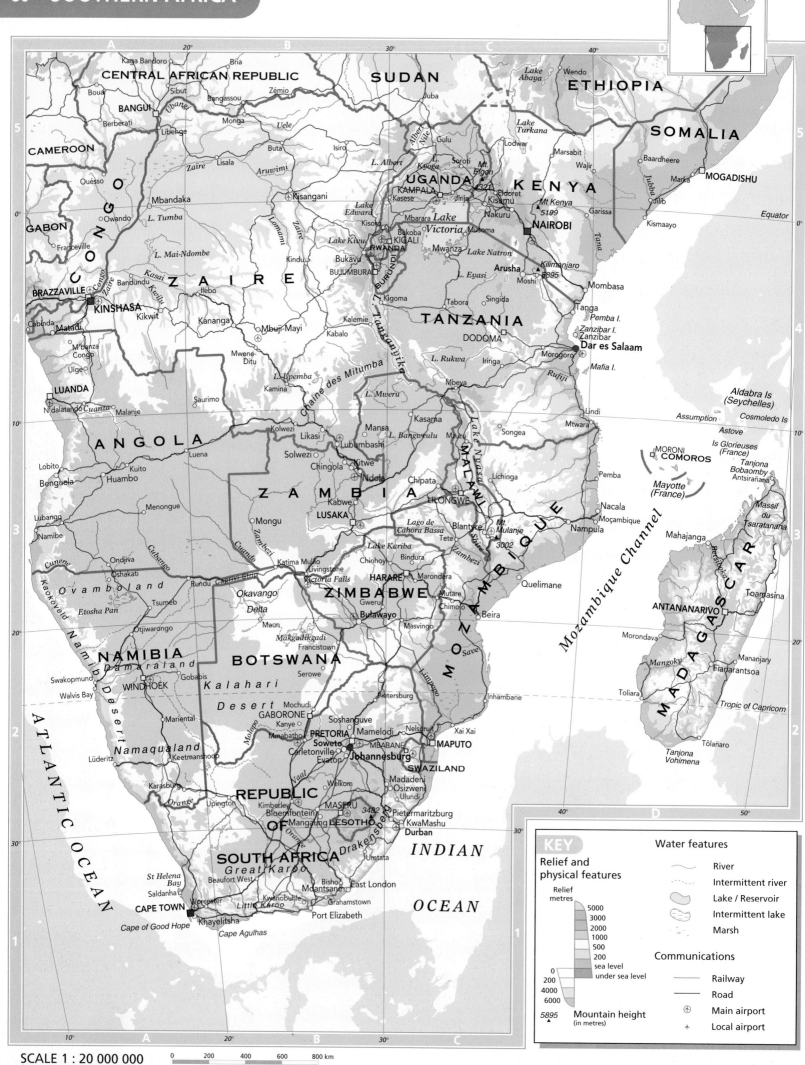

SCALE 1 : 20 000 000

| 0 | 200 | 400 | 600 | 800 km |

Bonne projection

KEY

Relief and physical features

Relief metres

5000
3000
2000
1000
500
200
sea level
under sea level

200
4000
6000

5895 Mountain height (in metres)

Water features

~~~ River
- - - Intermittent river
Lake / Reservoir
Intermittent lake
Marsh

Communications

Railway
Road
⊕ Main airport
✈ Local airport

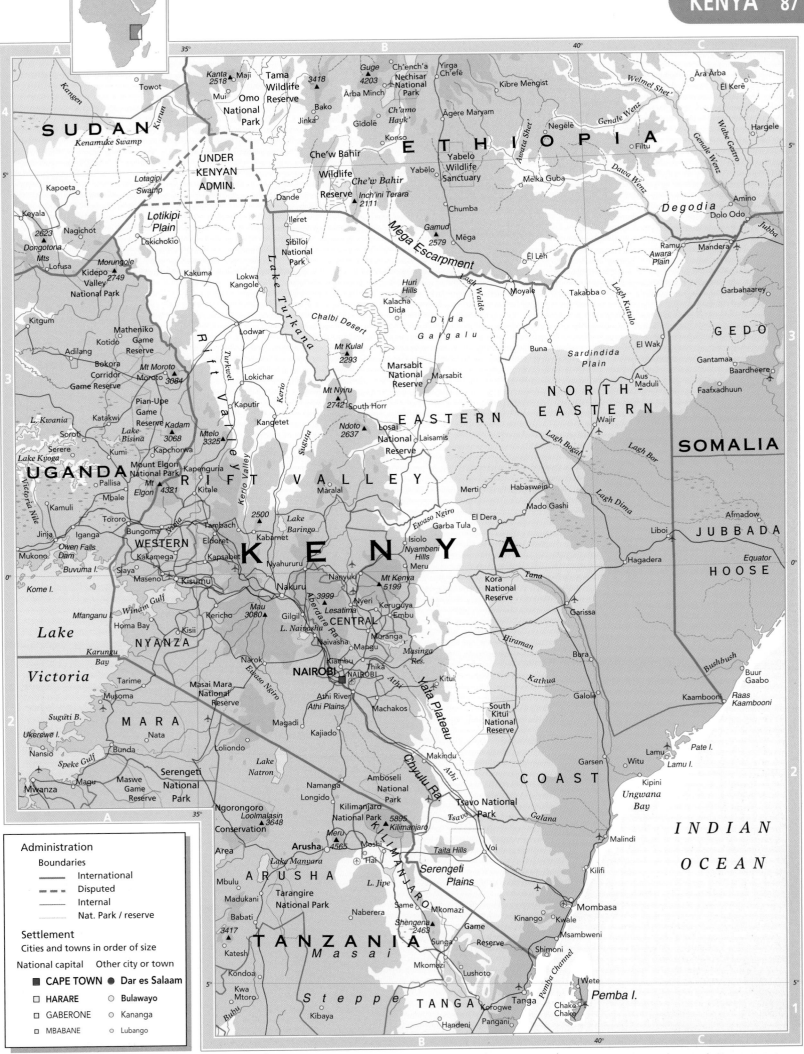

SUDAN

ETHIOPIA

SOMALIA

UGANDA

KENYA

TANZANIA

INDIAN OCEAN

Administration

Boundaries

——	International
– – –	Disputed
——	Internal
· · · · ·	Nat. Park / reserve

Settlement

Cities and towns in order of size

National capital   Other city or town

■	CAPE TOWN	●	Dar es Salaam
□	HARARE	○	Bulawayo
□	GABERONE	○	Kananga
□	MBABANE	○	Lubango

SCALE 1 : 5 000 000

0   50   100   150   200 km

Oblated Stereographic projection

1 POPULATION DENSITY

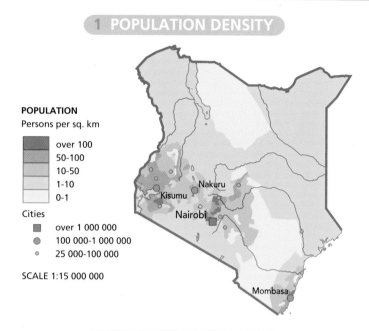

POPULATION

Persons per sq. km

- over 100
- 50-100
- 10-50
- 1-10
- 0-1

Cities

- over 1 000 000
- 100 000-1 000 000
- 25 000-100 000

SCALE 1:15 000 000

2 POPULATION CHANGE

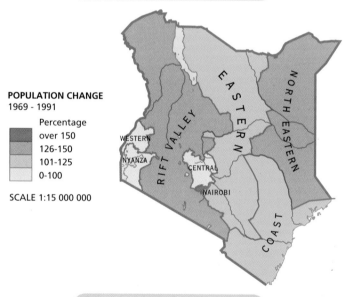

POPULATION CHANGE
1969 - 1991

Percentage
- over 150
- 126-150
- 101-125
- 0-100

SCALE 1:15 000 000

3 ECONOMIC ACTIVITY

INDUSTRY

- • Major industrial centre
- Iron / Steel
- Oil refineries
- Motor vehicles
- Mechanical engineering
- Publishing / Paper
- Chemicals
- Textiles / Clothing
- Food processing

CROPS

- Cash crop producing area

SCALE 1:15 000 000

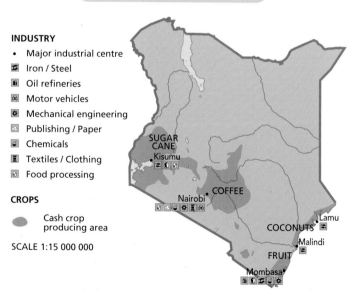

4 POPULATION GROWTH

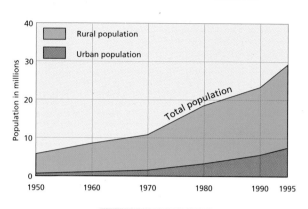

5 MAIN CITIES

City	1969 census	1991 census	% Increase
Nairobi	478 000	1 504 900	215
Mombasa	246 000	425 600	73
Kisumu	30 000	167 100	456
Nakuru	47 000	101 700	115
Machakos	4000	92 300	2300

6 TOURISM

- Hotel
- Lodge
- National game park
- National game reserve

SCALE 1:12 MILLION

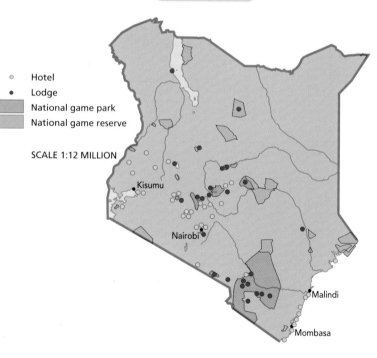

VISITORS TO KENYA 1993
Total 826 000

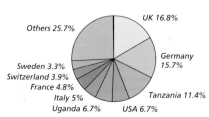

Others 25.7%
UK 16.8%
Germany 15.7%
Tanzania 11.4%
USA 6.7%
Uganda 6.7%
Italy 5%
France 4.8%
Switzerland 3.9%
Sweden 3.3%

TOURIST ARRIVALS
1984-1993

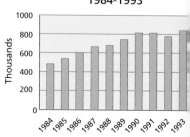

Thousands
1000
800
600
400
200
0
1984 1985 1986 1987 1988 1989 1990 1991 1992 1993

7 NAIROBI

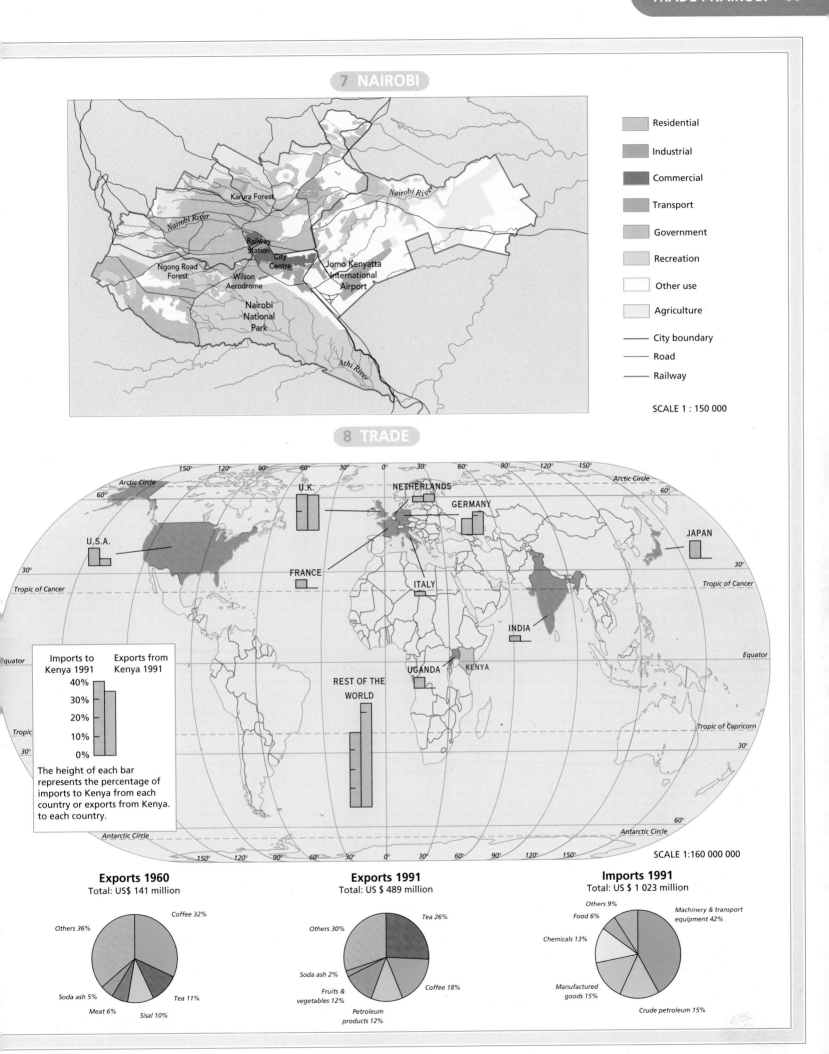

Karura Forest

Nairobi River

Nairobi River

Railway Station

City Centre

Ngong Road Forest

Wilson Aerodrome

Jomo Kenyatta International Airport

Nairobi National Park

Athi River

Residential

Industrial

Commercial

Transport

Government

Recreation

Other use

Agriculture

City boundary

Road

Railway

SCALE 1 : 150 000

8 TRADE

Arctic Circle

U.K.

NETHERLANDS

GERMANY

JAPAN

U.S.A.

FRANCE

ITALY

INDIA

UGANDA

KENYA

REST OF THE WORLD

Equator

Tropic of Cancer

Tropic of Capricorn

Antarctic Circle

SCALE 1:160 000 000

Imports to Kenya 1991

Exports from Kenya 1991

40%
30%
20%
10%
0%

The height of each bar represents the percentage of imports to Kenya from each country or exports from Kenya. to each country.

Exports 1960
Total: US$ 141 million

Coffee 32%

Others 36%

Soda ash 5%

Meat 6%

Sisal 10%

Tea 11%

Exports 1991
Total: US $ 489 million

Tea 26%

Others 30%

Soda ash 2%

Fruits & vegetables 12%

Petroleum products 12%

Coffee 18%

Imports 1991
Total: US $ 1 023 million

Others 9%

Food 6%

Chemicals 13%

Machinery & transport equipment 42%

Manufactured goods 15%

Crude petroleum 15%

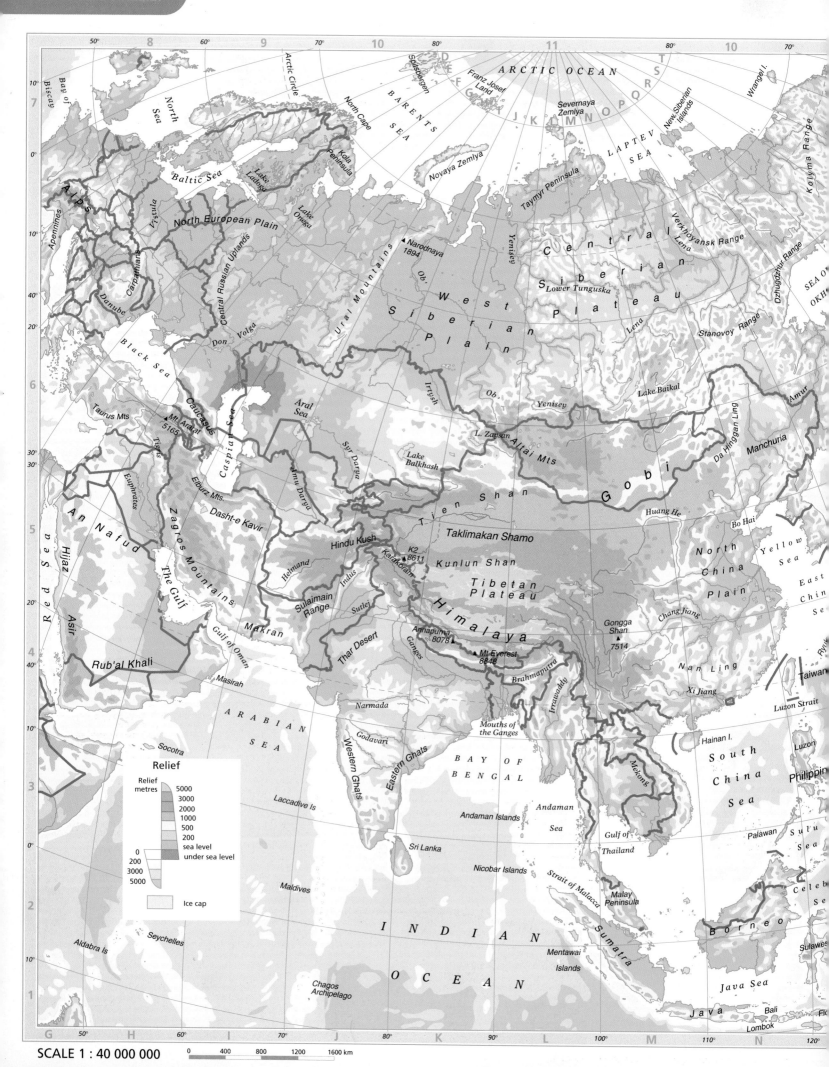

Relief

Relief
metres
5000
3000
2000
1000
500
200
0 sea level
under sea level
200
3000
5000

Ice cap

SCALE 1 : 40 000 000

0   400   800   1200   1600 km

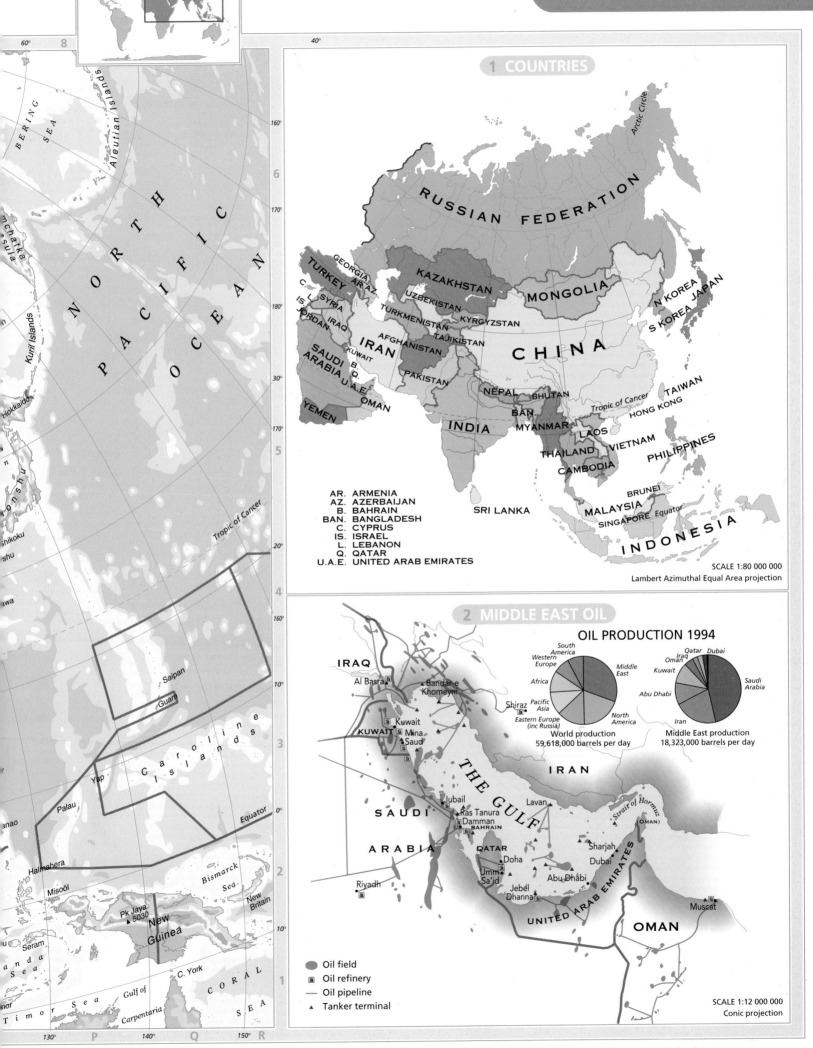

1 COUNTRIES

RUSSIAN FEDERATION

Arctic Circle

TURKEY
GEORGIA
AR.
AZ.
C. L
SYRIA
IS.
JORDAN
IRAQ
IRAN
KAZAKHSTAN
UZBEKISTAN
TURKMENISTAN
KYRGYZSTAN
AFGHANISTAN
TAJIKISTAN
MONGOLIA
CHINA
N KOREA
S KOREA
JAPAN
KUWAIT
B. Q.
SAUDI
ARABIA
U.A.E.
OMAN
YEMEN
PAKISTAN
NEPAL
BHUTAN
BAN.
INDIA
MYANMAR
Tropic of Cancer
TAIWAN
HONG KONG
LAOS
THAILAND
CAMBODIA
VIETNAM
PHILIPPINES
SRI LANKA
BRUNEI
MALAYSIA
SINGAPORE Equator
INDONESIA

AR. ARMENIA
AZ. AZERBAIJAN
B. BAHRAIN
BAN. BANGLADESH
C. CYPRUS
IS. ISRAEL
L. LEBANON
Q. QATAR
U.A.E. UNITED ARAB EMIRATES

SCALE 1:80 000 000
Lambert Azimuthal Equal Area projection

2 MIDDLE EAST OIL

OIL PRODUCTION 1994

South
America
Western
Europe
Africa
Pacific
Asia
Eastern Europe
(inc Russia)
Middle East
North
America
World production
59,618,000 barrels per day

Qatar Dubai
Iraq
Oman
Kuwait
Abu Dhabi
Iran
Saudi
Arabia
Middle East production
18,323,000 barrels per day

IRAQ
Al Basra
Bandar-e
Khomeyni
Shiraz
Kuwait
KUWAIT
Mina
Saud
IRAN
Jubail
Lavan
Strait of Hormuz
(OMAN)
Ras Tanura
Damman
BAHRAIN
SAUDI
ARABIA
THE GULF
Sharjah
Dubai
QATAR
Doha
Umm
Sa'id
Abu Dhabi
Riyadh
Jebel
Dhanna
UNITED ARAB EMIRATES
Muscat
OMAN

- Oil field
- Oil refinery
- Oil pipeline
- Tanker terminal

SCALE 1:12 000 000
Conic projection

NORTH PACIFIC OCEAN

BERING
SEA

Aleutian Islands

Kuril Islands

Hokkaido

Honshu

Shikoku

Kamchatka Peninsula

Tropic of Cancer

Saipan
Guam

Caroline Islands

Yap
Palau

Equator

Halmahera
Misoöl
Seram

Banda
Sea

Bismarck
Sea
New
Britain

Pk Jaya
5030
New
Guinea

C. York

Gulf of
Carpentaria

CORAL
SEA

Timor
Sea

Lambert Azimuthal Equal Area projection

1 TEMPERATURE : JANUARY

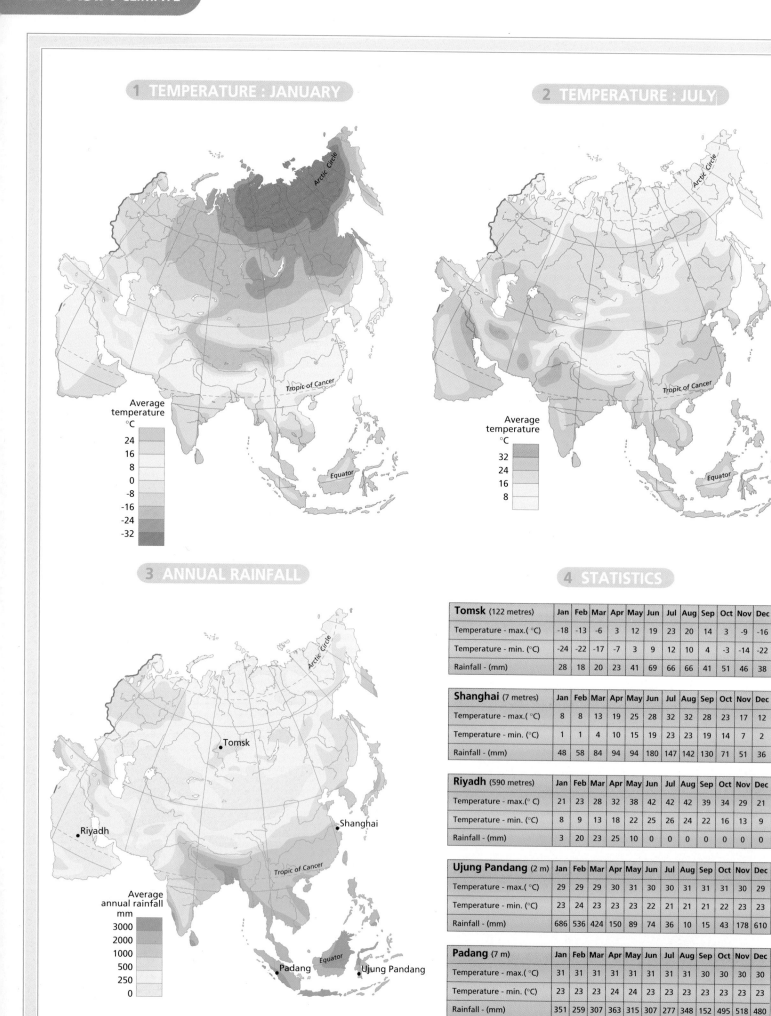

Average
temperature
°C

| 24 |
| 16 |
| 8 |
| 0 |
| -8 |
| -16 |
| -24 |
| -32 |

Tropic of Cancer

Equator

2 TEMPERATURE : JULY

Average
temperature
°C

| 32 |
| 24 |
| 16 |
| 8 |

Tropic of Cancer

Equator

3 ANNUAL RAINFALL

Tomsk

Riyadh

Shanghai

Tropic of Cancer

Padang   Equator   Ujung Pandang

Average
annual rainfall
mm

| 3000 |
| 2000 |
| 1000 |
| 500 |
| 250 |
| 0 |

4 STATISTICS

Tomsk (122 metres)	Jan	Feb	Mar	Apr	May	Jun	Jul	Aug	Sep	Oct	Nov	Dec
Temperature - max.(°C)	-18	-13	-6	3	12	19	23	20	14	3	-9	-16
Temperature - min. (°C)	-24	-22	-17	-7	3	9	12	10	4	-3	-14	-22
Rainfall - (mm)	28	18	20	23	41	69	66	66	41	51	46	38

Shanghai (7 metres)	Jan	Feb	Mar	Apr	May	Jun	Jul	Aug	Sep	Oct	Nov	Dec
Temperature - max.(°C)	8	8	13	19	25	28	32	32	28	23	17	12
Temperature - min. (°C)	1	1	4	10	15	19	23	23	19	14	7	2
Rainfall - (mm)	48	58	84	94	94	180	147	142	130	71	51	36

Riyadh (590 metres)	Jan	Feb	Mar	Apr	May	Jun	Jul	Aug	Sep	Oct	Nov	Dec
Temperature - max.(°C)	21	23	28	32	38	42	42	42	39	34	29	21
Temperature - min. (°C)	8	9	13	18	22	25	26	24	22	16	13	9
Rainfall - (mm)	3	20	23	25	10	0	0	0	0	0	0	0

Ujung Pandang (2 m)	Jan	Feb	Mar	Apr	May	Jun	Jul	Aug	Sep	Oct	Nov	Dec
Temperature - max.(°C)	29	29	29	30	31	30	30	31	31	31	30	29
Temperature - min. (°C)	23	24	23	23	23	22	21	21	21	22	23	23
Rainfall - (mm)	686	536	424	150	89	74	36	10	15	43	178	610

Padang (7 m)	Jan	Feb	Mar	Apr	May	Jun	Jul	Aug	Sep	Oct	Nov	Dec
Temperature - max.(°C)	31	31	31	31	31	31	31	31	30	30	30	30
Temperature - min. (°C)	23	23	23	24	24	23	23	23	23	23	23	23
Rainfall - (mm)	351	259	307	363	315	307	277	348	152	495	518	480

Lambert Azimuthal Equal Area projection

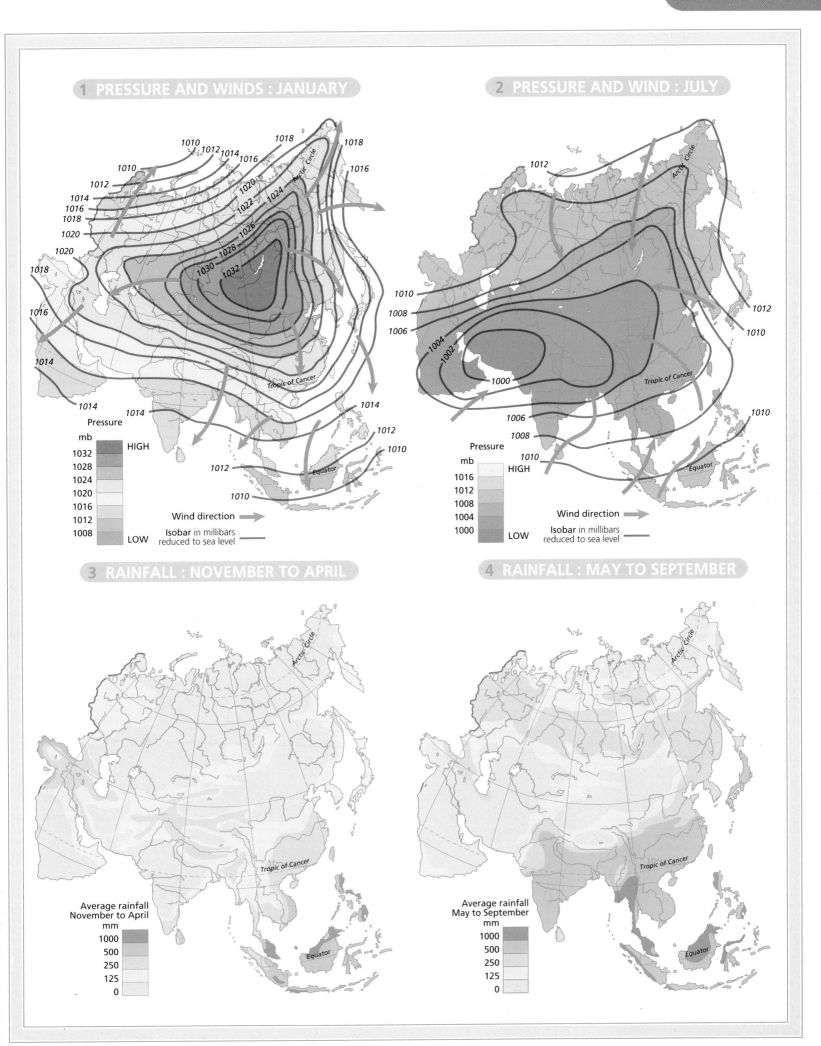

1 PRESSURE AND WINDS : JANUARY

1010 1012 1014 1016 1018
1018
1018
1010
1012
1014
1016
1018
1020
1020
1018
1016
1014
1014
1014

Arctic Circle

1020
1022
1024
1026
1028
1030 1032
1032

1014
1012
1010

Tropic of Cancer

1012

1010

Equator

Pressure

mb

1032	HIGH
1028	
1024	
1020	
1016	
1012	
1008	LOW

Wind direction →

Isobar in millibars
reduced to sea level

2 PRESSURE AND WIND : JULY

1012

Arctic Circle

1010
1008
1006

1004
1002

1000

1012
1010

Tropic of Cancer

1006
1008
1010

1010

Equator

Pressure

mb

1016	HIGH
1012	
1008	
1004	
1000	LOW

Wind direction →

Isobar in millibars
reduced to sea level

3 RAINFALL : NOVEMBER TO APRIL

Arctic Circle

Tropic of Cancer

**Average rainfall
November to April**

mm

1000	
500	
250	
125	
0	

Equator

4 RAINFALL : MAY TO SEPTEMBER

Arctic Circle

Tropic of Cancer

**Average rainfall
May to September**

mm

1000	
500	
250	
125	
0	

Equator

SCALE 1 : 100 000 000

Lambert Azimuthal Equal Area projection

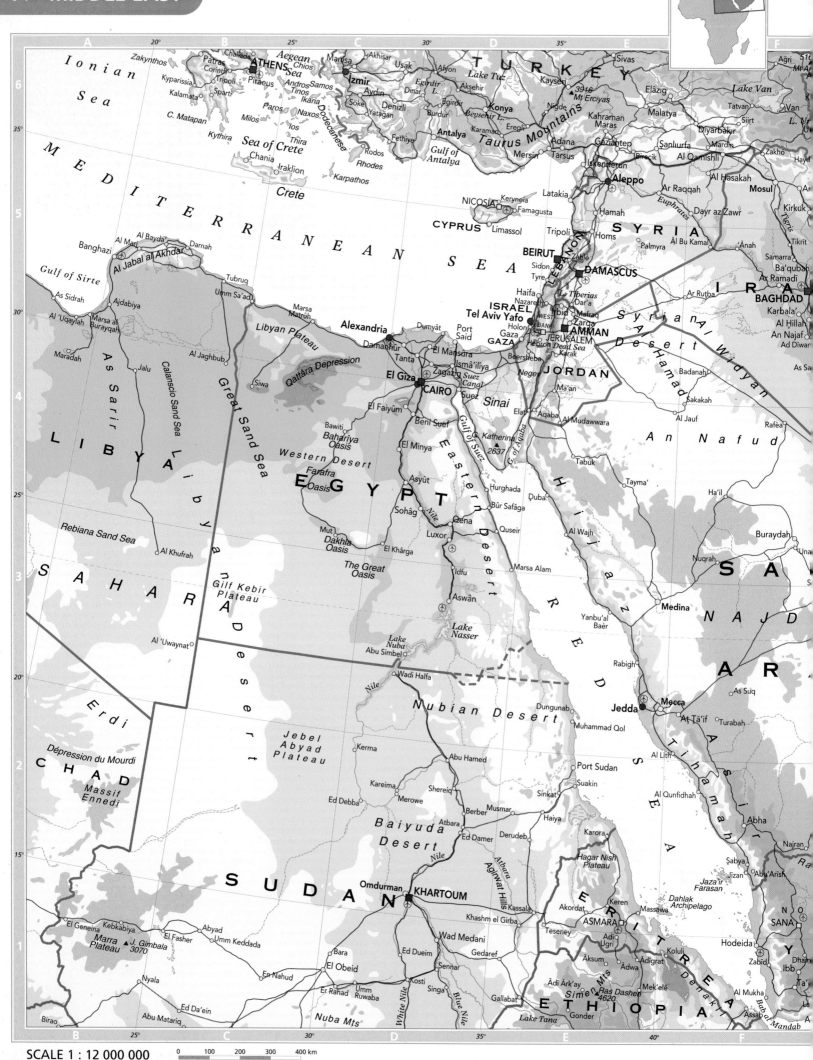

SCALE 1 : 12 000 000

0   100   200   300   400 km

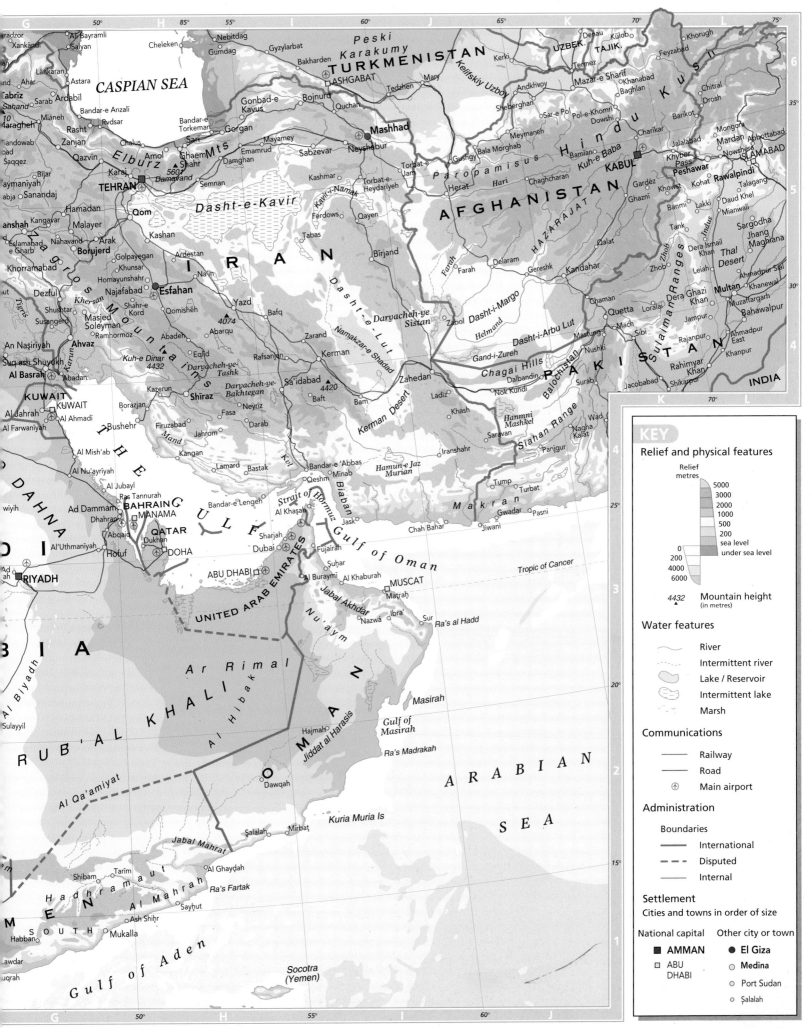

CASPIAN SEA

TURKMENISTAN

Peski Karakumy

UZBEK. TAJIK.

ASHGABAT

Hindu Kush

Mashhad

AFGHANISTAN

Paropamisus

Elburz Mts

ISLAMABAD

TEHRAN

Damavand 5601

KABUL

Peshawar

Rawalpindi

Dasht-e-Kavir

HAZARAJAT

Qom

I R A N

Kavir-i-Namak

Kabul

Kandahar

P A K I S T A N

Esfahan

Dasht-i-Margo

Zagros Mountains

Dasht-e-Lut

Namakzar-e Shadad

Quetta

Shiraz

Kerman

Kerman Desert

Zahedan

Chagai Hills

Siahan Range

KUWAIT

Bandar-e 'Abbas

Strait of Hormuz

Makran

Gulf of Oman

BAHRAIN G
MANAMA

QATAR U
DOHA L
F

Dubai

UNITED ARAB EMIRATES

ABU DHABI

MUSCAT

RIYADH

Tropic of Cancer

B I A

Ar Rimal

Al Hibak

O M A N

Masirah

Gulf of Masirah

RUB' AL KHALI

Jiddat al Harasis

Dawqah

A R A B I A N

S E A

Al Qa'amiyat

Kuria Muria Is

Salalah

Mirbat

Jabal Mahrat

Y E M E N

Hadhramaut

Al Mahrah

S O U T H

Gulf of Aden

Socotra (Yemen)

KEY

Relief and physical features

Relief metres

5000
3000
2000
1000
500
200
sea level
under sea level
200
4000
6000

▲ 8848 Mountain height (in metres)

Permanent ice

Water features

River
Intermittent river
Canal
Lake / Reservoir
Intermittent lake
Marsh

Communications

— Railway
— Road
⊕ Main airport

Administration

Boundaries

——— International
- - - Undefined or disputed
——— Internal

Settlement

Cities and towns in order of size

National capital   Other city or town

■ DHAKA   ● Bombay
□ PHNOM PENH   ○ Madurai
□ KATHMANDU   ○ Jaffna
□ THIMBU   ○ Farah

CALCUTTA

Kalyani
Jamuna
Mathura
Hugli Chunchura
Kunti
Ghia
Hugli
Bhatpara
Bhadreswar
Sunti
Barakpur
Shrirampur
Panihati
Madhyamgram
Dum Dum Airport
Nowai
Chakpara
Barahnagar
South Dum Dum
Kana Damodar
Salt Lake City
Haora
Calcutta
Dhapa
Manikpur
Garden Reach
Bhangar Kata
Uluberia
Bajbaj
South Suburb
Hugli
Bansdroni
Baruipur

Residential   Open space   Road
Industrial   Other use   Railway
Commercial   City boundary   Bridge
Transport   SCALE 1:600 000   Airport

SCALE 1:600 000
0   5   10   15   20km

Map labels (Pakistan, India and Bangladesh):

Sabzevar, Mashhad, TURKMEN-ISTAN, Andkhvoy, Termez, Mazar-e Sharif, TAJIKISTAN, Neyshabur, Sheberghan, Baghlan, Khorugh, Kashmar, Meymaneh, Hindu Kush, Chitral, Gilgit, Karakoram, Herat, AFGHANISTAN, Charikar, KABUL, Peshawar, Srinagar, JAMMU AND KASHMIR, Birjand, HAZARAJAT, Gardez, Rawalpindi, ISLAMABAD, Jammu, Dasht-e-Lut, Ghazni, Dera Ismail Khan, Gujranwala, Kerman, Zabol, Kandahar, Sargodha, Faisalabad, Amritsar, Lahore, Ludhiana, Chandigarh, PUNJAB, Chaman, Multan, Dasht-i-Margo, Quetta, Dera Ghazi Khan, Helmand, Jampur, Bahawalpur, Bam, Zahedan, Khash, Sibi, Rajanpur, Khanpur, HARYANA, NEW DELHI, Iranshahr, Jacobabad, Rahimyar Khan, Bikaner, Sikar, Larkana, Shikarpur, BALOCHISTAN, Sukkur, Jaisalmer, Chah Bahar, Bela, Khairpur, Pokaran, RAJASTHAN, Gwadar, Turbat, Nawabshah, Jodhpur, J, Tando Adam, Mirpur Khas, Barmer, Pali, Karachi, Hyderabad, Mouths of the Indus, Indus, PAKISTAN, Tropic of Cancer, Sur, Bhuj, Udaipur, Gandhidham, GUJARAT, Gandhinagar, Indore, OMAN, G. of Kachchh, Okha, Surendranagar, Ahmadabad, Jamnagar, Rajkot, Vadodara, Porbandar, Bhavnagar, Narmada, Satpura, Nandurbar, Khandwa, Surat, Diu, Gulf of Cambay, Daman, Dhule, Tapi, Jalgaon, ARABIAN SEA, Nasik, Manmad, Aurangabad, Bombay, MAHARASHTRA, Goda, Ahmadnagar, Deccan, Pune, Bhima, Sholapur, Kolhapur, Sangli, Gulbarga, Bijapur, Panaji, Dharwad, GOA, Hubli, KARNATAKA, Davangere, Chitradurga, Shimoga, Udupi, Bangalore, Mangalore, Mysore, LAKSHADWEEP, Laccadive Islands, Calicut, Malabar Coast, Coimbatore, KERALA, Cochin, Alleppey, Rajapalaiyam, Quilon, Trivandrum, Nagercoil, MALDIVES, MALE

SCALE 1 : 15 000 000

0   200   400   600   800 km

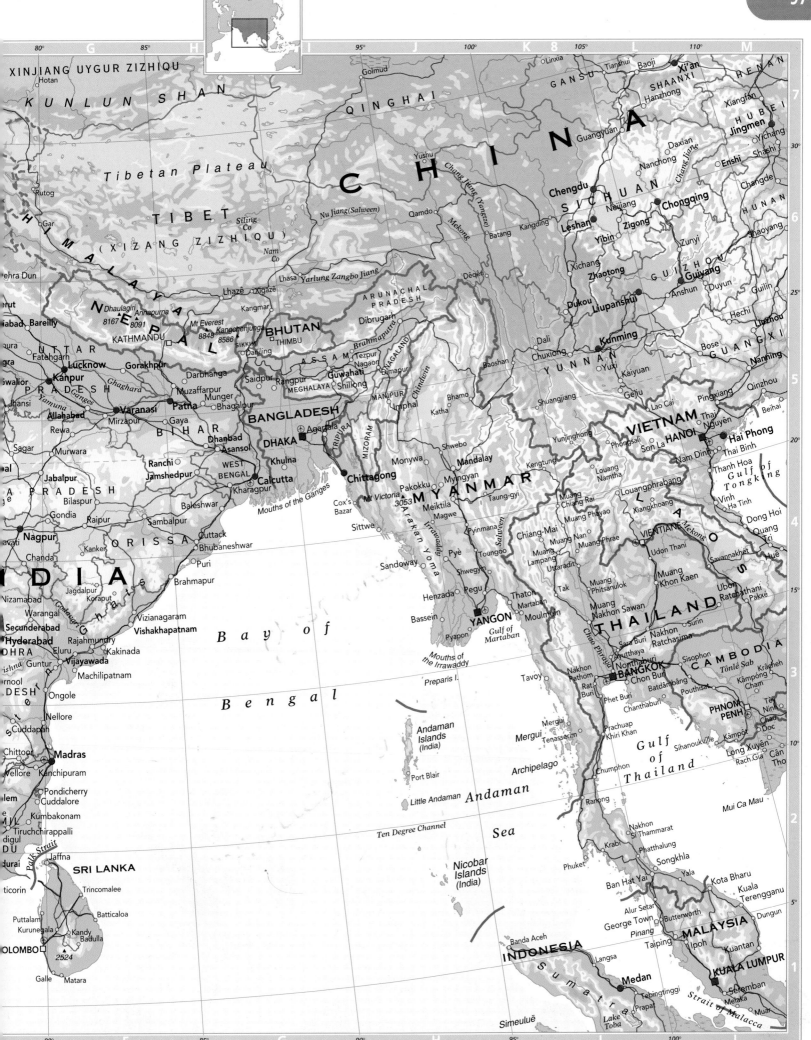

1 POPULATION DENSITY

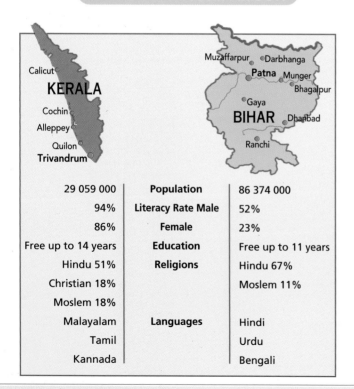

POPULATION
Persons per sq. km

- over 100
- 50-100
- 10-50
- 1-10
- 0-1

Cities

- over 5 000 000
- 1 000 000-5 000 000
- 500 000-1 000 000

Delhi

Calcutta

Bombay

Madras

SCALE 1:24 000 000

3 POPULATION GROWTH

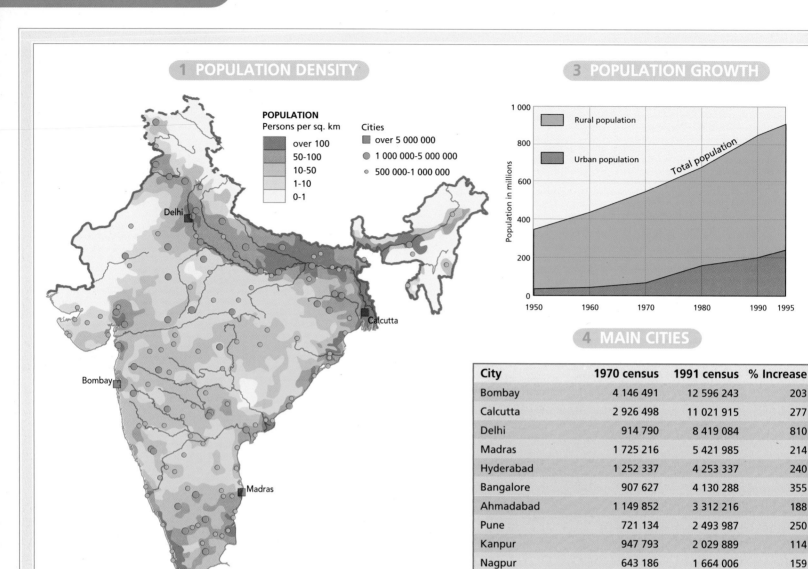

- Rural population
- Urban population

Total population

Population in millions

1 000
800
600
400
200
0

1950 1960 1970 1980 1990 1995

4 MAIN CITIES

City	1970 census	1991 census	% Increase
Bombay	4 146 491	12 596 243	203
Calcutta	2 926 498	11 021 915	277
Delhi	914 790	8 419 084	810
Madras	1 725 216	5 421 985	214
Hyderabad	1 252 337	4 253 337	240
Bangalore	907 627	4 130 288	355
Ahmadabad	1 149 852	3 312 216	188
Pune	721 134	2 493 987	250
Kanpur	947 793	2 029 889	114
Nagpur	643 186	1 664 006	159

2 REGIONAL COMPARISON

Calicut

KERALA

Cochin
Alleppey
Quilon
Trivandrum

Muzaffarpur • Darbhanga
Patna • Munger
• Bhagalpur
• Gaya
BIHAR Dhanbad
• Ranchi

29 059 000	**Population**	86 374 000
94%	**Literacy Rate Male**	52%
86%	**Female**	23%
Free up to 14 years	**Education**	Free up to 11 years
Hindu 51%	**Religions**	Hindu 67%
Christian 18%		Moslem 11%
Moslem 18%		
Malayalam	**Languages**	Hindi
Tamil		Urdu
Kannada		Bengali

5 POPULATION CHANGE

JAMMU AND KASHMIR

HIMACHAL PRADESH

PUNJAB

HARYANA

RAJASTHAN

UTTAR PRADESH

ARUNACHAL PRADESH

ASSAM

MEGHALAYA

BIHAR

WEST BENGAL

N.

MA

GUJARAT

MADHYA PRADESH

ORISSA

MAHARASHTRA

ANDHRA PRADESH

GOA

KARNATAKA

TAMIL NADU

KERALA

C.   CHANDIGARGH
D.   DELHI
MA. MANIPUR
MI. MIZORAM
N.   NAGALAND
S.   SIKKIM
T.   TRIPURA

POPULATION CHANGE
1970 - 1990

Percentage

- over 250
- 200-250
- 151-200
- 0-150

SCALE 1:30 000 000

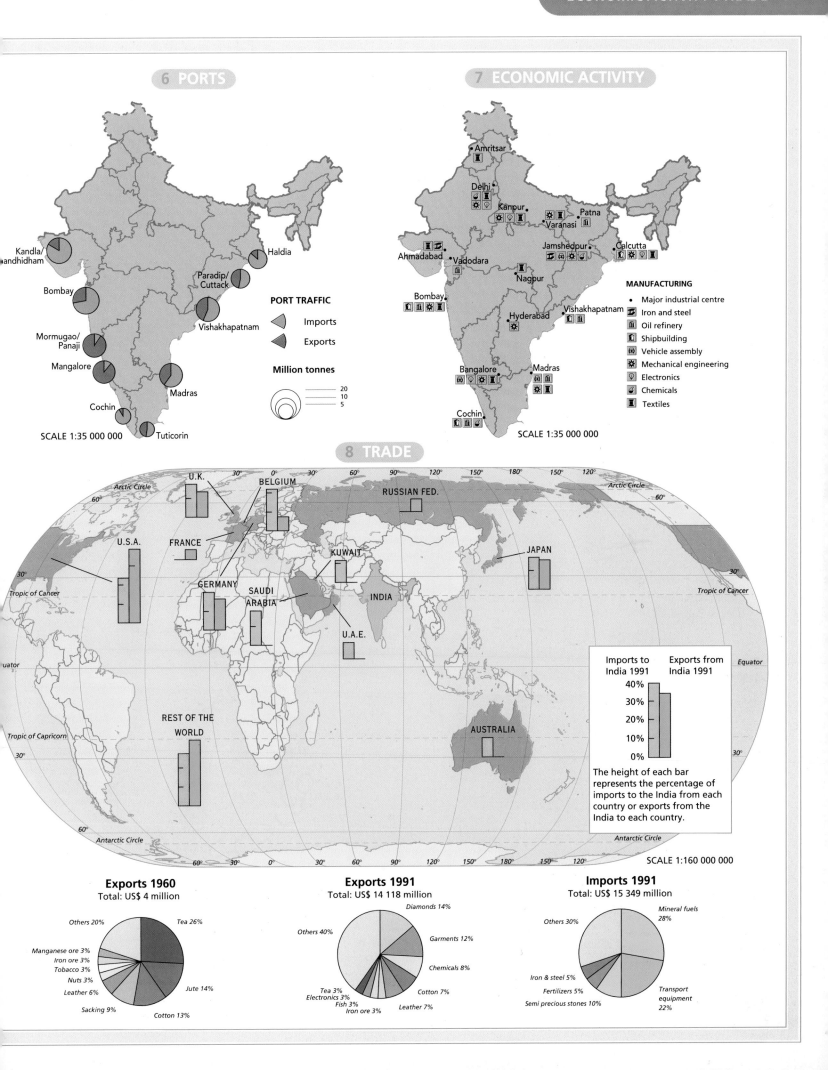

6 PORTS

Kandla/Gandhidham
Haldia
Bombay
Paradip/Cuttack
Vishakhapatnam
Mormugao/Panaji
Mangalore
Madras
Cochin
Tuticorin

PORT TRAFFIC

Imports

Exports

Million tonnes

20
10
5

SCALE 1:35 000 000

7 ECONOMIC ACTIVITY

Amritsar
Delhi
Kanpur
Patna
Varanasi
Ahmadabad
Jamshedpur
Calcutta
Vadodara
Nagpur
Bombay
Hyderabad
Vishakhapatnam
Bangalore
Madras
Cochin

MANUFACTURING

- Major industrial centre
- Iron and steel
- Oil refinery
- Shipbuilding
- Vehicle assembly
- Mechanical engineering
- Electronics
- Chemicals
- Textiles

SCALE 1:35 000 000

8 TRADE

U.K.
BELGIUM
RUSSIAN FED.
Arctic Circle
U.S.A.
FRANCE
KUWAIT
JAPAN
Tropic of Cancer
GERMANY
SAUDI ARABIA
INDIA
U.A.E.
REST OF THE WORLD
Tropic of Capricorn
AUSTRALIA
Antarctic Circle

Imports to India 1991   Exports from India 1991

40%
30%
20%
10%
0%

The height of each bar represents the percentage of imports to the India from each country or exports from the India to each country.

SCALE 1:160 000 000

Exports 1960
Total: US$ 4 million

Others 20%
Tea 26%
Manganese ore 3%
Iron ore 3%
Tobacco 3%
Nuts 3%
Leather 6%
Jute 14%
Sacking 9%
Cotton 13%

Exports 1991
Total: US$ 14 118 million

Diamonds 14%
Others 40%
Garments 12%
Chemicals 8%
Tea 3%
Electronics 3%
Cotton 7%
Fish 3%
Iron ore 3%
Leather 7%

Imports 1991
Total: US$ 15 349 million

Mineral fuels 28%
Others 30%
Iron & steel 5%
Fertilizers 5%
Transport equipment 22%
Semi precious stones 10%

1 POPULATION DENSITY

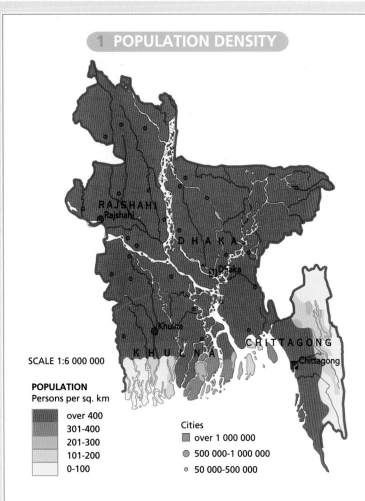

SCALE 1:6 000 000

POPULATION
Persons per sq. km

- over 400
- 301-400
- 201-300
- 101-200
- 0-100

Cities
- ■ over 1 000 000
- ● 500 000-1 000 000
- ○ 50 000-500 000

Forest
Dense forests known as the Sundarbans are found along the southwest
of Bangladesh. The same green on the right of the image is wooded fore
found on the highlands along the border with Myanmar.

Silt laden water
The red/browm area on the satellite image is the silt laden water at the
mouth of the Ganges. Silt carried down by the rivers Ganges and
Brahmaputra is deposited at the delta which is steadily growing out into
the Bay of Bengal.

Cultivated land
When silt is deposited on the deltaic plains extremely fertile ground is le
This is most suitable for the growing of rice, especially floating varieties
which are adapted to cope with seasonal flooding.

Rivers
Bangladesh has two major rivers, the Ganges and the Brahmaputra or
Jamuna, whose many tributaries criss cross the country.

Reservoir
In addition to its many small natural lakes, Bangladesh has a large
reservoir, the Karnafuli Reservoir, in the hills near Chittagong.

2 MAIN CITIES

City	1974 census	1991 census	% Increase
Dhaka	1 310 972	6 105 160	366
Chittagong	416 733	2 040 663	390
Khulna	436 000	877 388	101
Rajshahi	132 909	517 136	289

3 ECONOMIC ACTIVITY

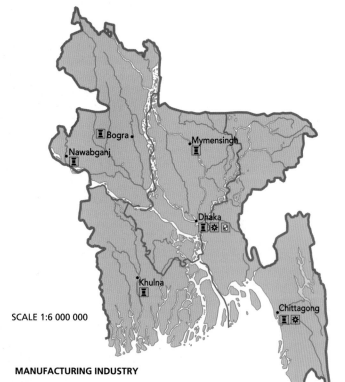

SCALE 1:6 000 000

MANUFACTURING INDUSTRY

- ▣ Food processing
- ✳ Mechanical engineering
- ▤ Textiles (jute processing / cotton milling)
- • Industrial centre

4 TRADE

PARTNERS 1993

Imports
Total: US$ 3950 million

- Japan 10.5%
- S. Korea 9.4%
- USA 7.0%
- Hong Kong 6.8%
- Singapore 6.6%
- India 6.3%
- China 5.3%
- Yemen 3.9%
- Others 44.2%

Exports
Total: US$ 2119 million

- USA 28.%
- Germar 9.6%
- UK 7.7%
- Italy 5.5%
- Belgium 4.5%
- Singapore 3.8%
- Japan 3.4%
- Netherlands 3.2%
- Others 33.4%

PRODUCTS 1993

Imports

- Textile yarns 20%
- Machinery and transport equipment 9%
- Petroleum 8%
- Chemicals 5%
- Iron & steel 3%
- Dairy products 2%
- Others 53%

Exports

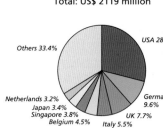

- Others 4%
- Tea 3%
- Raw jute 6%
- Leather 7%
- Fish and prawns 9%
- Ready mad garments 5
- Jute manufactures 15%

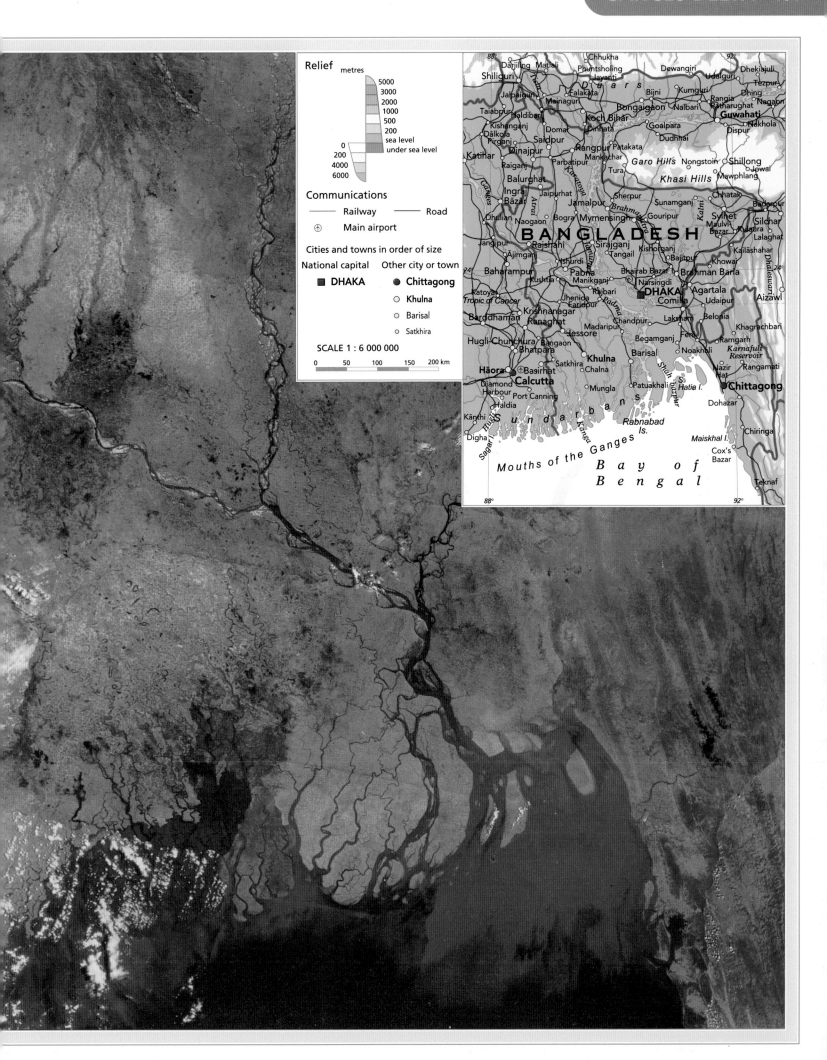

Relief

metres

5000
3000
2000
1000
500
200
sea level
0
under sea level
200
4000
6000

Communications

– – – – – Railway ———— Road

⊕ Main airport

Cities and towns in order of size

National capital   Other city or town

■ **DHAKA**   ● **Chittagong**

○ **Khulna**

○ Barisal

○ Satkhira

SCALE 1 : 6 000 000

0   50   100   150   200 km

Chhukha
Dārjiling Matiali Phuntsholing Dewangiri Udalguri Dhekiajuli
Shiliguri Jayanti
Jalpaiguri Falakata Bijni Kumguri Rangia Dhing Tezpur
Mainaguri Bongaigaon Nalbari Patharughat Nagaon
Taiabpur Haldibari Koch Bihar Goalpara Dudhnai **Guwahati** Nakhola
Kishanganj Domat Dinhata Dispur
Pirganj Saidpur Mankachar
Katihar Dinajpur Rangpur Patakata Garo Hills Nongstoin Shillong
Parbatipur Jowai
Raiganj Tura Khasi Hills Mawphlang Chhatak
Balurghat Sherpur
Ingraj Jaipurhat Jamalpur Sunamganj Gouripur Kalni Sylhet Badarpur
Bazar Maulvi
Dhulian Naogaon Bogra Mymensingh Bazar Silchar
Jangipur Rajshahi Lalaghat
Ajimganj Ishurdi Sirajganj Kishorganj Bajitpur Kailāshahar
Baharampur Tangail Khowai
Kushtia Pabna Bhairab Bazar Brahman Barla
Katoya Manikganj Narsingdi
Tropic of Cancer Rajbari **DHAKA** Agartala Aizawl
Barddhaman Jhenida Faridpur Comilla Udaipur
Krishnanagar Chandpur Laksham Belonia
Ranaghat Madaripur Begamganj Feni Khagrachhari
Hugli-Chunchura Bangaon Jessore Noakhali Ramgarh Karnafuli
Bhatpara Barisal Reservoir
Satkhira Rangamati
Hāora Basirhat **Khulna** Chalna Patuakhali Nazir Dohazar
Diamond **Calcutta** Mungla Hatia I.
Harbour Port Canning Maiskhal I.
Haldia Sundarbans Rabnabad Cox's
Kānthi Is. Bazar
Digha Mouths of the Ganges **Chittagong**
Chiringa
Bay of
Bengal
Teknaf

BANGLADESH

88°   92°   24°   88°   92°

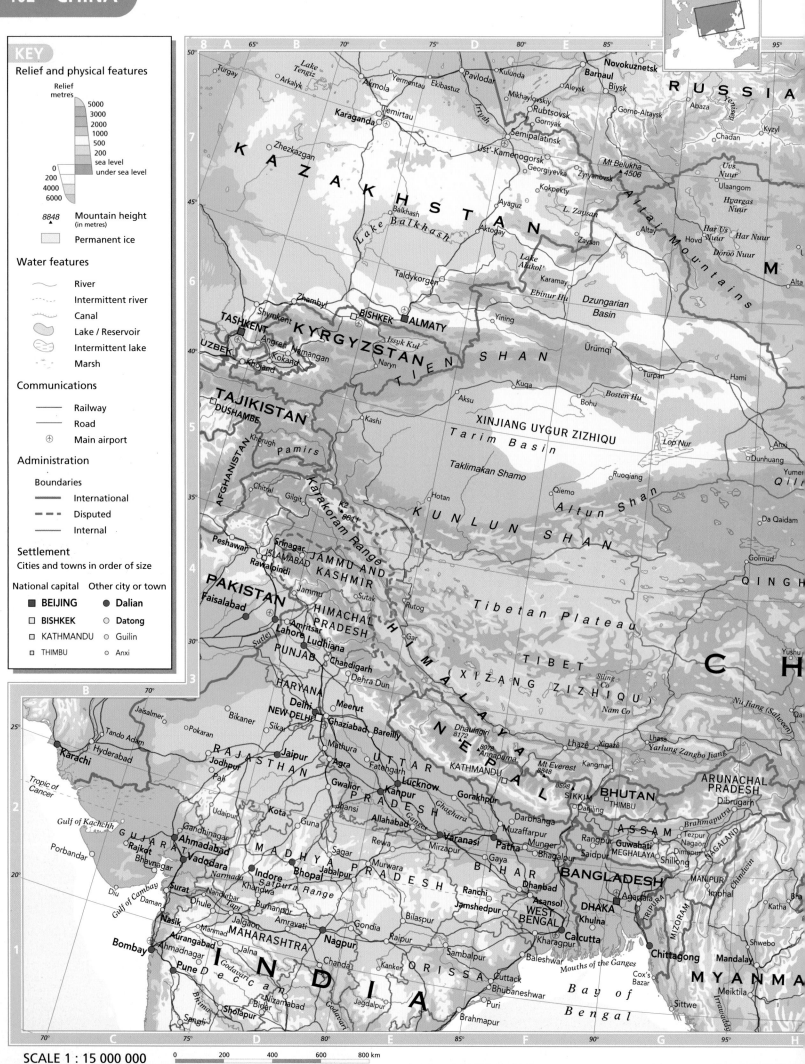

KEY

Relief and physical features

Relief metres
5000
3000
2000
1000
500
200
0 sea level
200 under sea level
400
6000

8848 ▲ Mountain height (in metres)

Permanent ice

Water features

River
Intermittent river
Canal
Lake / Reservoir
Intermittent lake
Marsh

Communications

Railway
Road
⊕ Main airport

Administration

Boundaries
International
Disputed
Internal

Settlement

Cities and towns in order of size

National capital | Other city or town
■ BEIJING | ● Dalian
□ BISHKEK | ○ Datong
□ KATHMANDU | ○ Guilin
□ THIMBU | ○ Anxi

SCALE 1 : 15 000 000

0   200   400   600   800 km

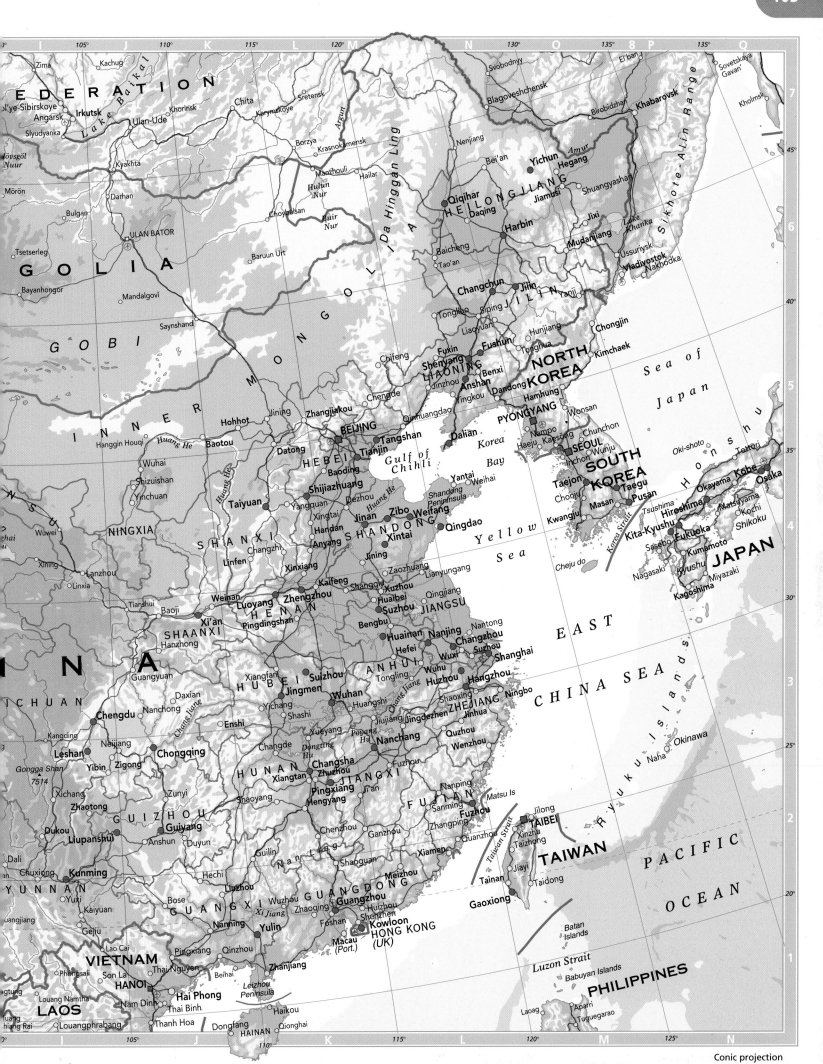

SCALE 1 : 15 000 000

0   200   400   600   800 km

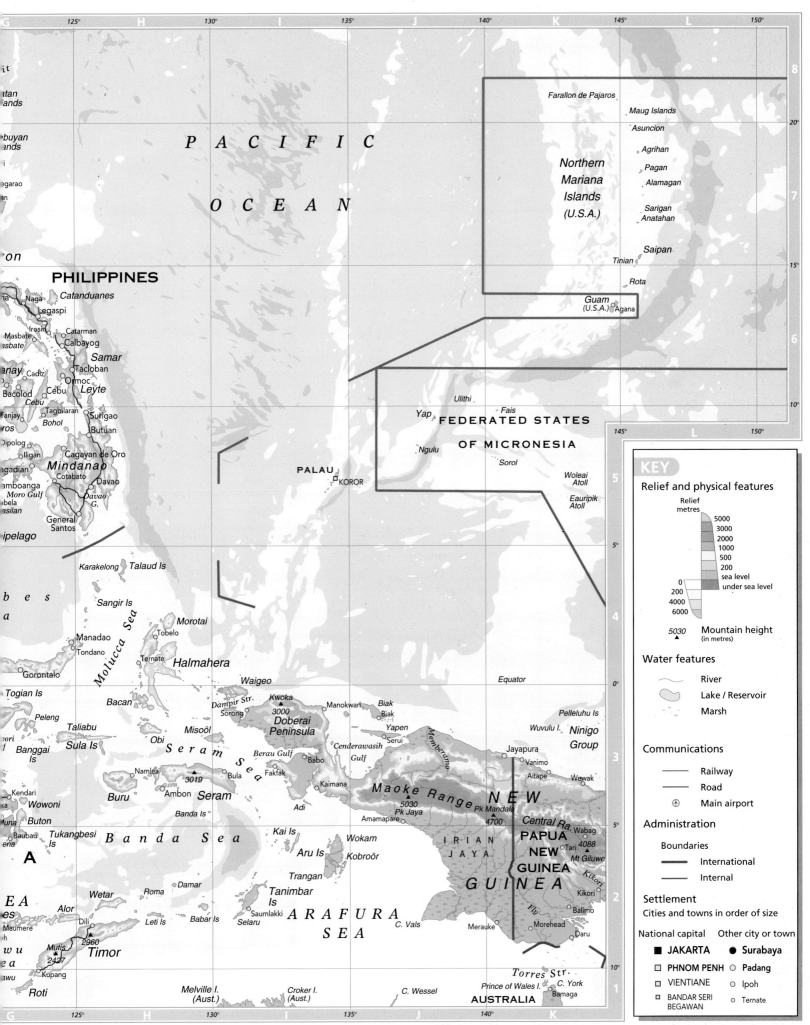

PACIFIC

OCEAN

PHILIPPINES

Catanduanes

Naga
Legaspi
Irosin
Masbate
Catarman
Calbayog

Samar

Cadiz
Cebu
Cebu
Tacloban
Ormoc
Leyte
Tagbilaran
Bohol
Surigao
Butuan

Dipolog
Illigan
Iligan
Cagayan de Oro
Mindanao
Cotabato
Davao
Zamboanga
Davao G.
General
Santos

Karakelong   Talaud Is

Sangir Is

Molucca Sea

Manadao
Tondano
Tobelo
Ternate   Halmahera

Gorontalo
Togian Is

Morotai

Waigeo

Bacan

Taliabu
Misoöl
Obi
Sula Is

Peleng

Banggai
Is

Namlea
3019
Bula

Buru
Ambon   Seram

Banda Is

Kendari
Wowoni
Buton

Baubau
Tukangbesi
Is

Banda   Sea

A

Farallon de Pajaros

Maug Islands

Asuncion

Agrihan

Pagan
Alamagan

Northern
Mariana
Islands
(U.S.A.)

Sarigan
Anatahan

Saipan

Tinian

Rota

Guam
(U.S.A.)   Agana

Ulithi
Fais

Yap   FEDERATED STATES

OF MICRONESIA

Ngulu
Sorol

PALAU   Woleai
Atoll
KOROR   Eauripik
Atoll

Kwoka
Sorong   3000
Dampir Str.
Doberai
Peninsula
Manokwari
Biak
Biak
Yapen
Serui
Berau Gulf
Babo
Fakfak
Cenderawasih
Gulf

Kaimana
Membramo
Maoke Range
5030
Pk Jaya
Amamapare   Pk Mandala
4700

Adi

IRIAN
JAYA

Pelleluhu Is
Wuvulu I.   Ninigo
Group

Jayapura
Vanimo

Aitape   Wewak

NEW

Central Ra.   Wabag
PAPUA   Tari   4088
NEW   Mt Giluwe
GUINEA
GUINEA   Kikori
Kikori

Equator

Kai Is

Aru Is
Kobroör

Trangan

Wokam

Tanimbar
Is
Saumlakki
Seluru
Selaru

Babar Is

ARAFURA

SEA

C. Vals

Amamapare

Merauke   Morehead
Daru

Wetar
Roma
Damar

Alor
Dili
Leti Is

Maumere
Mutis
2427   2960
Timor

Kupang
Roti

Melville I.
(Aust.)

Croker I.
(Aust.)

C. Wessel

Torres Str.

Prince of Wales I.   C. York
Bamaga
AUSTRALIA

Mercator projection

KEY

Relief and physical features

Relief
metres

5000
3000
2000
1000
500
200
sea level
under sea level

0
200
4000
6000

▲ 5030   Mountain height
(in metres)

Water features

～   River

⬭   Lake / Reservoir

Marsh

Communications

———   Railway

———   Road

⊕   Main airport

Administration

Boundaries

———   International

———   Internal

Settlement
Cities and towns in order of size

National capital   Other city or town

■ **JAKARTA**   ● **Surabaya**

□ PHNOM PENH   ○ Padang

□ VIENTIANE   ○ Ipoh

▢ BANDAR SERI   ○ Ternate
BEGAWAN

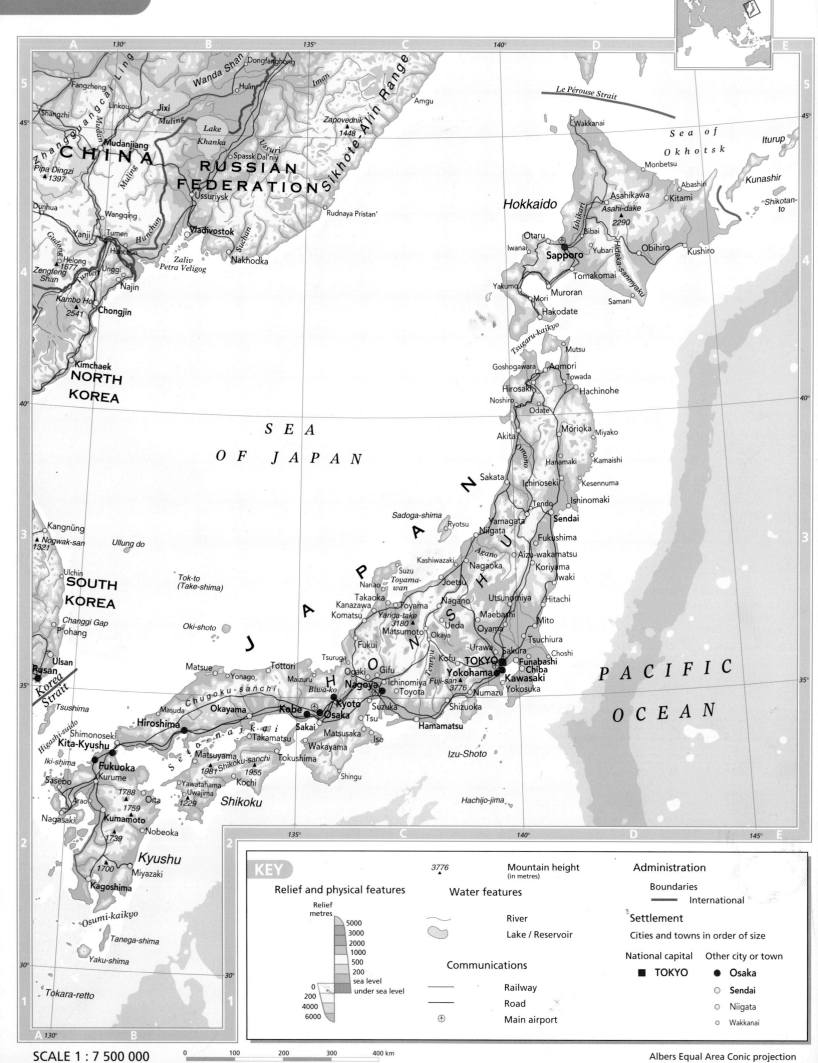

SCALE 1 : 7 500 000

0   100   200   300   400 km

Albers Equal Area Conic projection

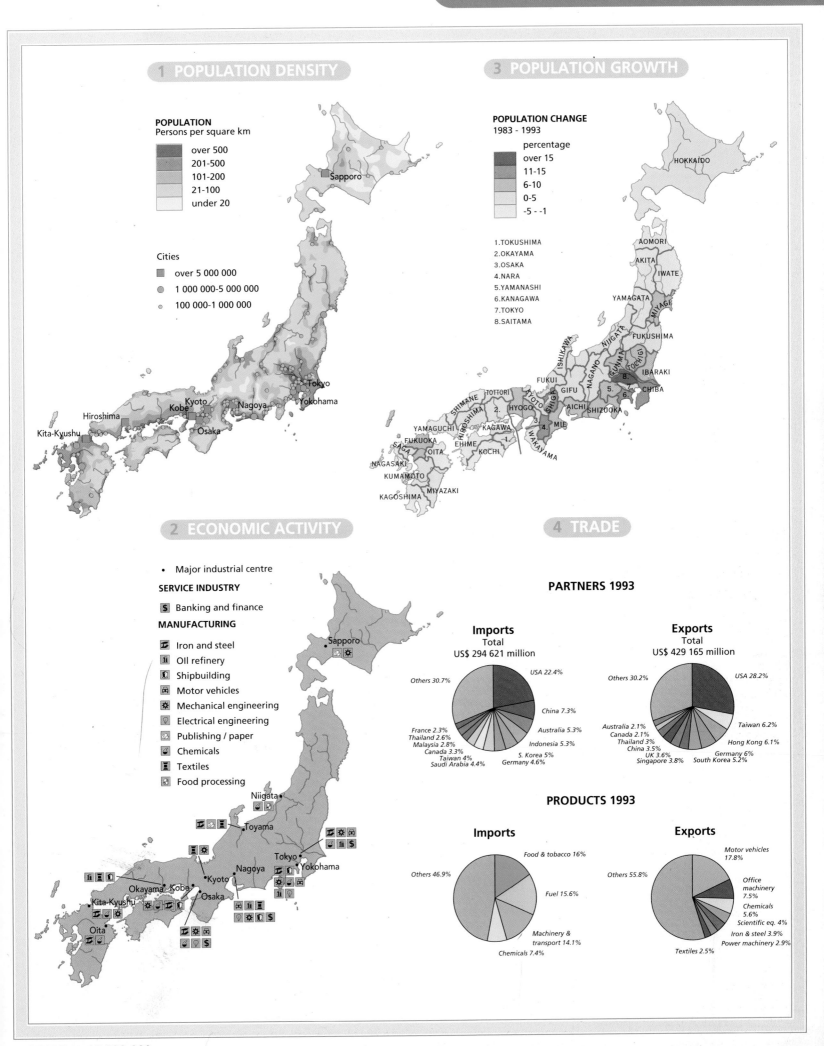

1 POPULATION DENSITY

POPULATION
Persons per square km

- over 500
- 201-500
- 101-200
- 21-100
- under 20

Cities

- over 5 000 000
- 1 000 000-5 000 000
- 100 000-1 000 000

Sapporo

Tokyo
Yokohama
Kyoto
Kobe
Nagoya
Hiroshima
Osaka
Kita-Kyushu

3 POPULATION GROWTH

POPULATION CHANGE
1983 - 1993

percentage

- over 15
- 11-15
- 6-10
- 0-5
- -5 - -1

1.TOKUSHIMA
2.OKAYAMA
3.OSAKA
4.NARA
5.YAMANASHI
6.KANAGAWA
7.TOKYO
8.SAITAMA

HOKKAIDO
AOMORI
AKITA
IWATE
YAMAGATA
MIYAGI
NIIGATA
FUKUSHIMA
ISHIKAWA
NAGANO
GUNMA
TOCHIGI
IBARAKI
FUKUI
GIFU
SHIGA
8.
CHIBA
SHIMANE
TOTTORI
KYOTO
AICHI
7.
TOKYO
HYOGO
5.
SHIZUOKA
YAMAGUCHI
HIROSHIMA
KAGAWA
3. 4.
MIE
6.
FUKUOKA
EHIME
1.
WAKAYAMA
SAGA
OITA
KOCHI
NAGASAKI
KUMAMOTO
MIYAZAKI
KAGOSHIMA

2 ECONOMIC ACTIVITY

- Major industrial centre

SERVICE INDUSTRY

- $ Banking and finance

MANUFACTURING

- Iron and steel
- Oil refinery
- Shipbuilding
- Motor vehicles
- Mechanical engineering
- Electrical engineering
- Publishing / paper
- Chemicals
- Textiles
- Food processing

Sapporo
Niigata
Toyama
Tokyo
Yokohama
Nagoya
Kyoto
Okayama
Kobe
Osaka
Kita-Kyushu
Oita

4 TRADE

PARTNERS 1993

Imports
Total
US$ 294 621 million

- USA 22.4%
- China 7.3%
- Australia 5.3%
- Indonesia 5.3%
- S. Korea 5%
- Germany 4.6%
- Saudi Arabia 4.4%
- Taiwan 4%
- Canada 3.3%
- Malaysia 2.8%
- Thailand 2.6%
- France 2.3%
- Others 30.7%

Exports
Total
US$ 429 165 million

- USA 28.2%
- Taiwan 6.2%
- Hong Kong 6.1%
- Germany 6%
- South Korea 5.2%
- Singapore 3.8%
- UK 3.6%
- China 3%
- Thailand 3%
- Canada 2.1%
- Australia 2.1%
- Others 30.2%

PRODUCTS 1993

Imports

- Food & tobacco 16%
- Fuel 15.6%
- Machinery & transport 14.1%
- Chemicals 7.4%
- Others 46.9%

Exports

- Motor vehicles 17.8%
- Office machinery 7.5%
- Chemicals 5.6%
- Scientific eq. 4%
- Iron & steel 3.9%
- Power machinery 2.9%
- Textiles 2.5%
- Others 55.8%

SCALE 1 : 15 000 000

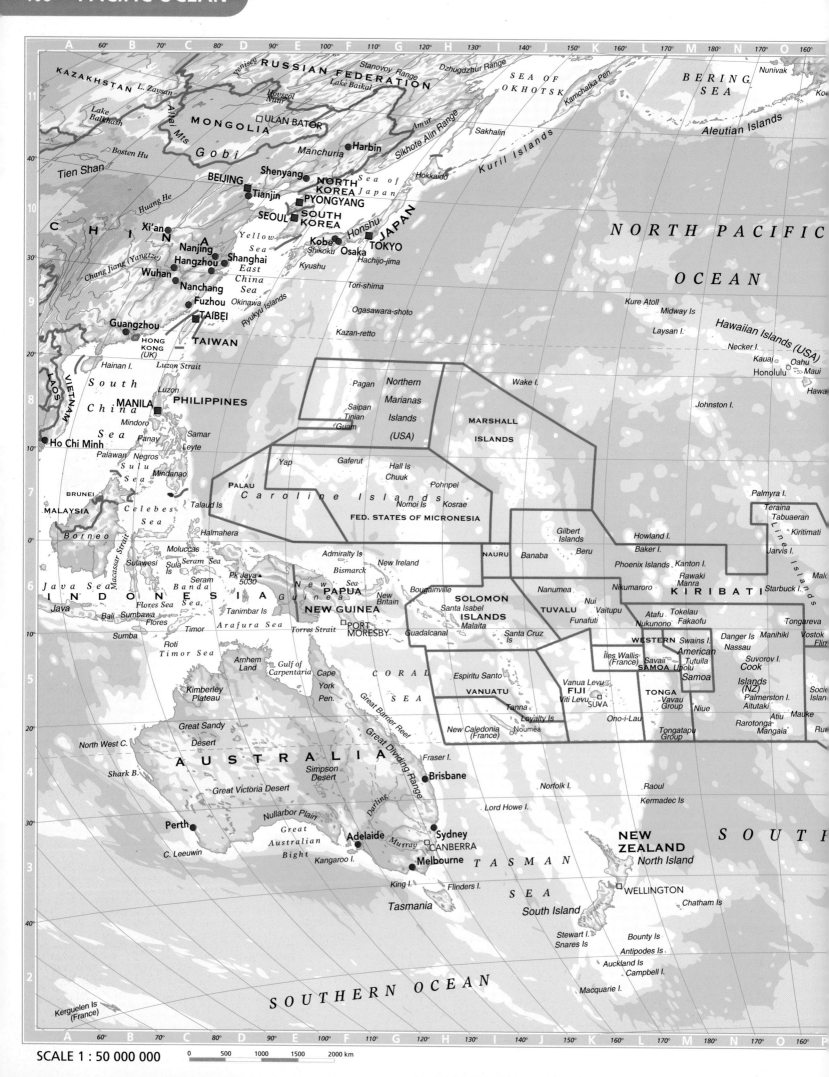

SCALE 1 : 50 000 000

0   500   1000   1500   2000 km

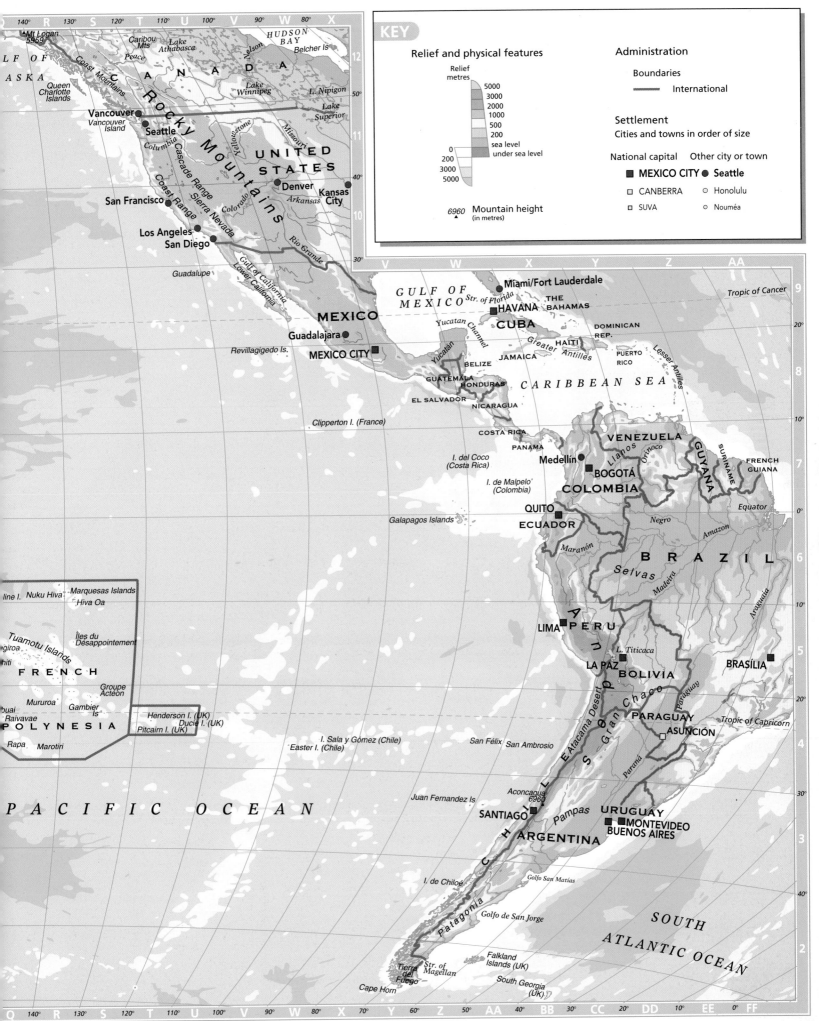

INDONESIA

Makassar Strait
Samarinda
Palu
Sulawesi
Peleng
Taliabu
Sula Is
Obi
Misoöl
Seram
Seram Sea
Berau Gulf
Cenderawasih Gulf
Jayapura
NEW GUINEA
Maoke Range
Pk Jaya 5030
Pk Mandala 4700
Banda Sea
Banggai Is
Towori Gulf
Buru
Ambon
Buton
Muna
Tukangbesi Is
Kabaena
Salayar
Ujung Pandang
2871
Bt Gandadiwata 3074
Parepare
Wowoni
Kai Is
Kobroör
Wokam
Aru Is
Trangan
Tanimbar Is
Selaru
C. Vals
Banda Is
Damar
3019
Central Ra.
Memberamo
PAPUA NEW GUINEA
Mt Giluwe
Kikori
Purari 4088
Umboi
Lae
New Britain
Bougainville Island
Solomon Sea
Woodlark I.
D'Entrecasteaux Is
New Ireland
Bismarck Sea
Mt Victoria 4073
Kerema
Balimo
Fly
PORT MORESBY
Owen Stanley Ra.
Gulf of Papua
Trobriand Is
Tagula I.
Rosse
Flores Sea
Wetar
Alor
Dili 2960
Leti Is
Timor
Kupang
Roti
Sawu Sea
Endeh
Flores
Raba
Waingapu
Sumba
Arafura Sea
Torres Strait
Prince of Wales I.
C. York
Timor Sea
C. Londonderry
Melville I.
Bathurst I.
Darwin
Wessel Is
C. Wessel
C. Arnhem
Cape York Peninsula
Gulf of Carpentaria
Wellesley Is
Cooktown
Cairns
CORAL SEA
CORAL SEA ISLANDS
TERRITORY
Great Barrier Reef
Joseph Bonaparte Gulf
Arnhem Land
Katherine
Collier Bay
Wyndham
Kimberley Plateau
Mt Ord 936
Derby
Hall's Creek
Broome
Eighty Mile Beach
Port Hedland
De Grey
Barrow I.
Dampier
Fortescue
Hamersley Range 1250
Ashburton
Daly
Victoria
Lake Argyle
NORTHERN TERRITORY
Tanami Desert
L. White
L. Wills
L. Mackay
Great Sandy Desert
L. Disappointment
Barkly Tableland
Leichhardt
Mount Isa
Normanton
Mitchell
Flinders
Selwyn Range
Georgina
Townsville
Mt Dalrymple 1277
Mackay
QUEENSLAND
Great Dividing Range
Barcaldine
Rockhampton
Capricorn Channel
Gladstone
Sandy Cape
Bundaberg
Fraser I.
Maryborough
WESTERN AUSTRALIA
Gibson Desert
1510 Mt Ziel
Macdonnell Ranges
Alice Springs
Ayers Rock 867
L. Amadeus
Musgrave Ranges
Simpson Desert
Diamantina
Cooper Creek
Warrego
L. Macleod
Gascoyne
L. Carnegie
L. Wells
Murchison
L. Barlee
Geraldton
L. Carey
L. Moore
L. Cowan
Great Victoria Desert
SOUTH AUSTRALIA
L. Eyre (North)
L. Eyre (South)
L. Blanche
Sturt Desert
Grey Range
Warburton
Bourke
Dirranbandi
Moree
Toowoomba
Brisbane
Gold Coast
Coolangatta
Southport
Lismore
Grafton
Coffs Harbour
Darling Downs
Kalgoorlie
Norseman
Nullarbor Plain
L. Gairdner
L. Torrens
L. Frome
Flinders Range
Broken Hill
NEW SOUTH WALES
Darling
Lachlan
Armidale
Round Mt 1615
Tamworth
Port Macquarie
Perth
Fremantle
Bunbury
Ravensthorpe
Esperance
Albany
C. Leeuwin
Hood Pt
Great Australian Bight
Port Augusta
Whyalla
Port Pirie
Port Lincoln
Cape Carnot
Spencer Gulf
Kangaroo I.
Adelaide
Murray Bridge
Murray
Mildura
Wagga Wagga
Dubbo
Bathurst
Maitland
Newcastle
Gosford
Sydney
Wollongong
Canberra
AUST. CAP. TER.
Goulburn
Albury
Mt Kosciusko 2230
Murrumbidgee
Hay
Bendigo
Horsham
Mt William 1167
Ballarat
Mount Gambier
Portland
VICTORIA
Melbourne
Geelong
Sale
Bairnsdale
Wilson's Promontory
Bass Strait
King I.
Flinders I.
Burnie
Devonport
Launceston
Mt Ossa 1617
TASMANIA
Hobart
South East Cape

SCALE 1 : 20 000 000

0   200   400   600   800 km

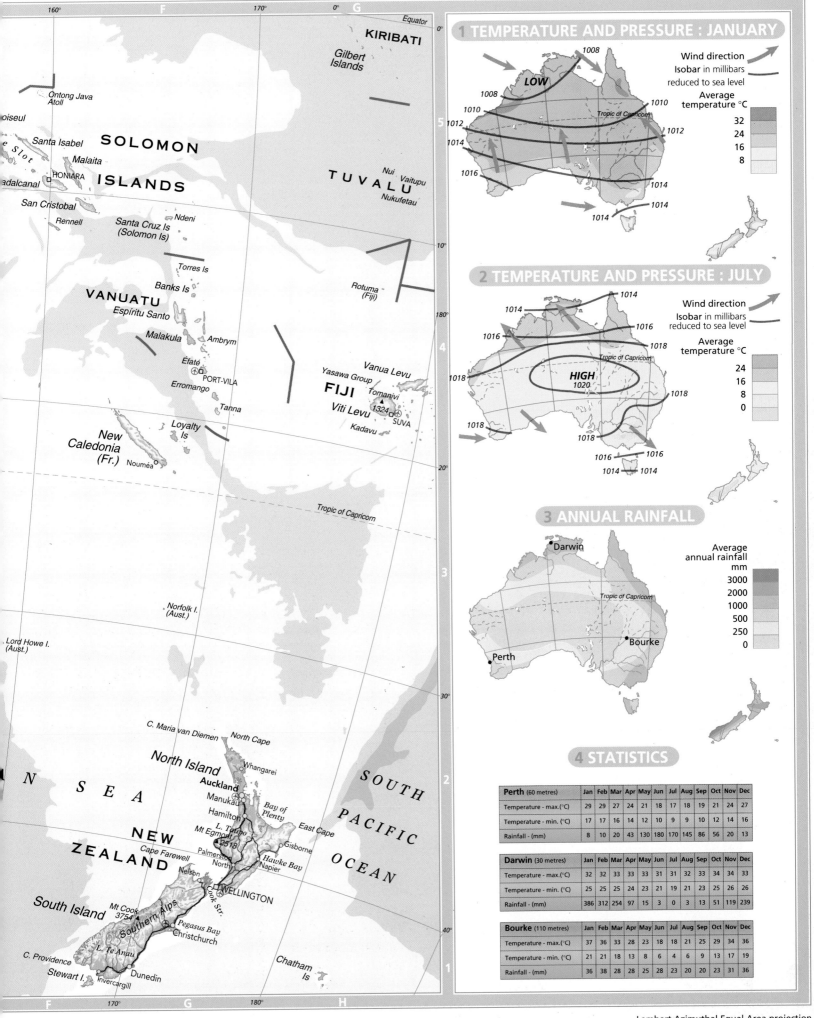

SOLOMON ISLANDS

Ontong Java Atoll

Santa Isabel

Malaita

HONIARA

San Cristobal

Rennell

Ndeni

Santa Cruz Is (Solomon Is)

Torres Is

Banks Is

VANUATU

Espíritu Santo

Malakula

Ambrym

Éfaté

PORT-VILA

Erromango

Tanna

New Caledonia (Fr.)

Nouméa

Loyalty Is

KIRIBATI

Gilbert Islands

Equator

TUVALU

Nui Vaitupu

Nukufetau

Rotuma (Fiji)

Vanua Levu

Yasawa Group

FIJI

Tomanivi

Viti Levu   1324

SUVA

Kadavu

Norfolk I. (Aust.)

Lord Howe I. (Aust.)

Tropic of Capricorn

TASMAN SEA

SOUTH PACIFIC OCEAN

C. Maria van Diemen   North Cape

North Island

Whangarei

Auckland

Manukau

Hamilton

Bay of Plenty

East Cape

L. Taupo

Mt Egmont 2518

Gisborne

NEW ZEALAND

Cape Farewell

Palmerston North

Hawke Bay

Napier

Nelson

WELLINGTON

Cook Str.

Mt Cook 3754

Southern Alps

Pegasus Bay

Christchurch

South Island

C. Providence

L. Te Anau

Dunedin

Stewart I.

Invercargill

Chatham Is

1 TEMPERATURE AND PRESSURE : JANUARY

1008

LOW

1008

1010

1012

1014

1016

Tropic of Capricorn

1010

1012

1014

1014

1014

Wind direction

Isobar in millibars reduced to sea level

Average temperature °C

	32
	24
	16
	8

2 TEMPERATURE AND PRESSURE : JULY

1014

1014

1016

1018

1016

1018

1018

HIGH 1020

Tropic of Capricorn

1018

1018

1018

1016   1016

1014   1014

Wind direction

Isobar in millibars reduced to sea level

Average temperature °C

	24
	16
	8
	0

3 ANNUAL RAINFALL

Darwin

Tropic of Capricorn

Bourke

Perth

Average annual rainfall mm

	3000
	2000
	1000
	500
	250
	0

4 STATISTICS

Perth (60 metres)	Jan	Feb	Mar	Apr	May	Jun	Jul	Aug	Sep	Oct	Nov	Dec
Temperature - max.(°C)	29	29	27	24	21	18	17	18	19	21	24	27
Temperature - min. (°C)	17	17	16	14	12	10	9	9	10	12	14	16
Rainfall - (mm)	8	10	20	43	130	180	170	145	86	56	20	13

Darwin (30 metres)	Jan	Feb	Mar	Apr	May	Jun	Jul	Aug	Sep	Oct	Nov	Dec
Temperature - max.(°C)	32	32	33	33	33	31	31	32	33	34	34	33
Temperature - min. (°C)	25	25	25	24	23	21	19	21	23	25	26	26
Rainfall - (mm)	386	312	254	97	15	3	0	3	13	51	119	239

Bourke (110 metres)	Jan	Feb	Mar	Apr	May	Jun	Jul	Aug	Sep	Oct	Nov	Dec
Temperature - max.(°C)	37	36	33	28	23	18	18	21	25	29	34	36
Temperature - min. (°C)	21	21	18	13	9	6	4	6	9	13	17	19
Rainfall - (mm)	36	38	28	28	25	28	23	20	20	23	31	36

Lambert Azimuthal Equal Area projection

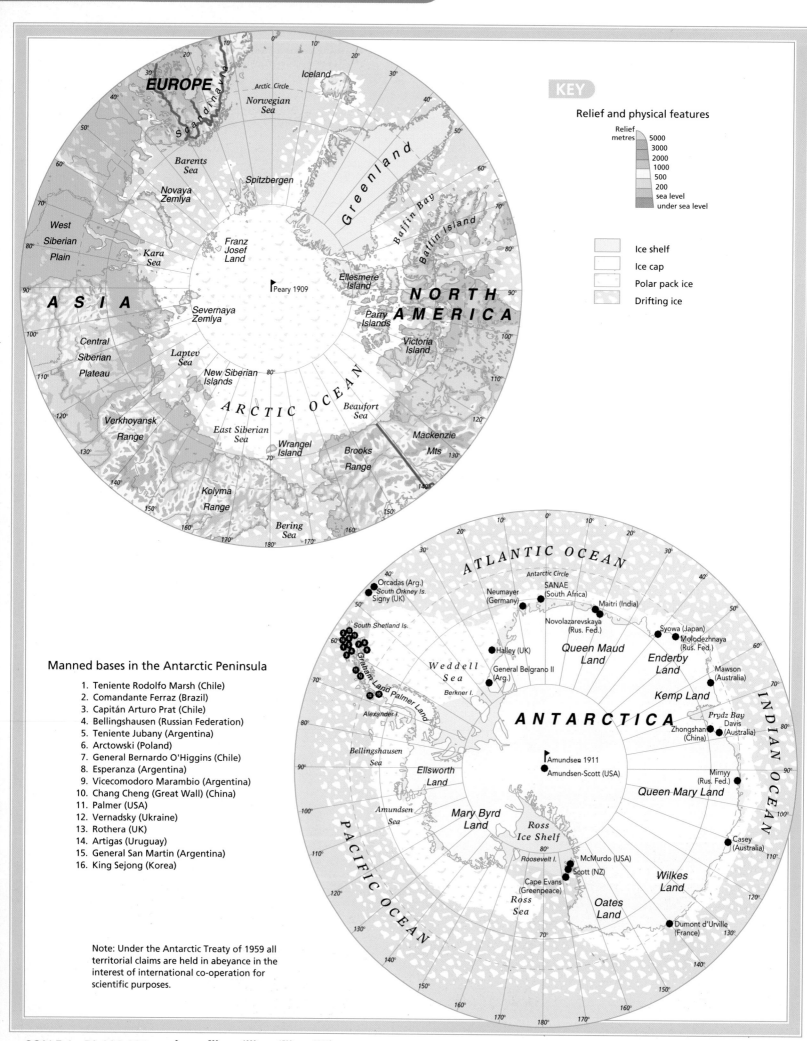

KEY

Relief and physical features

Relief metres
5000
3000
2000
1000
500
200
sea level
under sea level

Ice shelf
Ice cap
Polar pack ice
Drifting ice

Manned bases in the Antarctic Peninsula

1. Teniente Rodolfo Marsh (Chile)
2. Comandante Ferraz (Brazil)
3. Capitán Arturo Prat (Chile)
4. Bellingshausen (Russian Federation)
5. Teniente Jubany (Argentina)
6. Arctowski (Poland)
7. General Bernardo O'Higgins (Chile)
8. Esperanza (Argentina)
9. Vicecomodoro Marambio (Argentina)
10. Chang Cheng (Great Wall) (China)
11. Palmer (USA)
12. Vernadsky (Ukraine)
13. Rothera (UK)
14. Artigas (Uruguay)
15. General San Martin (Argentina)
16. King Sejong (Korea)

Note: Under the Antarctic Treaty of 1959 all territorial claims are held in abeyance in the interest of international co-operation for scientific purposes.

SCALE 1 : 50 000 000

0   500   1000   1500   2000 km

Polar Stereographic projection

1 TIME ZONES

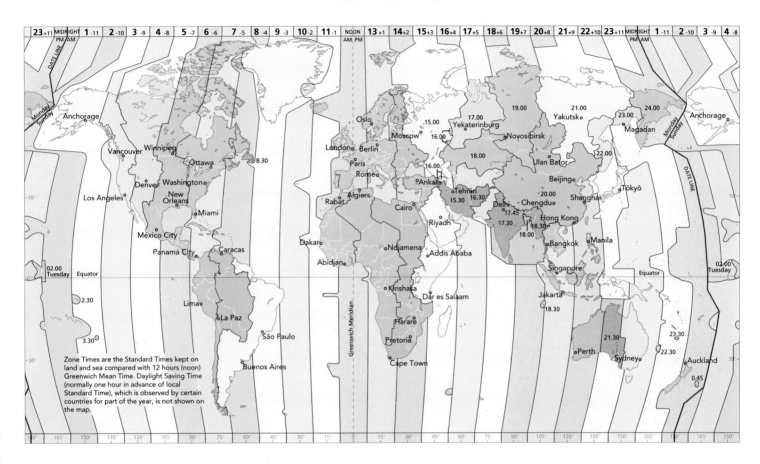

| 23 +11 | MIDNIGHT | 1 -11 | 2 -10 | 3 -9 | 4 -8 | 5 -7 | 6 -6 | 7 -5 | 8 -4 | 9 -3 | 10 -2 | 11 -1 | NOON | 13 +1 | 14 +2 | 15 +3 | 16 +4 | 17 +5 | 18 +6 | 19 +7 | 20 +8 | 21 +9 | 22 +10 | 23 +11 | MIDNIGHT | 1 -11 | 2 -10 | 3 -9 | 4 -8 |

Zone Times are the Standard Times kept on land and sea compared with 12 hours (noon) Greenwich Mean Time. Daylight Saving Time (normally one hour in advance of local Standard Time), which is observed by certain countries for part of the year, is not shown on the map.

2 INTERNATIONAL ORGANIZATIONS

THE UNITED NATIONS

The United Nations is the largest international group of countries. It was formed in 1945 in order to promote world peace and co-operation between nations. Its headquarters are in New York. Here the 184 members regularly meet in a General Assembly to settle disputes and agree on common policies to world problems. The work of the United Nations is carried out through its various agencies which include:

Agency:	Responsibility:
UNESCO	Science, education and culture.
UNICEF	Children's welfare.
UNDRO	Disaster relief.
UNHCR	Aid to refugees.
WHO	Health.
FAO	Food & agriculture.
UNEP	Environment.
UNDP	Development programme.

Council of Europe

Commonwealth of Independent States

Organization of African Unity (OAU)

Arab League

Organization of American States (OAS)

Commonwealth

Not a member of any of the organizations shown on the map

Note:- Countries represented by colour stripes are those which are members of more than one of the International Organizations shown on the map.

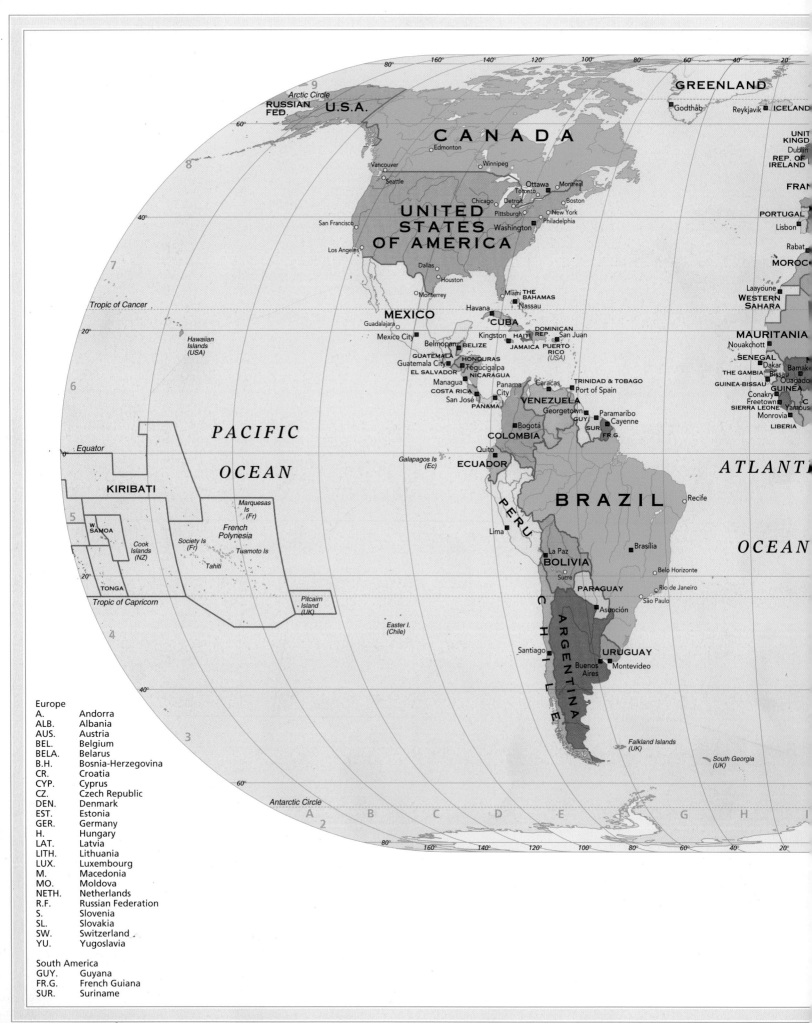

GREENLAND

RUSSIAN FED.   U.S.A.   Arctic Circle

Godthåb   Reykjavik   ICELAND

CANADA

Edmonton

UNIT KINGD

Dublin
REP. OF
IRELAND

Vancouver   Winnipeg

Seattle   Ottawa   Montreal

Chicago   Toronto   Boston   FRAN

Detroit

Pittsburgh   New York

Philadelphia

PORTUGAL

San Francisco   UNITED STATES OF AMERICA   Washington

Lisbon

Los Angeles

Rabat

Dallas   MOROC

Houston

Monterrey   Miami   THE BAHAMAS   Laayoune

Tropic of Cancer   WESTERN SAHARA

Havana   Nassau

MEXICO   CUBA   MAURITANIA

Guadalajara   Kingston   DOMINICAN REP.   San Juan   Nouakchott

Mexico City   HAITI   PUERTO RICO (USA)   SENEGAL

GUATEMALA   BELIZE   JAMAICA   Dakar   Bamak

Belmopan   Bissau

Guatemala City   Tegucigalpa   HONDURAS   THE GAMBIA

EL SALVADOR   NICARAGUA   GUINEA-BISSAU   GUINE

Managua   TRINIDAD & TOBAGO   Conakry   C

Hawaiian
Islands
(USA)   COSTA RICA   Panama
City   Caracas   Port of Spain   Freetown   Yamous

San José   SIERRA LEONE   Monrovia

PANAMA   VENEZUELA   LIBERIA

Georgetown   Paramaribo

GUY   Cayenne

COLOMBIA   Bogotá   SUR   FR. G.

Quito

PACIFIC   Galapagos Is   ATLANTI
(Ec)   ECUADOR

Equator   OCEAN

KIRIBATI   PERU   BRAZIL   Recife

Marquesas
Is
(Fr)

W
SAMOA   French
Polynesia   Lima

Cook
Islands
(NZ)   Society Is
(Fr)   Tuamoto Is   La Paz   Brasília

BOLIVIA   Belo Horizonte

Tahiti   Sucre   Rio de Janeiro

TONGA   PARAGUAY   São Paulo

Tropic of Capricorn   Pitcairn
Island
(UK)   Asunción

Easter I.
(Chile)

Santiago   URUGUAY

Buenos
Aires   Montevideo

Falkland Islands
(UK)   OCEAN

South Georgia
(UK)

Antarctic Circle

A   B   C   D   E   G   H

Europe
A.   Andorra
ALB.   Albania
AUS.   Austria
BEL.   Belgium
BELA.   Belarus
B.H.   Bosnia-Herzegovina
CR.   Croatia
CYP.   Cyprus
CZ.   Czech Republic
DEN.   Denmark
EST.   Estonia
GER.   Germany
H.   Hungary
LAT.   Latvia
LITH.   Lithuania
LUX.   Luxembourg
M.   Macedonia
MO.   Moldova
NETH.   Netherlands
R.F.   Russian Federation
S.   Slovenia
SL.   Slovakia
SW.   Switzerland
YU.   Yugoslavia

South America
GUY.   Guyana
FR.G.   French Guiana
SUR.   Suriname

SCALE 1 : 80 000 000   0   800   1600   2400   3200 km

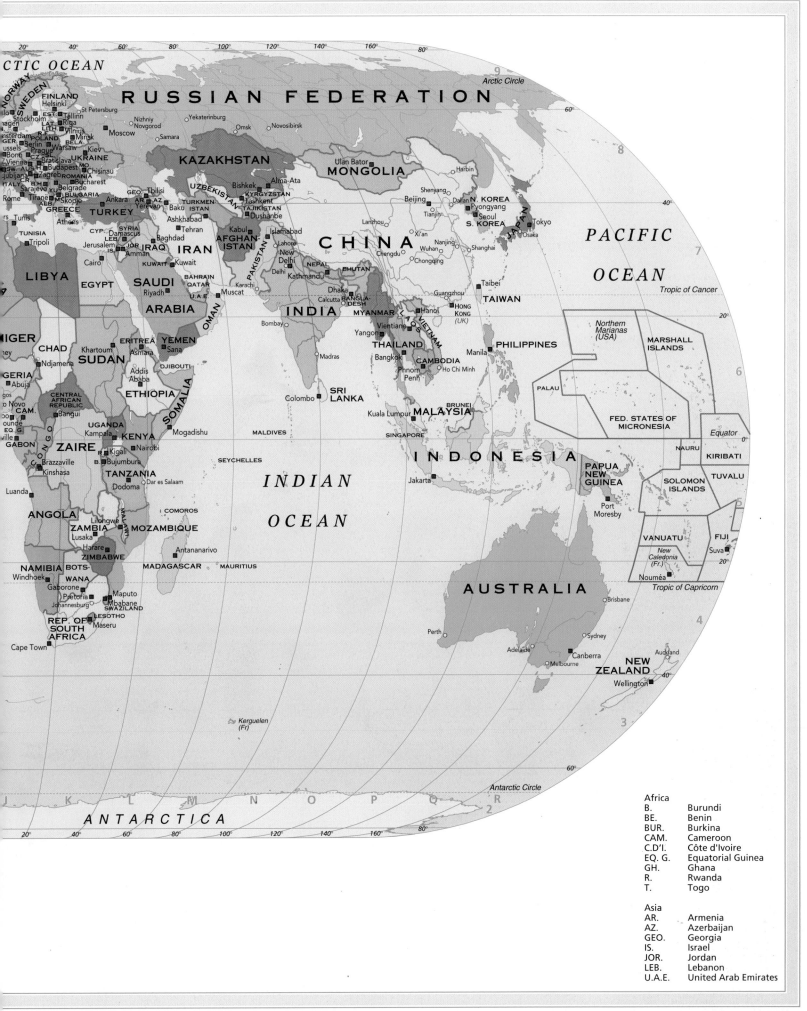

ARCTIC OCEAN

RUSSIAN FEDERATION

Arctic Circle

NORWAY
SWEDEN
FINLAND
Helsinki
Oslo
Stockholm
St Petersburg
Nizhniy Novgorod
Yekaterinburg
Omsk
Novosibirsk
EST.
Tallinn
LAT. Riga
LITH.
Vilnius
Minsk
Moscow
Samara

Amsterdam
Brussels
GER.
Bonn
Berlin
R.F.
POLAND
Warsaw
Kiev
BELA.
Vienna
Prague
CZ.
Bratislava
Budapest
SW. AUS-H.
UKRAINE
MO.
Chisinau

KAZAKHSTAN

MONGOLIA
Ulan Bator

Harbin

Ljubljana
Zagreb
ROMANIA
Bucharest
SW.
B-H.
Sarajevo
YU.
Belgrade
BULGARIA
Bishkek
UZBEKISTAN
Tashkent
KYRGYZSTAN
TAJIKISTAN
Dushanbe
Shenyang
Beijing
Dalian
N. KOREA
Pyongyang

Rome
Tirane
ALB.
MSkopje
GREECE
Athens
TURKEY
Ankara
GEO. Tbilisi
AR.
Yerevan
AZ.
Baku
TURKMEN-
ISTAN
Ashkhabad
Tianjin
Seoul
S. KOREA
JAPAN
Tokyo
Osaka

Tunis
TUNISIA
Tripoli
CYP.
SYRIA
Damascus
LEB.
Jerusalem
IS.
JOR.
Amman
IRAQ
Baghdad
IRAN
Tehran
AFGHAN-
ISTAN
Kabul
Islamabad
Lahore
New Delhi
CHINA
Lanzhou
Xi'an
Chengdu
Chongqing
Wuhan
Nanjing
Shanghai

LIBYA
EGYPT
Cairo
KUWAIT
Kuwait
SAUDI
Riyadh
ARABIA
BAHRAIN
QATAR
U.A.E.
Muscat
OMAN
PAKISTAN
Karachi
Delhi
NEPAL
Kathmandu
BHUTAN
Dhaka
BANGLA-
DESH
Calcutta
Guangzhou
HONG
KONG
(UK)
Taibei
TAIWAN

PACIFIC

OCEAN

Tropic of Cancer

NIGER
CHAD
Khartoum
ERITREA
Asmara
YEMEN
Sana
INDIA
Bombay
MYANMAR
Yangon
Hanoi
LAOS
VIETNAM
Vientiane

Northern
Marianas
(USA)
MARSHALL
ISLANDS

NGERIA
Abuja
SUDAN
Ndjamena
DJIBOUTI
Addis
Ababa
ETHIOPIA
Madras
THAILAND
Bangkok
CAMBODIA
Phnom
Penh
Ho Chi Minh
Manila
PHILIPPINES

PALAU

Porto Novo
CENTRAL
AFRICAN
REPUBLIC
CAM.
Bangui
SRI
LANKA
Colombo
BRUNEI
Kuala Lumpur
MALAYSIA

FED. STATES OF
MICRONESIA

Equator

Yaounde
EQ. G.
GABON
Libreville
UGANDA
Kampala
KENYA
Nairobi
Mogadishu
SOMALIA
MALDIVES
SINGAPORE

NAURU
KIRIBATI

ZAIRE
Brazzaville
Kinshasa
CONGO
Kigali
R.
B.
Bujumbura
TANZANIA
Dodoma
Dar es Salaam
SEYCHELLES

INDONESIA

PAPUA
NEW
GUINEA

SOLOMON
ISLANDS

TUVALU

Luanda
ANGOLA
ZAMBIA
Lusaka
MALAWI
Lilongwe
MOZAMBIQUE
COMOROS
Antananarivo

INDIAN

OCEAN

Jakarta

Port
Moresby

VANUATU

New
Caledonia
(Fr.)
Noumea

FIJI
Suva

NAMIBIA
Windhoek
BOTS-
WANA
Gaborone
Pretoria
Johannesburg
Maputo
Mbabane
SWAZILAND
ZIMBABWE
Harare
MADAGASCAR
MAURITIUS

Tropic of Capricorn

REP. OF
SOUTH
AFRICA
Cape Town
LESOTHO
Maseru

AUSTRALIA
Brisbane

Perth
Sydney
Adelaide
Canberra
Melbourne
Auckland
NEW
ZEALAND

Kerguelen
(Fr)

Wellington

ANTARCTICA

Antarctic Circle

Africa
B. Burundi
BE. Benin
BUR. Burkina
CAM. Cameroon
C.D'I. Côte d'Ivoire
EQ. G. Equatorial Guinea
GH. Ghana
R. Rwanda
T. Togo

Asia
AR. Armenia
AZ. Azerbaijan
GEO. Georgia
IS. Israel
JOR. Jordan
LEB. Lebanon
U.A.E. United Arab Emirates

Eckert iv projection

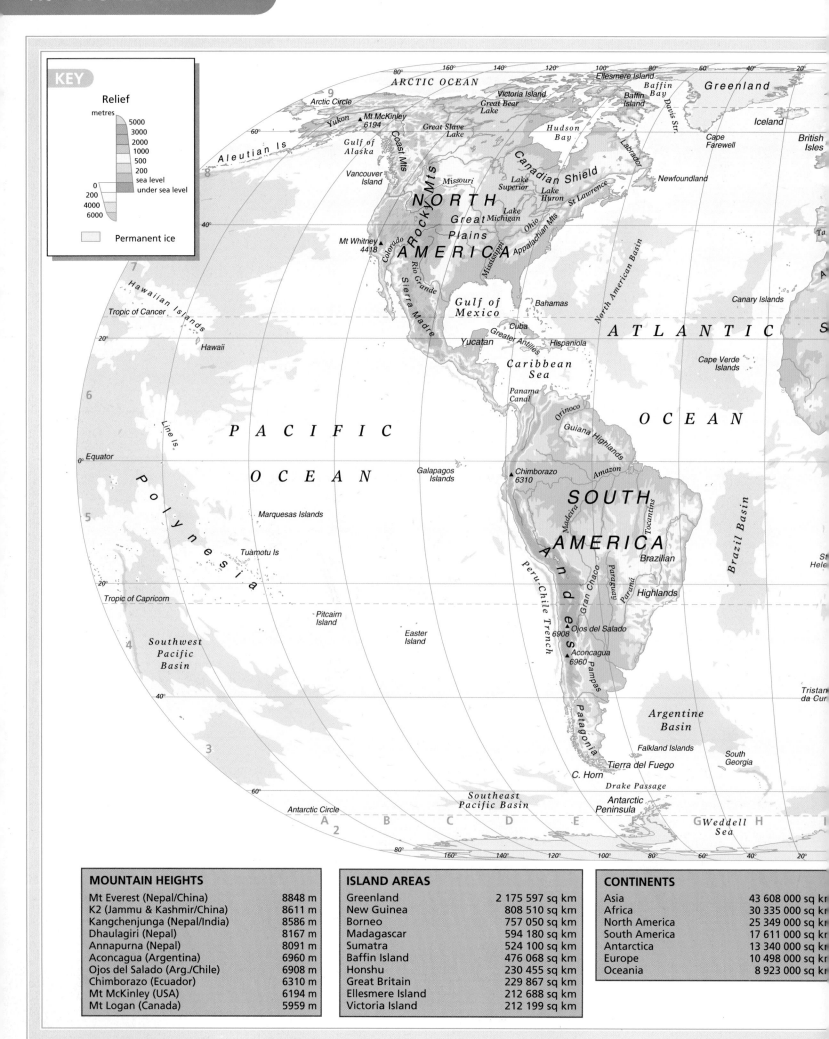

KEY

Relief

metres	
5000	
3000	
2000	
1000	
500	
200	
0	sea level
200	under sea level
4000	
6000	

Permanent ice

MOUNTAIN HEIGHTS

Mt Everest (Nepal/China)	8848 m
K2 (Jammu & Kashmir/China)	8611 m
Kangchenjunga (Nepal/India)	8586 m
Dhaulagiri (Nepal)	8167 m
Annapurna (Nepal)	8091 m
Aconcagua (Argentina)	6960 m
Ojos del Salado (Arg./Chile)	6908 m
Chimborazo (Ecuador)	6310 m
Mt McKinley (USA)	6194 m
Mt Logan (Canada)	5959 m

ISLAND AREAS

Greenland	2 175 597 sq km
New Guinea	808 510 sq km
Borneo	757 050 sq km
Madagascar	594 180 sq km
Sumatra	524 100 sq km
Baffin Island	476 068 sq km
Honshu	230 455 sq km
Great Britain	229 867 sq km
Ellesmere Island	212 688 sq km
Victoria Island	212 199 sq km

CONTINENTS

Asia	43 608 000 sq km
Africa	30 335 000 sq km
North America	25 349 000 sq km
South America	17 611 000 sq km
Antarctica	13 340 000 sq km
Europe	10 498 000 sq km
Oceania	8 923 000 sq km

SCALE 1 : 80 000 000

0   800   1600   2400   3200 km

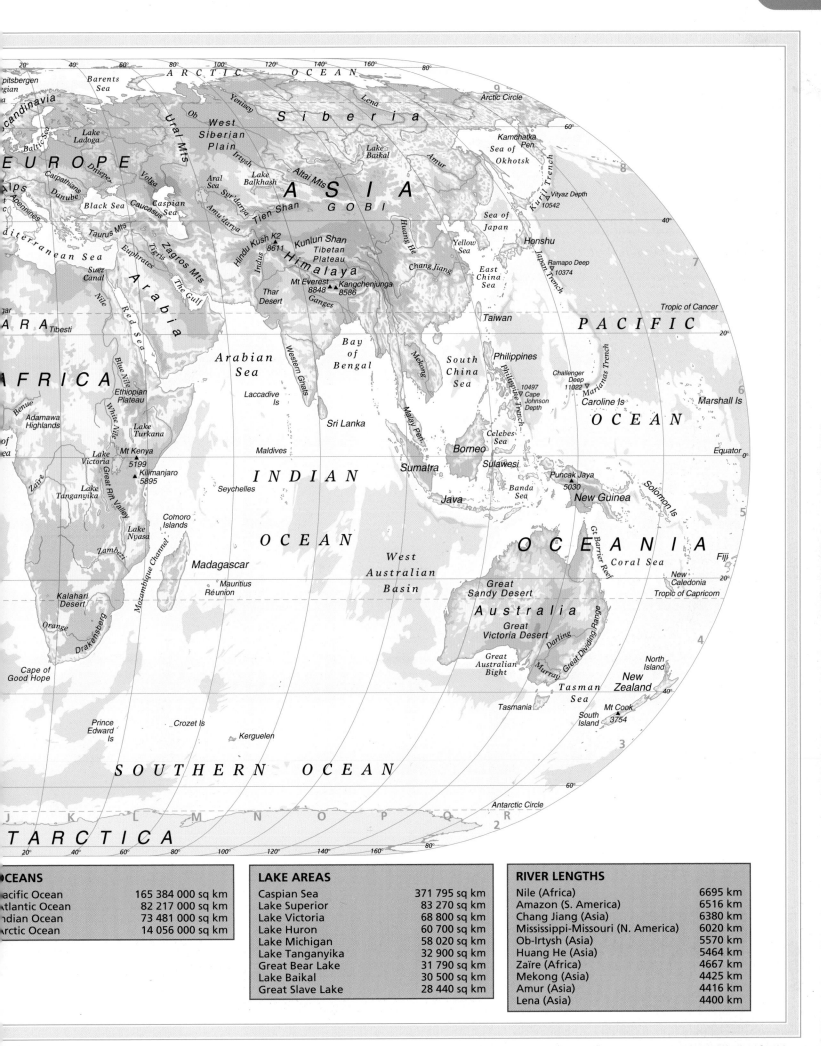

OCEANS

Pacific Ocean	165 384 000 sq km
Atlantic Ocean	82 217 000 sq km
Indian Ocean	73 481 000 sq km
Arctic Ocean	14 056 000 sq km

LAKE AREAS

Caspian Sea	371 795 sq km
Lake Superior	83 270 sq km
Lake Victoria	68 800 sq km
Lake Huron	60 700 sq km
Lake Michigan	58 020 sq km
Lake Tanganyika	32 900 sq km
Great Bear Lake	31 790 sq km
Lake Baikal	30 500 sq km
Great Slave Lake	28 440 sq km

RIVER LENGTHS

Nile (Africa)	6695 km
Amazon (S. America)	6516 km
Chang Jiang (Asia)	6380 km
Mississippi-Missouri (N. America)	6020 km
Ob-Irtysh (Asia)	5570 km
Huang He (Asia)	5464 km
Zaïre (Africa)	4667 km
Mekong (Asia)	4425 km
Amur (Asia)	4416 km
Lena (Asia)	4400 km

Eckert iv projection

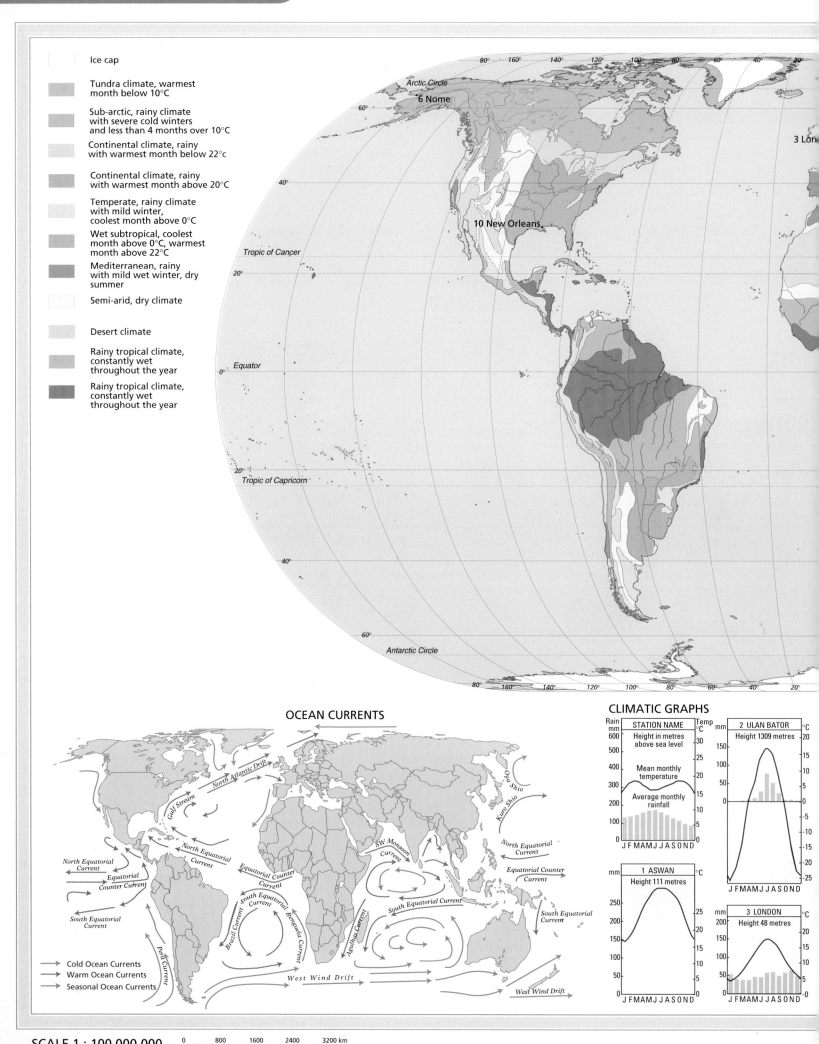

Ice cap

Tundra climate, warmest month below 10°C

Sub-arctic, rainy climate with severe cold winters and less than 4 months over 10°C

Continental climate, rainy with warmest month below 22°c

Continental climate, rainy with warmest month above 20°C

Temperate, rainy climate with mild winter, coolest month above 0°C

Wet subtropical, coolest month above 0°C, warmest month above 22°C

Mediterranean, rainy with mild wet winter, dry summer

Semi-arid, dry climate

Desert climate

Rainy tropical climate, constantly wet throughout the year

Rainy tropical climate, constantly wet throughout the year

Arctic Circle

6 Nome

3 Lon

40°

10 New Orleans

Tropic of Cancer

20°

0° Equator

20°

Tropic of Capricorn

40°

60°

Antarctic Circle

OCEAN CURRENTS

North Atlantic Drift

Gulf Stream

Kuro Shio

North Equatorial Current

North Equatorial Current

North Equatorial Current

Equatorial Counter Current

SW Monsoon Current

Equatorial Counter Current

Equatorial Counter Current

South Equatorial Current

South Equatorial Current

South Equatorial Current

South Equatorial Current

Brazil Current

Benguela Current

Peru Current

Agulhas Current

West Wind Drift

West Wind Drift

→ Cold Ocean Currents
→ Warm Ocean Currents
→ Seasonal Ocean Currents

CLIMATIC GRAPHS

| Rain mm | STATION NAME | Temp °C |
Height in metres above sea level
Mean monthly temperature
Average monthly rainfall
J F M A M J J A S O N D

2 ULAN BATOR
Height 1309 metres
J F M A M J J A S O N D

1 ASWAN
Height 111 metres
J F M A M J J A S O N D

3 LONDON
Height 48 metres
J F M A M J J A S O N D

SCALE 1 : 100 000 000

0   800   1600   2400   3200 km

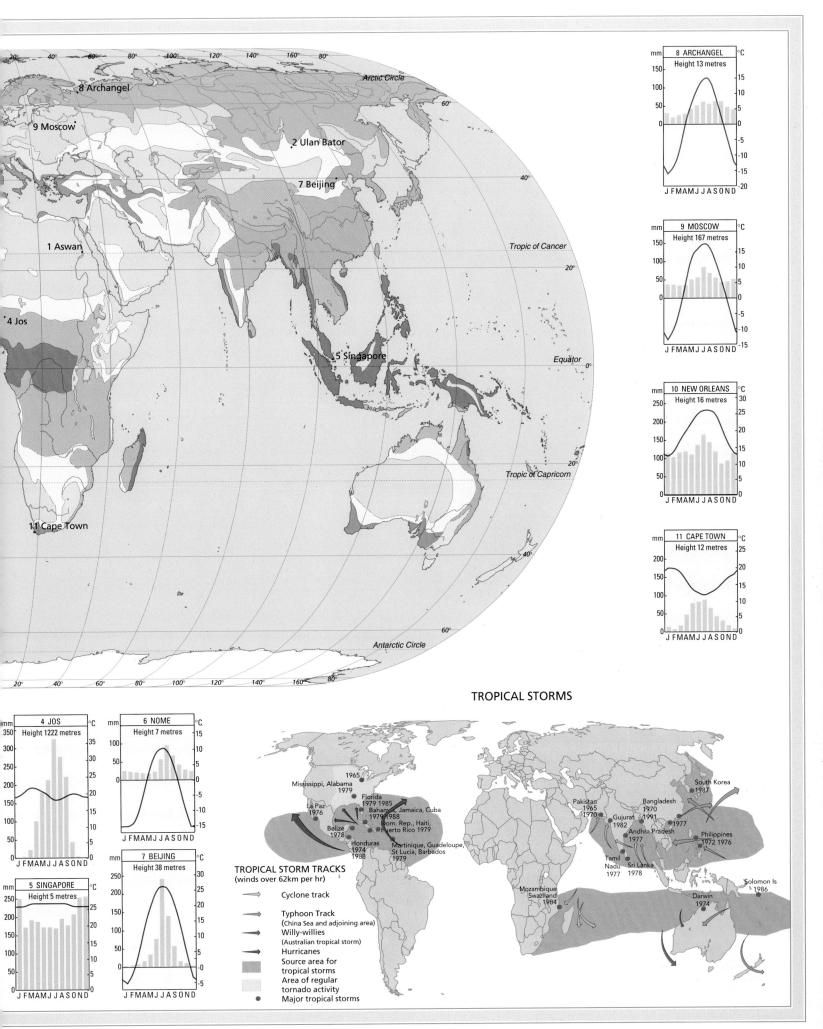

8 ARCHANGEL
Height 13 metres

9 MOSCOW
Height 167 metres

10 NEW ORLEANS
Height 16 metres

11 CAPE TOWN
Height 12 metres

4 JOS
Height 1222 metres

6 NOME
Height 7 metres

5 SINGAPORE
Height 5 metres

7 BEIJING
Height 38 metres

TROPICAL STORMS

Mississippi, Alabama 1979
Florida 1979 1985
La Paz 1976
Bahamas, Jamaica, Cuba 1979 1988
Belize 1978
Dom. Rep., Haiti, Puerto Rico 1979
Honduras 1974 1988
Martinique, Guadeloupe, St Lucia, Barbados 1979
1965

Pakistan 1965 1970
Bangladesh 1970 1991
South Korea 1987
Gujurat 1982
1977
Andhra Pradesh 1977
Philippines 1972 1976
Tamil Nadu 1977
Sri Lanka 1978
Mozambique Swaziland 1984
Darwin 1974
Solomon Is 1986

TROPICAL STORM TRACKS
(winds over 62km per hr)

→ Cyclone track

→ Typhoon Track
(China Sea and adjoining area)

→ Willy-willies
(Australian tropical storm)

→ Hurricanes

Source area for tropical storms

Area of regular tornado activity

• Major tropical storms

Eckert IV projection

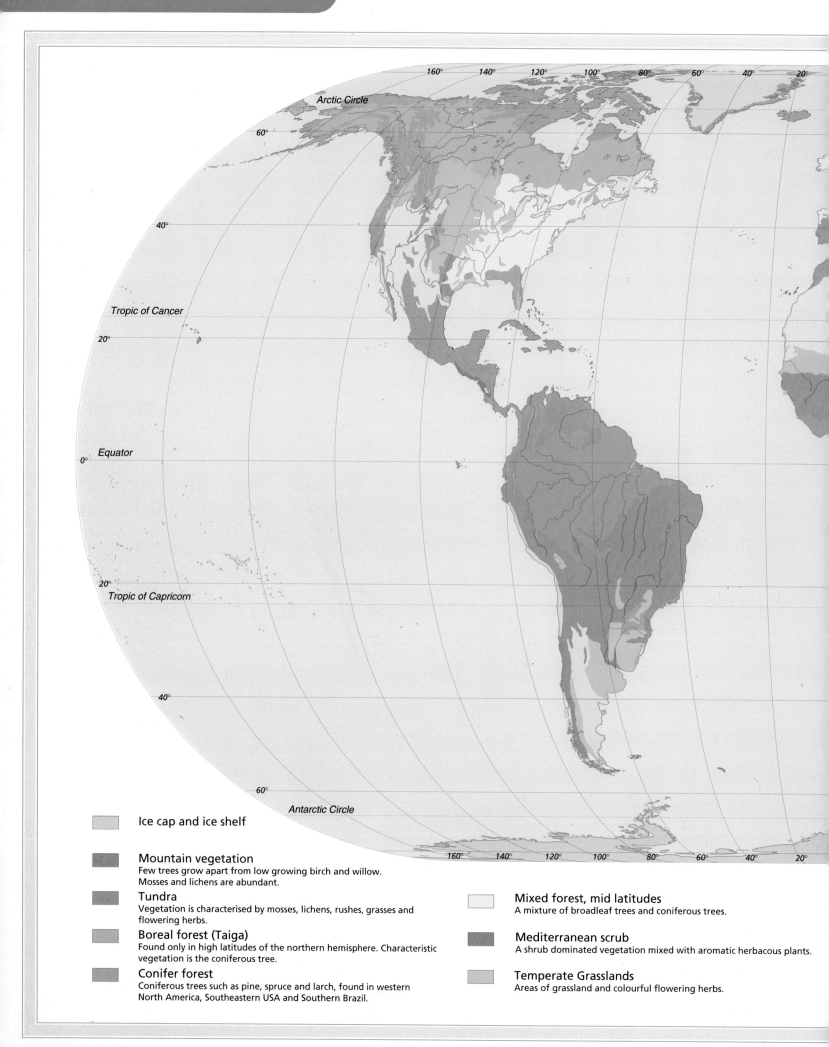

Arctic Circle

60°

40°

Tropic of Cancer

20°

Equator

0°

20°

Tropic of Capricorn

40°

60°

Antarctic Circle

160° 140° 120° 100° 80° 60° 40° 20°

Ice cap and ice shelf

Mountain vegetation
Few trees grow apart from low growing birch and willow.
Mosses and lichens are abundant.

Tundra
Vegetation is characterised by mosses, lichens, rushes, grasses and
flowering herbs.

Boreal forest (Taiga)
Found only in high latitudes of the northern hemisphere. Characteristic
vegetation is the coniferous tree.

Conifer forest
Coniferous trees such as pine, spruce and larch, found in western
North America, Southeastern USA and Southern Brazil.

Mixed forest, mid latitudes
A mixture of broadleaf trees and coniferous trees.

Mediterranean scrub
A shrub dominated vegetation mixed with aromatic herbacous plants.

Temperate Grasslands
Areas of grassland and colourful flowering herbs.

SCALE 1 : 80 000 000   0   800   1600   2400   3200 km

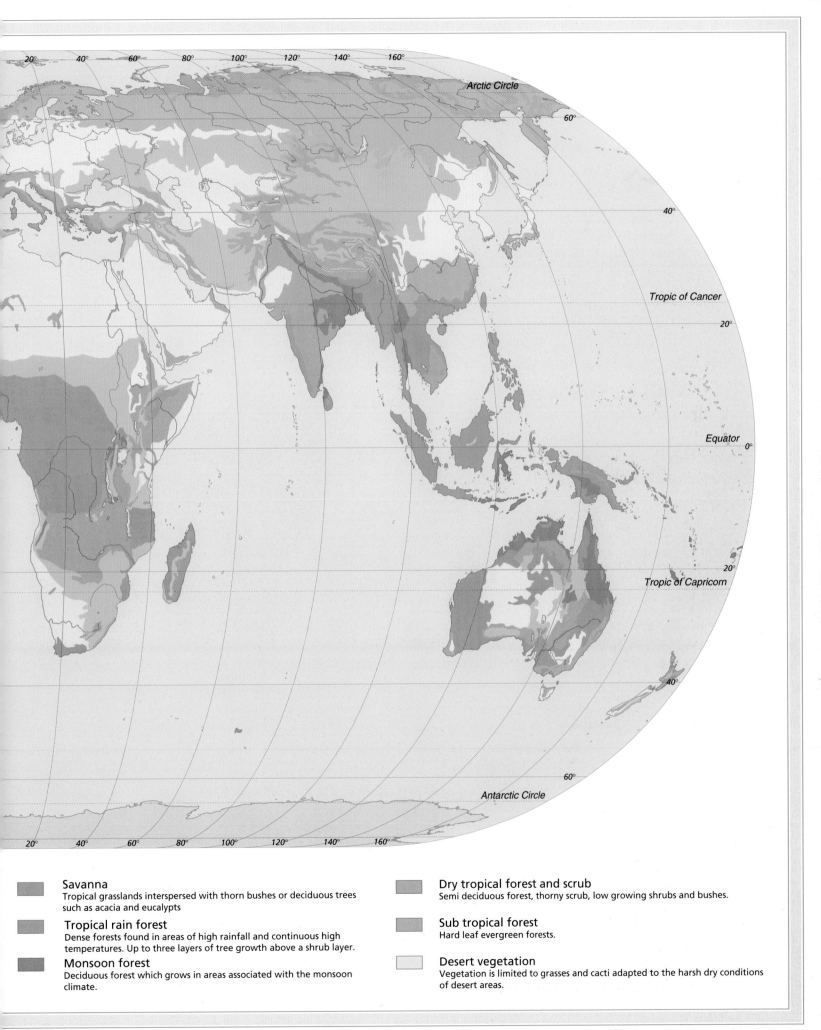

Savanna
Tropical grasslands interspersed with thorn bushes or deciduous trees
such as acacia and eucalypts

Tropical rain forest
Dense forests found in areas of high rainfall and continuous high
temperatures. Up to three layers of tree growth above a shrub layer.

Monsoon forest
Deciduous forest which grows in areas associated with the monsoon
climate.

Dry tropical forest and scrub
Semi deciduous forest, thorny scrub, low growing shrubs and bushes.

Sub tropical forest
Hard leaf evergreen forests.

Desert vegetation
Vegetation is limited to grasses and cacti adapted to the harsh dry conditions
of desert areas.

Eckert IV projection

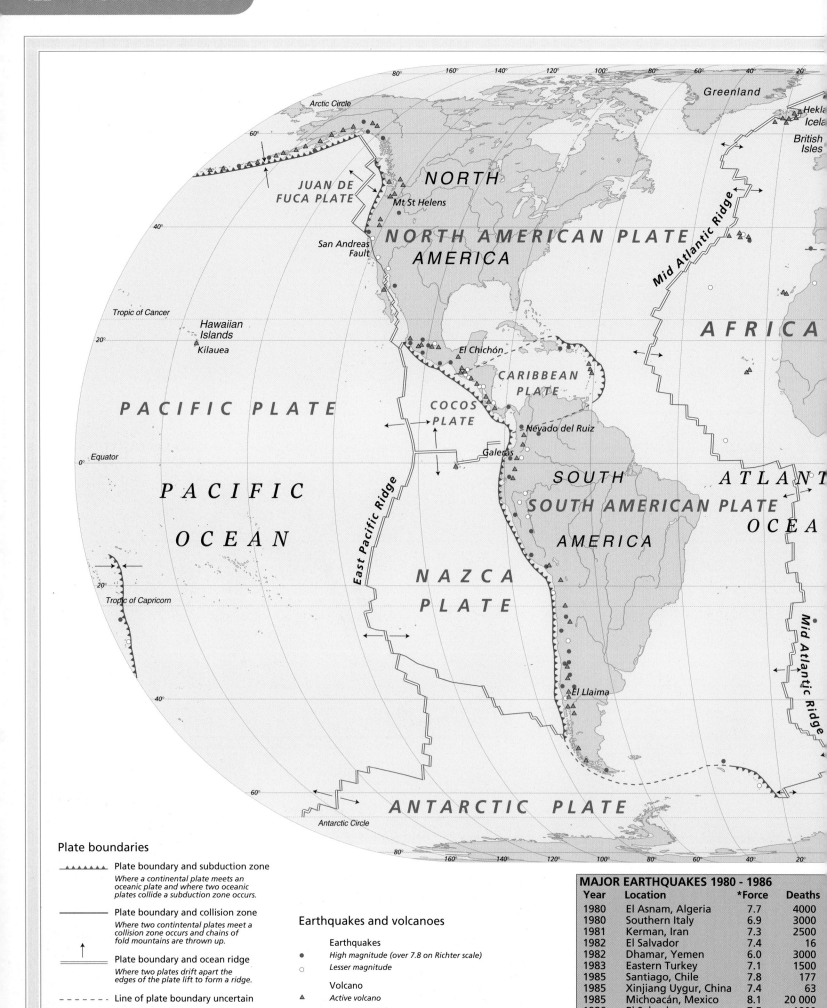

Plate boundaries

⌐⌐⌐⌐⌐⌐⌐ Plate boundary and subduction zone
Where a continental plate meets an oceanic plate and where two oceanic plates collide a subduction zone occurs.

──────── Plate boundary and collision zone
Where two contintental plates meet a collision zone occurs and chains of fold mountains are thrown up.

↑ ══════ Plate boundary and ocean ridge
Where two plates drift apart the edges of the plate lift to form a ridge.

- - - - - - Line of plate boundary uncertain

Earthquakes and volcanoes

Earthquakes

● High magnitude (over 7.8 on Richter scale)

○ Lesser magnitude

Volcano

▲ Active volcano

MAJOR EARTHQUAKES 1980 - 1986			
Year	Location	*Force	Deaths
1980	El Asnam, Algeria	7.7	4000
1980	Southern Italy	6.9	3000
1981	Kerman, Iran	7.3	2500
1982	El Salvador	7.4	16
1982	Dhamar, Yemen	6.0	3000
1983	Eastern Turkey	7.1	1500
1985	Santiago, Chile	7.8	177
1985	Xinjiang Uygur, China	7.4	63
1985	Michoacán, Mexico	8.1	20 000
1986	El Salvador	7.5	1000

SCALE 1 : 80 000 000

0   800   1600   2400   3200 km

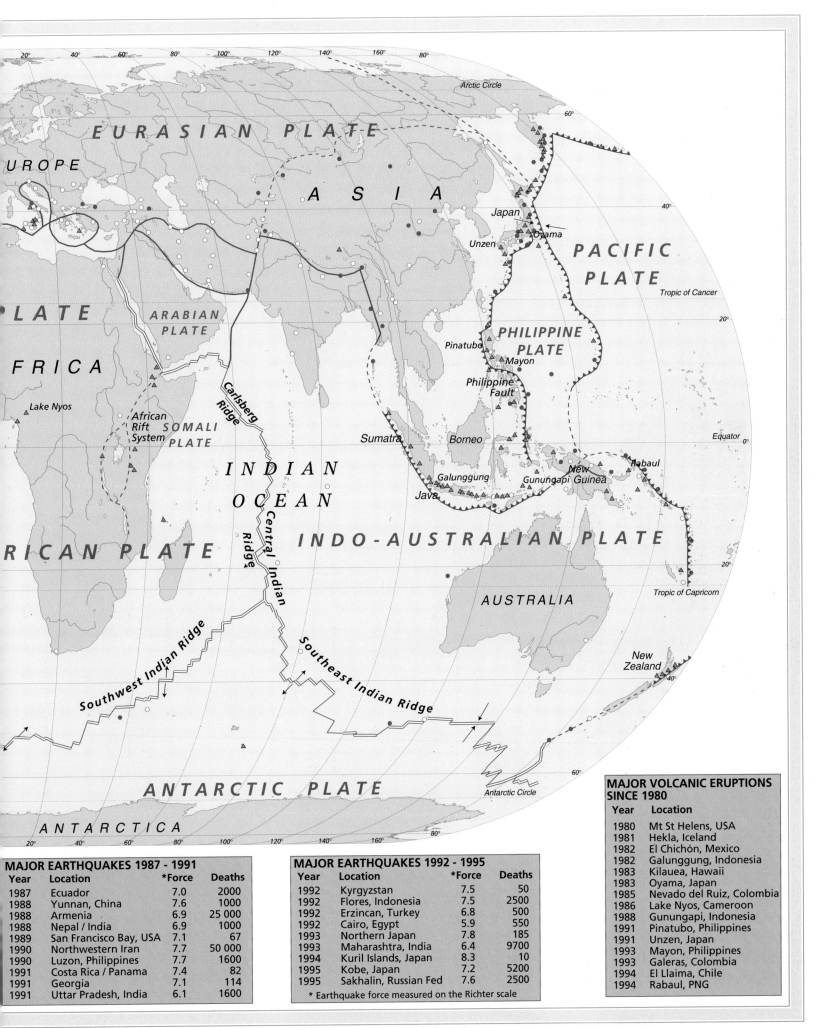

EURASIAN PLATE

EUROPE

ASIA

PLATE

ARABIAN
PLATE

AFRICA

Japan
Unzen Oyama

PACIFIC
PLATE

Tropic of Cancer

PHILIPPINE
PLATE

Pinatubo
Mayon

Philippine
Fault

Lake Nyos

African
Rift SOMALI
System PLATE

Carlsberg
Ridge

INDIAN
OCEAN

Sumatra

Borneo

Equator

Rabaul

Galunggung
Java

Gunungapi

New
Guinea

AFRICAN PLATE

Central Indian
Ridge

INDO-AUSTRALIAN PLATE

Southwest Indian Ridge

Southeast Indian Ridge

AUSTRALIA

Tropic of Capricorn

New
Zealand

ANTARCTIC PLATE

Antarctic Circle

ANTARCTICA

Arctic Circle

MAJOR EARTHQUAKES 1987 - 1991

Year	Location	*Force	Deaths
1987	Ecuador	7.0	2000
1988	Yunnan, China	7.6	1000
1988	Armenia	6.9	25 000
1988	Nepal / India	6.9	1000
1989	San Francisco Bay, USA	7.1	67
1990	Northwestern Iran	7.7	50 000
1990	Luzon, Philippines	7.7	1600
1991	Costa Rica / Panama	7.4	82
1991	Georgia	7.1	114
1991	Uttar Pradesh, India	6.1	1600

MAJOR EARTHQUAKES 1992 - 1995

Year	Location	*Force	Deaths
1992	Kyrgyzstan	7.5	50
1992	Flores, Indonesia	7.5	2500
1992	Erzincan, Turkey	6.8	500
1992	Cairo, Egypt	5.9	550
1993	Northern Japan	7.8	185
1993	Maharashtra, India	6.4	9700
1994	Kuril Islands, Japan	8.3	10
1995	Kobe, Japan	7.2	5200
1995	Sakhalin, Russian Fed	7.6	2500

* Earthquake force measured on the Richter scale

MAJOR VOLCANIC ERUPTIONS SINCE 1980

Year	Location
1980	Mt St Helens, USA
1981	Hekla, Iceland
1982	El Chichón, Mexico
1982	Galunggung, Indonesia
1983	Kilauea, Hawaii
1983	Oyama, Japan
1985	Nevado del Ruiz, Colombia
1986	Lake Nyos, Cameroon
1988	Gunungapi, Indonesia
1991	Pinatubo, Philippines
1991	Unzen, Japan
1993	Mayon, Philippines
1993	Galeras, Colombia
1994	El Llaima, Chile
1994	Rabaul, PNG

Eckert iv projection

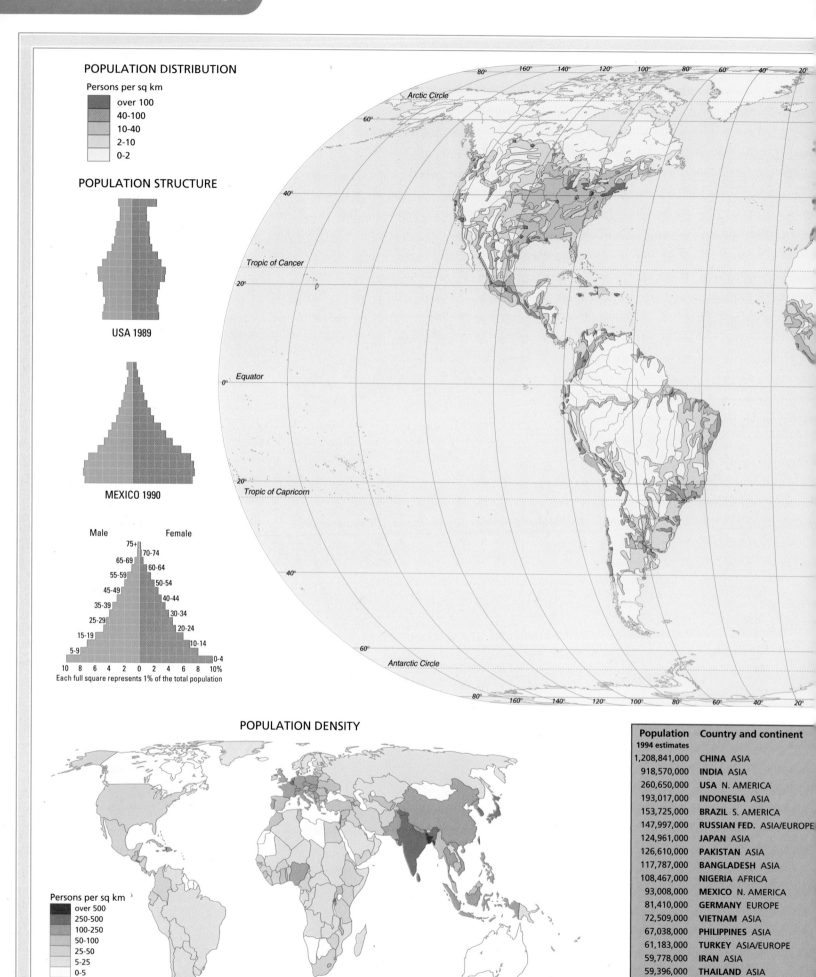

POPULATION DISTRIBUTION

Persons per sq km
- over 100
- 40-100
- 10-40
- 2-10
- 0-2

POPULATION STRUCTURE

USA 1989

MEXICO 1990

Male | Female

75+
70-74
65-69
60-64
55-59
50-54
45-49
40-44
35-39
30-34
25-29
20-24
15-19
10-14
5-9
0-4

10 8 6 4 2 0 0 2 4 6 8 10%
Each full square represents 1% of the total population

POPULATION DENSITY

Persons per sq km
- over 500
- 250-500
- 100-250
- 50-100
- 25-50
- 5-25
- 0-5
- no data

Population 1994 estimates	Country and continent
1,208,841,000	**CHINA** ASIA
918,570,000	**INDIA** ASIA
260,650,000	**USA** N. AMERICA
193,017,000	**INDONESIA** ASIA
153,725,000	**BRAZIL** S. AMERICA
147,997,000	**RUSSIAN FED.** ASIA/EUROPE
124,961,000	**JAPAN** ASIA
126,610,000	**PAKISTAN** ASIA
117,787,000	**BANGLADESH** ASIA
108,467,000	**NIGERIA** AFRICA
93,008,000	**MEXICO** N. AMERICA
81,410,000	**GERMANY** EUROPE
72,509,000	**VIETNAM** ASIA
67,038,000	**PHILIPPINES** ASIA
61,183,000	**TURKEY** ASIA/EUROPE
59,778,000	**IRAN** ASIA
59,396,000	**THAILAND** ASIA
58,326,000	**EGYPT** AFRICA
58,191,000	**UNITED KINGDOM** EUROPE
57,747,000	**FRANCE** EUROPE

SCALE 1 : 100 000 000

0   800   1600   2400   3200 km

Arctic Circle
Tropic of Cancer
Equator
Tropic of Capricorn
Antarctic Circle

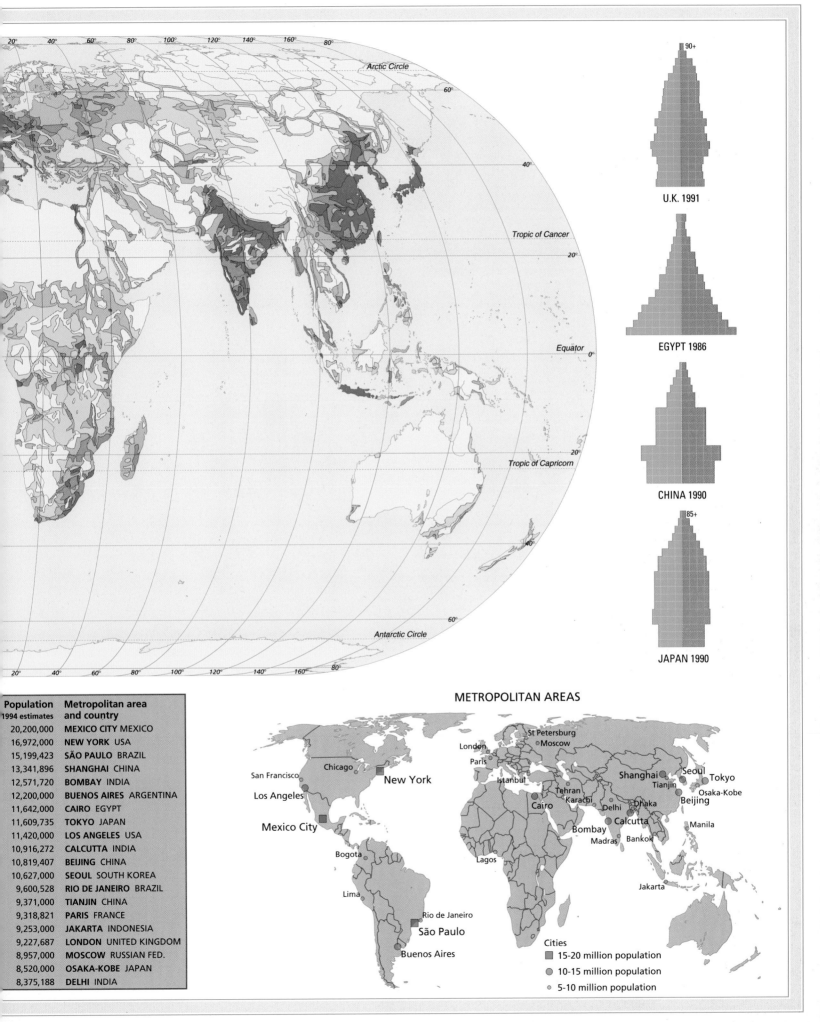

Arctic Circle

60°

40°

Tropic of Cancer

20°

Equator 0°

Tropic of Capricorn

20°

40°

60°

Antarctic Circle

90+
U.K. 1991

EGYPT 1986

CHINA 1990

85+
JAPAN 1990

Population 1994 estimates	Metropolitan area and country
20,200,000	**MEXICO CITY** MEXICO
16,972,000	**NEW YORK** USA
15,199,423	**SÃO PAULO** BRAZIL
13,341,896	**SHANGHAI** CHINA
12,571,720	**BOMBAY** INDIA
12,200,000	**BUENOS AIRES** ARGENTINA
11,642,000	**CAIRO** EGYPT
11,609,735	**TOKYO** JAPAN
11,420,000	**LOS ANGELES** USA
10,916,272	**CALCUTTA** INDIA
10,819,407	**BEIJING** CHINA
10,627,000	**SEOUL** SOUTH KOREA
9,600,528	**RIO DE JANEIRO** BRAZIL
9,371,000	**TIANJIN** CHINA
9,318,821	**PARIS** FRANCE
9,253,000	**JAKARTA** INDONESIA
9,227,687	**LONDON** UNITED KINGDOM
8,957,000	**MOSCOW** RUSSIAN FED.
8,520,000	**OSAKA-KOBE** JAPAN
8,375,188	**DELHI** INDIA

METROPOLITAN AREAS

St Petersburg
Moscow
London
Paris
San Francisco
Chicago
New York
Istanbul
Shanghai
Seoul
Tokyo
Tianjin
Tehran
Osaka-Kobe
Los Angeles
Karachi
Beijing
Cairo
Delhi
Dhaka
Mexico City
Bombay
Calcutta
Manila
Madras
Bankok
Bogota
Lagos
Lima
Jakarta
Rio de Janeiro
São Paulo
Buenos Aires

Cities
■ 15-20 million population
● 10-15 million population
● 5-10 million population

Eckert IV projection

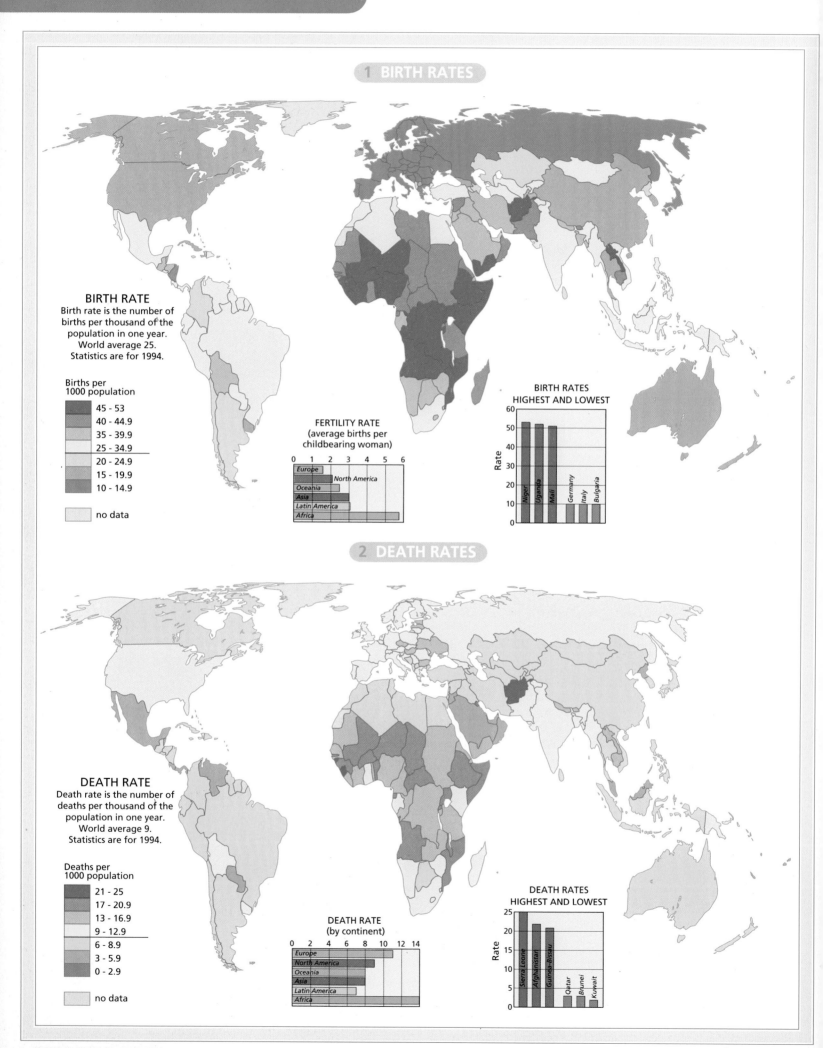

1 BIRTH RATES

BIRTH RATE
Birth rate is the number of births per thousand of the population in one year. World average 25. Statistics are for 1994.

Births per 1000 population

- 45 - 53
- 40 - 44.9
- 35 - 39.9
- 25 - 34.9
- 20 - 24.9
- 15 - 19.9
- 10 - 14.9

no data

FERTILITY RATE
(average births per childbearing woman)

Europe
North America
Oceania
Asia
Latin America
Africa

BIRTH RATES HIGHEST AND LOWEST

Niger
Uganda
Mali
Germany
Italy
Bulgaria

2 DEATH RATES

DEATH RATE
Death rate is the number of deaths per thousand of the population in one year. World average 9. Statistics are for 1994.

Deaths per 1000 population

- 21 - 25
- 17 - 20.9
- 13 - 16.9
- 9 - 12.9
- 6 - 8.9
- 3 - 5.9
- 0 - 2.9

no data

DEATH RATE
(by continent)

Europe
North America
Oceania
Asia
Latin America
Africa

DEATH RATES HIGHEST AND LOWEST

Sierra Leone
Afghanistan
Guinea-Bissau
Qatar
Brunei
Kuwait

SCALE 1 : 140 000 000

Eckert IV projection

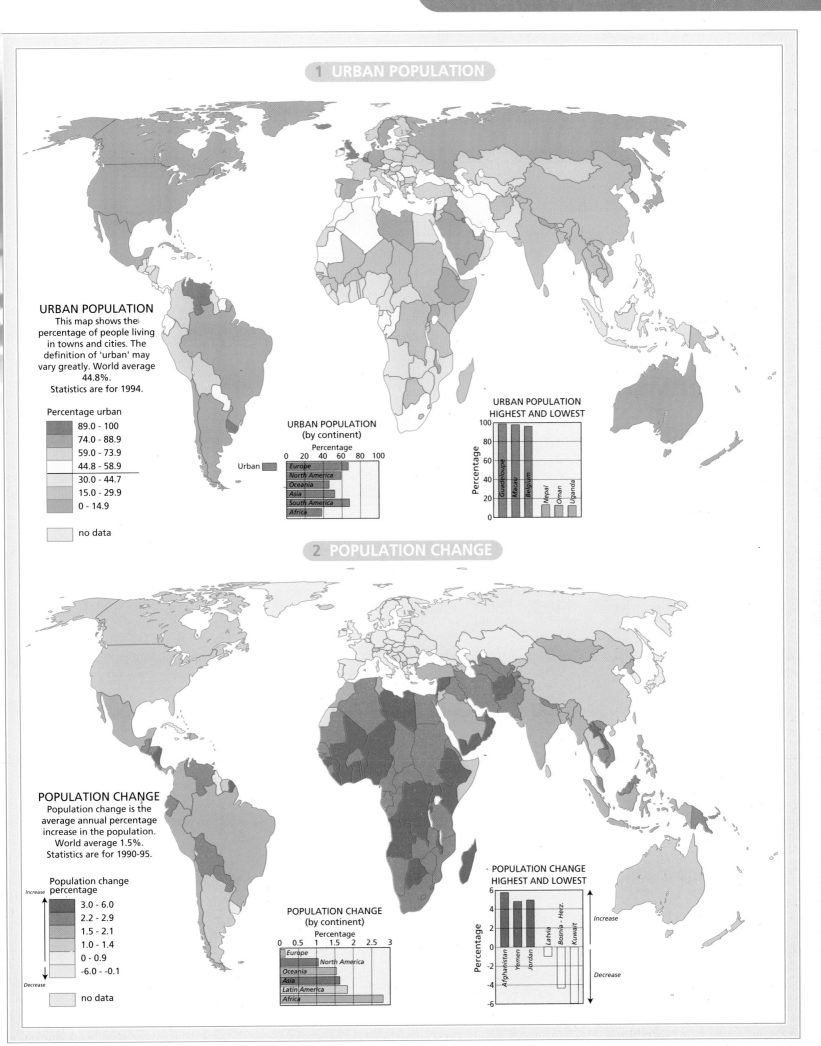

1 URBAN POPULATION

URBAN POPULATION
This map shows the percentage of people living in towns and cities. The definition of 'urban' may vary greatly. World average 44.8%.
Statistics are for 1994.

Percentage urban

- 89.0 - 100
- 74.0 - 88.9
- 59.0 - 73.9
- 44.8 - 58.9
- 30.0 - 44.7
- 15.0 - 29.9
- 0 - 14.9

no data

URBAN POPULATION (by continent)

Percentage

0 20 40 60 80 100

Urban

Europe
North America
Oceania
Asia
South America
Africa

URBAN POPULATION HIGHEST AND LOWEST

Percentage

Guadeloupe, Macau, Belgium, Nepal, Oman, Uganda

2 POPULATION CHANGE

POPULATION CHANGE
Population change is the average annual percentage increase in the population. World average 1.5%.
Statistics are for 1990-95.

Population change percentage

Increase

- 3.0 - 6.0
- 2.2 - 2.9
- 1.5 - 2.1
- 1.0 - 1.4
- 0 - 0.9
- -6.0 - -0.1

Decrease

no data

POPULATION CHANGE (by continent)

Percentage

0   0.5   1   1.5   2   2.5   3

Europe
North America
Oceania
Asia
Latin America
Africa

POPULATION CHANGE HIGHEST AND LOWEST

Percentage

Afghanistan, Yemen, Jordan, Latvia, Bosnia - Herz., Kuwait

Increase

Decrease

SCALE 1 : 140 000 000

Eckert IV projection

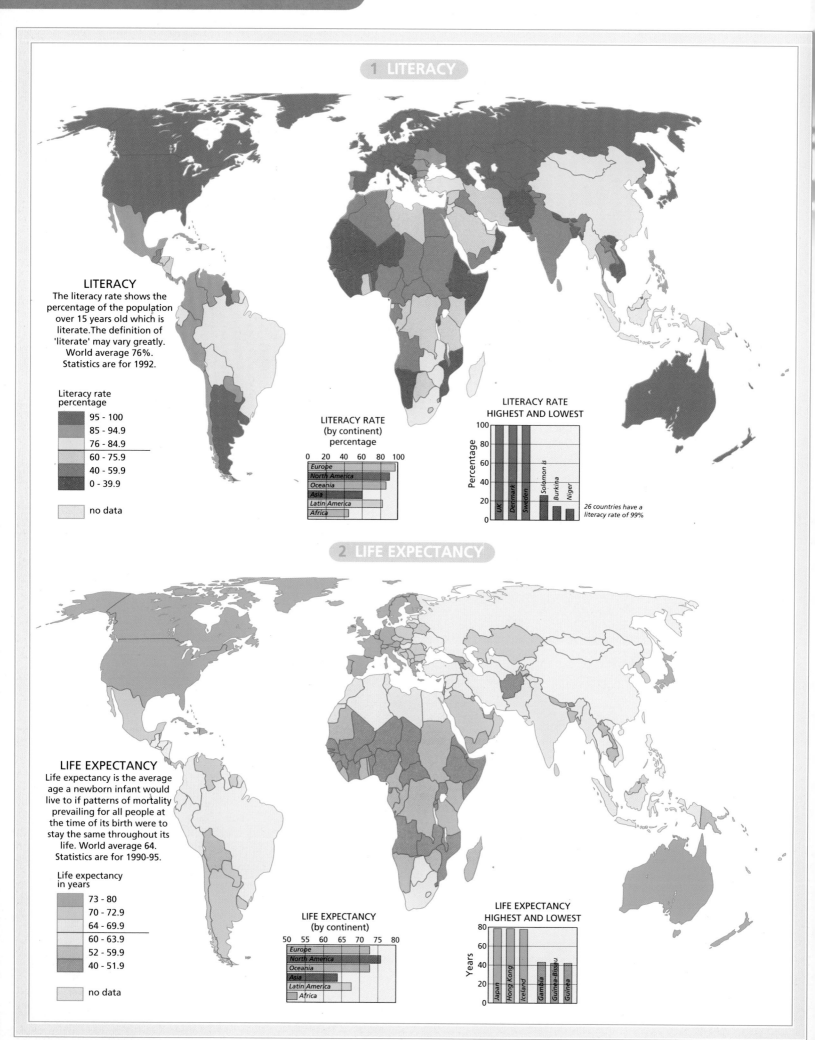

1 LITERACY

LITERACY

The literacy rate shows the percentage of the population over 15 years old which is literate. The definition of 'literate' may vary greatly. World average 76%. Statistics are for 1992.

Literacy rate percentage

- 95 - 100
- 85 - 94.9
- 76 - 84.9
- 60 - 75.9
- 40 - 59.9
- 0 - 39.9

no data

LITERACY RATE
(by continent) percentage

0 20 40 60 80 100

Europe
North America
Oceania
Asia
Latin America
Africa

LITERACY RATE HIGHEST AND LOWEST

Percentage
100
80
60
40
20
0

UK | Denmark | Sweden | Solomon Is | Burkina | Niger

26 countries have a literacy rate of 99%

2 LIFE EXPECTANCY

LIFE EXPECTANCY

Life expectancy is the average age a newborn infant would live to if patterns of mortality prevailing for all people at the time of its birth were to stay the same throughout its life. World average 64. Statistics are for 1990-95.

Life expectancy in years

- 73 - 80
- 70 - 72.9
- 64 - 69.9
- 60 - 63.9
- 52 - 59.9
- 40 - 51.9

no data

LIFE EXPECTANCY
(by continent)

50 55 60 65 70 75 80

Europe
North America
Oceania
Asia
Latin America
Africa

LIFE EXPECTANCY HIGHEST AND LOWEST

Years
80
60
40
20
0

Japan | Hong Kong | Iceland | Gambia | Guinea-Bissau | Guinea

SCALE 1 : 140 000 000

Eckert IV projection

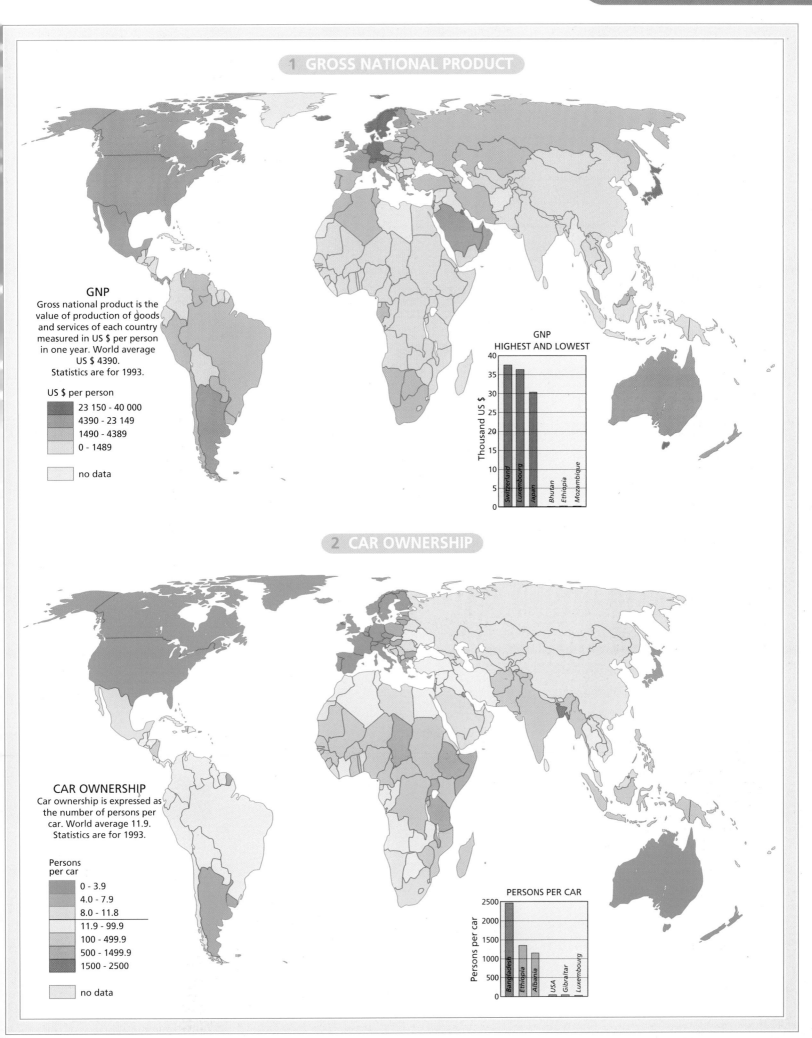

1 GROSS NATIONAL PRODUCT

GNP

Gross national product is the
value of production of goods
and services of each country
measured in US $ per person
in one year. World average
US $ 4390.
Statistics are for 1993.

US $ per person

- 23 150 - 40 000
- 4390 - 23 149
- 1490 - 4389
- 0 - 1489

no data

**GNP
HIGHEST AND LOWEST**

Thousand US $

Switzerland, Luxembourg, Japan, Bhutan, Ethiopia, Mozambique

2 CAR OWNERSHIP

CAR OWNERSHIP

Car ownership is expressed as
the number of persons per
car. World average 11.9.
Statistics are for 1993.

**Persons
per car**

- 0 - 3.9
- 4.0 - 7.9
- 8.0 - 11.8
- 11.9 - 99.9
- 100 - 499.9
- 500 - 1499.9
- 1500 - 2500

no data

PERSONS PER CAR

Persons per car

Bangladesh, Ethiopia, Albania, USA, Gibraltar, Luxembourg

SCALE 1 : 140 000 000

Eckert IV projection

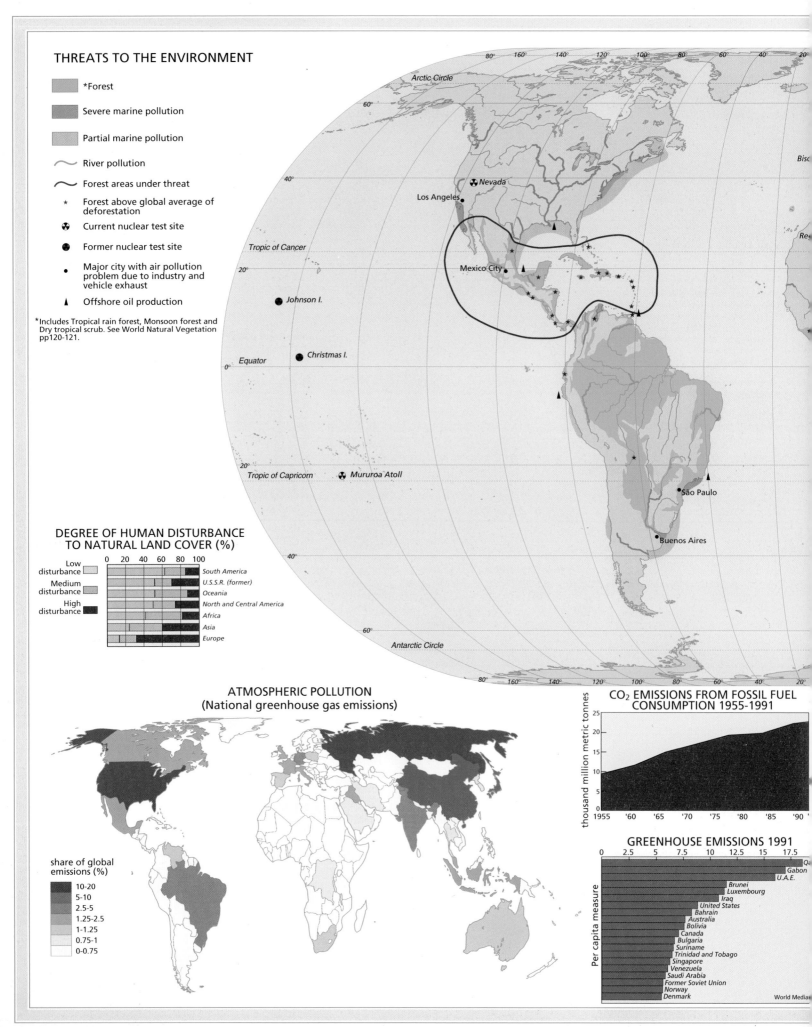

THREATS TO THE ENVIRONMENT

*Forest

Severe marine pollution

Partial marine pollution

River pollution

Forest areas under threat

★ Forest above global average of deforestation

☢ Current nuclear test site

● Former nuclear test site

• Major city with air pollution problem due to industry and vehicle exhaust

▲ Offshore oil production

*Includes Tropical rain forest, Monsoon forest and Dry tropical scrub. See World Natural Vegetation pp120-121.

Arctic Circle

Nevada

Los Angeles

Tropic of Cancer

Mexico City

Johnson I.

Christmas I.

Equator

Tropic of Capricorn   Mururoa Atoll

São Paulo

Buenos Aires

Antarctic Circle

Bisc

Re

DEGREE OF HUMAN DISTURBANCE TO NATURAL LAND COVER (%)

Low disturbance

Medium disturbance

High disturbance

0   20   40   60   80   100

South America
U.S.S.R. (former)
Oceania
North and Central America
Africa
Asia
Europe

ATMOSPHERIC POLLUTION
(National greenhouse gas emissions)

share of global emissions (%)

10-20
5-10
2.5-5
1.25-2.5
1-1.25
0.75-1
0-0.75

CO₂ EMISSIONS FROM FOSSIL FUEL CONSUMPTION 1955-1991

thousand million metric tonnes

25
20
15
10
5
0
1955 '60 '65 '70 '75 '80 '85 '90

GREENHOUSE EMISSIONS 1991

0   2.5   5   7.5   10   12.5   15   17.5

Qa
Gabon
U.A.E.
Brunei
Luxembourg
Iraq
United States
Bahrain
Australia
Bolivia
Canada
Bulgaria
Suriname
Trinidad and Tobago
Singapore
Venezuela
Saudi Arabia
Former Soviet Union
Norway
Denmark

Per capita measure

World Media

SCALE 1 : 100 000 000   0   1000   2000   3000   4000 km

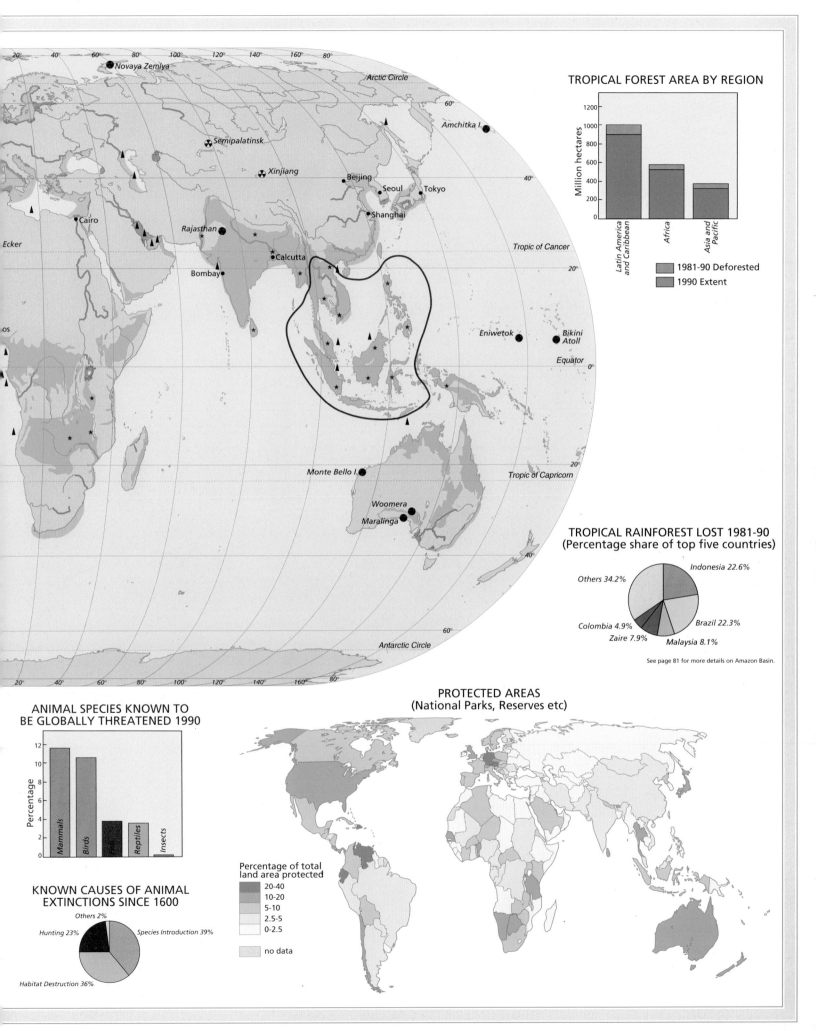

TROPICAL FOREST AREA BY REGION

Million hectares

- Latin America and Caribbean
- Africa
- Asia and Pacific

1981-90 Deforested
1990 Extent

TROPICAL RAINFOREST LOST 1981-90
(Percentage share of top five countries)

Others 34.2%
Indonesia 22.6%
Brazil 22.3%
Malaysia 8.1%
Zaire 7.9%
Colombia 4.9%

See page 81 for more details on Amazon Basin.

ANIMAL SPECIES KNOWN TO BE GLOBALLY THREATENED 1990

Percentage

Mammals, Birds, Fish, Reptiles, Insects

KNOWN CAUSES OF ANIMAL EXTINCTIONS SINCE 1600

Others 2%
Hunting 23%
Species Introduction 39%
Habitat Destruction 36%

PROTECTED AREAS
(National Parks, Reserves etc)

Percentage of total land area protected
- 20-40
- 10-20
- 5-10
- 2.5-5
- 0-2.5
- no data

Eckert IV projection

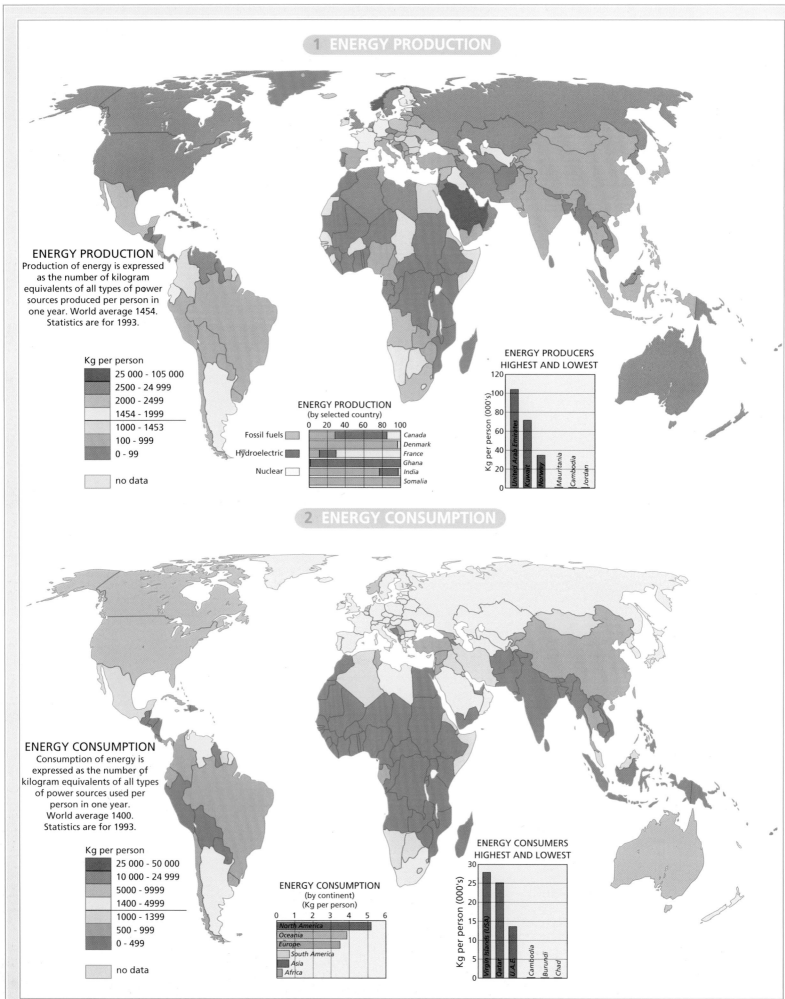

1 ENERGY PRODUCTION

ENERGY PRODUCTION

Production of energy is expressed as the number of kilogram equivalents of all types of power sources produced per person in one year. World average 1454. Statistics are for 1993.

Kg per person

- 25 000 - 105 000
- 2500 - 24 999
- 2000 - 2499
- 1454 - 1999
- 1000 - 1453
- 100 - 999
- 0 - 99

no data

ENERGY PRODUCTION
(by selected country)

0 20 40 60 80 100

Fossil fuels
Hydroelectric
Nuclear

Canada
Denmark
France
Ghana
India
Somalia

ENERGY PRODUCERS
HIGHEST AND LOWEST

Kg per person (000's)

United Arab Emirates
Kuwait
Norway
Mauritania
Cambodia
Jordan

2 ENERGY CONSUMPTION

ENERGY CONSUMPTION

Consumption of energy is expressed as the number of kilogram equivalents of all types of power sources used per person in one year. World average 1400. Statistics are for 1993.

Kg per person

- 25 000 - 50 000
- 10 000 - 24 999
- 5000 - 9999
- 1400 - 4999
- 1000 - 1399
- 500 - 999
- 0 - 499

no data

ENERGY CONSUMPTION
(by continent)
(Kg per person)

0 1 2 3 4 5 6

North America
Oceania
Europe
South America
Asia
Africa

ENERGY CONSUMERS
HIGHEST AND LOWEST

Kg per person (000's)

Virgin Islands (USA)
Qatar
U.A.E
Cambodia
Burundi
Chad

SCALE 1 : 140 000 000

Eckert IV projection

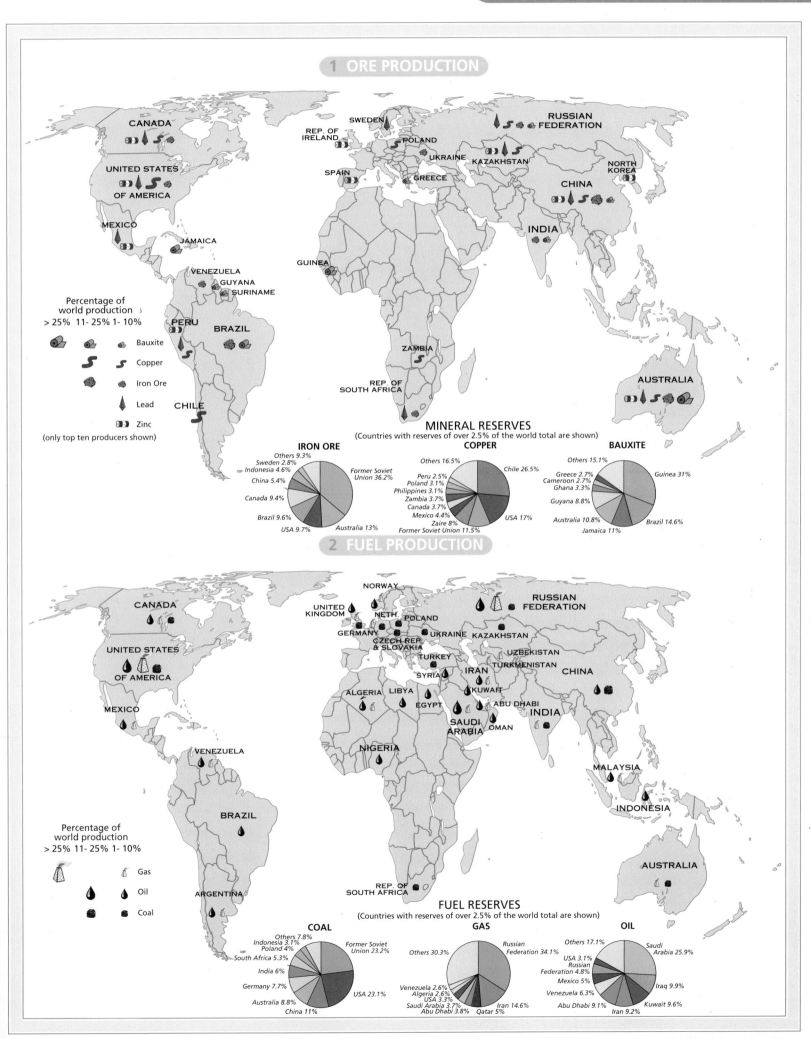

1 ORE PRODUCTION

CANADA

UNITED STATES OF AMERICA

MEXICO

JAMAICA

VENEZUELA
GUYANA
SURINAME

PERU

BRAZIL

CHILE

SWEDEN

REP. OF IRELAND

POLAND

SPAIN

UKRAINE

GREECE

GUINEA

ZAMBIA

REP. OF SOUTH AFRICA

RUSSIAN FEDERATION

KAZAKHSTAN

NORTH KOREA

CHINA

INDIA

AUSTRALIA

Percentage of world production
> 25%   11- 25%   1- 10%

Bauxite

Copper

Iron Ore

Lead

Zinc

(only top ten producers shown)

MINERAL RESERVES
(Countries with reserves of over 2.5% of the world total are shown)

IRON ORE
Others 9.3%
Sweden 2.8%
Indonesia 4.6%
China 5.4%
Canada 9.4%
Brazil 9.6%
USA 9.7%
Australia 13%
Former Soviet Union 36.2%

COPPER
Others 16.5%
Peru 2.5%
Poland 3.1%
Philippines 3.1%
Zambia 3.7%
Canada 3.7%
Mexico 4.4%
Zaire 8%
Former Soviet Union 11.5%
Chile 26.5%
USA 17%

BAUXITE
Others 15.1%
Greece 2.7%
Cameroon 2.7%
Ghana 3.3%
Guyana 8.8%
Australia 10.8%
Jamaica 11%
Guinea 31%
Brazil 14.6%

2 FUEL PRODUCTION

CANADA

UNITED STATES OF AMERICA

MEXICO

VENEZUELA

BRAZIL

ARGENTINA

NORWAY

UNITED KINGDOM

NETH.

GERMANY

CZECH REP. & SLOVAKIA

POLAND

UKRAINE

KAZAKHSTAN

TURKEY

SYRIA

ALGERIA   LIBYA

EGYPT

IRAN

KUWAIT

ABU DHABI

SAUDI ARABIA   OMAN

NIGERIA

RUSSIAN FEDERATION

UZBEKISTAN

TURKMENISTAN

CHINA

INDIA

MALAYSIA

INDONESIA

REP. OF SOUTH AFRICA

AUSTRALIA

Percentage of world production
> 25%   11- 25%   1- 10%

Gas

Oil

Coal

FUEL RESERVES
(Countries with reserves of over 2.5% of the world total are shown)

COAL
Others 7.8%
Indonesia 3.1%
Poland 4%
South Africa 5.3%
India 6%
Germany 7.7%
Australia 8.8%
China 11%
Former Soviet Union 23.2%
USA 23.1%

GAS
Others 30.3%
Venezuela 2.6%
Algeria 2.6%
USA 3.3%
Saudi Arabia 3.7%
Abu Dhabi 3.8%
Qatar 5%
Iran 14.6%
Russian Federation 34.1%

OIL
Others 17.1%
USA 3.1%
Russian Federation 4.8%
Mexico 5%
Venezuela 6.3%
Abu Dhabi 9.1%
Iran 9.2%
Kuwait 9.6%
Iraq 9.9%
Saudi Arabia 25.9%

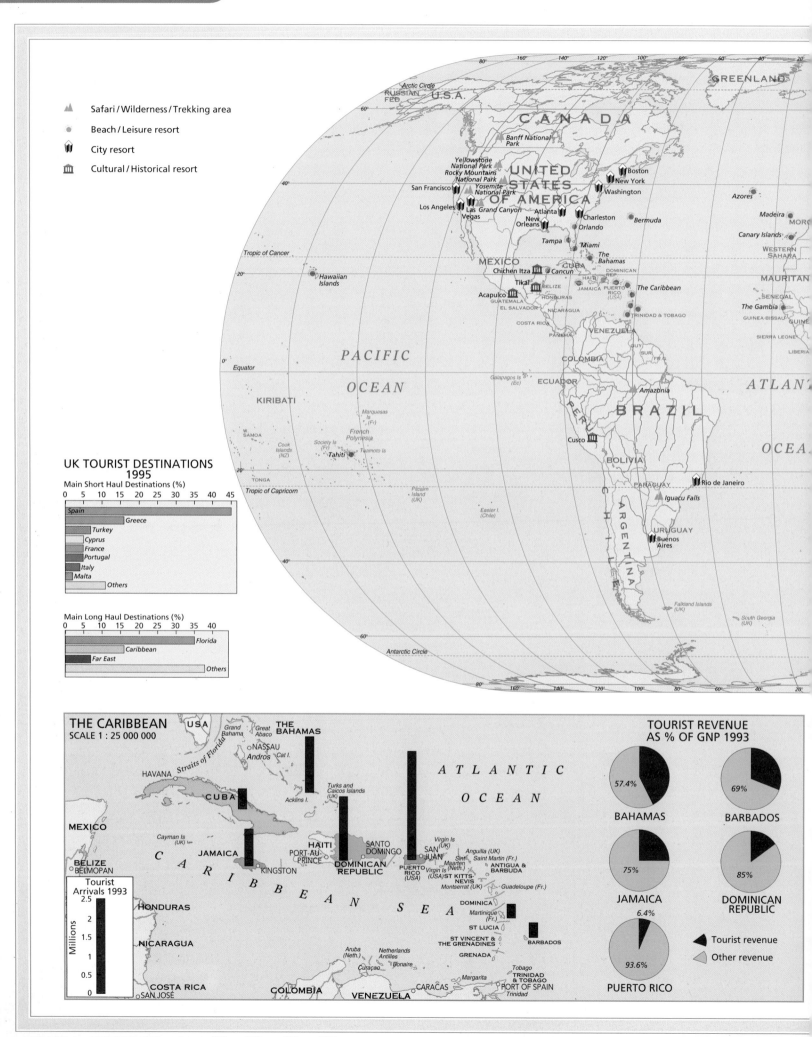

UK TOURIST DESTINATIONS 1995

Main Short Haul Destinations (%)

0 5 10 15 20 25 30 35 40 45

Spain
Greece
Turkey
Cyprus
France
Portugal
Italy
Malta
Others

Main Long Haul Destinations (%)

0 5 10 15 20 25 30 35 40

Florida
Caribbean
Far East
Others

THE CARIBBEAN
SCALE 1 : 25 000 000

USA
Grand Bahama
Great Abaco
THE BAHAMAS
NASSAU
Andros
Cat I.
HAVANA
Straits of Florida
CUBA
Acklins I.
Turks and Caicos Islands (UK)
ATLANTIC OCEAN
MEXICO
Cayman Is (UK)
JAMAICA
Kingston
HAITI
PORT-AU-PRINCE
SANTO DOMINGO
DOMINICAN REPUBLIC
PUERTO RICO (USA)
SAN JUAN
Virgin Is (UK)
Virgin Is (USA)
Anguilla (UK)
Saint Martin (Fr.)
Sint Maarten (Neth.)
ANTIGUA & BARBUDA
ST KITTS-NEVIS
Montserrat (UK)
Guadeloupe (Fr.)
BELIZE
BELMOPAN
C A R I B B E A N   S E A
HONDURAS
DOMINICA
Martinique (Fr.)
ST LUCIA
BARBADOS
NICARAGUA
ST VINCENT & THE GRENADINES
GRENADA
Aruba (Neth.)
Netherlands Antilles
Bonaire
Curaçao
Margarita
Tobago
TRINIDAD & TOBAGO
PORT OF SPAIN
Trinidad
COSTA RICA
SAN JOSÉ
COLOMBIA
VENEZUELA
CARACAS

Tourist Arrivals 1993
Millions
2.5
2
1.5
1
0.5
0

TOURIST REVENUE AS % OF GNP 1993

57.4% BAHAMAS

69% BARBADOS

75% JAMAICA

85% DOMINICAN REPUBLIC

6.4%
93.6% PUERTO RICO

■ Tourist revenue
▲ Other revenue

SCALE 1 : 100 000 000

0   1000   2000   3000   4000 km

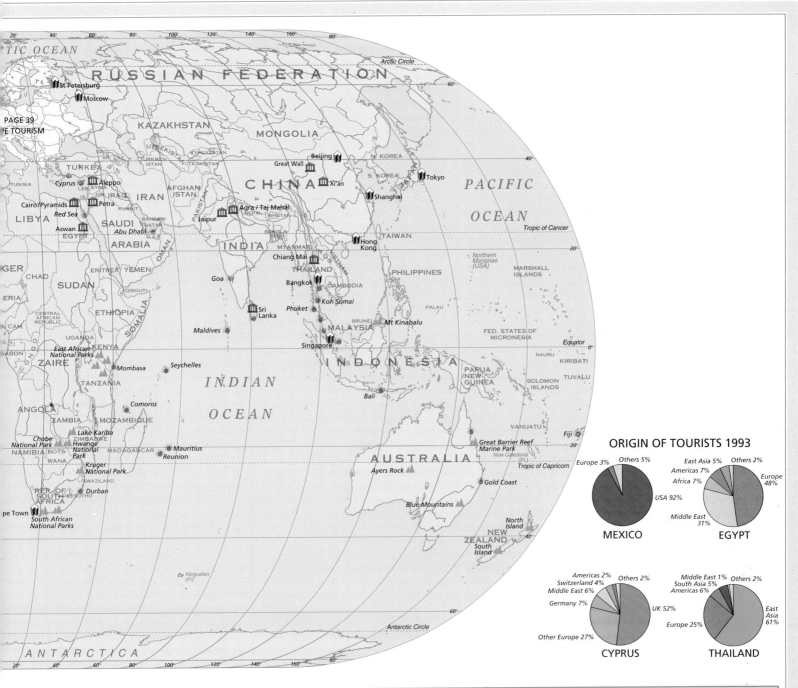

ORIGIN OF TOURISTS 1993

MEXICO
- Europe 3%
- Others 5%
- USA 92%

EGYPT
- East Asia 5%
- Others 2%
- Americas 7%
- Africa 7%
- Europe 48%
- Middle East 31%

CYPRUS
- Americas 2%
- Switzerland 4%
- Middle East 6%
- Germany 7%
- Others 2%
- UK 52%
- Other Europe 27%

THAILAND
- Middle East 1%
- South Asia 5%
- Americas 6%
- Others 2%
- East Asia 61%
- Europe 25%

ORIDA
ALE 1 : 12 000 000

Gulf of Mexico

- National Park
- Main expressway
- ★ Tourist attraction

Country	1984	1985	1986	1987	1988	1989	1990	1991	1992	1993	Importance of tourism 1993 Income as % of GNP
Bermuda	417	407	460	478	427	418	435	386	375	413	28.7
Cuba	207	240	276	282	298	315	327	418	455	544	36.0
Cyprus	666	770	828	949	1112	1378	1561	1385	1991	1841	21.2
Dom. Rep.	562	660	747	902	1116	1400	1533	1321	1524	1691	15.0
Egypt	N/A	1407	1236	1671	1833	2351	2411	2112	2944	2291	3.6
France	35 379	36 748	36 080	36 974	38 288	49 549	52 497	55 041	59 710	60 100	1.8
Greece	5523	6574	7025	7564	7923	8082	8873	8036	9331	9413	4.3
Martinique	184	193	183	234	280	312	282	315	321	366	8.3
Mexico	4654	4207	4625	5407	5692	14 962	17 174	16 066	17 273	16 534	2.0
Spain	27 176	27 477	29 910	32 900	35 000	38 867	37 441	38 539	39 638	40 085	3.5
Thailand	2347	2438	2818	3483	4231	4810	5299	5087	5136	5761	4.2
Trinidad & Tobago	191	187	191	202	188	190	195	220	235	249	1.6

GROWTH IN TOURISM - Tourist Arrivals (1000's)

KEY INFORMATION

POPULATION

FLAG	COUNTRY	CAPITAL CITY	TOTAL (in '000s 1994)	DENSITY (persons per sq km 1994)	BIRTH RATE (per 1000 population 1994)	DEATH RATE (per 1000 population 1994)	LIFE EXPEC-TANCY (in years 1990-95)	POP. CHANGE (average % per annum 1990 - 1995)	URBAN POP. (% 1994)
	AFGHANISTAN	Kabul	18 879	28.95	50	22	43	5.83	19.6
	ALBANIA	Tiranë	3414	118.76	24	6	72	0.9	37
	ALGERIA	Algiers	27 325	11.47	29	6	67	2.27	55
	ANGOLA	Luanda	10 674	8.56	51	19	46	3.72	31.5
	ARGENTINA	Buenos Aires	34 180	12.35	20	8	72	1.22	87.8
	ARMENIA	Yerevan	3548	119.06	21	6	73	1.42	68.4
	AUSTRALIA	Canberra	17 843	2.32	15	7	78	1.37	84.7
	AUSTRIA	Vienna	8031	95.77	12	11	76	0.67	55.5
	AZERBAIJAN	Baku	7472	86.28	23	6	71	1.2	55.5
	BAHAMAS	Nassau	272	19.51	19	5	73	1.51	86
	BAHRAIN	Manama	549	794.50	28	4	72	2.8	89.8
	BANGLADESH	Dhaka	117 787	817.98	35	12	56	2.16	17.7
	BARBADOS	Bridgetown	261	606.98	16	9	76	0.35	46.9
	BELARUS	Minsk	10 355	49.88	12	12	70	-0.14	70.3
	BELGIUM	Brussels	10 080	330.28	12	11	76	0.32	96.9
	BELIZE	Belmopan	211	9.19	35	5	74	2.64	46.9
	BENIN	Porto Novo	5246	46.58	49	18	48	3.1	30.8
	BHUTAN	Thimbu	1614	34.62	40	15	51	1.18	6.2
	BOLIVIA	La Paz	7237	6.59	36	10	72	2.41	59.8
	BOSNIA-HERZEGOVINA	Sarajevo	3527	68.98	13	7	72	-4.39	47.9
	BOTSWANA	Gaborone	1443	2.48	37	7	65	3.06	27.1
	BRAZIL	Brasília	153 725	18.06	25	7	66	1.72	77.6
	BRUNEI	Bandar Seri Begawan	280	48.57	24	3	74	2.06	57.7
	BULGARIA	Sofia	8443	76.07	10	13	71	-0.5	70.1
	BURKINA	Ouagadougou	9889	36.06	47	18	47	2.76	25.2
	BURUNDI	Bujumbura	6209	223.06	46	16	50	3	7.2
	CAMBODIA	Phnom Penh	9968	55.07	44	14	52	2.96	20.1
	CAMEROON	Yaoundé	12 871	27.07	41	12	56	2.76	44
	CANADA	Ottawa	29 248	2.93	15	8	77	1.17	76.6
	CAPE VERDE	Praia	381	94.47	36	9	65	2.77	52.5
	CENTRAL AFRICAN REPUBLIC	Bangui	3235	5.20	42	17	49	2.49	38.9
	CHAD	Ndjamena	6183	4.82	44	18	47	2.71	21.2
	CHILE	Santiago	13 994	18.49	22	6	66	1.62	83.8
	CHINA	Beijing	1 208 841	126.44	19	7	68	1.11	29.4
	COLOMBIA	Bogotá	34 520	30.23	24	6	69	1.66	72.2
	COMOROS	Moroni	630	338.35	48	12	56	3.68	30.1
	CONGO	Brazzaville	2516	7.36	45	15	51	2.98	57.8
	COSTA RICA	San José	3011	58.92	26	4	76	2.41	49.2
	CÔTE D'IVOIRE	Yamoussoukro	13 695	42.47	50	15	51	3.48	42.9
	CROATIA	Zagreb	4504	79.66	11	12	71	-0.1	63.5
	CUBA	Havana	10 960	98.86	17	7	75	0.82	75.5
	CYPRUS	Nicosia	734	79.34	19	8	77	1.11	53.5
	CZECH REPUBLIC	Prague	10 333	131.02	13	13	71	-0.02	65.3
	DENMARK	Copenhagen	5205	120.84	12	12	75	0.16	85.1

LAND / EDUCATION AND HEALTH / DEVELOPMENT

AREA ('000s sq km)	CULTIVATED AREA ('000s sq km 1993)	FOREST ('000s sq km 1993)	ADULT LITERACY (% 1992)	SCHOOL ENROLMENT (Secondary, gross % 1993)	PEOPLE PER DOCTOR (1991)	FOOD INTAKE (calories per capita per day 1992)	ENERGY CONSUMPTION (kg per cap oil eq 1993)	TRADE BALANCE (millions US $ 1994)	GNP PER CAPITA (US $ 1993 or earlier)	COUNTRY	TIME ZONES (+ OR - GMT)
652	81	19	28.9	6	5452	1523	30	-428	250	AFGHANISTAN	+4.5
29	7	10	85	79	583	2605	305		340	ALBANIA	+1
2382	79	40	57.4	59	1262	2897	1058	2489	1650	ALGERIA	+1
1247	35	519	42.5		15 298	1839	61	1849	490	ANGOLA	+1
2767	272	509	95.9	74	337	2880	1428	-5868	7290	ARGENTINA	-3
29.8	6	4	98.8		241		334	-56	660	ARMENIA	+4
7682	465	1450	99	83	467	3179	5310	-5853	17 510	AUSTRALIA	+8 to +10½
84	15	32	99	105.5	347	3497	2934	-10 313	23 120	AUSTRIA	+1
86.6	20	10	96.3		259		1768	-102	730	AZERBAIJAN	+4
14		3	98	93		2624	2134	-284	11 500	BAHAMAS	-5
0.691			83.5	99	758		12 325	-283	7870	BAHRAIN	+3
144	97	19	36.4	18.5	6615	2019	65	-2051	220	BANGLADESH	+6
			97	87		3207	1315	-427	6240	BARBADOS	-4
208	62	70	97.9		254		2928	-32	2840	BELARUS	+2
31	8	7	99	102.5	307	3681	4698	7275	21 210	BELGIUM	+1
23	1	21	96			2662	436	-114	2440	BELIZE	-6
113	19	34	32.9	12	19 899	2532	32	-110	420	BENIN	+1
47	1	31	39.2		10 643		35		170	BHUTAN	+6
1099	24	580	80.7	34	2331	2094	290	-177	770	BOLIVIA	-4
51	9	20					190		3200	BOSNIA-HERZEGOVINA	+1
581	4	265	67.2	54	8276	2266			2590	BOTSWANA	+2
8512	490	4880	81.9	33.5	729	2824	580	7561	3020	BRAZIL	-2 to -5
6		5	86.4	71.5	1556	2745	10 533	601	13 890	BRUNEI	+8
111	43	39	93	70	324	2831	2598	-733	1160	BULGARIA	+2
274	36	138	17.4	8.5	32 146	2387	20	-431	300	BURKINA	GMT
28	14	1	32.9	6.5		1941	14	-118	180	BURUNDI	+2
181	24	116	37.8		27 215	2021	17		280	CAMBODIA	+7
475	70	359	59.6	27.5	14 206	1981	68	640	770	CAMEROON	+1
9971	455	4940	99	107	463	3094	7624	10 427	20 670	CANADA	-3½ to -8
4			66.4	19.5		2805	97	-150	870	CAPE VERDE	-1
622	20	467	53.9	12	18 530	1690	26	-41	390	C.A.R.	+1
1284	33	324	44.9	7.5	60 415	1989	5	-77	200	CHAD	+1
757	43	165	94.5	70	946	2582	931	-286	3070	CHILE	-4 to -6
9561	960	1305	79.3	53.5	642	2727	603	5343	490	CHINA	+8
1142	55	500	90.3	61.5	1124	2677	583	-3484	1400	COLOMBIA	-5
2	1		55.6	18.5		1897	36	-47	520	COMOROS	+3
342	2	211	70.7		4542	2296	236	602	920	CONGO	+1
51.1	5	16	94.3	47	1179	2883	457	-810	2160	COSTA RICA	-6
322	37	71	36.6	24	23 900	2491	196	974	630	CÔTE D'IVOIRE	GMT
57	13	21					1394	-970	5600	CROATIA	+1
111	33	26	94.9	84	305	2833	809	-135	1370	CUBA	-5
9	2	1	94	94.5	604	3779	2059	-2053	10 380	CYPRUS	+2
79	33	26	99			3156	3849	-471	2730	CZECH REPUBLIC	+1
43	25	4	99	110	376	3664	3522	5979	26 510	DENMARK	+1

KEY INFORMATION			POPULATION						
FLAG	COUNTRY	CAPITAL CITY	TOTAL (in '000s 1994)	DENSITY (persons per sq km 1994)	BIRTH RATE (per 1000 population 1994)	DEATH RATE (per 1000 population 1994)	LIFE EXPEC-TANCY (in years 1990-95)	POP. CHANGE (average % per annum 1990 - 1995)	URBAN POP. (% 1994)
	DJIBOUTI	Djibouti	566	24.40	38	16	48	2.2	82.5
	DOMINICAN REPUBLIC	Santo Domingo	7769	160.38	27	6	70	1.91	63.8
	ECUADOR	Quito	11 221	41.25	28	6	69	2.2	57.7
	EGYPT	Cairo	58 326	58.31	29	8	64	2.22	44.5
	EL SALVADOR	San Salvador	5641	268.10	33	7	66	2.18	44.8
	EQUATORIAL GUINEA	Malabo	389	13.87	43	18	48	2.55	40.9
	ERITREA	Asmara	3437	29.28	43	15	50	2.72	16.9
	ESTONIA	Tallinn	1541	34.09	11	13	69	-0.58	72.8
	ETHIOPIA	Addis Ababa	54 938	48.45	48	18	47	2.98	13.1
	FIJI	Suva	771	42.06	24	5	71	1.52	40.4
	FINLAND	Helsinki	5095	15.07	13	10	76	0.48	62.8
	FRANCE	Paris	57 747	106.16	13	10	77	0.44	72.7
	GABON	Libreville	1283	4.79	37	15	54	2.83	49.2
	GAMBIA	Banjul	1081	95.71	44	19	45	3.83	24.9
	GEORGIA	Tbilisi	5450	78.19	16	9	73	0.14	58
	GERMANY	Berlin	81 410	227.49	10	12	76	0.55	86.3
	GHANA	Accra	16 944	71.03	42	12	56	3	35.8
	GREECE	Athens	10 426	79.01	10	10	78	0.41	64.7
	GUATEMALA	Guatemala City	10 322	94.79	39	8	65	2.88	41
	GUINEA	Conakry	6501	26.44	51	20	44	3.04	28.8
	GUINEA-BISSAU	Bissau	1050	29.07	43	21	44	2.14	21.7
	GUYANA	Georgetown	825	3.84	25	7	65	0.94	35.6
	HAITI	Port-au-Prince	7041	253.73	35	12	57	2.03	30.9
	HONDURAS	Tegucigalpa	5770	51.48	37	6	68	2.95	43.2
	HUNGARY	Budapest	10 261	110.30	12	15	69	-0.49	64.1
	ICELAND	Reykjavik	266	2.59	18	7	78	1.06	91.4
	INDIA	New Delhi	918 570	279.43	29	10	60	1.91	26.5
	INDONESIA	Jakarta	193 017	100.56	25	8	63	1.55	34.4
	IRAN	Tehran	59 778	36.27	35	7	67	2.65	58.5
	IRAQ	Baghdad	19 925	45.46	38	7	66	2.46	74.1
	ISRAEL	Jerusalem	5383	259.17	21	7	76	3.78	90.5
	ITALY	Rome	57 193	189.86	10	10	77	0.06	66.6
	JAMAICA	Kingston	2429	221.00	22	6	74	0.68	53.2
	JAPAN	Tokyo	124 961	330.82	10	8	79	0.25	77.5
	JORDAN	Amman	5198	58.27	39	5	68	4.89	70.8
	KAZAKHSTAN	Alma-Ata	17 027	6.27	20	8	70	0.52	59.3
	KENYA	Nairobi	27 343	46.93	45	12	56	3.59	26.8
	KUWAIT	Kuwait	1620	90.92	24	2	75	-6.52	96.8
	KYRGYZSTAN	Bishkek	4596	23.15	29	7	69	1.68	38.7
	LAOS	Vientiane	4742	20.03	45	15	51	3	21.1
	LATVIA	Riga	2548	40.00	11	13	69	-0.87	72.5
	LEBANON	Beirut	2915	278.89	27	7	69	3.27	86.6
	LESOTHO	Maseru	1996	65.76	37	10	60	2.69	22.3
	LIBERIA	Monrovia	2941	26.41	47	14	55	3.32	44.4

AREA ('000s sq km)	CULTIV-ATED AREA ('000s sq km 1993)	FOREST ('000s sq km 1993)	ADULT LITERACY (% 1992)	SCHOOL ENROL-MENT (Secondary, gross % 1993)	PEOPLE PER DOCTOR (1991)	FOOD INTAKE (calories per capita per day 1992)	ENERGY CONSU-MPTION (kg per cap oil eq 1993)	TRADE BALANCE (millions US $ 1994)	GNP PER CAPITA (US $ 1993 or earlier)	COUNTRY	TIME ZONES (+ OR - GMT)
23.2	2		43.2	13.5		2338	767	-203	780	DJIBOUTI	+3
48	15	6	80.7	50.5	978	2286	469	-2124	1080	DOMINICAN REPUBLIC	-4
272	30	156	88.4	56	977	2583	534	75	1170	ECUADOR	-5 to -6
1000	28		49.1	79.5	725	3335	486	-6808	660	EGYPT	+2
21	7	1	69.8	26.5	1641	2663	313	-1185	1320	EL SALVADOR	-6
28	2	13	75.3		69 600		111	2	360	EQUATORIAL GUINEA	+1
117	13	20				1610			110	ERITREA	+3
45.2	11	20	99	91	208		3288	-364	3040	ESTONIA	+2
1134	127	250	32.7	10.5	38 255	1610	21	-683	100	ETHIOPIA	+3
18	3	12	90.1	60.5		3089	334	-279	2140	FIJI	+12
338	26	232	99	124	519	3018	4786	6436	18 970	FINLAND	+2
544	194	149	99	102	393	3633	3800	5743	22 360	FRANCE	+1
268	5	199	58.9		2074	2500	622	1443	4050	GABON	+1
11	2	3	35.6	20.5	13 045	2360	67	-166	360	GAMBIA	GMT
69.7	10	27	99		178		696	-121	560	GEORGIA	+4
358	121	107	99	97	365	3344	4054	42 127	23 560	GERMANY	+1
239	43	79	60.7	38.5	25 047	2199	98	-257	430	GHANA	GMT
132	35	26	93.8	98	304	3815	2276	-13 235	7390	GREECE	+2
109	19	58	54.2	18.5	2570	2255	171	-1308	1110	GUATEMALA	-6
246	7	145	33	11.5	9065	2389	58		510	GUINEA	GMT
36	3	11	51.7	6.5	7910	2556	73	-30	220	GUINEA-BISSAU	GMT
215	5	165	97.5	57.5	7171	2384	426	-89	350	GUYANA	-4
28	9	1	42.6	21.5	6871	1706	31	-232	370	HAITI	-5
112	20	60	70.7	30.5	1879	2305	192	-213	580	HONDURAS	-6
93	50	18	99	82	323	3503	2316	-3916	3330	HUNGARY	+1
103		1	99	92	378	3058	4935	151	23 620	ICELAND	GMT
3287	1697	685	49.9	48.5	2494	2395	247	-1751	290	INDIA	+5½
1919	310	1118	82.5	43	7767	2752	331	8069	730	INDONESIA	+7 to +9
1648	182	114	64.9	62	3228	2860	1215	-2481	2230	IRAN	+3½
438	55	2	54.6	42.5	4273	2121	1145		1940	IRAQ	+3
21	4	1	95	86	392	3050	2297	-6892	13 760	ISRAEL	+2
301	119	68	97.4	77	235	3561	2820	21 971	19 620	ITALY	+1
11	2	2	83.7	62.5	2157	2607	1035	-1061	1390	JAMAICA	-5
378	45	251	99	97	613	2903	3357	121 825	31 450	JAPAN	+9
89	4	1	83.9	53	891	3022	709	-1958	1190	JORDAN	+2
2717	348	96	97.5		254		4763	581	1540	KAZAKHSTAN	+4 to +6
583	45	168	74.5	27	7358	2075	81	-598	270	KENYA	+3
18			76.9	55	739	2523	6337	5285	23 350	KUWAIT	+3
199	14	7	97		295		782	0	830	KYRGYZSTAN	+5
237	8	125	53.5	22	7418	2259	25	-81	290	LAOS	+7
63.7	17	28	99	85	200		1712	-251	2030	LATVIA	+2
10	3	1	91.4	69	770	3317	1028		1400	LEBANON	+2
30	3		68.6	26.5		2201			660	LESOTHO	+2
111	4	17	35.4	21.5	29 292	1640	41	124	390	LIBERIA	GMT

KEY INFORMATION

POPULATION

FLAG	COUNTRY	CAPITAL CITY	TOTAL (in '000s 1994)	DENSITY (persons per sq km 1994)	BIRTH RATE (per 1000 population 1994)	DEATH RATE (per 1000 population 1994)	LIFE EXPEC- TANCY (in years 1990-95)	POP. CHANGE (average % per annum 1990 - 1995)	URBAN POP. (% 1994)
	LIBYA	Tripoli	5225	2.97	42	8	63	3.47	85.4
	LITHUANIA	Vilnius	3721	57.07	13	11	70	-0.06	71.4
	LUXEMBOURG	Luxembourg	401	155.07	13	11	76	1.26	88.6
	MACEDONIA	Skopje	2142	83.30	15	7		1.11	59.4
	MADAGASCAR	Antananarivo	14 303	24.36	44	12	56	3.21	26.4
	MALAWI	Lilongwe	10 843	91.51	51	20	46	3.45	13.2
	MALAYSIA	Kuala Lumpur	19 489	58.53	29	5	71	2.37	52.9
	MALDIVES	Male	246	825.50	42	9	62	3.31	26.6
	MALI	Bamako	10 462	8.44	51	19	46	3.17	26.3
	MALTA	Valletta	364	1151.90	15	8	76	0.67	89
	MAURITANIA	Nouakchott	2211	2.15	40	14	51	2.54	52.5
	MAURITIUS	Port Louis	1104	541.18	21	7	70	1.1	40.5
	MEXICO	Mexico City	93 008	47.15	28	5	71	2.06	74.8
	MICRONESIA	Palikir	121	172.61			68	2.77	27.6
	MOLDOVA	Chisinau	4350	129.08	16	10	68	0.32	50.9
	MONGOLIA	Ulan Bator	2363	1.51	28	7	64	2.03	60.3
	MOROCCO	Rabat	26 590	59.55	29	8	63	2.1	47.9
	MOZAMBIQUE	Maputo	15 527	19.42	45	18	46	2.41	32.8
	MYANMAR	Yangon	45 555	67.33	33	11	58	2.14	25.8
	NAMIBIA	Windhoek	1500	1.82	37	11	59	2.65	36.3
	NEPAL	Kathmandu	21 360	145.13	39	13	54	2.59	13.1
	NETHERLANDS	Amsterdam	15 380	370.37	13	9	77	0.72	88.9
	NEW ZEALAND	Wellington	3493	12.91	17	8	76	1.24	85.8
	NICARAGUA	Managua	4401	33.85	40	7	67	3.74	62.3
	NIGER	Niamey	8846	6.98	53	19	47	3.37	16.6
	NIGERIA	Abuja	108 467	117.42	45	15	50	3	38.5
	NORTH KOREA	Pyongyang	23 483	194.82	24	5	71	1.88	60.9
	NORWAY	Oslo	4325	13.35	14	11	77	0.45	73
	OMAN	Muscat	2077	7.64	44	5	70	4.23	12.7
	PAKISTAN	Islamabad	126 610	157.49	41	9	62	2.83	34.1
	PANAMA	Panama City	2563	33.25	25	5	73	1.86	52.9
	PAPUA NEW GUINEA	Port Moresby	4205	9.09	33	11	56	2.27	15.8
	PARAGUAY	Asunción	4700	11.55	33	5	70	2.78	51.9
	PERU	Lima	23 088	17.96	27	7	66	1.93	71.7
	PHILIPPINES	Manila	67 038	223.46	30	6	66	2.12	53.1
	POLAND	Warsaw	38 544	123.27	13	10	71	0.14	64.3
	PORTUGAL	Lisbon	9830	110.52	12	11	75	-0.09	35.1
	QATAR	Doha	540	47.22	21	3	71	2.53	91.1
	REPUBLIC OF IRELAND	Dublin	3571	50.81	15	9	75	0.28	57.4
	REPUBLIC OF SOUTH AFRICA	Pretoria / Cape Town	40 436	33.17	31	9	63	2.24	50.4
	ROMANIA	Bucharest	22 736	95.73	11	11	70	-0.32	55
	RUSSIAN FEDERATION	Moscow	147 997	8.67	11	12	68	-0.12	75.6
	RWANDA	Kigali	7750	294.25	44	17	47	2.59	6
	SÃO TOMÉ AND PRÍNCIPE	São Tomé	130	134.85				2.2	45.8

LAND

EDUCATION AND HEALTH

DEVELOPMENT

AREA ('000s sq km)	CULTIV-ATED AREA ('000s sq km 1993)	FOREST ('000s sq km 1993)	ADULT LITERACY (% 1992)	SCHOOL ENROL-MENT (Secondary, gross % 1993)	PEOPLE PER DOCTOR (1991)	FOOD INTAKE (calories per capita per day 1992)	ENERGY CONSU-MPTION (kg per cap oil eq 1993)	TRADE BALANCE (millions US $ 1994)	GNP PER CAPITA (US $ 1993 or earlier)	COUNTRY	TIME ZONES (+ OR - GMT)
1760	22	8	72.4		862	3308	2163	5857	5350	LIBYA	+1
65.2	30	20	98.4	78.5	218		2368	185	1310	LITHUANIA	+2
3			99	71	537	3681	9694		35 850	LUXEMBOURG	+1
26	7	10					1567	-144	780	MACEDONIA	+1
587	31	232	81.4	15.5	9081	2135	26	-173	240	MADAGASCAR	+3
118	17	37	53.9	4	31 637	1825	26	-226	220	MALAWI	+2
333	49	223	81.5	60	2847	2888	1236	-826	3160	MALAYSIA	+8
.298				92.6		2580	151	-176	820	MALDIVES	+5
1240	25	69	27.2	7.5	23 370	2278	17	-93	300	MALI	GMT
.316			87	85		3486	1562	-930	7240	MALTA	+1
1031	2	44	36.2	15	11 912	2685	432	215	510	MAURITANIA	GMT
2.04	1		81.1	54		2690	456	-571	2980	MAURITIUS	+4
1973	247	487	88.6	56	663	3146	1311	-18 542	3750	MEXICO	-6 to -8
.701									1560	MICRONESIA	+10 to +11
33.7	22	4	96		255		1267	-7	1180	MOLDOVA	+2
1565	14	138	81.1	91	413	1899	1079		400	MONGOLIA	+8
447	99	90	40.6	34.5	5067	2984	274	-3198	1030	MOROCCO	GMT
799	32	140	36.9	7	45 778	1680	23	-823	80	MOZAMBIQUE	+2
677	101	324	82	23	3947	2598	38	-114	200	MYANMAR	+6.5
824	7	180	40	52.5	6338	2134			1660	NAMIBIA	+1
147	24	58	25.6	35.5	21 520	1957	22	-489	160	NEPAL	+5.75
42	9	4	99	116.5	417	3222	5167	15 313	20 710	NETHERLANDS	+1
271	38	74	99	91.5	373	3669	3871	283	12 900	NEW ZEALAND	+12 to +12¾
130	13	32	64.7	42.5	1856	2293	304	-479	360	NICARAGUA	-6
1267	36	25	12.4	6.5	48 325	2257	41	-43	270	NIGER	+1
924	324	113	52.5	23.5	5997	2124	160	2402	310	NIGERIA	+1
121	20	74	95		377	2833	3031		990	NORTH KOREA	+9
324	9	83	99	110.5	328	3244	5020	7380	26 340	NORWAY	+1
272	1		35	64.5	1079		1947	1630	5600	OMAN	+4
804	213	35	35.7	21	1874	2315	204	-1535	430	PAKISTAN	+5
77	7	33	89.6	61.5	857	2242	576	-1871	2580	PANAMA	-5
463	4	420	69.7	12.5	13 071	2613	190	1109	1120	PAPUA NEW GUINEA	+10
407	23	129	91.2	33.5	1687	2670	260	-1004	1500	PARAGUAY	-4
1285	34	848	87.3	63	989	1882	328	-2239	1490	PERU	-5
300	92	136	94	73	1195	2257	290	-4341	830	PHILIPPINES	+8
313	147	88	99	84	482	3301	2529	-4143	2270	POLAND	+1
89	32	33	86.2	81	381	3634	1463	-9084	7890	PORTUGAL	GMT
11			78.1	88.5	646		25 210	1290	15 140	QATAR	+3
70	9	3	99	103	676	3847	2904	8939	12 580	REPUBLIC OF IRELAND	GMT
1219	132	82	80.6	71	1597	2695	1888		2900	R.S.A.	+2
238	99	67	96.9	82	553	3051	1828	-294	1120	ROMANIA	+2
17 075	1339	7785	98.7		215	3332	4856	24 593	2350	RUSSIAN FED.	+2 to +12
26	12	6	56.8	10		1821	24	-220	200	RWANDA	+2
0.964			60			2129	197		330	SÃO TOMÉ & PRINCIPE	GMT

KEY INFORMATION

POPULATION

FLAG	COUNTRY	CAPITAL CITY	TOTAL (in '000s 1994)	DENSITY (persons per sq km 1994)	BIRTH RATE (per 1000 population 1994)	DEATH RATE (per 1000 population 1994)	LIFE EXPEC-TANCY (in years 1990-95)	POP. CHANGE (average % per annum 1990 - 1995)	URBAN POP. (% 1994)
	SAUDI ARABIA	Riyadh	17 451	7.93	35	5	70	2.16	79.7
	SENEGAL	Dakar	8102	41.19	43	16	49	2.52	41.7
	SIERRA LEONE	Freetown	4402	61.36	49	25	39	2.4	35.4
	SINGAPORE	Singapore	2930	4585.29	16	6	75	1.03	100
	SLOVAKIA	Bratislava	5347	109.04	14	11	71	0.36	58.3
	SLOVENIA	Ljubljana	1942	95.90	11	11	73	0.29	62.7
	SOLOMON ISLANDS	Honiara	366	12.90	37	4	70	3.32	16.6
	SOMALIA	Mogadishu	9077	14.23	50	18	47	1.28	25.4
	SOUTH KOREA	Seoul	44 453	447.78	16	6	71	0.97	80
	SPAIN	Madrid	39 193	77.64	10	9	78	0.18	76.2
	SRI LANKA	Colombo	17 865	272.29	21	6	72	1.27	22.1
	ST LUCIA	Castries	141	228.90				1.35	47.7
	ST VINCENT	Kingstown	111	285.35				0.88	45.8
	SUDAN	Khartoum	27 361	10.92	40	13	53	2.67	24.2
	SURINAME	Paramaribo	418	2.55	25	6	70	1.1	49.7
	SWAZILAND	Mbabane	879	50.62	38	11	58	2.78	30.2
	SWEDEN	Stockholm	8794	19.54	14	11	78	0.51	83.1
	SWITZERLAND	Bern	6994	169.37	13	9	78	1.05	60.5
	SYRIA	Damascus	13 844	74.76	41	6	66	3.43	51.9
	TAIWAN	Taibei	21 074	582.49					
	TAJIKISTAN	Dushanbe	5751	40.19	37	6	70	2.86	32.1
	TANZANIA	Dodoma	28 846	30.52	43	14	52	2.96	23.6
	THAILAND	Bangkok	59 396	115.76	19	6	69	1.12	19.7
	TOGO	Lomé	3928	69.17	45	13	55	3.18	30.3
	TRINIDAD AND TOBAGO	Port of Spain	1257	245.03	21	6	72	1.1	71.3
	TUNISIA	Tunis	8733	53.20	26	6	68	1.92	56.8
	TURKEY	Ankara	61 183	78.49	27	7	66	1.98	67.3
	TURKMENISTAN	Ashkhabad	4010	8.22	32	8	65	2.28	44.8
	UGANDA	Kampala	20 621	85.55	52	19	45	3.42	12.2
	UKRAINE	Kiev	51 910	85.99	11	13	69	-0.1	69.7
	UNITED ARAB EMIRATES	Abu Dhabi	1861	23.95	23	3	74	2.62	83.5
	UNITED KINGDOM	London	58 091	238.00	13	11	76	0.29	89.4
	UNITED STATES OF AMERICA	Washington	260 650	26.57	16	9	76	1.04	76
	URUGUAY	Montevideo	3167	17.97	17	10	72	0.58	90.1
	UZBEKISTAN	Tashkent	22 349	49.95	31	6	69	2.24	41.1
	VANUATU	Port-Vila	165	13.54	35	7	65	2.49	19.1
	VENEZUELA	Caracas	21 177	23.22	27	5	72	2.27	92.4
	VIETNAM	Hanoi	72 509	220.01	31	8	65	2.23	20.5
	WESTERN SAMOA	Apia	164	57.93	37	6	68	1.07	21
	YEMEN	Sana	13 873	26.28	49	15	50	4.97	32.7
	YUGOSLAVIA	Belgrade	10 515	102.91	14	10	72	1.32	55.9
	ZAIRE	Kinshasa	42 552	18.14	48	14	52	3.19	28.8
	ZAMBIA	Lusaka	9196	12.22	45	15	49	2.97	42.8
	ZIMBABWE	Harare	11 150	28.53	39	12	54	2.57	31.4

AREA ('000s sq km)	CULTIV-ATED AREA ('000s sq km 1993)	FOREST ('000s sq km 1993)	ADULT LITERACY (% 1992)	SCHOOL ENROL-MENT (Secondary, gross % 1993)	PEOPLE PER DOCTOR (1991)	FOOD INTAKE (calories per capita per day 1992)	ENERGY CONSU-MPTION (kg per cap oil eq 1993)	TRADE BALANCE (millions US $ 1994)	GNP PER CAPITA (US $ 1993 or earlier)	COUNTRY	TIME ZONES (+ OR - GMT)
2200	37	18	60.6	51	969	2735	4092	1979	7780	SAUDI ARABIA	+3
197	24	105	30.5	17	18 002	2262	116	-489	730	SENEGAL	GMT
72	5	20	28.7	16.5	13 837	1694	31	-34	140	SIERRA LEONE	GMT
0.639			89.9	70.5	950		6371	-5841	19 310	SINGAPORE	+8
49	16	20	99			3156	3019	29	1900	SLOVAKIA +	+1
20	3	10					2396	-428	6310	SLOVENIA +	+1
28	1	25	24	15.5		2173	147	-5	750	SOLOMON ISLANDS	+11
638	10	160	27	7	16 660	1499		-28	170	SOMALIA	+3
99	21	65	97.4	92.5	1076	3285	2438	-6305	7670	SOUTH KOREA	+9
505	197	161	98	108.5	280	3708	2031	-19 205	13 650	SPAIN	+1
66	19	21	89.3	74.5	7337	2273	104	-1290	600	SRI LANKA	+5½
0.616			93			2588	403	-190	3040	ST LUCIA	-4
0.389			98			2347	264	-92	2130	ST VINCENT	4
2506	130	442	42.7	21	11 620	2202	43	-551	400	SUDAN	+2
164	1	150	92.2	54	1927	2547	1374	0	1210	SURINAME	-3
17	2	1	74	49.5		2706			1050	SWAZILAND	+2
450	28	280	99	95.5	322	2972	4561	9669	24 830	SWEDEN	+1
41	5	13	99	91.5	334	3379	3321	2158	36 410	SWITZERLAND	+1
185	58	7	67.7	48.5	1439	3175	986	-1822	1100	SYRIA	+2
36					974				10 180	TAIWAN	+8
143	8	5	96.7		366		1067	28	470	TAJIKISTAN	+5
945	35	335	64.4	5.5	24 070	2018	26	-778	100	TANZANIA	+3
513	208	135	93.5	33	5080	2432	675	-8885	2040	THAILAND	+7
57	24	9	47.9	23.5	15 352	2242	53	-60	330	TOGO	GMT
5.13	1	2	97.4	79	1197	2585	4993	164	3730	TRINIDAD AND TOBAGO	-4
164	50	7	62.8	49	1897	3330	608	-1900	1780	TUNISIA	+1
779	275	202	80.5	50	1201	3429	793	-5155	2120	TURKEY	+2
488	15	40	97.7		296		3380	548	1380	TURKMENISTAN	+5
241	68	55	58.6	12	26 850	2159	19	-459	190	UGANDA	+3
604	344	103	95		234		3733	-281	1910	UKRAINE	+2 to +3
176	13	9	96.9	61.5	348	2750	585	-860	3910	URUGUAY	-3
77.7			77.7	72.5	673	3384	13 667	9415	22 470	U.A.E	+4
244	61	24	99	86.5	623	3317	3910	-22 183	17 970	UNITED KINGDOM	GMT
9809	1878	2862	99	94	408	3732	7570	-176 694	24 750	UNITED STATES	5 to -10
447	45	13	97.2		292	2079		-121	960	UZBEKISTAN	+5
12	1	9	65			2739	124	-65	1230	VANUATU	+11
912	39	300	90.4	34.5	605	2618	2379	7488	2840	VENEZUELA	-4
330	67	97	91.9	42.5	3108	2250	106	70	170	VIETNAM	+7
3	1	1	98			2828	269	-76	980	WESTERN SAMOA	-11
528	15	20	41.4		5982	2203	222	-1277	780	YEMEN	+3
102	40	27				3551	856		2490	YUGOSLAVIA	+1
2345	79	1738	74.1	22.5	26 982	2060	42	-39	240	ZAIRE	+1 to +2
753	53	287	75.2	19.5	9787	1931	137	187	370	ZAMBIA	+2
391	29	88	83.4	47	7537	1985	462	-775	540	ZIMBABWE	+2

How to use the Index

All the names on the maps in this atlas, except some of those on the special topic maps, are included in the index.

The names are arranged in **alphabetical order.** Where the name has more than one word the separate words are considered as one to decide the position of the name in the index:

Thetford
Thetford Mines
The Trossachs
The Wash
The Weald
Thiers

Where there is more than one place with the same name, the country name is used to decide the order:

London Canada
London England

If both places are in the same country, the country or state name is also used:

Avon *r.* Bristol England
Avon *r.* Dorset England

Each entry in the index starts with the name of the place or feature, followed by the name of the country or region in which it is located. This is followed by the number of the most appropriate page on which the name appears, usually the largest scale map. Next comes the alphanumeric reference followed by the latitude and longitude.

Names of physical features such as rivers, capes, mountains etc are followed by a description. The descriptions are usually shortened to one or two letters, these abbreviations are keyed below. Town names are followed by a description only when the name may be confused with that of a physical feature:

Big Spring *town*

To help to distinguish the different parts of each entry, different styles of type are used:

place name | country name or region name | alphanumeric grid reference

description (if any) | page number | latitude/ longitude

Thames *r.* England **15** **C2** 51.30N 0.05E

To use the **alphanumeric grid reference** to find a feature on the map, first find the correct page and then look at the white letters printed in the blue frame along the top and bottom of the map and the white numbers printed in the blue frame at the sides of the map. When you have found the correct letter and number follow the grid boxes up and along until you find the correct grid box in which the feature appears. You must then search the grid box until you find the name of the feature.

The **latitude and longitude reference** gives a more exact description of the position of the feature.

Page 6 of the atlas describes lines of latitude and lines of longitude, and explains how they are numbered and divided into degrees and minutes. Each name in the index has a different latitude and longitude reference, so the feature can be located accurately. The lines of latitude and lines of longitude shown on each map are numbered in degrees. These numbers are printed black along the top, bottom and sides of the map.

The drawing above shows part of the map on page 20 and the lines of latitude and lines of longitude.

The index entry for Wexford is given as follows

Wexford Rep. of Ire. **20** **E2** 52.20N 6.28W

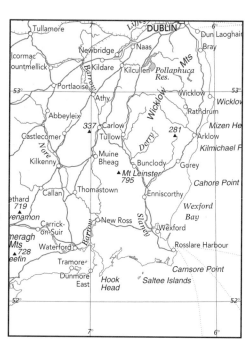

To locate Wexford, first find latitude 52N and estimate 20 minutes north from 52 degrees to find 52.20N, then find longitude 6W and estimate 28 minutes west from 6 degrees to find 6.28W. The symbol for the town of Wexford is where latitude 52.20N and longitude 6.28W meet.

On maps at a smaller scale than the map of Ireland, it is not possible to show every line of latitude and longitude. Only every 5 or 10 degrees of latitude and longitude may be shown. On these maps you must estimate the degrees and minutes to find the exact location of a feature.

Abbreviations

Afghan.	Afghanistan	Ill.	Illinois
Ala.	Alabama	*i.*, *I.*, *is.*, **Is.**	island, Island, islands, Islands
A. and B.	Argyll and Bute	I.o.M.	Isle of Man
Bangla.	Bangladesh	I.o.W.	Isle of Wight
b., **B.**	bay, Bay	*l.*, **L.**	lake, Lake
Bosnia.	Bosnia-Herzegovina	Lancs.	Lancashire
B.V.Is.	British Virgin Islands	Leics.	Leicestershire
Cambs.	Cambridgeshire	Liech.	Liechtenstein
c., **C.**	cape, Cape	Lincs.	Lincolnshire
Carib. Sea	Caribbean Sea	La.	Louisiana
C.A.R.	Central African Republic	Lux.	Luxembourg
Colo.	Colorado	Man.	Manitoba
Czech Rep.	Czech Republic	Med. Sea	Mediterranean Sea
d.	internal division eg. county, state	Miss.	Mississippi
		Mt.	Mount
Del.	Delaware	*mtn.*, **Mtn.**	mountain, Mountain'
Derbys.	Derbyshire	*mts.*, **Mts.**	mountains, Mountains
des.	desert	Neth.	Netherlands
Dom. Rep.	Dominican Republic	Neth. Ant.	Netherlands Antilles
D. and G.	Dumfries and Galloway	Nev.	Nevada
E. Sussex	East Sussex	N. Cal.	New Caledonia
E. Yorks.	The East Riding of Yorkshire	Nfld.	Newfoundland
Equat. Guinea	Equatorial Guinea	N. Mex.	New Mexico
est.	estuary	N.Y.	New York
f.	physical feature eg. valley, plain, geographic district	N. Ayr.	North Ayrshire
		N.C.	North Carolina
Fla.	Florida	N. Korea	North Korea
Ga.	Georgia	Northum.	Northumberland
Glos.	Gloucestershire	Notts.	Nottinghamshire
g., **G.**	Gulf	**Oc.**	Ocean
Hants.	Hampshire	Oreg.	Oregon
Herts.	Hertfordshire	Oxon.	Oxfordshire
High.	Highland	P.N.G.	Papua New Guinea

Pem.	Pembrokeshire
pen., **Pen.**	peninsula, Peninsula
P. and K.	Perth and Kinross
Phil.	Philadelphia
Pt.	Point
r., **R.**	river, River
Rep.of Ire.	Republic of Ireland
R.S.A.	Republic of South Africa
Resr.	Reservoir
Russian Fed.	Russian Federation
Shrops.	Shropshire
Somali Rep.	Somali Republic
Sd.	Sound
S.C.	South Carolina
S. Korea	South Korea
Staffs.	Staffordshire
str., **Str.**	strait, Strait
Switz.	Switzerland
Tex.	Texas
U.A.E.	United Arab Emirates
U.K.	United Kingdom
U.S.A.	United States of America
U.S. V.Is.	United States Virgin Islands
Va.	Virginia
Warwicks.	Warwickshire
W. Isles	Western Isles
W. Sahara	Western Sahara
W. Sussex	West Sussex
W. Va.	West Virginia
Wilts.	Wiltshire
Wyo.	Wyoming
Yugo.	Yugoslavia

A

Aachen Germany 48 C4 50.46N 6.06E
Aalen Germany 48 E3 48.50N 10.05E
Aalst Belgium 42 D2 50.57N 4.03E
Abadan Iran 95 G5 30.21N 48.15E
Abadeh Iran 95 H5 31.10N 52.40E
Abadla Algeria 84 D5 31.01N 2.45W
Abakan Russian Fed. 59 L3 53.43N 91.25E
Abancay Peru 76 C3 13.35S 72.55W
Abarqu Iran 95 H5 31.09N 53.18E
Abashiri Japan 106 D4 44.02N 144.17E
Abaya, L. Ethiopia 85 H2 6.20N 38.00E
Abaza Russian Fed. 102 G8 52.44N 90.12E
Abbeville France 44 D7 50.06N 1.51E
Abbeyfeale Rep. of Ire. 20 B2 52.24N 9.18W
Abbey Head Scotland 17 F2 54.45N 3.58W
Abbeyleix Rep. of Ire. 20 D2 52.55N 7.20W
Abbottabad Pakistan 95 L5 34.12N 73.15E
Abéché Chad 85 G3 13.49N 20.49E
Åbenrå Denmark 43 B1 55.03N 9.26E
Abeokuta Nigeria 84 E2 7.10N 3.26E
Aberaeron Wales 12 C4 52.15N 4.16W
Aberchirder Scotland 19 G2 57.33N 2.38W
Aberconwy and Colwyn d. Wales 12 D5 53.10N 3.45W
Aberdare Wales 12 D3 51.43N 3.27W
Aberdare Range mts. Kenya 87 B2 0.20S 36.07E
Aberdeen Scotland 19 G2 57.08N 2.07W
Aberdeen U.S.A. 64 G6 45.28N 98.30W
Aberdeen City d. Scotland 19 G2 57.08N 2.07W
Aberdeenshire d. Scotland 19 G2 57.22N 2.35W
Aberfeldy Scotland 17 F4 56.38N 3.52W
Aberford England 15 F2 53.51N 1.20W
Aberfoyle Scotland 16 E4 56.11N 4.23W
Abergavenny Wales 12 D3 51.49N 3.01W
Abergele Wales 12 D5 53.17N 3.34W
Aberporth Wales 12 C4 52.08N 4.33W
Abersoch Wales 12 C4 52.50N 4.31W
Abertillery Wales 12 D3 51.44N 3.09W
Aberystwyth Wales 12 C4 52.25N 4.06W
Abha Saudi Arabia 94 F2 18.13N 42.30E
Abidjan Côte d'Ivoire 84 D2 5.19N 4.01W
Abilene U.S.A. 64 G3 32.27N 99.45W
Abingdon England 10 D2 51.40N 1.17W
Abington Scotland 17 F3 55.29N 3.42W
Abitibi, L. Canada 65 K6 48.42N 79.45W
Aboyne Scotland 19 G2 57.05N 2.49W
Abqaiq Saudi Arabia 95 G4 25.55N 49.40E
Abu' Arīsh Saudi Arabia 94 F2 16.58N 42.50E
Abu Dhabi U.A.E. 95 H3 24.27N 54.23E
Abu Hamed Sudan 85 H3 19.32N 33.20E
Abuja Nigeria 84 E2 9.12N 7.11E
Abu Matariq Sudan 94 C1 10.58N 26.17E
Abunã r. Brazil 76 D4 9.41S 65.20W
Abu Simbel Egypt 94 D3 22.18N 31.40E
Abyad Sudan 94 C1 13.46N 26.28E
Acapulco Mexico 70 E4 16.51N 99.56W
Acarigua Venezuela 71 K2 9.35N 69.12W
Accra Ghana 84 D2 5.33N 0.15W
Accrington England 15 E2 53.46N 2.22W
Acheloös r. Greece 56 E3 38.20N 21.04E
Achill I. Rep. of Ire. 20 A3 53.57N 10.00W
Achinsk Russian Fed. 59 L3 56.10N 90.10E
A'Chralaig mtn. Scotland 18 D2 57.11N 5.09W
Acklins I. The Bahamas 71 J5 22.30N 74.10W
Acle England 11 G3 52.38N 1.33E
Aconcagua mtn. Argentina 75 B3 32.37S 70.00W
A Coruña Spain 46 A5 43.22N 8.24W
Acre d. Brazil 76 C4 8.50S 71.30W
Acre r. Brazil 76 D4 8.45S 67.23W
Actéon, Groupe is. French Polynesia 109 Q4 22.00S 136.00W
Adaja r. Spain 46 C4 41.32N 4.52W
Adamawa Highlands Nigeria/Cameroon 84 F2 7.05N 12.00E
Adana Turkey 57 L2 37.00N 35.19E
Adda r. Italy 50 C6 45.08N 9.55E
Ad Dahna des. Saudi Arabia 95 G2 26.00N 47.00E
Ad Dakhla W. Sahara 84 C4 23.43N 15.57W
Ad Dammam Saudi Arabia 95 H4 26.23N 50.08E
Adderbury England 10 D3 52.01N 1.19W
Ad Dir'iyah Saudi Arabia 95 G4 24.45N 46.32E
Addis Ababa Ethiopia 85 H2 9.03N 38.42E
Ad Dīwanīyah Iraq 94 F5 31.59N 44.57E
Adelaide Australia 110 C2 34.56S 138.36E
Aden Yemen 94 F1 12.50N 45.00E
Aden, G. of Indian Oc. 85 I3 13.00N 50.00E
Adi i. Indonesia 105 I3 4.10S 133.10E
Ādī Ārk'ay Ethiopia 94 E1 13.35N 37.57E
Adige r. Italy 50 E6 45.10N 12.20E
Ādīgrat Ethiopia 94 E1 14.18N 39.31E
Adilang Uganda 87 A3 2.44N 33.28E
Adi Ugri Eritrea 94 E1 14.55N 38.53E
Adıyaman Turkey 57 N2 37.46N 38.15E
Admiralty Is. P.N.G. 108 J6 2.30S 147.20E
Adour r. France 44 C3 43.28N 1.35W
Adriatic Sea Med. Sea 50 F5 42.30N 16.00E
Adwa Ethiopia 85 H3 14.12N 38.56E
Aegean Sea Med. Sea 56 G3 39.00N 25.00E
Afghanistan Asia 95 K5 33.00N 65.30E
Afmadow Somalia 87 C3 0.27N 42.05E
Africa 82
Afyon Turkey 57 J3 38.46N 30.32E
Agadez Niger 84 E3 17.00N 7.56E
Agadir Morocco 84 D5 30.26N 9.36W
Agana Guam 105 K6 13.28N 144.45E
Agano r. Japan 106 C3 37.58N 139.02E
Agartala India 97 I5 23.49N 91.15E
Agde France 44 E3 43.19N 3.28E
Agen France 44 D4 44.12N 0.38E
Āgere Maryam Ethiopia 87 B4 5.40N 38.11E
Aghla Mtn. Rep. of Ire. 16 A2 54.50N 8.10W
Agios Efstratios i. Greece 56 G3 39.30N 25.00E
Agirwat Hills Sudan 94 E2 16.00N 35.10E
Agra India 97 F6 27.09N 78.00E
Ağri Turkey 94 F6 39.44N 43.04E
Agrigento Italy 50 E2 37.19N 13.36E
Agrihan i. N. Mariana Is. 105 L7 18.44N 145.39E
Aguascalientes Mexico 70 D5 21.51N 102.18W
Aguascalientes d. Mexico 70 D4 22.00N 102.18W
Aguilar de Campóo Spain 46 C5 42.55N 4.15W
Aguilas Spain 46 E2 37.25N 1.35W
Agulhas, C. R.S.A. 86 B1 34.50S 20.00E
Agulhas Negras mtn. Brazil 72 F4 22.20S 44.43W
Ahar Iran 95 G6 38.25N 47.07E
Ahaus Germany 42 G4 52.04N 7.01E
Ahmadabad India 96 E5 23.03N 72.40E
Ahmadnagar India 96 E4 19.08N 74.48E
Ahmadpur East Pakistan 95 L4 29.09N 71.16E
Ahmadpur Sial Pakistan 95 L5 30.41N 71.46E
Ahvaz Iran 95 G5 31.17N 48.44E
Aigina i. Greece 56 F2 37.43N 23.30E
Ailsa Craig i. Scotland 16 D3 55.15N 5.07W
Aïn Beïda Algeria 52 E4 35.50N 7.27E
Aïn Sefra Algeria 84 D5 32.45N 0.35W
Aïr mts. Niger 84 E3 18.30N 8.30E
Airdrie Canada 62 G3 51.20N 114.00W
Airdrie Scotland 17 F3 55.52N 3.59W
Aisne r. France 44 E6 49.27N 2.51E
Aitape P.N.G. 105 K3 3.10S 142.17E
Aitutaki i. Cook Is. 108 P5 18.52S 159.46W
Aix-en-Provence France 44 F3 43.31N 5.27E
Aizu-wakamatsu Japan 106 C3 37.30N 139.58E
Ajaccio France 44 H2 41.55N 8.43E
Ajdabiya Libya 85 G5 30.48N 20.15E
Akhdar, Al Jabal al mts. Libya 85 G5 32.10N 22.00E
Akhdar, Jabal mts. Oman 95 I3 23.10N 57.25E
Akhisar Turkey 57 H3 38.54N 27.49E
Akimiski I. Canada 63 J3 53.00N 81.20W
Akita Japan 106 D3 39.44N 140.05E
Akkajaure l. Sweden 43 D4 67.40N 17.30E
Akmola Kazakhstan 102 C8 51.10N 71.28E
Akobo r. Sudan/Ethiopia 82 G5 8.30N 33.15E
Akordat Eritrea 85 H3 15.35N 37.55E
Akpatok I. Canada 63 L4 60.30N 68.30W
Akranes Iceland 43 X2 64.19N 22.05W
Akron U.S.A. 65 J5 41.04N 81.31W
Aksaray Turkey 94 D5 38.22N 34.02E
Akşehir Turkey 57 J3 38.22N 31.24E
Aksu China 102 E6 42.10N 80.00E
Āksum Ethiopia 94 E1 14.08N 38.48E
Aktau Kazakhstan 58 H2 43.37N 51.11E
Aktogay Kazakhstan 102 D7 46.59N 79.42E
Aktyubinsk Kazakhstan 58 H3 50.16N 57.13E
Akureyri Iceland 43 Y2 65.41N 18.04W
Alabama d. U.S.A. 65 I3 33.00N 87.00W
Alabama r. U.S.A. 65 I3 31.05N 87.55W
Alagoas d. Brazil 77 G4 9.30S 37.00W
Alagoinhas Brazil 77 G3 12.09S 38.21W
Al Ahmadi Kuwait 95 G4 29.05N 48.04E
Alakol', L. Kazakhstan 102 E7 46.00N 81.40E
Alakurtti Russian Fed. 43 G4 67.00N 30.23E
Alamagan i. N. Mariana Is. 105 L7 17.35N 145.50E
Åland is. Finland 43 E3 60.20N 20.00E
Alanya Turkey 57 J2 36.32N 32.02E
Al Artawīyah Saudi Arabia 95 G4 26.31N 45.21E
Alaska d. U.S.A. 62 C4 65.00N 153.00W
Alaska, G. of U.S.A. 62 D3 58.45N 145.00W
Alaska Pen. U.S.A. 62 C3 56.00N 160.00W
Alaska Range mts. U.S.A. 62 C4 62.10N 152.00W
Alausí Ecuador 76 C4 2.00S 78.50W
Alavus Finland 43 E3 62.35N 23.37E
Alaw Resr. Wales 12 C5 53.20N 4.25W
Albacete Spain 46 E3 39.00N 1.52W
Alba Iulia Romania 56 F7 46.04N 23.33E
Albania Europe 56 E4 41.00N 20.00E
Albany Australia 110 A2 34.57S 117.54E
Albany r. Canada 63 J3 52.10N 82.00W
Albany Ga. U.S.A. 65 J3 31.37N 84.10W
Albany N.Y. U.S.A. 65 L5 42.40N 73.49W
Al Basrah Iraq 95 G5 30.33N 47.50E
Al Bayda' Libya 85 G5 32.50N 21.50E
Albenga Italy 50 C6 44.03N 8.13E
Alberche r. Spain 46 C4 40.00N 4.45W
Albert France 42 B1 50.00N 2.40E
Albert, L. Africa 86 C5 1.45N 31.00E
Alberta d. Canada 62 G3 55.00N 115.00W
Albert Lea U.S.A. 65 H5 43.39N 93.22W
Albert Nile r. Uganda 85 H2 3.30N 32.00E
Albi France 44 E3 43.56N 2.08E
Al Biyadah f. Saudi Arabia 95 G3 22.00N 47.00E
Alboran, Isla de i. Spain 46 D1 35.55N 3.10W
Ålborg Denmark 43 B2 57.03N 9.56E
Āl Bu Kamal Syria 94 F5 34.27N 40.55E
Albuquerque U.S.A. 64 E4 35.05N 106.38W
Al Buraymi U.A.E. 95 I3 24.15N 55.45E
Albury Australia 110 D2 36.03S 146.53E
Alcalá de Henares Spain 46 D4 40.28N 3.22W
Alcalá la Real Spain 46 D2 37.28N 3.55W
Alcañiz Spain 46 E4 41.03N 0.09W
Alcázar de San Juan Spain 46 D3 39.24N 3.12W
Alcester England 10 D3 52.13N 1.52W
Alcoy Spain 46 E3 38.42N 0.29W
Alcúdia Spain 46 G3 39.51N 3.09E
Aldabra Is. Indian Oc. 86 D4 9.00S 47.00E
Aldan Russian Fed. 59 O3 58.44N 125.22E
Aldan r. Russian Fed. 59 P4 63.30N 130.00E
Aldbrough England 15 G2 53.50N 0.07W
Aldeburgh England 11 G3 52.09N 1.35E
Alderley Edge England 15 E2 53.18N 2.15W
Alderney i. Channel Is. 13 Z9 49.42N 2.11W
Aldershot England 10 E2 51.15N 0.47W
Aldingham England 14 D3 54.08N 3.08W
Aldridge England 10 D3 52.36N 1.55W
Aleksandrovsk-Sakhalinskiy Russian Fed. 59 Q3 50.55N 142.12E
Aleksin Russian Fed. 55 O6 54.31N 37.07E
Alençon France 44 D6 48.25N 0.05E
Aleppo Syria 94 E6 36.14N 37.10E
Alès France 44 F4 44.08N 4.05E
Alessandria Italy 50 C6 44.54N 8.37E
Ålesund Norway 43 A3 62.28N 6.11E
Aleutian Is. U.S.A. 108 N12 52.00N 176.00W
Aleutian Range mts. U.S.A. 62 C3 58.00N 156.00W
Alexander Archipelago is. U.S.A. 62 E3 56.30N 134.30W
Alexander I. Antarctica 112 72.00S 70.00W
Alexandra, C. South Georgia 75 F1 54.05S 37.58W
Alexandria Egypt 94 C5 31.13N 29.55E
Alexandria Scotland 16 E3 55.59N 4.35W
Alexandria La. U.S.A. 65 H3 31.19N 92.29W
Alexandria Va. U.S.A. 65 K4 38.48N 77.03W
Alexandroupoli Greece 56 G4 40.50N 25.53E
Aleysk Russian Fed. 102 E8 52.32N 82.17E
Al Farwanīyah Kuwait 95 G4 29.04N 47.50E
Alford England 15 H2 53.17N 0.11E
Alfreton England 15 F2 53.06N 1.22W
Algarve f. Portugal 46 A2 37.20N 8.00W
Algeciras Spain 46 C2 36.08N 5.27W
Algeria Africa 84 E4 28.00N 2.00E
Al Ghaydah Yemen 95 H2 16.12N 52.16E
Alghero Italy 50 C4 40.33N 8.20E
Algiers Algeria 84 E5 36.50N 3.00E
Al Hamad des. Asia 94 E5 31.45N 39.00E
Al Hamadah al Hamra' f. Libya 52 F2 29.00N 12.00E
Al Ḥasakah Syria 94 F6 36.29N 40.45E
Al Hibak f. Saudi Arabia 95 H3 21.00N 53.30E
Al Hillah Iraq 94 F5 32.28N 44.29E
Al Hoceima Morocco 46 D1 35.15N 3.55W
Aliakmonas r. Greece 56 F4 40.30N 22.38E
Ali Bayramli Azerbaijan 95 G6 39.56N 48.55E
Alicante Spain 46 E3 38.21N 0.29W
Alice Springs town Australia 110 C3 23.42S 133.52E
Alingsås Sweden 43 C2 57.55N 12.30E
Al Jaghbub Libya 85 E4 29.42N 24.38E
Al Jaharah Kuwait 95 G4 29.20N 47.41E
Al Jauf Saudi Arabia 94 E4 29.49N 39.52E
Al Jawsh Libya 52 F3 32.00N 11.40E
Al Jubayl Saudi Arabia 95 G4 26.59N 49.40E
Al Khaburah Oman 95 I3 23.58N 57.10E
Al Khaşab Oman 95 I4 26.14N 56.15E
Al Khufrah Libya 85 G4 24.09N 23.19E
Al Khums Libya 53 F3 32.39N 14.15E
Alkmaar Neth. 42 D4 52.37N 4.44E
Al Kut Iraq 95 G5 32.30N 45.51E
Allahabad India 97 G6 25.57N 81.50E
Allegheny Mts. U.S.A. 65 K5 38.00N 81.00W
Allen, Lough Rep. of Ire. 20 C4 54.07N 8.04W
Allendale Town England 15 E3 54.54N 2.15W
Allentown U.S.A. 65 K5 40.37N 75.30W
Alleppey India 96 F2 9.30N 76.22E
Aller r. Germany 48 D5 52.57N 9.11E
Alliance U.S.A. 64 F5 42.08N 103.00W
Allier r. France 44 E5 46.58N 3.04E
Al Lith Saudi Arabia 94 F3 20.09N 40.16E
Alloa Scotland 17 F4 56.07N 3.49W
Al Mahrah f. Yemen 95 H2 15.30N 51.00E
Almansa Spain 46 E3 38.52N 1.06W
Almanzor mtn. Spain 46 C4 40.20N 5.22W
Al Marj Libya 53 H3 32.30N 20.50E
Almaty Kazakhstan 102 D6 43.19N 76.55E
Almeirim Brazil 77 E4 1.30S 52.35W
Almelo Neth. 42 F4 52.21N 6.40E
Almería Spain 46 D2 36.50N 2.26W
Almina, Punta c. Morocco 46 C1 35.54N 5.17W
Al Mish'ab Saudi Arabia 95 G4 28.00N 48.48E
Almodôvar Portugal 46 A2 37.31N 8.03W
Almond r. Scotland 17 F4 56.25N 3.28W
Al Mudawwara Jordan 94 E5 29.20N 36.00E
Al Mukha Yemen 94 F1 13.19N 43.15E
Almuñécar Spain 46 D2 36.44N 3.41W
Al Nu'ayriyah Saudi Arabia 95 G4 27.27N 48.17E
Alnwick England 15 F4 55.25N 1.41W
Alor i. Indonesia 105 G2 8.20S 124.30E
Alpes Maritimes mts. France 44 G4 44.07N 7.08E
Alpine U.S.A. 64 F3 30.22N 103.40W
Alps mts. Europe 34 E2 46.00N 7.30E
Al Qa'amiyat f. Saudi Arabia 95 G2 18.30N 49.00E
Al Qaddahiyah Libya 53 G3 31.24N 15.12E
Al Qamishlī Syria 94 F6 37.05N 41.11E
Al Qunfidhah Saudi Arabia 94 F2 19.08N 41.15E
Alsager England 15 E2 53.07N 2.20W
Alston England 15 E3 54.48N 2.26W
Alta r. Norway 43 E5 70.00N 23.15E
Altai Mts. Mongolia 102 G7 46.30N 93.30E
Altamira Brazil 77 E4 3.12S 52.12W
Altamura Italy 50 G4 40.50N 16.32E
Altay China 102 F7 47.48N 88.07E
Altay Mongolia 102 H7 46.20N 97.00E
Altenburg Germany 48 F4 50.59N 12.27E
Altiplano f. Bolivia 76 D3 18.00S 67.30W
Altiplano Mexicano mts. N. America 60 I4 24.00N 105.00W
Alton England 10 E2 51.08N 0.59W
Altoona U.S.A. 65 K5 40.32N 78.23W
Altrincham England 15 E2 53.25N 2.21W
Altun Shan mts. China 102 F5 38.10N 87.50E
Al'Uqaylah Libya 53 G3 30.15N 19.12E
Alur Setar Malaysia 104 C5 6.06N 100.23E
Al'Uthmanīyah Saudi Arabia 95 G4 25.16N 49.24E
Al'Uwaynat Libya 94 B3 21.53N 24.51E
Alva U.S.A. 64 G4 36.48N 98.40W
Älvdalen Sweden 43 C3 61.14N 14.05E
Alveley England 10 C3 52.28N 2.20W
Älvsbyn Sweden 43 E4 65.41N 21.00E
Al Wajh Saudi Arabia 94 E4 26.16N 36.28E
Alwen Resr. Wales 12 D5 53.05N 3.35W
Al Widyan f. Iraq/Saudi Arabia 94 F5 31.00N 42.00E
Alyth Scotland 17 F4 56.38N 3.14W
Alytus Lithuania 55 I6 54.24N 24.03E
Amadeus, L. Australia 110 C3 24.50S 130.45E
Amadjuak L. Canada 63 K4 65.00N 71.00W
Amadora Portugal 46 A3 38.45N 9.13W
Åmål Sweden 43 C2 59.04N 12.41E
Amamapare Indonesia 105 J3 4.56S 136.43E
Amapá d. Brazil 77 E5 2.00N 52.00W
Amarillo U.S.A. 64 F4 35.14N 101.50W
Amasya Turkey 57 L4 40.37N 35.50E
Amazon r. Brazil 77 E4 2.00S 50.00W
Amazonas d. Brazil 76 D4 4.50S 64.00W
Amazon Delta f. Brazil 77 F5 0.00 50.00W
Ambarchik Russian Fed. 59 S4 69.39N 162.27E
Ambato Ecuador 76 C4 1.18S 78.36W
Ambergate England 15 F2 53.03N 1.29W
Ambergris Cay i. Belize 70 G4 18.00N 87.58W
Amble England 15 F4 55.20N 1.34W
Ambleside England 14 E3 54.26N 2.58W
Ambon Indonesia 105 H3 3.50S 128.10E
Amboseli Nat. Park Kenya 87 B2 2.40S 37.10E
Ambrym i. Vanuatu 111 F4 16.15S 168.10E
Ameland i. Neth. 42 E5 53.28N 5.48E
American Samoa is. Pacific Oc. 108 O5 14.20S 170.00W
Amersfoort Neth. 42 E4 52.10N 5.23E
Amersham England 11 E2 51.40N 0.38W
Amesbury England 10 D2 51.10N 1.46W
Amgu Russian Fed. 106 C5 45.48N 137.36E
Amgun r. Russian Fed. 59 P3 53.10N 139.47E
Amiens France 44 E6 49.54N 2.18E
Amino Ethiopia 87 C3 4.25N 41.52E
Amlwch Wales 12 C5 53.24N 4.21W
Amman Jordan 94 E5 31.57N 35.56E
Ammanford Wales 12 C3 51.48N 4.00W
Amol Iran 95 H6 36.26N 52.24E
Amorgos i. Greece 56 G2 36.49N 25.54E
Amos Canada 63 K2 48.35N 78.05W
Ampthill England 11 E3 52.03N 0.30W
Amravati India 97 F5 20.58N 77.50E
Amritsar India 96 E7 31.35N 74.56E
Amstelveen Neth. 42 D4 52.18N 4.51E
Amsterdam Neth. 42 D4 52.22N 4.54E
Amudar'ya r. Asia 90 H7 43.50N 59.00E
Amund Ringnes I. Canada 63 I5 78.00N 96.00W
Amundsen G. Canada 62 F5 70.30N 122.00W
Amundsen Sea Antarctica 112 70.00S 110.00W
Amuntai Indonesia 104 F3 2.24S 115.14E
Amur r. Russian Fed. 59 P3 53.17N 140.00E
Anabar r. Russian Fed. 59 N5 72.40N 113.30E
Anadyr Russian Fed. 59 T4 64.40N 177.32E
Anadyr r. Russian Fed. 59 T4 65.00N 176.00E
Anadyr, G. of Russian Fed. 59 U4 64.30N 177.50W
'Ānah Iraq 94 F5 34.29N 41.57E
Anambas Is. Indonesia 104 D4 3.00N 106.10E
Anamur Turkey 57 K2 36.06N 32.49E
Anápolis Brazil 77 F3 16.19S 48.58W
Anatahan i. N. Mariana Is. 105 L7 16.22N 145.38E
Anatolia f. Turkey 57 J3 38.30N 32.00E
Anchorage U.S.A. 62 D4 61.10N 150.00W
Ancona Italy 50 E5 43.37N 13.33E
Åndalsnes Norway 43 A3 62.33N 7.43E
Andaman Is. India 97 I3 12.00N 93.00E
Andaman Sea Indian Oc. 97 J3 11.00N 96.00E
Anderlecht Belgium 42 D2 50.51N 4.18E
Anderson r. Canada 62 F4 69.45N 129.00W
Anderson U.S.A. 62 D4 64.25N 149.10W
Andes mts. S. America 74 B5 15.00S 74.00W
Andfjorden est. Norway 43 D5 69.10N 16.20E
Andhra Pradesh d. India 97 F4 17.00N 79.00E
Andkhvoy Afghan. 95 K6 36.56N 65.05E
Andorra Europe 46 F5 42.30N 1.32E
Andorra La Vella Andorra 46 F5 42.30N 1.31E
Andover England 10 D2 51.13N 1.29W
Andøya i. Norway 43 C5 69.00N 15.30E
Andreas I.o.M. 14 C3 54.22N 4.26W
Andreas, C. Cyprus 57 L1 35.40N 34.35E
Andros i. Greece 56 G2 37.50N 24.50E
Andros i. The Bahamas 71 I5 24.30N 78.00W
Andújar Spain 46 C3 38.02N 4.03W
Anegada i. B.V.Is. 71 L4 18.46N 64.24W
Aneto, Pico de mtn. Spain 46 F5 42.40N 0.19E
Angara r. Russian Fed. 59 L3 58.00N 93.00E
Angarsk Russian Fed. 103 I8 52.31N 103.55E
Ånge Sweden 43 C3 62.31N 15.40E
Angel de la Guarda i. Mexico 70 B6 29.10N 113.20W
Ängelholm Sweden 43 C2 56.15N 12.50E
Angers France 44 C5 47.29N 0.32W
Anglesey d. Wales 12 C5 53.16N 4.25W
Angola Africa 86 A3 12.00S 18.00E
Angola Basin f. Atlantic Oc. 117 J5
Angoulême France 44 D4 45.40N 0.10E
Angren Uzbekistan 102 C6 41.01N 70.10E
Anguilla i. Leeward Is. 71 L4 18.14N 63.05W
Angus d. Scotland 19 G1 56.45N 3.00W
Anhui d. China 103 L4 31.30N 116.45E
Ankara Turkey 57 K3 39.55N 32.50E
Anlaby England 15 G2 53.45N 0.27W
Annaba Algeria 84 E5 36.55N 7.47E
An Nafud des. Saudi Arabia 94 F4 28.40N 41.30E
An Najaf Iraq 94 F5 31.59N 44.19E
Annalee r. Rep. of Ire. 20 D4 54.08N 7.25W
Annalong N. Ireland 16 D2 54.06N 5.55W
Annan Scotland 17 F2 54.59N 3.16W
Annan r. Scotland 17 F3 54.58N 3.16W
Annapurna mtn. Nepal 97 G6 28.34N 83.50E
Ann Arbor U.S.A. 65 J5 42.18N 83.45W
An Naşirīyah Iraq 95 G5 31.04N 46.16E
An Nawfaliyah Libya 53 G3 30.47N 17.50E
Annecy France 44 G4 45.54N 6.07E
Ansbach Germany 48 E3 49.18N 10.36E
Anshan China 103 M6 41.05N 122.58E
Anshun China 103 J3 26.15N 105.51E
Anstruther Scotland 17 G4 56.14N 2.42W
Antakya Turkey 57 M2 36.12N 36.10E
Antalya Turkey 57 J2 36.53N 30.42E
Antalya, G. of Turkey 57 J2 36.38N 31.00E
Antananarivo Madagascar 86 D3 18.52S 47.30E
Antarctica 112
Antarctic Pen. f. Antarctica 116 F2 65.00S 64.00W
An Teallach mtn. Scotland 18 D2 57.48N 5.16W
Antequera Spain 46 C2 37.01N 4.34W
Antibes France 44 G3 43.35N 7.07E
Anticosti, Île d' Canada 63 L2 49.20N 63.00W
Antigua i. Leeward Is. 71 L4 17.09N 61.49W
Antigua and Barbuda Leeward Is. 71 L4 17.30N 61.49W
Antikythira i. Greece 56 F1 35.52N 23.18E
Antipodes Is. Pacific Oc. 108 M2 49.42S 178.50E
Antofagasta Chile 76 C2 23.40S 70.23W
Antrim N. Ireland 16 C2 54.43N 6.14W
Antrim d. N. Ireland 16 C2 54.45N 6.15W
Antrim Hills N. Ireland 16 C2 55.00N 6.10W
Antsirañana Madagascar 86 D3 12.19S 49.17E
Antwerpen Belgium 42 D3 51.13N 4.25E
Antwerpen d. Belgium 42 D3 51.16N 4.45E
Anxi China 102 H6 40.32N 95.57E
Anyang China 103 K5 36.04N 114.20E
Anzhero-Sudzhensk Russian Fed. 58 K3 56.10N 86.10E
Aomori Japan 106 D4 40.50N 140.43E
Aosta Italy 50 B6 45.43N 7.19E
Apa r. Brazil/Paraguay 77 E2 22.08S 57.55W
Apalachee B. U.S.A. 65 J2 29.30N 84.00W
Apaporis r. Colombia 76 D4 1.40S 69.20W
Aparri Phil. 105 G7 18.22N 121.40E
Apatity Russian Fed. 43 H4 67.32N 33.21E
Apeldoorn Neth. 42 E4 52.13N 5.57E
Apennines mts. Italy 50 D6 44.00N 11.00E
Aporé r. Brazil 77 E3 19.30S 50.55W
Appalachian Mts. U.S.A. 65 K4 39.30N 78.00W
Appleby-in-Westmorland England 15 E3 54.35N 2.29W
Appledore England 13 C3 51.03N 4.12W
Appleton U.S.A. 65 I5 44.16N 88.25W
Apucarana Brazil 77 E2 23.34S 51.28W
Apurimac r. Peru 76 C3 10.43S 73.55W
Aqaba Jordan 94 E4 29.32N 35.00E
Aqaba, G. of Asia 94 D4 28.45N 34.45E
Āra Ārba Ethiopia 87 C4 5.50N 41.30E
Arabia Asia 117 L2 25.00N 45.00E
Arabian Sea Asia 96 C4 19.00N 65.00E
Aracaju Brazil 77 G3 10.54S 37.07W
Araçatuba Brazil 77 E2 21.12S 50.24W
Aracena, Sierra de mts. Spain 46 B2 37.50N 7.00W

Arad Romania 54 G2....46.12N 21.19E
Arafura Sea Austa. 105 I2....9.00S 135.00E
Aragón r. Spain 46 E5....42.20N 1.45W
Araguaia r. Brazil 77 F4....5.30S 48.05W
Araguaína Brazil 77 F4....7.16S 48.18W
Araguari Brazil 77 F3....18.38S 48.13W
Arak Iran 95 G5....34.06N 49.44E
Arakan Yoma mts. Myanmar 97 I5....20.00N 94.00E
Aral Sea Asia 58 H2....45.00N 60.00E
Aralsk Kazakhstan 58 I2....46.56N 61.43E
Aranda de Duero Spain 46 D4....41.40N 3.41W
Aran I. Rep. of Ire. 20 C5....55.00N 8.32W
Aran Is. Rep. of Ire. 20 B3....53.07N 9.38W
Aranjuez Spain 46 D4....40.02N 3.37W
Arao Japan 106 B2....33.00N 130.26E
Arapiraca Brazil 77 G4....9.45S 36.40W
Arapkir Turkey 57 N3....39.03N 38.29E
Araraquara Brazil 77 F2....21.46S 48.08W
Ararat, Mt. Turkey 90 G7....39.45N 44.15E
Ârba Minch Ethiopia 87 B4....6.02N 37.33E
Arbil Iraq 94 F6....36.12N 44.01E
Arboga Sweden 43 C2....59.24N 15.51E
Arbroath Scotland 17 G4....56.34N 2.35W
Arcachon France 44 C4....44.40N 1.11W
Archangel Russian Fed. 58 G4....64.32N 41.10E
Arctic Bay town Canada 63 J5....73.05N 85.20W
Arctic Ocean 112
Arctic Red r. Canada 62 E4....67.26N 133.48W
Ardabil Iran 95 H7....38.15N 48.18E
Ardas r. Greece 56 H4....41.39N 26.30E
Ardèche r. France 44 F4....44.31N 4.40E
Ardennes mts. Belgium 42 E2....50.10N 5.30E
Ardestan Iran 95 H5....33.22N 52.25E
Ardglass N. Ireland 16 D2....54.16N 5.37W
Ardila r. Portugal 46 B3....38.10N 7.30W
Ardnamurchan, Pt. of Scotland 18 C1....56.44N 6.14W
Ardrishaig Scotland 16 D3....56.00N 5.26W
Ardrossan Scotland 16 E3....55.38N 4.49W
Ards Pen. N. Ireland 16 D2....54.30N 5.30W
Ardvasar Scotland 18 D2....57.03N 5.54W
Arena, Pt. U.S.A. 64 B4....38.58N 123.44W
Arendal Norway 43 B2....58.27N 8.56E
Arenig Fawr mtn. Wales 12 D4....52.55N 3.26W
Arequipa Peru 76 C3....16.25S 71.32W
Arezzo Italy 50 D5....43.27N 11.52E
Arganda Spain 46 D4....40.19N 3.26W
Argentan France 44 C6....48.45N 0.01W
Argentina S. America 75 C3....35.00S 65.00W
Argentino, L. Argentina 75 B1....50.15S 72.25W
Argenton France 44 D5....46.36N 1.30E
Argos Greece 56 F2....37.37N 22.45E
Argun r. Russian Fed. 103 M8....53.30N 121.48E
Argyle, L. Australia 110 B4....16.20S 128.14E
Argyll f. Scotland 16 D4....56.12N 5.15W
Argyll and Bute d. Scotland 16 D4....56.15N 5.30W
Århus Denmark 43 B2....56.10N 10.13E
Arica Chile 76 C3....18.30S 70.20W
Ariège r. France 44 D3....43.31N 1.25E
Arienas, Loch Scotland 16 D4....56.38N 5.45W
Arinos r. Brazil 77 E3....10.20S 57.35W
Aripuanã r. Brazil 77 D4....5.05S 60.30W
Ariquemes Brazil 77 D4....9.56S 63.04W
Arisaig Scotland 18 D1....56.55N 5.51W
Arisaig, Sd. of Scotland 18 D1....56.50N 5.50W
Arizona d. U.S.A. 64 D3....34.00N 112.00W
Arkaig, Loch Scotland 18 D1....56.59N 5.10W
Arkalyk Kazakhstan 102 B8....50.17N 66.51E
Arkansas d. U.S.A. 65 H4....35.00N 92.00W
Arkansas r. U.S.A. 65 H3....33.50N 91.00W
Arkansas City U.S.A. 64 G4....37.03N 97.02W
Arklow Rep. of Ire. 20 E2....52.47N 6.10W
Arles France 44 F3....43.41N 4.38E
Arlit Niger 84 E3....19.00N 7.35E
Arlon Belgium 42 E2....49.41N 5.49E
Armagh N. Ireland 16 C2....54.21N 6.40W
Armagh d. N. Ireland 16 C2....54.15N 6.45W
Armavir Russian Fed. 53 L5....44.59N 41.10E
Armenia Asia 58 G2....40.00N 45.00E
Armenia Colombia 74 B7....4.32N 75.40W
Armidale Australia 110 E2....30.32S 151.40E
Armoy N. Ireland 16 C3....55.08N 6.20W
Arnauti, C. Cyprus 57 K1....35.06N 32.17E
Arnhem Neth. 42 E3....52.00N 5.55E
Arnhem, C. Australia 110 C4....12.10S 137.00E
Arnhem Land f. Australia 110 C4....13.00S 132.30E
Arno r. Italy 50 D5....43.43N 10.17E
Ar Ramadi Iraq 94 F5....33.27N 43.19E
Arran i. Scotland 16 D3....55.35N 5.14W
Ar Raqqah Syria 94 E6....35.57N 39.03E
Arras France 44 E7....50.17N 2.46E
Arrecife Canary Is. 46 Z2....28.57N 13.32W
Ar Rimal f. Saudi Arabia 95 H3....22.00N 53.00E
Arrochar Scotland 16 E4....56.12N 4.44W
Ar Ruṭba Iraq 94 F5....33.03N 40.18E
Arta Greece 56 E3....39.10N 20.57E
Artigas Uruguay 77 E1....30.24S 56.28W
Artois f. France 42 B2....50.16N 2.50E
Aruba i. Neth. Ant. 71 J3....12.30N 70.00W
Aru Is. Indonesia 105 I2....6.00S 134.30E
Arunachal Pradesh d. India 97 I6....28.40N 94.60E
Arundel England 11 E1....50.52N 0.32W
Arusha Tanzania 86 B4....3.21S 36.40E
Aruwimi r. Zaire 86 B5....1.20N 23.26E
Arviat Canada 63 I4....61.10N 94.15W
Arvidsjaur Sweden 43 D4....65.37N 19.10E
Arvika Sweden 43 C2....59.41N 12.38E
Asahi-dake mtn. Japan 106 D4....43.42N 142.54E
Asahikawa Japan 106 D4....43.46N 142.23E
Asansol India 97 H5....23.40N 87.00E
Ascension I. Atlantic Oc. 82 B4....8.00S 14.00W
Ascoli Piceno Italy 50 E5....42.52N 13.36E
Åsele Sweden 43 D4....64.10N 17.20E
Ashbourne England 15 F2....53.02N 1.44W
Ashbourne Rep. of Ire. 20 E3....53.31N 6.25W
Ashburton Australia 110 A3....21.15S 115.00E
Ashburton England 13 D2....50.31N 3.45W
Ashby de la Zouch England 10 D3....52.45N 1.29W
Ashford England 11 F2....51.08N 0.53E
Ashgabat Turkmenistan 95 I6....37.58N 58.24E
Ashington England 15 F4....55.11N 1.34W
Ashland U.S.A. 65 H6....46.34N 90.45W
Ash Shiḩr Yemen 95 G1....14.45N 49.36E
Ashton-under-Lyne England 15 E2....53.30N 2.08W
Asia 90-91
Asilah Morocco 46 B1....35.32N 6.00W
Asinara, G. of Med. Sea 50 C4....41.00N 8.32E

Asir f. Saudi Arabia 94 F2....19.00N 42.00E
Askern England 15 F2....53.37N 1.09W
Askim Norway 43 B2....59.33N 11.20E
Asmara Eritrea 85 H3....15.20N 38.58E
Åsnen l. Sweden 43 C2....56.40N 14.50E
Aspang Markt Austria 54 E2....47.34N 16.06E
Aspatria England 14 D3....54.45N 3.20W
Assab Eritrea 85 I3....13.01N 42.47E
Assam d. India 97 I6....26.30N 93.00E
As Samawah Iraq 94 G5....31.18N 45.18E
As Sarir f. Libya 53 H2....27.00N 21.20E
Assen Neth. 42 E4....53.00N 6.34E
As Sidrah Libya 53 G3....30.31N 18.34E
Assiniboine, Mt. Canada 62 G3....50.51N 115.39W
As Sulaymaniyah Iraq 95 G6....35.32N 45.27E
As Sulayyil Saudi Arabia 95 G3....20.27N 45.34E
Assumption i. Indian Oc. 86 D4....9.30S 47.20E
As Suq Saudi Arabia 94 F3....21.55N 42.02E
Assynt, Loch Scotland 18 D3....58.11N 5.03W
Astara Azerbaijan 95 G6....38.27N 48.53E
Asti Italy 50 C6....44.54N 8.13E
Astorga Spain 46 B5....42.30N 6.02W
Astoria U.S.A. 64 B6....46.12N 123.50W
Astove i. Indian Oc. 86 D3....10.05S 47.40E
Astrakhan' Russian Fed. 58 G2....46.22N 48.00E
Asuncion i. N. Mariana Is. 105 L7....19.34N 145.24E
Asunción Paraguay 77 E2....25.15S 57.40W
Aswân Egypt 94 D3....24.05N 32.56E
Asyût Egypt 94 D4....27.14N 31.07E
Atacama Desert S. America 76 D2....20.00S 69.00W
Atafu Pacific Oc. 108 N6....8.40S 172.40W
Atâr Mauritania 84 C4....20.32N 13.08W
Atbara Sudan 85 H3....17.42N 34.00E
Atbara r. Sudan 85 H3....17.47N 34.00E
Ath Belgium 42 C2....50.38N 3.45E
Athabasca r. Canada 62 G3....58.30N 111.00W
Athabasca, L. Canada 62 H3....59.30N 109.00W
Athboy Rep. of Ire. 20 E3....53.37N 6.55W
Athenry Rep. of Ire. 20 C3....53.18N 8.45W
Athens Greece 56 F2....37.59N 23.42E
Atherstone England 10 D3....52.35N 1.32W
Athi r. Kenya 87 B2....2.59S 38.29E
Athi Plains f. Kenya 87 B2....1.30S 36.50E
Athi River town Kenya 87 B2....1.28S 36.58E
Athlone Rep. of Ire. 20 D3....53.26N 7.57W
Athos, Mt. Greece 56 G4....40.09N 24.19E
Athy Rep. of Ire. 20 E2....53.00N 7.00W
Ati Chad 85 F3....13.11N 18.20E
Atlanta U.S.A. 65 J3....33.45N 84.23W
Atlantic City U.S.A. 65 L4....39.23N 74.27W
Atlantic Ocean 116
Atlas Mts. Africa 82 C8....33.00N 4.00W
At Ţā'if Saudi Arabia 94 F3....21.15N 40.21E
Attleborough England 11 G3....52.31N 1.01E
Atui r. Cook Is. 108 P4....20.00S 158.07W
Atyrau Kazakhstan 58 H2....47.08N 51.59E
Aube r. France 44 E6....48.30N 3.37E
Auchterarder Scotland 17 F4....56.18N 3.43W
Auchtermuchty Scotland 17 F4....56.17N 3.15W
Auckland New Zealand 111 G2....36.52S 174.45E
Auckland Is. Pacific Oc. 108 L1....50.35S 166.00E
Audlem England 15 E1....52.59N 2.31W
Aughnacloy N. Ireland 16 C2....54.25N 6.58W
Aughton England 15 F2....53.22N 1.18W
Augsburg Germany 48 E3....48.21N 10.54E
Augusta Ga. U.S.A. 65 J3....33.29N 82.00W
Augusta Maine U.S.A. 65 M5....44.20N 69.50W
Aulnoye-Aymeries France 42 C2....50.12N 3.50E
Aurangabad India 96 F4....19.52N 75.22E
Aurich Germany 42 G5....53.28N 7.29E
Aurora Colo. U.S.A. 64 F4....39.44N 104.52W
Aurora Ill. U.S.A. 65 I5....41.45N 88.20W
Auskerry i. Scotland 19 G4....59.02N 2.34W
Austin U.S.A. 64 G3....30.18N 97.47W
Australia Austa. 110 B3....25.00S 135.00E
Australian Capital Territory d. Australia 110 D2....35.30S 149.00E
Austria Europe 54 C2....47.30N 14.00E
Auvergne f. France 44 E4....45.20N 2.40E
Auxerre France 44 E5....47.48N 3.35E
Avallon France 44 E5....47.30N 3.54E
Avanos Turkey 57 L3....38.44N 34.51E
Aveiro Portugal 46 A4....40.40N 8.35W
Avellino Italy 50 F4....40.55N 14.46E
Avesta Sweden 43 D3....60.09N 16.10E
Aveyron r. France 44 D4....44.05N 1.16E
Avezzano Italy 50 E5....42.03N 13.26E
Aviemore Scotland 19 F2....57.11N 3.51W
Avignon France 44 F3....43.56N 4.48E
Ávila Spain 46 C4....40.39N 4.42W
Avilés Spain 46 C5....43.33N 5.55W
Avon r. Bristol England 10 C2....51.30N 2.43W
Avon r. Dorset England 10 D1....50.43N 1.45W
Avon r. Glos. England 10 C2....52.00N 2.10W
Avon r. Scotland 19 F2....57.25N 3.23W
Avonmouth England 10 C2....51.30N 2.42W
Awara Plain f. Kenya 87 C3....3.45N 41.05E
Awata Shet' r. Ethiopia 87 B3....4.55N 39.25E
Awe, Loch Scotland 16 D4....56.18N 5.24W
Axe r. England 13 D2....50.42N 3.03W
Axel Heiberg I. Canada 63 I5....79.30N 90.00W
Axminster England 13 E2....50.47N 3.01W
Ayacucho Peru 76 C3....13.10S 74.15W
Ayaguz Kazakhstan 102 E7....47.59N 80.27E
Ayan Russian Fed. 59 P3....56.29N 138.00E
Aydın Turkey 57 H2....37.52N 27.50E
Ayers Rock mtn. Australia 110 C3....25.20S 131.01E
Aylesbury England 10 E2....51.48N 0.49W
Aylesham England 11 G2....51.14N 1.12E
Aylsham England 11 G3....52.48N 1.16E
Ayr Scotland 16 E3....55.28N 4.37W
Ayr r. Scotland 16 E3....55.28N 4.38W
Ayr, Pt. of Wales 12 D5....53.21N 3.20W
Ayre, Pt. of I.o.M. 14 C3....54.25N 4.22W
Ayutthaya Thailand 104 C6....14.25N 100.30E
Ayvalık Turkey 56 H3....39.19N 26.42E
Azerbaijan Asia 58 G2....40.10N 47.50E
Azogues Ecuador 76 C4....2.35S 78.00W
Azores is. Atlantic Oc. 82 A8....38.00N 28.00W
Azov, Sea of Ukraine 53 K6....46.00N 36.30E
Azrou Morocco 52 B3....33.27N 5.14W
Azuero Pen. Panama 71 H2....7.30N 80.30W
Azul, Cordillera mts. Peru 76 C4....9.00S 76.30W

B

Baardeere Somalia 87 C3....2.18N 42.18E
Bab al Mandab str. Asia 94 F1....13.00N 43.10E
Babar Is. Indonesia 105 H2....8.00S 129.30E
Babati Tanzania 87 B2....4.14S 35.45E
Babbacombe B. England 13 D2....50.30N 3.28W
Babia Gora mtn. Slovakia/Poland 54 F3....49.38N 19.38E
Babo Indonesia 105 I3....2.33S 133.25E
Baboua C.A.R. 84 F2....5.49N 14.51E
Babruysk Belarus 55 K5....53.08N 29.10E
Babuyan Is. Phil. 105 G7....19.20N 121.30E
Bacabal Brazil 77 F4....4.15S 44.45W
Bacan i. Indonesia 105 H3....0.30S 127.30E
Bacău Romania 55 J2....46.32N 26.59E
Back r. Canada 63 I4....66.37N 96.00W
Backwater Resr. Scotland 19 F1....56.45N 3.16W
Bac Liêu Vietnam 104 D5....9.17N 105.44E
Bacolod Phil. 105 G6....10.38N 122.58E
Badajoz Spain 46 B3....38.53N 6.58W
Badanah Saudi Arabia 94 F5....30.59N 41.02E
Baden-Baden Germany 48 D3....48.45N 8.15E
Bad Neuenahr-Ahrweiler Germany 42 G2....50.33N 7.08E
Badulla Sri Lanka 97 G2....6.59N 81.03E
Baffin B. Canada 63 L5....74.00N 70.00W
Baffin I. Canada 63 L4....68.50N 70.00W
Bafoussam Cameroon 84 F2....5.31N 10.25E
Bafq Iran 95 I5....31.35N 55.21E
Bafra Turkey 57 L4....41.34N 35.56E
Baft Iran 95 I4....29.12N 56.36E
Bagé Brazil 77 E1....31.22S 54.06W
Baggy Pt. England 13 C3....51.08N 4.15W
Baghdad Iraq 94 F5....33.20N 44.26E
Baghlan Afghan. 95 K6....36.11N 68.44E
Baguio Phil. 104 G7....16.25N 120.37E
Baharîya Oasis Egypt 94 C4....28.10N 29.00E
Bahawalpur Pakistan 96 E6....29.24N 71.47E
Bahia d. Brazil 77 F3....12.30S 42.30W
Bahía Blanca Argentina 75 C3....38.45S 62.15W
Bahrain Asia 95 H4....26.00N 50.35E
Baia Mare Romania 55 H2....47.40N 23.35E
Baicheng China 103 M7....45.40N 122.52E
Baie Comeau Canada 63 L2....49.12N 68.10W
Baie-du-Poste town Canada 63 K3....50.20N 73.30W
Baikal, L. Russian Fed. 59 M3....53.30N 108.00E
Bailieborough Rep. of Ire. 20 E3....53.55N 6.58W
Bain r. England 15 G2....53.04N 0.12W
Bairnsdale Australia 110 D2....37.51S 147.38E
Baiyuda Desert Sudan 94 D3....17.10N 32.30E
Baja Hungary 54 F2....46.12N 18.58E
Baja California Norte d. Mexico 70 B6....30.00N 115.00W
Baja California Sur d. Mexico 70 B6....26.00N 112.00W
Baker U.S.A. 64 C5....44.46N 117.50W
Baker, Mt. U.S.A. 64 B6....48.48N 121.10W
Baker I. Kiribati 108 N6....0.14N 176.28W
Baker L. Canada 63 I4....64.10N 95.30W
Baker Lake town Canada 63 I4....64.20N 96.10W
Bakersfield U.S.A. 64 C4....35.25N 119.00W
Bakharden Turkmenistan 95 I6....38.25N 57.24E
Bakırköy Turkey 57 I4....40.59N 28.52E
Bako Ethiopia 87 B4....5.50N 36.40E
Baku Azerbaijan 58 G2....40.22N 49.53E
Bala Wales 12 D4....52.54N 3.36W
Bala, Cerros de mts. Bolivia 76 D3....14.00S 68.00W
Balabac Str. Malaysia/Phil. 104 F5....7.30N 117.00E
Bala L. Wales 12 D4....52.53N 3.38W
Bala Morghab Afghan. 95 J6....35.34N 63.20E
Balaton Hungary 54 E2....46.55N 17.50E
Balbina Reser. Brazil 77 E4....1.30S 60.00W
Balbriggan Rep. of Ire. 20 E3....53.36N 6.12W
Baldock England 11 E2....51.59N 0.11W
Balearic Is. Spain 46 G3....39.30N 2.30E
Baleia, Punta da c. Brazil 77 G3....17.41S 39.07W
Baleine r. Canada 63 L3....58.00N 67.50W
Baleshwar India 97 H5....21.31N 86.59E
Bali i. Indonesia 104 F2....8.30S 115.05E
Balige Indonesia 104 B4....2.20N 99.01E
Balıkesir Turkey 57 H3....39.38N 27.51E
Balikpapan Indonesia 104 F3....1.15S 116.50E
Balimo P.N.G. 105 K2....7.55S 143.20E
Balintore Scotland 19 F2....57.45N 3.55W
Bali Sea Indonesia 104 F2....7.30S 115.15E
Balkan Mts. Bulgaria 56 G5....42.50N 24.30E
Balkhash Kazakhstan 102 D7....46.51N 75.00E
Balkhash, L. Kazakhstan 102 D7....46.40N 75.00E
Ballachulish Scotland 16 D4....56.40N 5.08W
Ballagan Pt. Rep. of Ire. 16 C1....54.00N 6.07W
Ballantrae Scotland 16 E3....55.06N 5.01W
Ballarat Australia 110 D2....37.36S 143.58E
Ballater Scotland 19 F2....57.03N 3.04W
Ballena, Punta c. Chile 76 C2....22.50S 70.48W
Ballina Rep. of Ire. 20 B4....54.08N 9.10W
Ballinasloe Rep. of Ire. 20 C3....53.20N 8.15W
Ballybay Rep. of Ire. 16 C2....54.08N 6.56W
Ballybofey Rep. of Ire. 16 B2....54.47N 7.48W
Ballybunnion Rep. of Ire. 20 B2....52.36N 9.40W
Ballycastle N. Ireland 16 C3....55.12N 6.16W
Ballyclare N. Ireland 16 C2....54.45N 6.00W
Ballyhaunis Rep. of Ire. 20 C3....53.46N 8.46W
Ballymena N. Ireland 16 C2....54.52N 6.17W
Ballymoney N. Ireland 16 C3....55.04N 6.32W
Ballynahinch N. Ireland 16 D2....54.24N 5.54W
Ballyquintin Pt. N. Ireland 16 D2....54.20N 5.30W
Ballyshannon Rep. of Ire. 20 C4....54.30N 8.11W
Balochistan f. Pakistan 96 D6....29.00N 66.00E
Balsas r. Mexico 70 D4....18.10N 102.05W
Bălţi Moldova 55 J2....47.45N 27.59E
Baltic Sea Europe 43 D1....56.30N 19.00E
Baltimore U.S.A. 65 K4....39.18N 76.38W
Baltiysk Russian Fed. 54 F6....54.41N 19.59E
Bam Iran 95 I4....29.07N 58.20E
Bamako Mali 84 B3....12.40N 7.59W
Bamberg Germany 48 E3....49.54N 10.53E
Bamian Afghan. 95 K5....34.52N 67.45E
Bampton Devon England 13 D2....51.00N 3.29W
Bampton Oxon. England 10 D2....51.44N 1.33W
Banaba i. Kiribati 108 M6....0.52S 169.35E
Banagher Rep. of Ire. 20 D3....53.11N 7.58W
Bananal, Ilha do f. Brazil 77 E3....11.30S 50.15W
Banbridge N. Ireland 16 C2....54.21N 6.16W
Banbury England 10 D3....52.04N 1.21W
Banchory Scotland 19 G2....57.04N 2.28W
Banco Chinchorro is. Mexico 70 G4....18.30N 87.20W
Banda Aceh Indonesia 104 B5....5.35N 95.20E

Banda Is. Indonesia 105 H3....4.30S 129.55E
Bandar-e' Abbas Iran 95 H4....27.10N 56.15E
Bandar-e Anzali Iran 95 G6....37.26N 49.29E
Bandar-e Lengeh Iran 95 H4....26.34N 54.53E
Bandar-e Torkeman Iran 95 H6....36.55N 54.05E
Bandar Seri Begawan Brunei 104 E4....4.56N 114.58E
Banda Sea Indonesia 105 H2....5.00S 128.00E
Bandeiras mtn. Brazil 77 F2....20.25S 41.45W
Banderas B. Mexico 70 C5....20.27N 105.30W
Bandırma Turkey 57 H4....40.22N 28.00E
Bandon Rep. of Ire. 20 C1....51.45N 8.45W
Bandon r. Rep. of Ire. 20 C1....51.43N 8.38W
Bandundu Zaire 86 A4....3.20S 17.24E
Bandung Indonesia 104 D2....6.57S 107.34E
Banff Canada 64 C7....51.10N 115.34W
Banff Scotland 19 G2....57.40N 2.31W
Bangalore India 96 F3....12.58N 77.35E
Bangassou C.A.R. 85 G2....4.41N 22.48E
Banggai Is. Indonesia 105 G3....1.30S 123.10E
Banghazi Libya 85 G5....32.07N 20.05E
Bangka i. Indonesia 104 D3....2.20S 106.10E
Bangkok Thailand 104 C6....13.45N 100.35E
Bangladesh Asia 97 H5....24.00N 90.00E
Bangor N. Ireland 16 D2....54.39N 5.41W
Bangor U.S.A. 65 M5....44.49N 68.47W
Bangor Wales 12 C5....53.13N 4.09W
Bangui C.A.R. 85 F2....4.23N 18.37E
Bangweulu, L. Zambia 86 B3....11.15S 29.45E
Ban Hat Yai Thailand 104 C5....7.00N 100.28E
Bani r. Mali 82 C6....14.30N 4.15W
Bani Walid Libya 53 F3....31.43N 14.01E
Banja Luka Bosnia. 56 C6....44.47N 17.10E
Banjarmasin Indonesia 104 E3....3.22S 114.36E
Banjul The Gambia 84 C3....13.28N 16.39W
Banks I. Canada 62 E5....73.00N 122.00W
Banks Is. Vanuatu 111 F4....13.50S 167.30E
Banmi Pakistan 95 L5....32.59N 70.38E
Bann r. N. Ireland 16 C3....55.10N 6.47W
Banská Bystrica Slovakia 54 F3....48.44N 19.07E
Bantry Rep. of Ire. 20 B1....51.41N 9.27W
Bantry B. Rep. of Ire. 20 B1....51.45N 9.48W
Baoding China 103 L5....38.54N 115.26E
Baoji China 103 J4....34.23N 107.16E
Baoshan China 103 H3....25.07N 99.08E
Baotou China 103 J6....40.38N 109.59E
Ba'qubah Iraq 94 F5....33.45N 44.38E
Baquerizo Moreno Galapagos Is. 76 B4....0.54S 89.37W
Bar Yugo. 56 D5....42.05N 19.06E
Bara Sudan 94 D1....13.42N 30.22E
Baranavichi Belarus 55 I5....53.09N 26.00E
Barbacena Brazil 77 F2....21.13S 43.47W
Barbados Lesser Antilles 71 M3....13.20N 59.40W
Barbuda i. Leeward Is. 71 L4....17.41N 61.48W
Barcaldine Australia 110 D3....23.31S 145.15E
Barcelona Spain 46 G4....41.25N 2.10E
Barcelona Venezuela 71 L3....10.08N 64.43W
Barcelos Brazil 76 D4....0.59S 62.58W
Bárðarbunga mtn. Iceland 43 Y2....64.38N 17.34W
Bardney England 15 G2....53.13N 0.19W
Bardsey i. Wales 12 C4....52.45N 4.48W
Bardsey Sd. Wales 12 C4....52.45N 4.48W
Bareilly India 97 F6....28.20N 79.24E
Barents Sea Arctic Oc. 58 F5....73.00N 40.00E
Barham England 11 G2....51.12N 1.07E
Bari Italy 50 G4....41.08N 16.52E
Barikot Afghan. 95 L6....35.18N 71.36E
Barinas Venezuela 71 J2....8.36N 70.15W
Baringo, L. Kenya 87 B3....0.35N 36.04E
Barisan Range mts. Indonesia 104 C3....3.30S 102.30E
Barkly Tableland f. Australia 110 C4....19.00S 136.40E
Bârlad Romania 55 J2....46.14N 27.40E
Barlee, L. Australia 110 A3....29.30S 119.30E
Barletta Italy 50 G4....41.20N 16.15E
Barmer India 96 E5....25.45N 71.23E
Barmouth Wales 12 C4....52.44N 4.03W
Barmouth B. Wales 12 C4....52.42N 4.05W
Barnard Castle town England 15 F3....54.33N 1.55W
Barnaul Russian Fed. 58 K3....53.21N 83.15E
Barnet England 11 E2....51.39N 0.11W
Barnoldswick England 15 E2....53.55N 2.11W
Barnsley England 15 F2....53.33N 1.29W
Barnstaple England 13 C3....51.05N 4.03W
Barnstaple B. England 13 C3....51.04N 4.20W
Barquisimeto Venezuela 71 K3....10.03N 69.18W
Barra i. Scotland 18 B1....56.59N 7.28W
Barra, Sd. of Scotland 18 B2....57.03N 7.25W
Barra do Corda Brazil 77 F4....5.30S 45.15W
Barranquilla Colombia 71 J3....11.00N 74.50W
Barretos Brazil 77 F2....20.37S 48.38W
Barrhead Scotland 16 E3....55.47N 4.24W
Barrow r. Rep. of Ire. 20 D2....52.17N 7.00W
Barrow U.S.A. 62 C5....71.16N 156.50W
Barrow, Pt. U.S.A. 62 C5....71.30N 156.00W
Barrow I. Australia 110 A3....20.40S 115.27E
Barrow-in-Furness England 14 D3....54.08N 3.15W
Barry Wales 13 D3....51.23N 3.19W
Barstow U.S.A. 64 C3....34.55N 117.01W
Bartın Turkey 57 K4....41.37N 32.20E
Barton-upon-Humber England 15 G2....53.41N 0.27W
Bartoszyce Poland 54 G6....54.16N 20.49E
Baru mtn. Panama 71 H2....8.48N 82.33W
Baruun Urt Mongolia 103 K7....46.48N 113.18E
Barysaw Belarus 55 K6....54.09N 28.30E
Baschurch England 10 C3....52.48N 2.51W
Basel Switz. 44 G5....47.33N 7.36E
Basilan i. Phil. 105 G5....6.40N 122.10E
Basildon England 11 F2....51.34N 0.25E
Basingstoke England 10 D2....51.15N 1.05W
Bassein Myanmar 97 I4....16.45N 94.30E
Bassenthwaite L. England 14 D3....54.40N 3.13W
Bass Rock i. Scotland 17 G4....56.05N 2.38W
Bass Str. Australia 110 D2....39.45S 146.00E
Bastak Iran 95 H4....27.15N 54.26E
Bastia France 44 H3....42.41N 9.26E
Bastogne Belgium 42 E2....50.00N 5.43E
Bata Equat. Guinea 84 E2....1.51N 9.49E
Batabanó, G. of Cuba 71 H5....23.15N 82.30W
Batang China 103 H3....30.02N 99.01E
Batangas Phil. 105 G6....13.46N 121.01E
Batan Is. Phil. 105 G8....20.50N 121.55E
Batdâmbâng Cambodia 104 C6....13.06N 103.13E
Bath England 10 C2....51.22N 2.22W
Bath and North East Somerset d. England 10 C2....51.20N 2.30W
Bathgate Scotland 17 F3....55.55N 3.38W
Bathurst Australia 110 D2....33.27S 149.35E

Bathurst Canada 63 L2............47.37N 65.40W
Bathurst I. Australia 110 C4.....11.45S 130.15E
Bathurst I. Canada 63 H5.........76.00N 100.00W
Bathurst Inlet town Canada 62 H4...66.48N 108.00W
Batley England 15 F2.............53.43N 1.38W
Batna Algeria 84 E5..............35.34N 6.11E
Baton Rouge U.S.A. 65 H3.........30.30N 91.10W
Batticaloa Sri Lanka 97 G2.......7.43N 81.42E
Battle England 11 F1.............50.55N 0.30E
Batu Is. Indonesia 104 B3........0.30S 98.20E
Batumi Georgia 58 G2.............41.37N 41.36E
Baubau Indonesia 105 G2..........5.30S 122.37E
Bauchi Nigeria 84 E3.............10.16N 9.50E
Bauru Brazil 77 F2...............22.19S 49.07W
Bawean i. Indonesia 104 E2.......5.50S 112.35E
Bawiti Egypt 94 C4...............28.21N 28.51E
Bayamo Cuba 71 I5................20.23N 76.39W
Bayanhongor Mongolia 103 I7......46.42N 100.09E
Bayburt Turkey 57 O4.............40.15N 40.16E
Bay City U.S.A. 65 J5............43.35N 83.52W
Baydaratskaya B. Russian Fed. 58 I4...70.00N 66.00E
Bayonne France 44 C3.............43.30N 1.28W
Bayreuth Germany 48 E3...........49.56N 11.35E
Bayy al Kabir, Wadi r. Libya 53 G3...31.20N 16.00E
Baza Spain 46 D2.................37.30N 2.45W
Beachy Head England 11 F1........50.43N 0.15E
Beaconsfield England 10 E2.......51.37N 0.39W
Beaminster England 10 C1.........50.48N 2.44W
Bear I. Norway 58 D5.............74.30N 19.00E
Beata, C. Dom. Rep. 71 J4........17.41N 71.24W
Beata I. Dom. Rep. 71 J4.........17.38N 71.29W
Beaufort Sea N. America 62 D5....72.00N 141.00W
Beaufort West R.S.A. 86 B1.......32.20S 22.34E
Beauly Scotland 19 E2............57.29N 4.28W
Beauly Firth est. Scotland 19 E2...57.29N 4.20W
Beaumaris Wales 12 C5............53.16N 4.07W
Beaumont U.S.A. 65 H3............30.04N 94.06W
Beaune France 44 F5.............47.02N 4.50E
Beauvais France 44 E6............49.26N 2.05E
Beaver r. Canada 62 H3...........55.25N 107.45W
Beaver Creek town Canada 62 D4...62.20N 140.45W
Bebington England 14 E2..........53.23N 2.58W
Beccles England 11 G3............52.27N 1.33E
Béchar Algeria 84 D5.............31.35N 2.17W
Beckingham England 15 G2.........53.23N 0.50W
Bedale England 15 F3.............54.18N 1.35W
Bedele Ethiopia 85 H2............8.29N 36.19E
Bedford England 11 E3............52.08N 0.29W
Bedford Level f. England 11 E3...52.30N 0.06W
Bedfordshire d. England 11 E3....52.04N 0.28W
Bedlington England 15 F4.........55.08N 1.34W
Bedworth England 10 D3...........52.28N 1.29W
Beersheba Israel 94 D5...........31.15N 34.47E
Beeville U.S.A. 64 G2............28.25N 97.47W
Bei'an China 103 N7..............48.17N 126.33E
Beihai China 103 J2..............21.29N 109.10E
Beijing China 103 L5.............39.55N 116.25E
Beinn an Oir mtn. Scotland 16 C3...55.55N 6.00W
Beinn Dearg mtn. High. Scotland 18 E2...57.49N 4.55W
Beinn Dearg mtn. P. and K. Scotland 19 F1
..........................56.52N 3.54W
Beinn Heasgarnich mtn. Scotland 16 E4...56.31N 4.34W
Beira Mozambique 86 C3...........19.49S 34.52E
Beirut Lebanon 94 E5.............33.52N 35.30E
Beith Scotland 16 E3.............55.45N 4.37W
Beiuş Romania 54 H2..............46.40N 22.21E
Beja Portugal 46 B3..............38.01N 7.52W
Bejaïa Algeria 84 E5.............36.45N 5.05E
Béjar Spain 46 C4................40.24N 5.45W
Békéscsaba Hungary 54 G2.........46.41N 21.06E
Bela Pakistan 96 D6..............26.12N 66.20E
Belarus Europe 55 J5.............53.00N 28.00E
Belcher Is. Canada 63 K3.........56.00N 79.00W
Belém Brazil 77 F4...............1.27S 48.29W
Belen U.S.A. 64 E3...............34.39N 106.48W
Belfast N. Ireland 16 D2.........54.36N 5.57W
Belfast Lough N. Ireland 16 D2...54.41N 5.49W
Belford England 15 F4............55.36N 1.48W
Belgium Europe 42 D2.............51.00N 4.30E
Belgorod Russian Fed. 55 O4......50.38N 36.36E
Belgrade Yugo. 56 E6.............44.49N 20.28E
Belikh r. Syria 57 N1............35.58N 39.05E
Belitung i. Indonesia 104 D3.....3.00S 108.00E
Belize Belize 70 G4..............17.29N 88.20W
Belize C. America 70 G4..........17.00N 88.30W
Bellac France 44 D5..............46.07N 1.04E
Bellary India 96 F4..............15.11N 76.54E
Belle-Île France 44 B5...........47.20N 3.10W
Belle Isle, Str. of Canada 63 M3...50.45N 58.00W
Bellingham England 15 E4.........55.09N 2.15W
Bellingham U.S.A. 64 B6..........48.45N 122.29W
Bellingshausen Sea Antarctica 112...70.00S 88.00W
Bellinzona Switz. 44 H5..........46.11N 9.02E
Bello Colombia 71 I2.............6.20N 75.41W
Belmopan Belize 70 G4............17.25N 88.46W
Belmullet Rep. of Ire. 20 A4.....54.13N 10.00W
Belo Horizonte Brazil 77 F3......19.45S 43.53W
Belorechensk Russian Fed. 57 N4...44.46N 39.54E
Belper England 15 F2.............53.02N 1.29W
Belukha, Mt. Russian Fed. 58 K2...49.46N 86.40E
Belyy Russian Fed. 55 M6.........55.49N 32.58E
Bembridge England 10 D1..........50.41N 1.04W
Bemidji U.S.A. 65 H6.............47.29N 94.52W
Ben Alder mtn. Scotland 19 E1....56.49N 4.28W
Benavente Spain 46 C4............42.00N 5.40W
Benbane Head N. Ireland 16 C3....55.15N 6.29W
Benbecula i. Scotland 18 B2......57.26N 7.18W
Ben Cruachan mtn. Scotland 16 D4...56.26N 5.08W
Bend U.S.A. 64 B5................44.04N 121.20W
Bendigo Australia 110 D2.........36.48S 144.21E
Bengal, B. of Indian Oc. 97 H4...17.00N 89.00E
Bengbu China 103 L4.............32.56N 117.27E
Bengkulu Indonesia 104 C3........3.46S 102.16E
Benguela Angola 86 A3............12.34S 13.24E
Ben Hope mtn. Scotland 19 E3.....58.24N 4.36W
Beni r. Bolivia 76 D3............10.30S 66.00W
Benidorm Spain 46 E3.............38.33N 0.09W
Beni Mellal Morocco 84 D5........32.21N 6.21W
Benin Africa 84 E2...............9.00N 2.30E
Benin, Bight of Africa 84 E2.....5.30N 3.00E
Benin City Nigeria 84 E2.........6.19N 5.41E
Beni-Saf Algeria 52 E4...........35.19N 1.23W
Beni Suef Egypt 94 D4............29.05N 31.05E
Ben Klibreck mtn. Scotland 19 E3...58.15N 4.22W
Ben Lawers mtn. Scotland 16 E4...56.33N 4.14W

Ben Lomond mtn. Scotland 16 E4...56.12N 4.38W
Ben Loyal mtn. Scotland 19 E3....58.24N 4.26W
Ben Lui mtn. Scotland 16 E4......56.23N 4.49W
Ben Macdhui mtn. Scotland 19 F2...57.04N 3.40W
Ben More mtn. A. and B. Scotland 16 C4...56.26N 6.02W
Ben More mtn. Stirling Scotland 16 E4...56.23N 4.31W
Ben More Assynt mtn. Scotland 18 E3...58.07N 4.52W
Ben Nevis mtn. Scotland 18 D1....56.48N 5.00W
Bentley England 15 F2............53.31N 1.09W
Benue r. Nigeria 84 E2...........7.52N 6.45E
Ben Vorlich mtn. Scotland 16 E4...56.21N 4.13W
Ben Wyvis mtn. Scotland 19 E2....57.40N 4.35W
Benxi China 103 M6..............41.21N 123.45E
Berat Albania 56 D5.............40.42N 19.59E
Berau G. Indonesia 105 I3........2.20S 133.00E
Berber Sudan 94 D2..............18.01N 33.59E
Berbera Somalia 85 I3...........10.28N 45.02E
Berberati C.A.R. 86 A5..........4.19N 15.51E
Berdyans'k Ukraine 55 O2.........46.45N 36.47E
Berdychiv Ukraine 55 K3.........49.54N 28.39E
Berens River town Canada 62 I3...52.22N 97.00W
Berezivka Ukraine 55 L2.........47.12N 30.56E
Berezniki Russian Fed. 58 H3....59.26N 56.49E
Bergamo Italy 50 C6.............45.42N 9.40E
Bergen Norway 43 A3.............60.23N 5.20E
Bergerac France 44 D4...........44.50N 0.29E
Bergisch Gladbach Germany 48 C4...50.59N 7.10E
Bering Sea N. America/Asia 60 A7...60.00N 170.00E
Bering Str. Russian Fed./U.S.A. 59 U4
..........................65.00N 170.00W
Berkel r. Neth. 42 F4...........52.10N 6.12E
Berkeley England 10 C2..........51.42N 2.27W
Berkner I. Antarctica 112.......79.30S 50.00W
Berkshire d. England 10 D2......51.25N 1.03W
Berkshire Downs hills England 10 D2...51.30N 1.15W
Berlin Germany 48 F5............52.32N 13.25E
Bermejo r. Argentina 77 E2......26.47S 58.30W
Bermuda i. Atlantic Oc. 71 L7...32.18N 65.00W
Berne Switz. 44 G5..............46.57N 7.26E
Berneray i. W.Isles Scotland 18 B1...56.47N 7.38W
Berneray i. W.Isles Scotland 18 B2...57.43N 7.11W
Bernina Pass Switz. 50 D7.......46.25N 10.02E
Berry Head England 13 D2........50.24N 3.28W
Beru i. Kiribati 108 M6.........1.15S 176.00E
Berwick-upon-Tweed England 17 G3...55.46N 2.00W
Besançon France 44 G5...........47.14N 6.02E
Bessbrook N. Ireland 16 C2......54.12N 6.25W
Betanzos Spain 46 A5............43.17N 8.13W
Bethel U.S.A. 62 B4.............60.48N 161.46W
Bethesda Wales 12 C5............53.11N 4.03W
Béthune France 42 B2............50.32N 2.38E
Betsiboka r. Madagascar 86 D3...16.03S 46.36E
Betws-y-Coed Wales 12 D5........53.05N 3.48W
Beult r. England 11 F2..........51.13N 0.26E
Beverley England 15 G2..........53.52N 0.26W
Bewdley England 10 C3...........52.23N 2.19W
Bewl Water r. England 11 F2.....51.02N 0.22E
Bexhill England 11 F1...........50.51N 0.29E
Beykoz Turkey 57 I4.............41.09N 29.06E
Beyla Guinea 84 D2..............8.42N 8.39W
Beypazarı Turkey 57 J4..........40.10N 31.56E
Beyşehir L. Turkey 57 J2........37.47N 31.30E
Béziers France 44 E3............43.21N 3.13E
Bhagalpur India 97 H6...........25.14N 86.59E
Bhamo Myanmar 97 J5.............24.15N 97.15E
Bhavnagar India 96 E5...........21.46N 72.14E
Bhima r. India 96 F4............16.30N 77.10E
Bhopal India 97 F5..............23.17N 77.28E
Bhubaneshwar India 97 H5........20.15N 85.50E
Bhuj India 96 D5................23.12N 69.54E
Bhutan Asia 97 I6...............27.25N 90.00E
Biaban f. Iran 95 I4............26.00N 57.40E
Biak Indonesia 105 J3...........1.10S 136.05E
Biak i. Indonesia 105 J3........0.55S 136.00E
Biała Podlaska Poland 54 H5.....52.02N 23.06E
Białystok Poland 54 H5..........53.09N 23.10E
Biarritz France 44 C3...........43.29N 1.33W
Bibai Japan 106 D4..............43.21N 141.53E
Biberach Germany 48 D3..........48.06N 9.48E
Bicester England 10 D2..........51.53N 1.09W
Bidar India 96 F4...............17.54N 77.33E
Biddulph England 15 E2..........53.08N 2.11W
Bidean nam Bian mtn. Scotland 16 D4...56.39N 5.00W
Bideford England 13 C3..........51.01N 4.13W
Bideford Bay England 13 C3......51.04N 4.20W
Biel Switz. 44 G5...............47.09N 7.16E
Bielefeld Germany 48 D5.........52.02N 8.32E
Biella Italy 50 C6..............45.34N 8.03E
Bielsko-Biała Poland 54 F3......49.49N 19.02E
Bié Plateau f. Angola 82 E3.....13.00S 16.00E
Bifoun Gabon 84 E1..............0.20S 10.25E
Biga Turkey 56 H4...............40.13N 27.14E
Bigbury B. England 13 D2........50.15N 3.56W
Biggar Scotland 17 F3...........55.38N 3.31W
Biggleswade England 11 E3.......52.06N 0.16W
Big Hole r. U.S.A. 64 D6........45.52N 111.30W
Bighorn r. U.S.A. 64 E5.........46.05N 107.20W
Bighorn Mts. U.S.A. 64 E5.......44.00N 107.30W
Big Spring town U.S.A. 64 F3....32.15N 101.30W
Big Trout Lake town Canada 63 J3...53.45N 90.00W
Bihać Bosnia. 56 B6.............44.49N 15.53E
Bihar d. India 97 H5............24.15N 86.00E
Bijapur India 96 F4.............16.52N 75.47E
Bijar Iran 95 G5................35.52N 47.39E
Bikaner India 96 E6.............28.01N 73.22E
Bilaspur India 97 G5............22.03N 82.12E
Bilbao Spain 46 D5..............43.15N 2.56W
Bilecik Turkey 57 I4............40.10N 29.59E
Bilhorod-Dnistrovs'kyy Ukraine 55 L1...46.10N 30.19E
Billericay England 11 F2........51.38N 0.25E
Billingham England 15 F3........54.36N 1.18W
Billinge England 15 G2..........53.05N 0.18W
Billings U.S.A. 64 E6...........45.47N 108.30W
Billingshurst England 11 E2.....51.02N 0.28W
Bill of Portland c. England 10 C1...50.31N 2.27W
Biloxi U.S.A. 65 I3.............30.30N 88.53W
Bilston Scotland 17 F3..........55.53N 3.09W
Bilton England 15 G2............53.46N 0.13W
Bimini Is. The Bahamas 71 I6....25.44N 79.15W
Bindura Zimbabwe 86 C3..........17.18S 31.20E
Bingham England 10 D3...........52.57N 0.55W
Binghamton U.S.A. 65 K5.........42.06N 75.55W
Bingley England 15 F2...........53.51N 1.50W
Bintulu Malaysia 104 E4.........3.12N 113.01E
Bioco i. Equat. Guinea 84 E2....3.25N 8.45E

Birao C.A.R. 94 B1..............10.17N 22.47E
Birecik Turkey 57 N2............37.03N 37.59E
Birhan mtn. Ethiopia 85 H3......11.00N 37.50E
Birjand Iran 95 I5..............32.54N 59.10E
Birkenhead England 14 D2........53.24N 3.01W
Birmingham England 10 D3........52.30N 1.55W
Birmingham U.S.A. 65 I3.........33.30N 86.55W
Bîr Mogreïn Mauritania 84 C4....25.10N 11.35W
Birnin Konni Niger 84 E3........13.49N 5.19E
Birobidzhan Russian Fed. 103 O7...48.49N 132.54E
Birr Rep. of Ire. 20 D3.........53.06N 7.56W
Birstall England 10 D3..........52.42N 1.06W
Biržai Lithuania 55 I7..........56.10N 24.48E
Biscay, B. of France 44 B4......45.30N 3.00W
Bishkek Kyrgyzstan 102 C6.......42.53N 74.46E
Bisho R.S.A. 86 B1..............32.50S 27.30E
Bishop Auckland England 15 F3...54.40N 1.40W
Bishop's Lydeard England 13 D3...51.04N 3.12W
Bishop's Stortford England 11 F2...51.53N 0.09E
Bishop's Waltham England 10 D1...50.57N 1.13W
Bisina, L. Uganda 87 A3.........1.40N 34.00E
Biskra Algeria 84 E5............34.48N 5.40E
Bismarck U.S.A. 64 F6...........46.50N 100.48W
Bismarck Sea Pacific Oc. 110 D5...4.00S 146.30E
Bissau Guinea Bissau 84 C3......11.52N 15.39W
Bistriţa Romania 55 I2..........47.08N 24.30E
Bistriţa r. Romania 55 J2.......46.30N 26.54E
Bitburg Germany 42 F1...........49.58N 6.31E
Bitola Macedonia 56 E5..........41.02N 21.21E
Bitterroot Range U.S.A. 64 D6...47.06N 115.00W
Biwa-ko l. Japan 106 C3.........35.20N 136.10E
Biysk Russian Fed. 58 K3........52.35N 85.16E
Bizerte Tunisia 84 F5...........37.17N 9.51E
Black r. U.S.A. 65 H4...........35.30N 91.20W
Blackburn England 15 E2.........53.44N 2.30W
Black Combe mtn. England 14 D3...54.15N 3.20W
Blackfield England 10 D1........50.49N 1.22W
Black Forest f. Germany 48 D3...48.00N 8.00E
Black Head England 13 B2........49.59N 5.05W
Black Hill England 15 F2........53.30N 1.53W
Black Isle f. Scotland 19 E2....57.35N 4.15W
Blackpool England 14 D2.........53.48N 3.03W
Black Sea Europe 57 L5..........43.00N 35.00E
Blacksod B. Rep. of Ire. 20 A4...54.04N 10.00W
Black Volta r. Ghana 84 D2......8.14N 2.11W
Blackwater r. England 11 F2.....51.43N 0.42E
Blackwater r. Meath Rep. of Ire. 20 E3...53.39N 6.42W
Blackwater r. Waterford Rep. of Ire. 20 D1
..........................51.58N 7.52W
Blackwood Wales 12 D3...........51.38N 3.13W
Blaenau Ffestiniog Wales 12 D3...53.00N 3.57W
Blaenau Gwent d. Wales 12 D3....51.45N 3.10W
Blaenavon Wales 12 D3...........51.46N 3.05W
Blagdon England 10 C2...........51.20N 2.43W
Blagoevgrad Bulgaria 56 F5......42.02N 23.04E
Blagoveshchensk Russian Fed. 59 O3
..........................50.19N 127.30E
Blair Atholl Scotland 19 F1.....56.48N 3.50W
Blairgowrie Scotland 17 F4......56.36N 3.21W
Blanc, Mont mtn. Europe 44 G4...45.50N 6.52E
Blanca, Bahía b. Argentina 75 C3...39.15S 61.00W
Blanche, L. Australia 110 C3....29.15S 139.40E
Blanco, C. U.S.A. 64 B5.........42.50N 124.29W
Blandford Forum England 10 C1...50.52N 2.10W
Blanquilla i. Venezuela 71 L3...11.53N 64.38W
Blantyre Malawi 86 C3...........15.46S 35.00E
Blarney Rep. of Ire. 20 C1......51.56N 8.34W
Blaven mtn. Scotland 18 C2......57.13N 6.05W
Bletchley England 10 E2.........51.59N 0.45W
Blida Algeria 84 E5.............36.30N 2.50E
Bloemfontein R.S.A. 86 B2.......29.07S 26.14E
Blois France 44 D5..............47.36N 1.20E
Bloody Foreland c. Rep. of Ire. 20 C5...55.09N 8.17W
Bloomington U.S.A. 65 I5........40.29N 89.00W
Bluefield U.S.A. 65 J4..........37.14N 81.17W
Blue Mts. U.S.A. 64 C6..........45.00N 118.00W
Blue Nile r. Sudan 85 H3........15.45N 32.25E
Blue Stack Mts. Rep. of Ire. 20 C4...54.44N 8.09W
Blumenau Brazil 77 F2...........26.55S 49.07W
Blyth Northum. England 15 F4....55.07N 1.29W
Blyth Notts. England 15 F2......53.21N 1.03W
Bo Sierra Leone 84 C2...........7.58N 11.45W
Boa Vista Brazil 77 D5..........2.51N 60.43W
Boa Vista i. Cape Verde 84 B3...16.00N 22.55W
Bobo-Dioulasso Burkina 84 D3....11.11N 4.18W
Bóbr r. Poland 54 D4............52.04N 15.04E
Bocholt Germany 48 C4...........51.49N 6.37E
Boda C.A.R. 85 E2...............4.19N 17.26E
Boddam Scotland 19 H2...........57.28N 1.48W
Bodélé Depression f. Chad 85 F3...16.50N 17.10E
Boden Sweden 43 E4..............65.50N 21.44E
Bodenham England 10 C3..........52.09N 2.41W
Bodensee l. Europe 48 D2........47.40N 9.30E
Bodmin England 13 C2............50.28N 4.44W
Bodmin Moor England 13 C2.......50.35N 4.35W
Bodø Norway 43 C4...............67.18N 14.26E
Bodoquena, Serra de mts. Brazil 75 D4...21.00S 57.00W
Bogie r. Scotland 19 G2.........57.30N 2.47W
Bognor Regis England 10 E1......50.47N 0.40W
Bogor Indonesia 104 D2..........6.34S 106.45E
Bogotá Colombia 74 B7...........4.38N 74.05W
Bohain-en-Vermandois France 42 C1...49.59N 3.28E
Bohemian Forest mts. Germany/Czech Rep. 54 C3
..........................49.20N 13.10E
Bohol i. Phil. 105 G5...........9.45N 124.10E
Bohu China 102 F6...............41.48N 86.10E
Boise U.S.A. 64 C5..............43.38N 116.12W
Bojnurd Iran 95 I5..............37.28N 57.20E
Bokora Corridor Game Res. Uganda 87 A3
..........................2.30N 34.05E
Bolhrad Ukraine 55 K1...........45.42N 28.40E
Bolivia S. America 76 D3........17.00S 65.00W
Bollnäs Sweden 43 D3............61.20N 16.25E
Bolmen l. Sweden 43 C2..........57.00N 13.45E
Bologna Italy 50 D6.............44.30N 11.20E
Bolsena, L. Italy 50 D5.........42.36N 11.55E
Bolshevik i. Russian Fed. 59 M5...78.30N 102.00E
Bolshoi Lyakhovskiy i. Russian Fed. 59 Q5
..........................73.30N 142.00E
Bolsover England 15 F2..........53.14N 1.18W
Bolt Head c. England 13 D2......50.13N 3.48W
Bolton England 15 E2............53.35N 2.26W
Bolu Turkey 57 J4...............40.45N 31.38E

Bolus Head Rep. of Ire. 20 A1...51.48N 10.21W
Bolzano Italy 50 D7.............46.30N 11.20E
Boma Zaire 84 F1................5.50S 13.03E
Bombay India 96 E4..............18.56N 72.51E
Bømlo i. Norway 43 A2...........59.37N 5.13E
Bon, C. Tunisia 52 F4...........37.05N 11.03E
Bonaire i. Neth. Ant. 71 K3.....12.15N 68.27W
Bonar Bridge Scotland 19 E2.....57.53N 4.22W
Bonavista Canada 63 M2..........48.38N 53.08W
Bone, G. of Indonesia 104 G3....4.00S 120.50E
Bo'ness Scotland 17 F4..........56.01N 3.36W
Bonete mtn. Argentina 76 D2.....27.55S 68.41W
Bonifacio France 44 H2..........41.23N 9.10E
Bonifacio, Str. of Med. Sea 50 C4...41.18N 9.10E
Bonn Germany 48 C4..............50.44N 7.06E
Bonnyrigg Scotland 17 F3........55.52N 3.07W
Bontosunggu Indonesia 104 F2....5.42S 119.44E
Boothia, G. of Canada 63 J4.....70.00N 90.00W
Boothia Pen. Canada 63 I5.......70.30N 95.00W
Bootle England 14 D2............53.28N 3.01W
Borås Sweden 43 C2..............57.44N 12.55E
Borazjan Iran 95 H4.............29.14N 51.12E
Bordeaux France 44 C4...........44.50N 0.34W
Borden I. Canada 62 G5..........78.30N 111.00W
Borden Pen. Canada 63 J5........73.00N 83.00W
Bordj Messaouda Algeria 52 E3...30.10N 9.19E
Boreray i. Scotland 18 B2.......57.43N 7.17W
Borgarnes Iceland 43 X2.........64.33N 21.53W
Borger U.S.A. 64 F4.............35.39N 101.24W
Borken Germany 42 F3............51.50N 6.52E
Borkum i. Germany 48 C5.........53.35N 6.45E
Borlänge Sweden 43 C3...........60.29N 15.25E
Borneo i. Asia 104 E4...........1.00N 114.00E
Bornholm i. Denmark 43 C1.......55.02N 15.00E
Borodyanka Ukraine 55 K4........50.38N 25.59E
Boroughbridge England 15 F3.....54.06N 1.23W
Borujerd Iran 95 G5.............33.54N 48.47E
Boryslav Ukraine 54 H3..........49.18N 23.28E
Boryspil' Ukraine 55 L4.........50.21N 30.59E
Borzna Ukraine 55 M4............51.15N 32.25E
Borzya Russian Fed. 103 L8......50.24N 116.35E
Bosanska Dubica Croatia 56 C6...45.11N 16.50E
Bose China 103 J2...............23.58N 106.32E
Bosna r. Bosnia./Croatia 56 D6...45.04N 18.27E
Bosnia-Herzegovina Europe 56 C6...44.00N 18.00E
Bosporus str. Turkey 57 I4......41.07N 29.04E
Bosten Hu l. China 102 F6.......42.00N 87.00E
Boston England 15 G1............52.59N 0.02W
Boston Spa England 15 F2........53.54N 1.21W
Botevgrad Bulgaria 56 F5........42.55N 23.57E
Bothnia, G. of Europe 43 D3.....63.30N 20.30E
Botoşani Romania 55 J2..........47.44N 26.41E
Botswana Africa 86 B2...........22.00S 24.00E
Bottesford England 15 G2........52.32N 0.37W
Bouaké Côte d'Ivoire 84 D2......7.42N 5.00W
Bouar C.A.R. 86 A5..............5.58N 15.35E
Bouârfa Morocco 84 D5...........32.30N 1.59W
Bougainville i. P.N.G. 110 E5...6.00S 155.00E
Bouillon Belgium 42 E1..........49.48N 5.03E
Boulder U.S.A. 64 E5............40.02N 105.16W
Boulogne France 42 D3...........50.43N 1.37E
Boulogne-Billancourt France 44 E6...48.50N 2.15E
Bounty Is. Pacific Oc. 108 M2...48.00S 178.30E
Bourg-en-Bresse France 44 F5....46.12N 5.13E
Bourges France 44 E5............47.05N 2.23E
Bourke Australia 110 D2.........30.09S 145.59E
Bourne England 11 E3............52.46N 0.23W
Bournemouth England 10 D1.......50.43N 1.53W
Bou Saâda Algeria 52 D4.........35.12N 4.11E
Bowes England 15 E3.............54.31N 2.01W
Boxtel Neth. 42 E3..............51.36N 5.20E
Boyarka Ukraine 55 L4...........50.20N 30.26E
Boyle Rep. of Ire. 20 C3........53.58N 8.20W
Boyne r. Rep. of Ire. 20 E3.....53.43N 6.18W
Bozeman U.S.A. 64 D6............45.40N 111.00W
Bozüyük Turkey 57 J3............39.55N 30.03E
Braan r. Scotland 17 F4.........56.34N 3.36W
Brabant d. Belgium 42 D2........50.47N 4.30E
Brač i. Croatia 56 C5...........43.20N 16.38E
Bracadale, Loch Scotland 18 C2...57.20N 6.32E
Bräcke Sweden 43 C3.............62.44N 15.30E
Brackley England 10 D3..........52.02N 1.09W
Bracknell England 10 E2.........51.26N 0.46W
Brad Romania 56 F7..............46.06N 22.48E
Bradano r. Italy 50 G4..........40.23N 16.52E
Bradford England 15 F2..........53.47N 1.45W
Bradford-on-Avon England 10 C2...51.20N 2.15W
Braemar Scotland 19 F2..........57.00N 3.27W
Braga Portugal 46 A4............41.32N 8.26W
Bragança Brazil 77 F4...........1.03S 46.46W
Bragança Portugal 46 B4.........41.47N 6.46W
Brahmapur India 97 G4...........19.21N 84.51E
Brahmaputra r. Asia 97 H5.......23.50N 89.45E
Brăila Romania 55 J1............45.18N 27.58E
Braintree England 11 F2.........51.53N 0.32E
Bramön i. Sweden 43 D3..........62.15N 17.40E
Brampton England 14 E3.........54.56N 2.43W
Branco r. Brazil 77 D4..........1.30S 62.00W
Brandenburg Germany 48 F5.......52.25N 12.34E
Brandesburton England 15 G2.....53.55N 0.18W
Brandon Canada 62 I2...........49.50N 99.57W
Brandon England 11 F3...........52.27N 0.37E
Brandon Head Rep. of Ire. 20 A2...52.17N 10.11W
Brandon Mtn. Rep. of Ire. 20 A2...52.14N 10.15W
Bransgore England 10 D1.........50.47N 1.45W
Brasília Brazil 77 F3...........15.54S 47.50W
Braşov Romania 55 G6...........45.40N 25.35E
Bratislava Slovakia 54 E3.......48.10N 17.10E
Bratsk Russian Fed. 59 M3.......56.20N 101.15E
Bratsk Resr. Russian Fed. 90 M8...54.40N 100.00E
Braunschweig Germany 48 E5......52.15N 10.30E
Braunton England 13 C3..........51.06N 4.09W
Brawley U.S.A. 64 C3............33.10N 115.30W
Bray Rep. of Ire. 20 E3.........53.12N 6.07W
Bray Head Rep. of Ire. 20 A1....51.52N 10.28W
Brazil S. America 77 E3.........10.00S 52.00W
Brazil Basin f. Atlantic Oc. 116 H5...15.00S 25.00W
Brazilian Highlands Brazil 77 F3...17.00S 48.00W
Brazos r. U.S.A. 64 G2..........28.55N 95.20W
Brazzaville Congo 86 F1.........4.14S 15.14E
Brechin Scotland 19 G1..........56.44N 2.40W
Breckland f. England 11 F3......52.28N 0.40E
Břeclav Czech Rep. 54 E3........48.46N 16.53E
Brecon Wales 12 D3..............51.57N 3.23W
Brecon Beacons mts. Wales 12 D3...51.53N 3.27W

Breda Neth. 42 D3................................51.35N 4.46E
Bredhafjördhur est. Iceland 43 X2........65.15N 23.00W
Breidhdalsvik Iceland 43 Z2...............64.48N 14.00W
Bremen Germany 48 D5........................53.05N 8.48E
Bremerhaven Germany 48 D5................53.33N 8.35E
Brenner Pass Italy/Austria 50 D7.........47.00N 11.30E
Brentwood England 11 F2....................51.38N 0.18E
Brescia Italy 50 D6.............................45.33N 10.12E
Bressay i. Scotland 19 Y9...................60.08N 1.05W
Bressuire France 44 C5.......................46.50N 0.28W
Brest Belarus 55 H5............................52.08N 23.40E
Brest France 44 A6.............................48.23N 4.30W
Bretton Wales 12 E5...........................53.10N 3.00W
Bria C.A.R. 85 G2...............................6.32N 21.59E
Briançon France 44 G4.......................44.53N 6.39E
Bride r. Rep. of Ire. 20 D2..................52.06N 7.50W
Bridgend Wales 13 D3.........................51.30N 3.35W
Bridgend d. Wales 12 D3.....................51.33N 3.35W
Bridgeport U.S.A. 65 L5......................41.12N 73.12W
Bridgetown Barbados 71 M3.............13.06N 59.37W
Bridgnorth England 10 C3..................52.33N 2.25W
Bridgwater England 13 D3..................51.08N 3.00W
Bridgwater B. England 13 D3..............51.15N 3.10W
Bridlington England 15 G3..................54.06N 0.11W
Bridlington B. England 15 G3..............54.03N 0.10W
Bridport England 10 C1......................50.43N 2.45W
Brig Switz. 44 G5...............................46.19N 8.00E
Brigg England 15 G2..........................53.33N 0.30W
Brighstone England 10 D1..................50.38N 1.24W
Brightlingsea England 11 G2..............51.49N 1.01E
Brighton England 11 E1......................50.50N 0.09W
Brindisi Italy 50 G4............................40.38N 17.57E
Brisbane Australia 110 E3...................27.30S 153.00E
Bristol England 10 C2.........................51.26N 2.35W
Bristol d. England 10 C2.....................51.26N 2.35W
Bristol B. U.S.A. 62 C3......................58.00N 158.50W
Bristol Channel England/Wales 13 D3....51.17N 3.20W
British Columbia d. Canada 62 F3.......55.00N 125.00W
British Isles Europe 34 C5..................54.00N 5.00W
Briton Ferry town Wales 12 D3............51.37N 3.50W
Brittany f. France 44 B6.....................48.00N 3.00W
Brive-la-Gaillarde France 44 D4..........45.09N 1.32E
Brixham England 13 D2......................50.24N 3.31W
Brno Czech Rep. 54 E3.......................49.11N 16.39E
Broad B. Scotland 18 C3....................58.15N 6.15W
Broad Law mtn. Scotland 17 F3..........55.30N 3.21W
Broadstairs England 11 G2.................51.22N 1.27E
Broadview Canada 64 F7.....................50.20N 102.30W
Broadway England 10 D3....................52.02N 1.50W
Broadway England 10 C1....................50.39N 2.29W
Broadwindsor England 10 C1..............50.49N 2.48W
Brockenhurst England 10 D1...............50.49N 1.34W
Brock I. Canada 62 G5........................78.00N 114.30W
Brodeur Pen. Canada 63 J5.................73.00N 88.00W
Brodick Scotland 16 D3......................55.34N 5.09W
Broken Hill town Australia 110 D2.......31.57S 141.30E
Bromley England 11 F2........................51.24N 0.02E
Bromsgrove England 10 C3.................52.20N 2.03W
Bromyard England 10 C3.....................52.12N 2.30W
Brønderslev Denmark 43 B2................57.16N 9.58E
Brønnøysund Norway 43 C4.................65.38N 12.15E
Brooke England 11 G3........................52.32N 1.25E
Brooke's Point town Phil. 104 F5..........8.50N 117.52E
Brooks Range mts. U.S.A. 62 C4.........68.50N 152.00W
Broome Australia 110 B4....................17.58S 122.15E
Brora Scotland 19 F3..........................58.01N 3.52W
Brora r. Scotland 19 F3.......................57.59N 3.51W
Brosna r. Rep. of Ire. 20 D3................53.12N 7.59W
Brotton England 15 F3........................54.34N 0.55W
Brough Cumbria England 15 E3............54.32N 2.19W
Brough E.Yorks England 15 G2............53.42N 0.34W
Brough Head Scotland 19 F4................59.09N 3.19W
Brough Ness c. Scotland 19 F3.............58.44N 2.57W
Broughshane N. Ireland 16 C2.............54.54N 6.12W
Brownhills England 10 D3...................52.38N 1.57W
Broxburn Scotland 17 F3.....................55.57N 3.29W
Bruay-en-Artois France 42 B2.............50.29N 2.36E
Brue r. England 13 D3.........................51.13N 3.00W
Brugge Belgium 42 C3........................51.13N 3.14E
Brunei Asia 104 E4.............................4.56N 114.58E
Brunflo Sweden 43 C3........................63.04N 14.50E
Brunswick U.S.A. 65 J3......................31.09N 81.21W
Brussels Belgium 42 D2......................50.50N 4.23E
Bruton England 13 E3.........................51.06N 2.28W
Bryansk Russian Fed. 55 N5................53.15N 34.09E
Bryher i. England 13 A1......................49.57N 6.21W
Brynamman Wales 12 D3....................51.49N 3.52W
Brynmawr Wales 12 D3.......................51.48N 3.10W
Buca Turkey 56 H3.............................38.22N 27.10E
Bucaramanga Colombia 71 J2..............7.08N 73.01W
Bucharest Romania 56 H6...................44.25N 26.06E
Buckhaven Scotland 17 F4..................56.11N 3.03W
Buckie Scotland 19 G2.......................57.40N 2.58W
Buckingham England 10 E2.................52.00N 0.59W
Buckinghamshire d. England 10 E2......51.50N 0.48W
Buckley Wales 12 D5..........................53.11N 3.04W
Budapest Hungary 54 F2.....................47.30N 19.03E
Buddon Ness c. Scotland 17 G4...........56.29N 2.42W
Bude England 13 C2............................50.49N 4.33W
Bude B. England 13 C2.......................50.45N 4.40W
Buenaventura Colombia 74 B7............3.54N 77.02W
Buenos Aires Argentina 75 D3.............34.40S 58.30W
Buffalo N.Y. U.S.A. 65 K5..................42.52N 78.55W
Buffalo Wyo. U.S.A. 64 E5..................44.21N 106.40W
Bug r. Poland 54 G5...........................52.29N 21.11E
Bug r. Ukraine 55 L2...........................46.55N 31.59E
Buhayrat al Asad r. Syria 57 N2..........36.10N 38.20E
Builth Wells Wales 12 D4...................52.09N 3.24W
Buir Nur l. Mongolia 103 L7...............47.50N 117.40E
Bujumbura Burundi 86 B4....................3.22S 29.21E
Bukavu Zaire 86 B4............................2.30S 28.49E
Bukittinggi Indonesia 104 C3.............0.18S 100.20E
Bukoba Tanzania 86 C4.......................1.20S 31.49E
Bula Indonesia 105 I3.........................3.07S 130.27E
Bulawayo Zimbabwe 86 B2.................20.10S 28.43E
Bulgan Mongolia 103 I7......................48.34N 103.12E
Bulgaria Europe 56 G5........................42.30N 25.00E
Bulukumba Indonesia 104 G2.............5.35S 120.13E
Bulun Russian Fed. 59 O5..................70.50N 127.20E
Buna Kenya 87 B3...............................2.49N 39.27E
Bunbury Australia 110 A2...................33.20S 115.34E
Bunclody Rep. of Ire. 20 E2...............52.39N 6.39W
Buncrana Rep. of Ire. 20 D5................55.08N 7.28W
Bunda Tanzania 87 A2........................2.00S 33.57E
Bundaberg Australia 110 E3...............24.50S 152.21E

Bundoran Rep. of Ire. 20 C4...............54.28N 8.20W
Bungay England 11 G3.......................52.27N 1.26E
Bungoma Kenya 87 A3........................0.33N 34.33E
Buôn Mê Thuột Vietnam 104 D6.........12.41N 108.02E
Bura Kenya 87 B2..............................1.09S 39.55E
Buraydah Saudi Arabia 94 F4.............26.18N 43.58E
Burbage England 10 D2......................51.22N 1.40W
Burdur Turkey 57 J2...........................37.44N 30.17E
Bure r. England 11 G3........................52.36N 1.44E
Burford England 10 D2.......................51.48N 1.38W
Burgas Bulgaria 56 H5.......................42.30N 27.29E
Burgess Hill town England 11 E1.........50.57N 0.07W
Burghead Scotland 19 F2....................57.42N 3.30W
Burgh le Marsh England 15 H2............53.10N 0.15E
Burgos Spain 46 D5............................42.21N 3.41W
Burhanpur India 96 F5.......................21.18N 76.08E
Burkina Africa 84 D3..........................12.15N 1.30W
Burley U.S.A. 64 D5...........................42.32N 113.48W
Burlington U.S.A. 65 L5.....................44.25N 73.14W
Burnham England 10 E2......................51.35N 0.39W
Burnham-on-Crouch England 11 F2.....51.37N 0.50E
Burnham-on-Sea England 13 D3.........51.15N 3.00W
Burnie Australia 110 D1......................41.03S 145.55E
Burniston England 15 G3....................54.19N 0.27W
Burnley England 15 E2........................53.47N 2.15W
Burns Lake town Canada 62 F3...........54.14N 125.45W
Burntisland Scotland 17 F4.................56.03N 3.15W
Burntwood Green England 10 D3.........52.42N 1.54W
Burray i. Scotland 19 G3.....................58.51N 2.54W
Burrow Head Scotland 16 E2...............54.41N 4.24W
Burry Inlet Wales 12 C3......................51.40N 4.11W
Burry Port Wales 12 C3......................51.41N 4.17W
Bursa Turkey 57 I4.............................40.11N 29.04E
Bûr Safâga Egypt 94 D4.....................26.45N 33.55E
Burscough Bridge England 14 E2........53.37N 2.51W
Burton-in-Kendal England 14 E3.........54.12N 2.43W
Burton Latimer England 10 E3.............52.23N 0.41W
Burton upon Trent England 10 D3.......52.48N 1.39W
Buru i. Indonesia 105 H3....................3.30S 126.30E
Burundi Africa 86 B4..........................3.30S 30.00E
Burwash Landing Canada 62 E4..........61.21N 139.01W
Burwell England 11 F3........................52.17N 0.20E
Burwick Scotland 19 G3.....................58.44N 2.57W
Bury England 15 E2............................53.36N 2.19W
Bury St. Edmunds England 11 F3........52.15N 0.42E
Bush r. N. Ireland 16 C3.....................55.13N 6.33W
Bushbush r. Somalia 87 C2.................1.08S 41.52E
Bushehr Iran 95 H4............................28.57N 50.52E
Bushmills N. Ireland 16 C3.................55.12N 6.32W
Buta Zaire 86 B5................................2.49N 24.50E
Butaritari i. Kiribati 108 I8.................3.00N 172.30E
Butan Phil. 105 H5.............................8.56N 125.31E
Butterworth Malaysia 104 C5..............5.24N 100.22E
Buttevant Rep. of Ire. 20 C2...............52.13N 8.40W
Butt of Lewis c. Scotland 18 C3..........58.31N 6.15W
Butuan Phil. 105 H5...........................8.56N 125.31E
Buton i. Indonesia 105 G2..................5.00S 122.50E
Butte U.S.A. 64 D6.............................46.00N 112.31W
Buur Gaabo Somalia 87 C2.................1.10S 41.50E
Buvuma I. Uganda 87 A3.....................0.12N 33.17E
Buxton England 15 F2.........................53.16N 1.54W
Buzău Romania 56 H6.........................45.10N 26.49E
Byarezina r. Belarus 55 L5..................52.30N 30.20E
Bydgoszcz Poland 54 E5.....................53.16N 18.00E
Byfield England 10 D3........................52.10N 1.15W
Bylot I. Canada 63 K5.........................73.00N 78.30W
Byrranga Mts. Russian Fed. 59 M5......74.50N 101.00E
Bytom Poland 54 F4............................50.22N 18.54E

C

Caacupé Paraguay 77 E2....................25.23S 57.05W
Cabanatuan Phil. 104 G7...................15.30N 120.58E
Caban Coch Resr. Wales 12 D4...........52.17N 3.34W
Cabimas Venezuela 71 J3...................10.26N 71.27W
Cabinda Angola 84 F1.........................5.34S 12.12E
Cabonga, Réservoir Canada 65 K6.......47.20N 76.35W
Cabot Str. Canada 63 M2....................47.00N 59.00W
Cabrera, Sierra mts. Spain 46 B5.........42.10N 6.30W
Cabriel r. Spain 46 E3.........................39.13N 1.07W
Cáceres Brazil 77 E3..........................16.05S 57.40W
Cáceres Spain 46 B3..........................39.29N 6.23W
Cachimbo, Serra do mts. Brazil 77 E4...8.30S 55.00W
Cachoeiro de Itapemirim Brazil 77 F2....20.51S 41.07W
Cadera, C. Venezuela 71 K3...............10.40N 66.05W
Cadillac U.S.A. 65 I5..........................44.15N 85.23W
Cadiz Phil. 105 G6.............................10.57N 123.18E
Cádiz Spain 46 B2..............................36.32N 6.18W
Cádiz, G. of Spain 46 B2....................37.00N 7.10W
Caen France 44 C6.............................49.11N 0.22W
Caerleon Wales 12 E3........................51.36N 2.57W
Caernarfon Wales 12 C5.....................53.08N 4.17W
Caernarfon B. Wales 12 C5.................53.05N 4.25W
Caernarfonshire and Merionethshire d. Wales 12 D4
....53.00N 4.00W
Caerphilly Wales 12 D3......................51.34N 3.13W
Caerphilly d. Wales 12 D3..................51.34N 3.13W
Caersws Wales 12 D4.........................52.31N 3.26W
Cagayan de Oro Phil. 105 G5.............8.29N 124.40E
Cagliari Italy 50 C3............................39.14N 9.07E
Cagliari, G. of Med. Sea 50 C3............39.07N 9.15E
Caha Mts. Rep. of Ire. 20 B1...............51.44N 9.45W
Cahir Rep. of Ire. 20 D2......................52.23N 7.56W
Cahors France 44 D4..........................44.28N 0.26E
Cahul Moldova 55 K1.........................45.58N 28.10E
Caiabis, Serra dos mts. Brazil 77 E3....12.00S 56.30W
Caiapó, Serra mts. Brazil 77 E3...........17.10S 52.00W
Caicos Is. Turks & Caicos Is. 71 J5.......21.30N 72.00W
Cairn Gorm mtn. Scotland 19 F2..........57.06N 3.39W
Cairngorm Mts. Scotland 19 F2...........57.04N 3.30W
Cairnryan Scotland 16 D2...................54.58N 5.02W
Cairns Australia 110 D4......................16.51S 145.43E
Cairn Toul mtn. Scotland 19 F2...........57.04N 3.44W
Cairo Egypt 94 D4.............................30.03N 31.15E
Caister-on-Sea England 11 G3............52.38N 1.43E
Caistor England 15 G2.......................53.29N 0.20W
Caithness f. Scotland 19 F3................58.25N 3.25W
Calabar Nigeria 84 E2........................4.56N 8.22E
Calais France 44 D7...........................50.57N 1.50E
Calama Chile 76 D2...........................22.30S 68.55W
Calamian Group is. Phil. 104 F6..........12.00N 120.05E

Calamocha Spain 46 E4......................40.54N 1.18W
Calanscio Sand Sea f. Libya 53 H2.......27.00N 23.00E
Calapan Phil. 104 G6.........................13.23N 121.10E
Călăraşi Romania 56 H6.....................44.11N 27.21E
Calbayog Phil. 105 G6........................12.04N 124.58E
Calcanhar, Punta do c. Brazil 77 G4....5.06S 35.30W
Calcutta India 97 H5...........................22.35N 88.21E
Caldas da Rainha Portugal 46 A3........39.24N 9.08W
Caldey Island Wales 12 C3.................51.38N 4.43W
Caldicot Wales 12 E3.........................51.36N 2.45W
Calf of Man i. I.o.M. 14 C3.................54.03N 4.49W
Calgary Canada 62 G3.......................51.05N 114.05W
Cali Colombia 74 B7..........................3.24N 76.30W
Calicut India 96 F3.............................11.15N 75.45E
Caliente U.S.A. 64 D4........................37.36N 114.31W
California U.S.A. 64 B4......................37.00N 120.00W
California, G. of Mexico 70 B6............28.30N 112.30W
Callan Rep. of Ire. 20 D2....................52.33N 7.23W
Callander Scotland 16 E4....................56.15N 4.13W
Callanish Scotland 18 C3...................58.12N 6.45W
Callao Peru 76 C3..............................12.05S 77.08W
Callington England 13 C2...................50.30N 4.19W
Calne England 10 D2..........................51.26N 2.00W
Caltanissetta Italy 50 F2....................37.30N 14.05E
Calvi France 44 H3............................42.34N 8.44E
Cam r. England 11 F3.........................52.34N 0.21E
Camaçari Brazil 77 G3.......................12.44S 38.16W
Camagüey Cuba 71 I5.........................21.25N 77.55W
Camagüey, Archipelago de Cuba 71 I5
....22.30N 78.00W
Cambay, G. of India 96 E5..................20.30N 72.00E
Camberley England 10 E2...................51.21N 0.45W
Cambodia Asia 104 C6.......................12.00N 105.00E
Camborne England 13 B2...................50.12N 5.19W
Cambrai France 42 C2........................50.10N 3.14E
Cambrian Mts. Wales 12 D4...............52.33N 3.33W
Cambridge England 11 F3...................52.13N 0.08E
Cambridge Bay town Canada 62 H4.....69.09N 105.00W
Cambridgeshire d. England 11 E3........52.15N 0.05W
Camelford England 13 C2...................50.37N 4.41W
Cameroon Africa 84 F2......................6.00N 12.30E
Cameroun, Mt. Cameroon 84 E2.........4.20N 9.05E
Cametá Brazil 77 F4...........................2.12S 49.30W
Camlough N. Ireland 16 C2.................54.14N 6.26W
Campbell I. Pacific Oc. 108 L1............52.30S 169.02E
Campbell River town Canada 62 F3.....50.00N 125.18W
Campbellton Canada 65 M6................48.00N 66.40W
Campbeltown Scotland 16 D3.............55.25N 5.36W
Campeche Mexico 70 F4.....................19.50N 90.30W
Campeche d. Mexico 70 F4.................19.00N 90.00W
Campeche B. Mexico 70 F4................19.30N 94.00W
Campina Grande Brazil 77 G4.............7.15S 35.53W
Campinas Brazil 77 F2........................22.54S 47.06W
Campo Grande Brazil 77 E2................20.24S 54.35W
Campobasso Italy 50 F4.....................41.34N 14.39E
Campos Brazil 77 F2..........................21.46S 41.21W
Cam Ranh Vietnam 104 D6................11.54N 109.14E
Camrose Wales 12 B3.........................51.50N 5.01W
Canada N. America 62 H3...................60.00N 105.00W
Canadian r. U.S.A. 64 G4...................35.20N 95.40W
Canadian Shield f. N. America 60 K7....50.00N 80.00W
Çanakkale Turkey 56 H4.....................40.09N 26.26E
Canal du Midi France 44 D3...............43.18N 2.00E
Canary Is. Atlantic Oc. 46 X2..............29.00N 15.00W
Canaveral, C. U.S.A. 65 J2.................28.28N 80.28W
Canberra Australia 110 D2..................35.18S 149.08E
Cancún Mexico 70 G5.........................21.26N 86.51W
Caniapiscau r. Canada 63 L3..............57.40N 69.30W
Caniapiscau, Résr. Canada 63 K3........55.05N 72.40W
Canindé r. Brazil 77 F4.......................6.14S 42.51W
Canisp mtn. Scotland 18 D3................58.07N 5.03W
Çankaya Turkey 57 K3........................39.52N 32.52E
Çankırı Turkey 57 K4..........................40.35N 33.37E
Canna i. Scotland 18 C2.....................57.03N 6.30W
Cannes France 44 G3.........................43.33N 7.00E
Cannock England 10 C3.....................52.42N 2.02W
Canoas Brazil 77 E2..........................29.55S 51.10W
Canon City U.S.A. 64 E4....................38.27N 105.14W
Cantabrian Mts. Spain 46 B5..............43.00N 6.00W
Canterbury England 11 G2.................51.17N 1.05E
Cân Thơ Vietnam 104 D6...................10.03N 105.46E
Canvey Island town England 11 F2......51.32N 0.35E
Cao Bang Vietnam 104 D8..................22.40N 106.16E
Capbreton France 44 C3.....................43.38N 1.15W
Cape Breton I. Canada 63 L2..............46.00N 61.00W
Capel St. Mary England 11 G2............51.59N 1.02E
Cape Town R.S.A. 86 A1....................33.56S 18.28E
Cape Verde Atlantic Oc. 84 B3...........16.00N 24.00W
Cape York Pen. Australia 110 D4.........12.40S 142.20E
Cap Haïtien town Haiti 71 J4...............19.47N 72.17W
Capim r. Brazil 77 F4..........................1.40S 47.47W
Capraia i. Italy 50 C5.........................43.03N 9.50E
Caprera i. Italy 50 C4.........................41.48N 9.27E
Capri i. Italy 50 F4.............................40.33N 14.13E
Capricorn Channel str. Australia 110 E3
....23.00S 152.00E
Caprivi Strip f. Namibia 86 B3............17.50S 23.10E
Caquetá r. Colombia 76 C4.................1.20S 70.50W
Carabay, Cordillera de mts. Peru 76 C3
....13.50S 71.00W
Caracal Romania 56 G6......................44.08N 24.18E
Caracas Venezuela 71 K3...................10.35N 66.56W
Carajás, Serra dos mts. Brazil 77 E4....5.00S 51.00W
Caratasca Lagoon Honduras 71 H4......15.10N 84.00W
Caratinga Brazil 77 F3........................19.50S 42.06W
Caravaca de la Cruz Spain 46 E3.........38.06N 1.51W
Carbonara, C. Italy 50 C3..................39.06N 9.32E
Carcassonne France 44 E3.................43.13N 2.21E
Cardiff Wales 13 D3...........................51.28N 3.11W
Cardiff d. Wales 13 D3.......................51.30N 3.12W
Cardigan Wales 12 C4........................52.06N 4.41W
Cardigan B. Wales 12 C4....................52.30N 4.30W
Cardiganshire d. Wales 12 C4.............52.15N 4.00W
Carei Romania 54 H2.........................47.42N 22.28E
Carey, L. Australia 110 B3.................29.05S 122.15E
Cariacica Brazil 77 F2........................20.15S 40.23W
Caribbean Sea C. America 71 I4...........15.00N 75.00W
Caribou Mts. Canada 62 G3...............58.30N 115.00W
Cark Mtn. Rep. of Ire. 16 B2...............54.53N 7.53W
Carletonville R.S.A. 86 B2.................26.21S 27.23E
Carlingford Lough Rep. of Ire./N. Ireland 16 C2
....54.03N 6.09W
Carlisle England 14 E3.......................54.54N 2.55W
Carlow Rep. of Ire. 20 E2...................52.50N 6.54W
Carlow d. Rep. of Ire. 20 E2................52.43N 6.50W
Carluke Scotland 17 E3......................55.44N 3.51W

Carmacks Canada 62 E4.....................62.04N 136.21W
Carmarthen Wales 12 C3...................51.52N 4.20W
Carmarthen B. Wales 12 C3...............51.40N 4.30W
Carmarthenshire d. Wales 12 C3........52.00N 4.17W
Carmel Head Wales 12 C5..................53.24N 4.35W
Carndonagh Rep. of Ire. 16 B3...........55.15N 7.15W
Carnedd Llywelyn mtn. Wales 12 D5...53.10N 3.58W
Carnedd y Filiast mtn. Wales 12 D4.....52.56N 3.40W
Carnegie, L. Australia 110 B3.............26.15S 123.00E
Carn Eighe mtn. Scotland 18 D2.........57.17N 5.07W
Carnforth England 14 E3....................54.08N 2.47W
Carnic Alps mts. Italy/Austria 50 E7....46.40N 12.48E
Car Nicobar i. India 104 A5................9.06N 92.57E
Carnlough N. Ireland 16 D2................54.58N 6.00W
Carn nan Gabhar mtn. Scotland 19 F1...56.49N 3.44W
Carnot C.A.R. 84 F2...........................4.59N 15.56E
Carnot, C. Australia 110 C2...............34.57S 135.38E
Carnoustie Scotland 17 G4................56.30N 2.44W
Carnsore Pt. Rep. of Ire. 20 E2...........52.10N 6.21W
Caroline I. Kiribati 109 Q6.................10.00S 150.30W
Caroline Is. Pacific Oc. 108 J7............5.00N 150.00E
Carpathian Mts. Europe 34 F2............48.45N 23.45E
Carpentaria, G. of Australia 110 C4.....14.00S 140.00E
Carpentras France 44 F4....................44.03N 5.03E
Carra, Lough Rep. of Ire. 20 B3..........53.40N 9.15W
Carrara Italy 50 D6............................44.04N 10.06E
Carrauntuohill mtn. Rep. of Ire. 20 B2...52.00N 9.45W
Carrickfergus N. Ireland 16 D2...........54.43N 5.49W
Carrickmacross Rep. of Ire. 20 E3.......53.59N 6.44W
Carrick-on-Shannon Rep. of Ire. 20 C3...53.57N 8.06W
Carrick-on-Suir Rep. of Ire. 20 D2.......52.21N 7.26W
Carron r. Falkirk Scotland 17 F4..........56.01N 3.44W
Carron r. High. Scotland 19 F2............57.53N 4.22W
Carrowmore Lake Rep. of Ire. 20 B4....54.11N 9.48W
Carson City U.S.A. 64 C4...................39.10N 119.46W
Carsphairn Scotland 16 E3.................55.13N 4.15W
Cartagena Colombia 71 I3..................10.24N 75.33W
Cartagena Spain 46 E2......................37.36N 0.59W
Carter Bar pass Scotland/England 17 G3...55.21N 2.27W
Carterton England 10 D2...................51.46N 1.35W
Cartmel England 14 E3.......................54.12N 2.57W
Caruarú Brazil 77 G4.........................8.15S 35.55W
Carvin France 42 B2...........................50.30N 2.58E
Casablanca Morocco 84 D5................33.39N 7.35W
Cascade Range mts. U.S.A. 64 B5.......44.00N 121.30W
Cascavel Brazil 77 E2........................24.59S 53.29W
Caserta Italy 50 F4............................41.06N 14.21E
Caseyr, C. Somalia 85 J3....................12.00N 51.30E
Cashel Rep. of Ire. 20 D2...................52.31N 7.54W
Casper U.S.A. 64 E5...........................42.50N 106.20W
Caspian Depression f. Russian Fed./Kazakhstan 58 G2
....47.00N 48.00E
Caspian Sea Asia 90 H7.....................42.00N 51.00E
Cassiar Mts. Canada 62 F3.................60.00N 131.00W
Cassley r. Scotland 18 E3...................57.58N 4.35W
Castanhal Brazil 77 F4.......................1.16S 47.51W
Castelló de la Plana Spain 46 E3.........39.59N 0.03W
Castelbar Rep. of Ire. 20 B3...............53.52N 9.19W
Castleblayney Rep. of Ire. 20 E4.........54.08N 6.46W
Castle Cary England 13 E3.................51.06N 2.31W
Castlecomer Rep. of Ire. 20 D2...........52.48N 7.12W
Castleconnell Rep. of Ire. 20 C2..........52.43N 8.30W
Castlederg N. Ireland 16 B2...............54.43N 7.37W
Castle Donnington England 10 D3......52.51N 1.19W
Castle Douglas Scotland 17 F2...........54.56N 3.56W
Castleford England 15 F2...................53.43N 1.21W
Castleisland town Rep. of Ire. 20 B2....52.14N 9.29W
Castletown I.o.M. 14 C3....................54.04N 4.38W
Castres France 44 E3.........................43.36N 2.14E
Castries St. Lucia 71 L3.....................14.01N 60.59W
Catamarca Argentina 76 D2...............28.28S 65.46W
Catanduanes i. Phil. 105 G6...............13.45N 124.20E
Catania Italy 50 F2............................37.31N 15.05E
Catanzaro Italy 50 G3.......................38.55N 16.35E
Catarman Phil. 105 G6......................12.28N 124.50E
Caterham England 11 E2....................51.17N 0.04W
Cat I. The Bahamas 71 I5...................24.30N 75.30W
Catoche, C. Mexico 70 G5.................21.38N 87.08W
Catterick England 15 F3.....................54.23N 1.38W
Cauca r. Colombia 71 J2....................8.57N 74.30W
Caucaia Brazil 77 G4..........................3.45S 38.45W
Caucasus mts. Europe 58 G2..............43.00N 44.00E
Caudry France 42 C2.........................50.07N 3.25E
Cavan Rep. of Ire. 20 D3...................53.59N 7.22W
Cavan d. Rep. of Ire. 20 D3...............54.00N 7.15W
Cawston England 11 G3.....................52.46N 1.10E
Caxias Brazil 77 F4............................4.53S 43.20W
Caxias do Sul Brazil 77 E2.................29.14S 51.10W
Cayenne French Guiana 74 D7...........4.55N 52.18W
Cayman Brac i. Cayman Is. 71 I4.........19.44N 79.48W
Cayman Is. C. America 71 H4.............19.00N 81.00W
Cayos Miskito is. Nicaragua 71 H3......14.30N 82.40W
Ceará d. Brazil 77 G4..........................4.50S 39.00W
Cebu Phil. 105 G6.............................10.17N 123.56E
Cebu i. Phil. 105 G6..........................10.15N 123.45E
Cedar r. U.S.A. 65 H5........................41.15N 91.20W
Cedar City U.S.A. 64 D4....................37.40N 113.04W
Cedar Rapids town U.S.A. 65 H5........41.59N 91.31W
Cedros i. Mexico 64 C2......................28.15N 115.15W
Cefalù Italy 50 F3..............................38.01N 14.03E
Cegléd Hungary 54 F2........................47.10N 19.48E
Celaya Mexico 70 D5.........................20.32N 100.48W
Celebes Sea Indonesia 105 G4............3.00N 122.00E
Celje Slovenia 50 F7..........................46.15N 15.16E
Celle Germany 48 E5.........................52.37N 10.05E
Cenderawasih G. Indonesia 105 J3.......2.30S 135.20E
Central d. Kenya 87 B2......................1.00S 37.00E
Central, Cordillera mts. Bolivia 76 D3...20.00S 65.00W
Central, Cordillera mts. Colombia 74 B7...5.00N 75.30W
Central, Cordillera mts. Peru 76 C4....7.00S 79.00W
Central African Republic Africa 85 F2....6.30N 20.00E
Central Range mts. P.N.G. 105 K3.......5.00S 142.00E
Central Russian Uplands f. Russian Fed. 55 O5
....53.00N 37.00E
Central Siberian Plateau f. Russian Fed. 59 M4
....66.00N 108.00E
Cernavodă Romania 57 I6..................44.20N 28.02E
Cerralvo i. Mexico 70 C5....................24.17N 109.52W
Cervo Spain 46 B5.............................43.40N 7.25W
České Budějovice Czech Rep. 54 D3....49.00N 14.30E
Ceuta Spain 46 C1............................35.53N 5.19W
Cévennes mts. France 44 E4..............44.25N 3.30E
Ceyhan r. Turkey 57 L2......................36.54N 34.58E
Chad Africa 85 F3..............................13.00N 19.00E
Chad, L. Africa 84 F3.........................13.30N 14.00E

Chadan Russian Fed. 102 G8.................51.20N 91.39E
Chagai Hills Pakistan 95 J4.................29.10N 63.35E
Chaghcharan Afghan. 95 K5.................34.32N 65.15E
Chagos Archipelago is. Indian Oc. 90 J2...7.00S 72.00E
Chah Bahar Iran 95 J4.................25.17N 60.41E
Chake Chake Tanzania 87 B1.................5.13S 39.46E
Chalbi Desert Kenya 87 B3.................3.00N 37.20E
Chale England 10 D1.................50.36N 1.19W
Chalkida Greece 56 F3.................38.27N 23.36E
Challenger Deep Pacific Oc. 91 Q4...11.19N 142.15E
Châlons-sur-Marne France 44 F6.................48.58N 4.22E
Chalon-sur-Saône France 44 F5.................46.47N 4.51E
Chalus Iran 95 H6.................36.40N 51.25E
Chaman Pakistan 96 D7.................30.55N 66.27E
Chambéry France 44 F4.................45.34N 5.55E
Ch'amo Hayk' l. Ethiopia 87 B4.................5.49N 37.35E
Chamonix France 44 F4.................45.55N 6.52E
Champaqui mtn. Argentina 76 D1...31.59S 64.59W
Champlain, L. U.S.A. 65 L5.................44.45N 73.20W
Chañaral Chile 76 C2.................26.21S 70.37W
Chanda India 97 F4.................19.58N 79.21E
Chandalar r. U.S.A. 62 D4.................66.40N 146.00W
Chandeleur Is. U.S.A. 65 I2.................29.50N 88.50W
Chandigarh India 96 F7.................30.44N 76.54E
Changchun China 103 N6.................43.50N 125.20E
Changde China 103 K3.................29.03N 111.35E
Changgi Gap b. S. Korea 106 A3.................36.00N 129.30E
Chang Jiang r. China 103 M4.................31.40N 121.15E
Changsha China 103 K3.................28.10N 113.00E
Changzhi China 103 K5.................36.09N 113.12E
Changzhou China 103 L4.................31.45N 119.57E
Chania Greece 56 G1.................35.30N 24.02E
Channel Is. U.K. 13 Z9.................49.28N 2.13W
Channel-Port aux Basques town Canada 63 M2
.................47.35N 59.10W
Chanthaburi Thailand 104 C6.................12.38N 102.12E
Chantilly France 42 B1.................49.12N 2.28E
Chao Phraya r. Thailand 104 C6.................13.35N 100.37E
Chaouen Morocco 46 C1.................35.10N 5.16W
Chapada de Maracás f. Brazil 77 F3...13.20S 40.00W
Chapada Diamantina f. Brazil 77 F3...13.30S 42.30W
Chapala, Lago de l. Mexico 70 D5...20.00N 103.00W
Chapecó Brazil 77 E2.................27.14S 52.41W
Chapel-en-le-Firth England 15 F2.................53.19N 1.54W
Chapeltown England 15 F2.................53.28N 1.27W
Chapleau Canada 63 J2.................47.50N 83.24W
Chaplynka Ukraine 55 M2.................46.23N 33.32E
Chard England 13 E2.................50.52N 2.59W
Chari r. Chad 82 E6.................13.00N 14.30E
Charikar Afghan. 95 K6.................35.02N 69.13E
Charlbury England 10 D2.................51.53N 1.29W
Charleroi Belgium 42 D2.................50.25N 4.27E
Charleston U.S.A. 65 K3.................32.48N 79.58W
Charleston W.Va. U.S.A. 65 J4.................38.23N 81.20W
Charlestown Rep. of Ire. 20 C3.................53.57N 8.50W
Charleville-Mézières France 44 F6.................49.46N 4.43E
Charlotte U.S.A. 65 J4.................35.05N 80.50W
Charlottesville U.S.A. 65 K4.................38.02N 78.29W
Charlottetown Canada 63 L2.................46.14N 63.09W
Chartres France 44 D6.................48.27N 1.30E
Châteaubriant France 44 C5.................47.43N 1.22W
Châteaudun France 44 D6.................48.04N 1.20E
Châteauroux France 44 D5.................46.49N 1.41E
Château-Thierry France 44 E6.................49.03N 3.24E
Châtellerault France 44 D5.................46.49N 0.33E
Chatham England 11 F2.................51.23N 0.32E
Chatham Is. Pacific Oc. 111 H1.................44.00S 176.35W
Chattahoochee r. U.S.A. 65 J2.................30.52N 84.57W
Chattanooga U.S.A. 65 I4.................35.01N 85.18W
Chatteris England 11 F3.................52.27N 0.03E
Chaumont France 44 F6.................48.07N 5.08E
Chauny France 42 C1.................49.37N 3.13E
Cheadle England 10 D3.................52.59N 1.59W
Cheb Czech Rep. 54 C4.................50.04N 12.20E
Cheboksary Russian Fed. 58 G3.................56.08N 47.12E
Cheboygan U.S.A. 65 J6.................45.40N 84.28W
Cheddar England 13 E3.................51.16N 2.47W
Chekhov Russian Fed. 55 O6.................55.21N 37.31E
Cheleken Turkmenistan 95 H6.................39.26N 53.11E
Chełm Poland 55 H4.................51.10N 23.28E
Chelmer r. England 11 F2.................51.43N 0.42E
Chelmsford England 11 F2.................51.44N 0.28E
Cheltenham England 10 C2.................51.53N 2.07W
Chelyabinsk Russian Fed. 58 I3.................55.10N 61.25E
Chelyuskin, C. Russian Fed. 59 M5...77.20N 106.00E
Chemnitz Germany 48 F4.................50.50N 12.55E
Ch'ench'a Ethiopia 87 B4.................6.18N 37.37E
Chengde China 103 L6.................40.48N 118.06E
Chengdu China 103 I4.................30.37N 104.06E
Chenzhou China 103 K3.................25.45N 113.00E
Chepstow Wales 12 E3.................51.38N 2.40W
Cher r. France 44 D5.................47.21N 0.29E
Cherbourg France 44 C6.................49.38N 1.37W
Cherepovets Russian Fed. 58 F3.................59.05N 37.55E
Cherkasy Ukraine 55 M3.................49.27N 32.04E
Chernihiv Ukraine 55 L4.................51.30N 31.18E
Chernivtsi Ukraine 55 J3.................48.19N 25.52E
Chernyakhovsk Russian Fed. 54 G6...54.36N 21.48E
Cherskogo Range mts. Russian Fed. 59 Q4
.................65.50N 143.00E
Chervonohrad Ukraine 55 I4.................50.25N 24.10E
Cherwell r. England 10 D2.................51.45N 1.15W
Chesapeake B. U.S.A. 65 K4.................38.00N 76.00W
Chesham England 11 E2.................51.43N 0.38W
Cheshire d. England 14 E2.................53.14N 2.30W
Chëshskaya g. Russian Fed. 35 H4...67.20N 46.30E
Cheshunt England 11 E2.................51.43N 0.02W
Chesil Beach f. England 10 C1.................50.37N 2.33W
Chester England 14 E2.................53.12N 2.53W
Chesterfield England 15 F2.................53.14N 1.26W
Chester-le-Street England 15 F3.................54.53N 1.34W
Cheviot Hills U.K. 17 G3.................55.22N 2.24W
Chew Bahir l. Ethiopia 87 B3.................4.40N 36.50E
Che'w Bahir Wildlife Res. Ethiopia 87 B4
.................5.00N 36.50E
Chew Magna England 10 C2.................51.21N 2.37W
Chew Valley L. England 10 C2.................51.20N 2.37W
Cheyenne U.S.A. 64 F5.................41.08N 104.50W
Chiang Mai Thailand 104 B7.................18.48N 98.59E
Chiapas d. Mexico 70 F4.................16.30N 93.00W
Chiba Japan 106 D3.................35.38N 140.07E
Chibougamau Canada 63 K2.................49.56N 74.24W
Chicago U.S.A. 65 I5.................41.50N 87.45W
Chichester England 10 E1.................50.50N 0.47W
Chiclayo Peru 76 C4.................6.47S 79.47W

Chico U.S.A. 64 B4.................39.46N 121.50W
Chicoutimi Canada 63 K2.................48.26N 71.06W
Chidley, C. Canada 63 L4.................60.30N 65.00W
Chiemsee l. Germany 48 F2.................47.55N 12.30E
Chiengi Zambia 87 A2.................8.42S 29.10E
Chifeng China 103 L6.................41.17N 118.56E
Chihli, G. of China 103 L5.................38.30N 119.30E
Chihuahua Mexico 70 C6.................28.40N 106.06W
Chihuahua d. Mexico 70 C6.................28.40N 105.00W
Chile S. America 75 B3.................33.00S 71.00W
Chilham England 11 F2.................51.15N 0.57E
Chillán Chile 75 B3.................36.37S 72.10W
Chiloé, Isla de Chile 75 B2.................43.00S 73.00W
Chilpancingo Mexico 70 E4.................17.33N 99.30W
Chiltern Hills England 10 E2.................51.40N 0.53W
Chimborazo mtn. Ecuador 76 C4.................1.10S 78.50W
Chimbote Peru 74 B6.................8.58S 78.34W
Chimoio Mozambique 86 C3.................19.04S 33.29E
China Asia 103 H4.................33.00N 103.00E
Chindwin r. Myanmar 97 J5.................21.30N 95.12E
Chingola Zambia 86 B3.................12.31S 27.53E
Chinhoyi Zimbabwe 86 C3.................17.22S 30.10E
Chios Greece 56 H3.................38.22N 26.08E
Chios i. Greece 56 G3.................38.23N 26.04E
Chipata Zambia 86 C3.................13.37S 32.40E
Chippenham England 10 C2.................51.27N 2.07W
Chipping Campden England 10 D3...52.03N 1.46W
Chipping Norton England 10 D2.................51.56N 1.32W
Chipping Ongar England 11 F2.................51.43N 0.15E
Chipping Sodbury England 10 C2.................51.31N 2.23W
Chiriquí, G. of Panama 71 H2.................8.00N 82.20W
Chirk Wales 12 D3.................52.56N 3.03W
Chirnside Scotland 17 G3.................55.48N 2.12W
Chirripó mtn. Costa Rica 71 H2.................9.31N 83.30W
Chişinău Moldova 55 K2.................47.00N 28.50E
Chita Russian Fed. 59 N3.................52.03N 113.35E
Chitradurga India 96 F3.................14.16N 76.23E
Chitral Pakistan 96 E8.................35.52N 71.58E
Chittagong Bangla. 97 I5.................22.20N 91.48E
Chittoor India 97 F3.................13.13N 79.06E
Choiseul i. Solomon Is. 111 E5.................7.00S 157.00E
Chojnice Poland 54 E5.................53.42N 17.32E
Cholet France 44 C5.................47.04N 0.53W
Chon Buri Thailand 104 C6.................13.24N 100.59E
Chongjin N. Korea 103 N6.................41.55N 129.50E
Chongqing China 103 J3.................29.31N 106.35E
Chonju S. Korea 103 N5.................35.50N 127.05E
Chorley England 14 E2.................53.39N 2.39W
Chornobyl' Ukraine 55 L4.................51.17N 30.15E
Chortkiv Ukraine 55 I3.................49.01N 25.42E
Choshi Japan 106 D3.................34.53N 140.51E
Chott ech Chergui f. Algeria 52 D3...34.00N 0.30E
Chott el Hodna f. Algeria 52 D4.................35.40N 5.00E
Chott el Jerid f. Tunisia 84 E5.................33.30N 8.30E
Chott Melrhir f. Algeria 84 E5.................34.15N 7.00E
Choybalsan Mongolia 103 K7.................48.02N 114.32E
Christchurch England 10 D1.................50.44N 1.47W
Christchurch New Zealand 111 G1...43.32S 172.37E
Christmas I. Indian Oc. 104 D1.................10.30S 105.40E
Chuckchi Pen. Russian Fed. 59 U4...66.00N 174.30W
Chudovo Russian Fed. 54 L7.................59.10N 31.41E
Chugoku-sanchi mts. Japan 106 B3...35.30N 133.00E
Chuhuyiv Ukraine 55 O3.................49.51N 36.44E
Chukchi Sea Arctic Oc. 59 U4.................69.30N 172.00W
Chulmleigh England 13 D2.................50.55N 3.52W
Chumba Ethiopia 87 B3.................4.30N 38.15E
Chumphon Thailand 104 B6.................10.35N 99.14E
Chunchon S. Korea 103 N5.................37.53N 127.45E
Chur Switz. 44 H5.................46.52N 9.32E
Churchill Canada 63 I3.................58.45N 94.00W
Churchill r. Man. Canada 63 I3.................58.20N 94.15W
Churchill r. Nfld. Canada 63 L3.................53.20N 60.00W
Churchill, C. Canada 63 I3.................58.50N 93.00W
Church Stretton England 10 C3.................52.32N 2.49W
Chuuk i. Fed. States of Micronesia 108 K7
.................7.23N 151.46E
Chuxiong China 103 I3.................25.03N 101.33E
Chyulu Range mts. Kenya 87 B2.................2.40S 37.53E
Ciego de Avila Cuba 71 I5.................21.51N 78.47W
Cienfuegos Cuba 71 H5.................22.10N 80.27W
Cigüela r. Spain 46 D3.................39.08N 3.44W
Cihanbeyli Turkey 57 K3.................38.40N 32.55E
Cijara r. Spain 46 C3.................39.20N 4.50W
Cilacap Indonesia 104 D2.................7.44S 109.00E
Cinca r. Spain 46 F4.................41.22N 0.20E
Cincinnati U.S.A. 65 J4.................39.10N 84.30W
Cinderford England 10 C2.................51.49N 2.30W
Ciney Belgium 42 E2.................50.17N 5.06E
Cinto, Monte mtn. France 44 H3.................42.23N 8.57E
Cirebon Indonesia 104 D2.................6.46S 108.33E
Cirencester England 10 D2.................51.43N 1.59W
City of Edinburgh d. Scotland 17 F3...55.57N 3.13W
City of Glasgow d. Scotland 16 E3...55.52N 4.15W
Ciudad Bolívar Venezuela 71 L2.................8.06N 63.36W
Ciudad Camargo Mexico 70 C6.................27.41N 105.10W
Ciudad Delicias Mexico 70 C6.................28.10N 105.30W
Ciudad de Valles Mexico 70 E5.................22.00N 99.00W
Ciudad Guayana Venezuela 71 L2.................8.22N 62.40W
Ciudad Ixtepec Mexico 70 E4.................16.32N 95.10W
Ciudad Juárez Mexico 70 C7.................31.42N 106.29W
Ciudad Madero Mexico 70 E5.................22.19N 97.50W
Ciudad Obregón Mexico 70 C6.................27.28N 109.55W
Ciudad Real Spain 46 D3.................38.59N 3.55W
Ciudad-Rodrigo Spain 46 B4.................40.36N 6.33W
Ciudad Victoria Mexico 70 E5.................23.43N 99.10W
Ciutadella de Menorca Spain 46 G4...40.00N 3.50E
Civitavecchia Italy 50 D5.................42.06N 11.48E
Clackmannanshire d. Scotland 17 F4...56.10N 3.45W
Clacton-on-Sea England 11 G2.................51.47N 1.10E
Claerwen Resr. Wales 12 D4.................52.17N 3.40W
Claonaig Scotland 16 D3.................55.43N 5.24W
Clara Rep. of Ire. 20 D3.................53.21N 7.37W
Clare d. Rep. of Ire. 20 C2.................52.52N 8.55W
Clare r. Rep. of Ire. 20 B3.................53.20N 9.03W
Clare I. Rep. of Ire. 20 A3.................53.50N 10.00W
Claremorris Rep. of Ire. 20 C3.................53.44N 9.00W
Clarksville U.S.A. 65 I4.................36.31N 87.21W
Claro r. Brazil 77 E3.................19.05S 50.40W
Clay Cross England 15 F2.................53.11N 1.26W
Claydon England 11 G3.................52.06N 1.07E
Clay Head I.o.M. 14 C3.................54.12N 4.23W
Clayton U.S.A. 64 F4.................36.27N 103.12W
Clear, C. Rep. of Ire. 20 B1.................51.25N 9.31W
Clear I. Rep. of Ire. 20 B1.................51.26N 9.30W
Cleator Moor town England 14 D3...54.30N 3.32W
Cleethorpes England 15 G2.................53.33N 0.02W

Cleobury Mortimer England 10 C3...52.23N 2.28W
Clermont France 42 B1.................49.23N 2.24E
Clermont-Ferrand France 44 E4.................45.47N 3.05E
Clevedon England 10 C2.................51.26N 2.52W
Cleveland U.S.A. 65 J5.................41.30N 81.41W
Cleveland Hills England 15 F3.................54.25N 1.10W
Cleveleys England 14 D2.................53.52N 3.01W
Clew B. Rep. of Ire. 20 B3.................53.50N 9.47W
Cliffe England 11 F2.................51.28N 0.30E
Clifton England 15 E2.................53.52N 2.23W
Clipperton I. Pacific Oc. 109 U8...10.17N 109.13W
Clitheroe England 14 E2.................53.52N 2.23W
Clogher England 10 C3.................52.23N 2.23W
Clogher Head Rep. of Ire. 20 E3.................53.48N 6.13W
Clonakilty Rep. of Ire. 20 C1.................51.37N 8.55W
Clones Rep. of Ire. 20 D4.................54.11N 7.15W
Clonmel Rep. of Ire. 20 D2.................52.21N 7.44W
Cloud Peak mtn. U.S.A. 64 E5.................44.23N 107.11W
Clovis U.S.A. 64 F3.................34.14N 103.13W
Cluanie, Loch Scotland 18 D2.................57.08N 5.05W
Cluj-Napoca Romania 55 H2.................46.47N 23.37E
Clun England 10 B3.................52.26N 3.02W
Clydach Wales 12 D3.................51.42N 3.53W
Clyde r. Scotland 16 E3.................55.58N 4.53W
Clydebank Scotland 16 E3.................55.53N 4.23W
Clyde River town Canada 63 L5.................70.30N 68.30W
Coahuila d. Mexico 70 D6.................27.00N 103.00W
Coalville England 10 D3.................52.43N 1.21W
Coari Brazil 76 D4.................4.08S 63.07W
Coari r. Brazil 76 D4.................4.08S 63.07W
Coast d. Kenya 87 B2.................3.00S 40.00E
Coast Mts. Canada 62 F3.................55.30N 128.00W
Coast Range mts. U.S.A. 64 B5.................40.00N 123.00W
Coatbridge Scotland 17 E3.................55.52N 4.02W
Coats I. Canada 63 J4.................62.30N 83.00W
Coatzacoalcos Mexico 70 F4.................18.10N 94.25W
Cobh Rep. of Ire. 20 C1.................51.50N 8.18W
Cobija Bolivia 76 D3.................11.01S 68.45W
Coburg Germany 48 E4.................50.15N 10.58E
Cochabamba Bolivia 76 D3.................17.26S 66.10W
Cochin India 96 F2.................9.56N 76.15E
Cochrane Canada 65 J6.................49.00N 81.00W
Cochrane Chile 75 B2.................47.20S 72.30W
Cockburnspath Scotland 17 G3.................55.56N 2.22W
Cockburn Town Turks & Caicos Is. 71 J5
.................21.30N 71.30W
Cockermouth England 14 D3.................54.40N 3.22W
Coco r. Honduras 71 H3.................14.58N 83.15W
Coco, Isla del i. Pacific Oc. 60 K2...5.32N 87.04W
Cod, C. U.S.A. 65 L5.................42.08N 70.10W
Coddington England 15 G2.................53.04N 0.45W
Codó Brazil 77 F4.................4.28S 43.51W
Codsall England 10 C3.................52.37N 2.11W
Coffs Harbour Australia 110 E2.................30.19S 153.05E
Coggeshall England 11 F2.................51.53N 0.41E
Coiba, I. Panama 71 H2.................7.23N 81.45W
Coihaique Chile 75 B2.................45.35S 72.08W
Coimbatore India 96 F3.................11.00N 76.57E
Coimbra Portugal 46 A4.................40.12N 8.25W
Colatina Brazil 77 F3.................19.35S 40.37W
Colchester England 11 F2.................51.54N 0.55E
Cold Bay town U.S.A. 62 B3.................55.10N 162.47W
Coldstream Scotland 17 G3.................55.39N 2.15W
Coleford England 10 C2.................51.46N 2.38W
Coleraine N. Ireland 16 C3.................55.08N 6.41W
Colima Mexico 70 D4.................19.14N 103.41W
Colima d. Mexico 70 D4.................19.05N 104.00W
Colima mtn. Mexico 70 D4.................19.32N 103.36W
Coll i. Scotland 16 C4.................56.38N 6.34W
Collier B. Australia 110 B4.................16.10S 124.15E
Colmar France 44 G6.................48.05N 7.21E
Colne England 15 E2.................53.51N 2.11W
Colne r. England 11 F2.................51.50N 0.59E
Cologne Germany 48 C4.................50.56N 6.57E
Colombia S. America 74 B7.................5.00N 75.00W
Colombo Sri Lanka 97 F2.................6.55N 79.52E
Colón Panama 71 I2.................9.21N 79.54W
Colonsay i. Scotland 16 C4.................56.04N 6.13W
Colorado r. Argentina 75 C3.................39.50S 62.02W
Colorado d. U.S.A. 64 E4.................39.00N 106.00W
Colorado r. Tex. U.S.A. 64 G2.................28.30N 96.00W
Colorado r. U.S.A./Mexico 64 D3...31.45N 114.40W
Colorado Plateau f. U.S.A. 64 D4...36.00N 111.00W
Colorado Springs town U.S.A. 64 F4...38.50N 104.40W
Coltishall England 11 G3.................52.44N 1.22E
Columbia U.S.A. 65 J3.................34.00N 81.00W
Columbia r. U.S.A. 64 B6.................46.10N 123.30W
Columbia, Mt. Canada 62 G4.................52.09N 117.25W
Columbus Ga. U.S.A. 65 J3.................32.28N 84.59W
Columbus Ohio U.S.A. 65 J4.................39.59N 83.03W
Colville r. U.S.A. 62 C5.................70.06N 151.30W
Colwyn Bay town Wales 12 D5.................53.18N 3.43W
Combe Martin England 13 C3.................51.12N 4.02W
Comber N. Ireland 16 D2.................54.33N 5.45W
Comeragh Mts. Rep. of Ire. 20 D2...52.15N 7.35W
Comilla Bangla. 97 I5.................23.28N 91.10E
Comino i. Malta 90 J3.................8.04N 77.35E
Comodoro Rivadavia Argentina 75 C2...45.50S 67.30W
Comorin, C. India 90 J3.................8.04N 77.35E
Comoros Africa 86 D3.................12.15S 44.00E
Compiègne France 42 B1.................49.25N 2.50E
Comrie Scotland 17 F4.................56.23N 4.00W
Conakry Guinea 84 C2.................9.30N 13.43W
Concarneau France 44 B5.................47.53N 3.55W
Concepción Chile 75 B3.................36.50S 73.03W
Conception, Pt. U.S.A. 64 B3.................34.27N 120.26W
Conchos r. Chihuahua Mexico 70 D6...29.34N 104.30W
Conchos r. Tamaulipas Mexico 70 E6...25.00N 97.30W
Concord U.S.A. 65 L5.................43.13N 71.34W
Concordia Argentina 77 E1.................31.25S 58.00W
Condor, Cordillera del mts. Ecuador/Peru 76 C4
.................4.00S 78.30W
Congleton England 15 E2.................53.10N 2.12W
Congo Africa 84 F1.................1.00S 16.00E
Congo r. Congo 84 F1.................6.00S 12.30E
Coningsby England 15 G2.................53.07N 0.09W
Coniston England 14 D3.................54.22N 3.06W
Coniston Water l. England 14 D3.................54.20N 3.05W
Conn, Lough Rep. of Ire. 20 B4.................54.01N 9.15W
Connah's Quay town Wales 12 D5...53.13N 3.03W
Connecticut d. U.S.A. 65 L5.................41.30N 73.00W
Connemara f. Rep. of Ire. 20 B3.................53.30N 9.50W
Conon Bridge Scotland 19 E2.................57.33N 4.26W
Consett England 15 F3.................54.52N 1.50W
Con Son is. Vietnam 104 D5.................8.30N 106.30E
Constanța Romania 57 I6.................44.10N 28.31E

Constantine Algeria 84 E5.................36.22N 6.38E
Conwy Wales 12 D5.................53.17N 3.50W
Conwy r. Wales 12 D5.................53.17N 3.49W
Conwy B. Wales 12 D5.................53.19N 3.55W
Cook, Mt. New Zealand 111 G1.................43.36S 170.09E
Cook Is. Pacific Oc. 108 O5.................15.00S 160.00W
Cookstown N. Ireland 16 C2.................54.39N 6.46W
Cook Str. New Zealand 111 G1.................41.15S 174.30E
Cooktown Australia 110 D4.................15.29S 145.15E
Coolangatta Australia 110 E3.................28.10S 153.26E
Cooper Creek r. Australia 110 C3...28.33S 137.46E
Copenhagen Denmark 43 C1.................55.43N 12.34E
Copiapó Chile 76 C2.................27.20S 70.23W
Copinsay i. Scotland 19 G3.................58.54N 2.41W
Coppermine r. Canada 62 G4.................67.49N 115.12W
Coquimbo Chile 76 C1.................30.00S 71.25W
Coral Harbour town Canada 63 J4...64.10N 83.15W
Coral Sea Pacific Oc. 110 E4.................13.00S 150.00E
Coral Sea Islands Territory Austa. 110 E4
.................15.00S 153.00E
Corbie France 42 B1.................49.55N 2.31E
Corbridge England 15 E3.................54.58N 2.01W
Corby England 10 E3.................52.29N 0.41W
Córdoba Argentina 76 D1.................31.25S 64.11W
Córdoba Mexico 70 E4.................18.55N 96.55W
Córdoba Spain 46 C2.................37.53N 4.46W
Corfe Castle England 10 C1.................50.38N 2.04W
Corfu Greece 56 D3.................39.37N 19.50E
Corfu i. Greece 56 D3.................39.35N 19.50E
Corigliano Calabro Italy 50 G3.................39.36N 16.31E
Corinth Greece 56 F2.................37.56N 22.55E
Corinth, G. of Greece 56 F3.................38.15N 22.30E
Corixa Grande r. Brazil/Bolivia 77 E3...17.30S 57.55W
Cork Rep. of Ire. 20 C1.................51.54N 8.28W
Cork d. Rep. of Ire. 20 C1.................52.00N 8.40W
Çorlu Turkey 57 H4.................41.11N 27.48E
Corner Brook town Canada 63 M2...48.58N 57.58W
Corno, Monte mtn. Italy 50 E5.................42.29N 13.33E
Cornwall d. England 13 C2.................50.26N 4.40W
Cornwall, C. England 13 B2.................50.07N 5.44W
Cornwallis I. Canada 63 I5.................75.00N 95.00W
Coro Venezuela 71 K3.................11.27N 69.41W
Coronada B. Costa Rica 71 H2.................9.00N 83.50W
Coronation G. Canada 62 G4.................68.00N 112.00W
Coronel Oviedo Paraguay 77 E2...25.24S 56.30W
Coropuna mtn. Peru 76 C3.................15.31S 72.45W
Corpus Christi U.S.A. 64 G2.................27.47N 97.26W
Corralejo Canary Is. 48 Z2.................28.43N 13.53W
Corrib, Lough Rep. of Ire. 20 B3.................53.26N 9.14W
Corrientes Argentina 77 E2.................27.30S 58.48W
Corrientes r. Argentina 77 E2.................29.55S 59.32W
Corrientes, C. Mexico 70 C5.................20.25N 105.42W
Corse, Cap c. France 44 H3.................43.00N 9.21E
Corserine mtn. Scotland 16 E3.................55.09N 4.22W
Corsham England 10 C2.................51.25N 2.11W
Corsica i. France 44 H3.................42.00N 9.10E
Corte France 44 H3.................42.18N 9.08E
Cortegana Spain 46 B2.................37.55N 6.49W
Corton England 11 G3.................52.32N 1.44E
Çorum Turkey 57 L4.................40.31N 34.57E
Corumbá Brazil 77 E3.................19.00S 57.25W
Corwen Wales 12 D4.................52.59N 3.23W
Cosenza Italy 50 G3.................39.17N 16.14E
Cosmoledo Is. Indian Oc. 86 D4.................9.30S 49.00E
Cosne France 44 E5.................47.25N 2.55E
Costa Blanca f. Spain 46 E2.................38.30N 0.05E
Costa Brava f. Spain 46 G4.................41.30N 3.00E
Costa del Sol f. Spain 46 C2.................36.30N 4.00W
Costa Rica C. America 71 H3.................10.00N 84.00W
Cotabato Phil. 105 G5.................7.14N 124.15E
Côte d'Azur f. France 44 G3.................43.20N 6.45E
Côte d'Ivoire Africa 84 D2.................7.00N 5.30W
Cothi r. Wales 12 C3.................51.51N 4.10W
Cotonou Benin 84 E2.................6.24N 2.31E
Cotopaxi mtn. Ecuador 76 C4.................0.40S 78.30W
Cotswold Hills England 10 C2.................51.50N 2.00W
Cottbus Germany 48 G4.................51.43N 14.21E
Cottenham England 11 F3.................52.18N 0.08E
Cottesmore England 10 E3.................52.43N 0.39W
Coulogne France 42 A2.................50.55N 1.54E
Council Bluffs U.S.A. 64 G5.................41.14N 95.54W
Coupar Angus Scotland 17 F4.................56.33N 3.17W
Courland Lagoon Russian Fed. 54 G6...55.00N 21.00E
Coutances France 44 C6.................49.03N 1.29W
Coventry England 10 D3.................52.25N 1.31W
Covilhã Portugal 46 B4.................40.17N 7.30W
Cowan, L. Australia 110 B2.................32.00S 122.00E
Cowbridge Wales 13 D2.................51.28N 3.28W
Cowdenbeath Scotland 17 F4.................56.07N 3.21W
Cowes England 10 D1.................50.45N 1.18W
Cowfold England 11 E1.................50.59N 0.17W
Cow Green Resr. England 15 E3.................54.40N 2.19W
Cox's Bazar Bangla. 97 I5.................21.25N 91.59E
Cozumel i. Mexico 70 G5.................20.30N 87.00W
Craigavon N. Ireland 16 C2.................54.28N 6.25W
Craig Goch Resr. Wales 12 D4.................52.20N 3.35W
Craignure Scotland 16 D4.................56.28N 5.42W
Crail Scotland 17 G4.................56.16N 2.38W
Craiova Romania 56 F6.................44.18N 23.46E
Cramlington England 15 F4.................55.06N 1.33W
Cranbrook Canada 62 G2.................49.29N 115.48W
Cranleigh England 11 E2.................51.08N 0.29W
Crawley England 11 E2.................51.07N 0.10W
Creag Meagaidh mtn. Scotland 19 E1...56.57N 4.38W
Credenhill England 10 C3.................52.06N 2.49W
Crediton England 13 D2.................50.47N 3.39W
Cree L. Canada 62 H3.................57.20N 108.30W
Creil France 42 B1.................49.16N 2.29E
Cremona Italy 50 D6.................45.08N 10.03E
Crepy-en-Valois France 42 B1.................49.14N 2.54E
Cres i. Croatia 50 F6.................44.50N 14.20E
Crescent City U.S.A. 64 B5.................41.46N 124.13W
Creston U.S.A. 65 H5.................41.04N 94.20W
Creswell England 15 F2.................53.16N 1.12W
Crete i. Greece 56 G1.................35.15N 25.00E
Crete, Sea of Med. Sea 56 G1.................36.00N 25.00E
Creuse r. France 44 D5.................47.00N 0.35E
Crewe England 15 E2.................53.06N 2.28W
Crewkerne England 13 E2.................50.53N 2.48W
Crianlarich Scotland 16 E4.................56.23N 4.37W
Criccieth Wales 12 C4.................52.55N 4.15W
Criciúma Brazil 77 F2.................28.40S 49.23W
Crickhowell Wales 12 D3.................51.52N 3.08W
Crieff Scotland 17 F4.................56.23N 3.52W
Criffell mtn. Scotland 17 F2.................54.57N 3.38W
Crimea pen. Ukraine 55 N1.................45.30N 34.00E

Crimond Scotland 19 H2....................57.36N 1.55W
Cristóbal Colón mtn. Colombia 71 J3..10.53N 73.48W
Croatia Europe 56 C6........................45.30N 17.00E
Cromarty Scotland 19 E2....................57.40N 4.01W
Cromarty Firth est. Scotland 19 E2......57.41N 4.10W
Cromdale, Hills of Scotland 19 F2......57.18N 3.30W
Cromer England 11 G3........................52.56N 1.18E
Cronamuck Mtn. Rep. of Ire. 16 B2......54.54N 7.52W
Crook England 15 F3..........................54.43N 1.45W
Crooked I. The Bahamas 71 J5............22.45N 74.00W
Crooked Island Passage The Bahamas 71 J5
....22.45N 74.40W
Croom Rep. of Ire. 20 C2....................52.30N 8.42W
Crosby England 14 D2........................53.30N 3.02W
Cross Fell mtn. England 15 E3..............54.43N 2.28W
Crossgar N. Ireland 16 D2..................54.24N 5.45W
Crossmaglen N. Ireland 16 C2............54.05N 6.37W
Crotone Italy 50 G3............................39.05N 17.06E
Crouch r. England 11 F2......................51.37N 0.45E
Crowborough England 11 F2................51.03N 0.09E
Crowland England 11 E3......................52.41N 0.10W
Crowle England 15 G2........................53.36N 0.49W
Crowthorne England 10 E2..................51.23N 0.49W
Croyde England 13 C3........................51.07N 4.13W
Croydon England 11 E2......................51.23N 0.06W
Crozet Is. Indian Oc. 117 L2................47.00S 52.00E
Cruden Bay Scotland 19 H2................57.24N 1.51W
Crumlin N. Ireland 16 C2....................54.38N 6.13W
Crummock Water l. England 14 D3......54.33N 3.19W
Cruz, Cabo c. Cuba 71 I4..................19.52N 77.44W
Cruzeiro do Sul Brazil 76 C4..............7.40S 72.39W
Cuando r. Africa 86 B3........................18.30S 23.30E
Cuanza r. Angola 86 A4......................9.22S 13.09E
Cuba C. America 71 I5........................22.00N 79.00W
Cubango r. Botswana 86 B3................18.30S 22.04E
Cuckfield England 11 E2......................51.00N 0.08W
Cúcuta Colombia 71 J2........................7.55N 72.31W
Cuddalore India 97 F3........................11.43N 79.46E
Cuddapah India 97 F3........................14.30N 78.50E
Cuenca Ecuador 76 C4........................2.54S 79.00W
Cuenca Spain 46 D4............................40.04N 2.07W
Cuenca, Serrania de mts. Spain 46 E4..40.25N 2.00W
Cuernavaca Mexico 70 E4..................18.57N 99.15W
Cuiabá Brazil 77 E3............................15.32S 56.05W
Cuiabá r. Brazil 77 E3........................18.00S 57.25W
Cuilcagh mtn. Rep. of Ire. 16 B2........54.12N 7.50W
Cuillin Hills Scotland 18 C3................57.12N 6.13W
Culiacán Mexico 70 C5........................24.50N 107.23W
Cullen Scotland 19 G2........................57.42N 2.50W
Cullera Spain 46 E3............................39.10N 0.15W
Cullin Sound Scotland 18 C2..............57.05N 6.20W
Cullompton England 13 D2..................50.52N 3.23W
Cullybackey N. Ireland 16 C2..............54.53N 6.21W
Cul Mor mtn. Scotland 18 D3..............58.04N 5.10W
Culuene r. Brazil 77 E3........................12.56S 52.51W
Culzean B. Scotland 16 E3..................55.21N 4.50W
Cumaná Venezuela 71 L3....................10.29N 64.12W
Cumbal mtn. Colombia 76 C5..............0.59N 77.53W
Cumberland Sd. Canada 63 L4............65.00N 65.30W
Cumbernauld Scotland 17 F3..............55.57N 4.00W
Cumbria d. England 14 D3..................54.40N 3.00W
Cumnock Scotland 16 E3....................55.27N 4.15W
Cunene r. Angola 86 A3......................17.15S 11.50E
Cuneo Italy 50 B6..............................44.22N 7.32E
Cupar Scotland 17 F4........................56.19N 3.01W
Cupica, G. of Colombia 71 I2..............6.35N 77.25W
Curaçao i. Neth. Ant. 71 K3................12.15N 69.00W
Curaray r. Peru 76 C4........................2.20S 74.05W
Curitiba Brazil 77 F2..........................25.24S 49.16W
Curuá r. Brazil 77 E4..........................5.23S 54.22W
Cushendall N. Ireland 16 C3................55.05N 6.04W
Cuttack India 97 H5............................20.26N 85.56E
Cuxhaven Germany 48 D5..................53.52N 8.42E
Cuzco Peru 76 D3..............................13.32S 72.10W
Cwmbran Wales 12 D3........................51.39N 3.01W
Cyclades is. Greece 56 G2..................37.00N 25.00E
Cyprus Asia 57 K1..............................35.00N 33.00E
Cyrenaica f. Libya 53 H2....................28.00N 22.10E
Czech Republic Europe 54 D3............49.30N 15.00E
Częstochowa Poland 54 F4................50.49N 19.07E

D

Dabrowa Gornicza Poland 54 F4........50.22N 19.20E
Dagupan Phil. 104 G7........................16.02N 120.21E
Da Hinggan Ling mts. China 103 M7....50.00N 122.10E
Dahlak Archipelago is. Eritrea 94 F2....15.45N 40.30E
Dailly Scotland 16 E3..........................55.18N 4.43W
Dakar Senegal 84 C3..........................14.38N 17.27W
Dakhla Oasis Egypt 94 C4..................25.30N 29.00E
Dakol'ka r. Belarus 55 K5....................52.10N 29.00E
Dakovica Yugo. 56 E5........................42.22N 20.26E
Da Lat Vietnam 104 D6......................11.56N 108.25E
Dalbandin Pakistan 95 J4....................28.53N 64.25E
Dalbeattie Scotland 17 F2..................54.55N 3.49W
Dali China 103 I3................................25.42N 100.11E
Dalian China 103 M5..........................38.53N 121.37E
Dalkeith Scotland 17 F3......................55.54N 3.04W
Dallas U.S.A. 64 G3............................32.47N 96.48W
Dalmally Scotland 16 E4....................56.25N 4.58W
Dalmatia f. Croatia 56 C5..................43.30N 17.00E
Dalmellington Scotland 16 E3............55.19N 4.24W
Daloa Côte d'Ivoire 84 D2..................6.56N 6.28W
Dalry D. and G. Scotland 16 E3..........55.07N 4.10W
Dalry N.Ayr Scotland 16 E3................55.43N 4.43W
Dalrymple Scotland 16 E3..................55.24N 4.35W
Dalrymple, Mt. Australia 110 D3........21.02S 148.38E
Dalton-in-Furness England 14 D3......54.10N 3.11W
Daly r. Australia 110 C4......................13.20S 130.19E
Daman India 96 E5............................20.25N 72.58E
Damar i. Indonesia 105 H2..................7.10S 128.30E
Damaraland f. Namibia 86 A2............22.20S 16.00E
Damascus Syria 94 E5........................33.30N 36.19E
Damavand mtn. Iran 95 H6................35.47N 52.04E
Damghan Iran 95 H6..........................36.09N 54.22E
Dampier Australia 110 A3..................20.40S 116.42E
Dampir Str. Pacific Oc. 105 I3............0.30S 130.50E
Da Nang Vietnam 104 D7..................16.04N 108.14E
Dande Ethiopia 87 B3........................4.53N 36.20E
Dandong China 103 M6......................40.06N 124.25E
Dane r. England 15 E2........................53.16N 2.30W

Danger Is. Cook Is. 108 O5................10.53S 165.49W
Dankov Russian Fed. 55 P5................53.15N 39.08E
Danube r. Europe 35 F2......................45.26N 29.38E
Danube, Mouths of the f. Romania 55 K1
....45.05N 29.45E
Danville U.S.A. 65 K4........................36.34N 79.25W
Dapaong Togo 84 E3..........................10.58N 0.07E
Da Qaidam China 102 H5..................37.44N 95.08E
Daqing China 103 N7........................46.40N 125.00E
Dar'a Syria 94 E5................................32.37N 36.06E
Darab Iran 95 H4................................28.45N 54.34E
Darabani Romania 55 J3....................48.11N 26.35E
Daravica mtn. Yugo. 56 E5................42.32N 20.08E
Darbhanga India 97 H6......................26.10N 85.54E
Dardanelles str. Turkey 56 H4............40.15N 26.30E
Dar es Salaam Tanzania 86 C4............6.51S 39.18E
Darhan Mongolia 103 J7....................49.34N 106.23E
Darién, G. of Colombia 71 I2..............9.20N 77.00W
Darjiling India 97 H6..........................27.02N 88.20E
Darling r. Australia 110 D2................34.05S 141.57E
Darling Downs f. Australia 110 D3......28.00S 149.45E
Darlington England 15 F3..................54.33N 1.33W
Darmstadt Germany 48 D3................49.52N 8.30E
Darnah Libya 85 G5............................32.45N 22.39E
Dart r. England 13 D2........................50.24N 3.41W
Dartford England 11 F2......................51.27N 0.14E
Dartmoor hills England 13 D2............50.33N 3.55W
Dartmouth England 13 D2..................50.21N 3.35W
Darton England 15 F2........................53.36N 1.32W
Daru P.N.G. 105 K2............................9.05S 143.10E
Darwen England 15 E2......................53.42N 2.29W
Darwin Australia 110 C4....................12.23S 130.44E
Daryacheh-ye-Bakhtegan l. Iran 95 H4..29.20N 54.05E
Daryacheh-ye Sistan f. Iran 95 J5......31.00N 61.15E
Daryacheh-ye-Tashk l. Iran 95 H5......30.05N 54.00E
Dasht-e-Kavir des. Iran 95 H5............34.40N 55.00E
Dasht-e-Lut des. Iran 95 I5................31.30N 58.00E
Dasht-i-Arbu Lut des. Afghan. 95 J5....30.00N 65.00E
Dasht-i-Margo des. Afghan. 95 J5......30.45N 63.00E
Datong China 103 K5..........................40.12N 113.12E
Daud Khel Pakistan 96 D6..................32.53N 71.34E
Daugava r. Europe 43 F2....................57.03N 24.00E
Daugavpils Latvia 43 F1....................55.52N 26.31E
Dauphin Canada 62 H3......................51.09N 100.05W
Dauphiné f. France 44 F4....................45.00N 5.45E
Davangere India 96 F3......................14.30N 75.52E
Davao Phil. 105 H5............................7.05N 125.38E
Davao G. Phil. 105 H5........................6.30N 126.00E
Davenport U.S.A. 65 H5......................41.40N 90.36W
Daventry England 10 D3....................52.16N 1.10W
David Panama 71 H2..........................8.26N 82.26W
Davis Str. N. America 63 M4..............66.00N 58.00W
Dawa Wenz r. Ethiopia 87 C3............4.11N 42.06E
Dawlish England 13 D2......................50.34N 3.28W
Dawqah Oman 95 H2........................18.38N 54.05E
Dawson Canada 62 E4......................64.04N 139.24W
Dawson Creek town Canada 62 F3......55.44N 120.15W
Daxian China 103 J4..........................31.10N 107.28E
Dayr az Zawr Syria 94 F6..................35.20N 40.08E
Dayton U.S.A. 65 J4............................39.45N 84.10W
Daytona Beach town U.S.A. 65 J2......29.11N 81.01W
Dead Sea Jordan 94 E5......................31.25N 35.30E
Deal England 11 G2............................51.13N 1.25E
Death Valley f. U.S.A. 64 C4..............36.00N 116.45W
Debak Malaysia 104 E4......................1.30N 111.28E
Debar Macedonia 56 E4......................41.31N 20.30E
Debenham England 11 G3..................52.14N 1.10E
Debrecen Hungary 54 F2....................47.30N 21.37E
Decatur U.S.A. 65 I4..........................39.44N 88.57W
Deccan f. India 96 F4..........................18.00N 76.30E
Děčín Czech Rep. 54 D4......................50.48N 14.15E
Dee r. Scotland 19 G2........................57.07N 2.04W
Dee r. Wales 12 D5............................53.13N 3.05W
Deele r. Rep. of Ire. 16 B2..................54.51N 7.29W
Degodia r. Ethiopia 87 C3..................4.15N 41.30E
De Grey r. Australia 110 A3................20.12S 119.11E
Dehra Dun India 97 F7......................30.19N 78.00E
Dej Romania 55 H2............................47.08N 23.55E
Delano Peak mtn. U.S.A. 64 D4..........38.23N 112.22W
Delaram Afghan. 95 J5......................32.11N 63.25E
Delaware r. U.S.A. 65 K4....................39.00N 75.30W
Delft Neth. 42 D4..............................52.01N 4.23E
Delfzijl Neth. 42 F5............................53.20N 6.56E
Delhi India 96 F6................................28.40N 77.14E
Deliçe r. Turkey 57 L4........................40.27N 34.07E
De Longa Str. Russian Fed. 59 T5......70.00N 178.00E
Del Rio U.S.A. 64 F2..........................29.23N 100.56W
Demirkazik mtn. Turkey 57 L4............37.50N 35.10E
Dempo mtn. Indonesia 104 C3............4.02S 103.07E
Denakil f. Ethiopia/Eritrea 85 I3........13.00N 41.00E
Denau Uzbekistan 95 K6....................38.20N 67.54E
Denbigh Wales 12 D5........................53.11N 3.25W
Denbighshire d. Wales 12 D5............53.07N 3.20W
Den Burg Neth. 42 D5........................53.03N 4.47E
Dendermonde Belgium 42 D3............51.01N 4.07E
Den Helder Neth. 42 D4......................52.58N 4.46E
Denizli Turkey 57 I2............................37.46N 29.05E
Denmark Europe 43 B1......................56.00N 9.00E
Denmark Str. Greenland/Iceland 63 P4..66.00N 25.00W
Denny Scotland 17 F4........................56.02N 3.54W
Denpasar Indonesia 104 F2................8.40S 115.14E
D'Entrecasteaux Is. P.N.G. 110 E5......9.30S 150.40E
Denver U.S.A. 64 F4..........................39.45N 104.58W
Dêqên China 102 H3..........................28.45N 98.58E
Dera Ghazi Khan Pakistan 96 E7........30.05N 70.44E
Dera Ismail Khan Pakistan 96 E7........31.51N 70.56E
Derby Australia 110 B4......................17.19S 123.38E
Derby England 10 D3........................52.55N 1.28W
Derbyshire d. England 15 F2..............53.12N 1.28W
Derg r. N. Ireland 16 B2....................54.44N 7.27W
Derg, Lough Donegal Rep. of Ire. 16 B2..54.37N 7.55W
Derg, Lough Tipperary Rep. of Ire. 20 C2
....52.57N 8.18W
Derry r. Rep. of Ire. 20 E2..................52.35N 6.38W
Derryveagh Mts. Rep. of Ire. 20 C4....55.00N 8.10W
Dersingham England 11 F3................52.51N 0.30E
Derudeb Sudan 94 E3........................17.32N 36.06E
Derwent r. Derbys England 15 F2........53.24N 1.44W
Derwent Resr. Derbys England 15 F2..53.24N 1.44W
Derwent Resr. Durham England 15 F3..54.51N 2.00W
Derwent Water l. England 14 D3........54.35N 3.09W
Desaguadero r. Argentina 75 C3........34.00S 66.40W
Desappointement, Îles du is. Pacific Oc. 109 R5
....14.02S 141.24W
Desaquadero r. Bolivia 76 D3............18.24S 67.05W
Dese Ethiopia 85 H3..........................11.05N 39.40E

Deseado Argentina 75 C2..................47.44S 65.56W
Des Moines U.S.A. 65 H5..................41.35N 93.35W
Desna r. Russian Fed./Ukraine 55 L4..50.32N 30.37E
Dessau Germany 48 F4......................51.51N 12.15E
Detroit U.S.A. 65 J5............................42.23N 83.05W
Deva Romania 54 H1..........................45.54N 22.55E
Deventer Neth. 42 F4........................52.15N 6.10E
Deveron r. Scotland 19 G2..................57.40N 2.30W
Devils Lake town U.S.A. 64 G6..........48.08N 98.50W
Devizes England 10 D2......................51.21N 2.00W
Devon d. England 13 D2....................50.50N 3.40W
Devon r. England 15 G2....................53.04N 0.50W
Devon r. Scotland 17 F4....................56.07N 3.52W
Devon I. Canada 63 J5......................75.00N 86.00W
Devonport Australia 110 D1..............41.09S 146.16E
Devrez r. Turkey 57 L4......................41.07N 34.25E
Dewsbury England 15 F2..................53.42N 1.38W
Dezful Iran 95 G5..............................32.24N 48.27E
Dezhou China 103 L5........................37.29N 116.11E
Dhahran Saudi Arabia 95 H4..............26.18N 50.08E
Dhaka Bangla. 97 I5..........................23.42N 90.22E
Dhamar Yemen 94 F1........................14.33N 44.24E
Dhanbad India 97 H5........................23.47N 86.32E
Dhaulagiri mtn. Nepal 97 G6............28.39N 83.28E
Dhule India 96 E5..............................20.52N 74.50E
Diamantina r. Australia 110 C3..........26.45S 139.10E
Dibrugarh India 97 I6........................27.29N 94.56E
Dickinson U.S.A. 64 F6......................46.54N 102.48W
Dida Galgalu f. Kenya 87 B3..............3.00N 38.00E
Didcot England 10 D2........................51.36N 1.14W
Dieppe France 44 D6........................49.55N 1.05E
Digby Canada 65 M5..........................44.30N 65.47W
Digne-les-Bains France 44 G4............44.05N 6.14E
Dijon France 44 F5............................47.20N 5.02E
Diksmuide Belgium 42 B3..................51.01N 2.52E
Dili Indonesia 105 H2........................8.35S 125.35E
Dillon U.S.A. 64 D5............................45.14N 112.38W
Dimapur India 97 I6..........................25.54N 93.45E
Dimitrovgrad Bulgaria 56 G5............42.01N 25.34E
Dinan France 44 B6..........................48.27N 2.02W
Dinant Belgium 42 D2......................50.16N 4.55E
Dinar Turkey 57 J3............................38.05N 30.09E
Dinard France 44 B6..........................48.38N 2.04W
Dinaric Alps mts. Bosnia./Croatia 56 C6..44.00N 16.30E
Dindigul India 97 F3..........................10.23N 78.00E
Dingle Rep. of Ire. 20 A2....................52.08N 10.19W
Dingle B. Rep. of Ire. 20 A2................52.05N 10.12W
Dingwall Scotland 19 E2....................57.35N 4.26W
Dipolog Phil. 105 G5..........................8.34N 123.28E
Dire Dawa Ethiopia 85 I2..................9.35N 41.50E
Dirranbandi Australia 110 D3............28.35S 148.10E
Disappointment, C. South Georgia 75 F1
....54.53S 36.08W
Disappointment, L. Australia 110 B3..23.30S 122.55E
Disko I. Greenland 63 M4..................69.45N 53.00W
Diss England 11 G3..........................52.23N 1.06E
Distington England 14 D3..................54.36N 3.32W
District of Columbia d. U.S.A. 65 K4..38.55N 77.00W
Distrito Federal d. Brazil 77 F3..........15.45S 47.50W
Distrito Federal d. Mexico 70 E4........19.20N 99.10W
Diu India 96 E5..................................20.41N 70.59E
Divinópolis Brazil 77 F2....................20.08S 44.55W
Divriği Turkey 57 N3..........................39.23N 38.06E
Dixon Entrance str. Canada/U.S.A. 62 E3
....54.10N 133.30W
Diyarbakir Turkey 94 F6....................37.55N 40.14E
Djado Plateau f. Niger 84 F4..............22.00N 12.30E
Djelfa Algeria 84 E5..........................34.43N 3.14E
Djibouti Africa 85 I3..........................12.00N 42.50E
Djibouti town Djibouti 85 I3..............11.35N 43.11E
Dnieper r. Europe 55 M2....................46.30N 32.25E
Dniestr r. Europe 55 K2....................46.21N 30.20E
Dniprodzerzhyns'k Ukraine 55 N3......48.30N 34.37E
Dnipropetrovs'k Ukraine 55 N3........48.29N 35.00E
Dniprorudne Ukraine 55 N2..............47.24N 34.57E
Doberai Pen. Indonesia 105 I3............1.10S 132.30E
Doboj Bosnia. 56 D6..........................44.44N 18.02E
Dobrich Bulgaria 57 H5......................43.34N 27.52E
Dobrovelychkivka Ukraine 55 L3......48.23N 31.11E
Dochart r. Scotland 16 E4..................56.30N 4.17W
Docking England 11 F3......................52.55N 0.39E
Dodecanese is. Greece 53 I4..............37.00N 27.00E
Dodge City U.S.A. 64 F4....................37.45N 100.02W
Dodman Pt. England 13 C2................50.13N 4.48W
Dodoma Tanzania 86 C4....................6.10S 35.40E
Doetinchem Neth. 42 F3....................51.57N 6.17E
Doha Qatar 95 H4..............................25.15N 51.34E
Dokkum Neth. 42 E5..........................53.20N 6.00E
Dokkum r. Wales 12 C4......................52.58N 4.14W
Dole France 44 F5..............................47.05N 5.30E
Dolgellau Wales 12 D4......................52.44N 3.53W
Dolo Odo Ethiopia 87 C3..................4.13N 42.08E
Dolomites mts. Italy 50 D7................46.25N 11.50E
Dolyna Ukraine 55 H3........................49.00N 23.59E
Dolyns'ka Ukraine 55 M3..................48.06N 32.46E
Dominica Windward Is. 71 L4............15.30N 61.30W
Dominican Republic C. America 71 J4..18.00N 70.00W
Don r. Russian Fed. 35 G2..................47.06N 39.16E
Don r. Scotland 19 G2........................57.10N 2.05W
Donaghadee N. Ireland 16 D2............54.39N 5.34W
Don Benito Spain 46 C3....................38.57N 5.52W
Doncaster England 15 F2..................53.31N 1.09W
Donegal Rep. of Ire. 20 C4................54.39N 8.06W
Donegal d. Rep. of Ire. 20 C4............54.52N 8.00W
Donegal B. Rep. of Ire. 20 C4............54.32N 8.18W
Donegal Pt. Rep. of Ire. 20 B2..........52.42N 9.38W
Donets'k Ukraine 55 O2....................48.00N 37.50E
Dongfang China 103 J1......................19.04N 108.39E
Dongfangbong China 106 B5............46.20N 133.10E
Dong Hoi Vietnam 104 D7................17.32N 106.35E
Dongotona Mts. Sudan 87 A3............4.00N 33.00E
Dongting Hu l. China 103 K3............29.00N 113.00E
Donostia-San Sebastián Spain 46 E5..43.19N 1.59W
Doon r. Scotland 16 E3......................55.26N 4.38W
Doon, Loch Scotland 16 E3................55.15N 4.23W
Dorchester England 10 C1................50.43N 2.28W
Dordogne r. France 44 C4..................45.03N 0.34W
Dordrecht Neth. 42 D3......................51.48N 4.40E
Dore, Mont mtn. France 44 E4............45.32N 2.49E
Dorking England 11 E2......................51.14N 0.20W
Dornbirn Austria 50 C2......................47.25N 9.44E
Dornoch Scotland 19 E2....................57.52N 4.02W
Dornoch Firth est. Scotland 19 E2......57.50N 4.04W
Döröö Nuur l. Mongolia 102 G7........47.40N 93.30E

Dorset d. England 10 C1....................50.48N 2.25W
Dortmund Germany 48 C4................51.32N 7.27E
Dothan U.S.A. 65 I3..........................31.12N 85.25W
Douai France 44 E7..........................50.22N 3.05E
Douala Cameroon 84 E2....................4.05N 9.43E
Douglas I.o.M. 14 C3........................54.09N 4.29W
Douglas Scotland 17 F3....................55.33N 3.51W
Doullens France 42 B2......................50.09N 2.21E
Doune Scotland 17 E4......................56.11N 4.04W
Dourados Brazil 77 E2......................22.09S 54.52W
Douro r. Portugal 46 A4....................41.10N 8.40W
Dove r. Derbys England 10 D3............52.50N 1.34W
Dove r. Suffolk England 11 G3............52.21N 1.14E
Dover England 11 G2........................51.07N 1.19E
Dover U.S.A. 65 K4............................39.10N 75.32W
Dover, Str. of U.K./France 11 G1........51.00N 1.30E
Down d. N. Ireland 16 D2..................54.20N 6.00W
Downham Market England 11 F3........52.36N 0.22E
Downpatrick N. Ireland 16 D2............54.21N 5.43W
Downpatrick Head Rep. of Ire. 20 B4..54.20N 9.21W
Downton England 10 D1..................51.00N 1.44W
Dowshi Afghan. 95 K6......................35.38N 68.43E
Drachten Neth. 42 F5........................53.05N 6.06E
Drăgăşani Romania 56 G6................44.40N 24.16E
Draguignan France 44 G3................43.32N 6.28E
Drakensberg mts. R.S.A. 86 B1..........30.00S 29.00E
Drama Greece 56 G4..........................41.09N 24.11E
Drammen Norway 43 B2....................59.45N 10.15E
Dranmore Rep. of Ire. 20 C3..............53.16N 8.56W
Draperstown N. Ireland 16 C2............54.48N 6.46W
Drau r. see Drava r. Austria 54
Drava r. Yugo. 56 D6........................45.34N 18.56E
Drenthe d. Neth. 42 F4......................52.52N 6.30E
Dresden Germany 48 F4....................51.03N 13.45E
Dreux France 44 D6..........................48.44N 1.23E
Drobeta-Turnu-Severin Romania 56 F6..44.37N 22.39E
Drogheda Rep. of Ire. 20 E3..............53.43N 6.23W
Droitwich England 10 C3..................52.16N 2.10W
Dromore N. Ireland 16 C2..................54.24N 6.10W
Dronfield England 15 F2....................53.18N 1.29W
Drosh Pakistan 95 L6........................35.33N 71.48E
Drumheller Canada 62 G3................51.28N 112.40W
Drummore Scotland 16 E2................54.41N 4.54W
Druskininkai Lithuania 55 I5..............53.58N 23.58E
Druts' r. Belarus 55 L5......................53.03N 30.42E
Drygarn Fawr mtn. Wales 12 D4........52.13N 3.39W
Drymen Scotland 16 E4....................56.04N 4.27W
Duarte, Pico Dom. Rep. 71 J4............19.02N 70.59W
Quba Saudi Arabia 94 E4..................27.21N 35.40E
Dubai U.A.E. 95 H4............................25.13N 55.17E
Dubawnt L. Canada 62 H4................62.50N 102.00W
Dubbo Australia 110 D2....................32.16S 148.41E
Dublin Rep. of Ire. 20 E3..................53.21N 6.18W
Dublin d. Rep. of Ire. 20 E3..............53.20N 6.18W
Dublin B. Rep. of Ire. 20 E3..............53.20N 6.09W
Dubno Ukraine 55 I4..........................50.28N 25.40E
Dubrovnik Croatia 56 D5..................42.40N 18.07E
Dubrovytsya Ukraine 55 J4..............51.38N 26.40E
Ducie I. Pacific Oc. 109 S4................24.40S 124.48W
Dudinka Russian Fed. 59 K4..............69.27N 86.13E
Dudley England 10 C3......................52.30N 2.05W
Duero r. see Douro r. Spain 46
Dufftown Scotland 19 F2..................57.27N 3.11W
Dugi Otok i. Croatia 56 B6................44.04N 15.00E
Duisburg Germany 48 C4..................51.26N 6.45E
Dukhan Qatar 95 H4........................25.24N 50.47E
Dukou China 103 I3............................26.30N 101.40E
Dulce r. Argentina 76 D1..................30.40S 62.00W
Duluth U.S.A. 63 H6..........................46.50N 92.10W
Dulverton England 13 D3..................51.02N 3.33W
Dumbarton Scotland 16 E3................55.57N 4.35W
Dumfries Scotland 17 F3....................55.04N 3.37W
Dumfries and Galloway d. Scotland 17 F3
....55.05N 3.40W
Dumyât Egypt 94 D5........................31.26N 31.48E
Dunaff Head Rep. of Ire. 16 B3..........55.17N 7.31W
Dunany Pt. Rep. of Ire. 20 E3............53.51N 6.15W
Dunbar Scotland 17 G4....................56.00N 2.31W
Dunblane Scotland 17 F4..................56.12N 3.59W
Duncansby Head Scotland 19 F3......58.39N 3.01W
Dunchurch England 10 D3................52.21N 1.19W
Dundalk Rep. of Ire. 20 E3................54.01N 6.24W
Dundalk B. Rep. of Ire. 20 E3............53.55N 6.17W
Dundee Scotland 17 F4....................56.28N 3.00W
Dundee City d. Scotland 17 G4..........56.28N 3.00W
Dundonald N. Ireland 16 D2..............54.36N 5.48W
Dundrum B. N. Ireland 16 D2............54.12N 5.46W
Dunedin New Zealand 111 G1..........45.53S 170.31E
Dunfermline Scotland 17 F4..............56.04N 3.29W
Dungannon N. Ireland 16 C2............54.30N 6.47W
Dungarvan Rep. of Ire. 20 D2............52.06N 7.39W
Dungeness c. England 11 F1..............50.55N 0.58E
Dungiven N. Ireland 16 C2................54.56N 6.57W
Dungun Malaysia 104 C4..................4.44N 103.26E
Dungunab Sudan 94 E3....................21.06N 37.05E
Dunholme England 15 G2..................53.18N 0.29W
Dunhua China 106 A4........................43.25N 128.20E
Dunhuang China 102 G6..................40.00N 94.40E
Dunkerque France 44 E7....................51.02N 2.23E
Dunkery Beacon hill England 13 D3....51.11N 3.35W
Dun Laoghaire Rep. of Ire. 20 E3......53.17N 6.09W
Dunleer Rep. of Ire. 20 E3..................53.49N 6.24W
Dunloy N. Ireland 16 C3....................55.02N 6.24W
Dunmore East Rep. of Ire. 20 D2........52.09N 7.00W
Dunmurry N. Ireland 16 D2................54.33N 6.00W
Dunnet B. Scotland 19 F3..................58.38N 3.25W
Dunnet Head Scotland 19 F3............58.40N 3.23W
Dunoon Scotland 16 E3......................55.57N 4.57W
Duns Scotland 17 G3........................55.47N 2.20W
Dunstable England 11 E2..................51.53N 0.32W
Dunvegan, Loch Scotland 18 C2........57.30N 6.40W
Durance r. France 44 F3....................43.55N 4.48E
Durango Mexico 70 D5......................24.01N 104.00W
Durango d. Mexico 70 D5..................24.00N 104.00W
Durban R.S.A. 86 C2........................29.53S 31.00E
Düren Germany 42 F2........................50.48N 6.30E
Durham England 15 F3......................54.47N 1.34W
Durham d. England 15 F3..................54.42N 1.45W
Durham U.S.A. 65 K4........................36.00N 78.54W
Durness Scotland 18 E3....................58.33N 4.45W
Durrës Albania 56 D4........................41.19N 19.27E
Dursey Head Rep. of Ire. 20 A1..........51.35N 10.15W
Dursley England 10 C2......................51.41N 2.21W
Dushanbe Tajikistan 102 B5..............38.38N 68.51E
Düsseldorf Germany 48 C4................51.13N 6.47E

Duyun China 103 J3..............................26.16N 107.29E
Düzce Turkey 57 J4................................40.51N 31.09E
Dyat'kovo Russian Fed. 55 N5................53.35N 34.22E
Dyce Scotland 19 G2.............................57.12N 2.11W
Dyer, C. Canada 63 L4..........................67.45N 61.45W
Dyfi r. Wales 12 D4...............................52.33N 3.56W
Dymchurch England 11 G2......................51.02N 1.00E
Dymock England 10 C2...........................51.59N 2.26W
Dzerzhinsk Russian Fed. 58 G3..............56.15N 43.30E
Dzhankoy Ukraine 55 N1.........................45.42N 34.23E
Dzhigudzhak Russian Fed. 59 R4............64.33N 157.19E
Dzhugdzhur Range mts. Russian Fed. 59 P3
                                                       57.30N 138.00E
Dzisna r. Belarus 55 K6.........................55.30N 28.20E
Dzungarian Basin f. Asia 102 F7............45.20N 86.30E
Dzyarzhynsk Belarus 55 J5.....................53.40N 27.01E

E

Eagle Pass town U.S.A. 64 F2...............28.44N 100.31W
Ealing England 11 E2.............................51.31N 0.20W
Earn r. Scotland 17 F4............................56.21N 3.18W
Earn, Loch Scotland 16 E4.....................56.23N 4.12W
Easington England 15 F3........................54.47N 1.21W
Easingwold England 15 F3.....................54.08N 1.11W
East Anglian Heights hills England 11 F3
                                                       52.03N 0.15E
East Ayrshire d. Scotland 16 E3............55.25N 4.20W
Eastbourne England 11 F1......................50.46N 0.17E
East C. New Zealand 111 G2.................37.45S 178.30E
East China Sea Asia 103 N3.................29.00N 125.00E
East Dereham England 11 F3.................52.40N 0.57E
East Dunbartonshire d. Scotland 16 E3....56.00N 4.15W
Easter I. Pacific Oc. 109 U4..................27.08S 109.23W
Eastern d. Kenya 87 B3..........................1.00N 38.40E
Eastern Desert Egypt 94 D4.................28.15N 31.55E
Eastern Ghāts mts. India 97 G4............16.30N 80.30E
Eastern Sayan mts. Russian Fed. 59 L3...53.30N 98.00E
Easter Ross f. Scotland 19 E2...............57.46N 4.25W
East Falkland i. Falkland Is. 75 D1........51.45S 58.50W
East Fen f. England 15 H2.....................53.06N 0.02E
Eastfield England 15 G3.........................54.15N 0.25W
East Frisian Is. Germany 48 C5............53.45N 7.00E
East Grinstead England 11 E2...............51.08N 0.01W
East Kilbride Scotland 16 E3.................55.46N 4.09W
Eastleigh England 10 D1........................50.58N 1.21W
East Linton Scotland 17 G3...................55.59N 2.39W
East Loch Tarbert Scotland 18 C2.........57.52N 6.43W
East London R.S.A. 86 B1.....................33.00S 27.54E
East Looe England 13 C2.......................50.21N 4.26W
East Lothian d. Scotland 17 G3.............55.55N 2.40W
Eastmain Canada 63 K3.........................52.10N 78.30W
Eastmain r. Canada 63 K3......................52.10N 78.30W
Easton England 10 C1.............................50.32N 2.26W
East Renfrewshire d. Scotland 16 E3.....55.45N 4.20W
Eastry England 11 G2.............................51.15N 1.18E
East Siberian Sea Russian Fed. 59 S5....73.00N 160.00E
East Sussex d. England 11 F1.................50.56N 0.12E
Eastwood England 15 F2.........................53.02N 1.17W
Eaton Socon England 11 E3....................52.13N 0.18W
Eau Claire, Lac á l' Canada 63 K3........56.10N 74.30W
Eauripik Atoll i. Fed. States of Micronesia 105 K5
                                                       6.42N 143.04E
Ebbw Vale town Wales 12 D3.................51.47N 3.12W
Eberswalde Germany 48 F5....................52.50N 13.50E
Ebinur Hu i. China 102 E6......................45.00N 83.00E
Ebro r. Spain 46 F4.................................40.43N 0.54E
Ecclefechan Scotland 17 F3...................55.03N 3.18W
Eccleshall England 13 D2.......................52.52N 2.14W
Ech Chélif Algeria 84 E5.........................36.20N 1.30E
Écija Spain 46 C2...................................37.33N 5.04W
Eck, Loch Scotland 16 D4.......................56.05N 4.59W
Eckington England 15 F2.........................53.18N 1.22W
Ecuador S. America 76 C4......................2.00S 78.00W
Eday i. Scotland 19 G4............................59.11N 2.47W
Ed Da'ein Sudan 94 C1...........................11.26N 26.09E
Ed Damazin Sudan 85 H3........................11.52N 34.23E
Ed Damer Sudan 94 D2............................17.37N 33.59E
Ed Debba Sudan 94 D2............................18.03N 30.57E
Ed Dueim Sudan 94 D1...........................14.00N 32.19E
Eden r. England 14 E3.............................54.57N 3.02W
Edessa Greece 56 F4...............................40.47N 22.03E
Edinburgh Scotland 17 F3.......................55.57N 3.13W
Edirne Turkey 56 H4................................41.40N 26.35E
Edmonton Canada 62 G3.........................53.34N 113.25W
Edmundston Canada 63 L2......................47.22N 68.20W
Edremit Turkey 56 H3.............................39.35N 27.02E
Edson Canada 62 G3...............................53.36N 116.28W
Edward, L. Uganda/Zaire 86 B4............0.30S 29.30E
Edwards Plateau f. U.S.A. 64 F3............30.30N 100.30W
Éfaté i. Vanuatu 111 F4..........................17.40S 168.25E
Egilsay i. Scotland 19 G4.......................59.09N 2.56W
Egilsstadhir Iceland 43 Z2......................65.16N 14.25W
Eğirdir Turkey 57 J2................................37.52N 30.51E
Eğirdir L. Turkey 57 J3............................38.04N 30.55E
Eglinton N. Ireland 16 B3........................55.02N 7.12W
Egmont, Mt. New Zealand 111 G2...........39.20S 174.05E
Egremont England 14 D3.........................54.28N 3.33W
Egypt Africa 94 D4..................................26.30N 29.30E
Eifel f. Germany 48 C4............................50.10N 6.45E
Eigg i. Scotland 18 C1.............................56.53N 6.09W
Eighty Mile Beach f. Australia 110 B4......19.00S 121.00E
Eilean Shona i. Scotland 18 D1...............56.50N 5.48W
Eindhoven Neth. 42 E4............................51.26N 5.30E
Eisenhüttenstadt Germany 48 G5...........52.09N 14.41E
Eishort, Loch Scotland 18 D2.................57.09N 5.58W
Eisleben Germany 48 E4..........................51.32N 11.33E
Eivissa Spain 46 F3.................................38.55N 1.30E
Ekibastuz Kazakhstan 102 D8................51.45N 75.22E
Ekostrovskaya, Ozero l. Russian Fed. 43 H4
                                                       67.30N 33.00E
Eksjö Sweden 43 C2...............................57.40N 15.00E
Ekwan r. Canada 63 J3...........................53.30N 84.00W
Elat Israel 94 D4.....................................29.33N 34.56E
Elazığ Turkey 57 N3................................38.41N 39.14E
Elba i. Italy 50 D5....................................42.47N 10.17E
El'ban Russian Fed. 103 P8.....................50.05N 136.35E
Elbasan Albania 56 E4.............................41.07N 20.04E
Elbe r. Germany 48 E5.............................53.33N 10.00E
Elbistan Turkey 57 M3.............................38.14N 37.11E
Elblag Poland 54 F6................................54.10N 19.25E
Elbrus mtn. Russian Fed. 58 G2.............43.21N 42.29E

Elburz Mts. Iran 95 H6............................36.00N 52.30E
Elche Spain 46 E3...................................38.16N 0.41W
Elda Spain 46 E3.....................................38.29N 0.47W
El Dera Kenya 87 B3...............................0.39N 38.43E
Eldoret Kenya 87 B3................................0.31N 35.17E
El Eulma Algeria 52 E4............................36.09N 5.41E
Eleuthera i. The Bahamas 71 I6.............25.00N 76.00W
El Faiyūm Egypt 94 D4............................29.19N 30.50E
El Fasher Sudan 85 G3............................13.37N 25.22E
El Geneina Sudan 85 G3..........................13.27N 22.30E
Elgin Scotland 19 F2...............................57.39N 3.20W
Elgin U.S.A. 65 I5.....................................42.03N 88.19W
El Gîza Egypt 94 D5................................30.01N 31.12E
El Goléa Algeria 84 E5.............................30.35N 2.51E
Elgon, Mt. Kenya/Uganda 87 A3............1.07N 34.35E
El Hierro i. Canary Is. 46 X1...................27.45N 18.00W
Elista Russian Fed. 58 G2........................46.18N 44.14E
El Jadida Morocco 84 D5.........................33.16N 8.30W
Ełk Poland 54 H5.....................................53.50N 22.22E
El Kerē Ethiopia 87 C4.............................5.48N 42.10E
El Khârga Egypt 94 D4.............................25.27N 30.32E
Elkhovo Bulgaria 56 H5...........................42.09N 26.36E
Elko U.S.A. 64 C5....................................40.50N 115.46W
Ellef Ringnes I. Canada 62 H5...............78.30N 102.00W
Ellensburg U.S.A. 64 B6..........................47.00N 120.34W
Ellesmere England 13 D2........................52.55N 2.53W
Ellesmere I. Canada 63 J5.......................78.00N 82.00W
Ellesmere Port England 14 E2................53.17N 2.55W
Ellice r. Canada 62 H4............................67.30N 104.00W
Ellon Scotland 19 G2...............................57.22N 2.05W
Ellsworth Land Antarctica 112...............77.00S 100.00W
Elmalı Turkey 57 I2..................................36.43N 29.56E
El Mansûra Egypt 94 D5..........................31.03N 31.23E
El Meghaïer Algeria 52 E3......................33.58N 5.56E
El Minya Egypt 94 D4...............................28.06N 30.45E
El Muglad Sudan 85 G3............................11.01N 27.50E
El Obeid Sudan 85 H3.............................13.11N 30.10E
El Oued Algeria 52 E3.............................33.20N 6.53E
El Paso U.S.A. 64 E3...............................31.45N 106.30W
El Puerto de Santa María Spain 46 B2....36.36N 6.14W
El Salvador C. America 70 G3................13.30N 89.00W
Eluru India 97 G4....................................16.45N 81.10E
Elvas Portugal 46 B3...............................38.53N 7.10W
Elverum Norway 43 B3.............................60.54N 11.33E
El Wak Kenya 87 C3................................2.45N 40.52E
Ely England 11 F3...................................52.24N 0.16E
Emamrud Iran 95 I6.................................36.25N 55.00E
Embu Kenya 87 B2..................................0.32S 37.27E
Emden Germany 48 C5............................53.23N 7.13E
Emerson Canada 64 G6............................49.00N 97.12W
Emi Koussi mtn. Chad 85 F3...................19.58N 18.30E
Emmeloord Neth. 42 E4...........................52.43N 5.46E
Emmen Neth. 42 F4.................................52.48N 6.55E
Emory Peak mtn. U.S.A. 64 F2...............29.15N 103.19W
Emporia U.S.A. 64 G4.............................38.24N 96.10W
Ems r. Germany 48 C5.............................53.14N 7.25E
Encantada, Cerro la Mexico 70 A7........31.00N 115.23W
Encarnación Paraguay 77 E2..................27.20S 55.50W
Endeh Indonesia 105 G3..........................8.51S 121.40E
Enderby Land f. Antarctica 112...............67.00S 53.00E
Endicott Mts. U.S.A. 62 C4.....................68.00N 152.00W
Enfield England 11 E2.............................51.40N 0.05W
Engels Russian Fed. 58 G3......................51.30N 46.07E
Enggano i. Indonesia 104 C2..................5.20S 102.15E
England U.K. 10-15
English Channel France/U.K. 44 C7........50.15N 1.00W
Enköping Sweden 43 D2..........................59.38N 17.07E
En Nahud Sudan 94 C1...........................12.41N 28.28E
Ennerdale Water l. England 14 D3.........54.31N 3.21W
Ennis Rep. of Ire. 20 B2.........................52.51N 9.00W
Enniscorthy Rep. of Ire. 20 E2...............52.30N 6.35W
Enniskillen N. Ireland 16 B2...................54.20N 7.39W
Ennistymon Rep. of Ire. 20 B2...............52.56N 9.20W
Enns r. Austria 54 D3..............................48.14N 14.22E
Enschede Neth. 42 F4.............................52.13N 6.54E
Ensenada Mexico 70 A7..........................31.53N 116.35W
Enshi China 103 J4.................................30.18N 109.29E
Enugu Nigeria 84 E2................................6.20N 7.29E
Envira r. Brazil 76 C4..............................7.29S 70.00W
Épinal France 44 G6................................48.10N 6.28E
Epping England 11 F2.............................51.42N 0.07E
Epsom England 11 E2.............................51.20N 0.16W
Epworth England 15 G2..........................53.30N 0.50W
Eqlid Iran 95 H5.......................................30.55N 52.40E
Equatorial Guinea Africa 84 E2..............1.30N 10.30E
Erciyas, Mt. Turkey 57 L3.......................38.33N 35.25E
Erdi f. Chad 94 C3...................................19.00N 23.00E
Ereğli Turkey 57 I2..................................37.30N 34.02E
Erfurt Germany 48 E4..............................50.58N 11.02E
Ergani Turkey 57 N3................................38.17N 39.44E
Ergene r. Turkey 56 H4...........................40.52N 26.12E
Eriboll, Loch Scotland 18 E3..................58.28N 4.41W
Ericht, Loch Scotland 19 E1...................56.52N 4.20W
Erie U.S.A. 65 J5......................................42.07N 80.05W
Erie, L. U.S.A./Canada 65 J5..................42.15N 81.00W
Eriskay i. Scotland 18 B2........................57.04N 7.17W
Eritrea Africa 85 H3................................15.20N 38.50E
Erlangen Germany 48 E3........................49.36N 11.02E
Erode India 97 F3....................................11.21N 77.43E
Er Rachidia Morocco 84 D5.....................31.58N 4.25W
Er Rahad Sudan 85 H3............................12.42N 30.33E
Errigal mtn. Rep. of Ire. 20 C5...............55.02N 8.08W
Erris Head Rep. of Ire. 20 A4.................54.19N 10.00W
Errochty, Loch Scotland 19 E1...............56.45N 4.08W
Erromango i. Vanuatu 111 F4.................18.45S 169.00E
Erzincan Turkey 57 N3............................39.44N 39.30E
Erzurum Turkey 57 N3............................39.57N 41.17E
Esbjerg Denmark 43 B1..........................55.28N 8.28E
Escanaba U.S.A. 65 I6............................45.47N 87.04W
Esch-sur-Alzette Lux. 42 F1...................49.31N 6.01E
Eschweiler Germany 42 F2.....................50.49N 6.16E
Esfahan Iran 95 H5.................................32.42N 51.40E
Esha Ness c. Scotland 19 Y9.................60.29N 1.37W
Esk r. Dumfries Scotland 17 F3..............54.58N 3.08W
Esk r. Midlothian Scotland 17 F3...........55.56N 3.03W
Eske, L. Rep. of Ire. 16 A2....................54.42N 8.03W
Eskişehir Turkey 57 J3............................39.46N 30.30E
Esla r. Spain 46 B4.................................41.29N 6.03W
Eslamabade Gharb Iran 95 G5..............34.08N 46.35E
Esmeraldas Ecuador 76 C5....................0.56N 79.40W
Esperance Australia 110 B2....................33.49S 121.52E
Espigüete mtn. Spain 46 C5...................42.56N 4.48W
Espinhaç, Serra da mts. Brazil 77 F3......17.15S 43.10W

Espinosa Brazil 77 F3............................14.58S 42.49W
Espírito Santo d. Brazil 77 F3...............20.00S 40.30W
Espíritu Santo i. Mexico 70 B5..............24.30N 110.20W
Espíritu Santo i. Vanuatu 111 F4..........15.50S 166.50E
Espoo Finland 43 F3...............................60.13N 24.40E
Esquel Argentina 75 B2..........................42.55S 71.20W
Essen Germany 48 C4.............................51.27N 6.57E
Essequibo r. Guyana 74 D7....................6.48N 58.23W
Essex d. England 11 F2...........................51.46N 0.30E
Estats, Pic d' mtn. Spain 46 F5..............42.40N 1.23E
Estevan Canada 62 H2............................49.09N 103.00W
Estonia Europe 43 F2..............................58.45N 25.30E
Estrela, Serra da mts. Portugal 46 B4....40.20N 7.40W
Estrondo, Serra Brazil 77 E4.................9.00S 49.00W
Étaples France 44 D7..............................50.31N 1.39E
Ethiopia Africa 85 H3.............................10.00N 39.00E
Ethiopian Highlands Ethiopia 82 G6......10.00N 37.00E
Etive, Loch Scotland 16 D4...................56.27N 5.15W
Etna, Mt. Italy 50 F2...............................37.43N 14.59E
Etosha Pan f. Namibia 86 A3.................18.50S 16.30E
Ettelbruck Lux. 42 F1.............................49.51N 6.06E
Ettrick Forest f. Scotland 17 F3.............55.30N 3.00W
Ettrick Water r. Scotland 17 F3..............55.36N 2.49W
Etwall England 10 D3.............................52.54N 1.35W
Eugene U.S.A. 64 B5..............................44.03N 123.07W
Eugenia, Punta c. Mexico 70 A6............27.50N 115.50W
Euphrates r. Asia 95 G5.........................31.00N 47.27E
Eureka U.S.A. 64 B5...............................40.49N 124.10W
Europa, Picos de mts. Spain 46 C5........43.10N 4.40W
Europe 34-35
Evans, L. Canada 63 K3.........................50.50N 77.00W
Evansville U.S.A. 65 I4............................38.02N 87.24W
Evaton R.S.A. 86 B2................................26.32S 27.51E
Everest, Mt. Asia 97 H6..........................27.59N 86.56E
Evesham England 10 D3..........................52.06N 1.57W
Évora Portugal 46 B3...............................38.34N 7.54W
Évreux France 44 D6...............................49.03N 1.11E
Evvoia i. Greece 56 G3............................38.30N 23.50E
Ewaso Ngiro Rift Valley r. Kenya 87 B2....2.08S 36.03E
Ewaso Ngiro Eastern r. Kenya 87 B3.....1.06N 39.26E
Ewe, Loch Scotland 18 D2......................57.52N 5.40W
Exe r. England 13 D2...............................50.40N 3.28W
Exeter England 13 D2..............................50.43N 3.31W
Exminster England 13 D2.........................50.41N 3.29W
Exmoor hills England 13 D3....................51.08N 3.45W
Exmouth England 13 D2...........................50.37N 3.24W
Exuma Is. The Bahamas 71 I5................24.00N 76.00W
Exuma Sd. The Bahamas 71 I5...............24.10N 76.00W
Eyasi, L. Tanzania 86 C4........................3.40S 35.00E
Eye Cambs. England 11 E3.....................52.36N 0.11W
Eye Suffolk England 11 G3.....................52.19N 1.09E
Eyemouth Scotland 17 G3.......................55.52N 2.05W
Eye Pen. Scotland 18 C3.........................58.13N 6.12W
Eyre (North), L. Australia 110 C3...........28.30S 137.25E
Eyre (South), L. Australia 110 C3...........29.30S 137.25E
Ezine Turkey 56 H3.................................39.48N 26.12E

F

Faafxadhuun Somalia 87 C3...................2.14N 41.38E
Faeroes is. Europe 34 C4.......................62.00N 7.00W
Fagersta Sweden 43 C3..........................59.59N 15.49E
Fairbanks U.S.A. 62 D4..........................64.50N 147.50W
Fair Head N. Ireland 16 C3.....................55.14N 6.10W
Fair Isle Scotland 19 Y8..........................59.32N 1.38W
Fairweather, Mt. U.S.A. 62 E3................59.00N 137.30W
Fais i. Fed. States of Micronesia 105 K5....9.45N 140.31E
Faisalabad Pakistan 96 E7......................31.25N 73.09E
Fakaofo Pacific Oc. 108 O6....................9.30S 171.15W
Fakenham England 11 F3........................52.50N 0.51E
Fakfak Indonesia 105 I3..........................2.55S 132.17E
Fal r. England 13 C2...............................50.14N 4.58W
Falcon Lake U.S.A./Mexico 64 G2.........26.37N 99.11W
Falkenberg Sweden 43 C2......................56.55N 12.30E
Falkirk Scotland 17 F3.............................56.00N 3.48W
Falkland Is. S. America 75 C1.................52.00S 60.00W
Falköping Sweden 43 C2.........................58.10N 13.32E
Falmouth England 13 B2..........................50.09N 5.05W
Falmouth B. England 13 B2......................50.06N 5.05W
Falster i. Denmark 43 C1.........................54.30N 12.00E
Falun Sweden 43 C3...............................60.37N 15.40E
Famagusta Cyprus 57 K1.........................35.07N 33.57E
Famatina, Sierra de mts. Argentina 76 D2
                                                       28.30S 67.50W
Fanad Head Rep. of Ire. 16 B3..............55.17N 7.38W
Fane r. Rep. of Ire. 20 E3........................53.56N 6.22W
Fangzhong China 103 J4.........................45.50N 128.50E
Fannich, Loch Scotland 18 E2.................57.38N 4.58W
Farafra Oasis Egypt 94 C4......................27.00N 28.20E
Farah Afghan. 95 J5................................32.23N 62.07E
Farah r. Afghan. 95 J5.............................31.25N 61.30E
Farallon de Pajaros i. N. Mariana Is. 105 K8
                                                       20.33N 144.59E
Fareham England 10 D1...........................50.52N 1.11W
Farewell, C. Greenland 63 N3.................60.00N 44.20W
Farewell, C. New Zealand 111 G1..........40.30S 172.35E
Fargo U.S.A. 64 G6.................................46.52N 96.59W
Farnborough England 10 E2...................51.17N 0.46W
Farndon England 14 E2...........................53.06N 2.53W
Farne Is. England 15 F4..........................55.38N 1.36W
Farnham England 10 E2..........................51.13N 0.49W
Faro Portugal 46 B2................................37.01N 7.56W
Fårö i. Sweden 43 D2..............................57.55N 19.10E
Farsala Greece 56 F3..............................39.17N 22.22E
Fasa Iran 95 H4.......................................28.55N 53.38E
Fastiv Ukraine 55 K4...............................50.08N 29.59E
Fatehgarh India 97 F6.............................27.22N 79.38E
Faversham England 11 F2.......................51.18N 0.54E
Faxaflói b. Iceland 43 X2........................64.30N 22.50W
Fayetteville U.S.A. 65 H4.........................35.03N 78.53W
Fdérik Mauritania 84 C4.........................22.30N 12.30W
Feale r. Rep. of Ire. 20 B2......................52.28N 9.38W
Fear, C. U.S.A. 65 K3.............................33.51N 77.59W
Federated States of Micronesia Pacific Oc. 108 K7
                                                       7.50N 155.00E
Fehmarn i. Germany 48 E6......................54.30N 11.05E
Feijó Brazil 76 C4....................................8.09S 70.21W
Feira de Santana Brazil 77 G3................12.17S 38.53W
Felixstowe England 11 G2.......................51.58N 1.20E
Femunden l. Norway 43 B3......................62.05N 11.55E
Feniton England 13 D2............................50.47N 3.17W
Feodosiya Ukraine 55 N1........................45.03N 35.23E
Ferdows Iran 95 I5...................................34.00N 58.10E

Fergus Falls town U.S.A. 64 G6............46.18N 96.00W
Ferkessédougou Côte d'Ivoire 84 D2.....9.30N 5.10W
Fermanagh d. N. Ireland 16 B2..............54.15N 7.45W
Fermoy Rep. of Ire. 20 C2......................52.08N 8.17W
Fernando de Noronha i. Atlantic Oc. 72 G6
                                                       3.50S 32.25W
Ferndown England 10 D1........................50.48N 1.55W
Ferrara Italy 50 D6..................................44.49N 11.38E
Ferrol Spain 46 A5...................................43.29N 8.14W
Ferryhill England 15 F3............................54.41N 1.33W
Fethaland, Pt. of Scotland 19 Y9............60.38N 1.18W
Fethard Rep. of Ire. 20 D2.......................52.28N 7.41W
Fethiye Turkey 57 I2.................................36.37N 29.06E
Fetlar i. Scotland 19 Z9...........................60.37N 0.52W
Feuilles r. Canada 63 K3.........................58.47N 70.06W
Feyzabad Afghan. 95 L6...........................37.05N 70.40E
Fez Morocco 84 D5..................................34.05N 5.00W
Ffestiniog Wales 12 D4............................52.58N 3.56W
Fianarantsoa Madagascar 86 D2............21.27S 47.05E
Fife d. Scotland 17 F4.............................56.10N 3.10W
Fife Ness c. Scotland 17 G4...................56.17N 2.36W
Figeac France 44 E4................................44.32N 2.01E
Figueira da Foz Portugal 46 A4..............40.09N 8.51W
Figueras Spain 46 G5..............................42.16N 2.57E
Figuig Morocco 52 D3.............................32.10N 1.15E
Fiji Pacific Oc. 111 G4............................18.00S 178.00E
Filadélfia Paraguay 77 D2......................22.17S 60.03W
Filey England 15 G3................................54.13N 0.18W
Filton England 10 C2...............................51.28N 2.35W
Filtu Ethiopia 87 C4.................................5.05N 40.42E
Findhorn r. Scotland 19 F2......................57.37N 3.40W
Finisterre, C. Spain 46 A5.......................42.54N 9.16W
Finland Europe 43 F3..............................64.30N 27.00E
Finland, G. of Finland/Estonia 43 F2......60.00N 26.50E
Finlay r. Canada 62 F3............................56.30N 124.40W
Finn r. Rep. of Ire. 20 D4.........................54.50N 7.30W
Finspång Sweden 43 C2..........................58.42N 15.45E
Fintona N. Ireland 16 B2..........................54.29N 7.19W
Fionn Loch Scotland 18 D2.....................57.45N 5.27W
Fionnphort Scotland 16 C4......................56.19N 6.23W
Firth of Clyde est. Scotland 16 D3..........55.35N 5.00W
Firth of Forth est. Scotland 17 G4...........56.05N 3.00W
Firth of Lorn est. Scotland 16 D4.............56.20N 5.40W
Firth of Tay est. Scotland 17 F4...............56.24N 3.08W
Firuzabad Iran 95 H4...............................28.50N 52.35E
Fisher Str. Canada 63 J4.........................63.00N 84.00W
Fishguard Wales 12 C3...........................51.59N 4.59W
Fishguard B. Wales 12 C4.......................52.06N 4.54W
Fismes France 42 C1...............................49.18N 3.41E
Flagstaff U.S.A. 64 D4.............................35.12N 111.38W
Flamborough England 15 G3..................54.07N 0.07W
Flamborough Head England 15 G3.........54.06N 0.05W
Flannan Isles i. Scotland 18 B3..............58.16N 7.40W
Flåsjön l. Sweden 43 C4..........................64.05N 15.50E
Flathead L. U.S.A. 64 D6.........................47.50N 114.05W
Flat Holm i. England 13 D2......................51.23N 3.08W
Flattery, C. U.S.A. 64 B6.........................48.23N 124.43W
Fleet England 10 E2.................................51.16N 0.50W
Fleetwood England 14 D2........................53.55N 3.01W
Flensburg Germany 48 D6.......................54.47N 9.27E
Flevoland d. Neth. 42 E4.........................52.30N 5.40E
Flinders r. Australia 110 C4.....................15.12S 141.40E
Flinders I. Australia 110 D2......................40.00S 148.00E
Flinders Range mts. Australia 110 C2......31.00S 138.30E
Flin Flon Canada 62 H3...........................54.47N 101.51W
Flint U.S.A. 65 J5.....................................43.03N 83.40W
Flint Wales 12 D5....................................53.15N 3.07W
Flint r. U.S.A. 65 J3..................................30.52N 84.38W
Flint I. Kiribati 108 P5..............................11.26S 151.48W
Flintshire d. Wales 12 D5.........................53.12N 3.10W
Florence Italy 50 D5.................................43.46N 11.15E
Florence U.S.A. 65 K3.............................34.12N 79.44W
Florencia Colombia 74 B7.......................1.37N 75.37W
Flores i. Indonesia 105 G2......................8.40S 121.20E
Flores Sea Indonesia 104 G2.................7.00S 121.00E
Floresta Brazil 77 G4...............................8.33S 38.35W
Florianópolis Brazil 77 F2.......................27.35S 48.31W
Florida d. U.S.A. 65 J2.............................29.00N 82.00W
Florida, Straits of U.S.A. 71 H5..............24.00N 81.00W
Florida Keys U.S.A. 71 H5.......................25.00N 81.00W
Florina Greece 56 E4...............................40.48N 21.25E
Florø Norway 43 A3..................................61.45N 4.55E
Flotta i. Scotland 19 F3............................58.49N 3.07W
Fly r. P.N.G. 105 K2.................................8.22S 142.23E
Fochabers Scotland 19 F2.......................57.37N 3.07W
Focșani Romania 55 J1............................45.40N 27.12E
Foggia Italy 50 F4....................................41.28N 15.33E
Fogo i. Cape Verde 84 B3........................15.00N 24.28W
Foinaven mtn. Scotland 18 E3.................58.24N 4.53W
Foix France 44 D3....................................42.57N 1.35E
Foligno Italy 50 E5...................................42.56N 12.43E
Folkestone England 11 G2.......................51.05N 1.11E
Fonseca, G. of Honduras 70 G3.............13.10N 87.30W
Fontainebleau France 44 E6....................48.24N 2.42E
Fontur c. Iceland 43 Z2............................66.30N 14.30W
Førde Norway 43 A3................................61.28N 5.51E
Fordingbridge England 10 D1.................50.56N 1.48W
Foreland c. England 10 D1......................50.42N 1.06W
Foreland Pt. England 13 D3.....................51.15N 3.47W
Forest of Atholl f. Scotland 19 F1............56.53N 3.55W
Forest of Bowland hills England 14 E2....53.57N 2.30W
Forest of Dean f. England 10 C2.............51.48N 2.32W
Forfar Scotland 19 G1..............................56.38N 2.54W
Forlì Italy 50 E6.......................................44.13N 12.02E
Formby England 14 D2.............................53.34N 3.04W
Formentera i. Spain 46 F3.......................38.41N 1.30E
Formosa Argentina 77 E2........................26.06S 58.14W
Formosa, Serra mts. Brazil 77 E3...........12.00S 55.00W
Forres Scotland 19 F2..............................57.37N 3.38W
Forssa Finland 43 E3...............................60.49N 23.40E
Forst Germany 48 G4...............................51.46N 14.39E
Fort Albany Canada 63 J3........................52.15N 81.35W
Fortaleza Brazil 77 G4.............................3.45S 38.45W
Fort Augustus Scotland 18 E2.................57.09N 4.41W
Fort Chipewyan Canada 62 G3................58.46N 111.09W
Fort Collins U.S.A. 64 E5.........................40.35N 105.05W
Fort-de-France Martinique 71 L3.............14.36N 61.05W
Fortescue r. Australia 110 A3..................21.00S 116.06E
Fort Frances Canada 63 I2.......................48.37N 93.23W
Fort George Canada 63 K3.......................53.50N 79.01W
Fort Good Hope Canada 62 F4...............66.16N 128.37W
Forth r. Scotland 17 F4............................56.06N 3.48W
Fort Liard Canada 62 F4..........................60.14N 123.28W
Fort McMurray Canada 62 G3..................56.45N 111.27W
Fort McPherson Canada 62 E4................67.29N 134.50W
Fort Nelson Canada 62 F3.......................58.48N 122.44W
Fort Norman Canada 62 F4......................64.55N 125.29W

Fort Peck Resr. U.S.A. 64 E6.........47.55N 107.00W
Fortrose Scotland 19 E2.........57.34N 4.07W
Fort Rupert Canada 63 K3.........51.30N 79.45W
Fort Scott U.S.A. 65 H4.........37.52N 94.43W
Fort Severn Canada 63 J3.........56.00N 87.40W
Fort-Shevchenko Kazakhstan 58 H2.........44.31N 50.15E
Fort Simpson Canada 62 F4.........61.46N 121.15W
Fort Smith Canada 62 G4.........60.00N 111.51W
Fort Smith U.S.A. 65 H4.........35.22N 94.27W
Fort St. John Canada 62 F3.........56.14N 120.55W
Fortuneswell England 10 C1.........50.33N 2.27W
Fort Wayne U.S.A. 65 I5.........41.05N 85.08W
Fort William Scotland 18 D1.........56.49N 5.07W
Fort Worth U.S.A. 64 G3.........32.45N 97.20W
Fort Yukon U.S.A. 62 D4.........66.35N 145.20W
Foshan China 103 K2.........23.03N 113.08E
Fougères France 44 C6.........48.21N 1.12W
Foula i. Scotland 19 X9.........60.08N 2.05W
Foulness Pt. England 11 F2.........51.37N 0.57E
Fouta Djallon f. Guinea 84 C3.........11.30N 12.30W
Fowey r. England 13 C2.........50.22N 4.40W
Foxe Basin Canada 63 K4.........67.30N 79.00W
Foxe Channel Canada 63 J4.........65.00N 80.00W
Foxe Pen. Canada 63 K4.........65.00N 76.00W
Foxford Rep. of Ire. 20 B3.........53.59N 9.07W
Foyle r. N. Ireland 16 B2.........55.00N 7.20W
Foyle, Lough Rep. of Ire./N. Ireland 16 B3
.........55.07N 7.06W
Foz do Iguaçú Brazil 77 E2.........25.33S 54.31W
Framlingham England 11 G3.........52.14N 1.20E
Franca Brazil 77 F2.........20.33S 47.27W
France Europe 44 D5.........47.00N 2.00E
Franceville Gabon 84 F1.........1.40S 13.31E
Francistown Botswana 86 B2.........21.11S 27.32E
Frankfort U.S.A. 65 J4.........38.11N 84.53W
Frankfurt Germany 48 G5.........52.20N 14.32E
Frankfurt am Main Germany 48 D4.........50.06N 8.41E
Franklin D. Roosevelt L. U.S.A. 64 C6
.........47.55N 118.20W
Franz Josef Land is. Russian Fed. 58 H6
.........81.00N 54.00E
Fraser r. Canada 62 F2.........49.05N 123.00W
Fraserburgh Scotland 19 H2.........57.42N 2.00W
Fraser I. Australia 110 E3.........25.15S 153.10E
Freckleton England 14 E2.........53.45N 2.50W
Fredericia Denmark 43 B1.........55.34N 9.47E
Fredericksburg U.S.A. 65 K4.........38.18N 77.30W
Fredericton Canada 63 L2.........45.57N 66.40W
Frederikshavn Denmark 43 B2.........57.26N 10.32E
Fredrikstad Norway 43 B2.........59.15N 10.55E
Freeport City The Bahamas 71 I6.........26.40N 78.30W
Freetown Sierra Leone 84 C2.........8.30N 13.17W
Freiberg Germany 48 F4.........50.54N 13.20E
Freiburg im Breisgau Germany 48 C2.........48.00N 7.52E
Fréjus France 44 G3.........43.26N 6.44E
Fremantle Australia 110 A2.........32.07S 115.44E
French Guiana S. America 74 D7.........3.40N 53.00W
French Polynesia Pacific Oc. 109 Q5.........20.00S 140.00W
Freshwater England 10 D1.........50.40N 1.30W
Fresno U.S.A. 64 C4.........36.41N 119.57W
Fria Guinea 84 C3.........10.13N 13.48W
Friedrichshafen Germany 48 D2.........47.39N 9.29E
Friesland d. Neth. 42 E5.........53.05N 5.45E
Frinton-on-Sea England 11 G2.........51.50N 1.16E
Frio, Cabo c. Brazil 75 E4.........22.50S 42.10W
Frisa, Loch Scotland 16 C4.........56.33N 6.05W
Frisian Is. Europe 34 G3.........53.30N 6.00E
Frizington England 14 D3.........54.30N 3.30W
Frobisher B. Canada 63 L4.........63.00N 66.45W
Frodsham England 14 E2.........53.17N 2.45W
Frogmore England 10 E2.........51.20N 0.49W
Frohavet est. Norway 43 B3.........63.55N 9.05E
Frome England 13 E3.........51.16N 2.17W
Frome r. England 10 C1.........50.41N 2.05W
Frome, L. Australia 110 C2.........30.45S 139.45E
Frontera Canary Is. 46 W1.........27.46N 18.01W
Frosinone Italy 50 E4.........41.36N 13.21E
Frøya i. Norway 43 B3.........63.45N 8.30E
Fuenlabrada Spain 46 D4.........40.16N 3.49W
Fuerteventura i. Canary Is. 46 Y2.........28.20N 14.10W
Fujairah U.A.E. 95 I4.........25.10N 56.20E
Fujian d. China 103 L3.........26.30N 118.00E
Fuji-san mtn. Japan 106 C3.........35.23N 138.42E
Fukui Japan 106 C3.........36.04N 136.12E
Fukuoka Japan 106 B2.........33.39N 130.21E
Fukushima Japan 106 B3.........37.44N 140.28E
Fulda Germany 48 D4.........50.35N 9.45E
Fulford England 15 F2.........53.56N 1.04W
Fulham England 11 E2.........51.30N 0.14W
Fumay France 42 D1.........49.59N 4.42E
Funabashi Japan 106 C3.........35.42N 139.59E
Funafuti Tuvalu 108 M6.........8.31S 179.13E
Funchal Madeira Is. 84 C5.........32.38N 16.54W
Fundy, B. of N. America 65 M5.........44.30N 66.30W
Fürth Germany 48 E3.........49.28N 11.00E
Fushun China 103 M6.........41.51N 123.53E
Fuxin China 103 M6.........42.08N 121.39E
Fuzhou Fujian China 103 L3.........26.01N 119.20E
Fuzhou Jiangxi China 103 L3.........28.03N 116.15E
Fyn i. Denmark 43 B1.........55.10N 10.30E
Fyne, Loch Scotland 16 D3.........55.55N 5.23W

G

Gabès Tunisia 84 F5.........33.52N 10.06E
Gabès, G. of Tunisia 84 F5.........34.00N 11.00E
Gabon Africa 84 F1.........0.00 12.00E
Gaborone Botswana 86 B2.........24.45S 25.55E
Gadsden U.S.A. 65 I3.........34.00N 86.00W
Gaer Wales 12 D3.........51.54N 3.11W
Gaeta Italy 50 E4.........41.13N 13.35E
Gaeta, G. of Med. Sea 50 E4.........41.05N 13.30E
Gafsa Tunisia 84 E5.........34.28N 8.43E
Gagarin Russian Fed. 55 N6.........55.38N 35.00E
Gagnon Canada 63 L3.........51.56N 68.16W
Gagra Georgia 57 O5.........43.21N 40.16E
Gainesville Fla. U.S.A. 65 J2.........29.37N 82.31W
Gainesville Tex. U.S.A. 64 G3.........33.37N 97.08W
Gainsborough England 15 G2.........53.23N 0.46W
Gairdner, L. Australia 110 C2.........31.30S 136.00E
Gair Loch Scotland 18 D2.........57.43N 5.43W
Gairloch town Scotland 18 D2.........57.43N 5.41W
Galana r. Kenya 87 B2.........3.10S 40.10E

Galapagos Is. Pacific Oc. 76 A4.........0.30S 90.30W
Galashiels Scotland 17 G3.........55.37N 2.49W
Galati Romania 55 J1.........45.27N 27.59E
Gala Water r. Scotland 17 F3.........55.36N 2.48W
Gáldar Canary Is. 46 Y2.........28.09N 15.40W
Galdhøpiggen mtn. Norway 43 B3.........61.38N 8.19E
Gallabat Sudan 94 E1.........12.58N 36.09E
Galle Sri Lanka 97 G2.........6.01N 80.13E
Galley Head Rep. of Ire. 20 C1.........51.31N 8.57W
Gallinas Pt. Colombia 71 J3.........12.20N 71.30W
Gallipoli Italy 50 H4.........40.02N 18.01E
Gallipoli Turkey 56 H4.........40.25N 26.31E
Gällivare Sweden 43 E4.........67.10N 20.40E
Gallup U.S.A. 64 E4.........35.32N 108.46W
Galole Kenya 87 B2.........1.34S 40.01E
Galston Scotland 16 E3.........55.36N 4.23W
Galveston U.S.A. 65 H2.........29.17N 94.48W
Galveston B. U.S.A. 65 H2.........29.40N 94.40W
Galway Rep. of Ire. 20 B3.........53.17N 9.04W
Galway d. Rep. of Ire. 20 B3.........53.25N 9.00W
Galway B. Rep. of Ire. 20 B3.........53.12N 9.07W
Gambia r. The Gambia 82 B6.........13.28N 15.55W
Gambier Is. Pacific Oc. 109 R4.........23.10S 135.00W
Gamund mtn. Ethiopia 87 B3.........4.08N 38.04E
Gâncă Azerbaijan 58 G2.........40.39N 46.20E
Gandadiwata, Bukit mtn. Indonesia 104 F3
.........2.45S 119.25E
Gander Canada 63 M2.........48.58N 54.34W
Gandhidham India 96 E5.........23.07N 70.10E
Gandhinagar India 96 E5.........23.15N 72.45E
Gandía Spain 46 E3.........38.59N 0.11W
Gand-i-Zureh des. Afghan. 95 J3.........30.00N 62.00E
Ganges r. India 97 H5.........23.30N 90.25E
Ganges, Mouths of the India/Bangla. 97 H5
.........22.00N 89.35E
Gannett Peak mtn. U.S.A. 64 E5.........43.10N 109.38W
Gansu d. China 103 I5.........36.00N 103.00E
Gantamaa Somalia 87 C3.........2.25N 41.49E
Ganzhou China 103 K3.........25.52N 114.51E
Gao Mali 84 E3.........16.19N 0.09W
Gaoxiong Taiwan 103 M2.........22.36N 120.17E
Gap France 44 G4.........44.33N 6.05E
Gar China 102 E4.........32.10N 80.00E
Gara, Lough Rep. of Ire. 20 C3.........53.56N 8.28W
Garanhuns Brazil 77 G4.........8.53S 36.28W
Garbahaarey Somalia 87 C3.........3.20N 42.11E
Garba Tula Kenya 87 B3.........0.31N 38.30E
Gard r. France 44 F3.........43.52N 4.40E
Garda, L. Italy 50 D6.........45.40N 10.40E
Gardēz Afghan. 95 K5.........33.37N 69.07E
Garelochhead Scotland 16 E4.........56.05N 4.49W
Garforth England 15 F2.........53.48N 1.22W
Gargždai Lithuania 43 E1.........55.42N 21.21E
Garissa Kenya 87 B2.........0.27S 39.39E
Garmisch-Partenkirchen Germany 48 E2
.........47.30N 11.05E
Garonne r. France 44 C4.........45.00N 0.37W
Garoowe Somalia 85 I2.........8.17N 48.20E
Garoua Cameroon 84 F2.........9.17N 13.22E
Garron Pt. N. Ireland 16 D3.........55.03N 5.58W
Garry r. Scotland 18 E2.........57.05N 4.49W
Garry, Loch Scotland 19 E1.........56.47N 4.13W
Garsen Kenya 87 A2.........2.18S 40.08E
Garstang England 14 E2.........53.53N 2.47W
Garvagh N. Ireland 16 C2.........54.59N 6.42W
Gary U.S.A. 65 I5.........41.34N 87.20W
Gascony, G. of France 44 B3.........44.00N 2.40W
Gascoyne r. Australia 110 A3.........25.00S 113.40E
Gashua Nigeria 84 F3.........12.53N 11.05E
Gaspé Canada 63 L2.........48.50N 64.30W
Gaspé Pen. Canada 63 L2.........48.30N 65.00W
Gastonia U.S.A. 65 J4.........35.14N 81.12W
Gata, Cabo de c. Spain 46 D2.........36.45N 2.11W
Gatehouse of Fleet Scotland 16 E2.........54.53N 4.12W
Gateshead England 15 F3.........54.57N 1.35W
Gävle Sweden 43 D3.........60.41N 17.10E
Gaya India 97 H5.........24.48N 85.00E
Gaya Niger 84 E3.........11.52N 3.28E
Gaza Asia 94 D5.........31.20N 34.20E
Gaza town Gaza 94 D5.........31.30N 34.28E
Gaziantep Turkey 57 M2.........37.04N 37.21E
Gdańsk Poland 54 F5.........54.22N 18.38E
Gdańsk, G. of Poland 54 F5.........54.45N 19.15E
Gdynia Poland 54 F6.........54.31N 18.30E
Geal Charn mtn. Scotland 19 F2.........57.10N 3.31W
Gebze Turkey 57 I4.........40.48N 29.26E
Gedaref Sudan 85 H3.........14.01N 35.24E
Gediz Turkey 57 I3.........39.04N 29.25E
Gediz r. Turkey 56 H3.........38.37N 26.47E
Gedser Odde c. Denmark 54 C6.........54.35N 11.57E
Geel Belgium 42 E3.........51.10N 5.00E
Geelong Australia 110 D2.........38.10S 144.26E
Gejiu China 103 I2.........23.25N 103.05E
Gela Italy 50 F2.........37.03N 14.15E
Gelderland d. Neth. 42 E4.........52.05N 6.00E
Gelligaer Wales 12 D3.........51.40N 3.18W
Gelsenkirchen Germany 48 C4.........51.30N 7.05E
Gemlik Turkey 57 I4.........40.26N 29.10E
Genale Wenz r. Ethiopia 87 B3.........4.15N 42.10E
General Santos Phil. 105 H5.........6.05N 125.15E
Geneva, L. Switz. 44 G5.........46.13N 6.09E
Geneva, L. Switz. 44 G5.........46.30N 6.30E
Genil r. Spain 46 C2.........37.42N 5.20W
Genk Belgium 42 E2.........50.58N 5.34E
Genoa Italy 50 C6.........44.24N 8.54E
Genoa, G. of Italy 50 C5.........43.50N 8.55E
Gent Belgium 42 C3.........51.02N 3.42E
George r. Canada 63 L3.........58.30N 66.00W
Georgetown Guyana 74 D7.........6.48N 58.08W
George Town Malaysia 104 C5.........5.30N 100.16E
Georgia Asia 58 G2.........42.00N 43.30E
Georgia d. U.S.A. 65 J3.........33.00N 83.00W
Georgian B. Canada 63 J2.........45.15N 80.45W
Georgina r. Australia 110 C3.........23.12S 139.33E
Georgiyevka Kazakhstan 102 E7.........49.21N 81.63E
Gera Germany 48 F4.........50.51N 12.11E
Geral de Goiás, Serra mts. Brazil 77 F3.........13.00S 45.40W
Geraldton Australia 110 A3.........28.49S 114.36E
Gereshk Afghan. 95 J5.........31.48N 64.34E
Germany Europe 48 D4.........51.00N 10.00E
Gevgelija Macedonia 56 F4.........41.09N 22.30E
Gexto Spain 46 D5.........43.21N 3.01W
Geyik Dag mtn. Turkey 57 K2.........36.53N 32.12E
Geyve Turkey 57 J4.........40.32N 30.18E
Gezira f. Sudan 82 G6.........14.30N 33.00E

Ghadamis Libya 84 E5.........30.10N 9.30E
Ghaem Shahr Iran 95 H6.........36.28N 52.53E
Ghaghara r. India 97 G6.........25.45N 84.50E
Ghana Africa 84 D2.........8.00N 1.00E
Ghardaïa Algeria 84 E5.........32.20N 3.40E
Gharyan Libya 52 F3.........32.10N 13.01E
Ghazaouet Algeria 52 C4.........35.08N 1.50W
Ghaziabad India 97 F6.........28.40N 77.26E
Ghazni Afghan. 95 K5.........33.33N 68.28E
Giant's Causeway f. N. Ireland 16 C3.........55.14N 6.31W
Gibraltar Europe 46 C2.........36.07N 5.22W
Gibraltar, Str. of Africa/Europe 46 C1.........36.00N 5.25W
Gibson Desert Australia 110 B3.........23.10S 125.35E
Gidolē Ethiopia 87 B4.........5.38N 37.28E
Gien France 44 E5.........47.42N 2.38E
Giessen Germany 48 D4.........50.35N 8.40E
Gifu Japan 106 C3.........35.27N 136.50E
Gigha i. Scotland 16 D3.........55.41N 5.44W
Gijón Spain 46 C5.........43.32N 5.40W
Gila r. U.S.A. 64 D3.........32.45N 114.30W
Gilbert Is. Kiribati 111 G5.........2.00S 175.00E
Gilf Kebir Plateau f. Egypt 94 C3.........23.30N 26.00E
Gilgil Kenya 87 B2.........0.30S 36.19E
Gilgit Jammu & Kashmir 96 E8.........35.54N 74.20E
Gill, Lough Rep. of Ire. 20 C4.........54.15N 8.25W
Gillette U.S.A. 64 E5.........44.18N 105.30W
Gillingham Dorset England 10 C2.........51.02N 2.17W
Gillingham Kent England 11 F2.........51.24N 0.33E
Gilwern Wales 12 D3.........51.51N 3.06W
Gimbala, Jebel mtn. Sudan 85 G3.........13.00N 24.20E
Giresun Turkey 57 N4.........40.55N 38.25E
Girona Spain 46 G4.........41.59N 2.49E
Gironde r. France 44 C4.........45.35N 1.00W
Girvan Scotland 16 E3.........55.15N 4.51W
Gisborne New Zealand 111 G2.........38.41S 178.02E
Gisors France 42 A1.........49.17N 1.47E
Gizhiga Russian Fed. 59 S4.........62.00N 160.34E
Gizhiga G. Russian Fed. 59 R4.........61.00N 158.00E
Gjøvik Norway 43 B3.........60.47N 10.41E
Glace Bay town Canada 63 M2.........46.11N 60.00W
Glacier Peak mtn. U.S.A. 64 B6.........48.07N 121.06W
Gladstone Australia 110 E3.........23.52S 151.16E
Glanton England 15 F4.........55.25N 1.53W
Glasgow Scotland 16 E3.........55.52N 4.15W
Glasgow U.S.A. 64 E6.........48.12N 106.37W
Glass, Loch Scotland 19 E2.........57.43N 4.30W
Glastonbury England 13 E3.........51.09N 2.42W
Glenarm N. Ireland 16 D2.........54.58N 5.58W
Glen Coe f. Scotland 16 E4.........56.40N 4.55W
Glendale U.S.A. 64 D3.........33.32N 112.11W
Glendive U.S.A. 64 F6.........47.08N 104.42W
Glengad Head Rep. of Ire. 20 D5.........55.20N 7.11W
Glen Garry f. Scotland 18 D2.........57.03N 5.05W
Glengormley N. Ireland 16 D2.........54.41N 5.59W
Glenluce Scotland 16 E2.........54.53N 4.48W
Glen More f. Scotland 19 E2.........57.15N 4.30W
Glen Moriston f. Scotland 18 E2.........57.11N 4.52W
Glennallen U.S.A. 62 D4.........62.08N 145.38W
Glenrothes Scotland 17 F4.........56.12N 3.10W
Glenshee f. Scotland 18 F1.........56.50N 3.28W
Glinton England 11 E3.........52.39N 0.17W
Gliwice Poland 54 F4.........50.17N 18.40E
Głogów Poland 54 E4.........51.40N 16.06E
Glomfjord town Norway 43 C4.........66.49N 14.00E
Glorieuses, Is. Indian Oc. 86 D3.........11.34S 47.19E
Glossop England 15 F2.........53.27N 1.56W
Gloucester England 10 C2.........51.52N 2.15W
Gloucestershire d. England 10 C2.........51.45N 2.00W
Glusburn England 15 F2.........53.54N 2.00W
Glyder Fawr mtn. Wales 12 C5.........53.06N 4.01W
Glynneath Wales 12 D3.........51.45N 3.37W
Gmünd Austria 54 D3.........48.47N 14.59E
Gniezno Poland 54 E5.........52.32N 17.32E
Goa d. India 96 E4.........15.30N 74.00E
Goat Fell mtn. Scotland 16 D3.........55.37N 5.12W
Gobabis Namibia 86 A2.........22.30S 18.58E
Gobi des. Asia 103 I6.........43.30N 103.30E
Gobowen England 10 B3.........52.54N 3.02W
Goch Germany 42 E3.........51.41N 6.10E
Godalming England 11 E2.........51.11N 0.37W
Godavari r. India 97 G4.........16.40N 82.15E
Godmanchester England 11 E3.........52.19N 0.11W
Godthåb see Nuuk Greenland 63
Goes Neth. 42 C3.........51.30N 3.54E
Goiânia Brazil 77 F3.........16.43S 49.18W
Goiás d. Brazil 77 E3.........15.00S 48.00W
Gökçeada i. Turkey 56 G4.........40.10N 25.51E
Göksun Turkey 57 M3.........38.03N 36.30E
Gölcük Turkey 57 I4.........40.44N 29.50E
Gold Coast town Australia 110 E3.........28.00S 153.22E
Golmud China 102 G5.........36.23N 94.49E
Golpayegan Iran 95 H5.........33.23N 50.18E
Golspie Scotland 19 F2.........57.58N 3.58W
Gómez Palacio Mexico 70 D6.........25.39N 103.30W
Gonaïves Haiti 71 J4.........19.29N 72.42W
Gonbad-e Kavus Iran 95 I6.........37.15N 55.11E
Gondar Ethiopia 85 H3.........12.39N 37.29E
Gondia India 97 G5.........21.27N 80.12E
Gongga Shan mtn. China 103 I3.........29.30N 101.30E
Good Hope, C. of R.S.A. 86 A1.........34.20S 18.25E
Goodwick Wales 12 C4.........52.00N 5.00W
Goole England 15 G2.........53.42N 0.52W
Goose L. U.S.A. 64 B5.........41.55N 120.25W
Gorakhpur India 97 G6.........26.45N 83.23E
Gorebridge Scotland 17 F3.........55.51N 3.02W
Gorey Rep. of Ire. 20 E2.........52.40N 6.18W
Gorgan Iran 95 H6.........36.50N 54.29E
Goris Armenia 95 G6.........39.31N 46.22E
Gorizia Italy 50 E6.........45.58N 13.37E
Görlitz Germany 48 G4.........51.09N 15.00E
Gorno-Altaysk Russian Fed. 102 F8.........51.57N 85.58E
Gornyak Russian Fed. 102 E8.........50.59N 81.30E
Gorontalo Indonesia 105 G4.........0.33N 123.05E
Gort Rep. of Ire. 20 C3.........53.03N 8.50W
Gorzów Wielkopolski Poland 54 D5.........52.42N 15.12E
Gosberton England 11 E3.........52.52N 0.09W
Gosford Australia 110 E2.........33.25S 151.18E
Gosforth Cumbria England 14 D3.........54.26N 3.27W
Gosforth T. and W. England 15 F4.........55.02N 1.35W
Goshogawara Japan 106 D4.........40.48N 140.27E
Gospić Croatia 56 B6.........44.34N 15.23E
Gosport England 10 D1.........50.48N 1.08W
Göteborg Sweden 43 B2.........57.45N 12.00E
Gotha Germany 48 E4.........50.57N 10.43E
Gotland i. Sweden 43 D2.........57.30N 18.30E

Göttingen Germany 48 D4.........51.32N 9.57E
Gouda Neth. 42 D4.........52.01N 4.43E
Gouin, Résr. Canada 63 K2.........48.38N 74.54W
Goulburn Australia 110 D2.........34.47S 149.43E
Gourdon France 44 D4.........44.45N 1.22E
Governador Valadares Brazil 77 F3.........18.51S 42.00W
Gower pen. Wales 12 C3.........51.37N 4.10W
Gowna, L. Rep. of Ire. 20 D3.........53.50N 7.34W
Goya Argentina 77 E2.........29.10S 59.20W
Gozo i. Malta 50 F2.........36.03N 14.16E
Graciosa i. Canary Is. 46 Z2.........29.15N 13.30W
Gradaús, Serra dos mts. Brazil 77 E4.........8.00S 50.30W
Grafham Water l. England 11 E3.........52.19N 0.16W
Grafton Australia 110 E3.........29.40S 152.56E
Grafton U.S.A. 64 G6.........48.28N 97.25W
Graham Land f. Antarctica 112.........67.00S 60.00W
Grahamstown R.S.A. 86 B1.........33.19S 26.32E
Grain England 11 F2.........51.28N 0.43E
Granada Spain 46 D2.........37.10N 3.35W
Gran Canaria i. Canary Is. 46 Y1.........28.00N 15.30W
Gran Chaco f. S. America 75 C4.........23.30S 60.00W
Grand Bahama i. The Bahamas 71 I6.........26.35N 78.00W
Grand Canyon f. U.S.A. 64 D4.........36.15N 113.00W
Grand Canyon town U.S.A. 64 D4.........36.04N 112.07W
Grand Cayman i. Cayman Is. 71 H4.........19.20N 81.30W
Grande r. Bahia Brazil 77 F3.........11.05S 43.09W
Grande r. Minas Gerais Brazil 77 E3.........20.00S 51.00W
Grande, Bahía b. Argentina 75 C1.........50.45S 68.00W
Grande Prairie town Canada 62 G3.........55.10N 118.52W
Grand Falls town Canada 63 M2.........48.57N 55.40W
Grand Forks U.S.A. 64 G6.........47.57N 97.05W
Grand Island town U.S.A. 64 G5.........40.56N 98.21W
Grand Junction U.S.A. 64 E4.........39.04N 108.33W
Grand Manan I. Canada 65 M5.........44.40N 66.50W
Grand Rapids town U.S.A. 65 I5.........42.57N 85.40W
Grangemouth Scotland 17 F4.........56.01N 3.44W
Grange-over-Sands England 14 E3.........54.12N 2.55W
Gran Paradiso mtn. Italy 50 B6.........45.31N 7.15E
Grantham England 10 E3.........52.55N 0.39W
Grantown-on-Spey Scotland 19 F2.........57.19N 3.38W
Grants Pass town U.S.A. 64 B5.........42.26N 123.20W
Grasse France 44 G3.........43.40N 6.56E
Grassington England 15 F3.........54.04N 1.59W
Grave, Pointe de c. France 44 C4.........45.35N 1.04W
Gravelbourg England 11 F2.........51.27N 0.24E
Grays England 11 F2.........51.29N 0.20E
Graz Austria 54 D3.........47.05N 15.22E
Great Abaco i. The Bahamas 71 I6.........26.30N 77.00W
Great Australian Bight Australia 110 B2
.........33.20S 130.00E
Great Baddow England 11 F2.........51.43N 0.29E
Great Barrier Reef f. Australia 110 D4.........16.30S 146.30E
Great Basin f. U.S.A. 64 C4.........39.00N 115.30W
Great Bear L. Canada 62 G4.........66.00N 120.00W
Great Bend town U.S.A. 64 G4.........38.22N 98.47W
Great Bernera i. Scotland 18 C3.........58.13N 6.50W
Great Blasket I. Rep. of Ire. 20 A2.........52.05N 10.32W
Great Clifton England 14 D3.........54.38N 3.30W
Great Cumbrae i. Scotland 16 E3.........55.45N 4.57W
Great Dividing Range mts. Australia 110 D2
.........33.00S 151.00E
Great Driffield England 15 G3.........54.01N 0.26W
Great Dunmow England 11 F2.........51.53N 0.22E
Greater Antilles is. C. America 71 J4.........17.00N 70.00W
Greater London d. England 11 E2.........51.31N 0.06W
Greater Manchester d. England 15 E2.........53.30N 2.18W
Great Exuma i. The Bahamas 71 I5.........23.00N 76.00W
Great Falls town U.S.A. 64 D6.........47.30N 111.16W
Great Gonerby England 10 E3.........52.56N 0.40W
Greatham England 15 F3.........54.39N 1.14W
Great Harwood England 15 E2.........53.48N 2.24W
Great Inagua i. The Bahamas 71 J5.........21.00N 73.20W
Great Karoo f. R.S.A. 86 B1.........32.50S 22.30E
Great Linford England 10 E3.........52.03N 0.46W
Great Malvern England 10 C3.........52.07N 2.19W
Great Nicobar i. India 104 A5.........7.00N 93.50E
Great Ormes Head Wales 12 D5.........53.20N 3.52W
Great Ouse r. England 11 F3.........52.47N 0.23E
Great Plains f. N. America 60 I6.........45.00N 100.00W
Great Rhos mtn. Wales 12 D4.........52.16N 3.13W
Great Rift Valley f. Africa 82 G4.........7.00S 33.00E
Great Salt L. U.S.A. 64 D5.........41.10N 112.40W
Great Sand Sea f. Egypt/Libya 94 C4.........28.00N 25.00E
Great Sandy Desert Australia 110 B3.........21.00S 125.00E
Great Shelford England 11 F3.........52.09N 0.08E
Great Slave L. Canada 62 G4.........61.30N 114.20W
Great St. Bernard Pass Italy/Switz. 44 G4
.........45.52N 7.11E
Great Stour r. England 11 G2.........51.19N 1.15E
Great Torrington England 13 C2.........50.57N 4.09W
Great Victoria Desert Australia 110 B3.........29.00S 127.30E
Great Whernside mtn. England 15 F3.........54.09N 1.59W
Great Yarmouth England 11 G3.........52.36N 1.45E
Gréboun, Mt. Niger 82 D6.........19.55N 8.35E
Greco, Monte mtn. Italy 50 E4.........41.48N 14.00E
Gredos, Sierra de mts. Spain 46 C4.........40.18N 5.20W
Greece Europe 56 E3.........39.00N 22.00E
Greeley U.S.A. 64 F5.........40.26N 104.43W
Green r. U.S.A. 64 E4.........38.20N 109.53W
Green Bay town U.S.A. 65 I5.........44.30N 88.00W
Greenland N. America 63 N4.........68.00N 45.00W
Greenlaw Scotland 17 G3.........55.43N 2.28W
Greenock Scotland 16 E3.........55.57N 4.45W
Greensboro U.S.A. 65 K4.........36.03N 79.50W
Greenstone Pt. Scotland 18 D2.........57.55N 5.37W
Greenville Miss. U.S.A. 65 H3.........33.23N 91.03W
Greenville S.C. U.S.A. 65 J3.........34.52N 82.25W
Greifswald Germany 48 F6.........54.06N 13.24E
Grenå Denmark 43 B2.........56.25N 10.53E
Grenada C. America 71 L3.........12.15N 61.45W
Grenade France 44 D3.........43.47N 1.10E
Grenoble France 44 F4.........45.11N 5.43E
Greta r. England 15 F3.........54.31N 1.52W
Gretna Scotland 17 F2.........55.00N 3.04W
Grey Range mts. Australia 110 D3.........28.30S 142.15E
Grimsby England 15 G2.........53.35N 0.05W
Grímsey i. Iceland 43 Y2.........66.33N 18.00W
Grímsvötn mtn. Iceland 43 Y2.........64.30N 17.10W
Grodno Belarus 55 H5.........53.40N 23.50E
Grodzisk Wielkopolski Poland 54 E5.........52.14N 16.22E
Groningen Neth. 42 F5.........53.13N 6.35E
Groningen d. Neth. 42 F5.........53.15N 6.45E
Groote Eylandt i. Australia 110 C4.........14.00S 136.30E
Grosseto Italy 50 D5.........42.46N 11.08E

Gross Glockner mtn. Austria 54 C2........47.05N 12.50E
Groundhog r. Canada 63 J3........49.40N 82.06W
Groznyy Russian Fed. 58 G2........43.21N 45.42E
Grudziądz Poland 54 F5........53.29N 18.45E
Gruinard B. Scotland 18 D2........57.52N 5.26W
Guadalajara Mexico 70 D5........20.30N 103.20W
Guadalajara Spain 46 D4........40.37N 3.10W
Guadalcanal i. Solomon Is. 111 E5........9.30S 160.00E
Guadalete r. Spain 46 B2........36.37N 6.15W
Guadalope r. Spain 46 E4........41.15N 0.03W
Guadalquivir r. Spain 46 B2........36.50N 6.20W
Guadalupe i. Mexico 64 C2........29.00N 118.25W
Guadalupe, Sierra de mts. Spain 46 C3........39.30N 5.25W
Guadarrama, Sierra de mts. Spain 46 D4........41.00N 3.50W
Guadeloupe C. America 71 L4........16.20N 61.40W
Guadiana r. Portugal 46 B2........37.10N 7.36W
Guadix Spain 46 D2........37.19N 3.08W
Guajira Pen. Colombia 71 J3........12.00N 72.00W
Guam i. Pacific Oc. 105 K6........13.30N 144.40E
Guanajuato Mexico 70 D5........21.00N 101.16W
Guanajuato d. Mexico 70 D5........21.00N 101.00W
Guanare Venezuela 71 K2........9.04N 69.45W
Guangdong d. China 103 K2........23.00N 113.00E
Guangxi d. China 103 J2........23.50N 109.00E
Guangyuan China 103 J4........32.29N 105.55E
Guangzhou China 103 K2........23.20N 113.30E
Guanipa r. Venezuela 71 L2........10.00N 62.20W
Guantánamo Cuba 71 I5........20.09N 75.14W
Guaporé r. Brazil 76 D3........12.00S 65.15W
Guara, Sierra de mts. Spain 46 E5........42.20N 0.00
Guarapuava Brazil 77 E2........25.22S 51.28W
Guarda Portugal 46 B4........40.32N 7.17W
Guatemala C. America 70 F4........15.40N 90.00W
Guatemala City Guatemala 70 F3........14.38N 90.22W
Guaviare r. Colombia 74 C7........4.00N 67.35W
Guayaquil Ecuador 76 C4........2.13S 79.54W
Guayaquil, Golfo de g. Ecuador 76 B4........2.30S 80.00W
Guaymas Mexico 70 B6........27.59N 110.54W
Guba Ethiopia 85 H3........11.17N 35.20E
Gubkin Russian Fed. 55 O4........51.18N 37.32E
Gudbrandsdalen f. Norway 43 B3........62.00N 9.10E
Guelma Algeria 52 E4........36.28N 7.26E
Guelmine Morocco 84 D4........28.56N 10.04W
Guéret France 44 D5........46.10N 1.52E
Guernsey i. Channel Is. 13 Y9........49.27N 2.35W
Guerrero d. Mexico 70 D4........18.00N 100.00W
Guge mtn. Ethiopia 87 B4........6.16N 37.25E
Guiana Highlands S. America 74 D7........4.00N 59.00W
Guildford England 11 E2........51.14N 0.35W
Guilin China 103 K3........25.21N 110.11E
Guinea Africa 84 C3........10.30N 10.30W
Guinea, G. of Africa 82 D5........3.00N 3.00E
Guinea-Bissau Africa 84 C3........12.00N 15.30W
Guînes France 42 A2........50.52N 1.52E
Güiria Venezuela 71 L3........10.37N 62.21W
Guisborough England 15 F3........54.32N 1.02W
Guise France 42 C1........49.54N 3.39E
Guiyang China 103 J3........26.35N 106.40E
Guizhou d. China 103 J3........27.00N 106.30E
Gujarat d. India 96 E5........22.45N 71.30E
Gujranwala Pakistan 96 E7........32.06N 74.11E
Gujrat Pakistan 96 E7........32.35N 74.06E
Gulbarga India 96 F4........17.22N 76.47E
Gullane Scotland 17 G4........56.02N 2.49W
Gulu Uganda 86 C5........2.46N 32.21E
Gumdag Turkmenistan 95 H6........39.14N 54.33E
Gümüşhane Turkey 57 N4........40.26N 39.26E
Guna India 96 F5........24.39N 77.19E
Gunnbjørn Fjeld mtn. Greenland 63 P4........68.54N 29.48W
Guntur India 97 G4........16.20N 80.27E
Gurgueia r. Brazil 77 F4........6.45S 43.35W
Gurupi r. Brazil 77 F4........1.13S 46.06W
Gushgy Turkmenistan 95 J6........35.14N 62.15E
Guwahati India 97 I6........26.05N 91.55E
Guyana S. America 74 D7........5.00N 59.00W
Gwadar Pakistan 96 C6........25.09N 62.21E
Gwalior India 97 F6........26.12N 78.09E
Gweebarra B. Rep. of Ire. 20 C4........54.52N 8.30W
Gweru Zimbabwe 86 B3........19.25S 29.50E
Gydanskiy Pen. Russian Fed. 58 J5........70.00N 78.30E
Gyöngyös Hungary 54 F2........47.47N 19.56E
Győr Hungary 54 E2........47.41N 17.40E
Gypsumville Canada 62 I3........51.47N 98.38W
Gyzylarbat Turkmenistan 95 I6........39.00N 56.23E

H

Haapajärvi Finland 43 F3........63.45N 25.20E
Haapsalu Estonia 43 E2........58.58N 23.32E
Haarlem Neth. 42 D4........52.22N 4.38E
Habaswein Kenya 87 B3........1.06N 39.26E
Habban Yemen 95 G1........14.21N 47.04E
Hachijo-jima i. Japan 106 C2........33.00N 139.50E
Hachinohe Japan 106 D4........40.30N 141.30E
Haddington Scotland 17 G3........55.57N 2.47W
Haderslev Denmark 43 B1........55.15N 9.30E
Hadhramaut f. Yemen 95 G2........16.30N 49.30E
Hadleigh England 11 F3........52.03N 0.58E
Haeaebja Iraq 95 H5........35.11N 45.59E
Haeju N. Korea 103 N5........38.04N 125.40E
Hagadera Kenya 87 C3........0.01N 40.21E
Hagar Nish Plateau f. Eritrea 94 E2........17.00N 38.00E
Hagen Germany 42 G2........51.22N 7.27E
Hags Head Rep. of Ire. 20 B2........52.56N 9.29W
Hai Tanzania 87 B2........3.19S 37.08E
Haifa Israel 94 E5........32.49N 34.59E
Haikou China 103 K1........20.05N 110.25E
Ha'il Saudi Arabia 94 F4........27.31N 41.45E
Hailar China 103 M7........49.15N 119.41E
Hailsham England 11 F1........50.52N 0.17E
Hainan i. China 103 J1........18.30N 109.40E
Hainaut d. Belgium 42 C2........50.30N 3.45E
Haines U.S.A. 62 E3........59.11N 135.23W
Hai Phong Vietnam 104 D8........20.58N 106.41E
Haiti C. America 71 J4........19.00N 73.00W
Haiya Sudan 94 E2........18.17N 36.21E
Hajmah Oman 95 I2........19.55N 56.15E
Hakodate Japan 106 D4........41.46N 140.44E
Halden Norway 43 B2........59.08N 11.13E
Halesowen England 10 C3........52.27N 2.02W
Halesworth England 11 G3........52.21N 1.30E
Halifax Canada 63 L2........44.38N 63.35W
Halifax England 15 F2........53.43N 1.51W

Halkirk Scotland 19 F3........58.30N 3.30W
Halladale r. Scotland 19 F3........58.32N 3.53W
Hall Beach town Canada 63 J4........68.40N 81.30W
Halle Belgium 42 D2........50.45N 4.14E
Halle Germany 48 E4........51.28N 11.58E
Hall Is. Fed. States of Micronesia 108 K7........8.37N 152.00E
Hall's Creek town Australia 110 B4........18.13S 127.39E
Halmahera i. Indonesia 105 H4........0.45N 128.00E
Halmstad Sweden 43 C2........56.41N 12.55E
Halstead England 11 F2........51.57N 0.39E
Haltwhistle England 15 E3........54.58N 2.27W
Ham France 42 C1........49.45N 3.04E
Hamadan Iran 95 G5........34.47N 48.33E
Hamāh Syria 94 E6........35.09N 36.44E
Hamamatsu Japan 106 C2........34.42N 137.42E
Hamar Norway 43 B3........60.47N 10.55E
Hambleton Hills England 15 F3........54.15N 1.11W
Hamburg Germany 48 D5........53.33N 10.00E
Hämeenlinna Finland 43 F3........61.00N 24.25E
Hamersley Range mts. Australia 110 A3........22.00S 118.00E
Hamhung N. Korea 103 N5........39.54N 127.35E
Hami China 102 G6........42.40N 93.30E
Hamilton Bermuda 71 L7........32.18N 64.48W
Hamilton Canada 65 K5........43.15N 79.50W
Hamilton New Zealand 111 G2........37.47S 175.17E
Hamilton Scotland 16 E3........55.46N 4.02W
Hamim, Wadi al r. Libya 53 H3........32.06N 23.58E
Hamina Finland 43 F3........60.33N 27.15E
Hamm Germany 48 C4........51.40N 7.49E
Hammamet, G. of Tunisia 52 F4........36.05N 10.40E
Hammerdal Sweden 43 C3........63.35N 15.20E
Hammerfest Norway 43 E5........70.40N 23.44E
Hampshire d. England 10 D2........51.08N 1.20W
Hampshire Downs hills England 10 D2........51.18N 1.25W
Hamstreet England 11 F2........51.03N 0.52E
Hamun-e Jaz Murian l. Iran 95 I4........27.00N 59.20E
Hanamaki Japan 106 D3........39.23N 141.07E
Handa I. Scotland 18 D3........58.23N 5.12W
Handan China 103 K5........36.37N 114.26E
Handeni Tanzania 87 B2........5.26S 38.02E
Hanggin Houqi China 103 J6........40.52N 107.04E
Hangzhou China 103 M4........30.10N 120.07E
Hanmni Mashkel l. Pakistan 95 J4........28.15N 63.00E
Hannibal U.S.A. 65 H4........39.41N 91.25W
Hannover Germany 48 D5........52.23N 9.44E
Hanoi Vietnam 104 D8........21.01N 105.52E
Hantsavichy Belarus 55 J5........52.49N 26.29E
Hanzhong China 103 J4........33.08N 107.04E
Haparanda Sweden 43 F4........65.50N 24.05E
Happy Valley-Goose Bay town Canada 63 L3........53.16N 60.14W
Harare Zimbabwe 86 C3........17.43S 31.05E
Harbin China 103 N7........45.45N 126.41E
Hardangervidda f. Norway 43 A3........60.20N 8.00E
Harderwijk Neth. 42 E4........52.21N 5.37E
Haren Germany 42 G4........52.48N 7.15E
Hargele Ethiopia 87 C4........5.19N 42.04E
Hargeysa Somalia 85 I2........9.31N 44.02E
Har Hu l. China 102 H5........38.20N 97.40E
Hari r. Afghan. 95 J6........35.42N 61.12E
Harla Canary Is. 46 Z2........29.09N 13.30W
Harlech Wales 12 C4........52.52N 4.08W
Harleston England 11 G3........52.25N 1.18E
Harlingen Neth. 42 E5........53.10N 5.25E
Harlow England 11 F2........51.47N 0.08E
Harney Basin f. U.S.A. 64 C5........43.20N 119.00W
Härnösand Sweden 43 D3........62.37N 17.55E
Har Nuur l. Mongolia 102 G7........48.10N 93.30E
Harpenden England 11 E2........51.49N 0.22W
Harray, Loch of Scotland 19 F4........59.03N 3.15W
Harricana r. Canada 63 K3........51.10N 79.45W
Harris f. Scotland 18 C2........57.50N 6.55W
Harris, Sd. of Scotland 18 B2........57.43N 7.05W
Harrisburg U.S.A. 65 K5........40.35N 76.59W
Harrison, C. Canada 63 M3........55.00N 58.00W
Harrogate England 15 F2........53.59N 1.32W
Hârșova Romania 57 H6........44.41N 27.56E
Harstad Norway 43 C4........68.48N 16.30E
Hartfjäll mtn. Norway 43 A3........60.11N 7.05E
Harter Fell mtn. England 14 D3........54.27N 2.51W
Hart Fell mtn. Scotland 17 F3........55.25N 3.25W
Hartford U.S.A. 65 L5........41.40N 72.51W
Hartland England 13 C2........50.59N 4.29W
Hartland Pt. England 13 C3........51.01N 4.32W
Hartlepool England 15 F3........54.42N 1.11W
Hartlepool d. England 15 F3........54.42N 1.11W
Har Us Nuur l. Mongolia 102 G7........48.10N 92.10E
Harwich England 11 G2........51.56N 1.18E
Haryana d. India 96 F6........29.11N 76.00E
Haslemere England 10 E2........51.05N 0.41W
Hasselt Belgium 42 E2........50.56N 5.20E
Hassi Messaoud Algeria 84 E5........31.43N 6.03E
Hässleholm Sweden 43 C2........56.09N 13.45E
Hastings England 11 F1........50.51N 0.36E
Hatfield England 15 F2........53.36N 0.59W
Hatteras, C. U.S.A. 65 K4........35.14N 75.31W
Hattiesburg U.S.A. 65 I3........31.25N 89.19W
Haud f. Ethiopia 85 I2........8.00N 46.00E
Haugesund Norway 43 A2........59.25N 5.16E
Haukivesi l. Finland 43 G3........62.10N 28.30E
Haut Folin mtn. France 44 E5........47.00N 4.00E
Hauts Plateaux f. Algeria 52 C3........34.00N 0.10W
Havana Cuba 71 H5........23.07N 82.25W
Havant England 10 E1........50.51N 0.59W
Havel r. Germany 48 E5........52.51N 11.57E
Haverfordwest Wales 12 C3........51.48N 4.59W
Haverhill England 11 F3........52.06N 0.27E
Havre U.S.A. 64 E6........48.34N 109.45W
Havre-St.-Pierre Canada 63 L3........50.15N 63.36W
Hawaii i. Hawaiian Is. 108 P8........19.30N 155.30W
Hawaiian Is. Pacific Oc. 108 O9........21.00N 160.00W
Hawarden Wales 12 D5........53.11N 3.02W
Hawes England 15 E3........54.18N 2.12W
Haweswater Resr. England 14 E3........54.30N 2.45W
Hawick Scotland 17 G3........55.25N 2.47W
Hawke B. New Zealand 111 G2........39.18S 177.15E
Hawkhurst England 11 F2........51.02N 0.31E
Hawthorne U.S.A. 64 C4........38.31N 118.37W
Haxby England 15 F3........54.02N 1.06W
Hay Australia 110 D2........34.21S 144.31E
Hay r. Canada 62 G3........60.49N 115.52W
Haydarabad Iran 94 G6........37.09N 45.27E
Haydon Bridge England 15 E3........54.58N 2.14W

Hayle England 13 B2........50.12N 5.25W
Hay-on-Wye Wales 12 D4........52.04N 3.09W
Hay River town Canada 62 G4........60.51N 115.42W
Haywards Heath town England 11 E1........51.00N 0.05W
Hazarajat f. Afghan. 95 K5........33.00N 66.00E
Hazebrouck France 42 B2........50.43N 2.32E
Heacham England 11 F3........52.55N 0.30E
Headcorn England 11 F2........51.11N 0.37E
Heanor England 15 F2........53.01N 1.20W
Heathfield England 11 F1........50.58N 0.18E
Hebei d. China 103 L5........39.20N 117.15E
Hebron Jordan 94 E5........31.32N 35.06E
Hecate Str. Canada 62 E3........53.00N 131.00W
Hechi China 103 J2........24.42N 108.02E
Heckington England 15 G1........52.59N 0.18W
Hede Sweden 43 C3........62.27N 13.30E
Heerenveen Neth. 42 E4........52.57N 5.55E
Heerlen Neth. 42 E2........50.53N 5.59E
Hefei China 103 L4........31.55N 117.18E
Hegang China 103 O7........47.36N 130.30E
Heidelberg Germany 48 D3........49.25N 8.42E
Heighington England 15 G2........53.12N 0.28W
Heilbronn Germany 48 D3........49.08N 9.14E
Heilongjiang d. China 103 N7........47.00N 126.00E
Heinola Finland 43 F3........61.13N 26.05E
Hekla mtn. Iceland 43 Y2........64.00N 19.45W
Helena U.S.A. 64 D6........46.35N 112.00W
Helensburgh Scotland 16 E4........56.01N 4.44W
Heligoland B. Germany 48 D6........54.00N 8.15E
Hellín Spain 46 E3........38.31N 1.43W
Helmand r. Asia 95 J5........31.10N 61.20E
Helmond Neth. 42 E3........51.28N 5.40E
Helmsdale Scotland 19 F3........58.08N 3.40W
Helmsdale r. Scotland 19 F3........58.06N 3.40W
Helmsley England 15 F3........54.14N 1.04W
Helong China 106 A4........42.38N 128.58E
Helsingborg Sweden 43 C2........56.05N 12.45E
Helsingør Denmark 43 C2........56.03N 12.38E
Helsinki Finland 43 F3........60.08N 25.00E
Helston England 13 B2........50.07N 5.17W
Helvellyn mtn. England 14 D3........54.31N 3.00W
Hemel Hempstead England 11 E2........51.46N 0.28W
Henan d. China 103 K4........33.45N 113.00E
Henares r. Spain 46 D4........40.26N 3.35W
Henderson I. Pacific Oc. 109 S4........24.20S 128.20W
Hendon England 11 E2........51.35N 0.14W
Henfield England 11 E1........50.56N 0.17W
Hengelo Neth. 42 F4........52.16N 6.46E
Hengoed Wales 12 D3........51.39N 3.14W
Hengyang China 103 K3........26.58N 112.31E
Heniches'k Ukraine 55 N2........46.10N 34.49E
Henley-on-Thames England 10 E2........51.32N 0.53W
Hennef Germany 42 G2........50.47N 7.17E
Henrietta Maria, C. Canada 63 J3........55.00N 82.15W
Henzada Myanmar 97 J4........17.38N 95.35E
Herat Afghan. 95 J5........34.21N 62.10E
Hereford England 10 C3........52.04N 2.43W
Hereford and Worcester d. England 10 C3........52.10N 2.40W
Herm i. Channel Is. 13 Y9........49.28N 2.27W
Herma Ness c. Scotland 19 Z9........60.50N 0.54W
Hermosillo Mexico 70 B6........29.15N 110.59W
Herne Germany 42 G3........51.32N 7.12E
Herne Bay town England 11 G2........51.23N 1.10E
Herning Denmark 43 B2........56.08N 9.00E
Hertford England 11 E2........51.48N 0.05W
Hertfordshire d. England 11 E2........51.51N 0.05W
Heswall England 14 D2........53.20N 3.06W
Hetton England 15 E3........54.01N 2.05W
Hexham England 15 E3........54.58N 2.06W
Heysham England 14 E3........54.03N 2.53W
Heywood England 15 E2........53.36N 2.13W
Hidaka-sammyaku mts. Japan 106 D4........42.50N 143.00E
Hidalgo d. Mexico 70 E5........20.50N 98.30W
Hidalgo del Parral Mexico 70 C6........26.58N 105.40W
Higashi-suido str. Japan 106 A2........34.00N 129.30E
Higham Ferrers England 11 E3........52.18N 0.36W
Highbridge England 13 D3........51.22N 1.22W
Highclere England 10 D2........51.22N 1.22W
Highland d. Scotland 18 D2........57.42N 5.00W
High Peak mtn. England 15 F2........53.22N 1.48W
High Seat hill England 15 E3........54.23N 2.18W
Highworth England 10 D2........51.38N 1.42W
High Wycombe England 10 E2........51.38N 0.46W
Hiiumaa i. Estonia 43 E2........58.50N 22.30E
Hijaz f. Saudi Arabia 94 E4........26.00N 37.30E
Hildesheim Germany 48 D5........52.09N 9.58E
Hillerød Denmark 43 C1........55.56N 12.18E
Hillside Scotland 19 G1........56.45N 2.29W
Hilpsford Pt. England 14 D3........54.02N 3.10W
Hilversum Neth. 42 E4........52.14N 5.12E
Himachal Pradesh d. India 96 F7........31.45N 77.30E
Himalaya mts. Asia 97 G5........29.00N 84.00E
Hinckley England 10 D3........52.33N 1.21W
Hinderwell England 15 F3........54.32N 0.46W
Hindhead England 10 E2........51.06N 0.42W
Hindley England 14 E2........53.32N 2.35W
Hindu Kush mts. Asia 95 K6........36.40N 70.00E
Hinnøya i. Norway 43 C4........68.30N 16.00E
Hiraman r. Kenya 87 B2........1.05S 39.55E
Hirosaki Japan 106 D4........40.34N 140.28E
Hiroshima Japan 106 B2........34.30N 132.27E
Hirson France 42 D1........49.56N 4.05E
Hirwaun Wales 12 D3........51.43N 3.30W
Hispaniola i. C. America 71 J5........20.00N 71.00W
Hitachi Japan 106 D3........36.35N 140.40E
Hitchin England 11 E2........51.57N 0.16W
Hitra i. Norway 43 B3........63.30N 8.50E
Hiva Oa i. Marquesas Is. 109 R5........9.45S 139.00W
Hobart Australia 110 D1........42.54S 147.18E
Hobro Denmark 43 B2........56.38N 9.48E
Hồ Chí Minh Vietnam 104 D6........10.46N 106.43E
Hoddesdon England 11 E2........51.46N 0.01W
Hodeida Yemen 94 F1........14.50N 42.58E
Hodnet England 10 C3........52.51N 2.35W
Hoek van Holland Neth. 42 D3........51.59N 4.08E
Hof Germany 48 E3........50.19N 11.55E
Höfn Iceland 43 Z2........64.16N 15.10W
Hofsjökull i. Iceland 43 Y2........64.50N 19.00W
Hofuf Saudi Arabia 95 G4........25.20N 49.34E
Hoggar mts. Algeria 84 E4........24.00N 5.50E
Hohhot China 103 K6........40.49N 111.37E

Hokkaido i. Japan 106 D4........43.00N 144.00E
Holbæk Denmark 43 B1........55.42N 11.41E
Holbeach England 11 F3........52.48N 0.01E
Holbeach Marsh England 11 F3........52.50N 0.05E
Holbrook U.S.A. 64 E3........34.58N 110.00W
Holderness f. England 15 G2........53.45N 0.05W
Holguín Cuba 71 I5........20.54N 76.15W
Hollabrunn Austria 54 E3........48.34N 16.05E
Holland Fen f. England 11 F3........53.02N 0.12W
Hollesley B. England 11 G3........52.02N 1.33E
Hollington England 11 F1........50.51N 0.32E
Hollingworth England 15 F2........53.28N 1.59W
Holme-on-Spalding-Moor England 15 G2........53.50N 0.47W
Holmfirth England 15 F2........53.34N 1.48W
Holon Israel 94 E5........32.01N 34.46E
Holstebro Denmark 43 B2........56.22N 8.38E
Holsworthy England 13 C2........50.48N 4.21W
Holt England 11 G3........52.55N 1.04E
Holyhead Wales 12 C5........53.18N 4.38W
Holyhead B. Wales 12 C5........53.22N 4.40W
Holy I. England 15 F4........55.41N 1.47W
Holy I. Wales 12 C5........53.15N 4.38W
Holywell Wales 12 D5........53.17N 3.13W
Homa Bay town Kenya 87 A2........0.32S 34.27E
Homayunshahr Iran 95 H5........32.42N 51.28E
Homburg Germany 42 G1........49.19N 7.20E
Home B. Canada 63 L4........69.00N 66.00W
Homyel Belarus 55 L5........52.25N 31.00E
Hondo r. Mexico 70 G4........18.33N 88.22W
Honduras C. America 70 G4........15.00N 87.00W
Honduras, G. of Carib. Sea 60 K3........16.20N 87.30W
Hønefoss Norway 43 B3........60.10N 10.16E
Hong Kong Asia 103 K2........22.30N 114.10E
Honiara Solomon Is. 111 E5........9.27S 159.57E
Honiton England 13 D2........50.48N 3.13W
Honley England 15 F2........53.34N 1.46W
Honolulu Hawaiian Is. 108 P9........21.19N 157.50W
Honshu i. Japan 106 C3........36.00N 138.00E
Hood, Mt. U.S.A. 64 B6........45.23N 121.41W
Hood Pt. Australia 110 A2........34.23S 119.34E
Hoogeveen Neth. 42 F4........52.44N 6.29E
Hook England 10 E2........51.17N 0.55W
Hook Head Rep. of Ire. 20 E2........52.07N 6.55W
Hooper Bay town U.S.A. 62 B4........61.29N 166.10W
Hoorn Neth. 42 E4........52.38N 5.03E
Hope, Loch Scotland 19 E3........58.27N 4.38W
Hope, Pt. U.S.A. 59 V4........68.00N 167.00W
Hopedale Canada 63 L3........55.30N 60.10W
Horley England 11 E2........51.11N 0.11W
Horlivka Ukraine 55 P3........48.17N 38.05E
Hormuz, Str. of Asia 95 I4........26.35N 56.20E
Horn c. Iceland 43 X2........66.28N 22.27W
Horn, C. S. America 75 C1........55.47S 67.00W
Hornavan l. Sweden 43 D4........66.15N 17.40E
Horncastle England 15 G2........53.13N 0.08W
Hornepayne Canada 65 J6........49.14N 84.48W
Hornsea England 15 G2........53.55N 0.10W
Horodnya Ukraine 55 L4........51.54N 31.37E
Horodok Ukraine 55 H3........49.48N 23.39E
Horrabridge England 13 C2........50.30N 4.05W
Horsens Denmark 43 B1........55.53N 9.53E
Horsham Australia 110 D2........36.45S 142.15E
Horsham England 11 E2........51.04N 0.20W
Horten Norway 43 B2........59.25N 10.30E
Horwich England 14 E2........53.37N 2.33W
Hospitalet de Llobregat Spain 46 G4........41.20N 2.06E
Hotan China 102 E5........37.07N 79.57E
Houffalize Belgium 42 E2........50.08N 5.50E
Houghton-le-Spring England 15 F3........54.51N 1.28W
Houghton Regis England 11 E2........51.51N 0.30W
Hourn, Loch Scotland 18 D2........57.05N 5.35W
Houston U.S.A. 65 G2........29.45N 95.25W
Hovd Mongolia 102 G7........48.00N 91.45E
Hove England 11 E1........50.50N 0.10W
Hoveton England 11 G3........52.45N 1.23E
Howden England 15 G2........53.45N 0.52W
Howland I. Pacific Oc. 108 N7........0.48N 176.38W
Hoy i. Scotland 19 F3........58.51N 3.17W
Hoyanger Norway 43 A3........61.13N 6.05E
Hoyerswerda Germany 48 G4........51.26N 14.14E
Höysgöl Nuur l. Mongolia 103 I8........51.00N 100.30E
Hradec Králové Czech Rep. 54 E3........50.13N 15.50E
Huacho Peru 76 C3........11.05S 77.36W
Huaibei China 103 L4........33.58N 116.50E
Huainan China 103 L4........32.41N 117.06E
Huallaga r. Peru 76 C4........5.05S 75.30W
Huambo Angola 86 A3........12.47S 15.44E
Huancayo Peru 76 C3........12.15S 75.12W
Huang He r. China 103 L5........37.55N 118.46E
Huangshi China 103 L4........30.13N 115.05E
Huascaran mtn. Peru 74 B6........9.20S 77.36W
Hubei d. China 103 K4........31.15N 112.15E
Hubli India 96 E4........15.20N 75.14E
Hucknall England 15 F2........53.03N 1.12W
Huddersfield England 15 F2........53.38N 1.49W
Hudiksvall Sweden 43 D3........61.45N 17.10E
Hudson r. U.S.A. 65 L5........40.45N 74.00W
Hudson B. Canada 63 J3........58.00N 86.00W
Hudson Str. Canada 63 K4........62.00N 70.00W
Huê Vietnam 104 D7........16.28N 107.35E
Huelva Spain 46 B2........37.15N 6.56W
Huércal-Overa Spain 46 E2........37.23N 1.56W
Huesca Spain 46 E5........42.02N 0.25W
Huila mtn. Colombia 76 C5........3.00N 75.59W
Huizhou China 103 K2........23.05N 114.29E
Hulin China 106 B5........45.44N 132.59E
Hull Canada 65 K6........45.26N 75.45W
Hull d. England 15 G2........53.45N 0.20W
Hulun Nur l. China 103 L7........49.00N 117.20E
Humber, Mouth of the England 15 G2........53.40N 0.12W
Humphreys Peak mtn. U.S.A. 64 D4........35.21N 111.41W
Húnaflói b. Iceland 43 X2........65.45N 20.50W
Hunan d. China 103 K3........27.30N 111.30E
Hunchun China 106 A4........42.55N 130.28E
Hunchun r. China 106 B4........42.42N 130.10E
Hundested Denmark 43 B6........55.58N 11.52E
Hungarian Plain f. Hungary 34 E2........46.30N 19.00E
Hungary Europe 54 F2........47.30N 19.00E
Hungerford England 10 D2........51.25N 1.30W
Hunjiang China 103 N6........41.59N 126.30E
Hunmanby England 15 G3........54.11N 0.19W
Hunsrück mts. Germany 48 C3........49.44N 7.05E
Hunstanton England 11 F3........52.57N 0.30E
Huntingdon England 11 E3........52.20N 0.11W

Huntington U.S.A. **65 J4**..................38.25N 82.26W
Huntly Scotland **19 G2**..................57.27N 2.49W
Huntsville Ala. U.S.A. **65 I3**..........34.44N 86.35W
Huntsville Tex. U.S.A. **65 G3**........30.44N 95.35W
Hurghada Egypt **94 D4**..................27.17N 33.47E
Huri Hills Kenya **87 B3**..................3.30N 37.47E
Huron U.S.A. **64 G5**........................44.22N 98.12W
Huron, L. Canada/U.S.A. **65 J5**......45.00N 82.30W
Hurstpierpoint England **11 E1**.......50.56N 0.11W
Husum Germany **48 D6**..................54.29N 9.04E
Hutton Rudby England **15 F3**.........54.27N 1.17W
Hvannadalshnúkur mtn. Iceland **43 Y1**...64.02N 16.35W
Hvar i. Croatia **56 C5**.....................43.10N 16.45E
Hyargas Huur l. Mongolia **102 G7**...49.20N 93.40E
Hyderabad India **97 F4**..................17.22N 78.26E
Hyderabad Pakistan **96 D6**...........25.23N 68.24E
Hyères France **44 G3**.....................43.07N 6.08E
Hyrynsalmi Finland **43 G4**............64.41N 28.30E
Hythe Hants. England **10 D1**..........50.51N 1.24W
Hythe Kent England **11 G2**............51.04N 1.05E
Hyvinkää Finland **43 F3**.................60.37N 24.50E

I

Ialomiţa r. Romania **56 H6**.............44.41N 27.52E
Iar Connaught f. Rep. of Ire. **20 B3**...53.20N 9.20W
Iaşi Romania **55 J2**.......................47.09N 27.38E
Ibadan Nigeria **84 E2**....................7.23N 3.56E
Ibagué Colombia **74 B7**................4.25N 75.20W
Ibar r. Yugo. **56 E5**......................43.44N 20.44E
Ibarra Ecuador **76 C5**..................0.23N 77.50W
Ibb Yemen **94 F1**.........................13.58N 44.11E
Ibiapaba, Serra da mts. Brazil **77 F4**...5.30S 41.00W
Ibiza i. Spain **46 F3**.....................39.00N 1.23E
Ibra' Oman **95 I3**........................22.41N 58.32E
Ibstock England **10 D3**................52.42N 1.23W
Ica Peru **76 C3**...........................14.02S 75.48W
Iceland Europe **43 Y2**..................64.45N 18.00W
Ichinomiya Japan **106 C3**............35.18N 136.48E
Icklesham England **11 F1**.............50.54N 0.39E
Idaho d. U.S.A. **64 C6**..................45.00N 115.00W
Idaho Falls town U.S.A. **64 D5**.......43.30N 112.01W
Idar-Oberstein Germany **42 G1**.....49.43N 7.19E
Idfu Egypt **94 E3**.........................24.58N 32.50E
Idhan Awbari des. Libya **52 F2**......27.30N 11.30E
Idi mtn. Greece **56 G1**.................35.13N 24.45E
Idlib Syria **57 M1**.......................35.57N 36.38E
Ieper Belgium **42 B2**...................50.51N 2.53E
Igan Malaysia **104 E4**..................2.51N 111.43E
Iganga Uganda **87 A3**.................0.36N 33.29E
Iggesund Sweden **43 D3**............61.39N 17.10E
Iglesias Italy **50 C3**...................39.18N 8.32E
Iğneada, C. Turkey **57 I4**............41.50N 28.05E
Igoumenitsa Greece **56 E3**.........39.32N 20.14E
Iguaçu r. Brazil **77 E2**................25.33S 54.35W
Iguaçú Falls Brazil/Argentina **77 E2**...25.35S 54.22W
Iisalmi Finland **43 F3**.................63.34N 27.08E
IJmuiden Neth. **42 D4**................52.28N 4.37E
IJssel r. Neth. **42 E4**..................52.34N 5.50E
IJsselmeer l. Neth. **42 E4**...........52.45N 5.20E
Ikaria i. Greece **56 G2**...............37.35N 26.10E
Iki-shima i. Japan **106 A2**...........33.47N 129.43E
Ilagan Phil. **105 G7**...................17.07N 121.53E
Ilchester England **13 E3**.............51.00N 2.41W
Ilebo Zaire **86 B4**......................4.20S 20.35E
Ileret Kenya **87 B3**...................4.22N 36.13E
Ilford England **11 F2**.................51.33N 0.06E
Ilfracombe England **13 C3**........51.13N 4.08W
Ilhéus Brazil **77 G3**..................14.50S 39.06W
Iliamna L. U.S.A. **62 C3**.............59.30N 155.00W
Iligan Phil. **105 G5**...................8.12N 124.13E
Ilkeston England **15 F1**.............52.59N 1.19W
Ilkley England **15 F2**.................53.56N 1.49W
Illinois d. U.S.A. **65 I5**..............40.00N 89.00W
Illizi Algeria **84 E4**..................26.20N 8.20E
Ilminster England **13 E2**...........50.56N 2.56W
Iloilo Phil. **105 G6**...................10.45N 122.33E
Ilorin Nigeria **84 E2**................8.32N 4.34E
Iman r. Russian Fed. **106 B5**......45.55N 133.45E
Imandra, Ozero l. Russian Fed. **43 H4**...67.30N 32.45E
Imatra Finland **43 G3**..............61.14N 28.50E
Immingham England **15 G2**.....53.37N 0.12W
Imola Italy Brazil **77 F4**............5.32S 47.28W
Imphal India **97 I5**..................24.47N 93.55E
Inambari r. Peru **76 D3**............12.38S 69.50W
Inarijärvi l. Finland **43 F5**.........69.00N 28.00E
Inchard, Loch Scotland **18 D3**...58.27N 5.05W
Inch'ini Terara mtn. Ethiopia **87 B3**...4.32N 37.02E
Inchkeith i. Scotland **17 F4**.......56.02N 3.08W
Inchon S. Korea **103 N5**...........37.30N 126.38E
Indals r. Sweden **43 D3**...........62.30N 17.20E
India Asia **97 F4**....................20.00N 78.00E
Indiana d. U.S.A. **65 I5**............40.00N 86.00W
Indianapolis U.S.A. **65 I4**.........39.45N 86.10W
Indian Ocean **117 M5**
Indigirka r. Russian Fed. **59 Q5**...71.00N 148.45E
Indonesia Asia **104 F2**...........6.00S 118.00E
Indore India **96 E5**................22.42N 75.54E
Indre r. France **44 C5**..............47.16N 0.19W
Indus r. Asia **96 D5**................24.00N 67.33E
Indus, Mouths of the Pakistan **96 D5**...24.00N 67.00E
Inebolu Turkey **57 K4**...........41.57N 33.45E
İnegöl Turkey **57 I4**..............40.06N 29.31E
Infiernillo, L. Mexico **70 D4**....18.25N 102.00W
Infiesto Spain **46 C5**.............43.21N 5.21W
Ingatestone England **11 F2**....51.41N 0.22E
Ingenio Canary Is. **84 Y1**.......27.56N 15.26W
Ingleborough mtn. England **15 E3**...54.10N 2.23W
Ingleton England **15 E3**..........54.09N 2.29W
Ingoldmells England **15 H2**.....53.12N 0.21E
Ingolstadt Germany **48 E3**.......48.46N 11.27E
Inhambane Mozambique **86 C2**...23.51S 35.29E
Inhul r. Ukraine **55 M2**..........46.57N 32.00E
Inhulets' r. Ukraine **55 M2**......46.39N 32.38E
Inishbofin i. Rep. of Ire. **20 A3**...53.38N 10.15W
Inisheer i. Rep. of Ire. **20 B3**....53.04N 9.32W
Inishmaan i. Rep. of Ire. **20 B3**..53.06N 9.36W
Inishmore i. Rep. of Ire. **20 B3**..53.07N 9.45W
Inishmurray i. Rep. of Ire. **20 C4**...54.26N 8.40W
Inishowen pen. Rep. of Ire. **20 D5**...55.13N 7.17W
Inishowen Head Rep. of Ire. **16 C3**...55.15N 6.56W
Inishtrahull i. Rep. of Ire. **20 D5**...55.27N 7.14W
Inishtrahull Sd. Rep. of Ire. **16 B3**...55.25N 7.20W

Inishturk i. Rep. of Ire. **20 A3**...53.42N 10.09W
Inn r. Europe **54 C3**...............48.33N 13.26E
Inner Mongolia d. China **103 K6**...41.30N 112.00E
Inner Sound Scotland **18 D2**.....57.25N 5.55W
Innsbruck Austria **54 B2**.........47.17N 11.25E
Inny r. Rep. of Ire. **20 D3**.......53.32N 7.50W
Inowrocław Poland **54 F5**.......52.49N 18.12E
In Salah Algeria **84 E4**..........27.12N 2.29E
Insch Scotland **19 G2**............57.21N 2.36W
Inukjuak Canada **63 K3**.........58.25N 78.18W
Inuvik Canada **62 E4**.............68.16N 133.40W
Inveraray Scotland **16 D4**.......56.14N 5.05W
Inverbervie Scotland **19 G1**....56.51N 2.19W
Invercargill New Zealand **111 F1**...46.25S 168.21E
Inverclyde d. Scotland **16 E3**...55.55N 4.50W
Invergordon Scotland **19 E2**...57.42N 4.10W
Inverkeithing Scotland **17 F4**...56.02N 3.25W
Inverness Scotland **19 E2**......57.27N 4.15W
Inverurie Scotland **19 G2**.......57.17N 2.23W
Ioannina Greece **56 E3**.........39.39N 20.49E
Iona i. Scotland **16 C4**..........56.20N 6.25W
Ionian Is. Greece **56 E3**.......38.45N 20.00E
Ionian Sea Med. Sea **53 G4**...38.30N 18.45E
Ios i. Greece **56 G2**.............36.42N 25.20E
Iowa d. U.S.A. **65 H5**............42.00N 93.00W
Iowa City U.S.A. **65 H5**.........41.39N 91.30W
Ipatinga Brazil **77 F3**...........19.32S 42.32W
Ipoh Malaysia **104 C4**.........4.36N 101.02E
Ipswich England **11 G3**.......52.04N 1.09E
Iput' r. Belarus **55 L5**..........52.25N 31.00E
Iqaluit Canada **63 L4**...........63.45N 68.30W
Iquique Chile **76 C2**............20.15S 70.08W
Iquitos Peru **76 C4**.............3.51S 73.13W
Iraklion Greece **56 G1**.........35.20N 25.08E
Iran Asia **95 H5**..................32.00N 54.30E
Iran Range mts. Indonesia/Malaysia **104 F4**
...3.20N 115.00E
Iranshahr Iran **95 J4**...........27.14N 60.42E
Irapuato Mexico **70 D5**........20.40N 101.40W
Iraq Asia **94 F5**.................33.00N 44.00E
Irbid Jordan **94 E5**.............32.33N 35.51E
Ireland's Eye i. Rep. of Ire. **20 E3**...53.25N 6.04W
Irian Jaya d. Indonesia **105 J3**...4.00S 138.00E
Iringa Tanzania **86 C4**........7.49S 35.39E
Iriri r. Brazil **77 E4**............3.50S 52.40W
Irish Sea U.K./Rep. of Ire. **14 C1**...53.40N 5.00W
Irkutsk Russian Fed. **59 M3**...52.18N 104.15E
Iron Mountain town U.S.A. **65 I6**...45.51N 88.03W
Ironwood U.S.A. **65 I6**........46.25N 89.59W
Irosin Phil. **105 G6**............12.45N 124.02E
Irrawaddy r. Myanmar **97 J4**...17.45N 95.25E
Irrawaddy, Mouths of the Myanmar **97 I4**
...15.30N 95.00E
Irsha r. Ukraine **55 K4**........50.45N 29.30E
Irthing r. England **14 E3**......54.52N 2.50W
Irtysh r. Asia **58 I4**...........61.00N 68.40E
Irún Spain **46 E5**..............43.20N 1.48W
Irvine Scotland **16 E3**........55.37N 4.40W
Isabela Phil. **105 G5**.........6.40N 121.59E
Isabela, I. Galapagos Is. **76 A4**...0.40S 91.20W
Isabelia, Cordillera mts. Nicaragua **71 G3**
...13.30N 85.00W
Ísafjördhur Iceland **43 X2**....66.05N 23.06W
Isar r. Germany **48 F3**........48.48N 12.57E
Ischia i. Italy **50 E4**..........40.43N 13.54E
Ise Japan **106 C2**.............34.29N 136.41E
Isère, Pointe c. French Guiana **74 D7**...5.45N 53.53W
Ishikari r. Japan **106 D4**......43.15N 141.21E
Ishim r. Asia **58 J3**...........57.50N 71.00E
Ishinomaki Japan **106 D3**.....38.25N 141.18E
Ishinoseki Japan **106 D3**......38.55N 141.10E
Isiolo Kenya **87 B3**...........0.20N 37.36E
Isiro Zaire **86 B5**.............2.50N 27.40E
Iskenderun Turkey **57 M2**....36.37N 36.08E
Iskenderun, G. of Turkey **57 L2**...36.40N 35.50E
Iskür r. Bulgaria **56 G5**.......43.42N 24.27E
Isla r. Angus Scotland **17 F4**...56.32N 3.21W
Isla r. Moray Scotland **19 G2**...57.30N 2.47W
Islamabad Pakistan **96 E7**.....33.40N 73.08E
Island Magee pen. N. Ireland **16 D2**...54.49N 5.44W
Islay i. Scotland **16 C3**.......55.45N 6.20W
Isle of Ely f. England **11 F3**....52.25N 0.11E
Isle of Portland f. England **10 C1**...50.32N 2.25W
Isle of Purbeck f. England **10 C1**...50.40N 2.05W
Isle of Thanet f. England **11 G2**...51.22N 1.20E
Isle of Wight d. England **10 D1**...50.40N 1.17W
Isles of Scilly d. England **13 A1**...49.55N 6.20W
Ismâ'iliya Egypt **94 D5**.......30.36N 32.15E
Isparta Turkey **57 J2**.........37.46N 30.32E
Israel Asia **94 D5**.............32.00N 34.50E
Issyk Kul l. Kyrgyzstan **102 I3**...43.30N 77.20E
İstanbul Turkey **57 I4**.........41.02N 28.58E
Isthmus of Panama C. America **60 K2**...9.00N 80.00W
Istra pen. Croatia **56 A6**......45.12N 13.55E
Itabuna Brazil **77 G3**.........14.48S 39.18W
Itacoatiara Brazil **77 E4**......3.06S 58.22W
Itaituba Brazil **77 E4**.........4.17S 55.59W
Itajaí Brazil **77 F2**...........26.50S 48.39W
Italy Europe **50 D5**..........43.00N 12.00E
Itambé mtn. Brazil **77 F3**....18.23S 43.21W
Itapicuru r. Bahia Brazil **77 G3**...11.50S 37.30W
Itapicuru r. Maranhão Brazil **77 F4**...2.53S 44.15W
Itiquira r. Brazil **77 E3**.......18.01S 57.29W
Itui r. Brazil **76 C4**...........4.38S 70.19W
Iturup i. Russian Fed. **106 E4**...45.00N 147.30E
Ituxi r. Brazil **77 D4**.........7.20S 64.50W
Itzehoe Germany **48 D5**.....53.56N 9.32E
Ivaí r. Brazil **77 E2**..........23.20S 53.23W
Ivalo r. Finland **43 F5**.......68.41N 27.30E
Ivano-Frankivs'k Ukraine **55 I3**...48.55N 24.42E
Ivanovo Russian Fed. **58 G3**...57.00N 41.00E
Ivittuut Greenland **63 N4**....61.10N 48.00W
Ivybridge England **13 D2**....50.24N 3.56W
Iwaki Japan **106 D3**.........36.58N 140.58E
Iwanai Japan **106 D4**........43.01N 140.32E
Iwo Nigeria **84 E2**...........7.38N 4.11E
Ixworth England **11 F3**.......52.18N 0.50E
Izabal, L. Guatemala **70 G4**...15.30N 89.00W
Izmayil Ukraine **55 K1**........45.20N 28.50E
İzmir Turkey **56 H3**...........38.24N 27.09E
İzmir, G. of Turkey **56 H3**....38.30N 26.45E
Izozog Marshes f. Bolivia **77 D3**...18.30S 62.05W
Izu-Shoto is. Japan **106 C2**...34.20N 139.20E
Izyum Ukraine **55 O3**.........49.12N 37.19E

J

Jabal Mahrat mts. Yemen **95 H2**...17.00N 52.10E
Jabalón r. Spain **46 C3**.......38.55N 4.07W
Jabalpur India **97 F5**.........23.10N 79.59E
Jablah Syria **57 L1**...........35.22N 35.56E
Jaboatão Brazil **77 G4**.......8.05S 35.00W
Jaca Spain **46 E5**.............42.34N 0.33W
Jackson U.S.A. **65 H3**.......32.20N 90.11W
Jacksonville U.S.A. **65 J3**...30.20N 81.40W
Jacmel Haiti **71 J4**...........18.18N 72.32W
Jacobabad Pakistan **96 D6**...28.16N 68.30E
Jacui r. Brazil **77 E1**.........29.56S 51.13W
Jacuípe r. Brazil **77 G3**......12.44S 39.01W
Jaén Spain **46 D2**...........37.46N 3.48W
Jaffna Sri Lanka **97 G2**.......9.38N 80.02E
Jagdalpur India **97 G4**.......19.04N 82.05E
Jahrom Iran **95 H4**..........28.30N 53.30E
Jaipur India **96 F6**..........26.53N 75.50E
Jaisalmer India **96 E6**......26.55N 70.54E
Jakarta Indonesia **104 D2**...6.08S 106.45E
Jakobstad Finland **43 E3**...63.41N 22.40E
Jalalabad Afghan. **95 L5**....34.26N 70.28E
Jalapa Mexico **70 E4**.......19.45N 96.48W
Jalgaon India **96 F5**........21.01N 75.39E
Jalisco d. Mexico **70 D5**....21.00N 103.00W
Jalna India **96 F4**...........19.50N 75.58E
Jalón r. Spain **46 E4**........41.47N 1.02W
Jalu Libya **53 H2**...........29.02N 21.33E
Jamaica C. America **71 I4**...18.00N 77.00W
Jamanxim r. Brazil **77 E4**...4.43S 56.18W
Jambi Indonesia **104 C3**....1.36S 103.39E
James r. U.S.A. **64 G5**......42.50N 97.15W
James B. Canada **63 J3**.....53.00N 81.00W
Jamestown U.S.A. **64 G6**...46.54N 98.42W
Jammu Jammu & Kashmir **96 E7**...32.44N 74.52E
Jammu & Kashmir Asia **96 F7**...33.30N 76.00E
Jamnagar India **96 D5**.......22.28N 70.06E
Jampur Pakistan **96 E6**......28.45N 70.36E
Jämsänkoski Finland **43 F3**...61.54N 25.10E
Jamshedpur India **97 H5**.....22.47N 86.12E
Jan Mayen i. Arctic Oc. **34 C5**...72.00N 8.00W
Japan Asia **106 C3**..........36.00N 138.00E
Japan, Sea of Asia **106 C3**...40.00N 135.00E
Japan Trench f. Pacific Oc. **117 Q7**
Japurá r. Brazil **76 D4**........3.00S 64.30W
Jardines de la Reina is. Cuba **71 I5**...20.30N 79.00W
Järpen Sweden **43 C3**......63.20N 13.30E
Järvenpää Finland **43 F3**....60.29N 25.06E
Jarvis I. Pacific Oc. **108 P6**...0.23S 160.02W
Jatapu r. Brazil **77 E4**.......2.20S 58.10W
Jaú Brazil **77 F2**.............22.11S 48.35W
Java i. Indonesia **104 D2**....7.30S 110.00E
Java Sea Indonesia **104 D3**...5.00S 111.00E
Jayapura Indonesia **105 K3**...2.28S 140.38E
Jaza'ir Farasan is. Saudi Arabia **94 F2**...16.48N 41.54E
Jebel Abyad Plateau f. Sudan **94 C2**...19.00N 29.00E
Jedburgh Scotland **17 G3**...55.29N 2.33W
Jedda Saudi Arabia **94 E3**...21.30N 39.10E
Jefferson City U.S.A. **65 H4**...38.33N 92.10W
Jelenia Góra Poland **54 D4**...50.55N 15.45E
Jelgava Latvia **43 E2**........56.39N 23.40E
Jember Indonesia **104 E2**...8.07S 113.45E
Jena Germany **48 E4**........50.56N 11.35E
Jendouba Tunisia **52 E4**.....36.30N 8.45E
Jequié Brazil **77 F3**.........13.52S 40.06W
Jequitinhonha r. Brazil **77 G3**...16.46S 39.45W
Jérémie Haiti **71 I4**.........18.40N 74.09W
Jeréz de la Frontera Spain **46 B2**...36.41N 6.08W
Jersey i. Channel Is. **13 Z8**...49.13N 2.08W
Jerusalem Israel/Jordan **94 E5**...31.47N 35.13E
Jesi Italy **50 E5**............43.32N 13.15E
Jesup U.S.A. **65 J3**........31.36N 81.54W
Jhang Maghiana Pakistan **95 L5**...31.16N 72.20E
Jhansi India **97 F6**........25.27N 78.34E
Jiamusi China **103 O7**.....46.50N 130.21E
Ji'an China **103 L3**........27.08N 115.00E
Jiangsu d. China **103 L4**...33.00N 119.00E
Jiangxi d. China **103 L3**...27.25N 115.20E
Jiayi Taiwan **103 M2**.......23.28N 120.27E
Jibou Romania **54 H2**......47.15N 23.17E
Jiddat al Harasis f. Oman **95 I2**...19.50N 56.10E
Jiehkkevarri mtn. Norway **43 D5**...69.22N 19.55E
Jieśjávri l. Norway **43 F5**...69.40N 24.10E
Jihlava Czech Rep. **54 D3**...49.24N 15.35E
Jilib Somalia **86 D5**.......0.28N 42.50E
Jilin China **103 N6**.......43.53N 126.35E
Jilin d. China **103 N6**....43.00N 127.30E
Jilong Taiwan **103 M3**...25.10N 121.43E
Jimma Ethiopia **85 H2**...7.39N 36.47E
Jinan China **103 L5**.......36.50N 117.00E
Jingdezhen China **103 L3**...29.16N 117.11E
Jingmen China **103 K4**....31.02N 112.06E
Jinhua China **103 L3**......29.10N 119.40E
Jining Nei Monggol China **103 K6**...40.56N 113.00E
Jining Shandong China **103 L5**...35.25N 116.40E
Jinja Uganda **87 A3**.......0.27N 33.14E
Jinka Ethiopia **87 B4**.....5.45N 36.43E
Jinzhou China **103 M6**...41.07N 121.06E
Jiparaná r. Brazil **77 D4**...8.05S 62.52W
Jipe, L. Tanzania **87 B2**...3.35S 37.45E
Jiu, L. Romania **56 F5**.....43.44N 23.52E
Jiujiang China **103 L3**.....29.41N 116.03E
Jiwami Pakistan **95 J4**.....25.02N 61.50E
Jixi China **103 O7**.........45.17N 131.00E
Jizan Saudi Arabia **94 F2**...16.56N 42.33E
João Pessoa Brazil **77 G4**...7.06S 34.53W
Jodhpur India **96 E6**......26.18N 73.08E
Joensuu Finland **43 G3**...62.35N 29.46E
Joetsu Japan **106 C3**.....37.06N 138.15E
Johannesburg R.S.A. **86 B2**...26.10S 28.02E
John o' Groats Scotland **19 F3**...58.39N 3.04W
Johnston Wales **12 B3**...51.46N 5.00W
Johnstone Scotland **16 E3**...55.50N 4.30W
Johnston I. Pacific Oc. **108 P8**...16.45N 169.32W
Johor Bahru Malaysia **104 C4**...1.29N 103.40E
Joinville Brazil **77 F2**.......26.20S 48.49W
Jokkmokk Sweden **43 D4**...66.37N 19.50E
Jolo i. Phil. **105 G5**.......5.55N 121.20E
Jones Sd. Canada **63 J5**...76.00N 85.00W
Jönköping Sweden **43 C2**...57.45N 14.10E
Jonquière Canada **63 K2**...48.26N 71.06W
Joplin U.S.A. **65 H4**.......37.04N 94.31W
Jordan Asia **94 E5**.........31.00N 36.00E

Jörn Sweden **43 D4**.........65.04N 20.00E
Jos Nigeria **84 E3**..........9.54N 8.53E
Joseph Bonaparte G. Australia **110 B4**
...14.00S 128.30E
Jos Plateau f. Nigeria **82 D5**...10.00N 9.00E
Juan Fernandez Is. Chile **109 W3**...34.20S 80.00W
Juàzeiro Brazil **77 F4**.......9.25S 40.30W
Juàzeiro do Norte Brazil **77 G4**...7.10S 39.18W
Juba Sudan **85 H2**.........4.50N 31.35E
Jubba r. Somalia **85 I2**.....0.20S 42.53E
Júcar r. Spain **46 E3**.......39.10N 0.15W
Juchitán Mexico **70 F4**....16.27N 95.05W
Judenburg Austria **54 D2**...47.10N 14.40E
Juelsminde Denmark **54 A6**...55.43N 10.01E
Juist i. Germany **42 F5**.....53.43N 7.00E
Juiz de Fora Brazil **76 F2**...21.47S 43.23W
Juliaca Peru **76 C3**........15.29S 70.09W
Junction City U.S.A. **64 G4**...39.02N 96.51W
Juneau U.S.A. **62 E3**......58.20N 134.20W
Jungfrau mtn. Switz. **44 G5**...46.30N 8.00E
Jura mts. Europe **44 G5**...46.55N 6.45E
Jura i. Scotland **16 D4**....56.00N 5.55W
Jura, Sd. of Scotland **16 D3**...56.00N 5.45W
Juruá r. Brazil **76 D4**......2.30S 65.40W
Juruena r. Brazil **77 E4**....7.20S 57.30W
Jutaí r. Brazil **76 D4**.......2.35S 67.00W
Jyväskylä Finland **43 F3**...62.16N 25.50E

K

K2 mtn. Asia **96 F8**.........35.53N 76.32E
Kaambooni Somalia **87 C2**...1.36S 41.36E
Kabaena i. Indonesia **105 G2**...5.25S 122.00E
Kabarnet Kenya **87 B3**......0.28N 35.45E
Kabalo Zaire **86 B4**........6.02S 26.55E
Kabwe Zambia **86 B3**......14.29S 28.25E
Kachchh, G. of India **96 D5**...22.30N 69.30E
Kachug Russian Fed. **103 J8**...53.58N 105.55E
Kadam mtn. Uganda **87 A3**...1.45N 34.44E
Kadavu i. Fiji **111 G4**.......19.05S 178.15E
Kadirli Turkey **57 M2**......37.22N 36.05E
Kadugli Sudan **85 G3**......11.01N 29.43E
Kaduna Nigeria **84 E3**......10.28N 7.25E
Kaesong N. Korea **103 N5**...37.59N 126.30E
Kafireas, C. Greece **56 G3**...38.11N 24.30E
Kaga Bandoro C.A.R. **85 F2**...7.00N 19.10E
Kagoshima Japan **106 B2**...31.37N 130.32E
Kahraman Maraş Turkey **57 M2**...37.34N 36.54E
Kaifeng China **103 K4**......34.47N 114.20E
Kai Is. Indonesia **105 I2**....5.45S 132.55E
Kaimana Indonesia **105 I3**...3.39S 133.44E
Kairouan Tunisia **84 F5**.....35.40N 10.04E
Kaiserslautern Germany **48 C3**...49.27N 7.47E
Kaiyuan China **103 I2**......23.42N 103.09E
Kajaani Finland **43 F4**......64.14N 27.37E
Kajiado Kenya **87 B2**.......1.50S 36.48E
Kakamega Kenya **87 A3**....0.14N 34.46E
Kakhovka Resr. Ukraine **55 N2**...47.33N 34.40E
Kakinada India **97 G4**......16.59N 82.20E
Kaktovik U.S.A. **62 D5**.....70.08N 143.50W
Kakuma Kenya **87 A3**......3.38N 34.48E
Kalacha Dida Kenya **87 B3**...3.09N 37.30E
Kalahari Desert Botswana **86 B2**...23.55S 23.00E
Kalajoki Finland **43 E4**.....64.15N 24.00E
Kalamaria Greece **56 F4**...40.33N 22.55E
Kalamata Greece **56 F2**....37.02N 22.05E
Kalecik Turkey **57 K4**.......40.06N 33.22E
Kalemie Zaire **86 B4**.......5.57S 29.10E
Kalgoorlie Australia **110 B2**...30.49S 121.29E
Kaliakra, C. Bulgaria **57 I5**...43.23N 28.29E
Kalimantan f. Indonesia **104 E3**...1.00S 113.00E
Kaliningrad Russian Fed. **54 G6**...54.40N 20.30E
Kalininskaya Russian Fed. **57 N6**...45.31N 38.41E
Kalispell U.S.A. **64 D6**.....48.12N 114.19W
Kalisz Poland **54 F4**.......51.46N 18.02E
Kalix r. Sweden **43 E4**.....65.50N 23.10E
Kallavesi l. Finland **43 G3**...62.45N 28.00E
Kalmar Sweden **43 D2**.....56.39N 16.20E
Kaltag U.S.A. **62 C4**.......64.20N 158.44W
Kaluga Russian Fed. **58 O6**...54.31N 36.16E
Kalundborg Denmark **43 B1**...55.42N 11.06E
Kama r. Russian Fed. **58 H3**...55.30N 52.00E
Kamaishi Japan **106 D3**....39.16N 141.53E
Kambo Ho mtn. N. Korea **106 A4**...41.45N 129.20E
Kamchatka Pen. Russian Fed. **59 R3**...56.00N 160.00E
Kamen'-na-Obi Russian Fed. **102 K8**...53.46N 81.18E
Kamenskoye Russian Fed. **59 S4**...62.31N 165.15E
Kamensk-Ural'skiy Russian Fed. **58 I3**...56.29N 61.49E
Kamina Zaire **86 B4**.......8.46S 25.00E
Kamloops Canada **62 F3**...50.39N 120.24W
Kampala Uganda **86 C5**....0.19N 32.35E
Kampen Neth. **42 E4**......52.33N 5.55E
Kâmpóng Cham Cambodia **104 D6**...11.59N 105.26E
Kâmpôt Cambodia **104 C6**...10.37N 104.11E
Kamuli Uganda **87 A3**.....0.55N 33.08E
Kam"yanets'-Podil's'kyy Ukraine **55 J3**
...48.40N 26.36E
Kamyshin Russian Fed. **58 G3**...50.05N 45.24E
Kananga Zaire **86 B4**.......5.53S 22.26E
Kanazawa Japan **106 C3**...36.35N 136.40E
Kanchipuram India **97 F3**...12.50N 79.44E
Kandahar Afghan. **95 K5**...31.36N 65.47E
Kandalaksha Russian Fed. **43 H4**...67.09N 32.31E
Kandalakskaya G. Russian Fed. **43 H4**...66.30N 34.00E
Kandira Turkey **57 J4**......41.05N 30.08E
Kandy Sri Lanka **97 G2**....7.18N 80.43E
Kangan Iran **95 H4**........27.50N 52.07E
Kangaroo I. Australia **110 C2**...35.45S 137.30E
Kangchenjunga mtn. Asia **97 H6**...27.44N 88.11E
Kangding China **103 I4**....30.05N 102.04E
Kangean Is. Indonesia **104 F2**...7.00S 115.45E
Kangetet Kenya **87 B3**.....1.59N 36.05E
Kangiqsualujjuaq Canada **63 L3**...58.35N 65.59W
Kangiqsujuaq Canada **63 K4**...61.30N 72.00W
Kangmar China **102 E3**...28.35N 89.42E
Kangnŭng S. Korea **106 A3**...37.30N 129.02E
Kanin, C. Russian Fed. **58 G4**...68.38N 43.20E
Kanin Pen. Russian Fed. **58 G4**...68.00N 45.00E
Kankaanpää Finland **43 E3**...61.47N 22.25E
Kankakee U.S.A. **65 I5**.....41.08N 87.52W
Kankan Guinea **84 D3**......10.22N 9.11W
Kanker India **97 G5**.......20.17N 81.30E

Kano Nigeria 84 E3.................................12.00N 8.31E
Kanpur India 97 G6..............................26.27N 80.14E
Kansas d. U.S.A. 64 G4.........................38.00N 99.00W
Kansas City U.S.A. 65 H4.....................39.02N 94.33W
Kansk Russian Fed. 59 L3.....................56.11N 95.20E
Kanta mtn. Ethiopia 87 B4.....................6.12N 35.37E
Kanton I. Kiribati 108 N6......................2.50S 171.40W
Kanye Botswana 86 B2.........................24.58S 25.17E
Kaokoveld f. Namibia 86 A3..................18.30S 13.30E
Kaolack Senegal 84 C3........................14.09N 16.04W
Kapchorwa Uganda 87 A3.....................1.27N 34.32E
Kapenguria Kenya 87 A3........................1.13N 35.07E
Kapfenberg Austria 54 D2.....................47.27N 15.18E
Kapoeta Sudan 87 A3...........................4.47N 33.35E
Kaposvár Hungary 54 E2......................46.22N 17.47E
Kapsabet Kenya 87 B3...........................0.10N 35.07E
Kapuskasing Canada 63 J2...................49.25N 82.30W
Kaputir Kenya 87 B3.............................2.04N 35.30E
Kara Bogaz Gol B. Turkmenistan 58 H2...41.20N 53.40E
Karabük Turkey 57 K4..........................41.12N 32.36E
Karachi Pakistan 96 D5.........................24.51N 67.02E
Kara Dag mtn. Turkey 57 N4.................40.23N 39.02E
Karaganda Kazakhstan 102 C7.............49.53N 73.07E
Karaj Iran 95 H6.................................35.48N 50.58E
Karak Jordan 94 E5.............................31.11N 35.42E
Karakelong i. Indonesia 105 H4.............4.20N 126.50E
Karakoram Range mts. Jammu & Kashmir 96 F8
                                         35.30N 76.30E
Karaman Turkey 57 K2.........................37.11N 33.13E
Karamay China 102 E7........................45.48N 84.30E
Karand Iran 95 G6...............................34.16N 46.15E
Karasburg Namibia 86 A2....................28.00S 18.46E
Kara Sea Russian Fed. 58 I5................73.00N 65.00E
Karasuk Russian Fed. 58 J3.................53.45N 78.01E
Karbala Iraq 94 F5...............................32.37N 44.03E
Karcag Hungary 54 G2.........................47.19N 20.56E
Karditsa Greece 56 E3.........................39.22N 21.59E
Kärdla Estonia 43 E2.............................59.00N 22.42E
Kareima Sudan 85 H3..........................18.32N 31.48E
Kariba, L. Zimbabwe/Zambia 86 B3......16.50S 28.00E
Karimata Str. Indonesia 104 D3.............3.00S 109.00E
Karkinitskiy, G. of Ukraine 55 M1...........45.50N 32.45E
Karliyaka Turkey 56 H3........................38.24N 27.07E
Karlovac Croatia 56 B6.........................45.30N 15.34E
Karlovy Vary Czech Rep. 54 C4..............50.14N 12.53E
Karlshamn Sweden 43 C2....................56.10N 14.50E
Karlskoga Sweden 43 C2.....................59.19N 14.33E
Karlskrona Sweden 43 C2....................56.10N 15.35E
Karlsruhe Germany 48 D3.....................49.00N 8.24E
Karlstad Sweden 43 C2.........................59.24N 13.32E
Karmøy i. Norway 43 A2........................59.15N 5.05E
Karnataka d. India 96 F3.......................14.45N 76.00E
Karnobat Bulgaria 56 H5.......................42.40N 27.00E
Karora Sudan 85 H3.............................17.42N 38.22E
Karpathos i. Greece 56 H1....................35.35N 27.08E
Karstula Finland 43 F3...........................62.53N 24.50E
Kartal Turkey 57 I4...............................40.54N 29.12E
Karun r. Iran 95 G5..............................30.25N 48.12E
Karungu B. Kenya 87 A2.......................0.53S 34.07E
Karymskoye Russian Fed. 59 N3..........51.40N 114.20E
Kasai r. Zaire 86 A4...............................3.10S 16.13E
Kasama Zambia 86 C5..........................10.10S 31.11E
Kasese Uganda 86 C5............................0.14N 30.08E
Kashan Iran 95 H5...............................33.59N 51.31E
Kashi China 102 D5.............................39.29N 76.02E
Kashiwazaki Japan 106 C3....................37.22N 138.33E
Kashmar Iran 95 I6..............................35.12N 58.26E
Kasos i. Greece 56 H1..........................35.22N 26.56E
Kassala Sudan 85 H3...........................15.24N 36.30E
Kassel Germany 48 D4..........................51.18N 9.30E
Kasserine Tunisia 52 E4........................35.11N 8.48E
Kastamonu Turkey 57 K4.....................41.22N 33.47E
Kastoria Greece 56 E4...........................40.32N 21.15E
Kastsyukovichy Belarus 55 M5.............53.20N 32.01E
Katakwi Uganda 87 A3...........................1.54N 33.58E
Katerini Greece 56 F4..........................40.16N 22.30E
Katesh Tanzania 87 B2...........................4.32S 35.21E
Kates Needle mtn. Canada 62 E3.........57.02N 132.05W
Katha Myanmar 97 I5...........................24.11N 96.20E
Katherina, Gebel mtn. Egypt 94 D4.......28.30N 33.57E
Katherine Australia 110 C4...................14.29S 132.20E
Kathmandu Nepal 97 H6.......................27.42N 85.19E
Kathua r. Kenya 87 B2...........................1.34S 40.00E
Katima Mulilo Zambia 86 B3.................17.27S 24.10E
Katowice Poland 54 F4.........................50.15N 18.59E
Katrine, Loch Scotland 16 E4................56.15N 4.30W
Katrineholm Sweden 43 D2..................58.59N 16.15E
Katsina Nigeria 84 E3...........................13.00N 7.32E
Kattegat str. Denmark/Sweden 43 B2...57.00N 11.00E
Kauai i. Hawaiian Is. 108 P9.................22.05N 159.30W
Kauhajoki Finland 43 E3.......................62.26N 22.10E
Kaunas Lithuania 55 H6........................54.52N 23.55E
Kaura-Namoda Nigeria 84 E3..............12.39N 6.38E
Kavala Greece 56 G4...........................40.56N 24.24E
Kavir-i-Namak f. Iran 95 I5...................34.55N 58.00E
Kawasaki Japan 106 C3.......................35.30N 139.45E
Kayes Mali 84 C3.................................14.26N 11.28W
Kayseri Turkey 57 L3...........................38.42N 35.28E
Kazachye Russian Fed. 59 P5.............70.46N 136.15E
Kazakhstan Asia 115 M8......................48.00N 52.30E
Kazan Russian Fed. 58 G3...................55.45N 49.10E
Kazanlük Bulgaria 56 G5......................42.38N 25.26E
Kazan-retto is. Japan 108 J9................25.00N 141.00E
Kazerun Iran 95 H4.............................29.35N 51.39E
Kea i. Greece 56 G2.............................37.36N 24.20E
Keady N. Ireland 16 C2........................54.15N 6.43W
Kearney U.S.A. 64 G5..........................40.42N 99.04W
Keban Resr. Turkey 57 N3...................38.50N 39.00E
Kebkabiya Sudan 94 B1.......................13.39N 24.05E
Kebnekaise mtn. Sweden 43 D4..........67.55N 18.30E
Kebock Head Scotland 18 C3...............58.02N 6.22W
Keçiören Turkey 57 K4..........................39.57N 32.50E
Kecskemét Hungary 54 F2...................46.54N 19.42E
Kedainiai Lithuania 43 E1.....................55.17N 23.58E
Keen, Mt. Scotland 19 G1....................56.58N 2.56W
Keetmanshoop Namibia 86 A2.............26.36S 18.08E
Keewatin Canada 65 H6......................49.46N 94.34W
Kefallonia i. Greece 56 E3....................38.15N 20.33E
Keflavik Iceland 43 X2.........................64.01N 22.35W
Kegworth England 10 D3.....................52.50N 1.16W
Keighley England 15 F2.......................53.52N 1.54W
Keitele i. Finland 43 F3........................62.59N 26.00E
Keith Scotland 19 G2............................57.32N 2.57W
Kelifskiy Uzboy f. Turkmenistan 95 J6...37.40N 64.00E
Kelkit r. Turkey 57 M4.........................40.46N 36.32E
Kellett, C. Canada 62 F5......................72.00N 125.30W

Kells Rep. of Ire. 20 E3........................53.44N 6.53W
Kelo Chad 84 F2.................................9.21N 15.50E
Kelowna Canada 62 G2.......................49.50N 119.29W
Kelso Scotland 17 G3............................55.36N 2.26W
Keluang Malaysia 104 C4......................2.01N 103.18E
Kelvedon England 11 F2.....................51.50N 0.43E
Kem' Russian Fed. 58 F4.....................64.58N 34.39E
Kemerovo Russian Fed. 58 K3.............55.25N 86.10E
Kemi Finland 43 F4..............................65.45N 24.28E
Kemi r. Finland 43 F4..........................65.47N 24.28E
Kemijärvi Finland 43 F4.......................66.40N 27.21E
Kemijärvi r. Finland 43 F4....................66.36N 27.24E
Kemnay Scotland 19 G2......................57.14N 2.27W
Kemp Land f. Antarctica 112................69.00S 62.00E
Kempston England 11 E2....................52.07N 0.30W
Kempten Germany 48 E2.....................47.44N 10.19E
Kenai U.S.A. 62 C4.............................60.35N 151.19W
Kenamuke Swamp Sudan 87 A4..........5.30N 34.00E
Kendal England 14 E3.........................54.19N 2.44W
Kendari Indonesia 105 G3....................3.57S 122.36E
Kendawangan Indonesia 104 E3...........2.32S 110.13E
Kengtung Myanmar 97 J5....................21.16N 99.39E
Kenilworth England 10 D3...................52.22N 1.35W
Kenitra Morocco 84 D5.......................34.20N 6.34W
Kenmare Rep. of Ire. 20 B1..................51.53N 9.36W
Kenmare River est. Rep. of Ire. 20 B1....51.45N 10.00W
Kennet r. England 10 D2.....................51.28N 0.57W
Kennewick U.S.A. 64 C6.....................46.12N 119.07W
Kenora Canada 63 I2...........................49.47N 94.26W
Kent d. England 11 F2.........................51.12N 0.40E
Kent r. England 14 E3.........................54.14N 2.50W
Kentucky d. U.S.A. 65 I4......................38.00N 85.00W
Kenya Africa 87 B3................................0.00 38.00E
Kenya, Mt. Kenya 87 B2.......................0.10S 37.19E
Kerala d. India 96 F3...........................10.30N 76.30E
Kerch Ukraine 55 O1..........................45.22N 36.27E
Kerema P.N.G. 110 D5.........................7.59S 145.46E
Keren Eritrea 94 E2.............................15.46N 38.28E
Kerguelen Is. Indian Oc. 108 B2...........49.15S 69.10E
Kericho Kenya 87 A2.............................0.30S 35.15E
Kerinci, Gunung mtn. Indonesia 104 C3...1.45S 101.20E
Kerio r. Kenya 87 B3.............................3.00N 36.14E
Kerio Valley f. Kenya 87 B3....................1.10N 35.45E
Kerki Turkmenistan 95 K6....................37.53N 65.10E
Kerma Sudan 94 D2............................19.38N 30.25E
Kermadec Is. Pacific Oc. 108 N3...........30.00S 178.30W
Kerman Iran 95 I5...............................30.18N 57.05E
Kerman Desert Iran 95 I4.....................28.30N 58.00E
Kermanshah Iran 95 G5......................34.19N 47.04E
Kern r. U.S.A. 64 C4.............................35.25N 119.00W
Kerry d. Rep. of Ire. 20 B2....................52.07N 9.35W
Kerry Head Rep. of Ire. 20 B2...............52.24N 9.56W
Keruguya Kenya 87 B2..........................0.30S 37.16E
Kerynela Cyprus 57 K1........................35.20N 33.20E
Keşan Turkey 56 H4.............................40.51N 26.37E
Kesennuma Japan 106 D3...................38.54N 141.34E
Kessingland England 11 G3.................52.25N 1.41E
Keswick England 14 D3........................54.35N 3.09W
Ketapang Indonesia 104 E3..................1.50S 110.02E
Ketchikan U.S.A. 62 E3........................55.25N 131.40W
Kettering England 11 E3......................52.24N 0.44W
Keweenaw B. U.S.A. 65 I6....................47.00N 88.00W
Key, Lough Rep. of Ire. 20 C4...............54.00N 8.15W
Keyala Sudan 87 A3.............................4.27N 32.52E
Keynsham England 10 C2....................51.25N 2.30W
Khabarovsk Russian Fed. 59 P2...........48.32N 135.08E
Khairpur Pakistan 96 D6......................27.30N 68.50E
Khanabad Afghan. 95 K6......................36.42N 69.08E
Khandwa India 96 F5..........................21.49N 76.23E
Khanewal Pakistan 95 L5....................30.18N 71.56E
Khanka, L. Russian Fed. 59 P2.............45.00N 132.30E
Khanpur Pakistan 96 E6......................28.39N 70.39E
Khanty-Mansiysk Russian Fed. 58 I4...61.00N 69.00E
Kharagpur India 97 H5........................22.23N 87.22E
Kharkiv Ukraine 55 O4........................50.00N 36.15E
Khartoum Sudan 85 H3.......................15.33N 32.35E
Khash r. Afghan. 95 J5........................28.14N 61.15E
Khashm el Girba Sudan 94 E2..............14.58N 35.35E
Khaskovo Bulgaria 56 G4.....................41.57N 25.33E
Khatanga Russian Fed. 59 M5..............71.50N 102.31E
Khayelitsha R.S.A. 86 A1.....................34.03S 18.40E
Khenchela Algeria 52 F4......................35.26N 7.08E
Khenifra Morocco 52 B3.......................33.00N 5.40W
Khersan r. Iran 95 H4...........................31.29N 48.53E
Kherson Ukraine 55 M2.......................46.39N 32.38E
Khmel'nyts'kyy Ukraine 55 J3..............49.25N 27.02E
Khojand Tajikistan 102 B6....................40.14N 69.40E
Kholmsk Russian Fed. 59 Q2...............47.02N 142.03E
Khorinsk Russian Fed. 103 J8..............52.14N 109.52E
Khorramabad Iran 95 G5.....................33.29N 48.21E
Khorugh Tajikistan 95 L6.....................37.32N 71.32E
Khouribga Morocco 52 B3....................32.54N 6.57W
Khowst Afghan. 95 K5.........................33.22N 69.57E
Khulna Bangla. 97 H5..........................22.49N 89.34E
Khunsar Iran 95 H5.............................33.10N 50.19E
Khvoy Iran 94 F6.................................38.32N 45.02E
Khyber Pass Asia 95 L5.......................34.06N 71.05E
Kiambu Kenya 87 B2.............................1.10S 36.51E
Kiantajärvi i. Finland 43 G4.................65.05N 29.10E
Kibaya Tanzania 87 B1.........................5.19S 36.34E
Kibre Mengist Ethiopia 87 B4...............5.52N 39.00E
Kidderminster England 10 C3.............52.24N 2.13W
Kidepo Valley Nat. Park Uganda 87 A3...3.50N 33.45E
Kidlington England 10 D2....................51.50N 1.17W
Kidsgrove England 15 E2....................53.06N 2.15W
Kidwelly Wales 12 C3..........................51.44N 4.20W
Kiel Germany 48 E6.............................54.20N 10.08E
Kiel B. Germany 48 E6.........................54.30N 10.30E
Kiel Canal Germany 48 D6...................53.54N 9.12E
Kielce Poland 54 G4............................50.52N 20.37E
Kielder Water l. England 15 E4..............55.14N 2.30W
Kiev Ukraine 55 L4...............................50.28N 30.29E
Kiev Resr. Ukraine 55 L4......................51.00N 30.25E
Kigali Rwanda 86 C4............................1.59S 30.05E
Kigoma Tanzania 86 B4........................4.52S 29.36E
Kikinda Yugo. 56 E6.............................45.51N 20.30E
Kiklar Dagi mts. Turkey 57 M4.............40.35N 40.30E
Kikori P.N.G. 105 K2............................7.25S 144.13E
Kikori r. P.N.G. 105 K2.........................7.30S 144.20E
Kikwit Zaire 86 A4...............................5.02S 18.51E
Kilbrannan Sd. Scotland 16 D3............55.37N 5.25W
Kilcormac Rep. of Ire. 20 D3................53.10N 7.43W
Kilcullen Rep. of Ire. 20 E3...................53.08N 6.47W
Kildare Rep. of Ire. 20 E3.....................53.10N 6.55W
Kildare d. Rep. of Ire. 20 E3.................53.10N 6.50W
Kilifi Kenya 87 B2.................................3.36S 39.52E

Kilimanjaro mtn. Tanzania 87 B2...........3.02S 37.20E
Kilimanjaro Nat. Park Tanzania 87 B2....3.00S 37.20E
Kilis Turkey 57 M2..............................36.43N 37.07E
Kilkee Rep. of Ire. 20 B2......................52.41N 9.40W
Kilkeel N. Ireland 16 D2.......................54.04N 6.00W
Kilkenny Rep. of Ire. 20 D2..................52.39N 7.16W
Kilkenny d. Rep. of Ire. 20 D2...............52.35N 7.15W
Kilkis Greece 56 F4.............................40.59N 22.51E
Killala Rep. of Ire. 20 B4......................54.15N 9.10W
Killarney Rep. of Ire. 20 B2...................52.04N 9.32W
Killin Scotland 16 E4...........................56.29N 4.19W
Killybegs Rep. of Ire. 20 C4.................54.38N 8.29W
Kilmallock Rep. of Ire. 20 C2................52.25N 8.35W
Kilmarnock Scotland 16 E3..................55.37N 4.30W
Kilmelford Scotland 16 D4...................56.16N 5.29W
Kilmichael Pt. Rep. of Ire. 20 E2...........52.43N 6.10W
Kilrea N. Ireland 16 C2........................54.57N 6.34W
Kilrush Rep. of Ire. 20 B2.....................52.39N 9.30W
Kilsyth Scotland 16 E3.........................55.59N 4.04W
Kilwinning Scotland 16 E3...................55.40N 4.41W
Kimberley R.S.A. 86 B2........................28.45S 24.46E
Kimberley Plateau Australia 110 B4.......17.20S 127.20E
Kimchoaek N. Korea 103 N6................40.41N 129.12E
Kinabalu, Gunung mtn. Malaysia 104 F5
                                         6.10N 116.40E
Kinango Kenya 87 B2...........................4.06S 39.19E
Kinder Scout hill England 15 F2............53.23N 1.53W
Kindu Zaire 86 B4.................................3.00S 25.56E
King I. Australia 110 D1........................40.00S 144.00E
Kingsbridge England 13 D2.................50.17N 3.46W
Kingsclere England 10 D2...................51.20N 1.14W
Kingscourt Rep. of Ire. 20 E3................53.55N 6.48W
King's Lynn England 11 F3...................52.45N 0.25E
Kingsnorth England 11 F2...................51.06N 0.50E
Kings Peak U.S.A. 64 D5.....................40.46N 110.23W
Kingston Canada 65 K5........................44.14N 76.30W
Kingston Jamaica 71 I4........................17.58N 76.48W
Kingston upon Hull England 15 G2......53.45N 0.20W
Kingston-upon-Thames England 11 E2...51.25N 0.17W
Kingstown St. Vincent 71 L3.................13.12N 61.14W
Kingsville U.S.A. 64 G2........................27.31N 97.52W
Kingswood England 10 C2....................51.27N 2.29W
King's Worthy England 10 D2...............51.06N 1.18W
Kington England 10 B3........................52.12N 3.02W
Kingussie Scotland 19 E2.....................57.05N 4.04W
King William I. Canada 63 I4.................69.00N 97.30W
Kinlochleven town Scotland 18 E1.........56.43N 4.58W
Kinloss Scotland 17 F3........................57.38N 3.33W
Kinna Sweden 43 C2...........................57.32N 12.42E
Kinnegad Rep. of Ire. 20 D3................53.27N 7.07W
Kinross Scotland 17 F4........................56.13N 3.27W
Kinsale Rep. of Ire. 20 C1....................51.41N 8.32W
Kinshasa Zaire 86 A4...........................4.18S 15.18E
Kintore Scotland 19 G2.......................57.14N 2.21W
Kintyre pen. Scotland 16 D3................55.35N 5.35W
Kipini Kenya 87 B2...............................2.31S 40.37E
Kircubbin N. Ireland 16 D2..................54.29N 5.32W
Kirenga r. Russian Fed. 59 M3.............57.50N 108.00E
Kiribati Pacific Oc. 108 N6....................4.00S 175.00W
Kırıkkale Turkey 57 K3........................39.51N 33.32E
Kiritimati i. Kiribati 108 P7..................1.52N 157.20W
Kırkareli Turkey 56 H4.........................41.44N 27.12E
Kirkbean Scotland 17 F2.....................54.55N 3.36W
Kirkby England 14 E2..........................53.29N 2.54W
Kirkby in Ashfield England 15 F2...........53.06N 1.15W
Kirkby Lonsdale England 14 E3............54.13N 2.36W
Kirkbymoorside town England 15 G3.....54.16N 0.56W
Kirkby Stephen England 15 E3.............54.27N 2.23W
Kirkcaldy Scotland 17 F4.....................56.07N 3.10W
Kirkcolm Scotland 16 D2.....................54.58N 5.05W
Kirkconnel Scotland 17 F3...................55.23N 3.59W
Kirkcudbright Scotland 17 E2..............54.50N 4.03W
Kirkenes Norway 43 G5.......................69.44N 30.05E
Kirkham England 14 E2.......................53.47N 2.52W
Kirkintilloch Scotland 16 E3.................55.57N 4.10W
Kirkkonummi Finland 43 F3.................60.06N 24.20E
Kirkland Lake town Canada 63 J2.........48.10N 80.02W
Kirkuk Iraq 94 F6................................35.28N 44.26E
Kirkwall Scotland 19 G3......................58.59N 2.58W
Kirov Russian Fed. 55 N6....................54.01N 34.20E
Kirovohrad Ukraine 55 M3...................48.31N 32.15E
Kirovsk Russian Fed. 43 G4.................67.37N 33.39E
Kirovsk Russian Fed. 43 H4.................67.37N 33.39E
Kirriemuir Scotland 19 F1....................56.41N 3.01W
Kırşehir Turkey 57 L3...........................39.09N 34.08E
Kirton in Lindsey England 15 G2..........53.29N 0.35W
Kiruna Sweden 43 E4..........................67.53N 20.15E
Kisangani Zaire 86 B5...........................0.33N 25.14E
Kisii Kenya 87 A2.................................0.40S 34.45E
Kismaayo Somalia 85 I1.......................0.25S 42.31E
Kisoro Uganda 86 B4...........................1.19S 29.42E
Kisumu Kenya 87 A2............................0.03S 34.47E
Kita-Kyushu Japan 106 B2...................33.50N 130.50E
Kitale Kenya 87 B3..............................0.59N 35.01E
Kitami Japan 106 D4...........................43.51N 143.54E
Kitchener Canada 65 J5......................43.27N 80.30W
Kitgum Uganda 87 A3...........................3.17N 32.54E
Kitimat Canada 62 F3..........................54.05N 128.38W
Kittilä Finland 43 F4.............................67.40N 24.50E
Kitui Kenya 87 B2................................1.23S 38.00E
Kitwe Zambia 86 B3.............................12.48S 28.14E
Kiuruvesi Finland 43 F3.......................63.38N 26.40E
Kivu, L. Rwanda/Zaire 86 B4................1.50S 29.10E
Kızıl Irmak r. Turkey 57 L4....................41.45N 35.57E
Kladno Czech Rep. 54 D4....................50.10N 14.05E
Klagenfurt Austria 54 D2.....................46.38N 14.20E
Klaipeda Lithuania 54 G6....................55.43N 21.07E
Klamath Falls town U.S.A. 64 B5..........42.14N 121.47W
Klazienaveen Neth. 42 F4....................52.43N 7.00E
Kleve Germany 42 F3..........................51.47N 6.11E
Klimovo Russian Fed. 55 M5................52.24N 32.13E
Klintsy Russian Fed. 55 M5..................52.45N 32.15E
Klyuchevskaya Sopka mtn. Russian Fed. 59 S3
                                         56.00N 160.30E
Knaresborough England 15 F3.............54.01N 1.29W
Knighton Wales 12 D4.........................52.21N 3.02W
Knin Croatia 56 C6..............................44.02N 16.10E
Knockadoon Hd. Rep. of Ire. 20 D1......51.52N 7.51W
Knockalongy mtn. Rep. of Ire. 20 C4.....54.12N 8.45W
Knockboy mtn. Rep. of Ire. 20 B1.........51.48N 9.27W
Knocklayd mtn. N. Ireland 16 C3..........55.10N 6.15W
Knockmealdown Mts. Rep. of Ire. 20 D2...52.15N 7.55W
Knottingley England 15 F2..................53.42N 1.15W
Knowle England 10 D3.......................52.23N 1.43W

Knoxville U.S.A. 65 J4.........................36.00N 83.57W
Knutsford England 15 E2.....................53.18N 2.22W
Kobe Japan 106 C2.............................34.42N 135.15E
Koblenz Germany 48 C4......................50.21N 7.36E
Kobroör i. Indonesia 105 I2.................6.10S 134.30E
Kobryn Belarus 55 I5............................52.16N 24.22E
Kočani Macedonia 56 F4......................41.55N 22.24E
Kochi Japan 106 B2.............................33.33N 133.52E
Kodiak U.S.A. 62 C3............................57.49N 152.30W
Kodiak I. U.S.A. 62 C3.........................57.00N 153.50W
Kofu Japan 106 C3..............................35.44N 138.34E
Køge Denmark 43 C1...........................55.28N 12.12E
Kohat Pakistan 95 L5..........................33.37N 71.30E
Kokand Uzbekistan 102 C6.................40.33N 70.55E
Kokkola Finland 43 E3.........................63.50N 23.10E
Kokpekty Kazakhstan 102 E7..............48.45N 82.25E
Kokshetau Kazakhstan 58 I3...............53.18N 69.25E
Kola Russian Fed. 43 H5......................68.53N 33.01E
Kolaka Indonesia 105 G3.....................4.04S 121.38E
Kola Pen. Russian Fed. 58 F4..............67.00N 38.00E
Kolding Denmark 43 B1.......................55.29N 9.30E
Kolguyev i. Russian Fed. 58 G4............69.00N 49.00E
Kolhapur India 96 E4...........................16.43N 74.15E
Kołobrzeg Poland 54 D6......................54.10N 15.35E
Kolomna Russian Fed. 55 P6...............55.05N 38.45E
Kolomyya Ukraine 55 I3......................48.31N 25.00E
Koluli Eritrea 94 F1.............................14.26N 40.20E
Kolvitskoye, Ozero l. Russian Fed. 43 H4
                                         67.00N 33.20E
Kolwezi Zaire 86 B3.............................10.44S 25.28E
Kolyma r. Russian Fed. 59 S4..............68.50N 161.00E
Kolyma Range mts. Russian Fed. 59 R4
                                         63.00N 160.00E
Komatsu Japan 106 C3.......................36.24N 136.27E
Kome I. Uganda 87 A3...........................0.06S 32.43E
Komotini Greece 56 G4.......................41.07N 25.26E
Komsomolets i. Russian Fed. 59 L6......80.20N 96.00E
Komsomolsk-na-Amure Russian Fed. 59 P3
                                         50.32N 136.59E
Kondoa Tanzania 87 B2........................4.55S 35.48E
Kong Christian IX Land f. Greenland 63 O4
                                         68.20N 37.00W
Kong Frederik VI Coast f. Greenland 63 N4
                                         63.00N 44.00W
Kongsberg Norway 43 B2....................59.42N 9.39E
Kongsvinger Norway 43 C3.................60.13N 11.59E
Konin Poland 54 F5.............................52.13N 18.16E
Konotop Ukraine 55 M4......................51.15N 33.14E
Konso Ethiopia 87 B4............................5.18N 37.30E
Konstanz Germany 48 D2....................47.40N 9.10E
Konya Turkey 57 K2............................37.51N 32.30E
Köping Sweden 43 C2.........................59.31N 16.01E
Kora Nat. Res. Kenya 87 B2...................0.30S 39.00E
Koraput India 97 G4...........................18.49N 82.43E
Korçë Albania 56 E4............................40.37N 20.45E
Korcula i. Croatia 56 C5......................42.56N 16.53E
Korea B. Asia 103 M5..........................39.00N 124.00E
Korea Str. S. Korea/Japan 103 N4........35.00N 129.20E
Korenovsk Russian Fed. 57 N6............45.29N 39.28E
Körfez Turkey 57 I4.............................40.48N 29.55E
Koriyama Japan 106 D3......................37.23N 140.22E
Korkuteli Turkey 57 J2........................37.07N 30.11E
Korogwe Tanzania 87 B2.......................5.09S 38.29E
Koror Palau 105 I5..............................7.30N 134.30E
Korosten' Ukraine 55 K4.....................51.00N 28.30E
Korsør Denmark 43 B1.........................55.19N 11.09E
Kortrijk Belgium 42 C2.........................50.49N 3.17E
Koryak Range mts. Russian Fed. 59 T4
                                         62.20N 171.00E
Kos Greece 56 H2..............................36.53N 27.18E
Kos i. Greece 56 H2............................36.48N 27.10E
Kościerzyna Poland 54 E6...................54.08N 18.00E
Kosciusko, Mt. Australia 110 D2...........36.28S 148.17E
Košice Slovakia 54 G3.........................48.44N 21.15E
Kosovska Mitrovica Yugo. 56 E5...........42.54N 20.51E
Kosrae i. Fed. States of Micronesia 108 L7
                                         5.10N 163.05E
Kosti Sudan 85 H3..............................13.11N 32.38E
Kostroma Russian Fed. 58 G3..............57.46N 40.59E
Kostrzyn Poland 54 D5........................52.35N 14.40E
Kostyantynivka Ukraine 55 O3............48.33N 37.45E
Koszalin Poland 54 E6.........................54.12N 16.09E
Kota India 96 F6.................................25.11N 75.58E
Kota Bharu Malaysia 104 C5...............6.07N 102.15E
Kotabumi Indonesia 104 C3.................4.52S 104.59E
Kota Kinabalu Malaysia 104 F5............5.59N 116.04E
Kotel'nyy i. Russian Fed. 59 Q5............75.30N 141.00E
Kotido Uganda 87 B3............................3.01N 34.08E
Kotlas Russian Fed. 58 G4...................61.15N 46.28E
Kotlik U.S.A. 62 B4.............................63.02N 163.33W
Kötlutangi c. Iceland 43 Y1.................63.42N 18.40W
Kotor Yugo. 56 D5..............................42.28N 18.47E
Kotovs'k Ukraine 55 K2.......................47.42N 29.30E
Kotuy r. Russian Fed. 59 M5................71.40N 103.00E
Kotzebue U.S.A. 62 B4........................66.51N 162.40W
Kouvola Finland 43 F3.........................60.54N 26.45E
Kovel' Ukraine 55 I4............................51.12N 24.48E
Kowloon Hong Kong 103 K2...............22.20N 114.15E
Kozan Turkey 57 L2............................37.27N 35.47E
Kozani Greece 56 E4...........................40.18N 21.48E
Krabi Thailand 104 B5.........................8.04N 98.52E
Krâchéh Cambodia 104 D6.................12.30N 106.03E
Kragujevac Yugo. 56 E6......................44.01N 20.55E
Kraków Poland 54 F4..........................50.03N 19.55E
Kraljevo Yugo. 56 E5...........................43.44N 20.41E
Kramators'k Ukraine 55 O3..................48.43N 37.33E
Kramfors Sweden 43 D3......................62.55N 17.50E
Kranj Slovenia 54 D2...........................46.15N 14.21E
Krasnoarmiys'k Ukraine 55 O3.............48.17N 37.14E
Krasnodar Russian Fed. 57 N6............45.00N 39.15E
Krasnodar Resr. Russian Fed. 57 N6....45.00N 39.15E
Krasnohrad Ukraine 55 N3..................49.22N 35.28E
Krasnokamensk Russian Fed. 59 N3....50.10N 118.00E
Krasnovodsk Turkmenistan 58 H2........40.01N 53.00E
Krasnoyarsk Russian Fed. 59 L3..........56.05N 92.46E
Krefeld Germany 48 C4.......................51.20N 6.32E
Kremenchuk Ukraine 55 M3................49.03N 33.25E
Kremenchuk Resr. Ukraine 55 M3........49.20N 32.30E
Krishna r. India 97 G4.........................16.00N 81.00E
Kristiansand Norway 43 A2..................58.08N 7.59E
Kristianstad Sweden 43 C2.................56.02N 14.10E
Kristiansund Norway 43 A3.................63.15N 7.55E
Kristinehamn Sweden 43 C2...............59.17N 14.09E
Krk i. Croatia 56 B6.............................45.04N 14.36E
Kropotkin Russian Fed. 53 L6..............45.25N 40.35E
Krosno Poland 54 G3..........................49.42N 21.46E

Kruševac Yugo. 56 E5....43.34N 21.20E
Krychaw Belarus 55 L5....53.40N 31.44E
Krymsk Russian Fed. 57 M6....44.56N 38.00E
Kryvyy Rih' Ukraine 55 M2....47.55N 33.24E
Ksar El Boukhari Algeria 52 D4....35.53N 2.45E
Ksar el Kebir Morocco 52 B3....35.01N 5.54W
Kuala Lumpur Malaysia 104 C4....3.08N 101.42E
Kuala Terengganu Malaysia 104 C5....5.10N 103.10E
Kuantan Malaysia 104 C4....3.50N 103.19E
Kuban r. Russian Fed. 57 M6....45.20N 37.17E
Kuching Malaysia 104 E4....1.32N 110.20E
Kuh-e Baba Afghan. 95 K5....34.40N 67.30E
Kuh-e Dinar mtn. Iran 95 H5....30.45N 51.39E
Kuh-e Sahand mtn. Iran 95 G6....37.37N 46.27E
Kuhmo Finland 43 G4....64.04N 29.30E
Kuito Angola 86 A3....12.25S 16.58E
Kul r. Iran 95 I4....27.00N 55.45E
Kulal, Mt. Kenya 87 B3....2.44N 36.56E
Kuldiga Latvia 43 E2....56.58N 21.59E
Kulunda Russian Fed. 102 D8....52.34N 78.58E
Kumamoto Japan 106 B2....32.50N 130.42E
Kumanovo Macedonia 56 E5....42.08N 21.40E
Kumasi Ghana 84 D2....6.45N 1.35W
Kumbakonam India 97 F3....10.59N 79.24E
Kumi Uganda 87 A3....1.26N 33.54E
Kumla Sweden 43 C2....59.08N 15.09E
Kumluca Turkey 57 J2....36.23N 30.17E
Kumo Nigeria 84 F3....10.02N 11.50E
Kunashir i. Russian Fed. 106 E4....44.25N 146.00E
Kungrad Uzbekistan 58 H2....43.05N 58.23E
Kunlun Shan mts. China 102 E5....36.40N 85.00E
Kunming China 103 I3....25.04N 102.41E
Kuohijärvi l. Finland 43 F3....61.20N 24.10E
Kuopio Finland 43 F3....62.51N 27.30E
Kupa r. Croatia 56 C6....45.30N 16.20E
Kupang Indonesia 105 G1....10.13S 123.38E
Kup"yans'k Ukraine 55 O3....49.41N 37.37E
Kuqa China 102 E6....41.43N 82.58E
Kürdzhali Bulgaria 56 G4....41.39N 25.22E
Kure Atoll Hawaiian Is. 108 N9....28.25N 178.25W
Kuressaare Estonia 43 E2....58.12N 22.30E
Kurgan Russian Fed. 58 I3....55.20N 65.20E
Kuria Muria Is. Oman 95 I2....17.30N 56.00E
Kurikka Finland 43 E3....62.37N 22.25E
Kuril Is. Russian Fed. 59 R2....46.00N 150.30E
Kuril Trench f. Pacific Oc. 117 Q8
Kurmuk Sudan 85 H3....10.33N 34.17E
Kurnool India 97 F4....15.51N 78.01E
Kursk Russian Fed. 55 O4....51.45N 36.14E
Kuršumlija Yugo. 56 E5....43.09N 21.16E
Kurume Japan 106 B2....33.20N 130.29E
Kurun r. Sudan 87 A4....5.40N 33.50E
Kurunegala Sri Lanka 97 G2....7.28N 80.23E
Kushiro Japan 106 D4....42.58N 144.24E
Kuskokwim r. U.S.A. 62 B4....60.50N 161.00W
Kuskokwim B. U.S.A. 62 B3....59.45N 162.25W
Kuskokwim Mts. U.S.A. 62 C4....62.50N 156.00W
Kustanay Kazakhstan 58 I3....53.15N 63.40E
Kütahya Turkey 57 I3....39.25N 29.56E
Kuujjuaq Canada 63 L3....58.10N 68.15W
Kuusamo Finland 43 G4....65.57N 29.15E
Kuwait Asia 95 G4....29.20N 47.40E
Kuwait town Kuwait 95 G4....29.20N 48.00E
Kuznetsk Russian Fed. 58 G3....53.08N 46.36E
Kvaløya i. Norway 43 D5....69.45N 18.20E
Kwale Kenya 87 B2....4.10S 39.27E
KwaMashu R.S.A. 86 C2....29.45S 30.56E
Kwa Mtoro Tanzania 87 B1....5.14S 35.22E
Kwangju S. Korea 103 N5....35.07N 126.52E
Kwania, L. Uganda 87 A3....1.48N 32.45E
Kwanobuhle R.S.A. 86 B1....33.30S 25.26E
Kwilu r. Zaire 86 A4....3.18S 17.22E
Kwoka mtn. Indonesia 105 I3....1.30S 132.30E
Kyakhta Russian Fed. 103 J8....50.22N 106.30E
Kyle of Durness est. Scotland 18 E3....58.32N 4.50W
Kyle of Lochalsh town Scotland 18 D2....57.17N 5.43W
Kyle of Tongue est. Scotland 19 E3....58.27N 4.26W
Kyllini mtn. Greece 56 F2....37.56N 22.22E
Kyoga, L. Uganda 86 C5....1.30N 33.00E
Kyoto Japan 106 C2....35.04N 135.50E
Kyparissia Greece 56 E2....37.15N 21.40E
Kyrgyzstan Asia 102 C6....41.30N 75.00E
Kythira i. Greece 56 F2....36.15N 23.00E
Kythnos i. Greece 56 F2....37.25N 24.25E
Kyushu i. Japan 106 B2....32.00N 131.00E
Kyustendil Bulgaria 56 F5....42.18N 22.39E
Kyzyl Russian Fed. 59 L3....51.42N 94.28E
Kzyl-Orda Kazakhstan 58 J2....44.52N 65.28E

L

Laâyoune W. Sahara 84 C4....27.10N 13.11W
La Banda Argentina 75 C5....27.44S 64.14W
Labé Guinea 84 C3....11.17N 12.11W
Labrador f. Canada 63 L3....54.00N 61.30W
Labrador City Canada 63 L3....52.54N 66.50W
Labrador Sea Canada/Greenland 63 M4
....60.00N 55.00W
Laccadive Is. Indian Oc. 96 E3....11.00N 72.00E
Laceby England 15 G2....53.33N 0.10W
La Chaux-de-Fonds Switz. 44 G5....47.07N 6.51E
Lachlan r. Australia 110 D3....34.21S 143.58E
La Crosse U.S.A. 65 H5....43.48N 91.15W
La Demanda, Sierra de mts. Spain 46 D5
....42.10N 2.55W
Ladhar Bheinn mtn. Scotland 18 D2....57.04N 5.35W
Ladiz Iran 95 J4....28.57N 61.18E
Ladoga, L. Russian Fed. 58 F4....61.00N 32.00E
Ladybank Scotland 17 F4....56.17N 3.08W
Ladybower Resr. England 15 F2....53.23N 1.42W
Lae P.N.G. 110 D5....6.45S 146.30E
Læsø i. Denmark 43 B2....57.16N 11.01E
Lafayette U.S.A. 65 H3....30.12N 92.18W
Lagan r. N. Ireland 16 D2....54.37N 5.54W
Laggan, Loch Scotland 19 E1....56.57N 4.30W
Lagh Bogal r. Kenya 87 B3....1.04N 40.10E
Lagh Bor r. Kenya/Somalia 87 C3....0.30N 42.04E
Lagh Dima r. Kenya/Somalia 87 C3....0.30N 41.09E
Lagh Kutulu r. Kenya 87 C3....2.10N 40.53E
Laghouat Algeria 52 D3....33.49N 2.55E
Lagh Walde Kenya 87 B3....2.48N 38.54E
La Gomera i. Canary Is. 46 X2....28.08N 17.14W

Lagos Nigeria 84 E2....6.27N 3.28E
Lagos Portugal 46 A2....37.05N 8.40W
La Grande 2, Résr de Canada 63 K3....53.35N 77.10W
La Grande 3, Résr de Canada 63 K3....53.35N 74.55W
La Grande 4, Résr de Canada 63 K3....53.50N 73.30W
La Gran Sabana f. Venezuela 71 L2....5.20N 61.30W
Lahad Datu Malaysia 104 F5....5.05N 118.20E
Lahat Indonesia 104 C3....3.46S 103.32E
Lahij Yemen 94 F1....13.04N 44.53E
Lahore Pakistan 96 E7....31.34N 74.22E
Lahti Finland 43 F3....61.00N 25.40E
Laidon, Loch Scotland 16 E4....56.39N 4.38W
Laihia Finland 43 E3....62.58N 22.01E
Lainio r. Sweden 43 E4....67.26N 22.37E
Lairg Scotland 19 E3....58.01N 4.25W
Laisamis mtn. Kenya 87 B3....1.38N 37.47E
La Junta U.S.A. 64 F4....37.59N 103.34W
Lake City U.S.A. 65 J3....30.05N 82.40W
Lake District f. England 14 D3....54.30N 3.10W
Lakeland town U.S.A. 65 J2....28.02N 81.59W
Lakeview U.S.A. 64 B5....42.13N 120.21W
Lakki Pakistan 96 L5....32.35N 70.58E
Lakonia, G. of Greece 56 F2....36.35N 22.42E
Laksefjorden est. Norway 43 F5....70.40N 26.50E
Lakshadweep d. India 96 E3....11.00N 72.00E
La Línea de la Concepción Spain 46 C2....36.10N 5.21W
La Louvière Belgium 42 D2....50.29N 4.11E
La Mancha f. Spain 46 D3....39.00N 2.30W
Lamar U.S.A. 64 F4....38.04N 102.37W
Lamard Iran 95 H4....27.22N 53.20E
Lambay I. Rep. of Ire. 20 E3....53.30N 6.01W
Lambourn England 10 D2....51.31N 1.31W
Lambourn Downs hills England 10 D2....51.32N 1.36W
Lamego Portugal 46 B4....41.05N 7.49W
Lamia Greece 56 F3....38.53N 22.25E
Lamlash Scotland 16 D3....55.32N 5.08W
Lammermuir Hills Scotland 17 G3....55.51N 2.40W
Lampeter Wales 12 C4....52.06N 4.06W
Lamu Kenya 87 A2....2.20S 40.54E
Lamu I. Kenya 87 A2....2.17S 40.52E
La Nao, Cabo de c. Spain 46 F3....38.42N 0.15E
Lanark Scotland 17 F3....55.41N 3.47W
Lancashire d. England 14 E2....53.53N 2.30W
Lancaster England 14 E3....54.03N 2.48W
Lancaster Canal England 14 E2....54.00N 2.48W
Lancaster Sd. Canada 63 J5....74.00N 85.00W
Landes f. France 44 C4....44.40N 0.40W
Landguard Pt. England 11 G2....51.55N 1.18E
Land's End c. England 13 B2....50.03N 5.45W
Landshut Germany 48 F3....48.31N 12.10E
Lanesborough Rep. of Ire. 20 D3....53.40N 8.00W
Langavat, Loch Scotland 18 C2....57.48N 6.58W
Langavat, Loch Scotland 18 C4....58.04N 6.45W
Langeland i. Denmark 43 B1....54.50N 10.50E
Langholm Scotland 17 F3....55.09N 3.00W
Langoya i. Norway 43 C5....68.50N 15.00E
Langport England 13 E3....51.02N 2.51W
Langres France 44 F5....47.53N 5.20E
Langsa Indonesia 104 B4....4.28N 97.59E
Langstrothdale Chase hills England 15 E3
....54.13N 2.15W
Languedoc f. France 44 E3....43.30N 3.00E
Lanivet England 13 C2....50.27N 4.45W
Länkäran Azerbaijan 95 G6....38.45N 48.50E
Lannion France 44 B6....48.44N 3.27W
Lansing U.S.A. 65 J5....42.44N 84.34W
Lanzarote i. Canary Is. 46 Z2....29.00N 13.55W
Lanzhou China 103 I5....36.01N 103.45E
Laoag Phil. 104 G7....18.14N 120.36E
Lao Cai Vietnam 104 C8....22.30N 104.00E
Laois d. Rep. of Ire. 20 D2....53.00N 7.20W
Laon France 42 C1....49.34N 3.37E
Laos Asia 104 C7....19.00N 104.00E
La Palma i. Canary Is. 46 X2....28.50N 18.00W
La Palma del Condado Spain 46 B2....37.23N 6.33W
La Paz Bolivia 76 D3....16.30S 68.10W
La Paz Mexico 70 B5....24.10N 110.17W
La Perouse Str. Russian Fed. 106 D5....45.50N 142.30E
La Plata Argentina 75 D3....34.52S 57.55W
La Plata, Río de est. S. America 75 D3....35.15S 56.45W
Lappajärvi l. Finland 43 E3....63.05N 23.30E
Lappeenranta Finland 43 G3....61.04N 28.05E
Lappland f. Sweden/Finland 43 E5....68.10N 24.00E
Laptev Sea Russian Fed. 59 O5....74.30N 125.00E
Lapua Finland 43 E3....62.57N 23.00E
L'Aquila Italy 50 E5....42.22N 13.25E
Larache Morocco 46 B1....35.12N 6.10W
Laramie U.S.A. 64 E5....41.20N 105.38W
Laredo U.S.A. 64 G2....27.32N 99.22W
Largs Scotland 16 E3....55.48N 4.52W
La Rioja Argentina 76 D2....29.26S 66.50W
Larisa Greece 56 F3....39.36N 22.24E
Larkana Pakistan 96 D6....27.32N 68.18E
Larnaca Cyprus 57 K1....34.54N 33.39E
Larne N. Ireland 16 D2....54.51N 5.50W
Larne Lough N. Ireland 16 D2....54.50N 5.47W
La Rochelle France 44 C5....46.10N 1.10W
La Roche-sur-Yon France 44 C5....46.40N 1.25W
La Romana Dom. Rep. 71 K4....18.27N 68.57W
La Ronge Canada 62 H3....55.07N 105.18W
Larvik Norway 43 B2....59.04N 10.02E
La Sagra mtn. Spain 46 D2....37.57N 2.34W
Las Cruces U.S.A. 64 E3....32.18N 106.47W
La Seine, Baie de France 44 C6....49.40N 0.30W
La Selle mtn. Haiti 71 J4....18.23N 71.59W
La Serena Chile 76 C2....29.54S 71.16W
Las Marismas f. Spain 46 B2....37.05N 6.20W
Las Nieves, Pico de mtn. Canary Is. 46 Y1
....27.56N 15.34W
Las Palmas de Gran Canaria Canary Is. 46 Y2
....28.08N 15.27W
La Spezia Italy 50 C6....44.07N 9.49E
Las Vegas U.S.A. 64 C4....36.10N 115.10W
Latacunga Ecuador 76 C4....0.58S 78.36W
Latakia Syria 94 E6....35.31N 35.47E
Latheron Scotland 19 F3....58.17N 3.22W
Latina Italy 50 E4....41.28N 12.52E
La Tortuga i. Venezuela 71 K3....11.00N 65.20W
Latvia Europe 43 E2....57.00N 25.00E
Launceston Australia 110 D1....41.25S 147.07E
Launceston England 13 C2....50.38N 4.21W
Laurencekirk Scotland 19 G1....56.50N 2.30W
Lausanne Switz. 44 G5....46.32N 6.39E
Laut i. Indonesia 104 F3....3.45S 116.20E
Laval France 44 C6....48.04N 0.45W

Lavenham England 11 F3....52.06N 0.47E
Lawdar Yemen 95 G1....13.53N 45.53E
Laxey I.o.M. 14 C3....54.14N 4.24W
Laxford, Loch Scotland 18 D3....58.25N 5.06W
Laysan I. Hawaiian Is. 108 N9....25.46N 171.44W
Leane, L. Rep. of Ire. 20 B2....52.03N 9.33W
Leatherhead England 11 E2....51.18N 0.20W
Lebanon Asia 94 E5....34.00N 36.00E
Łebork Poland 54 E6....54.33N 17.44E
Lecce Italy 50 H4....40.21N 18.11E
Lech r. Germany 48 E3....48.45N 10.51E
Lechlade England 10 D2....51.42N 1.40W
Ledbury England 10 C3....52.03N 2.25W
Lee r. Rep. of Ire. 20 C1....51.53N 8.25W
Leech L. U.S.A. 65 H6....47.10N 94.30W
Leeds England 15 F2....53.48N 1.34W
Leek England 15 E2....53.07N 2.02W
Leeming England 15 F3....54.18N 1.33W
Leer Germany 48 C5....53.14N 7.27E
Leeuwarden Neth. 42 E5....53.12N 5.48E
Leeuwin, C. Australia 110 A2....34.00S 115.00E
Leeward Is. C. America 71 L4....18.00N 61.00W
Lefkada i. Greece 56 E3....38.44N 20.37E
Legaspi Phil. 105 G6....13.10N 123.45E
Legnica Poland 54 E4....51.12N 16.10E
Leh Jammu & Kashmir 97 F7....34.09N 77.35E
Le Havre France 44 D6....49.30N 0.06E
Leiah Pakistan 95 L5....30.58N 70.56E
Leicester England 10 D3....52.39N 1.09W
Leicestershire d. England 10 D3....52.30N 1.00W
Leichhardt r. Australia 110 C4....17.35S 139.48E
Leiden Neth. 42 D4....52.10N 4.30E
Leigh England 15 E2....53.30N 2.33W
Leighton Buzzard England 10 E2....51.55N 0.39W
Leinster, Mt. Rep. of Ire. 20 E2....52.37N 6.47W
Leipzig Germany 48 F4....51.20N 12.20E
Leiston England 11 G3....52.13N 1.35E
Leith Scotland 17 F3....55.59N 2.09W
Leith Hill England 11 E2....51.11N 0.21W
Leitrim d. Rep. of Ire. 20 C4....54.08N 8.00W
Leixlip Rep. of Ire. 20 E3....53.22N 6.30W
Leizhou Pen. China 103 J2....20.40N 109.30E
Lek r. Neth. 42 D3....51.55N 4.29E
Leksozero, Ozero l. Russian Fed. 43 G3
....63.40N 30.52E
Lelystad Neth. 42 E4....52.32N 5.29E
Le Mans France 44 D5....48.01N 0.10E
Lena r. Russian Fed. 59 O5....72.00N 127.10E
Leninsk-Kuznetskiy Russian Fed. 58 K3
....54.44N 86.13E
Lens France 44 E7....50.26N 2.50E
Leoben Austria 54 D2....47.23N 15.06E
Leominster England 10 C3....52.15N 2.43W
León Mexico 70 D5....21.10N 101.42W
León Spain 46 C5....42.35N 5.34W
Leova Moldova 55 K2....46.29N 28.12E
Lerum Sweden 43 C2....57.46N 12.12E
Lerwick Scotland 19 Y9....60.09N 1.09W
Lesatima mtn. Kenya 87 B2....0.17S 36.37E
Les Cayes Haiti 71 J4....18.15N 73.46W
Leshan China 103 I3....29.34N 103.42E
Leskovac Yugo. 56 E5....43.00N 21.56E
Lesotho Africa 86 B2....29.30S 28.00E
Les Sables-d'Olonne France 44 C5....46.30N 1.47W
Lesser Antilles is. C. America 71 K3....13.00N 67.00W
Lesser Slave L. Canada 62 G3....55.30N 115.00W
Lestijärvi l. Finland 43 F3....63.32N 24.40E
Lesvos i. Greece 56 G3....39.10N 26.16E
Leszno Poland 54 E4....51.51N 16.35E
Letchworth England 11 E2....51.58N 0.13W
Lethbridge Canada 62 G2....49.43N 112.48W
Leti Is. Indonesia 105 H2....8.20S 128.00E
Le Touquet-Paris-Plage France 42 A2....50.31N 1.36E
Letterkenny Rep. of Ire. 20 D4....54.56N 7.45W
Leuchars Scotland 17 G4....56.23N 2.53W
Leuser, Gunung mtn. Indonesia 104 B4....3.50N 97.10E
Leuven Belgium 42 D2....50.53N 4.45E
Leven England 15 G2....53.54N 0.18W
Leven Scotland 17 G4....56.12N 3.00W
Leven, Loch A. and B. Scotland 18 D1....56.43N 5.05W
Leven, Loch P. and K. Scotland 17 F4....56.13N 3.23W
Levens England 14 E3....54.16N 2.47W
Leverkusen Germany 48 C4....51.02N 6.59E
Lévis Canada 65 L6....46.47N 71.12W
Lewes England 11 F1....50.53N 0.02E
Lewis i. Scotland 18 C3....58.10N 6.40W
Lexington U.S.A. 65 J4....38.02N 84.30W
Leyburn England 15 F3....54.19N 1.50W
Leyland England 14 E2....53.41N 2.42W
Leyte i. Phil. 105 G6....10.40N 124.50E
L'gov Russian Fed. 55 N4....51.41N 35.16E
Lhasa China 102 F3....29.41N 91.10E
Lhazê China 102 F3....29.08N 87.43E
Lhokseumawe Indonesia 104 B5....5.09N 97.09E
Lianyungang China 103 L4....34.37N 119.10E
Liaoning d. China 103 M6....41.30N 123.00E
Liaoyuan China 103 M6....42.53N 125.10E
Liard r. Canada 62 F4....61.56N 120.35W
Libenge Zaire 86 A5....3.39N 18.39E
Liberal U.S.A. 64 F4....37.03N 100.56W
Liberec Czech Rep. 54 D4....50.48N 15.05E
Liberia Africa 84 C2....6.30N 9.30W
Libin Belgium 42 E1....49.58N 5.15E
Liboi Kenya 87 C3....0.23N 40.50E
Libourne France 44 C4....44.55N 0.14W
Libreville Gabon 84 E4....0.30N 9.25E
Libya Africa 84 F4....26.30N 17.00E
Libyan Desert Africa 85 G4....23.00N 26.10E
Libyan Plateau f. Africa 94 C5....30.45N 26.00E
Lichfield England 10 D3....52.40N 1.50W
Lichinga Mozambique 86 C3....13.19S 35.13E
Lida Belarus 55 I5....53.50N 25.19E
Liddel r. Scotland 17 G3....55.04N 2.57W
Lidköping Sweden 43 C2....58.30N 13.10E
Liechtenstein Europe 44 H5....47.08N 9.35E
Liège Belgium 42 E2....50.38N 5.35E
Liège d. Belgium 42 E2....50.32N 5.35E
Lieksa Finland 43 G3....63.13N 30.01E
Lienz Austria 54 C2....46.50N 12.47E
Liepaja Latvia 43 E2....56.30N 21.00E
Liévin France 42 B2....50.27N 2.49E
Liffey r. Rep. of Ire. 20 E3....53.21N 6.14W
Lifford Rep. of Ire. 20 D4....54.50N 7.29W
Ligurian Sea Med. Sea 50 C5....43.10N 9.00E

Likasi Zaire 86 B3....10.58S 26.47E
Lilla Edet Sweden 43 C2....58.10N 12.25E
Lille Belgium 42 D3....51.14N 4.50E
Lille France 44 E7....50.39N 3.05E
Lillehammer Norway 43 B3....61.06N 10.27E
Lilleshall England 10 C3....52.44N 2.24W
Lillestrøm Norway 43 B2....59.55N 11.05E
Lilongwe Malawi 86 C3....13.58S 33.49E
Lima Peru 76 C3....12.06S 77.03W
Limassol Cyprus 57 K1....34.40N 33.03E
Limavady N. Ireland 16 C2....55.03N 6.57W
Limburg d. Belgium 42 E3....51.00N 5.30E
Limburg d. Neth. 42 E3....51.15N 5.45E
Limeira Brazil 77 F2....22.34S 47.25W
Limerick Rep. of Ire. 20 C2....52.40N 8.37W
Limerick d. Rep. of Ire. 20 C2....52.30N 8.37W
Limingen l. Norway 43 C4....64.50N 13.40E
Limnos i. Greece 56 G3....39.55N 25.14E
Limoges France 44 D4....45.50N 1.15E
Limousin f. France 44 D4....45.30N 1.30E
Limoux France 44 E3....43.04N 2.14E
Limpopo r. Mozambique 86 C2....25.14S 33.33E
Linares Spain 46 D3....38.05N 3.38W
Lincoln England 15 G2....53.14N 0.32W
Lincoln U.S.A. 64 G5....40.49N 96.41W
Lincolnshire d. England 15 G2....53.14N 0.32W
Lincolnshire Wolds hills England 15 G2....53.22N 0.08W
Lindesnes c. Norway 43 A2....58.00N 7.05E
Lindfield England 11 E2....51.01N 0.05W
Lindi Tanzania 86 C4....10.00S 39.41E
Líndos Greece 57 I2....36.05N 28.05E
Line Is. Pacific Oc. 108 P6....3.00S 155.00W
Linfen China 103 K5....36.07N 111.34E
Lingen Germany 48 C5....52.32N 7.19E
Lingfield England 11 E2....51.11N 0.01W
Linhares Brazil 77 F3....19.22S 40.04W
Linköping Sweden 43 C2....58.25N 15.35E
Linkou China 103 N6....45.18N 130.17E
Linlithgow Scotland 17 F3....55.58N 3.36W
Linney Head Wales 12 B3....51.37N 5.05W
Linnhe, Loch Scotland 16 D4....56.35N 5.25W
Linosa i. Italy 50 E1....35.52N 12.50E
Linxia China 103 I5....35.31N 103.08E
Linz Austria 54 D3....48.19N 14.18E
Lions, G. of France 44 F3....43.00N 4.15E
Lipari Is. Italy 50 F3....38.35N 14.45E
Lipetsk Russian Fed. 55 P5....52.37N 39.36E
Liphook England 10 E2....51.05N 0.49W
Lipova Romania 54 G2....46.05N 21.40E
Lippe r. Germany 48 C4....51.38N 6.37E
Lisala Zaire 86 B5....2.08N 21.37E
Lisbon Portugal 46 A3....38.44N 9.08W
Lisburn N. Ireland 16 C2....54.31N 6.03W
Liscannor B. Rep. of Ire. 20 B2....52.55N 9.25W
Liskeard England 13 C2....50.27N 4.29W
Lismore Australia 110 E3....28.48S 153.17E
Lismore Rep. of Ire. 20 D2....52.08N 7.59W
Lisnaskea N. Ireland 16 B2....54.15N 7.28W
Liss England 10 E2....51.03N 0.53W
Listowel Rep. of Ire. 20 B2....52.27N 9.30W
Lithuania Europe 43 E2....55.00N 24.00E
Little Andaman i. India 97 I3....10.50N 92.38E
Littleborough England 15 E2....53.39N 2.05W
Little Cayman i. Cayman Is. 71 H4....19.40N 80.00W
Little Dart r. England 13 D2....50.54N 3.53W
Little Falls town U.S.A. 65 H6....45.59N 94.21W
Littlehampton England 11 E1....50.48N 0.32W
Little Inagua i. The Bahamas 71 J5....21.30N 73.00W
Little Karoo f. R.S.A. 86 B1....33.40S 21.40E
Little Minch str. Scotland 18 C2....57.40N 6.45W
Little Ouse r. England 11 F3....52.34N 0.20E
Littleport England 11 F3....52.27N 0.18E
Little Rock town U.S.A. 65 H3....34.42N 92.17W
Liupanshui China 103 I3....26.50N 104.45E
Liuzhou China 103 J2....24.17N 109.15E
Līvāni Latvia 55 J7....56.20N 26.12E
Liverpool England 14 E2....53.25N 3.00W
Livingston Scotland 17 F3....55.54N 3.31W
Livingstone Zambia 86 B3....17.50S 25.53E
Livny Russian Fed. 55 O5....52.25N 37.35E
Livorno Italy 50 D5....43.33N 10.18E
Lizard England 13 B1....49.58N 5.12W
Lizard Pt. England 13 B1....49.57N 5.15W
Ljubljana Slovenia 54 D2....46.04N 14.28E
Ljungan r. Sweden 43 D3....62.20N 17.19E
Ljungby Sweden 43 C2....56.49N 13.55E
Ljusdal Sweden 43 D3....61.49N 16.09E
Llanarth Wales 12 C4....52.12N 4.18W
Llanbadarn Fawr Wales 12 C4....52.24N 4.05W
Llanberis Wales 12 C5....53.07N 4.07W
Llandeilo Wales 12 C4....51.54N 4.00W
Llandovery Wales 12 D3....51.59N 3.49W
Llandrindod Wells Wales 12 D4....52.15N 3.23W
Llandudno Wales 12 D5....53.19N 3.49W
Llandwrog Wales 12 C5....53.04N 4.20W
Llandysul Wales 12 C4....52.03N 4.20W
Llanelli Wales 12 C3....51.41N 4.11W
Llanes Spain 46 C5....43.25N 4.45W
Llanfair Caereinion Wales 12 D4....52.39N 3.20W
Llanfairfechan Wales 12 D5....53.15N 3.58W
Llanfairpwllgwyngyll Wales 12 C5....53.12N 4.13W
Llanfair-yn-Neubwll Wales 12 C5....53.15N 4.33W
Llanfyllin Wales 12 D4....52.47N 3.17W
Llangadog Wales 12 D3....51.56N 3.53W
Llangefni Wales 12 C5....53.15N 4.20W
Llangeler Wales 12 C4....52.01N 4.24W
Llangelynin Wales 12 C5....52.38N 4.06W
Llangoed Wales 12 C5....53.18N 4.05W
Llangollen Wales 12 D4....52.58N 3.10W
Llanidloes Wales 12 D4....52.28N 3.31W
Llanilwchaiarn Wales 12 D4....52.33N 3.17W
Llanllyfni Wales 12 C5....53.03N 4.17W
Llanos f. Colombia/Venezuela 74 B7....5.30N 72.00W
Llanos de Mojos f. Bolivia 76 D3....15.00S 65.00W
Llanrumney Wales 13 D3....51.32N 3.07W
Llanrwst Wales 12 D5....53.08N 3.48W
Llansannan Wales 12 D5....53.11N 3.35W
Llantrisant Wales 12 D3....51.33N 3.23W
Llantwit Major Wales 13 D3....51.24N 3.29W
Llanwnda Wales 12 C5....53.05N 4.18W
Llanybydder Wales 12 C4....52.04N 4.10W
Llay Wales 12 D5....53.06N 2.58W
Lleida Spain 46 F5....41.37N 0.38E
Llerena Spain 46 C3....38.14N 6.00W

Lleyn Pen. Wales 12 C4 52.50N 4.35W
Lloydminster Canada 62 H3 53.18N 110.00W
Llullaillaco *mtn.* Chile/Argentina 76 D2 24.43S 68.30W
Llyn Brianne Resr. Wales 12 D4 52.09N 3.44W
Llyn Celyn *l.* Wales 12 D4 52.57N 3.40W
Llyn Trawsfynydd *l.* Wales 12 D4 52.55N 3.55W
Lobito Angola 86 A3 12.20S 13.34E
Lochaline Scotland 16 D4 56.32N 5.47W
Lochboisdale *town* Scotland 18 B2 57.09N 7.19W
Lochgelly Scotland 17 F4 56.08N 3.19W
Lochgilphead Scotland 16 D4 56.02N 5.26W
Lochinver *town* Scotland 18 D3 58.09N 5.13W
Lochmaben Scotland 17 F3 55.08N 3.27W
Lochmaddy *town* Scotland 18 B2 57.36N 7.10W
Lochnagar *mtn.* Scotland 19 F1 56.57N 3.15W
Lochranza Scotland 16 D3 55.42N 5.18W
Lochy, Loch Scotland 18 E1 56.58N 4.57W
Lockerbie Scotland 17 F3 55.07N 3.21W
Loddon England 11 G3 52.30N 1.29E
Lodwar Kenya 87 B3 3.07N 35.38E
Łódź Poland 54 F4 51.49N 19.28E
Lofoten *is.* Norway 43 C5 68.15N 13.50E
Lofusa Sudan 87 A3 3.44N 33.18E
Logan, Mt. Canada 62 D4 60.45N 140.00W
Loggerheads England 10 C3 52.55N 2.23W
Logone *r.* Cameroon/Chad 82 E6 12.10N 15.00E
Logroño Spain 46 D5 42.28N 2.26W
Loire *r.* France 44 C5 47.18N 2.00W
Loja Ecuador 76 C4 3.59S 79.16W
Loja Spain 46 C2 37.10N 4.09W
Lokan tekojärvi *resr.* Finland 43 F4 67.55N 27.40E
Lokeren Belgium 42 C3 51.06N 3.59E
Lokichar Kenya 87 B3 2.23N 35.40E
Lokichokio Kenya 87 A3 4.19N 34.16E
Løkken Norway 43 B3 63.06N 9.43E
Lokoja Nigeria 84 E2 7.49N 6.44E
Lokwa Kangole Kenya 87 B3 3.32N 35.50E
Loliondo Tanzania 87 B2 2.04S 35.38E
Lolland *i.* Denmark 43 B1 54.50N 11.30E
Lom Bulgaria 56 F5 43.49N 23.13E
Loman *r.* Zaire 86 B5 0.45N 24.10E
Lombok *i.* Indonesia 104 F2 8.30S 116.20E
Lomé Togo 84 E2 6.10N 1.21E
Lommel Belgium 42 E3 51.15N 5.18E
Lomond, Loch Scotland 16 E4 56.07N 4.36W
Łomża Poland 54 H5 53.11N 22.04E
London Canada 63 J2 42.58N 81.15W
London England 11 E2 51.32N 0.06W
Londonderry N. Ireland 16 B2 55.00N 7.20W
Londonderry *d.* N. Ireland 16 B2 55.00N 7.00W
Londonderry, C. Australia 110 B4 13.58S 126.55E
Long, Loch Scotland 16 E4 56.05N 4.52W
Long Ashton England 10 C2 51.26N 2.37W
Long Beach *town* U.S.A. 64 C3 33.57N 118.15W
Long Bennington England 15 G1 52.59N 0.45W
Long Eaton England 10 D3 52.54N 1.16W
Longford Rep. of Ire. 20 D3 53.44N 7.48W
Longford *d.* Rep. of Ire. 20 D3 53.42N 7.45W
Longhorsley England 15 F4 55.15N 1.46W
Longhoughton England 15 F4 55.26N 1.36W
Long I. The Bahamas 71 J5 23.00N 75.00W
Long I. U.S.A. 65 L5 40.50N 73.00W
Longido Tanzania 87 B2 2.43S 36.41E
Longlac *town* Canada 63 J2 49.47N 86.34W
Longmont U.S.A. 64 F5 40.10N 105.06W
Longridge England 14 E2 53.50N 2.37W
Long Stratton England 11 G3 52.29N 1.14E
Longton England 14 E2 53.44N 2.48W
Longtown England 14 E4 55.01N 2.58W
Longuyon France 42 E1 49.26N 5.36E
Long Xuyên Vietnam 104 D6 10.23N 105.25E
Lons-le-Saunier France 44 F5 46.40N 5.33E
Lookout, C. U.S.A. 65 K3 34.34N 76.34W
Loolmalasin *mtn.* Tanzania 87 B2 3.06S 35.46E
Loop Head Rep. of Ire. 20 B2 52.33N 9.56W
Lop Nur *l.* China 102 G6 40.30N 90.30E
Lopphavet *est.* Norway 43 E5 70.30N 21.00E
Loralai Pakistan 95 K5 30.22N 68.36E
Lorca Spain 46 E2 37.40N 1.41W
Lord Howe I. Pacific Oc. 111 E2 31.33S 159.06E
Lordsburg U.S.A. 64 E3 32.22N 108.43W
Lorient France 44 B5 47.45N 3.21W
Losai Nat. Res. Kenya 87 B3 1.30N 37.15E
Los Angeles Chile 75 B3 37.28S 72.21W
Los Angeles U.S.A. 64 C3 34.00N 118.17W
Los Canarios Canary Is. 46 X2 28.28N 17.52W
Los Canarreos, Archipiélago de Cuba 71 H5 21.40N 82.30W
Los Chonos, Archipielago de *is.* Chile 75 B2 45.00S 74.00W
Los Estados, I. de *i.* Argentina 75 C1 54.45S 64.00W
Los Llanos de Aridane Canary Is. 46 X2 28.39N 17.54W
Los Mochis Mexico 70 C6 25.45N 108.57W
Los Roques *is.* Venezuela 71 K3 12.00N 67.00W
Lossie *r.* Scotland 19 F2 57.43N 3.18W
Lossiemouth Scotland 19 F2 57.43N 3.18W
Los Taques Venezuela 71 J3 11.50N 70.16W
Los Teques Venezuela 71 K3 10.25N 67.01W
Los Testigos *i.* Lesser Antilles 71 L3 11.24N 63.07W
Lostwithiel England 13 C2 50.24N 4.41W
Lot *r.* France 44 D4 44.17N 0.22E
Lotagipi Swamp Kenya/Sudan 87 A3 4.40N 34.30E
Lotikipi Plain *f.* Kenya 87 A3 4.25N 34.30E
Lotta *r.* Russian Fed. 43 H5 68.36N 31.06E
Louang Namtha Laos 104 C8 21.01N 101.27E
Louangphrabang Laos 104 C7 19.53N 102.10E
Loughborough England 10 D3 52.47N 1.11W
Loughor *r.* Wales 12 C3 51.43N 4.04W
Loughrea Rep. of Ire. 20 C3 53.11N 8.36W
Loughton England 11 F2 51.39N 0.03E
Louisiana *d.* U.S.A. 65 H3 31.00N 92.30W
Louisville U.S.A. 65 I4 38.13N 85.45W
Loukhi Russian Fed. 43 H4 66.05N 33.04E
Lourdes France 44 C3 43.06N 0.02W
Louth England 15 H2 53.23N 0.00
Louth *d.* Rep. of Ire. 20 E3 53.45N 6.30W
Lověch Bulgaria 56 G5 43.08N 24.44E
Lovozero Russian Fed. 43 H5 68.01N 35.08E
Lowell U.S.A. 65 L5 42.39N 71.18W
Lower California *pen.* Mexico 70 B6 27.00N 113.00W
Lower Lough Erne N. Ireland 16 B2 54.28N 7.48W
Lower Tunguska *r.* Russian Fed. 59 K4 65.50N 88.00E
Lowestoft England 11 G3 52.29N 1.44E
Łowicz Poland 54 F5 52.06N 19.55E
Loyal, Loch Scotland 19 E3 58.23N 4.21W
Loyalty Is. N. Cal. 111 F3 21.00S 167.00E
Loyne, Loch Scotland 18 D2 57.06N 5.01W
Lozova Ukraine 55 O3 48.54N 36.20E
Luanda Angola 86 A4 8.50S 13.20E
Luarca Spain 46 B5 43.33N 6.31W
Lubango Angola 86 A3 14.55S 13.30E
Lubbock U.S.A. 64 F3 33.35N 101.53W
Lübeck Germany 48 E5 53.52N 10.40E
Lübeck B. Germany 48 E6 54.05N 11.00E
Lublin Poland 54 H4 51.18N 22.31E
Lubnaig, Loch Scotland 16 E4 56.17N 4.18W
Lubny Ukraine 55 M4 50.01N 33.00E
Lubuklinggau Indonesia 104 C3 3.24S 102.56E
Lubumbashi Zaire 86 B3 11.41S 27.29E
Luce B. Scotland 16 E2 54.45N 4.47W
Lucena Phil. 105 G6 13.56N 121.37E
Lucena Spain 46 C2 37.25N 4.29W
Lučenec Slovakia 54 F3 48.20N 19.40E
Lucknow India 97 G6 26.50N 80.54E
Lüderitz Namibia 86 A2 26.38S 15.10E
Ludgershall England 10 D2 51.15N 1.38W
Ludhiana India 96 F7 30.56N 75.52E
Ludlow England 10 C3 52.23N 2.42W
Ludvika Sweden 43 C3 60.08N 15.14E
Ludwigshafen Germany 48 D3 49.29N 8.27E
Luena Angola 86 A3 11.46S 19.55E
Lufkin U.S.A. 65 H3 31.21N 94.47W
Luga Russian Fed. 43 G2 58.42N 29.49E
Lugano Switz. 44 H5 46.01N 8.57E
Lugg *r.* England 10 C3 52.01N 2.38W
Lugo Spain 46 B5 43.00N 7.33W
Lugoj Romania 54 G1 45.42N 21.56E
Luhan'sk Ukraine 58 F2 48.35N 39.20E
Luing *i.* Scotland 16 D4 56.14N 5.38W
Lule *r.* Sweden 43 E4 65.40N 21.48E
Luleå Sweden 43 E4 65.35N 22.10E
Lüleburgaz Turkey 56 H4 41.25N 27.23E
Lumberton U.S.A. 65 K3 34.37N 79.03W
Lunan B. Scotland 19 G1 56.38N 2.30W
Lund Sweden 43 C1 55.42N 13.10E
Lundy I. England 13 C3 51.10N 4.41W
Lune *r.* England 14 E3 54.03N 2.49W
Lüneburg Germany 48 E5 53.15N 10.24E
Lunéville France 44 G6 48.36N 6.30E
Luninyets Belarus 55 J5 52.18N 26.50E
Luoyang China 103 K4 34.48N 112.25E
Lure France 44 G5 47.42N 6.30E
Lurgainn, Loch Scotland 18 D3 58.01N 5.12W
Lurgan N. Ireland 16 C2 54.28N 6.20W
Lusaka Zambia 86 B3 15.26S 28.20E
Lushoto Tanzania 87 B2 4.51S 38.19E
Luton England 11 E2 51.53N 0.25W
Luts'k Ukraine 55 I4 50.42N 25.15E
Lutterworth England 10 D3 52.28N 1.12W
Luxembourg *d.* Belgium 42 E1 49.58N 5.30E
Luxembourg Europe 42 F1 49.50N 6.15E
Luxembourg *town* Lux. 42 F1 49.37N 6.08E
Luxor Egypt 94 D4 25.41N 32.24E
Luzern Switz. 44 H5 47.03N 8.17E
Luziânia Brazil 77 F3 16.18S 47.57W
Luzon *i.* Phil. 105 G7 17.50N 121.00E
Luzon Str. Pacific Oc. 104 G8 20.20N 122.00E
L'viv Ukraine 55 I3 49.50N 24.03E
Lycksele Sweden 43 D4 64.34N 18.40E
Lydd England 11 F1 50.57N 0.56E
Lydford England 13 C2 50.39N 4.06W
Lydney England 10 C2 51.43N 2.32W
Lyepyel' Belarus 55 K6 54.48N 28.40E
Lyme B. England 10 C1 50.40N 2.55W
Lyme Regis England 10 C1 50.44N 2.57W
Lymington England 10 D1 50.46N 1.32W
Lynchburg U.S.A. 65 K4 37.24N 79.10W
Lyndhurst England 10 D1 50.53N 1.33W
Lynmouth England 13 D3 51.15N 3.50W
Lynn Lake *town* Canada 62 H3 56.51N 101.01W
Lynton England 13 D3 51.14N 3.50W
Lyon France 44 F4 45.46N 4.50E
Lyon *r.* Scotland 16 E4 56.37N 3.59W
Lysychans'k Ukraine 55 P3 48.53N 38.25E
Lytchett Minster England 10 C1 50.44N 2.04W
Lytham St. Anne's England 14 D2 53.45N 3.01W

M

Ma'an Jordan 94 E5 30.11N 35.43E
Maas *r.* Neth. 42 D3 51.44N 4.42E
Maaseik Belgium 42 E3 51.08N 5.48E
Maastricht Neth. 42 E2 50.51N 5.42E
Mablethorpe England 15 H2 53.21N 0.14W
Macaé Brazil 77 F2 22.21S 41.48W
Macapá Brazil 77 E5 0.01N 51.01W
Macas Ecuador 76 C4 2.22S 78.08W
Macau Asia 103 K2 22.13N 113.36E
Macclesfield England 15 E2 53.16N 2.09W
Macdonnell Ranges *mts.* Australia 110 C3 23.30S 132.00E
Macduff Scotland 19 G2 57.40N 2.30W
Macedo de Cavaleiros Portugal 46 B4 41.32N 6.58W
Macedonia Europe 56 E4 41.15N 21.15E
Maceió Brazil 77 G4 9.34S 35.47W
Macgillycuddy's Reeks *mts.* Rep. of Ire. 20 B2 52.00N 9.45W
Mach Pakistan 95 K4 29.52N 67.20E
Machakos Kenya 87 B2 1.31S 37.15E
Machala Ecuador 76 C4 3.20S 79.57W
Machilipatnam India 97 G4 16.13N 81.12E
Machrihanish Scotland 16 D3 55.25N 5.44W
Machynlleth Wales 12 D4 52.35N 3.51W
Mackay Australia 110 D3 21.10S 149.10E
Mackay, L. Australia 110 B3 22.30S 128.58E
Mackenzie *r.* Canada 62 E4 69.20N 134.00W
Mackenzie King I. Canada 62 G5 77.30N 112.00W
Mackenzie Mts. Canada 62 E4 64.00N 130.00W
MacLeod, L. Australia 110 A3 24.10S 113.35E
Macomer Italy 50 C4 40.16N 8.45E
Mâcon France 44 F5 46.18N 4.50E
Macon U.S.A. 65 J3 32.47N 83.37W
Macquarie I. Pacific Oc. 108 K1 54.29S 158.58E
Macroom Rep. of Ire. 20 C1 51.53N 8.59W
Madadeni R.S.A. 86 C2 27.43S 30.02E
Madagascar Africa 86 D2 20.00S 46.30E
Madeira *i.* Atlantic Oc. 84 C5 32.45N 17.00W
Madeira *r.* Brazil 77 E4 3.50S 58.30W
Madeley England 10 C3 52.39N 2.28W
Madhya Pradesh *d.* India 97 F5 23.00N 79.30E
Madīnat ath Thawrah Syria 57 N1 35.50N 38.35E
Madini *r.* Bolivia 76 D3 12.32S 66.50W
Madison U.S.A. 65 I5 43.04N 89.22W
Mado Gashi Kenya 87 B3 0.40N 39.11E
Madras India 97 G3 13.05N 80.18E
Madre, Sierra *mts.* C. America 60 K3 15.00N 90.00W
Madre de Dios *r.* Bolivia 76 D3 11.00S 66.30W
Madre del Sur, Sierra *mts.* Mexico 70 E4 17.00N 100.00W
Madre Lagoon Mexico 70 E5 25.00N 97.30W
Madre Occidental, Sierra *mts.* Mexico 70 C6 25.00N 105.00W
Madre Oriental, Sierra *mts.* Mexico 70 D5 24.00N 101.00W
Madrid Spain 46 D4 40.25N 3.43W
Madukani Tanzania 87 B2 3.52S 35.46E
Madura *i.* Indonesia 104 E2 7.00S 113.30E
Madurai India 97 F2 9.55N 78.07E
Maebashi Japan 106 C3 36.30N 139.04E
Maesteg Wales 12 D3 51.36N 3.40W
Maestra, Sierra *mts.* Cuba 71 I5 20.10N 76.30W
Mafia I. Tanzania 86 C4 7.50S 39.50E
Mafraq Jordan 94 E5 32.20N 36.12E
Magadan Russian Fed. 59 R3 59.38N 150.50E
Magadi Kenya 87 B2 1.52S 36.18E
Magdalena *r.* Colombia 74 B7 10.56N 74.58W
Magdalena Mexico 70 B7 30.38N 110.59W
Magdalena, B. Mexico 70 B5 24.30N 112.00W
Magdeburg Germany 48 E5 52.08N 11.36E
Magellan, Str. of Chile 75 B1 53.00S 71.00W
Magerøya *i.* Norway 43 F5 71.00N 25.50E
Maggiore, L. Italy 50 C7 46.00N 8.37E
Maghâgha Egypt 53 J2 28.39N 30.50E
Maghera N. Ireland 16 C2 54.51N 6.42W
Magherafelt N. Ireland 16 C2 54.45N 6.38W
Maghull England 14 E2 53.31N 2.56W
Magilligan Pt. N. Ireland 16 C3 55.11N 6.58W
Magnitogorsk Russian Fed. 58 H3 53.28N 59.06E
Magny-en-Vexin France 42 A1 49.09N 1.47E
Magu Tanzania 87 A2 2.35S 33.27E
Maguarinho, Cabo *c.* Brazil 77 F4 0.15S 48.23W
Magwe Myanmar 97 J5 20.10N 95.00E
Mahabad Iran 95 G6 36.44N 45.44E
Mahagi Zaire 85 H2 2.16N 30.59E
Mahajanga Madagascar 86 D3 15.40S 46.20E
Maharashtra *d.* India 96 E4 20.00N 75.00E
Mahé I. Seychelles 85 J1 4.41S 55.30E
Mahilyow Belarus 55 L5 53.54N 30.20E
Mahón Spain 46 H3 39.55N 4.18E
Maicao Colombia 71 J3 11.25N 72.10W
Maidenhead England 10 E2 51.32N 0.44W
Maidstone England 11 F2 51.17N 0.32E
Maiduguri Nigeria 84 F3 11.53N 13.16E
Main *r.* N. Ireland 16 C2 54.43N 6.19W
Mai-Ndombe, L. Zaire 86 A4 2.00S 18.20E
Maine *d.* U.S.A. 65 M6 45.00N 69.00W
Mainland *i.* Shetland Is. Scotland 19 Y9 60.15N 1.22W
Mainland *i.* Orkney Is. Scotland 19 F3 59.00N 3.10W
Mainz Germany 48 D3 50.00N 8.16E
Maio *i.* Cape Verde 84 B3 15.10N 23.10W
Maiquetía Venezuela 71 K3 10.03N 66.57W
Maitland Australia 110 E2 32.33S 151.33E
Maíz, Is. del Nicaragua 71 H3 12.12N 83.00W
Maizuru Japan 106 C3 35.30N 135.20E
Majene Indonesia 104 F3 3.33S 118.59E
Maji Ethiopia 87 B4 6.11N 35.38E
Makale Indonesia 104 F3 3.06S 119.53E
Makassar Str. Indonesia 104 F3 3.00S 118.00E
Makgadikgadi *f.* Botswana 86 B2 20.50S 25.45E
Makhachkala Russian Fed. 58 G2 42.59N 47.30E
Makindu Kenya 87 B2 2.18S 37.50E
Makiyivka Ukraine 55 P3 48.01N 38.00E
Makran *f.* Asia 95 J4 25.40N 62.00E
Makurdi Nigeria 84 E2 7.44N 8.35E
Malabar Coast *f.* India 96 F3 11.00N 75.00E
Malabo Equat. Guinea 84 E2 3.45N 8.48E
Malacca, Str. of Indian Oc. 104 C4 3.00N 100.30E
Maladzyechna Belarus 55 J6 54.16N 26.50E
Málaga Spain 46 C2 36.43N 4.25W
Malahide Rep. of Ire. 20 E3 53.27N 6.09W
Malaita *i.* Solomon Is. 111 F5 9.00S 161.00E
Malakal Sudan 85 H2 9.31N 31.40E
Malakula *i.* Vanuatu 111 F4 16.15S 167.30E
Malang Indonesia 104 E2 7.59S 112.45E
Malanje Angola 86 A4 9.36S 16.21E
Mala Pt. *c.* Panama 71 I2 7.30N 80.00W
Mälaren *l.* Sweden 43 D2 59.30N 17.00E
Malatya Turkey 57 N3 38.22N 38.18E
Malawi Africa 86 C3 13.00S 34.00E
Malaya *f.* Malaysia 104 C4 5.00N 102.00E
Malayer Iran 95 G5 34.19N 48.51E
Malaysia Asia 104 D5 5.00N 110.00E
Malbork Poland 54 F6 54.02N 19.01E
Malden I. Kiribati 108 P6 4.03S 154.49W
Maldives Indian Oc. 96 E2 6.20N 73.00E
Maldon England 11 F2 51.43N 0.41E
Maléa, C. Greece 56 F2 36.27N 23.11E
Malgomaj *l.* Sweden 43 D4 64.45N 16.00E
Mali Africa 84 D3 16.00N 3.00W
Malili Indonesia 104 G3 2.38S 121.06E
Malindi Kenya 87 A2 3.14S 40.07E
Malin Head Rep. of Ire. 20 D5 55.22N 7.24W
Mallaig Scotland 18 D1 57.00N 5.50W
Mallawi Egypt 53 J2 27.44N 30.50E
Mallorca *i.* Spain 46 G3 39.35N 3.00E
Mallow Rep. of Ire. 20 C2 52.08N 8.39W
Malmédy Belgium 42 F2 50.25N 6.02E
Malmesbury England 10 C2 51.35N 2.05W
Malmö Sweden 43 C1 55.35N 13.00E
Måløy Norway 43 A3 61.57N 5.06E
Malpas England 14 E2 53.01N 2.46W
Malpelo, I. de Pacific Oc. 60 K2 4.00N 81.35W
Malta Europe 50 F1 35.55N 14.25E
Maltby England 15 F2 53.25N 1.12W
Malton England 15 G3 54.09N 0.48W
Malvern Hills England 10 C3 52.07N 2.19W
Mamelodi R.S.A. 86 B2 25.41S 28.22E
Mamoré *r.* Brazil/Bolivia 76 D3 9.41S 65.20W
Mamuju Indonesia 104 F3 2.41S 118.55E
Man, Isle of U.K. 14 C3 54.15N 4.30W
Manacapuru Brazil 77 D4 3.16S 60.37W
Manacor Spain 46 G3 39.32N 3.12E
Manadao Indonesia 105 G4 1.30N 124.58E
Managua Nicaragua 70 G3 12.06N 86.18W
Managua, L. Nicaragua 70 G3 12.10N 86.30W
Manama Bahrain 95 H4 26.12N 50.36E
Mananjary Madagascar 86 D2 21.13S 48.20E
Manaus Brazil 77 E4 3.06S 60.00W
Manavgat Turkey 57 J2 36.47N 31.28E
Manchester England 15 E2 53.30N 2.15W
Manchester U.S.A. 65 L5 42.59N 71.28W
Manchuria *f.* Asia 90 O7 45.00N 125.00E
Mand *r.* Iran 95 H4 28.09N 51.16E
Mandala, Peak Indonesia 105 K3 4.45S 140.15E
Mandalay Myanmar 97 J5 21.57N 96.04E
Mandalgovĭ Mongolia 103 J7 45.40N 106.10E
Mandera Kenya 87 C3 3.55N 41.50E
Mandioré, Lagoa *l.* Brazil/Bolivia 77 E3 18.05S 57.30W
Manfredonia Italy 50 F4 41.38N 15.54E
Mangaia *i.* Cook Is. 108 P4 21.56S 157.56W
Mangalia Romania 57 I5 43.50N 28.35E
Mangalore India 96 E3 12.54N 74.51E
Mangaung R.S.A. 86 B2 29.30S 26.30E
Mangoky *r.* Madagascar 86 D2 21.20S 43.30E
Mangotsfield England 10 C2 51.29N 2.29W
Mangu Kenya 87 B2 0.58S 36.57E
Manihiki *i.* Cook Is. 108 O5 10.24S 161.01W
Maniitsoq Greenland 63 M4 65.40N 53.00W
Manila Phil. 104 G6 14.36N 120.59E
Manipur *d.* India 97 I5 25.00N 93.40E
Manisa Turkey 56 H3 38.37N 27.28E
Manitoba *d.* Canada 62 I3 54.00N 96.00W
Manitoba, L. Canada 62 I3 51.35N 99.00W
Manizales Colombia 74 B7 5.03N 75.32W
Manmad India 96 E5 20.15N 74.27E
Mannheim Germany 48 D3 49.30N 8.28E
Manningtree England 11 G2 51.56N 1.03E
Manokwari Indonesia 105 I3 0.53S 134.05E
Manorbier Wales 12 C3 51.39N 4.48W
Manorhamilton Rep. of Ire. 20 C4 54.18N 8.14W
Manra *i.* Kiribati 108 N6 4.29S 172.10W
Manresa Spain 46 F4 41.43N 1.50E
Mansa Zambia 86 B3 11.10S 28.52E
Mansel I. Canada 63 J4 62.00N 80.00W
Mansfield England 15 F2 53.09N 1.12W
Mansfield U.S.A. 65 J5 40.46N 82.31W
Manston England 10 C1 50.57N 2.16W
Manta Ecuador 76 B4 0.59S 80.44W
Mantua Italy 50 D6 45.09N 10.47E
Manukau New Zealand 111 G2 36.59S 174.53E
Manyara, L. Tanzania 87 B2 3.36S 35.44E
Manzanares Spain 46 D3 39.00N 3.23W
Manzhouli China 103 L7 49.36N 117.28E
Maoke Range *mts.* Indonesia 105 J3 4.00S 137.30E
Mapeura *r.* Brazil 77 E4 1.10S 57.00W
Maputo Mozambique 86 C2 25.58S 32.35E
Mar, Serra do *mts.* Brazil 77 F2 28.00S 49.40W
Maraba Brazil 77 F4 5.23S 49.10W
Maraca, Ilha de *i.* Brazil 77 E5 2.00N 50.30W
Maracaibo Venezuela 71 J3 10.44N 71.37W
Maracaibo, L. Venezuela 71 J2 10.00N 71.30W
Maracaju, Serra de *mts.* Brazil 77 E2 21.38S 55.10W
Maracay Venezuela 71 K3 10.20N 67.28W
Maradah Libya 85 F4 29.14N 19.13E
Maradi Niger 84 E3 13.29N 7.10E
Maragheh Iran 95 G6 37.25N 46.13E
Marajó, I. de Brazil 77 F4 1.00S 49.30W
Maralal Kenya 87 B3 1.04N 36.41E
Marand Iran 95 G6 38.25N 45.50E
Maranhão *d.* Brazil 77 F4 6.00S 45.30W
Marañón *r.* Peru 77 C4 4.00S 73.30W
Marathonas Greece 56 G3 38.10N 23.59E
Marazion England 13 B2 50.08N 5.29W
Marbella Spain 46 C2 36.31N 4.53W
Marburg Germany 48 D4 50.49N 8.36E
March England 11 F3 52.33N 0.05E
Marche-en-Famenne Belgium 42 E2 50.13N 5.21E
Mar Chiquita, L. Argentina 77 D1 30.42S 62.36W
Mardan Pakistan 95 L5 34.14N 72.05E
Mar del Plata Argentina 75 D3 38.00S 57.32W
Mardin Turkey 94 F6 37.19N 40.43E
Maree, Loch Scotland 18 D2 57.41N 5.28W
Maresfield England 11 F1 51.00N 0.05E
Margarita *i.* Venezuela 71 L3 11.00N 64.00W
Margate England 11 G2 51.23N 1.24E
Margery Hill England 15 F2 53.26N 1.42W
Marhanets' Ukraine 55 N2 47.37N 34.40E
Marianas Trench *f.* Pacific Oc. 117 Q6
Marianna U.S.A. 65 I3 30.45N 85.15W
Marías, I. *is.* Mexico 70 C5 21.25N 106.30W
Mariato Pt. *c.* Panama 71 H2 7.12N 80.52W
Maria van Diemen, C. New Zealand 111 G2 34.29S 172.39E
Ma'rib Yemen 94 G2 15.01N 45.30E
Maribor Slovenia 54 D2 46.35N 15.40E
Marie Galante *i.* Guadeloupe 71 L4 15.54N 61.11W
Mariehamn Finland 43 D3 60.05N 19.55E
Mariental Namibia 86 A2 24.38S 17.58E
Mariestad Sweden 43 C2 58.44N 13.50E
Marijampole Lithuania 54 H6 54.31N 23.20E
Marília Brazil 77 E2 22.13S 50.20W
Maringá Brazil 77 E2 23.36S 52.02W
Maritsa *r.* Bulgaria 56 H4 41.40N 26.25E
Mariupol' Ukraine 55 O2 47.05N 37.34E
Marka Somalia 86 D5 1.42N 44.47E
Markermeer *l.* Neth. 42 E4 52.30N 5.15E
Market Deeping England 11 E3 52.40N 0.20W
Market Drayton England 10 C3 52.55N 2.30W
Market Harborough England 10 E3 52.29N 0.55W
Markethill N. Ireland 16 C2 54.17N 6.31W
Market Rasen England 15 G2 53.24N 0.20W
Market Weighton England 15 G2 53.52N 0.40W
Markha *r.* Russian Fed. 59 O4 63.37N 119.00E
Marlborough England 10 D2 51.26N 1.44W
Marlborough Downs *hills* England 10 D2 51.28N 1.48W
Marlow England 10 E2 51.35N 0.48W
Marmande France 44 D4 44.30N 0.10E
Marmara *i.* Turkey 57 H4 40.38N 27.37E
Marmara, Sea of Turkey 57 I4 40.45N 28.15E
Marmaris Turkey 57 I2 36.52N 28.17E
Marne *r.* France 44 E6 48.50N 2.25E
Marne-la-Vallée France 44 E6 48.50N 2.30E
Marondera Zimbabwe 86 C3 18.11S 31.31E
Maroni *r.* French Guiana 74 D7 5.30N 54.00W
Marotiri *i.* French Polynesia 109 Q4 27.55S 143.26W
Maroua Cameroon 84 F3 10.35N 14.20E
Marple England 15 E2 53.23N 2.05W
Marquesas Is. Pacific Oc. 109 R6 9.00S 139.30W
Marquette U.S.A. 65 I6 46.33N 87.23W

Marrakesh Morocco 84 D5......................31.49N 8.00W
Marra Plateau Sudan 94 B1..................13.00N 23.50E
Marsa Alam Egypt 94 D4....................25.03N 34.44E
Marsa al Burayqah Libya 85 G4...........30.25N 19.35E
Marsabit Kenya 87 B3...........................2.20N 37.59E
Marsabit Nat. Res. Kenya 87 B3.............2.20N 37.58E
Marsala Italy 50 E2.............................37.48N 12.27E
Marsa Matrûh Egypt 94 C5................31.21N 27.15E
Marseille France 44 F3........................43.18N 5.22E
Marsfjället mtn. Sweden 43 C4..........65.10N 15.20E
Marshall Is. Pacific Oc. 108 L8.........10.00N 167.00E
Märsta Sweden 43 D2........................59.37N 17.52E
Martaban Myanmar 97 J4...................16.32N 97.35E
Martaban, G. of Indian Oc. 97 J4.......15.10N 96.30E
Martapura Indonesia 104 D3.............4.20S 104.22E
Martin Slovakia 54 F3.......................49.05N 18.55E
Martinique i. Windward Is. 71 L3......14.40N 61.00W
Martinsville U.S.A. 65 K4..................36.43N 79.53W
Martin Vaz is. Atlantic Oc. 72 H4....20.30S 28.51W
Martock England 13 E2.....................50.59N 2.46W
Martre, Lac La l. Canada 62 G4........63.15N 116.55W
Mary Turkmenistan 95 J6..................37.42N 61.54E
Maryborough Australia 110 E3.........25.32S 152.36E
Mary Byrd Land Antarctica 112.........80.00S 130.00W
Maryland d. U.S.A. 65 K4..................39.00N 76.30W
Maryport England 14 D3..................54.43N 3.30W
Masai Mara Nat. Res. Kenya 87 A2.....1.25S 35.05E
Masai Steppe f. Tanzania 87 B2.........5.00S 37.00E
Masan S. Korea 103 N5.....................35.10N 128.35E
Masbate Phil. 105 G6......................12.21N 123.36E
Masbate i. Phil. 105 G6...................12.00N 123.30E
Mascara Algeria 52 D4....................35.24N 0.08E
Maseno Kenya 87 A3........................0.00 34.32E
Maseru Lesotho 86 B2....................29.19S 27.29E
Mashhad Iran 95 I6.........................36.16N 59.34E
Masinga Resr. Kenya 87 B2...............1.10S 37.40E
Masirah i. Oman 95 I3.......................20.30N 58.50E
Masirah, G. of Oman 95 I2..............20.00N 58.10E
Masjed Soleyman Iran 95 G5............31.59N 49.18E
Mask, Lough Rep. of Ire. 20 B3.......53.38N 9.22W
Mason City U.S.A. 65 H5................43.10N 93.10W
Massachusetts d. U.S.A. 65 L5........42.20N 72.00W
Massakory Chad 84 F3....................13.02N 15.43E
Massawa Eritrea 85 H3....................15.36N 39.29E
Massif Central mts. France 44 E4......45.00N 3.30E
Massif Ennedi mts. Chad 94 B2.........17.00N 23.00E
Mastung Pakistan 95 K4.................29.48N 66.51E
Masuda Japan 106 B2.....................34.42N 131.51E
Masurian Lakes Poland 54 G5.........53.50N 21.40E
Masvingo Zimbabwe 86 C2.............20.10S 30.49E
Maswe Game Res. Tanzania 87 A2......2.30S 34.00E
Matadi Zaire 86 A4..........................5.50S 13.32E
Matam Senegal 84 C3.....................15.40N 13.18W
Matamoros Mexico 70 E6...............25.50N 97.31W
Matanzas Cuba 71 H5....................23.04N 81.35W
Matapan, C. Greece 56 F2...............36.22N 22.28E
Matara Sri Lanka 97 G7...................5.57N 80.32E
Mataram Indonesia 104 F2.............8.36S 116.07E
Mataró Spain 46 G4........................41.32N 2.27E
Matera Italy 50 G4.........................40.41N 16.36E
Matheniko Game Res. Uganda 87 A3...2.55N 34.25E
Mathura India 97 F6.........................27.30N 77.30E
Matlock England 15 F2....................53.08N 1.32W
Mato Grosso d. Brazil 77 E3.............13.00S 55.00W
Mato Grosso, Planalto do f. Brazil 77 E3
                                                        15.00S 55.00W
Mato Grosso do Sul d. Brazil 77 E2....20.00S 54.30W
Matrah Oman 95 I3.........................23.37N 58.33E
Matsue Japan 106 B3.....................35.29N 133.00E
Matsu Is. Taiwan 103 M3...............26.12N 120.00E
Matsumoto Japan 106 C3...............36.18N 137.58E
Matsusaka Japan 106 C2.................34.34N 136.32E
Matsuyama Japan 106 B2...............33.50N 132.47E
Matterhorn mtn. Switz. 44 G4..........45.58N 7.38E
Maturín Venezuela 71 L2.................9.45N 63.16W
Mau mtn. Kenya 87 B2.....................0.30S 35.50E
Maubeuge France 42 C2..................50.17N 3.58E
Mauchline Scotland 16 E3...............55.31N 4.23W
Maughold Head I.o.M. 14 C3...........54.18N 4.19W
Maug Is. N. Mariana Is. 105 L8.........20.02N 14.19E
Maui i. Hawaiian Is. 108 P9............20.45N 156.15W
Mauke i. Cook Is. 108 P5................19.49S 157.41W
Maumere Indonesia 105 G4.............8.35S 122.13E
Maun Botswana 86 B2.....................19.52S 23.40E
Mauritania Africa 84 C3.................20.00N 10.00W
May, Isle of Scotland 17 G4.............56.12N 2.32W
Maya r. Russian Fed. 59 P4.............60.25N 134.28E
Mayaguana i. The Bahamas 71 J5.....22.30N 73.00W
Mayagüez Puerto Rico 71 K4............18.13N 67.09W
Mayamey Iran 95 I6........................36.27N 55.40E
Maya Mts. Belize 70 G4.................16.30N 89.00W
Mayar mtn. Scotland 19 F1.............56.50N 3.16W
Maybole Scotland 16 E3.................55.21N 4.41W
Mayen Germany 42 G2....................50.19N 7.14E
Mayenne r. France 44 C5................47.30N 0.37W
Maykop Russian Fed. 53 L5.............44.37N 40.48E
Mayo Canada 62 E4.......................63.45N 135.45W
Mayo d. Rep. of Ire. 20 B3............53.47N 9.07W
Mayotte i. Indian Oc. 86 D3............12.50S 45.10E
Mazatlán Mexico 70 C5.................23.11N 106.25W
Mažeikiai Lithuania 54 H7..............56.06N 23.06E
Mazyr Belarus 55 K5.......................52.02N 29.10E
Mbabane Swaziland 86 C2.............26.20S 31.08E
Mbale Uganda 87 A3......................1.02N 34.11E
Mbandaka Zaire 86 A5...................0.03N 18.28E
M'banza Congo Angola 86 A4.........6.18S 14.16E
Mbarara Uganda 86 C4...................0.36S 30.40E
Mbeya Tanzania 86 C4....................8.54S 33.29E
Mbuji-Mayi Zaire 86 B4.................6.10S 23.39E
Mbulu Tanzania 87 B2....................3.51S 35.32E
McClintock Channel Canada 62 H5...71.20N 102.00W
McClure Str. Canada 62 F5.............74.30N 116.00W
McCook U.S.A. 64 F5.....................40.15N 100.45W
McGrath U.S.A. 62 C4....................62.58N 155.40W
McKinley, Mt. U.S.A. 62 C4............63.00N 151.00W
Mdantsane R.S.A. 86 B1.................32.54S 27.54E
Mead, L. U.S.A. 64 D4...................36.10N 114.25W
Mealasta i. Scotland 18 B3.............58.05N 7.07W
Meall a'Bhuiridh mtn. Scotland 16 E4...56.37N 4.50W
Meath d. Rep. of Ire. 20 E3............53.30N 6.30W
Meaux France 44 E6.......................48.58N 2.54E
Mecca Saudi Arabia 94 E3..............21.26N 39.49E
Mechelen Belgium 42 D3................51.01N 4.28E
Mecheria Algeria 52 C3.................33.33N 0.17E
Meckenheim Germany 42 G2..........50.37N 7.02E

Medan Indonesia 104 B4.................. 3.35N 98.39E
Medanosa, Punta c. Argentina 75 C2..48.08S 65.55W
Medellín Colombia 71 I2................6.15N 75.36W
Meden r. England 15 G2...............53.19N 0.55W
Medenine Tunisia 84 F5.................33.24N 10.25E
Medetsiz mtn. Turkey 57 L2............37.33N 34.38E
Medicine Hat Canada 62 G3.........50.03N 110.41W
Medina Saudi Arabia 94 E3............24.30N 39.35E
Medina del Campo Spain 46 C4......41.20N 4.55W
Mediterranean Sea 52-53
Medway r. England 11 F2.............. 51.24N 0.31E
Meerut India 97 F6.......................29.00N 77.42E
Mega Ethiopia 87 B3.....................4.02N 38.19E
Mega Escarpment f. Ethiopia 87 B3....4.00N 38.10E
Megara Greece 56 F3...................38.00N 23.21E
Meghalaya d. India 97 I6...............25.30N 91.00E
Meiktila Myanmar 97 J5.................20.53N 95.54E
Meiningen Germany 48 E4............50.34N 10.25E
Meissen Germany 48 F4................51.10N 13.28E
Meizhou China 103 L2..................24.20N 116.15E
Mejicana mtn. Argentina 76 D2......29.00S 67.50W
Mek'ele Ethiopia 94 E1.................13.33N 39.30E
Meknès Morocco 84 D5.................33.53N 5.37W
Mekong r. Asia 104 D6................10.00N 106.20E
Mekong, Mouths of the Vietnam 104 D6
                                                        10.00N 106.20E
Melaka Malaysia 104 C4................2.11N 102.16E
Melbourn England 11 F3...............52.05N 0.01E
Melbourne Australia 110 D2.........37.45S 144.58E
Melby Scotland 19 Y9..................60.19N 1.40W
Melilla Spain 84 D5......................35.17N 2.57W
Melitopol' Ukraine 55 N2.............46.51N 35.22E
Melka Guba Ethiopia 87 B3..........4.52N 39.18E
Melksham England 10 C2.............51.22N 2.09W
Melrose Scotland 17 G3...............55.36N 2.43W
Meltham England 15 F2...............53.36N 1.52W
Melton Mowbray England 10 E3....52.46N 0.53W
Melun France 44 E6.....................48.32N 2.40E
Melville i. Australia 110 C4...........11.30S 131.00E
Melville B. Greenland 63 L5..........75.00N 63.00W
Melville I. Australia 110 C4..........11.30S 131.00E
Melville I. Canada 62 G5..............75.30N 110.00W
Melville Pen. Canada 63 J4...........68.00N 84.00W
Melvin, Lough Rep. of Ire./N. Ireland 16 A2
                                                        54.25N 8.10W
Memberamo r. Indonesia 105 J3....1.45S 137.25E
Memmingen Germany 48 E2.........47.59N 10.11E
Memphis U.S.A. 65 I4...................35.05N 90.00W
Menai Bridge town Wales 12 C5......53.14N 4.11W
Menai Str. Wales 12 C5...............53.17N 4.20W
Mendawai r. Indonesia 104 E3......3.17S 113.20E
Mende France 44 E4.....................44.32N 3.30E
Menderes r. Turkey 56 H2.............37.30N 27.05E
Mendip Hills England 13 E3..........51.15N 2.40W
Mendoza Argentina 75 C3............33.00S 68.52W
Menongue Angola 86 A3..............14.40S 17.41E
Menorca i. Spain 46 H3................40.00N 4.00E
Mentawai is. Indonesia 104 B3......2.50S 99.00E
Mentok Indonesia 104 D3............2.04S 105.12E
Menzel Bourguiba Tunisia 52 E4.....37.10N 9.48E
Meppel Neth. 42 F4.......................52.42N 6.12E
Meppen Germany 42 G4................52.42N 7.17E
Merano Italy 50 D7......................46.41N 11.10E
Merauke Indonesia 105 K2.............8.30S 140.22E
Merced U.S.A. 64 B4....................37.17N 120.29W
Mere England 10 C2....................51.05N 2.16W
Mergui Myanmar 97 J3.................12.26N 98.34E
Mergui Archipelago is. Myanmar 97 J3...11.30N 98.30E
Mérida Mexico 70 G5...................20.59N 89.39W
Mérida Spain 46 B3.....................38.55N 6.20W
Mérida Venezuela 71 J2...............8.24N 71.08W
Mérida, Cordillera de mts. Venezuela 71 J2
                                                        8.00N 71.30W
Meridian U.S.A. 65 I3...................32.21N 88.42W
Merkys r. Lithuania 55 I6..............54.05N 24.03E
Merowe Sudan 85 H3..................18.30N 31.49E
Merrick mtn. Scotland 16 E3.........55.08N 4.29W
Mersch Lux. 42 F1.......................49.44N 6.05E
Mersey r. England 14 E2...............53.22N 2.37W
Merseyside d. England 14 E2.........53.28N 3.00W
Mersin Turkey 57 L2....................36.47N 34.37E
Merthyr Tydfil Wales 12 D3...........51.45N 3.23W
Merthyr Tydfil d. Wales 12 D3........51.45N 3.23W
Merti Kenya 87 B3.......................1.07N 38.39E
Méru France 42 B1......................49.14N 2.08E
Meru Kenya 87 B3........................0.03N 37.38E
Meru mtn. Tanzania 87 B2.............3.16S 36.53E
Merzifon Turkey 57 L4..................40.52N 35.28E
Merzig Germany 42 F1..................49.26N 6.39E
Mesolóngion Greece 56 E3...........38.23N 21.23E
Mesopotamia f. Iraq 85 I5.............33.30N 44.30E
Messina Italy 50 F3.....................38.13N 15.34E
Messina, G. of Greece 56 F2.........36.50N 22.05E
Mesta r. see Nestos r. Bulgaria 56
Meta r. Venezuela 74 C7...............6.10N 67.30W
Metheringham England 15 G2.......53.09N 0.22W
Methwold England 11 F3..............52.30N 0.33E
Metković Croatia 56 C5.................43.03N 17.38E
Metlika Slovenia 54 D1.................45.39N 15.19E
Metz France 44 G6......................49.07N 6.11E
Meuse r. see Maas r. Belgium 42
Mevagissey England 13 C2...........50.16N 4.48W
Mexborough England 15 F2...........53.29N 1.18W
Mexicali Mexico 70 A7.................32.26N 115.30W
México d. Mexico 70 E4................19.45N 99.30W
Mexico C. America 70 D5.............20.00N 100.00W
Mexico, G. of N. America 70 F5......25.00N 90.00W
Mexico City Mexico 70 E4............19.25N 99.10W
Meymaneh Afghan. 95 J6.............35.54N 64.43E
Mezen Russian Fed. 58 G3...........65.50N 44.20E
Mezen r. Russian Fed. 35 H4..........65.50N 44.18E
Mezha r. Russian Fed. 55 L5..........55.47N 31.24E
Mezitli Turkey 57 L2....................36.47N 34.36E
Mezquital r. Mexico 70 C5............21.58N 105.30W
Mfangani I. Kenya 87 A2...............0.27S 34.00E
Miami-Fort Lauderdale U.S.A. 65 J2...25.45N 80.10W
Miandowab Iran 95 G6.................36.57N 46.06E
Mīāneh Iran 95 G6.......................37.23N 47.45E
Mianwali Pakistan 95 L5...............32.32N 71.33E
Miass Russian Fed. 58 J3..............55.00N 60.00E
Michigan d. U.S.A. 65 I5...............45.00N 85.00W
Michigan, L. U.S.A. 65 I5..............44.00N 87.00W
Michipicoten I. Canada 65 I6.........47.40N 85.50W
Michipicoten River town Canada 65 J6...47.57N 84.55W
Michoacán d. Mexico 70 D4..........19.20N 101.00W

Michurinsk Russian Fed. 58 G3.......52.54N 40.30E
Middlesbrough England 15 F3........54.34N 1.13W
Middlesbrough d. England 15 F3.....54.33N 1.13W
Middleton England 15 E2..............53.33N 2.12W
Middleton-in-Teesdale England 15 E3...54.38N 2.05W
Middleton St. George England 15 F3...54.30N 1.28W
Middlewich England 15 E2............53.12N 2.28W
Midhurst England 10 E1...............50.59N 0.44W
Midland d. U.S.A. 64 F3...............32.00N 100.05W
Midleton Rep. of Ire. 20 C1...........51.55N 8.12W
Midlothian d. Scotland 17 F3.........55.50N 3.10W
Midway Is. Hawaiian Is. 108 N9......28.15N 177.25W
Miekojärvi l. Finland 43 F4.............66.35N 24.20E
Mikhaylovskiy Russian Fed. 102 D8...51.41N 79.47E
Mikkeli Finland 43 F3...................61.44N 27.15E
Milan Italy 50 C6.........................45.28N 9.16E
Milas Turkey 57 H2......................37.18N 27.48E
Milborne Port England 13 E2........50.58N 2.28W
Mildenhall England 11 F3.............52.20N 0.30E
Mildura Australia 110 D2..............34.14S 142.13E
Miles City U.S.A. 64 E6................46.24N 105.48W
Milford Haven town Wales 12 B3....51.43N 5.02W
Milk r. U.S.A. 64 E6.....................47.55N 106.15W
Millars r. Spain 46 E3..................39.58N 0.01W
Millau France 44 E4.....................44.06N 3.05E
Mille Lacs l. U.S.A. 65 H6.............46.15N 93.40W
Milleur Pt. Scotland 16 D3............55.01N 5.07W
Millom England 14 D3.................54.13N 3.16W
Millport Scotland 16 E3...............55.45N 4.56W
Milnthorpe England 14 E3............54.14N 2.47W
Milos i. Greece 56 G2..................36.40N 24.26E
Milton Keynes England 10 E3........52.03N 0.42W
Milwaukee U.S.A. 65 I5...............43.03N 87.56W
Mimizan France 44 C4.................44.12N 1.14W
Minab Iran 95 I4.........................27.07N 57.05E
Minas Gerais d. Brazil 77 F3..........18.00S 45.00W
Minatitlán Mexico 70 F4...............17.59N 94.32W
Mindanao i. Phil. 105 H5..............7.30N 125.00E
Mindelo Cape Verde 84 B3...........16.54N 25.00W
Mindoro i. Phil. 104 G6...............13.00N 121.00E
Mindoro Str. Pacific Oc. 104 G6.....12.30N 120.10E
Mindra, M. Romania 56 F6............45.20N 23.32E
Mingulay i. Scotland 18 B1............56.48N 7.37W
Minhead England 13 D3...............51.12N 3.29W
Minna Nigeria 84 E2.....................9.39N 6.32E
Minneapolis-St. Paul U.S.A. 65 H5...45.00N 93.15W
Minnesota d. U.S.A. 65 H5............46.00N 95.00W
Miño r. Spain 46 A4.....................41.50N 8.52W
Minot U.S.A. 64 F6......................48.16N 101.19W
Minsk Belarus 55 J5.....................53.51N 27.30E
Minsterley England 10 C3.............52.38N 2.56W
Mintlaw Scotland 19 H2...............57.31N 2.00W
Miranda r. Brazil 77 E2................19.22S 57.15W
Miranda de Ebro Spain 46 D5........42.41N 2.57W
Mirandela Portugal 46 B4.............41.28N 7.10W
Mirbat Oman 95 H2.....................17.00N 54.45E
Miri Malaysia 104 E4...................4.28N 114.00E
Mirim, Lagoa l. Brazil 75 D3..........33.10S 53.30W
Mirpur Khas Pakistan 96 D5..........25.33N 69.05E
Mirzapur India 97 G6...................25.09N 82.34E
Miskolc Hungary 54 G3...............48.07N 20.47E
Misoöl i. Indonesia 105 I3.............1.50S 130.10E
Misratah Libya 84 F5....................32.24N 15.04E
Missinaibi r. Canada 63 J3............50.44N 81.29W
Mississippi d. U.S.A. 65 I3............33.00N 90.00W
Mississippi r. U.S.A. 65 I2............28.55N 89.05W
Mississippi Delta U.S.A. 65 I2........29.00N 89.10W
Missoula U.S.A. 64 D6.................46.52N 114.00W
Missouri d. U.S.A. 65 H4..............39.00N 93.00W
Missouri r. U.S.A. 65 H4..............38.40N 90.20W
Mistassini, L. Canada 63 K3..........50.45N 73.40W
Mitchell r. Australia 110 D4...........15.12S 141.40E
Mitchell U.S.A. 64 G5..................43.40N 98.01W
Mitchell, Mt. U.S.A. 65 J4............35.57N 82.16W
Mitchelstown Rep. of Ire. 20 C2.....52.16N 8.19W
Mito Japan 106 D3......................36.30N 140.29E
Mitumba, Chaine des mts. Zaire 86 B4...8.00S 28.00E
Miyako Japan 106 D3..................39.40N 141.59E
Miyazaki Japan 106 B2................31.58N 131.50E
Mizdah Libya 52 F3.....................31.26N 12.59E
Mizen Head Cork Rep. of Ire. 20 B1...51.27N 9.50W
Mizen Head Wicklow Rep. of Ire. 20 E2...52.50N 6.03W
Mizoram d. India 97 I5.................23.40N 92.40E
Mjölby Sweden 43 C2..................58.19N 15.10E
Mkomazi Tanzania 87 B2.............4.41S 38.02E
Mkomazi Game Res. Tanzania 87 B2...4.00S 38.00E
Mljet i. Croatia 56 C5..................42.45N 17.30E
Mmabatho R.S.A. 86 B2...............25.46S 25.37E
Mobile U.S.A. 65 I3.....................30.40N 88.05W
Mobile B. U.S.A. 65 I3.................30.30N 87.50W
Mobridge U.S.A. 64 F6................45.31N 100.25W
Moçambique town Mozambique 86 D3...15.00S 40.55E
Mochudi Botswana 86 B2.............24.26S 26.07E
Modbury England 13 D2..............50.21N 3.53W
Modena Italy 50 D6....................44.39N 10.55E
Modica Italy 50 F2......................36.51N 14.51E
Moelfre Wales 12 C5...................53.21N 4.15W
Moel Sych mtn. Wales 12 D4.........52.52N 3.22W
Moffat Scotland 17 F3..................55.20N 3.27W
Mogadishu Somalia 85 I2..............2.02N 45.21E
Mohyliv Podil's'kyy Ukraine 55 J3...48.29N 27.49E
Mo i Rana Norway 43 C4.............66.20N 14.12E
Moji das Cruzes Brazil 77 F2.........23.33S 46.14W
Mold Wales 12 D5......................53.10N 3.08W
Moldova Europe 55 K2.................47.30N 28.30E
Mole r. England 10 E2.................51.12N 0.20W
Molde Norway 43 A3...................62.44N 7.08E
Molepolole R.S.A. 86 B2...............28.30S 20.07E
Molopo r. R.S.A. 86 B2................24.05S 24.00E
Moluccas is. Indonesia 108 H6.......2.00S 128.00E
Molucca Sea Pacific Oc. 105 H4......2.00N 126.30E
Mombasa Kenya 87 B2.................4.04S 39.40E
Møn i. Denmark 43 C1.................54.58N 12.20E
Monach, Sd. of Scotland 18 B2......57.34N 7.35W
Monach Is. Scotland 18 B2...........57.32N 7.38W
Monaco Europe 44 G3.................43.40N 7.25E
Monadhliath Mts. Scotland 19 E2....57.09N 4.08W
Monaghan Rep. of Ire. 20 E4........54.15N 6.58W
Monaghan d. Rep. of Ire. 20 E4......54.10N 7.00W
Mona I. Puerto Rico 71 K4............18.06N 67.54W
Mona Passage Dom. Rep. 71 K4.....18.10N 68.00W
Monar, Loch Scotland 18 D2.........57.25N 5.05W
Monbetsu Japan 106 D4..............44.21N 143.18E
Monchegorsk Russian Fed. 43 H4...67.55N 33.01E
Mönchengladbach Germany 48 C4...51.12N 6.25E
Monclova Mexico 70 D6..............26.55N 101.20W
Moncton Canada 63 L2...............46.06N 64.50W

Mondego r. Portugal 46 A4...........40.09N 8.52W
Mondovì Italy 50 B6...................44.24N 7.50E
Moneymore N. Ireland 16 C2........54.42N 6.41W
Monforte Spain 46 B5................42.32N 7.30W
Monga Zaire 88 B5....................4.05N 22.56E
Mongolia Asia 103 I7.................46.30N 104.00E
Mongora Pakistan 95 L5..............34.47N 72.22E
Mongu Zambia 86 B3..................15.10S 23.09E
Moniaive Scotland 17 F3.............55.12N 3.55W
Monmouth Wales 12 E3..............51.48N 2.43W
Monmouthshire d. Wales 12 E3......51.44N 2.50W
Monnow r. England/Wales 12 E3.....51.49N 2.42W
Monroe U.S.A. 65 H3..................32.31N 92.06W
Monrovia Liberia 84 C2...............6.20N 10.46W
Mons Belgium 42 C2..................50.27N 3.57E
Montana d. U.S.A. 64 D6.............47.00N 110.00W
Montargis France 44 E5...............48.00N 2.44E
Montauban France 44 D4............44.01N 1.20E
Montbéliard France 44 G5............47.31N 6.48E
Mont-de-Marsan town France 44 C3...43.54N 0.30W
Montdidier France 42 B1.............49.39N 2.34E
Monte Alegre town Brazil 77 E4.......2.01S 54.04W
Monte Carlo Monaco 44 G3..........43.44N 7.25E
Montecristo i. Italy 50 D5.............42.20N 10.19E
Montego Bay town Jamaica 71 I4....18.27N 77.56W
Montélimar France 44 F4.............44.33N 4.45E
Monte Lindo r. Paraguay 77 E3......23.57S 57.10W
Montemorelos Mexico 70 E6.........25.12N 99.50W
Montería Colombia 71 I2..............8.45N 75.54W
Monterrey Mexico 70 D6.............25.40N 100.20W
Monte Santu, C. Italy 50 C4..........40.05N 9.44E
Montes Claros Brazil 77 F3............16.45S 43.52W
Montevideo Uruguay 75 D3..........34.55S 56.10W
Montgomery U.S.A. 65 I3.............32.22N 86.20W
Montgomery Wales 12 D4............52.34N 3.09W
Montluçon France 44 E5..............46.20N 2.36E
Montmagny Canada 63 L2...........46.59N 70.33W
Montpelier U.S.A. 65 L5..............44.16N 72.34W
Montpellier France 44 E3.............43.36N 3.53E
Montréal Canada 63 K2...............45.30N 73.36W
Montreuil France 42 A2...............50.28N 1.46E
Montrose Scotland 19 G1............56.43N 2.29W
Montrose U.S.A. 64 E4................38.29N 107.53W
Montserrat i. Leeward Is. 71 L4......16.45N 62.14W
Monywa Myanmar 97 I5...............22.07N 95.11E
Monza Italy 50 C6......................45.35N 9.16E
Monzón Spain 46 F4...................41.52N 0.10E
Moore, L. Australia 110 A3...........29.30S 117.30E
Moorhead U.S.A. 64 G6..............46.51N 96.44W
Moose Jaw Canada 62 H3............50.23N 105.35W
Moosonee Canada 63 J3..............51.18N 80.40W
Mopti Mali 84 D3.......................14.29N 4.10W
Mora Sweden 43 C3...................61.00N 14.30E
Morar, Loch Scotland 18 D1.........56.56N 5.40W
Morava r. Yugo. 56 E6.................44.43N 21.02E
Moray d. Scotland 19 F2..............57.30N 3.20W
Moray Firth est. Scotland 19 F2.....57.45N 3.50W
Morbach Germany 42 G1.............49.48N 7.07E
Morden Canada 62 I2.................49.15N 98.10W
More, Loch Scotland 18 E3...........58.16N 4.51W
Morecambe England 14 E3...........54.03N 2.52W
Morecambe B. England 14 E3........54.05N 3.00W
Moree Australia 110 D3..............29.29S 149.53E
Morehead P.N.G. 105 K2.............8.55S 141.33E
Morelia Mexico 70 D4.................19.40N 101.11W
Morelos d. Mexico 70 E4.............18.40N 99.00W
Morena, Sierra mts. Spain 46 C3.....38.10N 5.00W
Moretonhampstead England 13 D2...50.39N 3.45W
Morgan City U.S.A. 65 H2............29.41N 91.13W
Mori Japan 106 D4.....................42.07N 140.30E
Morioka Japan 106 D3................39.43N 141.10E
Moriston r. Scotland 18 E2............57.12N 4.37W
Morlaix France 44 B6..................48.35N 3.50W
Morley England 15 F2.................53.45N 1.36W
Morocco Africa 84 D5.................31.00N 5.00W
Moro G. Phil. 105 G5..................6.30N 123.20E
Morogoro Tanzania 86 C4.............6.49S 37.40E
Mörön Mongolia 103 I7...............49.36N 100.08E
Morondava Madagascar 86 D2......20.17S 44.17E
Morón de la Frontera Spain 46 C2...37.08N 5.27W
Moroni Comoros 86 D3...............11.40S 43.19E
Morotai i. Indonesia 105 H4..........2.10N 128.30E
Moroto Uganda 87 A3.................2.30N 34.40E
Moroto, Mt. Uganda 87 A3...........2.30N 34.46E
Morpeth England 15 F4...............55.10N 1.40W
Morriston Wales 12 D3................51.40N 3.55W
Morro, Punta c. Chile 76 C2..........27.06S 71.00W
Morrosquillo, G. of Colombia 71 I2...9.30N 75.50W
Morte B. England 13 C3...............51.10N 4.14W
Mortehoe England 13 C3.............51.12N 4.12W
Mortes r. Brazil 77 E3..................11.59S 50.25W
Morungole mtn. Uganda 87 A3......3.50N 34.02E
Morvern f. Scotland 16 D4............56.37N 5.45W
Mosborough England 15 F2..........53.19N 1.21W
Moscow Russian Fed. 58 F3..........55.45N 37.42E
Moselle r. Germany 48 C4............50.23N 7.37E
Moshi Tanzania 87 B2.................3.20S 37.21E
Mosjøen Norway 43 C4...............65.50N 13.10E
Mosquitos, G. of Panama 71 H2.....9.00N 81.00W
Mosquitos Coast f. Nicaragua 71 H3...13.00N 84.00W
Moss Norway 43 B2....................59.26N 10.41E
Mossoró Brazil 77 G4..................5.10S 37.20W
Mostaganem Algeria 52 D4..........35.56N 0.05E
Mostar Bosnia. 56 C5..................43.20N 17.50E
Mosul Iraq 94 F6........................36.21N 43.08E
Møsvatnet l. Norway 43 A2...........59.55N 8.00E
Motala Sweden 43 C2.................58.34N 15.05E
Motherwell Scotland 17 F3...........55.48N 4.00W
Motril Spain 46 D2.....................36.45N 3.31W
Moulins France 44 E5.................46.34N 3.20E
Moulmein Myanmar 97 J4............16.30N 97.50E
Moundou Chad 84 F2..................8.36N 16.02E
Mount Gambier town Australia 110 D2...37.51S 140.50E
Mount Isa town Australia 110 C3....20.50S 139.29E
Mountmellick Rep. of Ire. 20 D3.....53.08N 7.21W
Mountrath Rep. of Ire. 20 D3........53.00N 7.28W
Mount's B. England 13 B2............50.05N 5.25W
Mountsorrel town England 10 D3.....52.44N 1.07W
Mourdi, Dépression du f. Chad 94 B2...18.00N 23.00E
Mourne r. N. Ireland 16 C2............54.50N 7.29W
Mourne Mts. N. Ireland 16 C2........54.10N 6.02W
Mousa i. Scotland 19 Y8..............60.00N 1.10W
Mouscron Belgium 42 C2.............50.46N 3.10E
Mouzon France 42 E1.................49.36N 5.05E
Moville Rep. of Ire. 16 B3.............55.11N 7.03W
Moy r. Rep. of Ire. 20 B4.............54.10N 9.09W

Moyale Kenya **87 B3** 3.31N 39.01E
Moyen Atlas *mts.* Morocco **52 B3** 33.30N 5.00W
Mozambique Africa **86 C3** 18.00S 35.00E
Mozambique Channel Indian Oc. **86 D3** 16.00S 42.30E
M'Saken Tunisia **52 F4** 35.42N 10.33E
Msambweni Kenya **87 B2** 4.27S 39.28E
Mt. Elgon Nat. Park Uganda **87 A3** 1.05N 34.20E
Mtelo *mtn.* Kenya **87 B3** 1.40N 35.23E
Mtsensk Russian Fed. **55 O5** 53.18N 36.35E
Mtwara Tanzania **86 D3** 10.17S 40.11E
Muang Chiang Rai Thailand **104 B7** 19.56N 99.51E
Muang Khon Kaen Thailand **104 C7** 16.25N 102.50E
Muang Lampang Thailand **104 B7** 18.16N 99.30E
Muang Nakhon Sawan Thailand **104 C7** 15.35N 100.10E
Muang Nan Thailand **104 C7** 18.45N 100.42E
Muang Phayao Thailand **104 B7** 19.10N 99.55E
Muang Phitsanulok Thailand **104 C7** 16.50N 100.15E
Muang Phrae Thailand **104 C7** 18.07N 100.09E
Muar Malaysia **104 C4** 2.01N 102.35E
Muarabungo Indonesia **104 C3** 1.29S 102.06E
Muchinga Mts. Zambia **82 G3** 12.00S 31.00E
Much Wenlock England **10 C3** 52.36N 2.34W
Muck *i.* Scotland **18 C1** 56.50N 6.14W
Muckish Mtn. Rep. of Ire. **16 A3** 55.06N 7.59W
Muckle Roe *i.* Scotland **19 Y9** 60.22N 1.26W
Mudanjiang China **103 N6** 44.36N 129.42E
Muğla Turkey **57 I2** 37.12N 28.22E
Muhammad Qol Sudan **94 E3** 20.53N 37.09E
Mühlhausen Germany **48 E4** 51.12N 10.27E
Muhos Finland **43 F4** 64.49N 26.00E
Mui Ethiopia **87 B4** 5.59N 35.29E
Mui Ca Mau *c.* Vietnam **104 C5** 8.30N 104.35E
Muine Bheag Rep. of Ire. **20 E2** 52.41N 6.59W
Muirkirk Scotland **16 E3** 55.31N 4.04W
Muirneag *mtn.* Scotland **18 C3** 58.24N 6.21W
Mukacheve Ukraine **54 H3** 48.26N 22.45E
Mukalla Yemen **95 G1** 14.34N 49.09E
Mukono Uganda **87 A3** 0.21N 32.27E
Mulanje, Mt. Malawi **86 C3** 15.57S 35.33E
Mulhacén *mtn.* Spain **46 D2** 37.04N 3.22W
Mulhouse France **44 G5** 47.45N 7.21E
Muling *r.* China **106 B5** 45.53N 133.40E
Mull *i.* Scotland **16 D4** 56.28N 5.56W
Mull, Sd. of *str.* Scotland **16 D4** 56.32N 5.55W
Mullaghareirk Mts. Rep. of Ire. **20 B2** 52.20N 9.10W
Mull Head Scotland **19 G4** 59.23N 2.53W
Mullingar Rep. of Ire. **20 D3** 53.31N 7.21W
Mull of Galloway *c.* Scotland **16 E2** 54.39N 4.52W
Mull of Kintyre *c.* Scotland **16 D3** 55.17N 5.45W
Mull of Oa *c.* Scotland **16 C3** 55.36N 6.20W
Multan Pakistan **96 E7** 30.10N 71.36E
Muna *i.* Indonesia **105 G2** 5.00S 122.30E
Mundesley England **11 G3** 52.53N 1.24E
Mundford England **11 F3** 52.31N 0.39E
Munger India **97 H6** 25.24N 86.29E
Munich Germany **48 E3** 48.08N 11.35E
Munim *r.* Brazil **77 F4** 2.51S 44.05W
Münster Germany **48 C4** 51.58N 7.37E
Muojärvi *l.* Finland **43 G4** 65.56N 29.40E
Muonio Finland **43 E4** 67.52N 23.45E
Muonio *r.* Sweden/Finland **43 E4** 67.13N 23.30E
Murallón *mtn.* Argentina/Chile **75 B2** 49.48S 73.26W
Muranga Kenya **87 B2** 0.43S 37.10E
Murchison *r.* Australia **110 A3** 27.30S 114.10E
Murcia Spain **46 E2** 37.59N 1.08W
Mureş *r.* Romania **54 G2** 46.16N 20.10E
Muret France **44 D3** 43.28N 1.19E
Müritz, L. Germany **48 F5** 53.25N 12.45E
Murmansk Russian Fed. **58 F4** 68.59N 33.08E
Murom Russian Fed. **58 G3** 55.04N 42.04E
Muroran Japan **106 D4** 42.21N 140.59E
Murray *r.* Australia **110 C2** 35.23S 139.20E
Murray Bridge *town* Australia **110 C2** 35.10S 139.17E
Murrumbidgee *r.* Australia **110 D2** 34.38S 143.10E
Mururoa *i.* French Polynesia **109 Q4** 22.00S 140.00W
Murwara India **97 G5** 23.49N 80.28E
Murzuq Libya **84 F4** 25.56N 13.57E
Muscat Oman **95 I3** 23.36N 58.37E
Musgrave Ranges *mts.* Australia **110 C3** 26.30S 131.10E
Muskegon U.S.A. **65 I5** 43.13N 86.10W
Muskogee U.S.A. **65 G4** 35.45N 95.21W
Musmar Sudan **94 E2** 18.13N 35.38E
Musoma Tanzania **87 A2** 1.29S 33.48E
Musselburgh Scotland **17 F3** 55.57N 3.04W
Mut Egypt **94 C4** 25.29N 28.59E
Mut Turkey **57 K2** 36.38N 33.27E
Mutare Zimbabwe **86 C3** 18.58S 32.38E
Mutis *mtn.* Indonesia **105 G2** 9.35S 124.15E
Mutsu Japan **106 D4** 41.16N 141.12E
Muzaffargarh Pakistan **95 L5** 30.04N 71.12E
Muzaffarpur India **97 H6** 26.07N 85.23E
Mwanza Tanzania **87 A2** 2.30S 32.54E
Mwene-Ditu Zaire **86 B4** 7.01S 23.27E
Mweru, L. Zambia/Zaire **86 B4** 9.00S 28.40E
Myanmar Asia **97 J5** 21.00N 95.00E
Myingyan Myanmar **97 J5** 21.25N 95.20E
Mykolayiv Ukraine **55 M2** 46.57N 32.00E
Mynydd Eppynt *mts.* Wales **12 D4** 52.06N 3.30W
Mysore India **96 F3** 12.18N 76.37E
My Tho Vietnam **104 D6** 10.21N 106.21E
Mytilini Greece **56 H3** 39.06N 26.34E
Mytishchi Russian Fed. **55 O6** 55.54N 37.47E
Mzuzu Malawi **86 C3** 11.26S 34.02E

N

Naas Rep. of Ire. **20 E3** 53.13N 6.41W
Naberera Tanzania **87 B2** 4.10S 36.57E
Naberezhnye Chelny Russian Fed. **58 H3** 55.42N 52.20E
Nabeul Tunisia **52 F4** 36.28N 10.44E
Nacala Mozambique **86 D3** 14.30S 40.37E
Nador Morocco **52 C4** 35.12N 2.55W
Næstved Denmark **43 B1** 55.14N 11.47E
Nafplio Greece **56 F2** 37.33N 22.47E
Naga Phil. **105 G6** 13.36N 123.12E
Nagaland *d.* India **97 I6** 26.10N 94.30E
Nagano Japan **106 C3** 36.39N 138.10E
Nagaoka Japan **106 C3** 37.30N 138.50E
Nagaon India **97 I6** 26.20N 92.41E
Nagasaki Japan **106 A2** 32.45N 129.52E
Nagercoil India **96 F2** 8.11N 77.30E
Nagha Kalat Pakistan **95 K4** 27.24N 65.08E
Nagichot Sudan **87 A3** 4.16N 33.34E
Nagoya Japan **106 C3** 35.08N 136.53E
Nagpur India **97 F5** 21.10N 79.12E
Nagykanizsa Hungary **54 E2** 46.27N 17.01E
Naha Japan **103 N3** 26.10N 127.40E
Nahanni *r.* Canada **62 F4** 61.00N 123.20W
Nahavand Iran **95 G5** 34.13N 48.23E
Nailsworth England **10 C2** 51.41N 2.12W
Nain Canada **63 L3** 56.30N 61.45W
Na'īn Iran **95 H5** 32.52N 53.05E
Nairn Scotland **19 F2** 57.35N 3.52W
Nairn *r.* Scotland **19 F2** 57.35N 3.52W
Nairobi Kenya **87 B2** 1.17S 36.50E
Nairobi *d.* Kenya **87 B2** 1.15S 36.50E
Naivasha Kenya **87 B2** 0.44S 36.26E
Naivasha, L. Kenya **87 B2** 0.45S 36.22E
Najafabad Iran **95 H5** 32.38N 51.23E
Najd *d.* Saudi Arabia **94 F3** 25.00N 43.00E
Najin N. Korea **106 B4** 42.10N 130.20E
Najran Saudi Arabia **94 F2** 17.28N 44.06E
Nakhodka Russian Fed. **59 P2** 42.53N 132.54E
Nakhon Pathom Thailand **97 J3** 13.50N 100.01E
Nakhon Ratchasima Thailand **104 C7** 15.02N 102.12E
Nakhon Si Thammarat Thailand **104 B5** 8.29N 99.55E
Naknek U.S.A. **62 C3** 58.45N 157.00W
Nakskov Denmark **43 B1** 54.50N 11.10E
Nakuru Kenya **87 B2** 0.16S 36.04E
Nalut Libya **84 F5** 31.53N 10.59E
Namakzar-e Shadad *f.* Iran **95 I5** 30.00N 59.00E
Namanga Kenya **87 B2** 2.31S 36.47E
Namangan Uzbekistan **102 C6** 40.59N 71.41E
Namaqualand *f.* Namibia **86 A2** 25.30S 17.00E
Nam Co *l.* China **102 G4** 30.40N 90.30E
Nam Dinh Vietnam **104 D8** 20.25N 106.12E
Namib Desert Namibia **86 A2** 22.50S 14.40E
Namibe Angola **86 A3** 15.10S 12.10E
Namibia Africa **86 A2** 22.00S 17.00E
Namlea Indonesia **105 H3** 3.15S 127.07E
Nampo N. Korea **103 N5** 38.40N 125.30E
Nampula Mozambique **86 C3** 15.09S 39.14E
Namsos Norway **43 B4** 64.28N 11.30E
Namur Belgium **42 D2** 50.28N 4.52E
Namur *d.* Belgium **42 D2** 50.20N 4.45E
Nanaimo Canada **64 B6** 49.08N 123.58W
Nanao Japan **106 C3** 37.03N 136.58E
Nanchang China **103 L3** 28.38N 115.56E
Nanchong China **103 J4** 30.54N 106.06E
Nancy France **44 G6** 48.42N 6.12E
Nandurbar India **96 E5** 21.22N 74.15E
Nanjing China **103 L4** 32.00N 118.40E
Nan Ling *mts.* China **103 K3** 25.20N 112.30E
Nanning China **103 J2** 22.50N 108.19E
Nanortalik Greenland **63 N4** 60.09N 45.15W
Nanping China **103 L3** 26.40N 118.07E
Nansio Tanzania **87 A2** 2.07S 33.03E
Nantes France **44 C5** 47.14N 1.35W
Nantong China **103 M4** 32.05N 120.59E
Nantucket I. U.S.A. **65 M5** 41.16N 70.00W
Nantwich England **14 E2** 53.05N 2.31W
Nant-y-moch Resr. Wales **12 D4** 52.28N 3.50W
Nanumea *i.* Tuvalu **108 M6** 5.40S 176.10E
Nanyuki Kenya **87 B2** 0.01N 37.08E
Napamute U.S.A. **62 C4** 61.31N 158.45W
Napier New Zealand **111 G2** 39.30S 176.54E
Naples Italy **50 F4** 40.50N 14.14E
Naples U.S.A. **65 J2** 26.09N 81.48W
Napo *r.* Peru **76 C4** 3.30S 73.10W
Narberth Wales **12 C3** 51.48N 4.45W
Narbonne France **44 E3** 43.11N 3.00E
Narborough Leics. England **10 D3** 52.35N 1.11W
Narborough Norfolk England **11 F3** 52.42N 0.35E
Nares Str. Canada **63 K5** 78.30N 72.00W
Narmada *r.* India **96 E5** 21.40N 73.00E
Narodnaya *mtn.* Russian Fed. **58 I4** 65.00N 61.00E
Narok Kenya **87 B2** 1.05S 35.55E
Närpes Finland **43 E3** 62.28N 21.19E
Narva Estonia **43 G2** 59.22N 28.17E
Narvik Norway **43 D5** 68.26N 17.25E
Naryan Mar Russian Fed. **58 H4** 67.37N 53.02E
Naryn Kyrgyzstan **102 D6** 41.24N 76.00E
Nashville U.S.A. **65 I4** 36.10N 86.50W
Näsijärvi *l.* Finland **43 E3** 61.30N 23.50E
Nasik India **96 E5** 20.00N 73.52E
Nassau *i.* Cook Is. **108 O5** 11.33S 165.25W
Nassau The Bahamas **71 I6** 25.03N 77.20W
Nasser, L. Egypt **94 D3** 22.40N 32.00E
Nässjö Sweden **43 C2** 57.39N 14.40E
Nata Tanzania **87 A2** 2.00S 34.28E
Natal Brazil **77 G4** 5.46S 35.15W
Natchez U.S.A. **65 H3** 31.22N 91.24W
Natron, L. Tanzania **87 B2** 2.18S 36.05E
Natuna Besar *i.* Indonesia **104 D4** 4.00N 108.20E
Natuna Is. Indonesia **104 D4** 3.00N 108.50E
Nauru Pacific Oc. **108 L6** 0.32S 166.55E
Navalmoral de la Mata Spain **46 C3** 39.54N 5.33W
Navan Rep. of Ire. **20 E3** 53.39N 6.42W
Navapolatsk Belarus **55 K6** 55.34N 28.40E
Naver *r.* Scotland **19 E3** 58.29N 4.12W
Naver, Loch Scotland **19 E3** 58.17N 4.20W
Navlya Russian Fed. **55 N5** 52.51N 34.30E
Navrongo Ghana **84 D3** 10.51N 1.03W
Nawabshah Pakistan **96 D6** 26.15N 68.26E
Naxçivan Azerbaijan **95 G6** 39.12N 45.22E
Naxos *i.* Greece **56 G2** 37.03N 25.30E
Nayarit *d.* Mexico **70 D5** 21.30N 105.00W
Nazareth Israel **94 E5** 32.41N 35.16E
Nazas *r.* Mexico **70 D6** 25.34N 103.25W
Nazca Peru **76 C3** 14.53S 74.54W
Nazilli Turkey **57 I2** 37.55N 28.20E
Nazret Ethiopia **85 H2** 8.32N 39.22E
Nazwá Oman **95 I3** 22.56N 57.33E
N'dalatando Angola **86 A4** 9.12S 14.54E
Ndélé C.A.R. **85 G2** 8.24N 20.39E
Ndeni *i.* Solomon Is. **111 F4** 10.30S 166.00E
Ndjamena Chad **84 F3** 12.10N 14.59E
Ndola Zambia **86 B3** 13.00S 28.39E
Ndoto *mtn.* Kenya **87 B3** 1.42N 37.10E
Neagh, Lough N. Ireland **16 C2** 54.36N 6.26W
Neath Wales **12 D3** 51.39N 3.49W
Neath *r.* Wales **12 D3** 51.39N 3.50W
Neath and Port Talbot *d.* Wales **12 D3** 51.42N 3.47W
Nebitdag Turkmenistan **95 H6** 39.31N 54.24E
Neblina, Pico da *mtn.* Colombia/Brazil **76 D5** 0.50N 66.00W
Nebraska *d.* U.S.A. **64 F5** 41.30N 100.00W
Nebrodi Mts. Italy **50 F2** 38.00N 14.50E
Nechisar Nat. Park Ethiopia **87 B4** 6.00N 37.50E
Neckar *r.* Germany **48 D3** 49.32N 8.26E
Necker I. Hawaiian Is. **108 O9** 23.35N 164.42W
Needham Market England **11 G3** 52.09N 1.02E
Needles U.S.A. **64 D3** 34.51N 114.36W
Neftekumsk Russian Fed. **58 G2** 44.46N 44.10E
Nefyn Wales **12 C4** 52.55N 4.31W
Negēlē Ethiopia **87 B4** 5.20N 39.36E
Negev *des.* Israel **94 D5** 30.42N 34.55E
Negotin Yugo. **56 F6** 44.14N 22.33E
Negra, Cordillera *mts.* Peru **76 C4** 10.00S 78.00W
Negra, Punta *c.* Peru **76 B4** 6.06S 81.09W
Negro *r.* Argentina **75 C2** 41.00S 62.48W
Negro *r.* Amazonas Brazil **77 D4** 3.30S 60.00W
Negro *r.* Mato Grosso do Sul Brazil **77 E3** 19.15S 57.15W
Negro, C. Morocco **46 C1** 35.41N 5.17W
Negros *i.* Phil. **105 G5** 10.00N 123.00E
Neijiang China **103 J3** 29.32N 105.03E
Neiva Colombia **74 B7** 2.58N 75.15W
Nek'emte Ethiopia **85 H2** 9.02N 36.31E
Neksø Denmark **54 D6** 55.04N 15.09E
Nelkan Russian Fed. **59 P3** 57.40N 136.04E
Nellore India **97 G3** 14.29N 80.00E
Nelson Canada **62 G2** 49.29N 117.17W
Nelson *r.* Canada **63 I3** 57.00N 93.20W
Nelson England **15 E2** 53.50N 2.14W
Nelson New Zealand **111 G1** 41.16S 173.15E
Nelspruit R.S.A. **86 C2** 25.27S 30.58E
Neman *r.* Europe **54 G6** 55.23N 21.15E
Neman Russian Fed. **54 H6** 55.02N 22.02E
Nementcha, Mts. de Algeria/Tunisia **52 E4** 35.00N 7.00E
Nenagh Rep. of Ire. **20 C2** 52.52N 8.13W
Nene *r.* England **11 F3** 52.49N 0.12E
Nenjiang China **103 N7** 49.10N 125.15E
Nepal Asia **97 G6** 28.00N 84.00E
Nephin *mtn.* Rep. of Ire. **20 B4** 54.00N 9.25W
Neris *r.* Lithuania **55 H6** 54.52N 23.55E
Ness *r.* Scotland **19 E2** 57.27N 4.15W
Ness, Loch Scotland **19 E2** 57.16N 4.30W
Neston England **14 D2** 53.17N 3.03W
Nestos *r.* Greece **56 G4** 40.51N 24.48E
Netherlands Europe **42 E4** 52.00N 5.30E
Netherlands Antilles *is.* S. America **71 K3** 12.30N 69.00W
Netley England **10 D1** 50.52N 1.19W
Nettilling L. Canada **63 K4** 66.30N 70.40W
Neubrandenburg Germany **48 F5** 53.33N 13.16E
Neuchâtel Switz. **44 G5** 47.00N 6.56E
Neuchâtel, Lac de *l.* Switz. **44 G5** 46.55N 6.55E
Neufchâteau Belgium **42 E1** 49.51N 5.26E
Neumünster Germany **48 E6** 54.05N 10.01E
Neunkirchen Germany **42 G1** 49.21N 7.12E
Neuquén Argentina **75 C3** 38.55S 68.55W
Neustrelitz Germany **48 F5** 53.22N 13.05E
Neuwied Germany **48 C4** 50.26N 7.28E
Nevada *d.* U.S.A. **64 C4** 39.00N 117.00W
Nevada, Sierra *mts.* Spain **46 D2** 37.04N 3.20W
Nevada, Sierra *mts.* U.S.A. **64 C4** 37.30N 119.00W
Nevers France **44 E5** 47.00N 3.09E
Nevėžis *r.* Lithuania **55 H6** 54.52N 23.55E
Nevis, Loch Scotland **18 D1** 57.00N 5.40W
Nevsehir Turkey **57 L3** 38.38N 34.43E
New Addington England **11 E2** 51.21N 0.01W
New Alresford England **10 D2** 51.06N 1.10W
Newark U.S.A. **65 L5** 40.44N 74.11W
Newark-on-Trent England **15 G2** 53.06N 0.48W
New Bedford U.S.A. **65 L5** 41.38N 70.55W
New Bern U.S.A. **65 K4** 35.05N 77.04W
Newbiggin-by-the-Sea England **15 F4** 55.11N 1.30W
Newbridge Rep. of Ire. **20 E3** 53.11N 6.48W
Newbridge Wales **12 D3** 51.41N 3.09W
New Britain *i.* P.N.G. **110 D5** 6.00S 143.00E
New Brunswick *d.* Canada **63 L2** 47.00N 66.00W
Newburgh Scotland **17 F4** 56.21N 3.15W
Newbury England **10 D2** 51.24N 1.19W
New Caledonia *i.* Pacific Oc. **111 F3** 22.00S 165.00E
Newcastle Australia **110 E2** 32.55S 151.46E
Newcastle N. Ireland **16 D2** 54.13N 5.54W
Newcastle Emlyn Wales **12 C4** 52.02N 4.29W
Newcastle-under-Lyme England **10 C3** 53.02N 2.15W
Newcastle upon Tyne England **15 F3** 54.58N 1.36W
Newcastle West Rep. of Ire. **20 B2** 52.27N 9.04W
New Cumnock Scotland **16 E3** 55.24N 4.11W
New Delhi India **96 F6** 28.37N 77.13E
Newent England **10 C2** 51.56N 2.24W
New Forest *f.* England **10 D1** 50.50N 1.35W
Newfoundland *d.* Canada **63 L3** 55.00N 60.00W
Newfoundland *i.* Canada **63 M2** 48.30N 56.00W
New Galloway Scotland **16 E3** 55.05N 4.09W
New Guinea *i.* Austa. **110 D5** 5.00S 140.00E
New Hampshire *d.* U.S.A. **65 L5** 44.00N 71.30W
New Haven U.S.A. **65 L5** 41.14N 72.50W
New Ireland *i.* P.N.G. **110 E5** 2.30S 151.30E
New Jersey *d.* U.S.A. **65 L5** 40.00N 74.30W
New Liskeard Canada **65 K6** 47.31N 79.41W
Newmarket England **11 F3** 52.15N 0.23E
Newmarket on-Fergus Rep. of Ire. **20 C2** 52.46N 8.55W
New Mexico *d.* U.S.A **64 E3** 34.00N 106.00W
New Milton England **10 D1** 50.45N 1.39W
Newnham England **10 C2** 51.48N 2.27W
New Orleans U.S.A. **65 H2** 30.00N 90.03W
New Pitsligo Scotland **19 G2** 57.35N 2.12W
Newport Essex England **11 F2** 51.58N 0.13E
Newport Hants. England **10 D1** 50.43N 1.18W
Newport Shrops. England **10 C3** 52.47N 2.22W
Newport *d.* Wales **12 E3** 51.33N 3.00W
Newport Newport Wales **12 E3** 51.34N 2.59W
Newport Pem. Wales **12 C4** 52.01N 4.51W
Newport B. Wales **12 C4** 52.03N 4.53W
Newport News U.S.A. **65 K4** 36.59N 76.26W
Newport Pagnell England **10 E3** 52.05N 0.42W
New Providence *i.* The Bahamas **71 I6** 25.03N 77.25W
Newquay England **13 B2** 50.24N 5.06W
New Quay Wales **12 C4** 52.13N 4.22W
New Romney England **11 F1** 50.59N 0.58E
New Ross Rep. of Ire. **20 E2** 52.23N 6.59W
Newry N. Ireland **16 C2** 54.11N 6.20W
Newry Canal N. Ireland **16 C2** 54.15N 6.22W
New Scone Scotland **17 F4** 56.25N 3.25W
New Siberian Is. Russian Fed. **59 Q5** 76.00N 144.00E
New South Wales *d.* Australia **110 D2** 33.45S 147.00E
Newton Abbot England **13 D2** 50.32N 3.37W
Newton Aycliffe England **15 F3** 54.36N 1.34W
Newtonhill Scotland **19 G2** 57.02N 2.08W
Newton-le-Willows England **14 E2** 53.28N 2.38W
Newton Mearns Scotland **16 E3** 55.46N 4.18W
Newtonmore Scotland **19 E2** 57.03N 4.10W
Newton Stewart Scotland **16 E2** 54.57N 4.29W
Newtown Wales **12 D4** 52.31N 3.19W
Newtownabbey N. Ireland **16 D2** 54.40N 5.57W
Newtownards N. Ireland **16 D2** 54.35N 5.42W
Newtown St. Boswells Scotland **17 G3** 55.35N 2.40W
Newtownstewart N. Ireland **16 B2** 54.43N 7.25W
New York U.S.A. **65 L5** 40.40N 73.50W
New York *d.* U.S.A. **65 K5** 43.00N 75.00W
New Zealand Austa. **111 G1** 41.00S 175.00E
Neyriz Iran **95 H4** 29.12N 54.17E
Neyshabur Iran **95 I6** 36.13N 58.49E
Ngaoundéré Cameroon **84 F2** 7.20N 13.35E
Ngorongoro Conservation Area Tanzania **87 B2** 3.00S 35.30E
Nguigmi Niger **84 F3** 14.00N 13.11E
Ngulu *i.* Fed. States of Micronesia **105 J5** 8.30N 137.30E
Nha Trang Vietnam **104 D6** 12.15N 109.10E
Niamey Niger **84 E3** 13.32N 2.05E
Niangara Zaire **85 G2** 3.45N 27.54E
Nias *i.* Indonesia **104 B4** 1.05N 97.30E
Nicaragua C. America **71 H3** 13.00N 85.00W
Nicaragua, L. Nicaragua **71 G3** 11.30N 85.30W
Nice France **44 G3** 43.42N 7.16E
Nicobar Is. India **97 I2** 8.00N 94.00E
Nicosia Cyprus **57 K1** 35.11N 33.23E
Nicoya, G. of Costa Rica **71 H2** 9.30N 85.00W
Nidd *r.* England **15 F3** 54.01N 1.12W
Nidzica Poland **54 G5** 53.22N 20.26E
Niers *r.* Neth. **42 E3** 51.43N 5.56E
Nieuwpoort Belgium **42 B3** 51.08N 2.45E
Niğde Turkey **57 L2** 37.58N 34.42E
Niger Africa **84 E3** 17.00N 10.00E
Niger *r.* Nigeria **84 E2** 4.15N 6.05E
Nigeria Africa **84 E2** 9.00N 9.00E
Nigg B. Scotland **19 E2** 57.42N 4.01W
Niigata Japan **106 C3** 37.58N 139.02E
Nijmegen Neth. **42 E3** 51.50N 5.52E
Nikel' Russian Fed. **43 G5** 69.20N 29.44E
Nikolayevsk-na-Amure Russian Fed. **59 Q3** 53.20N 140.44E
Nikopol' Ukraine **55 N2** 47.34N 34.25E
Niksar Turkey **57 M4** 40.35N 36.59E
Nikšić Yugo. **56 D5** 42.48N 18.56E
Nikumaroro *i.* Kiribati **108 N6** 4.40S 174.32W
Nile *r.* Egypt **94 D5** 31.30N 30.25E
Nilgiri Hills India **96 F3** 11.30N 77.30E
Nîmes France **44 F3** 43.50N 4.21E
Ningbo China **103 M3** 29.54N 121.33E
Ningxia *d.* China **103 J5** 37.00N 106.00E
Ninigo Group *is.* P.N.G. **105 K3** 2.00S 143.00E
Nioro Mali **84 D3** 15.12N 9.35W
Niort France **44 C5** 46.19N 0.27W
Nipigon Canada **63 J2** 49.02N 88.26W
Nipigon, L. Canada **63 J2** 49.50N 88.30W
Niš Yugo. **56 E5** 43.20N 21.54E
Niterói Brazil **77 F2** 22.45S 43.06W
Nith *r.* Scotland **17 F3** 55.00N 3.35W
Nitra Slovakia **54 F3** 48.20N 18.05E
Niue *i.* Cook Is. **108 O5** 19.02S 169.52W
Nivelles Belgium **42 D2** 50.36N 4.20E
Nizamabad India **97 F4** 18.40N 78.05E
Nizhneudinsk Russian Fed. **59 L3** 54.55N 99.00E
Nizhnevartovsk Russian Fed. **58 J4** 60.57N 76.40E
Nizhniy Novgorod Russian Fed. **58 G3** 56.20N 44.00E
Nizhniy Tagil Russian Fed. **58 I3** 58.00N 60.00E
Nizhyn Ukraine **55 L4** 51.03N 31.54E
Nizip Turkey **57 M2** 37.02N 37.47E
Nkongsamba Cameroon **84 E2** 4.59N 9.53E
Nobeoka Japan **106 B2** 32.36N 131.40E
Nogales Mexico **70 B7** 31.20N 111.00W
Nogent-le-Rotrou France **44 D6** 48.19N 0.50E
Nogent-sur-Oise France **42 B1** 49.17N 2.28E
Nogwak-san *mtn.* S. Korea **106 A3** 37.20N 128.50E
Nohfelden Germany **42 G1** 49.35N 7.09E
Noirmoutier, Île de *i.* France **44 B5** 47.00N 2.15W
Nok Kundi Pakistan **95 J4** 28.46N 62.46E
Nome U.S.A. **62 B4** 64.30N 165.30W
Nomoi Is. Fed. States of Micronesia **108 K7** 5.21N 153.42E
Nonthaburi Thailand **104 C6** 13.48N 100.31E
Noord-Brabant *d.* Neth. **42 E3** 51.37N 5.00E
Noord-Holland *d.* Neth. **42 D4** 52.37N 4.50E
Nordaustlandet Norway **58 E6** 80.00N 22.00E
Norden Germany **42 G5** 53.34N 7.13E
Nordhausen Germany **48 E4** 51.31N 10.48E
Nordhorn Germany **42 G4** 52.27N 7.05E
Nordvik Russian Fed. **59 N5** 73.40N 110.50E
Nore *r.* Rep. of Ire. **20 E2** 52.25N 6.58W
Norfolk *d.* England **11 F3** 52.39N 1.00E
Norfolk U.S.A. **65 K4** 36.54N 76.18W
Norfolk Broads *f.* England **11 G3** 52.43N 1.35E
Norfolk I. Pacific Oc. **111 F3** 28.58S 168.03E
Noril'sk Russian Fed. **59 K4** 69.21N 88.02E
Normandy *f.* France **44 C6** 48.50N 0.40W
Normanton Australia **110 D4** 17.40S 141.05E
Norra Storfjället *mtn.* Sweden **43 C4** 65.54N 15.10E
Norrköping Sweden **43 D2** 58.35N 16.10E
Norrtälje Sweden **43 D2** 59.46N 18.43E
Norseman Australia **110 B2** 32.15S 121.47E
Norte, C. Brazil **77 F5** 1.40N 49.55W
North *d.* Yemen **94 F2** 16.00N 44.00E
Northallerton England **15 F3** 54.20N 1.26W
North America 60
North American Basin *f.* Atlantic Oc. **116 G7**
Northampton England **10 E3** 52.14N 0.54W
Northamptonshire *d.* England **10 E3** 52.15N 1.00W
North Ayrshire *d.* Scotland **16 D3** 55.30N 5.00W
North Battleford Canada **62 H3** 52.47N 108.19W
North Bay *town* Canada **63 K2** 46.20N 79.28W
North Berwick Scotland **17 G4** 56.04N 2.43W
North C. New Zealand **111 G2** 34.28S 173.00E
North C. Norway **43 F5** 71.10N 25.45E
North Carolina *d.* U.S.A. **65 K4** 35.30N 79.00W
North Cave England **15 G2** 53.47N 0.39W
North Channel U.K. **16 D2** 55.00N 5.30W
North China Plain *f.* China **90 M6** 34.30N 117.00E
North Dakota *d.* U.S.A. **64 F6** 47.00N 100.00W
North Donets *r.* Ukraine/Russian Fed. **55 O3** 49.08N 37.28E

North Dorset Downs *hills* England **10 C1** 50.46N 2.25W
North Downs *hills* England **11 F2**............51.18N 0.40E
North Dvina *r.* Russian Fed. **58 G4**......64.40N 40.50E
North-Eastern *d.* Kenya **87 C3**............1.00N 40.00E
North East Lincolnshire *d.* England **15 G2** 53.33N 0.10W
Northern Ireland *d.* U.K. **16 C2**............54.40N 6.45W
Northern Mariana Is. Pacific Oc. **105 K7** 15.00N 145.00E
Northern Sporades *is.* Greece **56 F3**......39.00N 24.00E
Northern Territory *d.* Australia **110 C4**....20.00S 133.00E
North Esk *r.* Scotland **19 G1**............56.45N 2.25W
North European Plain *f.* Europe **34 F3**.... 56.00N 27.00E
North Foreland *c.* England **11 G2**......51.23N 1.26E
North Frisian Is. Germany **48 D6**......54.30N 8.00E
North Hykeham England **15 G2**......53.10N 0.36W
North I. New Zealand **111 G2**......39.00S 175.00E
North Korea Asia **103 N6**............40.00N 128.00E
North Lanarkshire *d.* Scotland **17 F3**....55.50N 3.50W
North Lincolnshire *d.* England **15 G2**....53.35N 0.40W
North Pacific Ocean 108 N10............35.00N 170.00E
North Platte U.S.A. **64 F5**............41.09N 100.45W
North Platte *r.* U.S.A. **64 F5**............41.09N 100.55W
North Ronaldsay *i.* Scotland **19 G4**......59.23N 2.26W
North Ronaldsay Firth *est.* Scotland **19 G4** 59.20N 2.25W
North Sea Europe **34 D3**............56.00N 4.00E
North Shields England **15 F4**............55.01N 1.26W
North Somercotes England **15 H2**......53.28N 0.08W
North Sunderland England **15 F4**......55.34N 1.39W
North Tidworth England **10 D2**......51.14N 1.40W
North Tyne *r.* England **15 E3**......54.59N 2.08W
North Uge *r.* Scotland **19 H2**......57.31N 1.48W
North Uist *i.* Scotland **18 B2**......57.35N 7.20W
Northumberland *d.* England **15 E4**......55.12N 2.00W
North Walsham England **11 G3**......52.49N 1.22E
North West C. Australia **108 G4**......21.48S 114.10E
North West Somerset *d.* England **10 C2**....51.20N 2.45W
Northwest Territories *d.* Canada **62 I4** 66.00N 110.00W
Northwich England **15 E2**............53.16N 2.30W
North York Moors *hills* England **15 G3**....54.21N 0.50W
North Yorkshire *d.* England **15 F3**......54.14N 1.14W
Norton England **15 G3**............54.08N 0.47W
Norton Fitzwarren England **13 D3**......51.02N 3.09W
Norton Sound *b.* U.S.A. **62 B4**......63.50N 164.00W
Norway Europe **43 B3**............65.00N 13.00E
Norway House *town* Canada **62 I3**......53.59N 97.50W
Norwegian Sea Europe **34 D4**......66.00N 2.00E
Norwich England **11 G3**............52.38N 1.17E
Nos de Cachi *mtn.* Argentina **76 D2**... 24.50S 66.25W
Noshiro Japan **106 D4**............40.13N 140.06E
Noss, Isle of Scotland **19 Y9**......60.08N 1.01W
Nottingham England **10 D3**............52.57N 1.10W
Nottinghamshire *d.* England **15 F2**......53.10N 1.00W
Nouâdhibou Mauritania **84 C4**......20.54N 17.01W
Nouakchott Mauritania **84 C3**......18.09N 15.58W
Nouméa N. Cal. **111 F3**............22.16S 166.27E
Noup Head Scotland **19 F4**............59.20N 3.04W
Nova Friburgo Brazil **77 F2**......22.16S 42.32W
Nova Iguaçu Brazil **77 F2**......22.45S 43.27W
Nova Kakhovka Ukraine **55 M2**......46.51N 33.26E
Novara Italy **50 C6**............45.27N 8.37E
Nova Scotia *d.* Canada **63 L2**......45.00N 64.00W
Novaya Sibir' *i.* Russian Fed. **59 Q5**....75.20N 148.00E
Novaya Zemlya *i.* Russian Fed. **58 H5**....74.00N 56.00E
Nové Zámky Slovakia **54 F2**............47.59N 18.11E
Novgorod Russian Fed. **58 F3**......58.30N 31.20E
Novi Pazar Yugo. **56 E5**............43.08N 20.28E
Novi Sad Yugo. **56 D6**............45.16N 19.52E
Novodvinsk Russian Fed. **58 G4**......64.25N 40.42E
Novo Hamburgo Brazil **77 E2**......29.37S 51.07W
Novohrad-Volyns'kyy Ukraine **55 J4**......50.34N 27.32E
Novokuznetsk Russian Fed. **58 K3**....53.45N 87.12E
Novomoskovsk Russian Fed. **55 P6**....54.06N 38.15E
Novomoskovs'k Ukraine **55 N3**......48.38N 35.15E
Novorossiysk Russian Fed. **58 F2**......44.44N 37.46E
Novosibirsk Russian Fed. **58 K3**......55.04N 82.55E
Novyy Oskol Russian Fed. **55 O4**......50.46N 37.52E
Nowshera Pakistan **95 L5**......34.01N 71.59E
Nowy Sacz Poland **54 G3**......49.39N 20.40E
Noyabr'sk Russian Fed. **58 J4**......63.10N 76.40E
Noyon France **42 C1**............49.35N 3.00E
Nu'aym *f.* Oman **95 I3**............22.30N 56.30E
Nuba, L. Egypt **94 D4**............22.20N 31.40E
Nuba Mts. Sudan **94 D1**............12.00N 31.00E
Nubian Desert Sudan **85 H4**......21.00N 34.00E
Nuevo Laredo Mexico **70 E6**......27.30N 99.30W
Nuevo León *d.* Mexico **70 E6**......26.00N 99.00W
Nui *i.* Tuvalu **111 G5**............7.12S 177.10E
Nu Jiang *r. see* Salween *r.* China **102**
Nukufetau *i.* Tuvalu **111 G5**......8.00S 178.25E
Nuku Hiva *i.* Marquesas Is. **109 Q6**......8.56S 140.00W
Nukunono *i.* Pacific Oc. **108 N6**......9.10S 171.55W
Nukus Uzbekistan **58 H2**............42.28N 59.07E
Nullarbor Plain *f.* Australia **110 B2**....31.30S 128.00E
Numazu Japan **106 C3**............35.08N 138.50E
Nuneaton England **10 D3**............52.32N 1.29W
Nunivak I. U.S.A. **62 B3**............60.00N 166.30W
Nuoro Italy **50 C4**............40.19N 9.20E
Nuqrah Saudi Arabia **94 F4**......25.35N 41.28E
Nurmes Finland **43 G3**............63.32N 29.10E
Nürnberg Germany **48 E3**......49.27N 11.05E
Nushki Pakistan **95 K4**............29.33N 66.01E
Nuuk Greenland **63 M4**......64.10N 51.40W
Nyahururu Kenya **87 B3**............0.02N 36.24E
Nyala Sudan **85 G3**............12.01N 24.50E
Nyambeni Hills Kenya **87 B3**......0.15N 38.00E
Nyanza *d.* Kenya **87 A2**............0.30S 34.20E
Nyasa, L. Africa **86 C3**............12.00S 34.30E
Nyborg Denmark **43 B1**............55.19N 10.49E
Nybro Sweden **43 C2**............56.44N 15.55E
Nyeri Kenya **87 B2**............0.25S 36.56E
Nyíregyháza Hungary **54 G2**......47.59N 21.43E
Nyiru, Mt. Kenya **87 B3**............2.09N 36.50E
Nykarleby Finland **43 E3**......63.22N 23.30E
Nykøbing Denmark **43 B1**......54.47N 11.53E
Nyköping Sweden **43 D2**............58.45N 17.03E
Nynäshamn Sweden **43 D2**......58.54N 17.55E
Nyurba Russian Fed. **59 N4**......63.18N 118.28E
Nzoia *r.* Kenya **87 A3**............0.03N 33.58E

O

Oadby England **10 D3**............52.37N 1.07W
Oahe, L. U.S.A. **64 F6**............45.45N 100.20W
Oahu *i.* Hawaiian Is. **108 P9**......21.30N 158.00W
Oakengates England **10 C3**......52.42N 2.29W
Oakham England **10 E3**............52.40N 0.43W
Oakland U.S.A. **64 B4**............37.50N 122.15W
Oaxaca Mexico **70 E4**............17.05N 96.41W
Oaxaca *d.* Mexico **70 E4**......17.30N 97.00W
Ob *r.* Russian Fed. **58 I4**......66.50N 69.00E
Ob, G. of Russian Fed. **58 J4**......68.30N 74.00E
Oban Scotland **16 D4**............56.26N 5.28W
Obi *i.* Indonesia **105 H3**......1.45S 127.30E
Óbidos Brazil **77 E4**............1.55S 55.31W
Obihiro Japan **106 D4**......42.55N 143.00E
Obninsk Russian Fed. **55 O6**......55.15N 36.41E
Oboyan' Russian Fed. **55 O4**......51.13N 36.17E
Occidental, Cordillera *mts.* Chile **76 D3** 20.00S 69.00W
Occidental, Cordillera Colombia **74 B7**.... 5.00N 76.15W
Occidental, Cordillera *mts.* Peru **76 C3**...14.00S 74.00W
Ocean Falls *town* Canada **62 F3**......52.24N 127.42W
Ochakiv Ukraine **55 L2**......46.37N 31.33E
Ochil Hills Scotland **17 F4**......56.16N 3.25W
October Revolution *i.* Russian Fed. **59 L5** 79.30N 96.00E
Ódádhahraun *mts.* Iceland **43 Y2**......65.00N 17.30W
Odate Japan **106 D4**......40.16N 140.34E
Ödemiş Turkey **57 I3**......38.12N 28.00E
Odense Denmark **43 B1**......55.24N 10.25E
Oder *r.* Poland/Germany **54 D5**......53.30N 14.36E
Odessa Ukraine **55 L2**......46.30N 30.46E
Odessa U.S.A. **64 F3**......31.50N 102.23W
Odintsovo Russian Fed. **55 O6**......55.38N 37.18E
Odorheiu Secuiesc Romania **55 I2**......46.18N 25.18E
Ofanto *r.* Italy **50 G4**......41.22N 16.12E
Offaly *d.* Rep. of Ire. **20 D3**......53.15N 7.30W
Offenbach am Main Germany **48 D4**...50.06N 8.46E
Offenburg Germany **48 C3**......48.29N 7.57E
Ogaden *f.* Ethiopia **85 I2**......7.50N 45.40E
Ogaki Japan **106 C3**......35.25N 136.36E
Ogasawara-shoto *is.* Japan **108 J9**......27.00N 142.10E
Ogbomoso Nigeria **84 E2**......8.05N 4.11E
Ogden U.S.A. **64 D5**......41.14N 111.59W
Ogilvie *r.* Canada **62 E4**......66.10N 134.10W
Oglio *r.* Italy **50 D6**......45.02N 10.39E
Ogoki *r.* Canada **65 I7**......51.35N 86.00W
Ogooué *r.* Gabon **84 E1**......1.00S 9.05E
Ogulin Croatia **56 B6**......45.17N 15.14E
O'Higgins, L. Chile **75 B2**......48.53S 73.10W
Ohio *d.* U.S.A. **65 J5**......40.00N 83.00W
Ohio *r.* U.S.A. **65 I4**......37.07N 89.10W
Ohrid Macedonia **56 E4**......41.06N 20.48E
Ohrid, L. Albania/Macedonia **56 E4**......41.00N 20.43E
Oich, Loch Scotland **18 E2**......57.04N 4.46W
Oil City U.S.A. **65 K5**......41.26N 79.30W
Oise *r.* France **44 E6**......49.00N 2.10E
Oita Japan **106 B2**......33.15N 131.40E
Oiti *mtn.* Greece **56 F3**......38.48N 22.15E
Ojinaga Mexico **70 D6**......29.35N 104.26W
Ojos del Salado *mtn.* Chile/Argentina **76 D2** 27.05S 68.05W
Okanogan *r.* U.S.A. **64 B6**......47.45N 120.05W
Okavango Delta Botswana **86 B3**......19.30S 23.00E
Okaya Japan **106 C3**......36.03N 138.00E
Okayama Japan **106 B2**......34.40N 133.54E
Okeechobee, L. U.S.A. **65 J2**......27.00N 80.45W
Okefenokee Swamp *f.* U.S.A. **65 J3**....30.40N 82.40W
Okehampton England **13 C2**......50.44N 4.01W
Okha India **96 D5**......22.25N 69.00E
Okha Russian Fed. **59 Q3**......53.35N 142.50E
Okhotsk Russian Fed. **59 Q3**......59.20N 143.15E
Okhotsk, Sea of Russian Fed. **59 Q3**....55.00N 150.00E
Okhtyrka Ukraine **55 N4**......50.19N 34.54E
Okinawa *i.* Japan **103 N3**......26.30N 128.00E
Oki-shoto *is.* Japan **106 B3**......36.10N 133.10E
Oklahoma *d.* U.S.A. **64 G4**......35.00N 97.00W
Oklahoma City U.S.A. **64 G4**......35.28N 97.33W
Oksskolten *mtn.* Norway **43 C4**......66.00N 14.24E
Öland *i.* Sweden **43 D2**......56.50N 16.50E
Olbia Italy **50 C4**......40.55N 9.29E
Old Crow Canada **62 E4**......67.34N 139.43W
Oldenburg Germany **48 D5**......53.08N 8.13E
Oldenzaal Neth. **42 F4**......52.19N 6.55E
Oldham England **15 E2**......53.33N 2.08W
Old Head of Kinsale *c.* Rep. of Ire. **20 C1** 51.37N 8.33W
Old Leake England **15 H2**......53.02N 0.06E
Oldmeldrum Scotland **19 G2**......57.20N 2.20W
Olean U.S.A. **65 K5**......42.05N 78.26W
Olekminsk Russian Fed. **59 N4**......60.25N 120.00E
Olenek Russian Fed. **59 N4**......68.38N 112.15E
Olenek *r.* Russian Fed. **59 O5**......73.00N 120.00E
Oléron, Île d' *i.* France **44 C4**......45.55N 1.16W
Olevs'k Ukraine **55 J4**......51.12N 27.35E
Olinda Brazil **77 G4**......8.00S 34.51W
Oliva, Cordillera de *mts.* Chile/Argentina **76 D2** 29.30S 70.00W
Olney England **10 E3**......52.09N 0.42W
Olomouc Czech Rep. **54 E3**......49.36N 17.16E
Olongapo Phil. **104 G7**......14.52N 120.16E
Oloron France **44 C3**......43.12N 0.35W
Olsztyn Poland **54 G5**......53.48N 20.29E
Olteniţa Romania **54 H6**......44.05N 26.31E
Oltet *r.* Romania **56 G6**......44.13N 24.28E
Olym *r.* Russian Fed. **55 P5**......52.25N 38.05E
Olympus *mtn.* Cyprus **57 K1**......34.55N 32.52E
Olympus *mtn.* Greece **56 F4**......40.04N 22.20E
Omagh N. Ireland **16 B2**......54.35N 7.20W
Omaha U.S.A. **64 G5**......41.15N 96.00W
Oman Asia **95 I4**......22.30N 57.30E
Oman, G. of Asia **95 I4**......25.00N 58.00E
Ombersley England **10 C3**......52.17N 2.14W
Ombrone *r.* Italy **50 E5**......42.40N 11.00E
Omdurman Sudan **85 H3**......15.37N 32.59E
Ommen Neth. **42 F4**......52.32N 6.25E
Omo Nat. Park Ethiopia **87 B4**......6.00N 35.40E
Omono *r.* Japan **106 D4**......39.44N 140.05E
Omsk Russian Fed. **58 J3**......55.00N 73.22E
Omulew *r.* Poland **54 G5**......53.05N 21.32E
Onchan I.o.M. **14 C3**......54.11N 4.27W
Ondjiva Angola **86 A3**......17.03S 15.41E

Onega, L. Russian Fed. **58 F4**......62.00N 35.30E
Onesti Romania **55 J2**......46.14N 26.44E
Ongole India **97 G4**......15.31N 80.04E
Onitsha Nigeria **84 E2**......6.10N 6.47E
Ono-i-Lau *i.* Fiji **108 N4**......19.00S 178.30W
Ontario *d.* Canada **63 J3**......52.00N 86.00W
Ontario, L. N. America **65 K5**......43.40N 78.00W
Ontong Java Atoll Solomon Is. **111 E5**...5.20S 159.30E
Oostende Belgium **42 B3**......51.13N 2.55E
Oosterschelde *est.* Neth. **42 C3**......51.35N 3.57E
Oost-Vlaanderen *d.* Belgium **42 C3**......51.00N 3.45E
Opochka Russian Fed. **43 G2**......56.41N 28.42E
Opole Poland **54 E4**......50.40N 17.56E
Oporto Portugal **46 A4**......41.09N 8.37W
Oradea Romania **54 G2**......47.03N 21.55E
Oran Algeria **84 D5**......35.45N 0.38W
Orange France **44 F4**......44.08N 4.48E
Orange *r.* R.S.A. **86 A2**......28.43S 16.30E
Orange, Cabo *c.* Brazil **74 D7**......4.25N 51.32W
Orangeburg U.S.A. **65 J3**......33.28N 80.53W
Orchila *i.* Venezuela **71 K3**......11.52N 66.10W
Orchy *r.* Scotland **16 E4**......56.26N 5.00W
Ord, Mt. Australia **110 B4**......17.19S 125.30E
Örebro Sweden **43 C2**......59.17N 15.13E
Oregon *d.* U.S.A. **64 B5**......44.00N 120.00W
Orel Russian Fed. **55 O5**......52.58N 36.04E
Ore Mts. Europe **48 F4**......50.30N 12.50E
Orenburg Russian Fed. **58 H3**......51.50N 55.00E
Orford Ness *c.* England **11 G3**......52.05N 1.36E
Orhei Moldova **55 K2**......47.24N 28.50E
Oriental, Cordillera *mts.* Colombia **74 B7** 5.00N 74.30W
Oriental, Cordillera *mts.* Peru/Bolivia **76 C3** 14.00S 70.00W
Orinoco *r.* Venezuela **74 C7**......9.00N 61.30W
Orinoco Delta *f.* Venezuela **74 C7**......9.00N 61.30W
Orissa *d.* India **97 G5**......20.15N 84.00E
Oristano Italy **50 C3**......39.53N 8.36E
Oristano, G. of Med. Sea **50 C3**......39.50N 8.30E
Orivesi *l.* Finland **43 G3**......62.20N 29.30E
Orizaba Mexico **70 E4**......18.51N 97.08W
Orkney *d.* Scotland **19 G3**......59.00N 3.00W
Orkney Is. Scotland **19 F4**......59.00N 3.00W
Orlando U.S.A. **65 J2**......28.33N 81.21W
Orléans France **44 D5**......47.54N 1.54E
Ormoc Phil. **105 G6**......11.01N 124.36E
Ormskirk England **14 E2**......53.35N 2.53W
Orne *r.* France **44 C6**......49.17N 0.10W
Örnsköldsvik Sweden **43 D3**......63.19N 18.45E
Oronsay *i.* Scotland **16 C4**......56.01N 6.14W
Orosei Italy **50 C4**......40.23N 9.40E
Orosei, G. of Med. Sea **50 C4**......40.15N 9.45E
Orrin *r.* Scotland **19 E2**......57.31N 4.28W
Orsha Belarus **55 L6**......54.30N 30.23E
Orsk Russian Fed. **58 H3**......51.13N 58.35E
Orşova Romania **56 F6**......44.42N 22.22E
Oruro Bolivia **76 C2**......18.05S 67.00W
Osaka Japan **106 C2**......34.40N 135.30E
Osa Pen. Costa Rica **71 H2**......8.20N 83.30W
Oshakati Namibia **86 A3**......17.47S 15.30E
Oshawa Canada **63 K2**......43.53N 78.51W
Osizweni R.S.A. **86 C2**......27.45S 30.11E
Ösjön *l.* Sweden **43 C3**......63.48N 15.40E
Oskarshamn Sweden **43 D2**......57.16N 16.25E
Oskil *r. see* Oskil *r.* Russian Fed. **55**
Oskol *r.* Ukraine **55 O3**......49.08N 37.10E
Oslo Norway **43 B2**......59.56N 10.45E
Osmancık Turkey **57 L4**......40.58N 34.50E
Osmaniye Turkey **57 M2**......37.04N 36.15E
Osnabrück Germany **48 D5**......52.17N 8.03E
Osorno Chile **75 B2**......40.35S 73.14W
Osorno Spain **46 C5**......42.24N 4.22W
Oss Neth. **42 E3**......51.46N 5.31E
Ossa *mtn.* Greece **56 F4**......39.47N 22.41E
Ossa, Mt. Australia **110 D1**......41.52S 146.04E
Österdal *r.* Sweden **43 C3**......61.03N 14.30E
Østerdalen *f.* Norway **43 B3**......62.00N 11.00E
Östersund Sweden **43 C3**......63.10N 14.40E
Ostrava Czech Rep. **54 F3**......49.50N 18.15E
Ostrogozhsk Russian Fed. **55 P4**......50.52N 39.03E
Ostrov Russian Fed. **43 G2**......57.22N 28.22E
Ostrów Mazowiecka Poland **54 G5**......52.50N 21.56E
Ostrzeszów Poland **54 F4**......51.25N 17.55E
Osum *r.* Bulgaria **56 G5**......43.41N 24.51E
Osumi-kaikyo *str.* Japan **106 B2**......30.30N 131.00E
Osuna Spain **46 C2**......37.14N 5.06W
Oswestry England **10 B3**......52.52N 3.03W
Otaru Japan **106 D4**......43.14N 140.59E
Otjiwarongo Namibia **86 A2**......20.30S 16.39E
Otley England **15 F2**......53.54N 1.41W
Otranto Italy **50 H4**......40.09N 18.30E
Otranto, Str. of Med. Sea **56 D4**......40.10N 19.00E
Otta Norway **43 B3**......61.46N 9.33E
Ottawa Canada **63 K2**......45.25N 75.43W
Ottawa *r.* Canada **63 K2**......45.23N 73.55W
Ottawa Is. Canada **63 J3**......59.50N 80.00W
Otter *r.* England **13 D2**......50.38N 3.19W
Otterburn *town* England **15 E4**......55.14N 2.10W
Ottery *r.* England **13 C2**......50.39N 4.20W
Ottignies Belgium **42 D2**......50.40N 4.34E
Oturkpo Nigeria **84 E2**......7.16N 8.16E
Ouachita *r.* U.S.A. **65 H3**......31.52N 91.48W
Ouachita Mts. U.S.A. **65 H3**......34.40N 94.30W
Ouagadougou Burkina **84 D3**......12.20N 1.40W
Ouargla Algeria **84 E5**......32.00N 5.16E
Ouarzazate Morocco **84 D5**......30.57N 6.50W
Oudenaarde Belgium **42 C2**......50.50N 3.37E
Ouésso Congo **86 B4**......1.38N 16.03E
Ouezzane Morocco **52 B3**......34.52N 5.35W
Oughter, Lough Rep. of Ire. **20 D4**......54.01N 7.28W
Ouistreham France **44 C6**......49.17N 0.15W
Oujda Morocco **84 D5**......34.41N 1.45W
Oulainen Finland **43 F4**......64.17N 24.50E
Oulton England **11 G3**......52.28N 1.45E
Oulu Finland **43 F4**......65.02N 25.27E
Oulujärvi *l.* Finland **43 F4**......64.30N 27.00E
Oulujoki *r.* Finland **43 F4**......65.02N 25.20E
Oundle England **11 E3**......52.29N 0.29W
Oupeye Belgium **42 E2**......50.42N 5.39E
Ourense Spain **46 B5**......42.20N 7.52W
Ourthe *r.* E.Sussex England **11 F1**......50.46N 0.03E
Ouse *r.* N.Yorks. England **15 G2**......53.41N 0.42W
Outer Hebrides *is.* Scotland **18 B2**......58.00N 7.00W
Outokumpu Finland **43 G3**......62.43N 29.05E
Out Skerries *is.* Scotland **19 Z9**......60.20N 0.45W
Ovamboland *f.* Namibia **86 A3**......17.45S 17.00E

Overijssel *d.* Neth. **42 F4**......52.25N 6.30E
Overton Wales **12 E4**......52.58N 2.56W
Övertorneå Sweden **43 E4**......66.22N 23.40E
Oviedo Spain **46 C5**......43.21N 5.50W
Ovruch Ukraine **55 K4**......51.20N 28.50E
Owando Congo **86 A4**......0.30S 15.48E
Owen Falls Dam Uganda **87 A3**......0.27N 33.10E
Owensboro U.S.A. **65 I4**......37.46N 87.07W
Owen Sound *town* Canada **63 J2**......44.34N 80.56W
Owen Stanley Range *mts.* P.N.G. **110 D5** 9.30S 148.00E
Oxelösund Sweden **43 D2**......58.40N 17.10E
Oxford England **10 D2**......51.45N 1.15W
Oxfordshire *d.* England **10 D2**......51.46N 1.20W
Oxnard U.S.A. **64 C3**......34.12N 119.11W
Oxted England **11 F2**......51.16N 0.01E
Oyama Japan **106 C3**......36.18N 139.48E
Oykel *r.* Scotland **19 E2**......57.52N 4.22W
Ozark Plateau U.S.A. **65 H4**......36.00N 93.35W
Özd Hungary **54 G3**......48.14N 20.18E

P

Paamiut Greenland **63 N4**......62.05N 49.30W
Pabbay *i.* W.Isles Scotland **18 B1**......56.51N 7.35W
Pabbay *i.* W.Isles Scotland **18 B2**......57.46N 7.14W
Pachuca Mexico **70 E5**......20.10N 98.44W
Pacific Ocean 109
Padang Indonesia **104 C3**......0.55S 100.21E
Padangpanjang Indonesia **104 C3**......0.30S 100.26E
Paderborn Germany **48 D4**......51.43N 8.44E
Padiham England **15 E2**......53.49N 2.19W
Padre *i.* U.S.A. **64 G2**......27.00N 97.20W
Padstow England **13 C2**......50.33N 4.57W
Padua Italy **50 D6**......45.27N 11.52E
Pag *i.* Croatia **56 B6**......44.28N 15.00E
Pagadian Phil. **105 G5**......7.50N 123.30E
Pagan *i.* N. Mariana Is. **105 L7**......18.08N 145.46E
Paget, Mt. South Georgia **75 F1**......54.23S 36.45W
Paignton England **13 D2**......50.26N 3.34W
Päijänne *l.* Finland **43 F3**......61.30N 25.30E
Painswick England **10 C2**......51.47N 2.11W
Paisley Scotland **16 E3**......55.50N 4.26W
Pakistan Asia **96 D6**......30.00N 70.00E
Pakokku Myanmar **97 J5**......21.20N 95.10E
Pakxé Laos **104 D7**......15.05N 105.50E
Palana Russian Fed. **59 R3**......59.05N 159.59E
Palau Pacific Oc. **105 I5**......7.00N 134.25E
Palawan *i.* Phil. **104 F5**......9.30N 118.30E
Palembang Indonesia **104 C3**......2.59S 104.50E
Palencia Spain **46 C5**......42.01N 4.34W
Palermo Italy **50 F3**......38.09N 13.22E
Pali India **96 E6**......25.46N 73.20E
Palk Str. India/Sri Lanka **97 F2**......10.00N 79.40E
Pallisa Uganda **87 A3**......1.08N 33.43E
Palma de Mallorca Spain **46 G3**......39.36N 2.39E
Palmas, C. Liberia **84 D2**......4.30N 7.55W
Palmer Land *f.* Antarctica **112**......74.00S 66.00W
Palmerston I. Cook Is. **108 O5**......18.04S 163.10W
Palmerston North New Zealand **111 G1** 40.21S 175.37E
Palmi Italy **50 F3**......38.22N 15.50E
Palmira Colombia **74 B7**......3.33N 76.17W
Palmyra Syria **94 E5**......34.36N 38.15E
Palmyra I. Pacific Oc. **108 O7**......5.52N 162.05W
Palopo Indonesia **104 G3**......3.01S 120.12E
Palos, Cabo de *c.* Spain **46 E2**......37.38N 0.41W
Palu Indonesia **104 F3**......0.54S 119.52E
Pamiers France **44 D3**......43.07N 1.36E
Pamirs *mts.* Tajikistan **102 C5**......37.50N 73.30E
Pampa U.S.A. **64 F4**......35.32N 100.58W
Pampas *f.* Argentina **75 C3**......35.00S 63.00W
Pamplona Spain **46 E5**......42.49N 1.39W
Panaji India **96 E4**......15.29N 73.50E
Panama C. America **71 H2**......9.00N 80.00W
Panamá, G. of Panama **71 I2**......8.30N 79.00W
Panama Canal Panama **71 I2**......9.21N 79.54W
Panama City Panama **71 I2**......8.57N 79.30W
Panama City U.S.A. **65 I3**......30.10N 85.41W
Panay *i.* Phil. **105 G6**......11.10N 122.30E
Panevėžys Lithuania **55 I6**......55.44N 24.24E
Pangani Tanzania **87 B2**......5.26S 38.58E
Pangkalanbuun Indonesia **104 E3**......2.43S 111.38E
Pangkalpinang Indonesia **104 D3**......2.05S 106.09E
Pangnirtung Canada **63 L4**......66.05N 65.45W
Panjgur Pakistan **95 J4**......26.58N 64.06E
Pantelleria *i.* Italy **50 E2**......36.48N 12.00E
Paola Italy **50 G3**......39.21N 16.03E
Papa Stour *i.* Scotland **19 Y9**......60.20N 1.42W
Papa Westray *i.* Scotland **19 G4**......59.22N 2.54W
Papenburg Germany **42 G5**......53.05N 7.25E
Paphos Cyprus **57 K1**......34.45N 32.25E
Papua, G. of P.N.G. **110 D5**......8.50S 145.00E
Papua New Guinea Austa. **110 D5**......6.00S 148.00E
Par England **13 C2**......50.21N 4.43W
Pará *d.* Brazil **77 E4**......4.00S 53.00W
Paracel Is. S. China Sea **104 E7**......16.20N 112.00E
Paragua *r.* Bolivia **77 D3**......13.28S 61.50W
Paraguai *r. see* Paraguay *r.* Brazil **77**
Paraguay *r.* Argentina **77 E2**......27.30S 58.50W
Paraguay S. America **77 E2**......23.00S 58.00W
Paraíba *d.* Brazil **77 G4**......7.30S 36.30W
Paraíba *r.* Brazil **77 F2**......21.45S 41.10W
Parakow Benin **84 E2**......9.23N 2.40E
Paramaribo Suriname **74 D7**......5.52N 55.14W
Paraná Argentina **77 D1**......31.45S 60.30W
Paraná *r.* Argentina **75 D3**......34.00S 58.30W
Paraná *d.* Brazil **77 E3**......12.30S 48.10W
Paranaguá Brazil **77 F2**......25.32S 48.36W
Paranaíba Brazil **77 E3**......20.00S 51.00W
Paranapanema *r.* Brazil **77 E2**......22.30S 53.03W
Paranapiacaba, Serra *mts.* Brazil **77 F2**...24.30S 49.15W
Parczew Poland **54 H4**......51.39N 22.54E
Pardo *r.* Bahia Brazil **77 G3**......15.39N 38.38W
Pardo *r.* Mato Grosso do Sul Brazil **77 E2** 21.56S 52.07W
Pardubice Czech Rep. **54 D4**......50.03N 15.45E
Parecis, Serra dos *mts.* Brazil **77 E3**......13.30S 60.00W
Parepare Indonesia **104 F3**......4.03S 119.40E
Paria Pen. Venezuela **71 L3**......10.45N 62.30W
Pariñas, Punta *c.* Peru **76 B4**......4.45S 81.22W

Parintins Brazil 77 E4..............2.36S 56.44W
Paris France 44 E6..............48.52N 2.20E
Parma Italy 50 D5..............44.48N 10.18E
Parnaíba Brazil 77 F4..............2.58S 41.46W
Parnaíba r. Brazil 77 F4..............3.00S 42.00W
Parnassos mtn. Greece 56 F3..............38.33N 22.35E
Pärnu Estonia 43 F2..............58.28N 24.30E
Paropamisus Afghan. 95 J5..............35.00N 63.00E
Paros i. Greece 56 G2..............37.04N 25.11E
Parrett r. England 13 E3..............51.10N 3.00W
Parry, C. Canada 62 F5..............70.10N 124.33W
Parry, C. Greenland 63 K5..............76.50N 71.00W
Parry Is. Canada 62 H5..............76.00N 106.00W
Parsęta r. Poland 54 D6..............54.12N 15.33E
Parthenay France 44 C5..............46.39N 0.14W
Partry Mts. Rep. of Ire. 20 B3..............53.40N 9.30W
Paru r. Brazil 77 E4..............1.33S 52.38W
Pasadena U.S.A. 64 C3..............34.10N 118.09W
Pasado, C. Ecuador 76 B4..............0.22S 80.30W
Pashkovskiy Russian Fed. 57 N6..............45.01N 39.06E
Pasig Phil. 104 G6..............14.30N 120.54E
Pasni Pakistan 95 J4..............25.16N 63.28E
Passau Germany 48 F3..............48.35N 13.28E
Passero, C. Italy 50 F2..............36.40N 15.08E
Passo Fundo Brazil 77 E2..............28.16S 52.20W
Pastavy Belarus 55 J6..............55.07N 26.50E
Pastaza r. Peru 76 C4..............4.50S 76.25W
Pasto Colombia 74 B7..............1.12N 77.17W
Patagonia f. Argentina 75 C2..............45.00S 68.00W
Patchway England 10 C2..............51.30N 2.34W
Pate i. Kenya 87 A2..............2.07S 41.08E
Paterson U.S.A. 65 L5..............40.55N 74.10W
Pathfinder Resr. U.S.A. 64 E5..............42.25N 106.55W
Patna India 97 H6..............25.37N 85.12E
Patos, Lagoa dos l. Brazil 77 E1..............31.00S 51.10W
Patos de Minas Brazil 77 F3..............18.35S 46.32W
Patras Greece 56 E3..............38.15N 21.45E
Patras, G. of Med. Sea 56 E3..............38.15N 21.35E
Patrington England 15 G2..............53.41N 0.02W
Pau France 44 C3..............43.18N 0.22E
Paulo Afonso Brazil 77 G4..............9.25S 38.15W
Pavia Italy 50 C6..............45.10N 9.10E
Pavlodar Kazakhstan 102 D8..............52.21N 76.59E
Pavlohrad Ukraine 55 N3..............48.34N 35.50E
Pavlovskaya Russian Fed. 53 K6..............46.18N 39.48E
Pazardzhik Bulgaria 56 G5..............42.12N 24.20E
Peace r. Canada 62 G3..............59.00N 111.26W
Peacehaven England 11 E1..............50.45N 0.01W
Peace River town Canada 62 G3..............56.15N 117.18W
Peale, Mt. U.S.A. 64 E4..............38.26N 109.14W
Pearl r. U.S.A. 65 I3..............30.15N 89.25W
Peć Yugo. 56 E5..............42.40N 20.17E
Pechora r. Russian Fed. 58 H4..............68.10N 54.00E
Pechora G. Russian Fed. 58 H4..............69.00N 56.00E
Pecos U.S.A. 64 F3..............31.25N 103.30W
Pecos r. U.S.A. 64 F2..............29.45N 101.25W
Pécs Hungary 54 F2..............46.05N 18.14E
Pedro Juan Caballero Paraguay 77 E2..............22.30S 55.44W
Peebles Scotland 17 F3..............55.39N 3.12W
Peel r. Canada 62 E4..............68.13N 135.00W
Peel I.o.M. 14 C3..............54.14N 4.42W
Pegasus B. New Zealand 111 G1..............43.15S 173.00E
Pegu Myanmar 97 J4..............17.18N 96.31E
Pegwell B. England 11 G2..............51.18N 1.25E
Peiphólsfjöll mtn. Iceland 43 X2..............65.40N 22.25W
Peipus, L. Europe 43 F2..............58.30N 27.30E
Pekalongan Indonesia 104 D2..............6.54S 109.37E
Pelat, Mont mtn. France 44 G4..............44.17N 6.41E
Peleng i. Indonesia 105 G3..............1.30S 123.10E
Pelleluhu Is. P.N.G. 105 K3..............1.09S 144.23E
Pello Finland 43 E4..............66.47N 23.55E
Pelotas Brazil 77 E1..............31.45S 52.20W
Pemba Mozambique 86 D3..............13.02S 40.30E
Pemba Channel Tanzania 87 B2..............5.00S 39.20E
Pemba I. Tanzania 87 B1..............5.10S 39.45E
Pembrey Wales 12 C3..............51.42N 4.16W
Pembroke Wales 12 C3..............51.41N 4.57W
Pembroke Dock Wales 12 C3..............51.42N 4.56W
Pembrokeshire d. Wales 12 B3..............51.50N 5.00W
Pembury England 11 F2..............51.07N 0.19E
Peña Nevada, Cerro mtn. Mexico 70 E5..............23.49N 99.51W
Peñaranda de Bracamonte Spain 46 C4..............40.54N 5.13W
Penarth Wales 13 D3..............51.26N 3.11W
Penas, Golfo de g. Chile 75 B2..............47.20S 75.00W
Pendine Wales 12 C3..............51.44N 4.33W
Pendlebury England 15 E2..............53.32N 2.21W
Pendle Hill England 15 E2..............53.52N 2.18W
Penicuik Scotland 17 F3..............55.49N 3.13W
Peninsular Malaysia d. Malaysia 104 C4..............5.00N 102.00E
Penitente, Serra do mts. Brazil 77 F4..............9.00S 46.15W
Penkridge England 10 C3..............54.44N 2.07W
Pennsylvania d. U.S.A. 65 K5..............41.00N 78.00W
Penny Icecap f. Canada 63 L4..............67.10N 66.50W
Penrhyn Mawr c. Wales 12 C4..............52.51N 4.46W
Penrith England 14 E3..............54.40N 2.45W
Penryn England 13 B2..............50.10N 5.07W
Pensacola U.S.A. 65 I3..............30.30N 87.12W
Penticton Canada 64 C6..............49.29N 119.38W
Pentire Pt. England 13 B2..............50.35N 4.55W
Pentland Firth str. Scotland 19 F3..............58.40N 3.00W
Pentland Hills Scotland 17 F3..............55.50N 3.20W
Pentland Skerries Scotland 19 G3..............58.41N 2.55W
Penygadair mtn. Wales 12 D4..............52.40N 3.55W
Pen-y-Ghent mtn. England 15 E3..............54.10N 2.14W
Penza Russian Fed. 58 G3..............53.11N 45.00E
Penzance England 13 B2..............50.07N 5.32W
Penzhina, G. of Russian Fed. 59 S4..............61.00N 163.00E
Peoria U.S.A. 65 I5..............40.43N 89.38W
Pereira Colombia 74 B7..............4.47N 75.46W
Périgueux France 44 D4..............45.12N 0.44E
Perija, Sierra de mts. Venezuela 71 J2..............10.00N 73.00W
Perito Moreno Argentina 75 B2..............46.35S 71.00W
Perlas Pt. c. Nicaragua 71 H3..............12.23N 83.30W
Perm Russian Fed. 58 H3..............58.01N 56.10E
Pernambuco d. Brazil 77 G4..............8.00S 39.00W
Pernik Bulgaria 56 F5..............42.35N 23.03E
Péronne France 42 B1..............49.56N 2.57E
Perpignan France 44 E3..............42.42N 2.54E
Perranporth England 13 B2..............50.21N 5.09W
Pershore England 10 C3..............52.07N 2.04W
Perth Australia 110 A2..............31.58S 115.49E
Perth Scotland 17 F4..............56.24N 3.28W
Perth and Kinross d. Scotland 17 F4..............56.30N 3.40W
Peru S. America 76 C4..............10.00S 75.00W

Perugia Italy 50 E5..............43.06N 12.24E
Pervouralsk Russian Fed. 58 H3..............56.59N 59.58E
Pesaro Italy 50 E5..............43.54N 12.54E
Pescara Italy 50 F5..............42.27N 14.13E
Pescara r. Italy 50 F5..............42.28N 14.13E
Peshawar Pakistan 96 E7..............34.01N 71.40E
Peshkopi Albania 56 E4..............41.41N 20.25E
Peski Karakumy f. Turkmenistan 95 I6..............37.45N 60.00E
Peterborough Canada 63 K2..............44.18N 78.19W
Peterborough England 11 E3..............52.35N 0.14W
Peterhead Scotland 19 H2..............57.30N 1.46W
Peterlee England 15 F3..............54.45N 1.18W
Petersfield England 10 E2..............51.00N 0.56W
Petersville U.S.A. 62 C4..............62.30N 150.48W
Petrich Bulgaria 56 F4..............41.25N 23.13E
Petrolina Brazil 77 F4..............9.22S 40.30W
Petropavlovsk-Kamchatskiy Russian Fed. 59 R3..............53.03N 158.43E
Petroșani Romania 56 F6..............45.25N 23.22E
Petrozavodsk Russian Fed. 58 F4..............61.46N 34.19E
Petworth England 11 E1..............50.59N 0.37W
Pevensey England 11 F1..............50.49N 0.20E
Pewsey England 10 D2..............51.20N 1.46W
Pforzheim Germany 48 D3..............48.53N 8.41E
Phan Thiêt Vietnam 104 D6..............10.56N 108.06E
Phatthalung Thailand 104 C5..............7.38N 100.05E
Phet Buri Thailand 104 B6..............13.01N 99.55E
Philadelphia U.S.A. 65 K5..............39.55N 75.10W
Philippeville Belgium 42 D2..............50.12N 4.32E
Philippines Asia 105 G6..............13.00N 123.00E
Philippine Trench f. Pacific Oc. 117 P6............
Phnom Penh Cambodia 104 C6..............11.35N 104.55E
Phoenix U.S.A. 64 D3..............33.30N 111.55W
Phoenix Is. Kiribati 108 N6..............4.00S 172.00W
Phôngsali Laos 104 C8..............21.40N 102.06E
Phuket Thailand 104 B5..............8.00N 98.28E
Piacenza Italy 50 C6..............45.03N 9.42E
Pianosa i. Italy 50 D5..............42.35N 10.05E
Pian-Upe Game Res. Uganda 87 A3..............1.30N 34.40E
Piatra-Neamț Romania 55 J2..............46.56N 26.22E
Piauí d. Brazil 77 F4..............7.45S 42.30W
Piave r. Italy 50 E6..............45.33N 12.45E
Picardie f. France 44 D6..............49.47N 2.00E
Pickering England 15 G3..............54.15N 0.46W
Piedras Negras Mexico 70 D6..............28.40N 100.32W
Pieksämäki Finland 43 F3..............62.18N 27.10E
Pielinen l. Finland 43 G3..............63.20N 29.50E
Pierre U.S.A. 64 F5..............44.23N 100.20W
Pietermaritzburg R.S.A. 86 C2..............29.36S 30.24E
Pietersburg R.S.A. 86 B2..............23.54S 29.23E
Pihlajavesi l. Finland 43 G3..............61.45N 29.10E
Piła Poland 54 E5..............53.09N 16.44E
Pilar Paraguay 77 E2..............26.52S 58.23W
Pilcomayo r. Argentina/Paraguay 77 E2............25.15S 57.43W
Pilica r. Poland 54 G4..............51.52N 21.17E
Pimperne England 10 C1..............50.53N 2.09W
Pinang i. Malaysia 104 C5..............5.30N 100.10E
Pinar del Río Cuba 71 H5..............22.24N 83.42W
Pindaré r. Brazil 77 F4..............3.10S 44.40W
Pindus Mts. Albania/Greece 56 E4..............39.40N 21.00E
Pine Bluff town U.S.A. 65 H3..............34.13N 92.00W
Pinega Russian Fed. 58 G4..............64.42N 43.28E
Pineios r. Greece 56 F3..............39.51N 22.37E
Pinerolo Italy 50 A6..............44.53N 7.21E
Pines, I. of Cuba 71 H5..............21.40N 82.40W
Pingdingshan China 103 K4..............33.38N 113.30E
Pingxiang Guangxi China 103 J2..............22.05N 106.46E
Pingxiang Jiangxi China 103 K3..............27.36N 113.48E
Pinsk Belarus 55 J5..............52.08N 26.01E
Piombino Italy 50 D5..............42.56N 10.30E
Piotrków Trybunalski Poland 54 F4..............51.25N 19.42E
Pipa Dingzi mtn. China 106 A4..............44.00N 128.10E
Piracicaba Brazil 77 F2..............22.20S 47.40W
Piraeus Greece 56 F2..............37.56N 23.38E
Pirot Yugo. 56 F5..............43.10N 22.32E
Pisa Italy 50 D5..............43.43N 10.24E
Pisco Peru 76 C3..............13.46S 76.12W
Písek Czech Rep. 54 D3..............49.19N 14.10E
Pisuerga r. Spain 46 C4..............41.35N 5.40W
Pisz Poland 54 G5..............53.38N 21.49E
Pitcairn I. Pacific Oc. 109 R4..............25.04S 130.06W
Piteå Sweden 43 E4..............65.19N 21.30E
Pitești Romania 56 G6..............44.52N 24.51E
Pitlochry Scotland 19 F1..............56.44N 3.47W
Pittsburgh U.S.A. 65 K5..............40.26N 79.58W
Piura Peru 76 B4..............5.15S 80.38W
Plasencia Spain 46 B4..............40.02N 6.05W
Platí, C. Greece 56 F4..............40.26N 23.59E
Platinum U.S.A. 62 B3..............59.00N 161.50W
Plauen Germany 48 F4..............50.29N 12.08E
Playa Blanca Canary Is. 46 Z2..............28.51N 13.49W
Plenty, B. of New Zealand 111 G2..............37.40S 176.50E
Pleven Bulgaria 56 G5..............43.25N 24.39E
Pljevlja Yugo. 56 D5..............43.22N 19.22E
Płock Poland 54 F5..............52.33N 19.43E
Ploiești Romania 56 H6..............44.57N 26.02E
Plomb du Cantal mtn. France 44 E4..............45.04N 2.45E
Plovdiv Bulgaria 56 G5..............42.09N 24.45E
Plunge Lithuania 54 G6..............55.52N 21.49E
Plymouth England 13 C2..............50.23N 4.09W
Plympton England 13 C2..............50.24N 4.02W
Plymstock England 13 C2..............50.21N 4.05W
Plynlimon mtn. Wales 12 D4..............52.28N 3.47W
Plzeň Czech Rep. 54 C3..............49.45N 13.22E
Po r. Italy 50 E6..............44.51N 12.30E
Pobeda, Mt. Russian Fed. 59 Q4..............65.20N 145.50E
Pocatello U.S.A. 64 D5..............42.53N 112.26W
Pochep Russian Fed. 55 M5..............52.55N 33.29E
Pocklington England 15 G2..............53.56N 0.48W
Poços de Caldas Brazil 77 F2..............21.48S 46.33W
Podgorica Yugo. 56 D5..............42.30N 19.16E
Podol'sk Russian Fed. 55 O6..............55.23N 37.32E
P'ohang S. Korea 106 A3..............36.00N 129.26E
Pohnpei i. Fed. States of Micronesia 108 K7..............6.55N 158.15E
Pointe-à-Pitre Guadeloupe 71 L4..............16.14N 61.32W
Pointe Noire town Congo 84 F1..............4.46S 11.53E
Poitiers France 44 D5..............46.35N 0.20E
Pokaran India 96 E6..............26.55N 71.55E
Poland Europe 54 F5..............52.30N 19.00E
Polatlı Turkey 57 K3..............39.34N 32.08E
Polatsk Belarus 55 J6..............55.30N 28.43E
Polegate England 11 F1..............50.49N 0.15E
Pol-e-Khomrī Afghan. 95 K6..............35.55N 68.45E

Policastro, G. of Med. Sea 50 F3..............40.00N 15.35E
Pollino, Monte mtn. Italy 50 G3..............39.53N 16.11E
Polperro England 13 C2..............50.19N 4.31W
Poltava Ukraine 55 N3..............49.35N 34.35E
Pombal Portugal 46 A3..............39.55N 8.38W
Ponce Puerto Rico 71 K4..............18.00N 66.40W
Pondicherry India 97 F3..............11.59N 79.50E
Pond Inlet town Canada 63 K5..............72.40N 77.59W
Ponferrada Spain 46 B5..............42.32N 6.31W
Ponta do Sol Cape Verde 84 B3..............17.12N 25.03W
Ponta Grossa Brazil 77 E2..............25.07S 50.09W
Pontardawe Wales 12 D3..............51.44N 3.51W
Pontefract England 15 F2..............53.42N 1.19W
Ponteland England 15 F4..............55.03N 1.43W
Pontevedra Spain 46 A5..............42.25N 8.39W
Pontianak Indonesia 104 D3..............0.05S 109.16E
Pontine Is. Italy 50 E4..............40.56N 12.58E
Pontine Mts. Turkey 57 M4..............40.32N 38.00E
Pontoise France 44 E6..............49.03N 2.05E
Pont-Ste.-Maxence France 42 B1..............49.18N 2.37E
Pontycymer Wales 12 D3..............51.36N 3.35W
Pontypool Wales 12 D3..............51.42N 3.01W
Pontypridd Wales 12 D3..............51.36N 3.21W
Poole England 10 D1..............50.42N 1.58W
Poole B. England 10 D1..............50.40N 1.55W
Pooley Bridge town England 14 E3..............54.37N 2.49W
Poopó, L. Bolivia 76 D3..............19.00S 67.00W
Popayán Colombia 74 B7..............2.27N 76.32W
Poplar Bluff town U.S.A. 65 H4..............36.40N 90.25W
Popocatépetl mtn. Mexico 70 E4..............19.02N 98.38W
Poprad Slovakia 54 G3..............49.03N 20.18E
Porbandar India 96 D5..............21.40N 69.40E
Porcupine r. U.S.A. 62 D4..............66.25N 145.20W
Pori Finland 43 E3..............61.28N 21.45E
Porlock England 13 D3..............51.14N 3.36W
Poronaysk Russian Fed. 59 Q2..............49.13N 142.55E
Porsangen est. Norway 43 F5..............70.30N 25.45E
Porsgrunn Norway 43 B2..............59.10N 9.40E
Porsuk r. Turkey 57 J3..............39.41N 31.56E
Portadown N. Ireland 16 C2..............54.25N 6.27W
Portaferry N. Ireland 16 D2..............54.23N 5.33W
Portage la Prairie town Canada 62 I2..............49.58N 98.20W
Portalegre Portugal 46 B3..............39.17N 7.25W
Port Angeles U.S.A. 64 B6..............48.06N 123.26W
Port Arthur U.S.A. 65 H2..............29.55N 93.56W
Port Askaig Scotland 16 C3..............55.51N 6.07W
Port Augusta Australia 110 C2..............32.30S 137.46E
Port-au-Prince Haiti 71 J4..............18.33N 72.20W
Portavogie N. Ireland 16 D2..............54.26N 5.27W
Port Blair India 97 I3..............11.40N 92.30E
Port-de-Paix Haiti 71 J4..............19.57N 72.50W
Port Elizabeth R.S.A. 86 B1..............33.58S 25.36E
Port Ellen Scotland 16 C3..............55.38N 6.12W
Port Erin I.o.M. 14 C3..............54.05N 4.45W
Port-Gentil Gabon 84 E1..............0.40S 8.50E
Port Glasgow Scotland 16 E3..............55.56N 4.40W
Port Harcourt Nigeria 84 E2..............4.43N 7.05E
Port Hawkesbury Canada 65 N6..............45.37N 61.21W
Port Hedland Australia 110 A3..............20.24S 118.36E
Porthleven England 13 B2..............50.05N 5.20W
Port Hope Simpson Canada 63 M3..............52.18N 55.51W
Portimão Portugal 46 A2..............37.08N 8.32W
Port Isaac B. England 13 C2..............50.36N 4.50W
Portishead England 10 C2..............51.29N 2.46W
Portknockie Scotland 19 G2..............57.42N 2.52W
Portland Australia 110 D2..............38.21S 141.38E
Portland Maine U.S.A. 65 L5..............43.41N 70.18W
Portland Oreg. U.S.A. 64 B6..............45.32N 122.40W
Portlaoise Rep. of Ire. 20 D3..............53.03N 7.20W
Portlethen Scotland 19 G2..............57.03N 2.07W
Port Lincoln Australia 110 C2..............34.43S 135.49E
Port Macquarie Australia 110 E2..............31.28S 152.25E
Port Moresby P.N.G. 110 D5..............9.30S 147.07E
Portnahaven Scotland 16 C3..............55.41N 6.31W
Pôrto Alegre Brazil 77 E1..............30.03S 51.10W
Porto-Novo Benin 84 E2..............6.30N 2.47E
Porto Torres Italy 50 C4..............40.49N 8.24E
Porto-Vecchio France 44 H2..............41.35N 9.16E
Pôrto Velho Brazil 76 D4..............8.45S 63.54W
Portoviejo Ecuador 76 B4..............1.07S 80.28W
Port Pirie Australia 110 C2..............33.11S 138.01E
Portree Scotland 18 C2..............57.24N 6.12W
Portrush N. Ireland 16 C3..............55.12N 6.40W
Port Said Egypt 94 D5..............31.17N 32.18E
Portsmouth England 10 D1..............50.48N 1.06W
Portsoy Scotland 19 G2..............57.42N 2.42W
Portstewart N. Ireland 16 C3..............55.10N 6.43W
Port Sudan Sudan 85 H3..............19.39N 37.01E
Port Talbot Wales 12 D3..............51.35N 3.48W
Portugal Europe 46 A3..............39.30N 8.05W
Portumna Rep. of Ire. 20 C3..............53.06N 8.13W
Port-Vila Vanuatu 111 F4..............17.44S 168.19E
Port William Scotland 16 E2..............54.46N 4.35W
Posadas Argentina 77 E2..............27.25S 55.48W
Poso Indonesia 104 G3..............1.23S 120.45E
Potenza Italy 50 F4..............40.40N 15.47E
Potosí Bolivia 76 D3..............19.34S 65.45W
Potsdam Germany 48 F5..............52.24N 13.04E
Poulton-le-Fylde England 14 E2..............53.51N 3.00W
Pouthisat Cambodia 104 C6..............12.33N 103.55E
Powell, L. U.S.A. 64 D4..............37.30N 110.45W
Powick England 10 C3..............52.10N 2.14W
Powys d. Wales 12 D4..............52.26N 3.26W
Poyang Hu l. China 103 L3..............29.05N 116.20E
Požarevac Yugo. 56 E6..............44.38N 21.12E
Poza Rica Mexico 70 E5..............20.34N 97.26W
Poznań Poland 54 E5..............52.25N 16.53E
Pozoblanco Spain 46 C3..............38.23N 4.51W
Prabumulih Indonesia 104 C3..............3.29S 104.14E
Prachuap Khiri Khan Thailand 104 B6..............11.50N 99.49E
Prague Czech Rep. 54 D4..............50.05N 14.25E
Praia Cape Verde 84 B3..............14.53N 23.30W
Prapat Indonesia 104 B4..............2.42N 98.56E
Prato Italy 50 D5..............43.52N 11.06E
Prawle Pt. England 13 D2..............50.13N 3.43W
Pregel r. Russian Fed. 54 G6..............54.41N 20.22E
Preparis I. Myanmar 97 I3..............14.40N 93.40E
Prescott U.S.A. 64 D3..............34.34N 112.28W
Presidente Prudente Brazil 77 E2..............22.09S 51.24W
Prespa, L. Europe 56 E4..............40.53N 21.02E

Presque Isle town U.S.A. 65 M6..............46.42N 68.01W
Prestatyn Wales 12 D5..............53.20N 3.24W
Presteigne Wales 12 D4..............52.17N 3.00W
Preston Dorset England 10 C1..............50.39N 2.25W
Preston Lancs. England 14 E2..............53.46N 2.42W
Prestonpans Scotland 17 G3..............55.57N 3.00W
Prestwick Scotland 16 E3..............55.30N 4.36W
Pretoria R.S.A. 86 B2..............25.45S 28.12E
Preveza Greece 56 E3..............38.58N 20.43E
Pribilof Is. U.S.A. 62 A3..............57.00N 170.00W
Prievidza Slovakia 54 F3..............48.47N 18.35E
Prilep Macedonia 56 E4..............41.20N 21.32E
Prince Albert Canada 62 H3..............53.13N 105.45W
Prince Alfred, C. Canada 62 F5..............74.30N 125.00W
Prince Charles I. Canada 63 K4..............67.50N 76.00W
Prince Edward Is. Indian Oc. 117 K3..............47.00S 37.00E
Prince Edward Island d. Canada 63 L2..............46.15N 63.10W
Prince George Canada 62 F3..............53.55N 122.49W
Prince of Wales I. Australia 110 D4..............10.55S 142.05E
Prince of Wales I. Canada 63 I5..............73.00N 99.00W
Prince of Wales I. U.S.A. 62 E3..............55.00N 132.30W
Prince Patrick I. Canada 62 G5..............77.00N 120.00W
Prince Rupert Canada 62 E3..............54.09N 130.20W
Princes Risborough England 10 E2..............51.43N 0.50W
Príncipe i. São Tomé & Príncipe 84 E2..............1.37N 7.27E
Pripet r. Europe 55 L4..............51.08N 30.30E
Pripet Marshes f. Belarus 55 J5..............52.15N 29.00E
Pristina Yugo. 56 E5..............42.39N 21.10E
Privas France 44 F4..............44.44N 4.36E
Prizren Yugo. 56 E5..............42.13N 20.42E
Probolinggo Indonesia 104 E2..............7.45S 113.09E
Probus England 13 C2..............50.17N 4.57W
Providence U.S.A. 65 L5..............41.50N 71.30W
Providence, C. New Zealand 111 F1..............46.01S 166.28E
Providencia, I. de Colombia 71 H3..............13.21N 81.22W
Provins France 44 E6..............48.34N 3.18E
Provo U.S.A. 64 D5..............40.15N 111.40W
Prudhoe Bay town U.S.A. 62 D5..............70.20N 148.25W
Prüm Germany 42 F2..............50.12N 6.25E
Pruszków Poland 54 G5..............52.11N 20.48E
Prut r. Europe 55 K1..............45.29N 28.14E
Pruzhany Belarus 55 I5..............52.23N 24.28E
Prydz B. Antarctica 112..............68.30S 74.00E
Pryluky Ukraine 55 M4..............50.35N 32.24E
Przemyśl Poland 54 H3..............49.48N 22.48E
Psara i. Greece 56 G3..............38.34N 25.35E
Psel r. Ukraine/Russian Fed. 55 M3..............49.00N 33.30E
Pskov Russian Fed. 58 E3..............57.48N 28.00E
Ptsich r. Belarus 55 K5..............52.09N 28.52E
Pucallpa Peru 76 C4..............8.21S 74.33E
Pudsey England 15 F2..............53.47N 1.40W
Puebla Mexico 70 E4..............19.03N 98.10W
Puebla d. Mexico 70 E4..............18.30N 98.00W
Pueblo U.S.A. 64 F4..............38.17N 104.38W
Puente-Genil Spain 46 C2..............37.24N 4.46W
Puerto de la Cruz Canary Is. 46 X2..............28.24N 16.33W
Puerto del Rosario Canary Is. 46 Z2..............28.29N 13.52W
Puertollano Spain 46 C3..............38.41N 4.07W
Puerto Maldonado Peru 76 D3..............12.37S 69.11W
Puerto Montt Chile 75 B2..............41.28S 73.00W
Puerto Natales Chile 75 B1..............51.41S 72.15W
Puerto Peñasco Mexico 70 B7..............31.20N 113.35W
Puerto Princesa Phil. 104 F5..............9.46N 118.45E
Puerto Rico C. America 71 K4..............18.20N 66.30W
Pula Croatia 56 A6..............44.52N 13.53E
Pulborough England 11 E1..............50.58N 0.30W
Pułtusk Poland 54 G5..............52.42N 21.02E
Pune India 96 E4..............18.34N 73.58E
Punjab d. India 96 F7..............30.30N 75.15E
Punta Arenas town Chile 75 B1..............53.10S 70.56W
Puntjak Jaya mtn. Indonesia 105 J3..............4.00S 137.15E
Pur r. Russian Fed. 58 J4..............67.30N 75.30E
Purari r. P.N.G. 110 D5..............7.50S 145.01E
Puri India 97 H4..............19.49N 85.54E
Purmerend Neth. 42 D4..............52.30N 4.56E
Purus r. Brazil 76 D4..............3.15S 61.30W
Pusan S. Korea 103 N5..............35.05N 129.02E
Puting, Tanjung c. Indonesia 104 E3..............3.35S 111.52E
Puttalam Sri Lanka 97 F2..............8.02N 79.50E
Putumayo r. Brazil 76 D4..............3.00S 67.30W
Puvurnituq Canada 63 K3..............60.10N 77.20W
Puy de Dôme mtn. France 44 E4..............45.46N 2.56E
Pwllheli Wales 12 C4..............52.53N 4.25W
Pyaozero, Ozero Russian Fed. 43 G4..............66.00N 31.00E
Pyapon Myanmar 97 J4..............16.15N 95.40E
Pyasina r. Russian Fed. 59 K5..............73.10N 84.55E
Pyè Myanmar 97 J4..............18.50N 95.14E
Pyhä r. Finland 43 F4..............64.30N 24.20E
Pyhäselkä l. Finland 43 G3..............62.25N 29.55E
Pyinmana Myanmar 97 J4..............19.45N 96.12E
Pyle Wales 13 D3..............51.32N 3.42W
Pyongyang N. Korea 103 N5..............39.00N 125.47E
Pyramid L. U.S.A. 64 C5..............40.00N 119.35W
Pyrenees mts. France/Spain 46 F5..............42.40N 0.30E
Pyrgos Greece 56 E2..............37.42N 21.27E
Pyryatyn Ukraine 55 M4..............50.14N 32.31E

Q

Qaanaaq Greenland 63 L5..............77.30N 69.29W
Qalat Afghan. 95 K5..............32.07N 66.54E
Qamdo China 102 H4..............31.11N 97.18E
Qasigiannguit Greenland 63 M4..............68.50N 51.00W
Qatar Asia 95 H4..............25.20N 51.10E
Qattâra Depression f. Egypt 94 C4..............30.00N 27.30E
Qayen Iran 95 I5..............33.44N 59.07E
Qazvīn Iran 95 G6..............36.16N 50.00E
Qena Egypt 94 D4..............26.08N 32.42E
Qeshm Iran 95 I4..............26.58N 56.17E
Qiemo China 102 F5..............38.08N 85.33E
Qilian Shan mts. China 102 H5..............38.30N 99.20E
Qingdao China 103 M5..............36.04N 120.22E
Qinghai d. China 103 I5..............36.40N 100.00E
Qinghai Hu l. China 102 H5..............36.15N 100.00E
Qingjiang China 103 L4..............33.30N 119.15E
Qinhuangdao China 103 L5..............39.55N 119.37E
Qinzhou China 103 J2..............21.58N 108.34E
Qiqihar China 103 M7..............47.23N 124.00E
Qom Iran 95 H5..............34.40N 50.57E
Qomishēh Iran 95 H5..............32.01N 51.55E
Quang Ngai Vietnam 104 D7..............15.09N 108.50E
Quang Tri Vietnam 104 D7..............16.46N 107.11E
Quantock Hills England 13 D3..............51.06N 3.12W

Quanzhou China **103 L2** 24.57N 118.36E
Quchan Iran **95 I6** 37.04N 58.29E
Québec Canada **63 K2** 46.50N 71.15W
Québec *d.* Canada **63 K3** 51.00N 70.00W
Queenborough England **11 F2** 51.24N 0.46E
Queen Charlotte Is. Canada **62 E3** 53.00N 132.30W
Queen Charlotte Sd. Canada **62 F3** 51.00N 129.00W
Queen Elizabeth Is. Canada **63 I5** 78.30N 99.00W
Queen Mary Land Antarctica **112** 72.00S 100.00E
Queen Maud G. Canada **62 H4** 68.30N 100.00W
Queen Maud Land *f.* Antarctica **112** 74.00S 20.00E
Queensland *d.* Australia **110 D3** 23.30S 144.00E
Quelimane Mozambique **86 C3** 17.53S 36.51E
Querétaro Mexico **70 D5** 20.38N 100.23W
Querétaro *d.* Mexico **70 D5** 21.03N 100.00W
Quetta Pakistan **96 D7** 30.15N 67.00E
Quezaltenango Guatemala **70 F3** 14.50N 91.30W
Quezon City Phil. **104 G6** 14.39N 121.01E
Quibdó Colombia **71 I2** 5.40N 76.38W
Quilon India **96 F2** 8.53N 76.38E
Quimper France **44 A5** 48.00N 4.06W
Quincy U.S.A. **65 H4** 39.55N 91.22W
Qui Nhon Vietnam **104 D6** 13.47N 109.11E
Quintana Roo *d.* Mexico **70 G4** 19.00N 88.00W
Quito Ecuador **76 C4** 0.14S 78.30W
Quoich, Loch Scotland **18 D2** 57.04N 5.15W
Quoile *r.* N. Ireland **16 D2** 54.20N 5.42W
Quseir Egypt **94 D4** 26.04N 34.15E
Quzhou China **103 L3** 28.57N 118.52E

R

Raahe Finland **43 F4** 64.42N 24.30E
Raalte Neth. **42 F4** 52.22N 6.17E
Raasay *i.* Scotland **18 C2** 57.25N 6.02W
Raasay, Sd. of Scotland **18 C2** 57.25N 6.05W
Raas Kaambooni *c.* Somalia **87 C2** 1.36S 41.36E
Raba Indonesia **104 F2** 8.27S 118.45E
Rabat Morocco **84 D5** 34.02N 6.51W
Rabigh Saudi Arabia **94 E3** 22.48N 39.01E
Rach Gia Vietnam **104 D6** 10.02N 105.05E
Radom Poland **54 G4** 51.26N 21.10E
Radomsko Poland **54 F4** 51.05N 19.25E
Radstock England **10 C2** 51.17N 2.25W
Rafḥa Saudi Arabia **94 F4** 29.36N 43.32E
Rafsanjan Iran **95 I5** 30.24N 56.00E
Raglan Wales **12 E3** 51.46N 2.51W
Ragusa Italy **50 F2** 36.56N 14.44E
Rahimyar Khan Pakistan **96 E6** 28.25N 70.18E
Raichur India **96 F4** 16.15N 77.20E
Rainier, Mt. U.S.A. **64 B6** 46.52N 121.45W
Raipur India **97 G5** 21.16N 81.42E
Raivavae *i.* Pacific Oc. **109 Q4** 23.52S 147.40W
Rajahmundry India **97 G4** 17.01N 81.52E
Rajanpur Pakistan **96 E6** 29.06N 70.19E
Rajapalaiyam India **96 F2** 9.26N 77.36E
Rajasthan *d.* India **96 E6** 27.00N 74.00E
Rajkot India **96 E5** 22.18N 70.53E
Rakhiv Ukraine **55 I3** 48.02N 24.10E
Rakitnoye Russian Fed. **55 N4** 50.52N 35.51E
Rakvere Estonia **43 F2** 59.22N 26.28E
Raleigh U.S.A. **65 K4** 35.46N 78.39W
Rame Head England **13 C2** 50.18N 4.13W
Ramhormoz Iran **95 G5** 31.14N 49.37E
Ramlat Dahm *f.* Yemen **94 F2** 17.00N 45.00E
Râmnica Vâlcea Romania **56 G6** 45.06N 24.22E
Ramsbottom England **15 E2** 53.38N 2.20W
Ramsey England **11 E3** 52.27N 0.06W
Ramsey I.o.M. **14 C3** 54.19N 4.23W
Ramsey B. I.o.M. **14 C3** 54.20N 4.20W
Ramsey I. Wales **12 B3** 51.53N 5.21W
Ramsgate England **11 G2** 51.20N 1.25E
Ramu Kenya **87 C3** 3.55N 41.09E
Rancagua Chile **75 B3** 34.10S 70.45W
Ranchi India **97 H5** 23.22N 85.20E
Randalstown N. Ireland **16 C2** 54.45N 6.20W
Randers Denmark **43 B2** 56.28N 10.03E
Rangiroa *i.* Pacific Oc. **109 Q5** 15.00S 147.40W
Rangpur Bangla. **97 H6** 25.45N 89.15E
Rankin Inlet *town* Canada **63 I4** 62.52N 92.00W
Rannoch, Loch Scotland **19 E1** 56.41N 4.20W
Rannoch Moor *f.* Scotland **16 E4** 56.38N 4.40W
Ranong Thailand **104 B5** 9.58N 98.35E
Rantauprapat Indonesia **104 B4** 2.05N 99.46E
Raoul *i.* Pacific Oc. **108 N4** 29.15S 177.55W
Rapa *i.* Pacific Oc. **109 Q4** 27.35S 144.20W
Rapallo Italy **50 C6** 44.20N 9.14E
Raphoe Rep. of Ire. **16 B2** 54.52N 7.36W
Rapid City U.S.A. **64 F5** 44.06N 103.14W
Rarotonga *i.* Cook Is. **108 P4** 21.14S 159.46W
Ra's al Hadd *c.* Oman **95 I3** 22.32N 59.49E
Ra's al Hilal *c.* Libya **53 H3** 33.00N 22.10E
Ras Dashan *mtn.* Ethiopia **85 H3** 13.20N 38.10E
Ra's Fartak *c.* Yemen **95 H2** 15.38N 52.15E
Rasht Iran **95 G6** 37.18N 49.38E
Ra's Madrakah *c.* Oman **95 I2** 19.00N 57.50E
Ras Muhammad *c.* Egypt **53 J2** 27.42N 34.13E
Ras Tannurah Saudi Arabia **95 H4** 26.40N 50.05E
Rat Buri Thailand **104 B6** 13.30N 99.50E
Rathdrum Rep. of Ire. **20 E2** 52.55N 6.14W
Rathenow Germany **48 F5** 52.37N 12.21E
Rathfriland N. Ireland **16 C2** 54.14N 6.10W
Rathkeale Rep. of Ire. **20 C2** 52.32N 8.56W
Rathlin I. N. Ireland **16 C3** 55.18N 6.12W
Rath Luirc Rep. of Ire. **20 C2** 52.20N 8.40W
Raton U.S.A. **64 F4** 36.54N 104.27W
Rattray Head Scotland **19 H2** 57.37N 1.50W
Rättvik Sweden **43 C3** 60.56N 15.10E
Rauma Finland **43 E3** 61.09N 21.30E
Raunds England **11 E3** 52.21N 0.33W
Ravenna Italy **50 E6** 44.25N 12.12E
Ravensthorpe Australia **110 B2** 33.35S 120.02E
Rawaki *i.* Kiribati **108 N6** 3.43S 170.43W
Rawalpindi Pakistan **96 E7** 33.40N 73.08E
Rawicz Poland **54 E4** 51.37N 16.52E
Rawlins U.S.A. **64 E5** 41.46N 107.16W
Rawson Argentina **75 C2** 43.15S 65.53W
Rawtenstall England **15 E2** 53.42N 2.18W
Rayleigh England **11 F2** 51.36N 0.36E
Razgrad Bulgaria **56 H5** 43.32N 26.30E
Ré, Île de *i.* France **44 C5** 46.10N 1.26W
Reading England **10 E2** 51.27N 0.57W
Rebiana Sand Sea *f.* Libya **94 B3** 24.00N 22.00E
Reboly Russian Fed. **43 G3** 63.50N 30.49E
Rechytsa Belarus **55 L5** 52.21N 30.24E
Recife Brazil **77 G4** 8.06S 34.53W
Reconquista Argentina **77 E2** 29.08S 59.38W
Red *r.* U.S.A. **65 H3** 31.10N 91.35W
Red Bluff U.S.A. **64 B5** 40.11N 122.16W
Redcar England **15 F3** 54.37N 1.04W
Redcar and Cleveland *d.* England **15 G3** 54.35N 1.00W
Red Deer Canada **62 G3** 52.15N 113.48W
Redding U.S.A. **64 B5** 40.35N 122.24W
Redditch England **10 D3** 52.18N 1.57W
Redhill England **11 E2** 51.14N 0.11W
Red Lake *town* Canada **63 I3** 50.59N 93.40W
Red Lakes U.S.A. **65 H6** 48.00N 95.00W
Redruth England **13 B2** 50.14N 5.14W
Red Sea Africa/Asia **85 H4** 20.00N 39.00E
Red Wharf B. Wales **12 C5** 53.20N 4.10W
Ree, Lough Rep. of Ire. **20 D3** 53.31N 7.58W
Regensburg Germany **48 F3** 49.01N 12.07E
Reggane Algeria **84 E4** 26.30N 0.30E
Reggio Italy **50 D6** 44.40N 10.37E
Reggio di Calabria Italy **50 F3** 38.07N 15.38E
Regina Canada **62 H3** 50.30N 104.38W
Reigate England **11 E2** 51.14N 0.13W
Reims France **44 F6** 49.15N 4.02E
Reindeer L. Canada **62 H3** 57.00N 102.20W
Reinosa Spain **46 C5** 43.01N 4.09W
Reliance Canada **62 H4** 62.45N 109.08W
Relizane Algeria **52 D4** 35.45N 0.33E
Rena Norway **43 B3** 61.06N 11.20E
Renfrewshire *d.* Scotland **16 E3** 55.50N 4.30W
Reni Moldova **55 K1** 45.28N 28.17E
Rennell *i.* Solomon Is. **111 F4** 11.45S 16.00E
Rennes France **44 C6** 48.06N 1.40W
Reno *r.* Italy **50 E6** 44.36N 12.17E
Reno U.S.A. **64 C4** 39.32N 119.49W
Republic of Ireland Europe **20 D3** 53.00N 8.00W
Republic of South Africa Africa **86 B1** 30.00S 27.00E
Repulse Bay *town* Canada **63 J4** 66.35N 86.20W
Resistencia Argentina **77 E2** 27.28S 59.00W
Reşiţa Romania **56 E6** 45.17N 21.53E
Resolute Canada **63 I5** 74.40N 95.00W
Resolution I. Canada **63 L4** 61.30N 65.00W
Retford England **15 G2** 53.19N 0.55W
Rethel France **42 D1** 49.31N 4.22E
Rethymno Greece **56 G1** 35.22N 24.29E
Reus Spain **46 F4** 41.10N 1.06E
Reutlingen Germany **48 D3** 48.30N 9.13E
Revillagigedo Is. Mexico **70 B4** 19.00N 111.00W
Rewa India **97 G5** 24.32N 81.18E
Reykjavík Iceland **43 X2** 64.09N 21.58W
Reynosa Mexico **70 E6** 26.09N 97.10W
Rezekne Latvia **43 F2** 56.30N 27.22E
Rhayader Wales **12 D4** 52.19N 3.30W
Rheine Germany **42 G4** 52.17N 7.26E
Rhine *r.* Europe **34 D3** 51.53N 6.03E
Rhode Island *d.* U.S.A. **65 L5** 41.30N 71.30W
Rhodes *i.* Greece **57 I2** 36.12N 28.00E
Rhodope Mts. Bulgaria **56 G4** 41.35N 24.35E
Rhondda Wales **12 D3** 51.39N 3.30W
Rhondda Cynon Taff *d.* Wales **12 D3** 51.38N 3.25W
Rhône *r.* France **44 F3** 43.25N 4.45E
Rhosllanerchrugog Wales **12 D5** 53.03N 3.04W
Rhyl Wales **12 D5** 53.19N 3.29W
Riau Is. Indonesia **104 C4** 0.50N 104.00E
Ribble *r.* England **14 E2** 53.45N 2.44W
Ribe Denmark **43 B1** 55.19N 8.47E
Ribeira *r.* Brazil **77 F2** 24.44S 47.31W
Ribeirão Prêto Brazil **77 F2** 21.09S 47.48W
Riberalta Bolivia **76 D3** 10.59S 66.06W
Richmond England **15 F3** 54.24N 1.43W
Richmond U.S.A. **65 K4** 37.34N 77.27W
Rifstangi *c.* Iceland **43 Y2** 66.32N 16.10W
Rift Valley *d.* Kenya **87 B2** 1.05N 35.45E
Rift Valley *f.* Kenya **87 B3** 2.00N 35.30E
Riga Latvia **43 F2** 56.53N 24.08E
Riga, G. of Latvia **43 E2** 57.30N 23.50E
Rigside Scotland **17 F3** 55.35N 3.46W
Riihimäki Finland **43 F3** 60.45N 24.45E
Rijeka Croatia **56 B6** 45.20N 14.25E
Rimini Italy **50 E6** 44.01N 12.34E
Rimouski Canada **63 L2** 48.27N 68.32W
Rimsdale, Loch Scotland **19 E3** 58.18N 4.10W
Ringkøbing Denmark **43 B2** 56.06N 8.15E
Ringsted Denmark **54 B6** 55.27N 11.49E
Ringvassøy *i.* Norway **43 D5** 70.00N 19.00E
Ringwood England **10 D1** 50.50N 1.48W
Riobamba Ecuador **76 C4** 1.44S 78.40W
Rio Branco Brazil **76 D3** 10.00S 67.49W
Río Cuarto *town* Argentina **75 C3** 33.08S 64.20W
Rio de Janeiro Brazil **77 F2** 22.50S 43.17W
Rio de Janeiro *d.* Brazil **77 F2** 22.00S 42.30W
Rio Gallegos Argentina **75 C1** 51.35S 69.15W
Rio Grande *town* Brazil **77 E1** 32.03S 52.18W
Rio Grande *r.* N. America **64 G2** 25.55N 97.08W
Rio Grande *r.* Nicaragua **71 H3** 12.48N 83.30W
Rio Grande do Norte *d.* Brazil **77 G4** 6.00S 36.30W
Rio Grande do Sul *d.* Brazil **77 E2** 30.00S 53.30W
Ríohacha Colombia **71 J3** 11.34N 72.58W
Rio Verde *town* Brazil **77 E3** 17.50S 50.55W
Ripley England **15 F2** 53.03N 1.24W
Ripon England **15 F3** 54.08N 1.31W
Risca Wales **12 D3** 51.36N 3.06W
Rivera Uruguay **77 E1** 30.54S 55.31W
Rivière-du-Loup *town* Canada **63 L2** 47.50N 69.32W
Rivne Ukraine **55 J4** 50.39N 26.10E
Riyadh Saudi Arabia **95 G3** 24.39N 46.44E
Rize Turkey **57 O4** 41.03N 40.31E
Roadford Resr. England **13 C2** 50.42N 4.14W
Roanne France **44 F5** 46.02N 4.05E
Roanoke U.S.A. **65 K4** 37.15N 79.58W
Roanoke *r.* U.S.A. **65 K4** 36.00N 76.35W
Robertsfors Sweden **43 E4** 64.12N 20.50E
Roberval Canada **63 K2** 48.31N 72.16W
Roca, Cabo da *c.* Portugal **46 A3** 38.40N 9.31W
Rocha Uruguay **75 D3** 34.30S 54.22W
Rochdale England **15 E2** 53.36N 2.10W
Rochefort Belgium **42 E2** 50.10N 5.13E
Rochefort France **44 C4** 45.57N 0.58W
Rochester England **11 F2** 51.22N 0.30E
Rochester U.S.A. **65 K5** 43.12N 77.37W
Rochford England **11 F2** 51.36N 0.43E
Rockford U.S.A. **65 I5** 42.16N 89.06W
Rockhampton Australia **110 E3** 23.22S 150.32E
Rockingham Forest *f.* England **11 E3** 52.30N 0.30W
Rock Springs U.S.A. **64 E5** 41.35N 109.13W
Rocky Mts. N. America **60 I6** 42.30N 109.30W
Rodel Scotland **18 C2** 57.47N 6.58W
Rodez France **44 E4** 44.21N 2.34E
Rodos *town* Greece **57 I2** 36.24N 28.15E
Roe *r.* N. Ireland **16 C3** 55.06N 7.00W
Roermond Neth. **42 E3** 51.12N 6.00E
Roeselare Belgium **42 C2** 50.57N 3.06E
Rogaguado, Lago *l.* Bolivia **76 D3** 13.00S 65.40W
Rokiškis Lithuania **43 F1** 55.59N 25.32E
Rolla U.S.A. **65 H4** 37.56N 91.55W
Roma *i.* Indonesia **105 H2** 7.45S 127.20E
Romain, C. U.S.A. **65 K3** 33.01N 79.23W
Romania Europe **53 H6** 46.30N 24.00E
Rombas France **42 F1** 49.15N 6.10E
Rome Italy **50 E4** 41.54N 12.29E
Romford England **11 F2** 51.35N 0.11E
Romney Marsh *f.* England **11 F2** 51.03N 0.55E
Romny Ukraine **55 M4** 50.45N 33.30E
Romsey England **10 D1** 51.00N 1.29W
Rona *i.* Scotland **18 D2** 57.33N 5.59W
Ronas Hill Scotland **19 Y9** 60.32N 1.26W
Ronda Spain **46 C2** 36.45N 5.10W
Rondônia *d.* Brazil **76 D3** 12.10S 62.30W
Rondonópolis Brazil **77 E3** 16.29S 54.37W
Rønne Denmark **43 C1** 55.07N 14.43E
Ronneby Sweden **54 D6** 56.12N 15.18E
Ronse Belgium **42 C2** 50.45N 3.36E
Roosendaal Neth. **42 D3** 51.32N 4.28E
Roosevelt, Mt. Canada **62 F3** 58.26N 125.20W
Roosevelt I. Antarctica **112** 79.00S 161.00W
Roquefort France **44 C4** 44.02N 0.19W
Roraima *d.* Brazil **77 D5** 2.00N 62.00W
Roraima, Mt. Guyana **74 C7** 5.11N 60.44W
Røros Norway **43 B3** 62.35N 11.23E
Rosa, Monte *mtn.* Italy/Switz. **44 G4** 45.56N 7.51E
Rosario Argentina **75 C3** 33.00S 60.40W
Roscoff France **44 A6** 48.44N 4.00W
Roscommon Rep. of Ire. **20 C3** 53.38N 8.13W
Roscommon *d.* Rep. of Ire. **20 C3** 53.38N 8.11W
Roscrea Rep. of Ire. **20 D2** 52.57N 7.49W
Roseau Dominica **71 L4** 15.18N 61.23W
Roseburg U.S.A. **64 B5** 43.13N 123.21W
Rosenheim Germany **48 F2** 47.51N 12.09E
Roskilde Denmark **54 C6** 55.39N 12.05E
Roslavl' Russian Fed. **55 M5** 53.55N 32.53E
Rossel I. P.N.G. **110 E4** 11.27S 154.05E
Ross Ice Shelf Antarctica **112** 82.00S 170.00W
Rossington England **15 F2** 53.29N 1.01W
Rosslare Harbour Rep. of Ire. **20 E2** 52.17N 6.23W
Rosso Mauritania **84 C3** 16.29N 15.53W
Ross of Mull *pen.* Scotland **16 C4** 56.19N 6.10W
Ross-on-Wye England **10 C2** 51.55N 2.36W
Ross Sea Antarctica **112** 73.00S 170.00W
Røssvatnet *l.* Norway **43 C4** 65.50N 14.00E
Rostock Germany **48 F6** 54.06N 12.09E
Rostov-na-Donu Russian Fed. **58 F2** 47.15N 39.45E
Rota *i.* N. Mariana Is. **105 L6** 14.10N 145.15E
Rothbury England **15 F4** 55.19N 1.54W
Rother *r.* England **11 E1** 50.57N 0.32W
Rotherham England **15 F2** 53.26N 1.21W
Rothes Scotland **19 F2** 57.31N 3.14W
Rothesay Scotland **16 D3** 55.50N 5.03W
Rothwell England **10 E3** 52.25N 0.48W
Roti *i.* Indonesia **105 G1** 10.30S 123.10E
Rotterdam Neth. **42 D3** 51.55N 4.29E
Rotuma *i.* Fiji **111 G4** 11.00S 176.00E
Roubaix France **44 E7** 50.42N 3.10E
Rouen France **44 D6** 49.26N 1.05E
Round Hill England **15 F3** 54.24N 1.03W
Round Mt. Australia **110 E2** 30.26S 152.15E
Rousay *i.* Scotland **19 F4** 59.10N 3.02W
Rovaniemi Finland **43 F4** 66.29N 25.40E
Royale, Isle U.S.A. **65 I6** 48.00N 88.45W
Royal Leamington Spa England **10 D3** 52.18N 1.32W
Royal Tunbridge Wells England **11 F2** 51.07N 0.16E
Royan France **44 C4** 45.37N 1.01W
Roye France **42 B1** 49.42N 2.48E
Royston England **11 E3** 52.03N 0.01W
Royton England **15 E2** 53.34N 2.08W
Rozdil'na Ukraine **55 L2** 46.50N 30.02E
Ruabon Wales **12 D4** 52.59N 3.03W
Rub'al Khali *des.* Saudi Arabia **95 H3** 20.20N 52.30E
Rubha Coigeach *c.* Scotland **18 D3** 58.06N 5.25W
Rubha Hunish *c.* Scotland **18 C2** 57.42N 6.21W
Rubha Reidh *c.* Scotland **18 D2** 57.51N 5.49W
Rubtsovsk Russian Fed. **58 K3** 51.29N 81.10E
Rudnaya Pristan' Russian Fed. **106 C4** 43.46N 135.14E
Rudnya Russian Fed. **55 L6** 54.55N 31.07E
Rudnyy Kazakhstan **58 I3** 53.00N 63.05E
Rufiji *r.* Tanzania **86 C4** 8.02S 39.17E
Rugby England **10 D3** 52.23N 1.16W
Rugby U.S.A. **64 G6** 48.24N 99.59W
Rugeley England **10 D3** 52.47N 1.56W
Rügen *i.* Germany **48 F6** 54.30N 13.30E
Ruhr *r.* Germany **48 C4** 51.27N 6.41E
Rukwa, L. Tanzania **86 C4** 8.00S 32.20E
Rum *i.* Scotland **18 C1** 57.00N 6.20W
Ruma Yugo. **56 D6** 44.59N 19.51E
Rum Cay *i.* The Bahamas **71 J5** 23.41N 74.53W
Runcorn England **14 E2** 53.20N 2.44W
Rundu Namibia **86 A3** 17.52S 19.49E
Ruoqiang China **102 F5** 39.00N 88.00E
Rurutu *i.* Pacific Oc. **108 P4** 22.25S 151.20W
Ruse Bulgaria **56 G5** 43.50N 25.59E
Rushden England **11 E3** 52.17N 0.36W
Russian Federation Europe/Asia **58 J4** 62.00N 80.00E
Ruteng Indonesia **104 G2** 8.35S 120.28E
Ruthin Wales **12 D5** 53.07N 3.18W
Rutland Water *l.* England **10 E3** 52.39N 0.40W
Rutog China **102 D4** 33.30N 79.40E
Ruza Russian Fed. **55 O6** 55.40N 36.12E
Rvdsar Iran **95 H6** 37.12N 50.00E
Rwanda Africa **86 B4** 2.00S 30.00E
Ryan, Loch Scotland **16 D2** 54.56N 5.02W
Ryazan' Russian Fed. **55 P6** 54.37N 39.43E
Ryazhsk Russian Fed. **55 Q5** 53.40N 40.07E
Rybinsk Russian Fed. **58 F3** 58.01N 38.52E
Rybinsk Resr. Russian Fed. **58 F3** 58.30N 38.25E
Rybnik Poland **54 F4** 50.06N 18.32E
Ryde England **10 D1** 50.44N 1.09W
Rye England **11 F1** 50.57N 0.46E
Rye *r.* England **15 G3** 54.10N 0.42W
Rye B. England **11 F1** 50.53N 0.48E
Ryotsu Japan **106 C3** 38.06N 138.28E
Ryukyu Is. Japan **103 N3** 26.00N 126.00E
Rzeszów Poland **54 H4** 50.04N 22.00E

S

Saale *r.* Germany **48 E4** 51.58N 11.53E
Saarbrücken Germany **48 C3** 49.15N 6.58E
Saaremaa *i.* Estonia **43 E2** 58.30N 22.30E
Saarlouis Germany **42 F1** 49.21N 6.45E
Šabac Yugo. **56 D6** 44.45N 19.41E
Sabadell Spain **46 G4** 41.33N 2.07E
Sabah *d.* Malaysia **104 F5** 5.00N 117.00E
Sabana, Archipiélago de Cuba **71 H5** 23.30N 80.00W
Sabha Libya **84 F4** 27.04N 14.25E
Sabinas Mexico **70 D6** 27.51N 101.10W
Sabkhat al Hayshah *f.* Libya **53 G3** 31.30N 15.15E
Sable, C. Canada **63 L2** 43.30N 65.50W
Sable, C. U.S.A. **65 J2** 25.00N 81.20W
Sable I. Canada **63 M2** 44.00N 60.00W
Şabya Saudi Arabia **94 F2** 17.09N 42.37E
Sabzevar Iran **95 I6** 36.13N 57.38E
Sachs Harbour Canada **62 F5** 72.00N 124.30W
Sacramento U.S.A. **64 B4** 38.32N 121.30W
Sacramento Mts. U.S.A. **64 E3** 33.10N 105.50W
Sado *r.* Portugal **46 A3** 38.29N 8.55W
Sadoga-shima *i.* Japan **106 C3** 38.00N 138.20E
Säffle Sweden **43 C2** 59.08N 12.55E
Saffron Walden England **11 F3** 52.02N 0.15E
Safi Morocco **84 D5** 32.20N 9.17W
Safonovo Russian Fed. **55 M6** 55.08N 33.16E
Sagar India **97 F5** 23.50N 78.44E
Sagunto Spain **46 E3** 39.40N 0.17W
Sahara *des.* Africa **84 F3** 24.00N 12.00E
Saharan Atlas *mts.* Algeria **84 E5** 34.20N 2.00E
Sa'idabad Iran **95 I4** 29.28N 55.43E
Saidpur Bangla. **97 H6** 25.48N 89.00E
Saimaa *l.* Finland **43 F3** 61.20N 28.00E
St. Abb's Head Scotland **17 G3** 55.54N 2.07W
St. Agnes England **13 B2** 50.18N 5.13W
St. Agnes *i.* England **13 A1** 49.53N 6.20W
St. Albans England **11 E2** 51.46N 0.21W
St. Alban's Head England **10 C1** 50.35N 2.04W
St.-Amand-les-Eaux France **42 C2** 50.27N 3.26E
St.-Amand-Montrond *town* France **44 E5** 46.43N 2.29E
St. Andrews Scotland **17 G4** 56.20N 2.48W
St. Anne Channel Is. **13 Z9** 49.43N 2.12W
St. Ann's Head Wales **12 B3** 51.41N 5.11W
St. Anthony Canada **63 M3** 51.24N 55.37W
St. Asaph Wales **12 D5** 53.16N 3.26W
St. Augustine U.S.A. **65 J2** 29.54N 81.19W
St. Austell England **13 C2** 50.20N 4.48W
St. Austell B. England **13 C2** 50.16N 4.43W
St. Barthélémy *i.* Leeward Is. **71 L4** 17.55N 62.50W
St. Bees England **14 D3** 54.29N 3.36W
St. Bees Head England **14 D3** 54.31N 3.39W
St. Brelade Channel Is. **13 Z8** 49.12N 2.13W
St. Brides B. Wales **12 B3** 51.48N 5.03W
St.-Brieuc France **44 B6** 48.31N 2.45W
St. Catharines Canada **65 K5** 43.10N 79.15W
St. Catherine's Pt. England **10 D1** 50.34N 1.18W
St. Clears Wales **12 C3** 51.48N 4.30W
St. Cloud U.S.A. **65 H6** 45.34N 94.10W
St. Columb Major England **13 C2** 50.26N 4.56W
St. Croix *r.* U.S.A. **65 H5** 44.40N 92.42W
St. Croix *i.* U.S.V.Is. **71 L4** 17.45N 64.35W
St. David's Wales **12 B3** 51.54N 5.16W
St. David's Head Wales **12 B3** 51.55N 5.19W
St.-Dié France **44 G6** 48.17N 6.57E
St.-Dizier France **44 F6** 48.38N 4.58E
Saintes France **44 C4** 45.44N 0.38W
St.-Étienne France **44 F4** 45.26N 4.26E
Saintfield N. Ireland **16 D2** 54.28N 5.50W
St. Gallen Switz. **44 H5** 47.25N 9.23E
St.-Gaudens France **44 D3** 43.07N 0.44E
St. George's Grenada **71 L3** 12.04N 61.44W
St. George's Channel U.K./Rep. of Ire. **20 E1** 52.00N 6.00W
St. Germans England **13 C2** 50.24N 4.18W
St. Govan's Head Wales **12 C3** 51.36N 4.55W
St. Helena *i.* Atlantic Oc. **116 I5** 16.00S 6.00W
St. Helena B. R.S.A. **86 A1** 32.35S 18.00E
St. Helens England **14 E2** 53.28N 2.43W
St. Helens, Mt. U.S.A. **64 B6** 46.12N 122.11W
St. Helier Channel Is. **13 Z8** 49.12N 2.07W
St. Ives Cambs. England **11 E3** 52.20N 0.05W
St. Ives Cornwall England **13 B2** 50.13N 5.29W
St. Ives B. England **13 B2** 50.14N 5.26W
St.-Jean, L. Canada **65 L6** 48.35N 72.00W
St. John Canada **63 L2** 45.16N 66.03W
St. John *r.* Canada **63 L2** 45.30N 66.05W
St. John Channel Is. **13 Z8** 49.15N 2.08W
St. John *i.* U.S.V. Is. **71 K4** 18.21N 64.48W
St. John's Antigua **71 L4** 17.07N 61.51W
St. John's Canada **63 M2** 47.34N 52.41W
St. John's Pt. N. Ireland **16 D2** 54.13N 5.39W
St. Jordi, G. of Spain **46 F4** 40.50N 1.10E
St. Joseph U.S.A. **65 H4** 39.45N 94.51W
St. Joseph, Lac *l.* Canada **63 I3** 51.05N 90.35W
St. Just England **13 B2** 50.07N 5.41W
St. Keverne England **13 B2** 50.03N 5.05W
St. Kilda *i.* Scotland **18 A2** 57.49N 8.34W
St. Kitts-Nevis Leeward Is. **71 L4** 17.20N 62.45W
St. Lawrence *r.* Canada/U.S.A. **63 L2** 48.45N 68.30W
St. Lawrence, G. of Canada **63 L2** 48.00N 62.00W
St. Lawrence I. U.S.A. **62 A4** 63.00N 170.00W
St.-Lô France **44 C6** 49.07N 1.05W
St. Louis Senegal **84 C3** 16.01N 16.30W
St. Louis U.S.A. **65 H4** 38.40N 90.15W
St. Lucia Windward Is. **71 L3** 14.05N 61.00W
St. Magnus B. Scotland **19 Y9** 60.25N 1.35W
St.-Malo France **44 B6** 48.39N 2.00W
St.-Malo, Golfe de *g.* France **44 B6** 49.00N 2.00W
St. Margaret's Hope Scotland **19 G3** 58.50N 2.57W
St. Martin Guernsey Channel Is. **13 Y9** 49.27N 2.34W
St. Martin Jersey Channel Is. **13 Z8** 49.13N 2.03W
St. Martin *i.* Leeward Is. **71 L4** 18.05N 63.05W
St. Martin's *i.* England **13 A1** 49.57N 6.16W
St. Mary's *i.* England **13 A1** 49.55N 6.16W
St. Matthew I. U.S.A. **62 A4** 60.30N 172.45W
St. Maurice *r.* Canada **65 L6** 46.21N 72.31W
St. Mawes England **13 B2** 50.10N 5.01W
St. Moritz Switz. **44 H5** 46.30N 9.51E
St.-Nazaire France **44 B5** 47.17N 2.12W

St. Neots England 11 E3............52.14N 0.16W
St.-Niklaas Belgium 42 D3............51.10N 4.09E
St.-Omer France 42 B2............50.45N 2.15E
St. Ouen Channel Is. 13 Z8............49.13N 2.14W
St. Peter Port Channel Is. 13 Y9............49.27N 2.32W
St. Petersburg Russian Fed. 58 F3............59.55N 30.25E
St. Pierre and Miquelon is. N. America 63 M2............47.00N 56.15W
St. Pölten Austria 54 D3............48.13N 15.37E
St.-Quentin France 44 E6............49.51N 3.17E
St. Sampson Channel Is. 13 Y9............49.29N 2.31W
St. Vincent, C. Portugal 46 A2............37.01N 8.59W
St. Vincent and the Grenadines C. America 71 L3............13.10N 61.15W
St.-Vith Belgium 42 F2............50.15N 6.08E
St. Wendel Germany 42 G1............49.27N 7.10E
Saipan i. N. Mariana Is. 105 L7............15.12N 145.43E
Sajama mtn. Bolivia 76 D3............18.06S 69.00W
Sakai Japan 106 C3............34.37N 135.28E
Sakakah Saudi Arabia 94 F5............29.59N 40.12E
Sakakawea, L. U.S.A. 64 F6............47.30N 102.20W
Sakarya Turkey 57 J4............40.45N 30.23E
Sakarya r. Turkey 57 J4............41.08N 30.36E
Sakata Japan 106 C3............38.55N 139.51E
Sakhalin i. Russian Fed. 59 Q3............50.00N 143.00E
Sakura Japan 106 D3............35.43N 140.13E
Sal i. Cape Verde 84 B3............16.45N 23.00W
Sala Sweden 43 D2............59.55N 16.38E
Salado r. Argentina 77 D1............31.40S 60.41W
Salado r. Mexico 70 E6............26.46N 98.55W
Salalah Oman 95 I2............17.00N 54.04E
Salamanca Spain 46 C4............40.58N 5.40W
Salar de Arizaro f. Argentina 76 D2............24.50S 67.40W
Salar de Atacama f. Chile 76 D2............23.30S 68.46W
Salar de Coipasa l. Bolivia 76 D3............19.20S 68.00W
Salar de Uyuni l. Bolivia 76 D2............20.30S 67.45W
Salavat Russian Fed. 58 H3............53.22N 55.50E
Salayar i. Indonesia 104 G2............6.07S 120.28E
Salcombe England 13 D2............50.14N 3.47W
Saldanha R.S.A. 86 A1............33.00S 17.56E
Sale Australia 110 D2............38.06S 147.06E
Sale England 15 E2............53.26N 2.19W
Salehurst England 11 F1............50.58N 0.29E
Salekhard Russian Fed. 58 I4............66.33N 66.35E
Salem India 97 F3............11.38N 78.08E
Salem U.S.A. 64 B5............44.57N 123.01W
Salerno Italy 50 F4............40.41N 14.45E
Salerno, G. of Med. Sea 50 F4............40.30N 14.45E
Salford England 15 E2............53.30N 2.17W
Salgado r. Brazil 77 G4............4.27S 37.46W
Salihli Turkey 57 I3............38.29N 28.08E
Salihorsk Belarus 55 J5............52.41N 27.29E
Salina U.S.A. 64 G4............38.50N 97.37W
Salinas U.S.A. 64 B4............36.40N 121.38W
Salinas Grandes f. Argentina 76 D2............29.37S 64.56W
Salinosó Lachay, Punto c. Peru 76 C3............11.20S 77.29W
Salisbury England 10 D2............51.04N 1.48W
Salisbury U.S.A. 65 K4............38.22N 75.37W
Salisbury Plain f. England 10 D2............51.15N 1.55W
Salitre r. Brazil 77 F4............9.23S 40.35W
Salluit Canada 63 K4............62.10N 75.40W
Salmon r. U.S.A. 64 C6............45.50N 116.50W
Salmon Arm Canada 62 G3............50.41N 119.18W
Salmon River Mts. U.S.A. 64 D5............44.30N 114.30W
Salo Finland 43 E3............60.23N 23.10E
Sal'sk Russian Fed. 53 L6............46.30N 41.33E
Salta Argentina 76 D2............24.46S 65.28W
Saltash England 13 C2............50.25N 4.13W
Saltcoats Scotland 16 E3............55.37N 4.47W
Saltee Is. Rep. of Ire. 20 E2............52.08N 6.36W
Saltillo Mexico 70 D6............25.30N 101.00W
Salt Lake City U.S.A. 64 D5............40.45N 111.55W
Salto Uruguay 77 E1............31.23S 57.58W
Salton Sea l. U.S.A. 64 C3............33.25N 115.45W
Salvador Brazil 77 G3............12.58S 38.20W
Salween r. Myanmar 97 J4............16.30N 97.33E
Salyan Azerbaijan 95 G6............39.36N 48.59E
Salzburg Austria 54 C2............47.54N 13.03E
Salzgitter Germany 48 E5............52.02N 10.22E
Samandağı Turkey 57 L2............36.07N 35.55E
Samani Japan 106 D4............42.09N 142.50E
Samar i. Phil. 105 H6............11.45N 125.15E
Samara Russian Fed. 58 H3............53.10N 50.15E
Samara r. Ukraine 55 N3............48.27N 35.07E
Samarinda Indonesia 104 F3............0.30S 117.09E
Samarra' Iraq 95 F5............34.13N 43.52E
Sambalpur India 97 G5............21.28N 84.04E
Sambas Indonesia 104 D4............1.20N 109.15E
Sambre r. Belgium 42 D2............50.29N 4.52E
Same Tanzania 87 B2............4.04S 37.44E
Samos i. Greece 56 H2............37.44N 26.45E
Samothraki i. Greece 56 G4............40.26N 25.35E
Sampit Indonesia 104 E3............2.34S 112.59E
Samsø i. Denmark 54 B6............55.52N 10.37E
Samsun Turkey 57 M4............41.17N 36.22E
San Mali 84 D3............13.21N 4.57W
Sana Yemen 94 F2............15.23N 44.14E
San Ambrosio i. Chile 109 X4............26.28S 79.53W
Sanandaj Iran 95 G6............35.18N 47.01E
San Andrés, I. de Colombia 71 H3............12.35N 81.42W
San Antonio U.S.A. 64 G2............29.25N 98.30W
San Antonio, C. Cuba 71 H5............21.50N 84.57W
San Benedicto, I. Mexico 70 B5............19.20N 110.50W
San Bernardino U.S.A. 64 C3............34.07N 117.18W
San Blas, C. U.S.A. 64 I4............29.40N 85.25W
San Cristobal i. Solomon Is. 111 F4............10.40S 162.00E
San Cristóbal Venezuela 71 J2............7.46N 72.15W
San Cristóbal i. Galapagos Is. 76 B4............0.50S 89.30W
San Cristóbal de la Laguna Canary Is. 46 X2............28.29N 16.19W
Sanda I. Scotland 16 D3............55.17N 5.34W
Sandakan Malaysia 104 F5............5.52N 118.04E
Sandane Norway 43 A3............61.47N 6.14E
Sanday i. Scotland 19 G4............59.15N 2.33W
Sanday Sd. Scotland 19 G4............59.11N 2.35W
Sandbach England 15 E2............53.09N 2.23W
Sandhurst England 10 D2............51.20N 0.49W
San Diego U.S.A. 64 C3............32.45N 117.10W
Sandnes Norway 43 A2............58.51N 5.45E
Sandnessjøen Norway 43 C4............66.01N 12.40E
Sandoway Myanmar 97 H4............18.28N 94.20E
Sandown England 10 D1............50.39N 1.09W
Sandpoint town U.S.A. 64 C6............48.17N 116.34W
Sandviken Sweden 43 D3............60.38N 16.50E
Sandwich England 11 G2............51.16N 1.21E

Sandy England 11 E3............52.08N 0.18W
Sandy C. Australia 110 E3............24.42S 153.17E
Sandy Lake town Canada 63 I3............53.00N 93.00W
San Felipe Mexico 70 B7............31.03N 114.52W
San Félix i. Chile 109 W4............26.23S 80.05W
San Fernando Phil. 104 G7............16.39N 120.19E
San Fernando Spain 46 B2............36.28N 6.12W
San Fernando de Apure Venezuela 71 K2............7.53N 67.15W
San Francisco U.S.A. 64 B4............37.45N 122.27W
San Francisco, C. de Ecuador 76 B5............0.38N 80.08W
San Francisco de Paula, C. Argentina 75 C2............49.44S 67.38W
Sangha r. Congo 82 E4............1.10S 16.47E
Sangir i. Indonesia 105 H4............2.45N 125.20E
Sangkulirang Indonesia 104 F4............1.00N 117.58E
Sangli India 96 E4............16.55N 74.37E
Sangmélima Cameroon 84 F2............2.57N 11.56E
Sangre de Cristo Range mts. U.S.A. 64 E4............37.30N 106.00W
Sangue r. Brazil 77 E3............11.00S 58.30W
San Jorge, Golfo de g. Argentina 75 C2............46.00S 66.00W
San José Costa Rica 71 H3............9.59N 84.04W
San José i. Mexico 70 B6............25.00N 110.38W
San Jose U.S.A. 64 B4............37.20N 121.55W
San Juan Argentina 76 D1............31.33S 68.31W
San Juan r. Costa Rica 71 H3............10.50N 83.40W
San Juan r. Puerto Rico 71 K4............18.29N 66.08W
San Juan r. U.S.A. 64 D4............37.20N 110.05W
San Juan Bautista Paraguay 77 E2............26.37S 57.06W
San Juan Mts. U.S.A. 64 E4............37.30N 107.00W
Şanlıurfa Turkey 57 N2............37.08N 38.45E
Sanlúcar de Barrameda Spain 46 B2............36.46N 6.21W
San Lucas, C. Mexico 70 B5............22.50N 110.00W
San Luis, Lago de l. Bolivia 76 D3............13.40S 64.00W
San Luis Obispo U.S.A. 64 B4............35.16N 120.40W
San Luis Potosi Mexico 70 D5............22.10N 101.00W
San Luis Potosi d. Mexico 70 D5............23.00N 100.00W
San Marino Europe 50 E5............43.55N 12.27E
San Marino town San Marino 50 E5............43.55N 12.27E
San Martin, L. Argentina 75 B2............49.00S 72.30W
San Matias, Golfo g. Argentina 75 C2............41.30S 64.00W
San Miguel r. Bolivia 76 D3............12.25S 64.25W
San Miguel El Salvador 70 G3............13.28N 88.10W
San Miguel de Tucumán Argentina 76 D2............26.47S 65.15W
Sanming China 103 L3............26.25N 117.35E
Sanndray i. Scotland 18 B1............56.53N 7.31W
San Pablo Phil. 104 G6............13.58N 121.10E
San Pedro Paraguay 77 E2............24.08S 57.08W
San Pedro, Sierra de mts. Spain 46 B3............39.20N 6.20W
San Pedro Sula Honduras 70 G4............15.26N 88.01W
San Pietro i. Italy 50 C3............39.09N 8.16E
Sanquhar Scotland 17 F3............55.22N 3.56W
San Quintin, C. Mexico 64 C3............30.20N 116.00W
San Remo Italy 50 B5............43.48N 7.46E
San Salvador El Salvador 70 G3............13.40N 89.10W
San Salvador i. The Bahamas 71 J5............24.00N 74.32W
San Salvador de Jujuy Argentina 76 D2............24.10S 65.20W
San Sebastian de la Gomera Canary Is. 46 X2............28.06N 17.06W
San Severo Italy 50 F4............41.40N 15.24E
Santa Ana El Salvador 70 G3............14.00N 89.31W
Santa Ana U.S.A. 64 C3............33.44N 117.54W
Santa Barbara U.S.A. 64 C3............34.25N 119.41W
Santa Catarina d. Brazil 77 E2............27.00S 50.00W
Santa Clara Cuba 71 H5............22.25N 79.58W
Santa Cruz Bolivia 76 D3............17.58S 63.14W
Santa Cruz, I. Galapagos Is. 76 A4............0.40S 90.20W
Santa Cruz de la Palma Canary Is. 46 X2............28.41N 17.46W
Santa Cruz de Tenerife Canary Is. 46 X2............28.27N 16.14W
Santa Cruz do Sul Brazil 77 E2............29.42S 52.25W
Santa Cruz Is. Solomon Is. 111 F4............10.30S 166.00E
Santa Elena, B. de Ecuador 76 B4............2.10S 80.50W
Santa Elena, C. Costa Rica 70 G3............10.54N 85.56W
Santa Fé Argentina 77 D1............31.38S 60.43W
Santa Fe U.S.A. 64 E4............35.41N 105.57W
Santa Isabel i. Solomon Is. 111 E5............8.00S 159.00E
Santa Maria Brazil 77 E2............29.40S 53.47W
Santa Maria r. Mexico 70 C7............31.10N 107.05W
Santa Maria U.S.A. 64 B3............34.56N 120.25W
Santa Maria di Leuca, C. Italy 50 H3............39.47N 18.24E
Santa Marta Colombia 71 J3............11.18N 74.10W
Santander Spain 46 D5............43.28N 3.48W
Santarém Brazil 76 E4............2.26S 54.41W
Santarém Portugal 46 A3............39.14N 8.40W
Santa Rosa Argentina 75 C3............36.00S 64.40W
Santa Rosa U.S.A. 64 B4............38.26N 122.34W
Santa Rosalía Mexico 70 B6............27.20N 112.20W
Santiago Chile 75 B3............33.30S 70.40W
Santiago Dom. Rep. 71 J4............19.30N 70.42W
Santiago de Cuba Cuba 71 I5............20.00N 75.49W
Santo André Brazil 77 F2............23.39S 46.29W
Santo Antão i. Cape Verde 84 B3............17.00N 25.10W
Santo Domingo Dom. Rep. 71 K4............18.30N 69.57W
Santoña Spain 46 D5............43.27N 3.26W
Santos Brazil 77 F2............23.56S 46.22W
San Valentín mtn. Chile 75 B2............46.33S 73.20W
São Carlos Brazil 77 F2............22.01S 47.54W
São Francisco r. Brazil 77 G3............10.10S 36.40W
São José do Rio Prêto Brazil 77 F2............20.50S 49.20W
São Luís Brazil 77 F4............2.34S 44.16W
São Marcos, Baia de b. Brazil 77 F4............2.30S 44.15W
Saône r. France 44 F4............45.46N 4.52E
São Paulo Brazil 77 F2............23.33S 46.39W
São Roque, C. de Brazil 77 G4............5.00S 35.00W
São Sebastião, I. de Brazil 77 F2............23.53S 45.17W
São Tiago i. Cape Verde 84 B3............15.00N 23.40W
São Tomé i. São Tomé & Príncipe 84 E2............0.19N 6.43E
São Tomé, Cabo de c. Brazil 75 G4............21.54S 40.59W
São Tomé & Príncipe Africa 84 E2............1.00N 7.00E
São Vicente Brazil 77 F2............23.57S 46.23W
Sã Paulo d. Brazil 77 F2............22.05S 48.00W
Sapporo Japan 106 D4............43.05N 141.21E
Sapri Italy 50 F4............40.04N 15.38E
Saqqaq Greenland 63 M5............70.00N 52.00W
Saqqez Iran 95 G6............36.14N 46.15E
Sarab Iran 95 G6............37.56N 47.35E
Sara Buri Thailand 104 C6............14.32N 100.53E
Sarajevo Bosnia. 56 D5............43.52N 18.26E

Sarandë Albania 56 E3............39.52N 20.00E
Saransk Russian Fed. 58 G3............54.12N 45.10E
Sarasota U.S.A. 65 J2............27.20N 82.32W
Saratov Russian Fed. 58 G3............51.30N 45.55E
Saravan Iran 95 J4............27.25N 62.17E
Sarawak d. Malaysia 104 E4............3.00N 114.00E
Sardindida Plain f. Kenya 87 C3............2.30N 40.00E
Sardinia i. Italy 50 C4............40.00N 9.00E
Sarektjåkkå mtn. Sweden 43 D4............67.25N 17.45E
Sar-e Pol Afghan. 95 K6............36.13N 65.55E
Sargodha Pakistan 96 E7............32.01N 72.40E
Sarh Chad 85 F2............9.08N 18.22E
Sarī Iran 95 H6............36.33N 53.06E
Sarigan i. N. Mariana Is. 105 L7............16.43N 145.47E
Sarıyer Turkey 57 I4............41.11N 29.03E
Sark i. Channel Is. 13 Y9............49.26N 2.22W
Şarkışla Turkey 57 M3............39.21N 36.27E
Sarny Ukraine 55 J4............51.21N 26.31E
Saros, G. of Turkey 56 H4............40.32N 26.25E
Sarpsborg Norway 43 B2............59.17N 11.06E
Sarrebourg France 44 G6............48.43N 7.03E
Sarria Spain 46 B5............42.47N 7.25W
Sarthe r. France 44 C5............47.29N 0.30W
Sasebo Japan 106 A2............33.10N 129.42E
Saskatchewan d. Canada 62 H3............55.00N 105.00W
Saskatchewan r. Canada 62 H3............53.25N 100.15W
Saskatoon Canada 62 H3............52.10N 106.40W
Sassandra Côte d'Ivoire 84 D2............4.58N 6.08W
Sassari Italy 50 C4............40.43N 8.33E
Sassnitz Germany 48 F6............54.32N 13.40E
Satpura Range mts. India 96 F5............21.50N 76.00E
Satu Mare Romania 54 H2............47.48N 22.52E
Saudhárkrókur Iceland 43 Y2............65.45N 19.39W
Saudi Arabia Asia 94 F3............25.00N 44.00E
Sault Sainte Marie Canada 63 J2............46.32N 84.20W
Sault Sainte Marie U.S.A. 65 J6............46.30N 84.21W
Saumlaki Indonesia 105 I2............7.59S 131.22E
Saundersfoot Wales 12 C3............51.43N 4.42W
Saurimo Angola 86 B4............9.38S 20.20E
Sava r. Yugo. 56 E6............44.50N 20.26E
Savaii i. W. Samoa 108 N5............13.36S 172.27W
Savannah U.S.A. 65 J3............32.09N 81.01W
Savannah r. U.S.A. 65 J3............32.10N 81.00W
Savannakhét Laos 104 C7............16.34N 104.55E
Save r. Mozambique 86 C2............21.00S 35.01E
Savona Italy 50 C6............44.18N 8.28E
Sawel Mt. N. Ireland 16 B2............54.49N 7.03W
Sawston England 11 E3............52.07N 0.11E
Sawtry England 11 E3............52.26N 0.17W
Sawu i. Indonesia 105 G1............10.30S 121.50E
Sawu Sea Pacific Oc. 105 G2............9.30S 122.30E
Saxilby England 15 G2............53.17N 0.40W
Saxmundham England 11 G3............52.13N 1.29E
Sayhut Yemen 95 H2............15.12N 51.12E
Saylac Somalia 85 I3............11.21N 43.30E
Saynshand Mongolia 103 K6............44.58N 110.10E
Scafell Pike mtn. England 14 D3............54.27N 3.12W
Scalasaig Scotland 16 C4............56.04N 6.12W
Scalby England 15 G3............54.18N 0.26W
Scalp mtn. Donegal Rep. of Ire. 16 B3............55.05N 7.22W
Scalp mtn. Galway Rep. of Ire. 20 C3............53.00N 8.29W
Scalpay i. High. Scotland 18 D2............57.18N 5.58W
Scalpay i. W.Isles Scotland 18 C2............57.52N 6.40W
Scandinavia f. Europe 34 A6............65.00N 18.00E
Scapa Flow str. Scotland 19 F3............58.53N 3.05W
Scarba i. Scotland 16 D4............56.11N 5.42W
Scarborough England 15 G3............54.17N 0.24W
Scarp i. Scotland 18 B3............58.02N 7.07W
Schaffhausen Switz. 44 H5............47.42N 8.38E
Schagen Neth. 42 D4............52.47N 4.47E
Schefferville Canada 63 L3............54.50N 67.00W
Schelde r. Belgium 42 D3............51.13N 4.25E
Schiehallion mtn. Scotland 19 E1............56.40N 4.08W
Schiermonnikoog i. Neth. 42 F5............53.28N 6.15E
Schleswig Germany 48 D6............54.32N 9.34E
Schwaner Mts. Indonesia 104 E3............0.45S 113.20E
Schwedt Germany 48 G5............53.04N 14.17E
Schweinfurt Germany 48 E4............50.03N 10.16E
Schwerin Germany 48 E5............53.38N 11.25E
Scilly, Isles of England 13 A1............49.55N 6.20W
Scole England 11 G3............52.22N 1.10E
Scotland U.K. 8-9
Scottish Borders d. Scotland 17 G3............55.30N 2.53W
Scottsbluff U.S.A. 64 F5............41.52N 103.40W
Scourie Scotland 18 D3............58.20N 5.09W
Scranton U.S.A. 65 K5............41.25N 75.40W
Scridain, Loch Scotland 16 C4............56.22N 6.06W
Scunthorpe England 15 G2............53.35N 0.38W
Scuol Switz. 44 G5............46.48N 10.18E
Seaford England 11 F1............50.46N 0.08E
Seamer England 15 G3............54.14N 0.27W
Seascale England 14 D3............54.24N 3.29W
Seaton Cumbria England 14 D3............54.41N 3.31W
Seaton Devon England 13 D2............50.43N 3.05W
Seaton Delaval England 15 F4............55.05N 1.31W
Seattle U.S.A. 64 B6............47.35N 122.20W
Sebastián Vizcaíno B. Mexico 70 B6............28.20N 114.45W
Sechura, Bahía de b. Peru 76 B4............5.30S 81.00W
Sedan France 44 F6............49.42N 4.57E
Sedbergh England 14 E3............54.20N 2.31W
Seefin mtn. Rep. of Ire. 20 D2............52.13N 7.36W
Segovia Spain 46 C4............40.57N 4.07W
Segura, Sierra de mts. Spain 46 D3............38.00N 2.50W
Seiland i. Norway 43 E5............70.30N 23.00E
Seinäjoki Finland 43 E3............62.45N 22.55E
Seine r. France 44 D6............49.28N 0.25E
Sekondi-Takoradi Ghana 84 D2............4.59N 1.43W
Selaru i. Indonesia 105 I2............8.15S 131.00E
Selatan, Tanjung c. Indonesia 104 E3............4.20S 114.45E
Selatan i. Indonesia 104 C3............3.00S 100.18E
Selattyn England 10 B3............52.54N 3.05W
Selawik U.S.A. 62 C4............66.35N 160.10W
Selby England 15 F2............53.47N 1.05W
Selkirk Canada 62 I3............50.10N 96.52W
Selkirk Scotland 17 G3............55.33N 2.51W
Sellindge England 11 G2............51.07N 1.00E
Selsey England 10 E1............50.44N 0.47W
Selsey Bill c. England 10 E1............50.44N 0.47W
Selvas f. Brazil 77 D4............8.00S 68.00W
Selwyn Mts. Canada 62 E4............63.00N 130.00W
Selwyn Range mts. Australia 110 C4............21.35S 140.35E
Seman r. Albania 56 D4............40.53N 19.25E
Semarang Indonesia 104 E2............6.58S 110.29E
Semenivka Ukraine 55 M5............52.08N 32.36E

Seminoe Resr. U.S.A. 64 E5............42.05N 106.50W
Semipalatinsk Kazakhstan 102 E8............50.26N 80.16E
Semnan Iran 95 H6............35.31N 53.24E
Semois r. France/Belgium 42 D1............49.53N 4.45E
Sendai Japan 106 A3............38.20N 140.50E
Senegal Africa 84 C3............14.15N 14.15W
Sénégal r. Senegal/Mauritania 84 C3............16.00N 16.28W
Senja i. Norway 43 D5............69.20N 17.30E
Senlis France 42 B1............49.12N 2.35E
Sennar Sudan 85 H3............13.31N 33.38E
Sens France 44 E6............48.12N 3.18E
Seoul S. Korea 103 N5............37.30N 127.00E
Sept-Îles town Canada 63 L3............50.13N 66.22W
Seram i. Indonesia 105 H3............3.10S 129.30E
Seram Sea Pacific Oc. 105 H3............2.50S 128.00E
Serang Indonesia 104 D2............6.07S 106.09E
Seremban Malaysia 104 C4............2.42N 101.54E
Serengeti Nat. Park Tanzania 87 A2............2.20S 34.55E
Serengeti Plains f. Kenya 87 B2............3.30S 37.50E
Serere Uganda 87 A3............1.31N 33.25E
Seret r. Ukraine 55 I3............48.38N 25.52E
Sergipe d. Brazil 77 G3............11.00S 37.00W
Seria Brunei 104 E4............4.39N 114.23E
Serov Russian Fed. 58 I3............59.42N 60.32E
Serowe Botswana 86 B2............22.25S 26.44E
Serpukhov Russian Fed. 55 O6............54.53N 37.25E
Serranías del Burro mts. Mexico 70 D6............28.30N 102.00W
Serres Greece 56 F4............41.04N 23.32E
Serui Indonesia 105 J3............1.53S 136.15E
Sestroretsk Russian Fed. 43 G3............60.09N 29.58E
Sète France 44 E4............43.25N 3.43E
Sete Lagoas Brazil 77 F3............19.29S 44.15W
Setesdal f. Norway 43 A2............59.20N 7.25E
Sétif Algeria 84 E5............36.09N 5.26E
Seto-naikai str. Japan 106 B2............34.00N 132.30E
Settat Morocco 84 D5............33.04N 7.37W
Settle England 15 E3............54.05N 2.18W
Setúbal Portugal 46 A3............38.31N 8.54W
Setúbal, B. of Portugal 46 A3............38.20N 9.00W
Seul, Lac l. Canada 65 H7............50.20N 92.30W
Sevastopol' Ukraine 55 M1............44.36N 33.31E
Seven Heads Rep. of Ire. 20 C1............51.34N 8.42W
Sevenoaks England 11 F2............51.16N 0.12E
Severn r. Canada 63 J3............56.00N 87.40W
Severn r. England 10 C2............51.50N 2.21W
Severnaya Zemlya is. Russian Fed. 59 L5............80.00N 96.00E
Severo-Kurilsk Russian Fed. 59 R3............50.40N 156.01E
Seville Spain 46 C2............37.24N 5.59W
Seward U.S.A. 62 D4............60.05N 149.34W
Seward Pen. U.S.A. 62 B4............65.00N 164.10W
Seychelles Indian Oc. 85 J1............5.00S 55.00E
Seydhisfjördhur Iceland 43 Z2............65.16N 14.02W
Seydişehir Turkey 57 J2............37.25N 31.51E
Seym r. Russian Fed. 55 M4............51.30N 32.30E
Sfântu Gheorghe Romania 56 G6............45.52N 25.50E
Sfax Tunisia 84 F5............34.45N 10.43E
Sgurr Dhomhnuill mtn. Scotland 18 D1............56.45N 5.25W
Sgurr Mor mtn. Scotland 18 D2............57.41N 5.01W
Shaanxi d. China 103 J4............34.00N 109.00E
Shabeelle r. Somalia 85 I2............0.30N 43.10E
Shaftesbury England 10 C2............51.00N 2.12W
Shahr-e Kord Iran 95 H5............32.40N 50.52E
Shandong d. China 103 L5............35.45N 117.30E
Shandong Pen. China 103 M5............37.00N 121.30E
Shanghai China 103 M4............31.13N 121.25E
Shangqiu China 103 L4............34.21N 115.40E
Shangzhi China 106 A5............45.13N 127.59E
Shanklin England 10 D1............50.38N 1.10W
Shannon r. Rep. of Ire. 20 C2............52.39N 8.43W
Shannon, Mouth of the est. Rep. of Ire. 20 B2............52.29N 9.57W
Shantar Is. Russian Fed. 59 P3............55.00N 138.00E
Shanxi d. China 103 K5............36.45N 112.00E
Shaoguan China 103 K2............24.54N 113.33E
Shaoxing China 103 M3............30.02N 120.35E
Shaoyang China 103 K3............27.43N 111.24E
Shap England 14 E3............54.32N 2.40W
Shapinsay i. Scotland 19 G4............59.03N 2.51W
Shaqra Saudi Arabia 94 G3............25.17N 45.14E
Sharjah U.A.E. 95 I4............25.20N 55.26E
Shark B. Australia 108 G4............25.30S 113.30E
Shashemene Ethiopia 85 H2............7.13N 38.33E
Shashi China 103 K4............30.16N 112.20E
Shasta, Mt. U.S.A. 64 B5............41.35N 122.12W
Shawinigan Canada 65 L6............46.33N 72.45W
Shchigry Russian Fed. 55 O4............51.52N 36.54E
Sheberghan Afghan. 95 K6............36.40N 65.42E
Sheelin, Lough Rep. of Ire. 20 D3............53.48N 7.20W
Sheep Haven b. Rep. of Ire. 16 B3............55.12N 7.52W
Sheerness England 11 F2............51.26N 0.47E
Sheffield England 15 F2............53.23N 1.28W
Shelby U.S.A. 64 D6............48.30N 111.52W
Shelikof Str. U.S.A. 62 C3............58.00N 153.45W
Shengena mtn. Tanzania 87 B2............4.17S 37.52E
Shenyang China 103 M6............41.50N 123.26E
Shenzhen China 103 K2............22.32N 114.08E
Shepetivka Ukraine 55 J4............50.12N 27.01E
Sheppey, Isle of England 11 F2............51.24N 0.50E
Shepshed England 15 F3............52.46N 1.17W
Shepton Mallet England 13 E3............51.11N 2.31W
Sherborne England 10 C1............50.56N 2.31W
Sherbrooke Canada 63 L2............45.24N 71.54W
Shereiq Sudan 94 D2............18.44N 33.37E
Sheridan U.S.A. 64 E5............44.48N 107.05W
Sheringham England 11 G3............52.56N 1.11E
's-Hertogenbosch Neth. 42 E3............51.42N 5.19E
Sherwood Forest England 15 G2............53.10N 0.55W
Shetland d. Scotland 19 Y9............60.20N 1.15W
Shetland Is. Scotland 19 Y9............60.20N 1.15W
Shiant Is. Scotland 18 C2............57.54N 6.20W
Shibam Yemen 95 G2............15.56N 48.38E
Shibîn el Kôm Egypt 53 J3............30.33N 31.00E
Shiel, Loch Scotland 18 D1............56.50N 5.35W
Shieldaig Scotland 18 D2............57.31N 5.40W
Shifnal England 10 C3............52.40N 2.23W
Shijiazhuang China 103 K5............38.04N 114.28E
Shikarpur Pakistan 96 D6............27.58N 68.42E
Shikoku i. Japan 106 B2............33.30N 133.00E
Shikoku-sanchi mts. Japan 106 B2............34.00N 134.00E
Shikotan-to i. Russian Fed. 106 E4............43.47N 148.45E
Shildon England 15 F3............54.37N 1.39W
Shillong India 97 H5............25.34N 91.53E
Shimoga India 96 F3............13.56N 75.31E
Shimoni Kenya 87 B2............4.38S 39.20E

Shimonoseki Japan 106 B2.................34.02N 130.58E
Shin, Loch Scotland 19 E3.................58.06N 4.32W
Shingu Japan 106 C2.................33.44N 135.59E
Shining Tor hill England 15 E2.................53.16N 2.01W
Shipley England 15 F2.................53.50N 1.47W
Shipston on Stour England 10 D3.................52.04N 1.38W
Shīrāz Iran 95 H4.................29.36N 52.33E
Shire r. Mozambique 86 C3.................17.44S 35.17E
Shizuishan China 103 J5.................39.17N 106.52E
Shizuoka Japan 106 C2.................35.00N 138.28E
Shklow Belarus 55 L6.................54.16N 30.16E
Shkodër Albania 56 D5.................42.03N 19.30E
Shkodër, L. Albania/Yugo. 56 D5.................42.10N 19.18E
Sholapur India 96 F4.................17.43N 75.56E
Shostka Ukraine 55 M4.................51.53N 33.30E
Shpola Ukraine 55 L3.................49.00N 31.25E
Shreveport U.S.A. 65 H3.................32.30N 93.46W
Shrewsbury England 10 C3.................52.42N 2.45W
Shropshire d. England 10 C3.................52.35N 2.40W
Shuangjiang China 103 H2.................23.25N 99.49E
Shuangyashan China 103 O7.................46.37N 131.22E
Shumagin is. U.S.A. 62 C3.................55.00N 160.00W
Shumen Bulgaria 56 H5.................43.15N 26.55E
Shuqrah Yemen 95 G1.................13.21N 45.42E
Shushtar Iran 95 G5.................32.04N 48.53E
Shwebo Myanmar 97 J5.................22.35N 95.42E
Shwegyin Myanmar 97 J4.................17.56N 96.59E
Shymkent Kazakhstan 102 B6.................42.16N 69.05E
Siahan Range mts. Pakistan 95 J4.................27.30N 64.30E
Siaya Kenya 87 A3.................0.05N 34.18E
Šibenik Croatia 56 B5.................43.45N 15.55E
Siberia f. Asia 117 O9.................62.00N 110.00E
Siberut i. Indonesia 104 B3.................1.30S 99.00E
Sibi Pakistan 96 D6.................29.31N 67.54E
Sibiloi Nat. Park Kenya 87 B3.................4.00N 36.30E
Sibiu Romania 56 G6.................45.47N 24.09E
Sibolga Indonesia 104 B4.................1.42N 98.48E
Sibsey England 15 H2.................53.02N 0.01E
Sibu Malaysia 104 E4.................2.18N 111.49E
Sibut C.A.R. 85 F2.................5.46N 19.06E
Sichuan d. China 103 I4.................30.30N 103.00E
Sicily i. Italy 50 F2.................37.30N 14.00E
Sidi bel Abbès Algeria 84 D5.................35.15N 0.39W
Sidi Kacem Morocco 52 B3.................34.15N 5.39W
Sidlaw Hills Scotland 17 F4.................56.31N 3.10W
Sidmouth England 13 D2.................50.40N 3.13W
Sidoan Indonesia 104 G4.................0.19N 120.12E
Sidon Lebanon 94 E6.................33.32N 35.22E
Siedlce Poland 54 H5.................52.10N 22.18E
Siegen Germany 48 D4.................50.52N 8.02E
Siena Italy 50 D5.................43.19N 11.20E
Sierra Leone Africa 84 C2.................8.30N 12.00W
Sierra Nevada del Cocuy mtn. Colombia 71 J2
.................6.30N 72.21W
Siglufjördhur Iceland 43 Y2.................66.09N 18.55W
Sigüenza Spain 46 D4.................41.04N 2.38W
Sihanoukville Cambodia 104 C6.................10.32N 103.28E
Siilinjärvi Finland 43 F3.................63.05N 27.40E
Siirt Turkey 94 F6.................37.56N 41.56E
Sikar India 96 F6.................27.33N 75.12E
Sikasso Mali 84 D3.................11.18N 5.38W
Sikeston U.S.A. 65 I4.................36.53N 89.35W
Sikhote-Alin Range mts. Russian Fed. 59 P2
.................45.20N 136.50E
Sikkim d. India 97 H6.................27.30N 88.30E
Sil r. Spain 46 B5.................42.24N 7.15W
Silesian Plateau mts. Poland 54 F4.................50.30N 19.30E
Silifke Turkey 57 K2.................36.22N 33.57E
Siling Co l. China 102 F4.................31.40N 88.30E
Silistra Bulgaria 56 H6.................44.07N 27.17E
Siljan l. Sweden 43 C3.................60.50N 14.40E
Šilutė Lithuania 54 G6.................55.18N 21.30E
Silver City U.S.A. 64 E3.................32.47N 108.16W
Silverstone England 10 D3.................52.05N 1.03W
Silverton England 13 D2.................50.49N 3.29W
Simanggang Malaysia 104 E4.................1.10N 111.32E
Simbirsk Russian Fed. 58 G3.................54.19N 48.22E
Simen Mts. Ethiopia 94 E3.................13.30N 37.50E
Simeuluë i. Indonesia 104 B4.................2.30N 96.00E
Simferopol' Ukraine 55 N1.................44.57N 34.05E
Simojärvi l. Finland 43 F4.................66.06N 27.03E
Simplon Pass Switz. 44 H5.................46.15N 8.03E
Simpson Desert Australia 110 C3.................25.00S 136.50E
Sinai pen. Egypt 94 D4.................29.00N 34.00E
Sinaloa d. Mexico 70 C5.................25.00N 107.30W
Sincelejo Colombia 71 I2.................9.17N 75.23W
Sinclair's B. Scotland 19 F3.................58.30N 3.07W
Sines Portugal 46 A2.................37.58N 8.52W
Singa Sudan 94 D1.................13.09N 33.56E
Singapore Asia 104 C4.................1.20N 103.45E
Singapore town Singapore 104 C4.................1.20N 103.45E
Singaraja Indonesia 104 F2.................8.06S 115.07E
Singida Tanzania 86 C4.................4.45S 34.42E
Singkawang Indonesia 104 D4.................0.57N 108.57E
Sinj Croatia 56 C5.................43.42N 16.38E
Sinkat Sudan 94 E2.................18.50N 36.50E
Sinop Turkey 57 L5.................42.02N 35.09E
Sint Maarten i. Neth. Antilles 71 L4.................18.05N 63.05W
Sion Mills N. Ireland 16 B2.................54.47N 7.30W
Sioux City U.S.A. 64 G5.................42.30N 96.28W
Sioux Falls town U.S.A. 64 G5.................43.34N 96.42W
Sioux Lookout town Canada 63 I3.................50.07N 91.54W
Sipacate Guatemala 70 F3.................13.56N 91.10W
Siping China 103 M6.................43.15N 124.25E
Sipora i. Indonesia 104 B3.................2.10S 99.40E
Sira r. Norway 43 A2.................58.13N 6.13E
Siracusa Italy 50 F2.................37.05N 15.17E
Siret r. Romania 55 J1.................45.28N 27.56E
Sirte Libya 85 F5.................31.10N 16.39E
Sirte, G. of Libya 85 F5.................31.45N 17.50E
Sisak Croatia 56 C6.................45.30N 16.21E
Sisimiut Greenland 63 M4.................66.55N 53.30W
Sisophon Cambodia 104 C6.................13.37N 102.58E
Sisteron France 44 F4.................44.16N 5.56E
Siteia Greece 56 H1.................35.13N 26.06E
Sitka U.S.A. 62 E3.................57.05N 135.20W
Sittard Neth. 42 E2.................51.00N 5.52E
Sittingbourne England 11 F2.................51.20N 0.43E
Sittwe Myanmar 97 I5.................20.09N 92.55E
Sivas Turkey 57 M3.................39.44N 37.01E
Siverek Turkey 57 N2.................37.46N 39.19E
Sivrihisar Turkey 57 J3.................39.29N 31.32E
Siwa Egypt 94 C4.................29.11N 25.31E
Sjælland i. Denmark 43 B1.................55.30N 12.00E
Skaftárós b. Iceland 43 Y1.................63.40N 17.48W

Skagen Denmark 43 B2.................57.44N 10.36E
Skagerrak str. Denmark/Norway 43 B2.................57.45N 8.55E
Skagway U.S.A. 62 E3.................59.23N 135.20W
Skaill Scotland 19 G3.................58.57N 2.43W
Skara Sweden 43 C2.................58.23N 13.25E
Skarzysko-Kamienna Poland 54 G4.................51.08N 20.53E
Skegness England 15 H2.................53.09N 0.20E
Skellefte r. Sweden 43 E4.................64.44N 21.07E
Skellefteå Sweden 43 E4.................64.45N 21.00E
Skelmersdale England 14 E2.................53.34N 2.49W
Skerries Rep. of Ire. 20 E3.................53.34N 6.07W
Ski Norway 43 B2.................59.43N 10.52E
Skibbereen Rep. of Ire. 20 B1.................51.33N 9.15W
Skiddaw mtn. England 14 D3.................54.40N 3.09W
Skien Norway 43 B2.................59.14N 9.37E
Skikda Algeria 84 E5.................36.50N 6.58E
Skipton England 15 E2.................53.57N 2.01W
Skive Denmark 43 B2.................56.34N 9.03E
Skokholm I. Wales 12 B3.................51.42N 5.17W
Skomer I. Wales 12 B3.................51.45N 5.18W
Skopje Macedonia 56 E4.................41.58N 21.27E
Skövde Sweden 43 C2.................58.24N 13.52E
Skovorodino Russian Fed. 59 O3.................54.00N 123.53E
Skye i. Scotland 18 C2.................57.20N 6.15W
Skyros i. Greece 56 G3.................38.50N 24.33E
Slamet mtn. Indonesia 104 D2.................7.10S 109.10E
Slaney r. Rep. of Ire. 20 E2.................52.21N 6.30W
Slatina Romania 56 G6.................44.26N 24.23E
Slave r. Canada 62 G4.................61.10N 113.30W
Slave Lake town Canada 62 G3.................55.17N 114.43W
Slavyansk-na-Kubani Russian Fed. 57 N6
.................45.14N 38.08E
Sleaford England 15 G2.................53.00N 0.22W
Sleat, Sd. of Scotland 18 D2.................57.07N 5.45W
Sleights England 15 G3.................54.26N 0.40W
Slieve Anierin mtn. Rep. of Ire. 16 B2.................54.06N 7.58W
Slieve Beagh mtn. N. Ireland 16 B2.................54.21N 7.12W
Slievecallan mtn. Rep. of Ire. 20 B2.................52.50N 9.20W
Slieve Car mtn. Rep. of Ire. 20 B4.................54.04N 9.39W
Slieve Donard mtn. N. Ireland 16 D2.................54.11N 5.56W
Slievenamon mtn. Rep. of Ire. 20 D2.................52.26N 7.37W
Slieve Snaght mtn. Rep. of Ire. 20 D5.................55.12N 7.20W
Sligo Rep. of Ire. 20 C4.................54.17N 8.28W
Sligo d. Rep. of Ire. 20 C4.................54.10N 8.35W
Sligo B. Rep. of Ire. 20 C4.................54.18N 8.40W
Sliven Bulgaria 56 H5.................42.41N 26.19E
Slobozia Romania 56 H6.................44.34N 27.23E
Slough England 11 E2.................51.30N 0.35W
Slovakia Europe 54 F3.................49.00N 19.00E
Slovenia Europe 54 F3.................46.00N 14.30E
Slov"yans'k Ukraine 55 O3.................48.51N 37.36E
Slovyechna r. Belarus 55 K4.................51.41N 29.41E
Sluch r. Belarus/Ukraine 55 J5.................52.08N 27.31E
Słupsk Poland 54 E6.................54.28N 17.01E
Slutsk Belarus 55 J5.................53.02N 27.31E
Slyne Head Rep. of Ire. 20 A3.................53.25N 10.12W
Słyudyanka Russian Fed. 103 I8.................51.40N 103.40E
Smallwood Resr. Canada 63 L3.................54.00N 64.00W
Smarhon' Belarus 55 J6.................54.28N 26.20E
Smila Ukraine 55 L3.................49.15N 31.54E
Smoky r. Canada 62 G3.................56.10N 117.21W
Smøla i. Norway 43 A3.................63.20N 8.00E
Smolensk Russian Fed. 55 M6.................54.49N 32.04E
Smolikas mtn. Greece 56 E4.................40.06N 20.55E
Smolyan Bulgaria 56 G4.................41.34N 24.45E
Snaefell mtn. Iceland 43 Z2.................64.48N 15.34W
Snaefell mtn. I.o.M. 14 C3.................54.16N 4.28W
Snaith England 15 F2.................53.42N 1.01W
Snake r. U.S.A. 64 C6.................46.15N 119.00W
Snettisham England 11 F3.................52.53N 0.30E
Snizort, Loch Scotland 18 C2.................57.35N 6.30W
Snøtinden mtn. Norway 43 C4.................66.30N 14.00E
Snov r. Ukraine 55 L4.................51.45N 31.45E
Snowdon mtn. Wales 12 C5.................53.05N 4.05W
Soay i. Scotland 18 C2.................57.09N 6.13W
Sobral Brazil 77 F4.................3.45S 40.20W
Sochi Russian Fed. 57 N6.................43.35N 39.46E
Society Is. Pacific Oc. 108 P5.................17.00S 150.00W
Socorro, I. Mexico 70 B4.................18.45N 110.58W
Socotra i. Yemen 85 J3.................12.30N 54.00E
Sodankylä Finland 43 F2.................67.21N 26.31E
Söderhamn Sweden 43 D3.................61.19N 17.10E
Södertälje Sweden 43 D2.................59.11N 17.39E
Sodo Ethiopia 85 H2.................6.52N 37.47E
Södra Kvarken str. Sweden/Finland 43 D3
.................60.20N 19.00E
Sofia Bulgaria 56 F5.................42.41N 23.19E
Sognefjorden est. Norway 43 A3.................61.10N 5.50E
Sohâg Egypt 94 D4.................26.33N 31.42E
Soham England 11 F3.................52.20N 0.20E
Soignies Belgium 42 D2.................50.35N 4.04E
Soissons France 44 E6.................49.23N 3.20E
Söke Turkey 56 H2.................37.46N 27.26E
Sokhumi Georgia 57 O5.................43.01N 41.01E
Sokółka Poland 54 H5.................53.25N 23.31E
Sokoto Nigeria 84 E3.................13.02N 5.15E
Sokoto r. Nigeria 84 E3.................11.23N 4.05E
Solihull England 10 D3.................52.26N 1.47W
Solikamsk Russian Fed. 58 H3.................59.40N 56.45E
Sollefteå Sweden 43 D3.................63.09N 17.15E
Solomon Is. Pacific Oc. 111 F5.................8.00S 160.00E
Solomon Sea Pacific Oc. 110 E5.................7.00S 153.00E
Sölvesborg Sweden 43 C1.................56.03N 14.33E
Solway Firth est. England/Scotland 17 F2
.................54.52N 3.30W
Solwezi Zambia 86 B3.................12.11S 26.23E
Soma Turkey 57 H3.................39.10N 27.36E
Somalia Africa 85 I2.................5.30N 47.00E
Sombor Yugo. 56 D6.................45.48N 19.08E
Somerset d. England 13 D3.................51.09N 3.00W
Somerset I. Canada 63 I5.................73.00N 93.30W
Somerton England 13 E3.................51.03N 2.44W
Sommen l. Sweden 43 C2.................58.05N 15.15E
Songea Tanzania 86 C3.................10.42S 35.39E
Songkhla Thailand 104 C5.................7.13N 100.37E
Son La Vietnam 104 C8.................21.20N 103.55E
Sono r. Brazil 77 E4.................9.58S 48.11W
Sonora d. Mexico 70 B6.................29.20N 110.40W
Sonora r. Mexico 70 B6.................28.45N 111.55W
Soria Spain 46 D4.................41.46N 2.28W
Soroca Moldova 55 K3.................48.08N 28.12E
Sorocaba Brazil 77 F2.................23.30S 47.32W
Sorol i. Fed. States of Micronesia 105 K5
.................8.09N 140.25E
Sorong Indonesia 105 I3.................0.50S 131.17E

Soroti Uganda 87 A3.................1.42N 33.37E
Sørøya i. Norway 43 E5.................70.30N 22.30E
Sorraia r. Portugal 46 A3.................39.00N 8.51E
Sorsele Sweden 43 D4.................65.32N 17.34E
Sortavala Russian Fed. 43 G3.................61.40N 30.40E
Soshanguve R.S.A. 86 B2.................25.38S 28.11E
Sosna r. Russian Fed. 55 P5.................52.38N 38.50E
Sosnowiec Poland 54 F4.................50.18N 19.08E
Souk Ahras Algeria 52 E4.................36.17N 7.57E
Souris r. Canada 64 G6.................49.38N 99.35W
Sousse Tunisia 84 F5.................35.48N 10.38E
South d. Yemen 95 G1.................14.30N 47.30E
South America 74
Southampton England 10 D1.................50.54N 1.23W
Southampton I. Canada 63 J4.................64.30N 84.00W
South Anston England 15 F2.................53.22N 1.13W
South Australia d. Australia 110 C3.................29.00S 135.00E
South Ayrshire d. Scotland 16 E3.................55.15N 4.40W
South Bank England 15 F3.................54.35N 1.10W
South Bend U.S.A. 65 I5.................41.40N 86.15W
South Carolina d. U.S.A. 65 J3.................34.00N 81.00W
South Cave England 15 G2.................53.46N 0.37W
South China Sea Asia 104 E6.................12.30N 115.00E
South Dakota d. U.S.A. 64 F5.................44.30N 100.00W
South Dorset Downs hills England 10 C1
.................50.40N 2.25W
South Downs hills England 11 E1.................50.54N 0.34W
South East C. Australia 110 D1.................43.38S 146.48E
Southeast Pacific Basin f. Pacific Oc. 116 D2
Southend-on-Sea England 11 F2.................51.32N 0.43E
Southern Alps mts. New Zealand 111 G1
.................43.20S 170.45E
Southern Ocean 108 F1.................66.00S 0.00
Southern Uplands hills Scotland 17 F3.................55.30N 3.30W
Southery England 11 F3.................52.32N 0.23E
South Esk r. Scotland 19 G1.................56.43N 2.32W
South Georgia i. Atlantic Oc. 75 F1.................54.00S 37.00W
South Gloucestershire d. England 10 C2
.................51.35N 2.40W
South Horr Kenya 87 B3.................2.10N 36.55E
South I. New Zealand 111 G1.................43.00S 171.00E
South Kirkby England 15 F2.................53.35N 1.25W
South Kitui Nat. Res. Kenya 87 B2.................1.45S 38.40E
South Korea Asia 103 N5.................36.00N 128.00E
South Lanarkshire d. Scotland 17 F3.................55.40N 3.45W
Southminster England 11 F2.................51.40N 0.51E
South Molton England 13 D3.................51.01N 3.50W
South Ockendon England 11 F2.................51.32N 0.18E
South Orkney Is. Atlantic Oc. 112.................60.50S 45.00W
South Pacific Ocean 109 R3.................35.00S 140.00W
South Platte r. U.S.A. 64 G5.................41.09N 100.55W
Southport Australia 110 E3.................27.58S 153.20E
Southport England 14 D2.................53.38N 3.01W
South Ronaldsay i. Scotland 19 G3.................58.47N 2.56W
South Sandwich Is. Atlantic Oc. 72 H1.................58.00S 27.00W
South Saskatchewan r. Canada 62 H3
.................53.15N 105.05W
South Shetland Is. Antarctica 112.................62.00S 60.00W
South Shields England 15 F4.................55.00N 1.24W
South Tyne r. England 15 E4.................54.59N 2.08W
South Uist i. Scotland 18 B2.................57.15N 7.20W
South Walls i. Scotland 19 F3.................58.45N 3.07W
Southwell England 15 G2.................53.05N 0.58W
Southwest Pacific Basin f. Pacific Oc. 116 A4
Southwold England 11 G3.................52.19N 1.41E
South Woodham Ferrers England 11 F2.................51.39N 0.36E
South Wootton England 11 F3.................52.47N 0.26E
South Yorkshire d. England 15 F2.................53.28N 1.25W
Sovetsk Russian Fed. 54 G6.................55.02N 21.50E
Sovetskaya Gavan' Russian Fed. 103 Q7
.................48.57N 140.16E
Soweto R.S.A. 86 B2.................26.16S 27.51E
Spain Europe 46 C4.................40.00N 4.00W
Spalding England 11 E3.................52.47N 0.09W
Span Head hill England 13 D3.................51.09N 3.51W
Sparti Greece 56 F2.................37.04N 22.28E
Spartivento, C. Calabria Italy 50 F3.................37.55N 16.04E
Spartivento, C. Sardinia Italy 50 C3.................38.53N 8.51E
Spassk Dal'niy Russian Fed. 106 B4.................44.37N 132.37E
Spátha, C. Greece 56 F1.................35.42N 23.43E
Speke G. Tanzania 87 A2.................2.18S 33.25E
Spencer G. Australia 110 C2.................34.30S 136.10E
Spennymoor town England 15 F3.................54.43N 1.35W
Sperrin Mts. N. Ireland 16 B2.................54.48N 7.06W
Spey r. Scotland 19 F2.................57.40N 3.06W
Speyer Germany 48 D3.................49.19N 8.26E
Spijkenisse Neth. 42 D3.................51.52N 4.19E
Spilsby England 15 H2.................53.10N 0.06E
Spitsbergen is. Arctic Oc. 58 D5.................78.00N 19.00E
Split Croatia 56 C5.................43.32N 16.27E
Spofforth England 15 F2.................53.57N 1.26W
Spokane U.S.A. 64 C6.................47.40N 117.25W
Spratly Is. S. China Sea 104 E5.................9.00N 112.50E
Spree r. Germany 48 F5.................52.32N 13.15E
Springfield Ill. U.S.A. 65 I4.................39.49N 89.39W
Springfield Miss. U.S.A. 65 H4.................37.11N 93.19W
Springhill Canada 65 N6.................45.39N 64.03W
Sprowston England 11 G3.................52.38N 1.22E
Spurn Head England 15 H2.................53.35N 0.08E
Srebrenica Bosnia. 56 D6.................44.06N 19.20E
Srednekolymsk Russian Fed. 59 R4.................67.27N 153.35E
Sretensk Russian Fed. 103 L8.................52.15N 117.52E
Sri Lanka Asia 97 G2.................7.30N 80.50E
Srinagar Jammu & Kashmir 96 E7.................34.08N 74.50E
Stadskanaal Neth. 42 F4.................52.58N 6.56E
Staffa i. Scotland 16 C4.................56.26N 6.21W
Stafford England 10 C3.................52.49N 2.09W
Staffordshire d. England 10 C3.................52.50N 2.00W
Staines England 11 E2.................51.29N 0.31W
Stalbridge England 10 C1.................50.57N 2.22W
Stalham England 11 G3.................52.46N 1.31E
Stalowa Wola Poland 54 H4.................50.40N 22.05E
Stamford England 11 E3.................52.39N 0.29W
Stamford Bridge town England 15 G2.................53.59N 0.53W
Standish England 14 E2.................53.36N 2.41W
Stanley England 15 F3.................54.53N 1.42W
Stanley Falkland Is. 75 D1.................51.45S 57.56W
Stanley, Mt. Uganda/Zaire 82 G5.................0.20N 30.50E
Stannington England 15 F4.................55.06N 1.40W
Stanovoy Range mts. Russian Fed. 59 O3
.................56.00N 125.40E
Stansted Mountfitchet England 11 F2.................51.55N 0.12E
Stanton England 11 F3.................52.19N 0.53E

Stara Zagora Bulgaria 56 G5.................42.26N 25.37E
Starbuck I. Kiribati 108 P6.................5.37S 155.55W
Stargard Szczecinski Poland 54 D5.................53.21N 15.01E
Starokostyantyniv Ukraine 55 J3.................49.48N 27.10E
Start B. England 13 D2.................50.17N 3.35W
Start Pt. England 13 D2.................50.13N 3.38W
Staryy Oskol Russian Fed. 55 O4.................51.20N 37.50E
Stavanger Norway 43 A2.................58.58N 5.45E
Staveley England 15 F2.................53.16N 1.20W
Stavropol' Russian Fed. 53 L6.................45.03N 41.59E
Stavropol Highlands Russian Fed. 58 G2
.................45.00N 42.30E
Steenwijk Neth. 42 F4.................52.47N 6.07E
Steep Holm i. England 13 D3.................51.20N 3.06W
Stefansson I. Canada 62 H5.................73.30N 105.30W
Steinfurt Germany 42 G4.................52.09N 7.21E
Steinkjer Norway 43 B3.................64.00N 11.30E
Stenness, Loch of Scotland 19 F4.................59.00N 3.15W
Sterling U.S.A. 64 F5.................40.37N 103.13W
Sterlitamak Russian Fed. 58 H3.................53.40N 55.59E
Stevenage England 11 E2.................51.54N 0.11W
Stewart r. Canada 62 E4.................63.40N 139.25W
Stewart I. New Zealand 111 F1.................47.02S 167.51E
Stewarton Scotland 16 E3.................55.41N 4.31W
Steyning England 11 E1.................50.54N 0.19W
Steyr Austria 54 E3.................48.04N 14.25E
Stikine r. Canada 62 E3.................56.45N 132.30W
Stilton England 11 E3.................52.29N 0.17W
Stinchar r. Scotland 16 E3.................55.06N 5.00W
Stirling Scotland 17 F4.................56.07N 3.57W
Stirling d. Scotland 16 E4.................56.10N 4.20W
Stjørdalshalsen Norway 43 B3.................63.30N 10.59E
Stob Choire Claurigh mtn. Scotland 18 E1
.................56.50N 4.49W
Stockholm Sweden 43 D2.................59.20N 18.05E
Stockport England 15 E2.................53.25N 2.11W
Stockton U.S.A. 64 B4.................37.59N 121.20W
Stockton-on-Tees England 15 F3.................54.34N 1.20W
Stockton-on-Tees d. England 15 F3.................54.34N 1.20W
Stoer, Pt. of Scotland 18 D3.................58.16N 5.23W
Stoke on Trent England 10 C3.................53.01N 2.11W
Stokesay England 10 C3.................52.25N 2.49W
Stokesley England 15 F3.................54.27N 1.12W
Stolin Belarus 55 J4.................51.52N 26.51E
Stone England 10 C3.................52.55N 2.10W
Stonehaven Scotland 19 G1.................56.58N 2.13W
Stony Rapids town Canada 62 H3.................59.14N 103.48W
Stony Tunguska r. Russian Fed. 59 L4.................61.40N 90.00E
Stora Lulevatten l. Sweden 43 D4.................67.00N 19.30E
Storavan l. Sweden 43 D4.................65.45N 18.10E
Store Bælt str. Denmark 43 B1.................55.30N 11.00E
Støren Norway 43 B3.................63.03N 10.16E
Stornoway Scotland 18 C3.................58.12N 6.23W
Storrington England 11 E1.................50.55N 0.28W
Storsjön l. Sweden 43 C3.................63.10N 14.20E
Storskrymten mtn. Norway 43 B3.................62.15N 9.03E
Storuman Sweden 43 D4.................65.05N 17.10E
Storuman l. Sweden 43 D4.................65.14N 16.50E
Stotfold England 11 E3.................52.02N 0.13W
Stour r. Dorset England 10 D1.................50.43N 1.47W
Stour r. Suffolk England 11 G2.................51.56N 1.03E
Stour r. Warwicks England 10 D3.................52.11N 1.43W
Stourbridge England 10 C3.................52.28N 2.08W
Stourport-on-Severn England 10 C3.................52.21N 2.16W
Stowbtsy Belarus 55 J5.................53.30N 26.44E
Stowmarket England 11 F3.................52.11N 1.00E
Stow-on-the-Wold England 10 D2.................51.55N 1.42W
Strabane N. Ireland 16 B2.................54.50N 7.29W
Stradbroke England 11 G3.................52.19N 1.16E
Stralsund Germany 48 F6.................54.18N 13.06E
Stranda Norway 43 A3.................62.18N 6.56E
Strangford Lough N. Ireland 16 D2.................54.28N 5.35W
Stranorlar Rep. of Ire. 16 B2.................54.48N 7.47W
Stranraer Scotland 16 D2.................54.54N 5.02W
Strasbourg France 44 G6.................48.35N 7.45E
Stratford-upon-Avon England 10 D3.................52.12N 1.42W
Strathaven town Scotland 16 E3.................55.41N 4.05W
Strathbeg, Loch of Scotland 19 H2.................57.37N 1.53W
Strathbogie f. Scotland 19 G2.................57.24N 2.50W
Strathmore r. Angus Scotland 17 F4.................56.34N 3.10W
Strathmore f. High. Scotland 18 E3.................58.25N 4.38W
Strathspey r. Scotland 19 F2.................57.25N 3.25W
Strathy Pt. Scotland 19 E3.................58.35N 4.01W
Stratton England 13 C2.................50.49N 4.31W
Stratton St. Margaret England 10 D2.................51.35N 1.45W
Straubing Germany 48 F3.................48.53N 12.35E
Straumnes c. Iceland 43 X2.................66.30N 23.05W
Streatley England 10 D2.................51.32N 1.10W
Street England 13 E3.................51.07N 2.43W
Stretham England 11 F3.................52.21N 0.14E
Stroma, I. of Scotland 19 F3.................58.41N 3.09W
Stromboli i. Italy 50 F3.................38.48N 15.14E
Stromness Scotland 19 F3.................58.58N 3.19W
Strömsund Sweden 43 C3.................63.51N 15.35E
Stronsay i. Scotland 19 G4.................59.07N 2.36W
Stronsay Firth est. Scotland 19 G4.................59.05N 2.45W
Stroud England 10 C2.................51.44N 2.12W
Struer Denmark 43 B2.................56.30N 8.37E
Strule r. N. Ireland 16 B2.................54.43N 7.25W
Struma r. Greece 56 F4.................40.45N 23.51E
Strumble Head Wales 12 B4.................52.03N 5.05W
Strumica Macedonia 56 F4.................41.26N 22.39E
Stryy Ukraine 55 I3.................49.16N 23.51E
Stryy r. Ukraine 55 I3.................49.16N 24.18E
Studley England 10 D3.................52.16N 1.52W
Stupino Russian Fed. 55 P6.................54.53N 38.07E
Sturry England 11 G2.................51.18N 1.07E
Sturt Desert Australia 110 D3.................28.30S 141.12E
Stuttgart Germany 48 D3.................48.47N 9.12E
Styr r. Belarus/Ukraine 55 J5.................52.07N 26.35E
Suakin Sudan 85 H3.................19.04N 37.22E
Subotica Yugo. 56 D7.................46.04N 19.41E
Suceava Romania 55 J2.................47.39N 26.19E
Suchan r. Russian Fed. 106 B4.................42.53N 132.56E
Suck r. Rep. of Ire. 20 C3.................53.16N 8.03W
Sucre Bolivia 76 D3.................19.05S 65.15W
Sudak Ukraine 55 N1.................44.52N 34.57E
Sudan Africa 85 G3.................14.00N 30.00E
Sudbury Canada 63 J2.................46.30N 81.01W
Sudbury England 11 F3.................52.03N 0.44E
Sudd f. Sudan 85 H2.................7.50N 30.00E
Sudeten Mts. Czech Rep./Poland 54 E4.................50.30N 16.30E
Suez Egypt 94 D4.................29.59N 32.33E
Suez, G. of Egypt 94 D4.................28.48N 33.00E
Suez Canal Egypt 94 D5.................30.40N 32.20E

Suffolk d. England 11 F3 52.16N 1.00E
Suguta r. Kenya 87 B3 0.36N 36.04E
Suguti B. Tanzania 87 A2 1.44S 33.36E
Şuḩar Oman 95 I3 24.23N 56.43E
Suhl Germany 48 E4 50.37N 10.43E
Suir r. Rep. of Ire. 20 D2 52.17N 7.00W
Suizhou China 103 K4 31.46N 113.22E
Sukabumi Indonesia 104 D2 6.55S 106.50E
Sukadana Indonesia 104 E3 1.15S 110.00E
Sukhinichi Russian Fed. 55 N6 54.07N 35.21E
Sukkur Pakistan 96 D6 27.42N 68.54E
Sula i. Norway 43 A3 61.10N 4.50E
Sulaiman Ranges mts. Pakistan 90 I5 30.00N 68.00E
Sula Is. Indonesia 105 H3 1.50S 125.10E
Sulawesi i. Indonesia 104 G3 2.00S 120.30E
Sulina Romania 55 K1 45.08N 29.40E
Sullana Peru 76 B4 4.52S 80.39W
Sulmona Italy 50 E5 42.04N 13.57E
Sulu Archipelago Phil. 105 G5 5.30N 121.00E
Sulu Sea Pacific Oc. 104 G5 8.00N 120.00E
Sumatra i. Indonesia 104 C3 2.00S 102.00E
Sumba i. Indonesia 104 F2 9.30S 119.55E
Sumbawa i. Indonesia 104 F2 8.45S 117.50E
Sumburgh Scotland 19 Y8 59.53N 1.16W
Sumburgh Head Scotland 19 Y8 59.51N 1.16W
Summer Isles is. Scotland 18 D3 58.01N 5.26W
Sumqayıt Azerbaijan 58 G2 40.35N 49.38E
Sumy Ukraine 55 N4 50.55N 34.49E
Sunart, Loch Scotland 18 D1 56.42N 5.45W
Sunda Str. Indonesia 104 C2 6.00S 105.50E
Sunderland England 15 F3 54.55N 1.22W
Sundsvall Sweden 43 D3 62.22N 17.20E
Sunga Tanzania 87 B2 4.25S 38.04E
Sungaipenuh Indonesia 104 C3 2.00S 101.28E
Sungurlu Turkey 57 L4 40.10N 34.23E
Suolijärvet l. Finland 43 F4 66.18N 28.00E
Suonenjoki Finland 43 F3 62.40N 27.06E
Superior U.S.A. 65 H6 46.42N 92.05W
Superior, L. N. America 65 I6 48.00N 88.00W
Suq ash Shuyukh Iraq 95 G5 30.53N 46.28E
Sur Oman 95 I3 22.23N 59.32E
Surab Pakistan 95 K4 28.29N 66.16E
Surabaya Indonesia 104 E2 7.14S 112.45E
Surakarta Indonesia 104 E2 7.32S 110.50E
Surat India 96 E5 21.10N 72.54E
Surendranagar India 96 E5 22.42N 71.41E
Surgut Russian Fed. 58 J4 61.13N 73.20E
Surigao Phil. 105 H5 9.47N 125.29E
Surin Thailand 104 C6 14.53N 103.29E
Suriname S. America 74 D7 4.00N 56.00W
Surrey d. England 11 E2 51.16N 0.30W
Surtsey i. Iceland 43 X1 63.18N 20.37W
Susangerd Iran 95 G5 31.40N 48.06E
Sutak Jammu & Kashmir 97 F7 33.12N 77.28E
Sutherland f. Scotland 19 E3 58.20N 4.20W
Sutlej r. Pakistan 96 E6 29.26N 71.09E
Sutterton England 11 E3 52.54N 0.06W
Sutton England 11 F3 52.23N 0.07E
Sutton Bridge England 11 F3 52.46N 0.12E
Sutton Coldfield England 10 D3 52.33N 1.50W
Sutton in Ashfield England 15 F2 53.08N 1.16W
Suva Fiji 111 G4 18.08S 178.25E
Suvorov I. Cook Is. 108 O5 13.15S 163.05W
Suwałki Poland 54 H6 54.07N 22.56E
Suzhou Anhui China 103 L4 33.38N 117.02E
Suzhou Jiangsu China 103 M4 31.21N 120.40E
Suzu Japan 106 C3 37.20N 137.15E
Suzuka Japan 106 C2 34.51N 136.35E
Svalbard is. Norway 58 D5 76.00N 15.00E
Svapa r. Russian Fed. 55 N4 51.44N 34.56E
Sveg Sweden 43 C3 62.02N 14.20E
Svendborg Denmark 43 B1 55.04N 10.38E
Svetogorsk Russian Fed. 43 G3 61.07N 28.50E
Svitavy Czech Rep. 54 E3 49.45N 16.27E
Svitlovods'k Ukraine 55 M3 49.04N 33.15E
Svobodnyy Russian Fed. 59 O3 51.24N 128.05E
Swabian Alps mts. Germany 48 D3 48.20N 9.30E
Swadlincote England 10 D3 52.47N 1.34W
Swaffham England 11 F3 52.38N 0.42E
Swains I. Samoa 108 N5 11.03S 171.06W
Swakopmund Namibia 86 A2 22.40S 14.34E
Swale r. England 15 F3 54.05N 1.20W
Swanage England 10 D1 50.36N 1.59W
Swan Is. Honduras 71 H4 17.25N 83.55W
Swanley England 11 F2 51.24N 0.12E
Swansea Wales 12 D3 51.37N 3.57W
Swansea d. Wales 12 C3 51.35N 4.10W
Swansea B. Wales 12 D3 51.33N 3.50W
Swaziland Africa 86 C2 26.30S 31.30E
Sweden Europe 43 C2 63.00N 16.00E
Sweetwater U.S.A. 64 F3 32.37N 100.25W
Swift Current town Canada 62 H3 50.17N 107.49W
Swilly, Lough Rep. of Ire. 20 D5 55.10N 7.32W
Swindon England 10 D2 51.33N 1.47W
Swineshead England 11 E3 52.57N 0.10W
Świnoujście Poland 54 D5 53.55N 14.18E
Switzerland Europe 44 G5 47.00N 8.00E
Swords Rep. of Ire. 20 E3 53.28N 6.13W
Sybil Pt. Rep. of Ire. 20 A2 52.10N 10.27W
Sydney Australia 110 E2 33.55S 151.10E
Sydney Mines town Canada 63 L2 46.10N 60.10W
Syktyvkar Russian Fed. 58 H4 61.42N 50.45E
Sylarna mtn. Norway/Sweden 43 C3 63.01N 12.13E
Sylt i. Germany 43 B1 54.50N 8.20E
Syracuse U.S.A. 65 K5 43.03N 76.10W
Syrdar'ya r. Asia 58 I2 46.00N 61.12E
Syria Asia 94 E5 35.00N 38.00E
Syrian Desert Asia 94 E5 32.00N 39.00E
Syzran Russian Fed. 58 G3 53.10N 48.29E
Szczecin Poland 54 D5 53.25N 14.32E
Szczecinek Poland 54 E5 53.42N 16.41E
Szczytno Poland 54 G5 53.34N 21.00E
Szeged Hungary 54 G2 46.16N 20.08E
Székesfehérvár Hungary 54 F2 47.12N 18.25E
Szekszárd Hungary 54 F2 46.22N 18.44E
Szombathely Hungary 54 E2 47.12N 16.38E

T

Tabas Iran 95 I5 33.36N 56.55E
Tabasco d. Mexico 70 F4 18.30N 93.00W
Tabatinga, Serra da mts. Brazil 77 F3 10.00S 44.00W
Tábor Czech Rep. 54 D3 49.25N 14.41E
Tabora Tanzania 86 C4 5.02S 32.50E
Tabrīz Iran 95 G6 38.05N 46.18E
Tabuaeran i. Kiribati 108 P7 3.52N 159.20W
Tabuk Saudi Arabia 94 E4 28.25N 36.35E
Täby Sweden 43 D2 59.29N 18.04E
Tacloban Phil. 105 G6 11.15N 124.59E
Tacna Peru 76 C3 18.01S 70.15W
Tacoma U.S.A. 64 B6 47.16N 122.30W
Tacuarembó Uruguay 77 E1 31.42S 56.00W
Tadcaster England 15 F2 53.53N 1.16W
Taegu S. Korea 103 N5 35.52N 128.36E
Taejon S. Korea 103 N5 36.20N 127.26E
Taf r. Wales 12 C3 51.45N 4.29W
Taganrog Russian Fed. 53 K6 47.14N 38.55E
Taganrog, G. of Ukraine/Russian Fed. 53 K6 47.00N 38.30E
Tagbilaran Phil. 105 G5 9.38N 123.53E
Tagula I. P.N.G. 110 E4 11.30S 153.30E
Tagus r. Portugal 46 A3 39.00N 8.57W
Tahat, Mt. Algeria 84 E4 23.20N 5.40E
Tahiti i. Îs. de la Société 109 Q5 17.37S 149.27W
Taibei Taiwan 103 M2 25.05N 121.32E
Taidong Taiwan 103 M2 22.49N 121.10E
Tain Scotland 19 E2 57.49N 4.02W
Tainan Taiwan 103 M2 23.01N 120.14E
Taiping Malaysia 104 C4 4.54N 100.42E
Taita Hills Kenya 87 B2 3.20S 38.17E
Taivalkoski Finland 43 G4 65.35N 28.20E
Taivaskero mtn. Finland 43 E5 68.02N 24.00E
Taiwan Asia 103 M2 23.30N 121.00E
Taiwan Str. China/Taiwan 103 M2 25.00N 120.00E
Taiyuan China 103 K5 37.50N 112.30E
Taizhong Taiwan 103 M2 24.09N 120.40E
Ta'izz Yemen 94 F1 13.35N 44.02E
Tajikistan Asia 102 C5 39.00N 70.30E
Tak Thailand 104 B7 16.47N 99.10E
Takabba Kenya 87 C3 3.25N 40.11E
Takamatsu Japan 106 B2 34.28N 134.05E
Takaoka Japan 106 C3 36.47N 137.00E
Take-shima i. see Tok-to i. Japan 106 B3
Taklimakan Shamo des. China 102 E5 38.10N 82.00E
Talagang Pakistan 95 L5 32.55N 72.25E
Talara Peru 76 B4 4.38S 81.18W
Talaud Is. Indonesia 105 H4 4.20N 126.50E
Talavera de la Reina Spain 46 C3 39.58N 4.50W
Talca Chile 75 B3 35.28S 71.40W
Talcahuano Chile 75 B3 36.40S 73.10W
Taldykorgan Kazakhstan 102 D6 45.02N 78.23E
Talgarth Wales 12 D3 51.59N 3.15W
Taliabu i. Indonesia 105 G3 1.50S 124.55E
Tallahassee U.S.A. 65 J3 30.28N 84.19W
Tallinn Estonia 43 F2 59.22N 24.48E
Taloyoak Canada 63 I4 69.30N 93.20W
Talsi Latvia 43 E2 57.15N 22.36E
Taltson r. Canada 62 G4 61.35N 112.12W
Tamale Ghana 84 D2 9.26N 0.49W
Tamanrasset Algeria 84 E4 22.50N 5.31E
Tamar r. England 13 C2 50.28N 4.13W
Tamaulipas d. Mexico 70 E5 24.00N 98.20W
Tama Wildlife Res. Ethiopia 87 B4 6.00N 36.00E
Tambach Kenya 87 B3 0.32N 35.32E
Tambacounda Senegal 84 C3 13.45N 13.40W
Tambelan Is. Indonesia 104 D4 0.59N 107.35E
Tambov Russian Fed. 58 G3 52.44N 41.28E
Tambre r. Spain 46 A5 42.50N 8.55W
Tâmega r. Portugal 46 A4 41.04N 8.17W
Tamiahua Lagoon Mexico 70 E5 21.30N 97.20W
Tamil Nadu d. India 97 F3 11.15N 79.00E
Tampa-St. Petersburg U.S.A. 65 J2 27.58N 82.38W
Tampere Finland 43 E3 61.32N 23.45E
Tampico Mexico 70 E5 22.18N 97.52W
Tamworth Australia 110 E2 31.07S 150.57E
Tamworth England 10 D3 52.38N 1.42W
Tana r. Kenya 87 C2 2.32S 40.32E
Tana, L. Ethiopia 85 H3 12.00N 37.20E
Tanafjorden est. Norway 43 G5 70.40N 28.30E
Tanami Desert Australia 110 C4 19.50S 130.50E
Tanana U.S.A. 62 C4 65.11N 152.10W
Tanaro r. Italy 50 C6 45.01N 8.46E
Tando Adam Pakistan 96 D6 25.46N 68.40E
Tandragee N. Ireland 16 C1 54.21N 6.26W
Tanega-shima i. Japan 106 B2 30.32N 131.00E
Tanga Tanzania 87 B1 5.07S 39.05E
Tanganyika, L. Africa 86 B4 5.37S 29.30E
Tangier Morocco 84 D5 35.48N 5.45W
Tangshan China 103 L5 39.37N 118.05E
Tanimbar Is. Indonesia 105 I2 7.50S 131.30E
Tanjay Phil. 105 G5 9.31N 123.10E
Tanjona Bobaomby c. Madagascar 86 D3 11.58S 49.14E
Tanjona Vohimena c. Madagascar 86 D2 25.34S 45.10E
Tanjungkarang Telukbetung Indonesia 104 D2 5.28S 105.16E
Tanjungpandan Indonesia 104 D3 2.44S 107.36E
Tanjungredeb Indonesia 104 F4 2.09N 117.29E
Tank Pakistan 95 L5 32.13N 70.23E
Tanna i. Vanuatu 111 F4 19.30S 169.20E
Tanta Egypt 94 D5 30.48N 31.00E
Tanzania Africa 86 C4 5.00S 35.00E
Tao'an China 103 M7 45.25N 122.46E
Taourirt Morocco 52 C3 34.25N 2.53W
Tapachula Mexico 70 F3 14.54N 92.15W
Tapajós r. Brazil 77 E4 2.40S 55.30W
Tapauá r. Brazil 76 D4 5.40S 64.20W
Tapi r. India 96 E5 21.05N 72.45E
Taquari r. Brazil 77 E3 19.00S 57.27W
Tar r. Rep. of Ire. 20 D2 52.15N 7.48W
Tara r. Yugo. 56 D5 43.23N 18.47E
Tarakan Indonesia 104 F4 3.20N 117.38E
Tarancón Spain 46 D4 40.01N 3.01W
Tarangire Nat. Park Tanzania 87 B2 4.00S 36.00E
Taranto Italy 50 G4 40.28N 17.14E
Taranto, G. of Italy 50 G4 40.00N 17.20E
Tarapoto Peru 76 C4 6.31S 76.23W
Tarbat Ness c. Scotland 19 F2 57.52N 3.46W
Tarbert A. and B. Scotland 16 D3 55.57N 5.45W
Tarbert A. and B. Scotland 16 D3 55.51N 5.25W
Tarbert W.Isles Scotland 18 C2 57.55N 6.50W
Tarbes France 44 D3 43.14N 0.05E
Târgu-Jiu Romania 56 F6 45.03N 23.17E
Târgu Mureş Romania 55 I2 46.33N 24.34E
Târgu Secuiesc Romania 55 J2 46.00N 26.08E
Tari P.N.G. 105 K2 5.52S 142.58E
Tarija Bolivia 76 D2 21.33S 64.45W
Tarīm Yemen 95 G2 16.03N 49.00E
Tarim Basin f. China 102 E5 40.00N 82.00E
Tarime Tanzania 87 A2 1.20S 34.20E
Tarleton England 14 E2 53.41N 2.50W
Tarn r. France 44 D4 44.15N 1.15E
Tarnica mtn. Poland 54 H3 49.05N 22.44E
Tarnów Poland 54 G4 50.01N 20.59E
Taroudannt Morocco 52 B3 30.31N 8.55W
Tarragona Spain 46 F4 41.07N 1.15E
Tarsus Turkey 57 L2 36.52N 34.52E
Tartary, G. of Russian Fed. 59 Q2 47.40N 141.00E
Tartu Estonia 43 F2 58.20N 26.44E
Ţarţūs Syria 57 L1 34.55N 35.52E
Tashkent Uzbekistan 102 B6 41.16N 69.13E
Tasiilaq Greenland 63 O4 65.40N 38.00W
Tasikmalaya Indonesia 104 D2 7.20S 108.16E
Tasmania d. Australia 110 D1 42.00S 147.00E
Tasman Sea Pacific Oc. 111 F2 38.00S 160.00E
Tatarbunary Ukraine 55 K1 45.49N 29.34E
Tatarsk Russian Fed. 58 J3 55.14N 76.00E
Tatvan Turkey 94 F6 38.31N 42.15E
Taubaté Brazil 77 F2 23.00S 45.36W
Taung-gyi Myanmar 97 J5 20.49N 97.01E
Taunton England 13 D3 51.01N 3.07W
Taunus mts. Germany 48 D4 50.07N 8.10E
Taupo, L. New Zealand 111 G2 38.45S 175.30E
Taurus Mts. Turkey 57 K2 37.15N 34.00E
Taverham England 11 G3 52.40N 1.13E
Tavira Portugal 46 B2 37.07N 7.39W
Tavistock England 13 C2 50.33N 4.09W
Tavoy Myanmar 97 J3 14.07N 98.18E
Tavy r. England 13 C2 50.27N 4.10W
Taw r. England 13 C3 51.05N 4.05W
Tawau Malaysia 104 F4 4.16N 117.54E
Tawe r. Wales 12 D3 51.38N 3.56W
Tawitawi i. Phil. 104 G5 5.05N 120.00E
Tay r. Scotland 17 F4 56.21N 3.18W
Tay, Loch Scotland 16 E4 56.32N 4.08W
Tayma' Saudi Arabia 94 E4 27.37N 38.30E
Taymyr, L. Russian Fed. 59 M5 74.20N 101.00E
Taymyr Pen. Russian Fed. 59 L5 75.30N 99.00E
Tayport Scotland 17 G4 56.27N 2.53W
Taytay Phil. 104 F6 10.47N 119.32E
Taz r. Russian Fed. 58 J4 67.30N 78.50E
Taza Morocco 52 C3 34.16N 4.01W
Te Anau, L. New Zealand 111 F1 45.25S 167.43E
Tébessa Algeria 52 E4 35.22N 8.08E
Tebingtinggi Indonesia 104 B4 3.20N 99.08E
Tecuci Romania 55 J1 45.49N 27.27E
Tedzhen Turkmenistan 95 J6 37.26N 60.30E
Tees r. England 15 F3 54.35N 1.11W
Tees B. England 15 F3 54.40N 1.07W
Tefé r. Brazil 76 D4 3.35S 64.47W
Tegucigalpa Honduras 70 G3 14.05N 87.14W
Teguise Canary Is. 46 Z2 29.03N 13.36W
Tehran Iran 95 H6 35.40N 51.26E
Tehuantepec, G. of Mexico 70 F4 16.00N 95.00W
Teide, Pico del mtn. Canary Is. 46 X2 28.17N 16.39W
Teifi r. Wales 12 C4 52.05N 4.41W
Teign r. England 13 D2 50.32N 3.36W
Teignmouth England 13 D2 50.33N 3.30W
Teith r. Scotland 17 E4 56.09N 4.00W
Tekirdağ Turkey 56 H4 40.59N 27.30E
Tel Aviv Yafo Israel 94 D5 32.05N 34.46E
Teles Pires r. Brazil 77 E4 7.20S 57.30W
Telford England 10 C3 52.42N 2.30W
Teme r. England 10 C3 52.10N 2.13W
Temirtau Kazakhstan 102 C8 50.05N 72.55E
Temple U.S.A. 64 G3 31.06N 97.22W
Temple Ewell England 11 G2 51.09N 1.16E
Templemore Rep. of Ire. 20 D2 52.48N 7.51W
Temryuk Russian Fed. 57 M6 45.16N 37.24E
Temuco Chile 75 B3 38.45S 72.40W
Tena Ecuador 76 C4 1.00S 77.48W
Tenasserim Myanmar 97 J3 12.05N 99.00E
Tenbury Wells England 10 C3 52.18N 2.35W
Tenby Wales 12 C3 51.40N 4.42W
Ten Degree Channel Indian Oc. 97 I2 10.00N 92.30E
Tendo Japan 106 D3 38.22N 140.22E
Tenerife i. Canary Is. 46 X2 28.10N 16.30W
Tengiz, L. Kazakhstan 102 B8 50.30N 69.00E
Tennessee d. U.S.A. 65 I4 36.00N 86.00W
Tennessee r. U.S.A. 65 I4 37.10N 88.25W
Tenryu r. Japan 106 C2 34.42N 137.44E
Tenterden England 11 F2 51.04N 0.42E
Teófilo Otôni Brazil 77 F3 17.52S 41.31W
Tepic Mexico 70 D5 21.30N 104.51W
Teplice Czech Rep. 54 C4 50.40N 13.50E
Teraina i. Kiribati 108 O7 4.30N 160.02W
Teramo Italy 50 E5 42.40N 13.43E
Terebovlya Ukraine 55 I3 49.18N 25.44E
Teresina Brazil 77 F4 4.50S 42.50W
Tergnier France 42 C1 49.39N 3.18E
Termez Uzbekistan 95 K6 37.15N 67.15E
Terminillo, Monte mtn. Italy 50 E5 42.29N 13.00E
Términos Lagoon Mexico 70 F4 18.30N 91.30W
Termoli Italy 50 F4 41.58N 14.59E
Tern r. England 10 C3 52.40N 2.38W
Ternate Indonesia 105 H4 0.48N 127.23E
Terneuzen Neth. 42 C3 51.20N 3.50E
Terni Italy 50 E5 42.34N 12.44E
Ternopil' Ukraine 55 I3 49.35N 25.39E
Terrace Canada 62 F3 54.31N 128.32W
Terrassa Spain 46 F4 41.34N 2.00E
Terre Haute U.S.A. 65 I4 39.27N 87.24W
Terrington Marsh England 11 F3 52.47N 0.15E
Terschelling i. Neth. 42 E5 53.25N 5.25E
Teseney Eritrea 94 E2 15.05N 36.41E
Teslin Canada 62 E4 60.10N 132.42W
Test r. England 10 D1 50.55N 1.29W
Tetas, Punta c. Chile 76 C2 23.32S 70.39W
Tetbury England 10 C2 51.37N 2.09W
Tete Mozambique 86 C3 16.10S 33.30E
Tetney England 15 G2 53.30N 0.01W
Tétouan Morocco 84 D5 35.34N 5.22W
Teviot r. Scotland 17 G3 55.36N 2.26W
Teviothead Scotland 17 G3 55.20N 2.56W
Tewkesbury England 10 C2 51.59N 2.09W
Texarkana U.S.A. 65 H3 33.28N 94.02W
Texas d. U.S.A. 64 G3 32.00N 100.00W
Texel i. Neth. 42 D5 53.05N 4.47E
Texoma, L. U.S.A. 64 G3 34.00N 96.40W
Tezpur India 97 I6 26.38N 92.49E
Thai Binh Vietnam 104 D8 20.27N 106.20E
Thailand Asia 104 C7 16.00N 101.00E
Thailand, G. of Asia 104 C6 11.00N 101.00E
Thai Nguyên Vietnam 104 D8 21.31N 105.55E
Thal Desert Pakistan 95 L5 31.30N 71.40E
Thame England 10 E2 51.44N 0.58W
Thame r. England 10 D2 51.38N 1.10W
Thames r. England 11 F2 51.30N 0.05E
Thanh Hoa Vietnam 104 D7 19.50N 105.48E
Thar Desert India 96 E6 28.00N 72.00E
Thasos i. Greece 56 G4 40.40N 24.39E
Thatcham England 10 D2 51.25N 1.15W
Thaton Myanmar 97 J4 16.56N 97.20E
Thaxted England 11 F2 51.57N 0.21E
The Bahamas C. America 71 I5 23.30N 75.00W
The Calf mtn. England 14 E3 54.21N 2.32W
The Cheviot mtn. England 15 E4 55.29N 2.10W
The East Riding of Yorkshire d. England 15 G2 53.48N 0.35W
The Everglades f. U.S.A. 65 J2 26.00N 80.30W
The Gambia Africa 84 C3 13.30N 15.00W
The Great Oasis Egypt 94 D3 24.30N 30.40E
The Grenadines is. Windward Is. 71 L3 12.35N 61.20W
The Gulf Asia 95 H4 27.00N 50.00E
The Hague Neth. 42 D4 52.05N 4.16E
Thelon r. Canada 62 I4 64.23N 96.15W
The Marsh f. England 11 F3 52.50N 0.10E
The Minch str. Scotland 18 D3 58.10N 5.50W
The Mullet pen. Rep. of Ire. 20 A4 54.10N 10.05W
The Mumbles Wales 12 C3 51.34N 4.00W
The Naze c. England 11 G2 51.53N 1.17E
The Needles c. England 10 D1 50.39N 1.35W
The North Sd. Scotland 19 G4 59.18N 2.45W
Theodore Roosevelt r. Brazil 77 D4 7.33S 60.24W
The Old Man of Coniston mtn. England 14 D3 54.22N 3.08W
The Pas Canada 62 H3 53.50N 101.15W
The Pennines hills England 15 E3 54.40N 2.20W
The Rhinns of Galloway f. Scotland 16 D2 54.50N 5.02W
The Slot str. Solomon Is. 111 E5 7.30S 157.00E
The Snares is. New Zealand 108 L2 48.00S 166.30E
The Solent str. England 10 D1 50.45N 1.20W
The Sound England 13 C2 50.20N 4.10W
Thessaloniki Greece 56 F4 40.38N 22.56E
Thessaloniki, G. of Med. Sea 56 F4 40.10N 23.00E
The Storr mtn. Scotland 18 C2 57.30N 6.11W
Thet r. England 11 F3 52.25N 0.44E
Thetford England 11 F3 52.25N 0.44E
Thetford Mines Canada 65 L6 46.05N 71.18W
The Trossachs f. Scotland 16 E4 56.15N 4.25W
The Wash b. England 11 F3 52.55N 0.15E
The Weald f. England 11 F2 51.05N 0.20E
Thiers France 44 E4 45.51N 3.33E
Thiès Senegal 84 A3 14.48N 16.56W
Thika Kenya 87 B2 1.04S 37.04E
Thimbu Bhutan 97 H6 27.29N 89.40E
Thionville France 44 G6 49.22N 6.11E
Thira i. Greece 56 G2 36.24N 25.27E
Thirlmere l. England 14 D3 54.32N 3.04W
Thirsk England 15 F3 54.15N 1.20W
Thisted Denmark 43 B2 56.57N 8.42E
Thomastown Rep. of Ire. 20 D2 52.31N 7.08W
Thompson Canada 62 I3 55.45N 97.54W
Thornaby-on-Tees England 15 F3 54.34N 1.18W
Thornbury England 10 C2 51.36N 2.31W
Thorne England 15 G2 53.36N 0.56W
Thornhill Scotland 17 F3 55.15N 3.46W
Thornton England 14 E2 53.53N 3.00W
Thrapston England 11 E3 52.24N 0.32W
Thuin Belgium 42 D2 50.21N 4.20E
Thule see Qaanaaq Greenland 63
Thun Switz. 44 G5 46.46N 7.38E
Thunder Bay town Canada 63 J2 48.25N 89.14W
Thüringian Forest mts. Germany 48 E4 50.40N 10.50E
Thurles Rep. of Ire. 20 D2 52.41N 7.50W
Thursby England 14 D3 54.51N 3.03W
Thurso Scotland 19 F3 58.35N 3.32W
Thurso r. Scotland 19 F3 58.35N 3.32W
Thurso B. Scotland 19 F3 58.35N 3.32W
Tianjin China 103 L5 39.08N 117.12E
Tianshui China 103 J4 34.25N 105.58E
Tiaret Algeria 52 D4 35.28N 1.21E
Tibaji r. Brazil 77 E2 22.45S 51.01W
Tibati Cameroon 84 F2 6.25N 12.33E
Tiber r. Italy 50 E4 41.45N 12.16E
Tiberias, L. Israel 94 E5 32.49N 35.36E
Tibesti mts. Chad 85 F4 21.00N 17.30E
Tibet d. China 102 F4 32.20N 86.00E
Tibetan Plateau f. China 102 F4 34.00N 86.15E
Tiburón i. Mexico 70 B6 29.00N 112.25W
Ticehurst England 11 F2 51.02N 0.23E
Tidjikja Mauritania 84 C3 18.29N 11.31W
Tiel Neth. 42 E3 51.53N 5.26E
Tielt Belgium 42 C3 51.00N 3.20E
Tienen Belgium 42 D2 50.49N 4.56E
Tien Shan mts. Asia 102 D6 42.00N 80.30E
Tierra del Fuego i. S. America 75 C1 54.00S 68.30W
Tiétar r. Spain 46 C3 39.50N 6.00W
Tiflis Georgia 58 G2 41.43N 44.48E
Tighina Moldova 55 K2 46.50N 29.29E
Tigre r. Peru 76 C4 4.30S 74.05W
Tigre r. Venezuela 71 L2 9.20N 62.30W
Tigris r. Asia 95 G5 31.00N 47.27E
Tihamah f. Saudi Arabia 94 F2 20.00N 40.30E
Tijuana Mexico 70 A7 32.29N 117.10W
Tikhoretsk Russian Fed. 53 L6 45.52N 40.07E
Tikrīt Iraq 94 F5 34.36N 43.42E
Tiksi Russian Fed. 59 O5 71.40N 128.45E
Tilburg Neth. 42 E3 51.34N 5.05E
Tilbury England 11 F2 51.28N 0.23E
Tilehurst England 10 D2 51.27N 1.02W
Till r. England 15 E4 55.41N 2.12W
Tillabéri Niger 84 E3 14.28N 1.27E
Tillicoultry Scotland 17 F4 56.09N 3.45W
Timashevsk Russian Fed. 53 K6 45.38N 38.56E
Timiş r. Yugo./Romania 56 E6 44.49N 20.28E
Timişoara Romania 54 G1 45.47N 21.15E
Timmins Canada 63 J2 48.30N 81.20W
Timon Brazil 77 F4 5.08S 42.52W
Timor i. Indonesia 105 H2 9.30S 125.00E
Timor Sea Austa. 110 B4 13.00S 122.00E
Timrå Sweden 43 D3 62.29N 17.20E
Tindouf Algeria 84 D4 27.42N 8.10W
Tinian i. N. Mariana Is. 105 L6 14.58N 145.38E
Tinos i. Greece 56 G2 37.36N 25.08E
Tintagel England 13 C2 50.40N 4.45W
Tinto mtn. Scotland 17 F3 55.36N 3.40W
Tipperary Rep. of Ire. 20 C2 52.29N 8.10W
Tipperary d. Rep. of Ire. 20 D2 52.37N 7.55W

Tiptree England 11 F2............51.48N 0.46E
Tiracambu, Serra do mts. Brazil 77 F4.... 4.00S 46.30W
Tiranë Albania 56 D4............41.20N 19.48E
Tiraspol Moldova 55 K2.........46.50N 29.38E
Tiree i. Scotland 16 C4..........56.30N 6.50W
Tirga Mor mtn. Scotland 18 C2...58.00N 6.59W
Tirso r. Italy 50 C3............39.52N 8.33E
Tiruchchirappalli India 97 F3....10.50N 78.43E
Tiruppur India 96 F3............11.05N 77.20E
Tisa r. Yugo. 56 E6............45.09N 20.16E
Tisza r. see Tisa r. Hungary 54
Titicaca, L. Bolivia/Peru 76 D3....16.00S 69.00W
Titovo Užice Yugo. 56 D5......43.52N 19.51E
Tiverton England 13 D2.........50.54N 3.30W
Tivoli Italy 50 E4............41.58N 12.48E
Tizi Ouzou Algeria 52 D4.......36.44N 4.05E
Tiznit Morocco 84 D4..........29.43N 9.44W
Tkhab mtn. Russian Fed. 57 N6...44.34N 38.23E
Tlaxcala Mexico 70 E4..........19.20N 98.12W
Tlaxcala Mexico 70 E4..........19.45N 98.20W
Tlemcen Algeria 84 D5.........34.53N 1.21W
Toamasina Madagascar 86 D3....18.10S 49.23E
Toba, L. Indonesia 104 C4......2.45N 98.50E
Tobago i. S. America 71 L3....11.15N 60.40W
Tobelo Indonesia 105 H4......1.45N 127.59E
Tobermory Scotland 16 C4....56.37N 6.04W
Tobooali Indonesia 104 D3....3.00S 106.30E
Tobol r. Russian Fed. 58 I3....58.15N 68.12E
Tobol'sk Russian Fed. 58 I3....58.15N 68.12E
Tocantins d. Brazil 77 F3......10.15S 48.30W
Tocantins r. Brazil 77 F4......2.40S 49.20W
Tocopilla Chile 76 C2..........22.05S 70.12W
Todmorden England 15 E2......53.43N 2.07W
Toft Scotland 19 Y9...........60.27N 1.11W
Togian Is. Indonesia 105 G3....0.20S 122.00E
Togo Africa 84 E2............8.30N 1.00E
Tok U.S.A. 62 D4............63.20N 143.10W
Tokara-retto is. Japan 106 A1...29.30N 129.00E
Tokat Turkey 57 M4...........40.20N 36.35E
Tokelau i. Pacific Oc. 108 N6...9.00S 171.45W
Tokmak Ukraine 55 N2.........47.13N 35.43E
Tok-to i. Japan 106 B3........30.51N 130.28E
Tokushima Japan 106 B2.......34.03N 134.34E
Tokyo Japan 106 C3..........35.40N 139.45E
Tôlaňaro Madagascar 86 D2....25.01S 47.00E
Toledo Spain 46 C3..........39.52N 4.02W
Toledo U.S.A. 65 J5..........41.40N 83.35W
Toledo, Montes de mts. Spain 46 C3...39.35N 4.30W
Tolentino Italy 50 E4.........43.12N 13.17E
Toliara Madagascar 86 D2.....23.20S 43.41E
Tolitoli Indonesia 104 G4.....1.05N 120.50E
Tollesbury England 11 F2......51.44N 0.51E
Tolsta Head Scotland 18 C3....58.20N 6.10W
Toluca Mexico 70 E4..........19.20N 99.40W
Tomanivi mtn. Fiji 111 U4......17.36S 178.09E
Tomaszów Lubelski Poland 55 H4...50.28N 23.25E
Tomaszów Mazowiecki Poland 54 G4...51.32N 20.01E
Tombigbee r. U.S.A. 65 K2....31.05N 87.55W
Tombouctou Mali 84 D3........16.49N 2.59W
Tomelloso Spain 46 D3.........39.09N 3.01W
Tomini G. Indonesia 104 G3....0.30S 120.45E
Tomsk Russian Fed. 58 K3......56.30N 85.05E
Tona, G. of Russian Fed. 59 P5...72.00N 136.10E
Tonbridge England 11 F2......51.12N 0.16E
Tondano Indonesia 105 G4.....1.19N 124.56E
Tone r. England 13 D2.........51.04N 2.56W
Tonga Pacific Oc. 108 N5......20.00S 175.00W
Tongareva i. Cook Is. 108 P6...9.00S 158.00W
Tongatapu Group is. Tonga 108 N4...21.10S 175.10W
Tongeren Belgium 42 E2.......50.47N 5.28E
Tonghua China 103 N6.........41.40N 126.52E
Tongking, G. of Asia 104 D8...20.00N 107.50E
Tongliao China 103 M6........43.37N 122.15E
Tongling China 103 L4.........30.57N 117.40E
Tongue Scotland 19 E3.........58.28N 4.26W
Tônlé Sab l. Cambodia 104 C6...12.50N 104.00E
Tønsberg Norway 43 B2........59.16N 10.25E
Toowoomba Australia 110 E3....27.35S 151.54E
Topeka U.S.A. 65 G4..........39.03N 95.41W
Topozero, Ozero l. Russian Fed. 43 H4...65.45N 32.00E
Topsham England 13 D2.......50.40N 3.27W
Tor B. England 13 D2.........50.25N 3.30W
Torbat-e-Heydarīyeh Iran 95 I6...35.16N 59.13E
Torbat-e Jam Iran 95 J6......35.15N 60.37E
Tordesillas Spain 46 C4.......41.30N 5.00W
Torfaen d. Wales 12 D3.......51.42N 3.01W
Tori-shima i. Japan 108 J9....30.28N 140.18E
Tormes r. Spain 46 B4........41.18N 6.29W
Torne r. Sweden 43 E4........67.13N 23.30E
Torneträsk l. Sweden 43 D5....68.15N 19.20E
Tornio Finland 43 F4.........65.52N 24.10E
Toronto Canada 63 K2........43.42N 79.25W
Tororo Uganda 87 A3.........0.39N 34.10E
Torpoint town England 13 C2...50.23N 4.12W
Torquay England 13 D2.......50.27N 3.31W
Torre del Greco Italy 50 F4....40.44N 14.22E
Torremolinos Spain 46 C2.....36.37N 4.30W
Torrens, L. Australia 110 C2...31.00S 137.50E
Torreón Mexico 70 D6.........25.34N 103.25W
Torres Is. Vanuatu 111 F4.....13.45S 166.30E
Torres Str. Pacific Oc. 110 D4...10.30S 142.20E
Torres Vedras Portugal 46 A3....39.05N 9.15W
Torrevieja Spain 46 E2.......37.59N 0.40W
Torridge r. England 13 C2.....51.01N 4.12W
Torridon Scotland 18 D2......57.32N 5.30W
Torridon, Loch Scotland 18 D2...57.35N 5.50W
Torshavn Faeroes 58 A4......62.02N 6.47W
Tortolas, Cerro las mtn. Chile/Argentina 76 D2...29.55S 69.55W
Tortosa Spain 46 F4..........40.49N 0.31E
Toruń Poland 54 F5..........53.01N 18.35E
Tory I. Rep. of Ire. 20 C5....55.15N 8.15W
Tosno Russian Fed. 43 G2....59.38N 30.46E
Totland England 10 D1.......50.40N 1.32W
Totnes England 13 D2........50.26N 3.41W
Totton England 10 D2........50.55N 1.29W
Tottori Japan 106 B3.........35.32N 134.12E
Toubkal mtn. Morocco 84 D5...31.03N 7.57W
Touggourt Algeria 84 E5......33.08N 6.04E
Toulon France 44 F3.........43.07N 5.53E
Toulouse France 44 D3.......43.33N 1.24E
Toungoo Myanmar 97 J4......19.00N 96.30E
Touraine f. France 44 D5.....47.00N 1.00E
Tournai Belgium 42 C2.......50.36N 3.23E

Tournon-sur-Rhône France 44 F4...45.04N 4.50E
Tours France 44 D5..........47.23N 0.42E
Tove r. England 10 E3........52.03N 0.42W
Towada Japan 106 D4........40.36N 140.47E
Towcester England 10 E3.....52.07N 0.56W
Townsville Australia 110 D4...19.13S 146.48E
Towori G. Indonesia 105 G3....2.00S 122.30E
Towot Sudan 87 M4..........6.11N 34.28E
Toyama Japan 106 C3........36.42N 137.14E
Toyama-wan b. Japan 106 C3...37.00N 137.20E
Toyota Japan 106 C3.........35.05N 137.09E
Tozeur Tunisia 52 E3.........33.55N 8.08E
Trabzon Turkey 57 N4........41.00N 39.43E
Trafalgar, C. Spain 46 B2....36.10N 6.02W
Tralee Rep. of Ire. 20 B2.....52.16N 9.42W
Tralee B. Rep. of Ire. 20 B2...52.18N 9.55W
Tramore Rep. of Ire. 20 D2...52.10N 7.10W
Tranås Sweden 43 C2.........58.03N 15.00E
Trangan i. Indonesia 105 I2...6.30S 134.15E
Transylvanian Alps mts. Romania 34 F2...45.35N 24.40E
Trapani Italy 50 E3..........38.02N 12.30E
Trasimeno, Lago l. Italy 50 E5...43.09N 12.07E
Traverse City U.S.A. 65 I5....44.46N 85.38W
Travnik Bosnia. 56 C6.......44.14N 17.40E
Trebišov Slovakia 54 G3......48.40N 21.47E
Tredegar Wales 12 D3........51.47N 3.16W
Tregaron Wales 12 D4.......52.14N 3.56W
Treig, Loch Scotland 18 E1...56.48N 4.41W
Trelleborg Sweden 43 C1....55.22N 13.10E
Tremadoc B. Wales 12 C4....52.52N 4.14W
Trent r. England 15 G2.......53.41N 0.41W
Trento Italy 50 D7..........46.04N 11.08E
Trenton U.S.A. 65 L5.........40.15N 74.43W
Tresco i. England 13 A1......49.57N 6.20W
Tres Picos mtn. Argentina 75 C3...38.13S 61.50W
Treviso Italy 50 E6..........45.40N 12.14E
Trier Germany 48 C3.........49.45N 6.39E
Trieste Italy 50 E7..........45.40N 13.47E
Trikala Greece 56 E3........39.34N 21.46E
Trim Rep. of Ire. 20 E3......53.34N 6.47W
Trincomalee Sri Lanka 97 G2...8.34N 81.13E
Trindade i. Atlantic Oc. 72 H4...20.30S 29.15W
Tring England 10 E2.........51.48N 0.40W
Trinidad Bolivia 76 D5.......15.00S 64.50W
Trinidad i. S. America 71 L3...10.20N 61.10W
Trinidad U.S.A. 64 F4........37.11N 104.31W
Trinidad & Tobago S. America 71 L3...10.30N 61.20W
Tripoli Greece 56 F2.........37.31N 22.21E
Tripoli Lebanon 94 E5.......34.27N 35.50E
Tripoli Libya 84 F5..........32.58N 13.12E
Tripolitania f. Libya 52 F3...31.00N 12.00E
Tripura d. India 97 I5........23.45N 91.45E
Tristan da Cunha i. Atlantic Oc. 116 I4...38.00S 12.00W
Trivandrum India 96 F2......8.41N 76.57E
Trnava Slovakia 54 E3.......48.23N 17.35E
Trobriand Is. P.N.G. 110 E5...8.35S 151.05E
Troisdorf Germany 42 G2....50.50N 7.07E
Trois Rivières town Canada 63 K2...46.21N 72.34W
Troitsko-Pechorsk Russian Fed. 58 H4...62.40N 56.08E
Trollhättan Sweden 43 C2....58.17N 12.20E
Trombetas r. Brazil 77 E4....2.00S 55.40W
Tromsø Norway 43 D5........69.42N 19.00E
Trondheim Norway 43 B3.....63.36N 10.23E
Troon Scotland 16 E3........55.33N 4.40W
Trostan mtn. N. Ireland 16 C3...55.03N 6.10W
Troup Head Scotland 19 G2...57.41N 2.18W
Trout L. Canada 63 H7.......51.13N 93.20W
Trowbridge England 10 C2....51.18N 2.12W
Troyes France 44 F6.........48.18N 4.05E
Trubchevsk Russian Fed. 55 M5...52.36N 33.46E
Trujillo Peru 74 B6.........8.06S 79.00W
Truro Canada 63 L2.........45.24N 63.18W
Truro England 13 B2.........50.17N 5.02W
Tsaratanana, Massif du mts. Madagascar 86 D3...14.00S 49.00E
Tsavo r. Kenya 87 B2........2.59S 38.28E
Tsavo Nat. Park Kenya 87 B2...3.00S 38.30E
Tsetserleg Mongolia 103 I7...47.26N 101.22E
Tsimlyansk Resr. Russian Fed. 35 H2...48.00N 43.00E
Tsna r. Belarus 55 J5........52.10N 27.03E
Tsu Japan 106 C3...........34.43N 136.35E
Tsuchiura Japan 106 C3......36.05N 140.12E
Tsugaru-kaikyo str. Japan 106 D4...41.30N 140.50E
Tsumeb Namibia 86 A3.......19.13S 17.42E
Tsuruga Japan 106 C3.......35.40N 136.05E
Tsushima i. Japan 106 A2....34.30N 129.20E
Tuam Rep. of Ire. 20 C3.....53.32N 8.52W
Tuamotu Is. Pacific Oc. 109 Q5...17.00S 142.00W
Tuapse Russian Fed. 53 K3...44.06N 39.05E
Tuban Indonesia 104 E2......6.55S 112.01E
Tubbercurry Rep. of Ire. 20 C4...54.03N 8.47W
Tübingen Germany 48 D3....48.31N 9.02E
Tubruq Libya 85 G5.........32.06N 23.58E
Tubuai i. Pacific Oc. 109 Q4...23.23S 149.27W
Tucson U.S.A. 64 D3........32.15N 110.57W
Tucumcari U.S.A. 64 F4......35.11N 103.44W
Tucuruí Brazil 77 F4........3.42S 49.44W
Tucuruí Resr. Brazil 77 F4....4.35S 49.33W
Tudela Spain 46 E5.........42.04N 1.37W
Tuguegarao Phil. 105 G7....17.36N 121.44E
Tui Spain 46 A5............42.03N 8.38W
Tuineje Canary Is. 46 Y2....28.18N 14.03W
Tukangbesi Is. Indonesia 105 G2...5.30S 124.00E
Tukums Latvia 43 E2........56.58N 23.10E
Tula Russian Fed. 55 O6.....54.11N 37.38E
Tulcea Romania 55 K1.......45.10N 28.50E
Tul'chyn Ukraine 55 K3......48.40N 28.49E
Tullamore Rep. of Ire. 20 D3...53.17N 7.31W
Tulle France 44 D4.........45.16N 1.46E
Tullow Rep. of Ire. 20 E2....52.48N 6.43W
Tullybrack mtn. N. Ireland 16 B2...54.22N 7.50W
Tulsa U.S.A. 64 G4.........36.07N 95.58W
Tumaco Colombia 76 C5.....1.51N 78.46W
Tumba, L. Zaïre 86 A4.......0.45S 18.00E
Tumbes Peru 76 B4.........3.37S 80.27W
Tumen China 106 B4........42.59N 129.47E
Tumen r. China/N. Korea 106 B4...42.19N 130.40E
Tumkur India 96 F3.........13.20N 77.06E
Tummel r. Scotland 17 F4....56.39N 3.40W
Tummel, Loch Scotland 19 F1...56.43N 3.55W
Tump Pakistan 95 J4........26.06N 62.24E
Tumucumaque, Serra mts. S. America 77 E5...2.20N 54.50W
Tunceli Turkey 57 N3.......39.07N 39.34E

Tundzha r. Bulgaria 56 H5....42.00N 26.35E
Tunis Tunisia 84 F5.........36.47N 10.10E
Tunisia Africa 84 E5.........34.00N 9.00E
Tunja Colombia 71 J2........5.33N 73.23W
Tunnsjøen l. Norway 43 C4...64.45N 13.25E
Tupelo U.S.A. 65 I3.........34.15N 88.43W
Tupinambarama, Ilha i. Brazil 77 E4...3.00S 58.00W
Tura Russian Fed. 59 M4....64.05N 100.00E
Turabah Saudi Arabia 94 F3...21.13N 41.39E
Turbarkas Lithuania 54 H6...55.05N 22.48E
Turbat Pakistan 95 J4.......25.59N 63.04E
Turgay Kazakhstan 102 A7....49.38N 63.25E
Turgutlu Turkey 57 H3.......38.30N 27.43E
Turhal Turkey 57 M4........40.23N 36.05E
Turin Italy 50 B6...........45.04N 7.40E
Turkana, L. Kenya 87 B3.....4.00N 36.00E
Turkey Asia 57 K3..........39.00N 33.00E
Turkmenistan Asia 115 L7....40.00N 60.00E
Turks and Caicos Is. C.America 71 J5...21.30N 71.50W
Turks Is. Turks & Caicos Is. 71 J5...21.30N 71.10W
Turku Finland 43 E3.........60.27N 22.15E
Turkwel r. Kenya 87 B3......3.08N 35.39E
Turneffe Is. Belize 70 G4....17.30N 87.45W
Turnhout Belgium 42 D3.....51.19N 4.57E
Türnovo Bulgaria 56 G5.....43.04N 25.39E
Turnu Măgurele Romania 56 G5...43.43N 24.53E
Turpan China 102 F6........42.55N 89.06E
Turquino mtn. Cuba 71 I5....20.05N 76.50W
Turriff Scotland 19 G2......57.32N 2.29W
Tuscaloosa U.S.A. 65 I3.....33.12N 87.33W
Tutbury England 10 D3......52.52N 1.40W
Tuticorin India 96 F2.......8.48N 78.10E
Tuttlingen Germany 48 D2...47.59N 8.49E
Tutuila i. Samoa 108 N5.....14.18S 170.42W
Tuvalu i. Pacific Oc. 111 G5...8.00S 178.00E
Tuxford England 15 G2......53.14N 0.54W
Tuxtla Gutiérrez Mexico 70 F4...16.45N 93.09W
Tuz, L. Turkey 57 K3........38.45N 33.24E
Tuzla Bosnia. 56 D6........44.33N 18.41E
Tver Russian Fed. 58 F3.....56.47N 35.57E
Tweed r. Scotland 17 G3....55.46N 2.00W
Twin Falls town U.S.A. 64 D5...42.34N 114.30W
Twyford England 10 E2......51.29N 0.51W
Tyler U.S.A. 65 G3..........32.22N 95.18W
Tynda Russian Fed. 59 O3....55.11N 124.34E
Tyne r. England 15 F4.......55.00N 1.25W
Tyne and Wear d. England 15 F3...54.57N 1.35W
Tynemouth England 15 F4....55.01N 1.24W
Tynset Norway 43 B3........62.17N 10.47E
Tyre Lebanon 94 E5.........33.16N 35.12E
Tyrone d. N. Ireland 16 B2...54.30N 7.15W
Tyrrhenian Sea Med. Sea 50 D4...40.00N 12.00E
Tyumen Russian Fed. 58 I3...57.11N 65.29E
Tywi r. Wales 12 C3.........51.46N 4.22W

U

Uaupés Brazil 76 D4.........0.00 67.10W
Ubangi r. Congo/Zaïre 86 A4...0.25S 17.50E
Úbeda Spain 46 D3..........38.01N 3.22W
Uberaba Brazil 77 F3........19.47S 47.57W
Uberlândia Brazil 77 F3......18.57S 48.17W
Ubon Ratchathani Thailand 104 C7...15.15N 104.50E
Ucayali r. Peru 76 C4.......4.00S 73.30W
Uckfield England 11 F1......50.58N 0.06E
Udaipur India 96 E5.........24.36N 73.47E
Uddevalla Sweden 43 B2.....58.20N 11.56E
Uddjaure l. Sweden 43 D4....65.55N 17.50E
Udine Italy 50 E7...........46.03N 13.15E
Udipi India 96 E3...........13.21N 74.45E
Ueda Japan 106 C3.........36.27N 138.13E
Uele r. Zaïre 86 B5.........4.08N 22.25E
Uelzen Germany 48 E5......52.58N 10.34E
Ufa Russian Fed. 58 H3......54.45N 55.58E
Uganda Africa 86 B5........1.00N 33.00E
Uglegorsk Russian Fed. 59 Q2...49.01N 142.04E
Ugra r. Russian Fed. 55 N6...54.30N 36.10E
Uig Scotland 18 C2.........57.35N 6.22W
Uíge Angola 86 A4.........7.40S 15.09E
Uinta Mts. U.S.A. 64 D5.....40.45N 110.30W
Ujung Pandang Indonesia 104 F2...5.09S 119.28E
Ukerewe I. Tanzania 87 A2...2.00S 33.00E
Ukhta Russian Fed. 58 H4...63.33N 53.44E
Ukiah U.S.A. 64 B4.........39.09N 123.12W
Ukraine Europe 55 L3.......49.00N 30.00E
Ulaangom Mongolia 102 G7...49.59N 92.00E
Ulan Bator Mongolia 103 J7...47.54N 106.52E
Ulan-Ude Russian Fed. 59 M3...51.55N 107.40E
Ulchin S. Korea 106 A3......37.00N 129.26E
Uliastay Mongolia 102 H7....47.42N 96.52E
Ulithi i. Fed. States of Micronesia 105 J6...10.00N 139.40E
Ullapool Scotland 18 D2.....57.54N 5.10W
Ullswater l. England 14 E3...54.34N 2.52W
Ullung do i. S. Korea 106 B3...37.30N 130.55E
Ulm Germany 48 E3.........48.24N 10.00E
Ulsan S. Korea 106 A3......35.32N 129.21E
Ulster Canal Rep. of Ire. 16 B2...54.14N 7.00W
Ulundi R.S.A. 86 C2........28.17S 31.28E
Ulva i. Scotland 16 C4......56.29N 6.12W
Ulverston England 14 D3....54.13N 3.07W
Uman' Ukraine 55 L3.........48.45N 30.10E
Umboi i. P.N.G. 110 D5......5.35S 148.00E
Ume r. Sweden 43 E3.........63.43N 20.20E
Umeå Sweden 43 E3.........63.50N 20.15E
Umm Keddada Sudan 94 C2...13.33N 26.35E
Umm Ruwaba Sudan 94 D1...12.54N 31.13E
Umm Sa'ad Libya 94 B1.....31.33N 25.03E
Umtata R.S.A. 86 B1........31.35S 28.47E
Umuarama Brazil 77 E2......24.00S 53.20W
Una r. Croatia/Bosnia. 56 C6...45.16N 16.55E
Unayzah Saudi Arabia 94 F4...26.05N 43.57E
Ungava B. Canada 63 L3.....59.00N 67.30W
Unggi N. Korea 106 B4.......42.19N 130.24E
Ungwana B. Kenya 87 A2....2.40S 40.23E
Unimak I. U.S.A. 62 B3......54.50N 164.00W
Unini r. Brazil 77 D4........1.40S 61.40W
United Arab Emirates Asia 95 H3...24.00N 54.00E
United States of America N. America 64...39.00N 100.00W
Unst i. Scotland 19 Z9......60.45N 0.55W
Upa r. Russian Fed. 55 O5...54.00N 36.15E

Upavon England 10 D2......51.17N 1.49W
Upemba, L. Zaïre 86 B4.....8.35S 26.28E
Upernavik Greenland 63 M5...72.50N 56.00W
Upington R.S.A. 86 B2......28.26S 21.12E
Upolu i. W. Samoa 108 N5...13.55S 171.45W
Upper Lough Erne N. Ireland 16 B2...54.13N 7.32W
Upper Tean England 10 D3...52.57N 1.59W
Uppingham England 10 E3...52.36N 0.43W
Uppsala Sweden 43 D2......59.55N 17.38E
Upton upon Severn England 10 C3...52.04N 2.12W
Ural r. Russian Fed./Kazakhstan 58 H2...47.00N 52.00E
Ural Mts. Russian Fed. 58 H3...60.00N 59.00E
Ural'sk Kazakhstan 58 H3....51.19N 51.20E
Uranium City Canada 62 H3...59.32N 108.43W
Urawa Japan 106 C3........35.51N 139.39E
Ure r. England 15 F3........54.05N 1.20W
Urengoy Russian Fed. 58 J4...65.59N 78.30E
Urie r. Scotland 19 G2......57.16N 2.22W
Urmia Iran 94 G6...........37.32N 45.02E
Urmia, L. Iran 94 G6........37.40N 45.28E
Uruapán Mexico 70 D4......19.26N 102.04W
Urubamba r. Peru 76 C3.....10.43S 73.55W
Urucara Brazil 77 E4........2.32S 57.45W
Uruguaiana Brazil 77 E2.....29.45S 57.05W
Uruguay S. America 75 D3...33.00S 55.00W
Uruguay r. Uruguay 75 D3...34.00S 58.30W
Ürümqi China 102 F6........43.43N 87.38E
Uşak Turkey 57 I3...........38.42N 29.25E
Ushuaia Argentina 75 C1....54.47S 68.20W
Usk Wales 12 D3...........51.42N 2.53W
Usk r. Wales 12 D3.........51.34N 2.59W
Usk Resr. Wales 12 D3......51.56N 3.42W
Usol'ye-Sibirskoye Russian Fed. 59 M3...52.48N 103.40E
Ussuri r. Russian Fed. 106 B5...45.36N 133.20E
Ussuriysk Russian Fed. 59 P2...43.48N 131.59E
Ustica i. Italy 50 E3........38.42N 13.11E
Ust-Ilimsk Russian Fed. 59 M3...58.05N 102.40E
Ust-Kamchatsk Russian Fed. 59 S3...56.14N 162.28E
Ust-Kamenogorsk Kazakhstan 102 E8...50.00N 82.40E
Ust-Kut Russian Fed. 59 M3...56.40N 105.50E
Ust-Maya Russian Fed. 59 P4...60.25N 134.28E
Ust Olenek Russian Fed. 59 N5...72.59N 120.00E
Ust Urt Plateau f. Asia 58 H2...43.30N 55.00E
Utah d. U.S.A. 64 D4.......39.00N 112.00W
Utara i. Indonesia 105 J2....2.42S 100.05E
Utica U.S.A. 65 K5.........43.06N 75.05W
Utiel Spain 46 E3...........39.33N 1.13W
Utrecht Neth. 42 E4........52.04N 5.07E
Utrecht d. Neth. 42 E4......52.04N 5.10E
Utrera Spain 46 C2.........37.10N 5.47W
Utsunomiya Japan 106 C3...36.40N 139.52E
Uttaradit Thailand 104 C7...17.20N 100.05E
Uttar Pradesh d. India 97 G6...27.40N 80.00E
Uttoxeter England 10 D3....52.53N 1.50W
Uusikaupunki Finland 43 E3...60.48N 21.30E
Uvs Nuur l. Mongolia 102 G8...50.30N 92.30E
Uwajima Japan 106 B2......33.13N 132.32E
Uxbridge England 11 E2....51.33N 0.30W
Uzbekistan Asia 115 M8....42.00N 63.00E
Uzhhorod Ukraine 54 H3....48.38N 22.15E
Uzlovaya Russian Fed. 55 P5...53.55N 38.11E

V

Vaal r. R.S.A. 86 B2.........29.04S 23.37E
Vaasa Finland 43 E3........63.06N 21.36E
Vác Hungary 54 F2.........47.49N 19.10E
Vadodara India 96 E5.......22.19N 73.14E
Vadsø Norway 43 G5........70.05N 29.47E
Vaduz Liech. 44 H5.........47.08N 9.32E
Værøy i. Norway 43 C4......67.40N 12.40E
Váh r. Slovakia 54 F2.......47.40N 18.09E
Vaitupu i. Tuvalu 111 G5....7.28S 178.41E
Valdai Hills Russian Fed. 35 G3...57.10N 33.00E
Valday Russian Fed. 55 M4...57.59N 33.10E
Valdepeñas Spain 46 D3....38.46N 3.24W
Valdés, Pen. Argentina 75 C2...42.30S 64.00W
Valdez U.S.A. 62 D4........61.07N 146.17W
Valdivia Chile 75 B3.........39.46S 73.15W
Val d'Or town Canada 63 K2...48.07N 77.47W
Valdosta U.S.A. 65 J3.......30.51N 83.51W
Valdres f. Norway 43 B3.....61.00N 9.10E
Valence France 44 F4.......44.56N 4.54E
Valencia Spain 46 E3........39.29N 0.24W
Valencia Venezuela 71 K3....10.14N 67.59W
Valencia, G. of Spain 46 F3...39.38N 0.20E
Valencia de Alcántara Spain 46 B3...39.25N 7.14W
Valenciennes France 44 E7...50.22N 3.32E
Vale of Evesham f. England 10 D3...52.05N 1.55W
Vale of Glamorgan d. Wales 12 D3...51.27N 3.22W
Vale of Pickering f. England 15 G3...54.11N 0.45W
Vale of York f. England 15 F3...54.12N 1.25W
Valera Venezuela 71 J2......9.21N 70.38W
Valier, Mont mtn. France 44 D3...42.48N 1.04E
Valinco, G. of Med. Sea 44 H2...41.40N 8.50E
Valjevo Yugo. 56 D6........44.16N 19.56E
Valka Latvia 43 F2..........57.44N 26.00E
Valkeakoski Finland 43 F3...61.17N 24.05E
Valkenswaard Neth. 42 E3...51.21N 5.27E
Valladolid Spain 46 C4......41.39N 4.45W
Valledupar Colombia 71 J3...10.10N 73.16W
Valletta Malta 50 E2........35.53N 14.31E
Valley town Wales 12 C5....53.17N 4.34W
Valley City U.S.A. 64 G6....46.57N 97.58W
Valparaíso Chile 75 B3......33.05S 71.40W
Vals, C. Indonesia 105 J2...8.30S 137.30E
Vammala Finland 43 E3......61.20N 22.54E
Van Turkey 94 F6...........38.28N 43.20E
Van, L. Turkey 94 F6........38.35N 42.52E
Vancouver Canada 62 F2....49.13N 123.06W
Vancouver I. Canada 62 F2...50.00N 126.00W
Vänern l. Sweden 43 C2.....59.00N 13.15E
Vänersborg Sweden 43 C2...58.23N 12.19E
Vanimo P.N.G. 105 K3......2.40S 141.17E
Vännäs Sweden 43 E3.......63.56N 19.50E
Vannes France 44 B5.......47.40N 2.44W
Vantaa Finland 43 F3.......60.18N 25.01E
Vanua Levu i. Fiji 111 G4...16.33S 179.15E
Vanuatu Pacific Oc. 111 F4...16.00S 167.00E
Varanasi India 97 G6.......25.20N 83.00E

Varangerfjorden *est.* Norway 43 G5....... 70.00N 29.30E
Varaždin Croatia 56 C7........................ 46.18N 16.20E
Varberg Sweden 43 C2.......................... 57.06N 12.15E
Vardar *r.* Greece 56 F4....................... 40.31N 22.43E
Varese Italy 50 C6.............................. 45.48N 8.48E
Vârful Bihor *mtn.* Romania 54 H2............ 46.26N 22.43E
Vârful Moldoveanu *mtn.* Romania 56 G6
                                            45.36N 24.32E
Varkaus Finland 43 F3........................... 62.15N 27.45E
Varna Bulgaria 57 H5............................ 43.13N 27.57E
Värnamo Sweden 43 C2........................... 57.11N 14.03E
Várpalota Hungary 54 F2........................ 47.12N 18.09E
Vasa Barris *r.* Brazil 77 G3.................. 11.07S 37.08W
Vaslui Romania 55 J2............................ 46.38N 27.44E
Västerås Sweden 43 D2.......................... 59.36N 16.32E
Västerdal *r.* Sweden 43 C3................... 60.32N 15.02E
Västervik Sweden 43 D2........................ 57.45N 16.40E
Vasyl'kiv Ukraine 55 L4........................ 50.12N 30.15E
Vatersay *i.* Scotland 18 B1.................. 56.56N 7.32W
Vatnajökull *mts.* Iceland 43 Y2............. 64.20N 17.00W
Vättern *l.* Sweden 43 C3...................... 58.30N 14.30E
Vavau Group *is.* Tonga 108 N5............... 19.50S 174.30W
Växjö Sweden 43 C2.............................. 56.52N 14.50E
Vaygach *i.* Russian Fed. 58 H5.............. 70.00N 59.00E
Vechte *r.* Neth. 42 F4......................... 52.39N 6.01E
Veendam Neth. 42 F5............................. 53.08N 6.52E
Veenendaal Neth. 42 E4......................... 52.03N 5.32E
Vega *i.* Norway 43 B4.......................... 65.40N 11.55E
Vejle Denmark 43 B1............................. 55.43N 9.33E
Velen Germany 42 F3............................. 51.53N 6.59E
Veles Macedonia 56 E4........................... 41.43N 21.49E
Vélez-Málaga Spain 46 C2....................... 36.48N 4.05W
Velhas *r.* Brazil 74 E5....................... 17.10S 44.49W
Velikiye Luki Russian Fed. 58 F3............. 56.19N 30.31E
Velino, Monte *mtn.* Italy 50 E5.............. 42.09N 13.23E
Velizh Russian Fed. 55 L6...................... 55.36N 31.13E
Vellore India 97 F3............................. 12.56N 79.09E
Vel'sk Russian Fed. 58 G4...................... 61.05N 42.06E
Venachar, Loch Scotland 16 E4................ 56.13N 4.19W
Vendôme France 44 D5........................... 47.48N 1.04E
Venezuela S. America 74 C7.................... 7.00N 65.00W
Venezuela, G. of Venezuela 71 J3............ 11.30N 71.00W
Venice Italy 50 E6.............................. 45.26N 12.20E
Venice, G. of Med. Sea 50 E6.................. 45.20N 13.00E
Venray Neth. 42 E3.............................. 51.32N 5.58E
Venta *r.* Latvia 43 E2........................ 57.22N 21.31E
Ventnor England 10 D1.......................... 50.36N 1.11W
Ventspils Latvia 43 E2......................... 57.22N 21.31E
Vera Spain 46 E2................................. 37.15N 1.51W
Veracruz Mexico 70 E4.......................... 19.11N 96.10W
Veracruz *d.* Mexico 70 E4.................... 18.00N 95.00W
Vercelli Italy 50 C6............................ 45.19N 8.26E
Verdalsøra Norway 43 B3........................ 63.47N 11.23E
Verde *r.* Brazil 77 E2........................ 21.18S 51.50W
Verde *r.* Paraguay 77 E2..................... 23.00S 57.45W
Verde *r.* U.S.A. 64 D3........................ 33.22N 112.20W
Verdun France 44 F6............................ 49.10N 5.24E
Verín Spain 46 B4.............................. 41.55N 7.26W
Verkhoyansk Russian Fed. 59 P4.............. 67.25N 133.25E
Verkhoyansk Range *mts.* Russian Fed. 59 O4
                                            66.00N 130.00E
Vermont *d.* U.S.A. 65 L5...................... 44.00N 72.30W
Verona Italy 50 D6.............................. 45.27N 10.59E
Versailles France 44 E6........................ 48.48N 2.08E
Verviers Belgium 42 E2......................... 50.36N 5.52E
Vervins France 42 C1........................... 49.50N 3.55E
Verwood England 10 D1.......................... 50.53N 1.53W
Vesoul France 44 G5............................ 47.38N 6.09E
Vesterålen *is.* Norway 43 C5................. 68.55N 15.00E
Vestfjorden *est.* Norway 43 C4.............. 68.10N 15.00E
Vestmannaeyjar *is.* Iceland 43 X1.......... 63.30N 20.20W
Vesturhorn *c.* Iceland 43 Z2................ 64.17N 14.54W
Vesuvius *mtn.* Italy 50 F4................... 40.48N 14.25E
Vettore, Monte *mtn.* Italy 50 E5............ 42.50N 13.18E
Veurne Belgium 42 B3........................... 51.04N 2.40E
Vézère *r.* France 44 D4....................... 44.53N 0.55E
Viana do Castelo Portugal 46 A4............. 41.41N 8.50W
Viborg Denmark 43 B2........................... 56.28N 9.25E
Vibo Valentia Italy 50 G3..................... 38.40N 16.06E
Vic Spain 46 G4................................. 41.56N 2.15E
Vicenza Italy 50 D6............................. 45.33N 11.32E
Vichy France 44 E5.............................. 46.07N 3.25E
Victoria *d.* Australia 110 D2............... 37.20S 144.10E
Victoria *r.* Australia 110 B4............... 15.12S 129.43E
Victoria Canada 62 F2.......................... 48.26N 123.20W
Victoria U.S.A. 64 G2.......................... 28.48N 97.00W
Victoria, L. Africa 86 C4...................... 1.00S 33.00E
Victoria, Mt. Myanmar 97 I5................... 21.12N 93.55E
Victoria, Mt. P.N.G. 110 D5................... 8.55S 147.35E
Victoria de las Tunas Cuba 71 I5............ 20.58N 76.59W
Victoria Falls *f.* Zimbabwe/Zambia 86 B3
                                            17.58S 25.45E
Vidin Bulgaria 56 F5........................... 43.58N 22.51E
Viedma Argentina 75 C3........................ 40.45S 63.00W
Viedma, L. Argentina 75 B2.................... 49.40S 72.30W
Vienna Austria 54 E3........................... 48.13N 16.22E
Vienne France 44 F4............................ 45.32N 4.54E
Vienne *r.* France 44 D5....................... 47.13N 0.05W
Vientiane Laos 104 C7.......................... 18.01N 102.48E
Vierzon France 44 E5........................... 47.14N 2.03E
Vietnam Asia 104 D6............................ 15.00N 108.00E
Vignemale, Pic de *mtn.* France 44 C3....... 42.46N 0.08W
Vigo Spain 46 A5............................... 42.15N 8.44W
Vijayawada India 97 G4......................... 16.34N 80.40E
Vik Iceland 43 Y1.............................. 63.25N 19.00W
Vikna *i.* Norway 43 B4........................ 64.59N 11.00E
Vilagarcía Spain 46 A5......................... 42.35N 8.45W
Vilaine *r.* France 44 B5...................... 47.30N 2.25W
Vila Real Portugal 46 B4....................... 41.17N 7.45W
Vila Velha Brazil 77 F2........................ 20.20S 40.17W
Vilcabamba, Cordillera *mts.* Peru 76 C3
                                            12.40S 73.20W
Vilhelmina Sweden 43 D4....................... 64.38N 16.40E
Viljandi Estonia 43 Y1......................... 58.22N 25.30E
Vilkaviškis Lithuania 54 H6................... 54.39N 23.02E
Villach Austria 54 C2.......................... 46.37N 13.51E
Villahermosa Mexico 70 F4..................... 18.00N 92.53W
Villaputzu Italy 50 C3......................... 39.28N 9.35E
Villarrica Paraguay 77 E2...................... 25.45S 56.28W
Villarobledo Spain 46 D3....................... 39.16N 2.36W
Villavicencio Colombia 76 C7.................. 4.09N 73.38W
Villefranche-sur-Saône France 44 F5......... 46.00N 4.43E
Villena Spain 46 E3............................ 38.39N 0.52W
Villeneuve France 44 D4........................ 44.25N 0.43E
Villers-Cotterêts France 42 C1............... 49.15N 3.05E

Villeurbanne France 44 F4..................... 45.46N 4.54E
Vilnius Lithuania 55 I6........................ 54.40N 25.19E
Vilvoorde Belgium 42 D2....................... 50.56N 4.25E
Vilyuysk Russian Fed. 59 O4................... 63.46N 121.35E
Viña del Mar Chile 75 B3...................... 33.02S 71.35W
Vindel *r.* Sweden 43 D3...................... 63.56N 19.54E
Vinh Vietnam 104 D7............................ 18.42N 105.41E
Vinkovci Croatia 56 D6......................... 45.17N 18.49E
Vinnytsya Ukraine 55 K3........................ 49.11N 28.30E
Vırânşehir Turkey 57 N2........................ 37.13N 39.45E
Vire France 44 C6............................... 48.50N 0.53W
Virginia *d.* U.S.A. 65 K4.................... 37.30N 79.00W
Virgin Is. (British) C. America 71 L4....... 18.30N 64.30W
Virgin Is. (U.S.A.) C. America 74 C8........ 18.30N 65.00W
Virton Belgium 42 E1........................... 49.35N 5.32E
Vis *i.* Croatia 56 C5......................... 43.03N 16.10E
Visby Sweden 43 D2............................. 57.37N 18.20E
Viscount Melville Sd. Canada 62 H5.......... 74.30N 104.00W
Viseu Portugal 46 B4........................... 40.40N 7.55W
Visginas Lithuania 55 J6....................... 55.34N 26.20E
Vishakhapatnam India 97 G4.................... 17.42N 83.24E
Viso, Monte *mtn.* Italy 50 B6............... 44.38N 7.05E
Vistula *r.* Poland 54 F6...................... 54.23N 18.52E
Viterbo Italy 50 E5............................ 42.26N 12.07E
Viti Levu *i.* Fiji 111 G4.................... 18.00S 178.00E
Vitim *r.* Russian Fed. 59 N3................. 59.30N 112.36E
Vitória da Conquista Brazil 77 F3........... 14.53S 40.52W
Vitória Espírito Santo Brazil 77 F2......... 20.19S 40.21W
Vitoria-Gasteiz Spain 46 D5................... 42.51N 2.40W
Vitsyebsk Belarus 55 L6........................ 55.10N 30.14E
Vittel France 44 F6............................ 48.12N 5.57E
Vizcaíno, Sierra *mts.* Mexico 70 B6........ 27.20N 114.30W
Vizianagaram India 97 G4...................... 18.07N 83.30E
Vlaardingen Neth. 42 D3........................ 51.55N 4.20E
Vladimir Russian Fed. 58 G3................... 56.08N 40.25E
Vladivostok Russian Fed. 59 P2............... 43.09N 131.53E
Vlieland *i.* Neth. 42 D5..................... 53.15N 5.00E
Vlissingen Neth. 42 C3......................... 51.27N 3.35E
Vlorë Albania 56 D4............................ 40.28N 19.27E
Vltava *r.* Czech Rep. 54 D4.................. 50.22N 14.28E
Voe Scotland 19 Y9............................. 60.21N 1.15W
Voi Kenya 87 B2................................ 3.23S 38.34E
Volda Norway 43 A3............................. 62.09N 6.05E
Volga *r.* Russian Fed. 58 G2................. 45.45N 47.50E
Volga Uplands *hills* Russian Fed. 35 H3.... 53.15N 45.45E
Volgograd Russian Fed. 58 G2.................. 48.45N 44.30E
Völklingen Germany 42 F1...................... 49.15N 6.50E
Volnovakha Ukraine 55 O2...................... 47.36N 37.32E
Volodymyr-Volyns'kyy Ukraine 55 I4.......... 50.51N 24.19E
Vologda Russian Fed. 58 F3.................... 59.10N 39.55E
Volokonovka Russian Fed. 55 O4.............. 50.28N 37.52E
Volos Greece 56 F3............................. 39.22N 22.57E
Volta, L. Ghana 84 E2.......................... 7.00N 0.00
Volta Redonda Brazil 77 F2.................... 22.31S 44.05W
Volzhskiy Russian Fed. 58 G2.................. 48.48N 44.45E
Vorkuta Russian Fed. 58 I4.................... 67.27N 64.00E
Voronezh Russian Fed. 55 P4................... 51.40N 39.13E
Vosges *mts.* France 44 G5.................... 48.00N 7.00E
Voss Norway 43 A3.............................. 60.39N 6.26E
Vostok I. Kiribati 108 P5..................... 10.05S 152.23W
Vouziers France 42 D1.......................... 49.24N 4.42E
Voznesens'k Ukraine 55 L2..................... 47.34N 31.21E
Vranje Yugo. 56 E5............................. 42.34N 21.52E
Vratsa Bulgaria 56 F5.......................... 43.12N 23.33E
Vrbas *r.* Bosnia./Croatia 56 C6............ 45.06N 17.29E
Vršac Yugo. 56 E6.............................. 45.08N 21.18E
Vung Tau Vietnam 104 D6....................... 10.21N 107.04E
Vuollerim Sweden 43 E4........................ 66.26N 20.40E
Vyatka *r.* Russian Fed. 58 G3................ 56.38N 49.38E
Vyaz'ma Russian Fed. 55 N6.................... 55.12N 34.17E
Vyborg Russian Fed. 43 G3..................... 60.45N 28.41E
Vychegda *r.* Russian Fed. 35 H4............ 61.15N 46.28E
Vyrnwy, L. Wales 12 D4......................... 52.46N 3.30W

W

Wa Ghana 84 D3................................. 10.07N 2.28W
Wabag P.N.G. 105 K2............................ 5.28S 143.40E
Wabasca *r.* Canada 62 G3..................... 58.22N 115.20W
Wabash *r.* U.S.A. 65 I4...................... 38.25N 87.45W
Wabe Gestro *r.* Ethiopia 87 C3.............. 4.11N 42.09E
Wabush Canada 63 L3........................... 53.00N 66.50W
Waco U.S.A. 64 G3.............................. 31.33N 97.10W
Wad Pakistan 95 K4............................ 27.21N 66.30E
Waddan Libya 85 F4............................ 29.06N 16.03E
Waddenzee Neth. 42 E5......................... 53.15N 5.05E
Waddington England 15 F2...................... 53.10N 0.32W
Waddington, Mt. Canada 62 F3................. 51.30N 125.00W
Wadebridge England 13 C2...................... 50.31N 4.51W
Wadhurst England 11 F2........................ 51.03N 0.21E
Wadi Halfa Sudan 85 H4........................ 21.55N 31.20E
Wad Medani Sudan 85 H3........................ 14.24N 33.30E
Wagga Wagga Australia 110 D2................. 35.07S 147.24E
Wahpeton U.S.A. 64 G6......................... 46.16N 96.36W
Waigeo *i.* Indonesia 105 I3................. 0.05S 130.30E
Wainfleet All Saints England 15 H2.......... 53.07N 0.16E
Waingapu Indonesia 104 G2..................... 9.30S 120.10E
Waini Pt. *c.* Guyana 74 D7................... 8.24N 59.48W
Wainwright U.S.A. 62 C5....................... 70.39N 160.00W
Wajir Kenya 87 C3............................. 1.46N 40.05E
Wakayama Japan 106 C2......................... 34.12N 135.10E
Wakefield England 15 F2....................... 53.41N 1.31W
Wake I. Pacific Oc. 108 L8.................... 19.17N 166.36E
Wakkanai Japan 106 D4......................... 45.26N 141.43E
Wałbrzych Poland 54 E4........................ 50.48N 16.19E
Wales *d.* U.K. 8-9
Wallasey England 14 D2........................ 53.26N 3.02W
Wallingford England 10 D2.................... 51.36N 1.07W
Wallis, Îles *is.* Pacific Oc. 108 N5....... 13.16S 176.15W
Walney, Isle of England 14 D3................ 54.05N 3.12W
Walsall England 10 D3......................... 52.36N 1.59W
Waltham on the Wolds England 10 E3.......... 52.49N 0.49W
Walton on Thames England 11 E2.............. 51.23N 0.23W
Walvis Bay *town* Namibia 86 A2............. 22.50S 14.31E
Wandsworth England 11 E2...................... 51.27N 0.11W
Wangqing China 106 A4......................... 43.20N 129.48E
Wantage England 10 D2......................... 51.35N 1.25W
Warangal India 97 F4.......................... 18.00N 79.35E
Warboys England 11 E3......................... 52.24N 0.06W
Warburton *r.* Australia 110 C3............. 27.55S 137.15E
Ward Hill Scotland 19 F3...................... 58.54N 3.20W
Ward's Stone *mtn.* England 14 E3........... 54.03N 2.36W
Wareham England 10 C1......................... 50.41N 2.08W

Waremme Belgium 42 E2......................... 50.42N 5.15E
Warlingham England 11 E2...................... 51.19N 0.04W
Warminster England 10 C2...................... 51.12N 2.11W
Warrego *r.* Australia 110 D3................ 30.25S 145.18E
Warrenpoint N. Ireland 16 C2................. 54.06N 6.15W
Warri Nigeria 84 E2........................... 5.36N 5.46E
Warrington England 14 E2...................... 53.25N 2.38W
Warsaw Poland 54 G5........................... 52.15N 21.00E
Warsop England 15 F2.......................... 53.13N 1.08W
Warta *r.* Poland 54 D5....................... 52.45N 15.09E
Warwick England 10 D3......................... 52.17N 1.36W
Warwickshire *d.* England 10 D3............. 52.10N 1.30W
Washington England 15 F3...................... 54.55N 1.30W
Washington *d.* U.S.A. 64 B6................. 47.00N 120.00W
Washington U.S.A. 65 K4....................... 38.55N 77.00W
Washington, Mt. U.S.A. 65 L5................. 44.17N 71.19W
Wast Water *l.* England 14 D3................ 54.25N 3.18W
Watampone Indonesia 104 G3................... 4.33S 120.20E
Watchet England 13 D3......................... 51.10N 3.20W
Waterford Rep. of Ire. 20 D2................. 52.16N 7.08W
Waterford *d.* Rep. of Ire. 20 D2........... 52.10N 7.40W
Watergate B. England 13 B2................... 50.28N 5.06W
Waterloo U.S.A. 65 H5......................... 42.30N 92.20W
Waterlooville England 10 D1.................. 50.53N 1.02W
Water of Saughs *r.* Scotland 19 G1......... 56.47N 2.36W
Watertown U.S.A. 64 G5........................ 44.54N 97.08W
Watford England 11 E2......................... 51.40N 0.25W
Watlington England 10 D2...................... 51.38N 1.00W
Watson Lake *town* Canada 62 F4............. 60.07N 128.49W
Watten, Loch Scotland 19 F3.................. 58.29N 3.20W
Watton England 11 F3.......................... 52.35N 0.50E
Wau Sudan 85 G2............................... 7.40N 28.04E
Waveney *r.* England 11 G3................... 52.29N 1.46E
Wear *r.* England 15 F3....................... 54.55N 1.22W
Weddell Sea Antarctica 112................... 73.00S 42.00W
Wedmore England 13 E3......................... 51.14N 2.50W
Weener Germany 42 G5.......................... 53.11N 7.21E
Weert Neth. 42 E3............................. 51.14N 5.40E
Weifang China 103 L5.......................... 36.44N 119.10E
Weihai China 103 M5........................... 37.30N 122.04E
Weinan China 103 J4........................... 34.25N 109.30E
Weldiya Ethiopia 85 H3........................ 11.50N 39.36E
Welkom R.S.A. 86 B2........................... 27.59S 26.44E
Welland *r.* England 11 E3.................... 52.53N 0.00
Wellesley Is. Australia 110 C4.............. 16.42S 139.30E
Wellingborough England 10 E3................. 52.18N 0.41W
Wellington Shrops. England 10 C3............ 52.42N 2.31W
Wellington Somerset England 13 D2........... 50.58N 3.13W
Wellington New Zealand 111 G1............... 41.17S 174.46E
Wells England 13 E3........................... 51.12N 2.39W
Wells, L. Australia 110 B3.................... 26.50S 123.20E
Wells-next-the-Sea England 11 F3............ 52.57N 0.51E
Welmel Shet' *r.* Ethiopia 87 C4............ 5.37N 41.00E
Welshpool Wales 12 D4......................... 52.40N 3.09W
Welwyn Garden City England 11 E2............ 51.48N 0.13W
Wem England 10 C3............................. 52.52N 2.45W
Wembley England 11 E2......................... 51.34N 0.18W
Wemyss Bay *town* Scotland 16 E3............ 55.52N 4.52W
Wendo Ethiopia 85 H2.......................... 6.40N 38.27E
Wendover England 10 E2........................ 51.46N 0.46W
Wenlock Edge *hill* England 10 C3........... 52.33N 2.40W
Wensleydale *f.* England 15 E3.............. 54.19N 2.04W
Wensum *r.* England 11 G3.................... 52.37N 1.20E
Wenzhou China 103 M3.......................... 28.02N 120.40E
Wesel Germany 42 F3........................... 51.39N 6.37E
Weser *r.* Germany 48 D5...................... 53.15N 8.30E
Wessel, C. Australia 110 C4.................. 10.59S 136.46E
Wessel Is. Australia 110 C4.................. 11.30S 136.25E
West Australian Basin *f.* Indian Oc. 117 O5
                                            23.00N 87.40E
West Bengal *d.* India 97 H5................. 23.00N 87.40E
West Bridgford England 10 D3................. 52.56N 1.08W
West Bromwich England 10 D3.................. 52.32N 1.59W
West Burra *i.* Scotland 19 Y9.............. 60.05N 1.21W
Westbury England 10 C2........................ 51.16N 2.11W
West Calder Scotland 17 F3................... 55.51N 3.34W
West Dunbartonshire *d.* Scotland 16 E3.... 55.58N 4.30W
Western *d.* Kenya 87 A3..................... 0.30N 34.30E
Western Australia *d.* Australia 110 B3.... 25.00S 123.00E
Western Desert Egypt 94 C4................... 27.30N 28.00E
Western Ghats *mts.* India 96 E4............ 15.30N 74.30E
Western Isles *d.* Scotland 18 B2........... 57.40N 7.10W
Western Sahara Africa 84 C4.................. 25.00N 13.30W
Western Sayan *mts.* Russian Fed. 59 L3
                                            53.00N 92.00E
Wester Ross *f.* Scotland 18 D2............. 57.37N 5.20W
Westerschelde *est.* Neth. 42 C3............ 51.25N 3.40E
West Falkland *i.* Falkland Is. 75 C1....... 51.40S 60.00W
West Fen *f.* Cambs. England 11 E3.......... 52.32N 0.00
West Fen *f.* Lincs. England 15 G2.......... 53.03N 0.02E
West Frisian Is. Neth. 42 D5................. 53.20N 5.00E
Westhill Scotland 19 G2....................... 57.09N 2.16W
West Kirby England 14 D2...................... 53.22N 3.11W
West Lavington England 10 D2................. 51.17N 2.00W
West Linton Scotland 17 F3................... 55.45N 3.21W
West Loch Roag Scotland 18 C3............... 58.17N 6.52W
West Lothian *d.* Scotland 17 F3............ 55.55N 3.30W
West Malling England 11 F2................... 51.18N 0.25E
Westmeath *d.* Rep. of Ire. 20 D3........... 53.30N 7.30W
West Mersea England 11 F2.................... 51.46N 0.55E
West Midlands *d.* England 10 D3............ 52.25N 2.00W
Weston-super-Mare England 10 C2............. 51.20N 2.59W
West Palm Beach *town* U.S.A. 65 J2......... 26.42N 80.05W
Westport Rep. of Ire. 20 B3.................. 53.48N 9.32W
Westray *i.* Scotland 19 G4.................. 59.18N 2.58W
Westray Firth Scotland 19 F4................. 59.13N 3.00W
West Siberian Plain *f.* Russian Fed. 58 J4
                                            60.00N 75.00E
West Sussex *d.* England 11 E1.............. 50.58N 0.30W
West Terschelling Neth. 42 E5............... 53.22N 5.13E
West Virginia *d.* U.S.A. 65 J4............. 39.00N 80.30W
West-Vlaanderen *d.* Belgium 42 B2......... 51.00N 3.00E
Westward Ho! England 13 C3................... 51.02N 4.15W
West Yorkshire *d.* England 15 F2........... 53.45N 1.40W
Wetar *i.* Indonesia 105 H2.................. 7.45S 126.00E
Wetherby England 15 F2........................ 53.56N 1.23W
Wete Tanzania 87 B1........................... 5.03S 39.44E
Wetzlar Germany 48 D4......................... 50.33N 8.30E
Wewak P.N.G. 105 K3........................... 3.35S 143.35E
Wexford Rep. of Ire. 20 E2................... 52.20N 6.28W
Wexford *d.* Rep. of Ire. 20 E2............. 52.25N 6.30W
Wexford B. Rep. of Ire. 20 E2................ 52.25N 6.15W
Weybridge England 11 E2....................... 51.23N 0.28W
Weyburn Canada 64 F6.......................... 49.41N 103.52W
Weymouth England 10 C1........................ 50.36N 2.28W
Whalsay *i.* Scotland 19 Z9.................. 60.22N 0.59W

Whangarei New Zealand 111 G2................. 35.43S 174.20E
Wharfe *r.* England 15 F2.................... 53.50N 1.07W
Wheeler Peak *mtn.* Nev. U.S.A. 64 D4....... 38.59N 114.29W
Wheeler Peak *mtn.* N.Mex. U.S.A. 64 E4
                                            36.34N 105.25W
Whernside *mtn.* England 15 E3.............. 54.14N 2.25W
Whitburn Scotland 17 F3....................... 55.52N 3.41W
Whitby England 15 G3.......................... 54.29N 0.37W
Whitchurch England 10 C3..................... 52.58N 2.42W
Whitchurch Wales 13 D3........................ 51.32N 3.14W
White *r.* U.S.A. 65 H3...................... 33.53N 91.10W
Whitecourt Canada 62 G3...................... 54.10N 115.38W
Whitehaven England 14 D3..................... 54.33N 3.35W
Whitehead N. Ireland 16 D2................... 54.45N 5.43W
Whitehill England 10 D2....................... 51.08N 0.50W
Whitehorse Canada 62 E4...................... 60.41N 135.08W
White L. Australia 110 B3.................... 21.05S 129.00E
White Mt. Peak U.S.A. 64 C4.................. 37.40N 118.15W
White Nile *r.* Sudan 85 H3................. 15.45N 32.25E
Whitesand B. England 13 C2.................. 50.20N 4.20W
White Sea Russian Fed. 58 F4................ 65.30N 38.00E
White Volta *r.* Ghana 84 D2................ 9.13N 1.15W
Whitfield England 11 G2...................... 51.09N 1.15E
Whithorn Scotland 16 E2...................... 54.44N 4.25W
Whitland Wales 12 C3.......................... 51.49N 4.38W
Whitley Bay *town* England 15 F4........... 55.03N 1.25W
Whitney, Mt. U.S.A. 64 C4.................... 36.35N 118.17W
Whitstable England 11 G2...................... 51.21N 1.02E
Whittlesey England 11 E3..................... 52.33N 0.08W
Whyalla Australia 110 C2..................... 33.04S 137.34E
Wichita U.S.A. 64 G4.......................... 37.43N 97.20W
Wichita Falls *town* U.S.A. 64 G3........... 33.55N 98.30W
Wick Scotland 19 F3........................... 58.26N 3.06W
Wick *r.* Scotland 19 F3..................... 58.26N 3.06W
Wickford England 11 F2........................ 51.38N 0.31E
Wickham England 10 D1......................... 50.54N 1.11W
Wickham Market England 11 G3................. 52.09N 1.21E
Wicklow Rep. of Ire. 20 E2................... 52.59N 6.03W
Wicklow *d.* Rep. of Ire. 20 E3............. 53.00N 6.25W
Wicklow Head Rep. of Ire. 20 E2............. 52.58N 6.00W
Wicklow Mts. Rep. of Ire. 20 E2............. 53.06N 6.20W
Widecombe in the Moor England 13 D2........ 50.35N 3.48W
Wide Firth Scotland 19 F4.................... 59.02N 3.00W
Widnes England 14 E2......................... 53.22N 2.44W
Wieluń Poland 54 F5.......................... 51.14N 18.34E
Wiener Neustadt Austria 54 E2............... 47.49N 16.15E
Wiesbaden Germany 48 D4...................... 50.05N 8.15E
Wigan England 14 E2.......................... 53.33N 2.38W
Wigston England 10 D3........................ 52.35N 1.08W
Wigton England 14 D3......................... 54.50N 3.09W
Wigtown Scotland 16 E2....................... 54.52N 4.26W
Wigtown B. Scotland 16 E2.................... 54.47N 4.15W
Wijchen Neth. 42 E3.......................... 51.48N 5.44E
Wildhorn *mtn.* Switz. 44 G5................ 46.22N 7.22E
Wilhelmshaven Germany 48 D5................. 53.32N 8.07E
Wilkes Land *f.* Antarctica 112............ 69.00S 130.00E
Willebroek Belgium 42 D3..................... 51.04N 4.22E
William, Mt. Australia 110 D2............... 37.20S 142.41E
Williams Lake *town* Canada 62 F3.......... 52.08N 122.09W
Williamsport U.S.A. 65 K5.................... 41.16N 77.03W
Willingdon England 11 F1.................... 50.47N 0.15E
Williston U.S.A. 64 F6....................... 48.09N 103.39W
Williston L. Canada 62 F3.................... 55.00N 126.00W
Williton England 13 D3....................... 51.09N 3.20W
Willmar U.S.A. 65 G6......................... 45.06N 95.00W
Wills, L. Australia 110 B3................... 21.15S 128.40E
Wilmington Del. U.S.A. 65 K4................ 39.46N 75.31W
Wilmington N.C. U.S.A. 65 K3................ 34.14N 77.55W
Wilmslow England 15 E2....................... 53.19N 2.14W
Wilson's Promontory *c.* Australia 110 D2
                                            39.06S 146.23E
Wilton England 10 D2......................... 51.05N 1.52W
Wiltshire *d.* England 10 C2................ 51.20N 2.00W
Wiltz Lux. 42 E1............................. 49.59N 5.53E
Wimbledon England 11 F3...................... 52.31N 0.06E
Wimborne Minster England 10 C1.............. 50.48N 2.00W
Wimereux France 42 A2........................ 50.46N 1.37E
Winam *d.* Kenya 87 A3....................... 0.15S 34.30E
Wincanton England 13 E3...................... 51.03N 2.24W
Winchester England 10 D2..................... 51.04N 1.19W
Windermere England 14 E3.................... 54.24N 2.56W
Windermere *l.* England 14 E3............... 54.20N 2.56W
Windhoek Namibia 86 A2....................... 22.34S 17.06E
Windrush *r.* England 10 D2................. 51.42N 1.25W
Windsor Canada 63 J5......................... 42.18N 83.00W
Windsor England 11 E2........................ 51.29N 0.38W
Windward Is. C. America 71 L3............... 13.00N 60.00W
Windward Passage *str.* Carib. Sea 71 J4
                                            20.00N 74.00W
Wingate England 15 F3........................ 54.44N 1.23W
Winisk *r.* Canada 63 J3.................... 55.20N 85.20W
Winkleigh England 13 D2...................... 50.49N 3.57W
Winnebago, L. U.S.A. 65 I5.................. 44.00N 88.25W
Winnipeg Canada 62 I2........................ 49.53N 97.10W
Winnipeg, L. Canada 62 I3................... 52.45N 98.00W
Winnipegosis, L. Canada 62 H3............... 52.00N 100.00W
Winsford England 15 E2....................... 53.12N 2.31W
Winslow England 10 E2........................ 51.57N 0.54W
Winston-Salem U.S.A. 65 J4.................. 36.05N 80.05W
Winterswijk Neth. 42 F3...................... 51.58N 6.44E
Winterthur Switz. 44 H5...................... 47.30N 8.45E
Winterton England 15 G2...................... 53.39N 0.37W
Wirksworth England 15 F2.................... 53.05N 1.34W
Wirral *f.* England 14 D2................... 53.18N 3.02W
Wisbech England 11 F3........................ 52.39N 0.10E
Wisconsin *d.* U.S.A. 65 H5................. 45.00N 90.00W
Wishaw Scotland 17 F3........................ 55.47N 3.55W
Wismar Germany 48 E5......................... 53.54N 11.28E
Witham England 11 F2......................... 51.48N 0.38E
Witham *r.* England 15 H1.................... 52.56N 0.04E
Witheridge England 13 D2.................... 50.55N 3.42W
Withernsea England 15 H2.................... 53.43N 0.02E
Witney England 10 D2......................... 51.47N 1.29W
Wittenberge Germany 48 E5................... 52.59N 11.45E
Wittlich Germany 42 F1....................... 49.59N 6.54E
Witu Kenya 87 A2............................. 2.25S 40.27E
Wiveliscombe England 13 D2.................. 51.02N 3.20W
Wivenhoe England 11 F2....................... 51.51N 0.59E
Wkra *r.* Poland 54 G5....................... 52.27N 20.44E
Włocławek Poland 54 F5....................... 52.39N 19.01E
Wokam *i.* Indonesia 105 I2................. 5.45S 134.30E
Woking England 11 E2......................... 51.20N 0.34W
Wokingham England 10 E2..................... 51.25N 0.50W
Woleai Atoll *i.* Fed. States of Micronesia 105 K5
                                            7.24N 143.52E
Wolfsburg Germany 48 E5...................... 52.27N 10.49E

Wollaston L. Canada 62 H3................. 58.15N 103.30W
Wollongong Australia 110 E2............... 34.25S 150.52E
Wolsingham England 15 F3................ 54.44N 1.52W
Wolvega Neth. 42 E4....................... 52.53N 6.00E
Wolverhampton England 10 C3............ 52.35N 2.06W
Wombwell England 15 F2.................. 53.31N 1.23W
Wonsan N. Korea 103 N5................. 39.07N 127.26E
Woodbridge England 11 G3.............. 52.06N 1.19E
Woodcote England 10 D2................. 51.32N 1.04W
Woodhall Spa England 15 G2............ 53.10N 0.12W
Woodlark I. P.N.G. 110 E5............... 9.05S 152.50E
Woods, L. of the Canada 63 I2.......... 49.15N 94.45W
Woodstock England 10 D2............... 51.51N 1.20W
Wooler England 15 E4.................... 55.33N 2.01W
Wootton Bassett England 10 D2......... 51.32N 1.55W
Worcester England 10 C3................ 52.12N 2.12W
Worcester R.S.A. 86 A1................. 33.39S 19.26E
Worcester U.S.A. 65 L5................. 42.14N 71.48W
Workington England 14 D3............... 54.39N 3.34W
Worksop England 15 F2.................. 53.19N 1.09W
Worland U.S.A. 64 E5................... 44.01N 107.58W
Worms Germany 48 D3................... 49.38N 8.23E
Worms Head Wales 12 C3............... 51.34N 4.18W
Worth England 11 E2.................... 51.03N 0.08W
Worthing England 11 E1................. 50.49N 0.21W
Worthington U.S.A. 64 G5.............. 43.37N 95.36W
Wowoni i. Indonesia 105 G3............ 4.10S 123.10E
Wragby England 15 G2.................. 53.17N 0.18W
Wrangel I. Russian Fed. 59 U5......... 71.00N 180.00
Wrangell U.S.A. 62 E3.................. 56.28N 132.23W
Wrangle England 15 H2................. 53.03N 0.09E
Wrath, C. Scotland 18 D3.............. 58.37N 5.01W
Wrexham Wales 12 E5.................. 53.05N 3.00W
Wrexham d. Wales 12 D5............... 53.00N 3.00W
Wrigley Canada 62 F4.................. 63.16N 123.39W
Wrocław Poland 54 E4.................. 51.05N 17.00E
Wuhai China 103 J5.................... 39.50N 106.40E
Wuhan China 103 K4................... 30.35N 114.19E
Wuhu China 103 L4..................... 31.23N 118.25E
Wunju S. Korea 103 N5................ 37.24N 127.52E
Wuppertal Germany 48 C4.............. 51.15N 7.10E
Würzburg Germany 48 D3.............. 49.48N 9.57E
Wuvulu I. P.N.G. 105 K3............... 1.44S 142.50E
Wuwei China 103 I5................... 38.00N 102.54E
Wuxi China 103 M4.................... 31.35N 120.19E
Wuzhou China 103 K2................. 23.30N 111.21E
Wye England 11 F2.................... 51.11N 0.56E
Wye r. U.K. 12 E3..................... 51.37N 2.40W
Wylye r. England 10 D2................ 51.04N 1.48W
Wymondham England 11 G3............ 52.34N 1.07E
Wyndham Australia 110 B4............ 15.29S 128.05E
Wyoming d. U.S.A. 64 E5.............. 43.00N 108.00W
Wythall England 10 D3................ 52.22N 1.52W
Wytheville U.S.A. 65 J4............... 36.57N 81.07W

X

Xai Xai Mozambique 86 C2............ 25.05S 33.38E
Xankändi Azerbaijan 95 G6............ 39.48N 46.45E
Xanthi Greece 56 G4.................. 41.07N 24.55E
Xavantes, Serra dos mts. Brazil 77 F3... 12.00S 49.00W
Xiamen China 103 L2.................. 24.26N 118.07E
Xi'an China 103 J4.................... 34.16N 108.54E
Xiangfan China 103 K4.:.............. 32.20N 112.05E
Xiangkhoang Laos 104 C7............. 19.11N 103.23E
Xiangtan China 103 K3................ 27.55N 112.47E
Xichang China 103 I3.................. 27.52N 102.16E
Xigazê China 102 F3.................. 29.18N 88.50E
Xi Jiang r. China 90 M5............... 22.23N 113.20E
Xingtai China 103 K5................. 37.08N 114.29E
Xingu r. Brazil 77 E4................. 2.00S 52.30W
Xining China 103 I5................... 36.35N 101.55E
Xinjiang Uygur Zizhiqu d. China 102 E6
.... 41.15N 87.00E
Xintai China 103 L5.................. 35.56N 117.49E
Xinxiang China 103 K5................ 35.16N 113.51E

Xinzhu Taiwan 103 M2................ 24.48N 120.59E
Xizang Zizhiqu d. see Tibet d. China 102
Xuzhou China 103 L4................. 34.17N 117.18E

Y

Yabēlo Ethiopia 87 B3................ 4.54N 38.05E
Yabelo Wildlife Sanctuary Ethiopia 87 B3
.... 5.00N 38.20E
Yablonovy Range mts. Russian Fed. 59 N3
.... 53.20N 115.00E
Yacuma r. Bolivia 76 D3.............. 13.40S 65.20W
Yaghargradzor Armenia 95 G6........ 39.44N 45.19E
Yagodnoye Russian Fed. 59 Q4...... 62.34N 149.33E
Yakima U.S.A. 64 B6................. 46.37N 120.30W
Yakumo Japan 106 D4............... 42.14N 140.19E
Yaku-shima i. Japan 106 B2......... 30.20N 130.40E
Yakutsk Russian Fed. 59 O4......... 62.10N 129.20E
Yala Thailand 104 C5................ 6.32N 101.15E
Yalta Ukraine 55 N1................. 44.30N 34.09E
Yamagata Japan 106 D3............. 38.16N 140.19E
Yamal Pen. Russian Fed. 58 I5....... 70.20N 70.00E
Yaman Tau mtn. Russian Fed. 58 H3... 54.20N 58.10E
Yamoussoukro Côte d'Ivoire 84 D2... 6.49N 5.17W
Yamuna r. India 97 G6............... 25.20N 81.49E
Yana r. Russian Fed. 59 P5.......... 71.30N 135.00E
Yanbu'al Baēr Saudi Arabia 94 E3... 24.07N 38.04E
Yangon Myanmar 97 J4.............. 16.45N 96.20E
Yangquan China 103 K5............. 37.52N 113.29E
Yangtze r. see Chang Jiang r. China 103
Yanji China 103 N6.................. 42.45N 129.25E
Yantai China 103 M5................ 37.30N 121.22E
Yaoundé Cameroon 84 F2............ 3.51N 11.31E
Yap i. Fed. States of Micronesia 105 J5... 9.30N 138.09E
Yapen i. Indonesia 105 J3............ 1.45S 136.10E
Yaqui r. Mexico 70 B6............... 27.40N 110.30W
Yare r. England 11 G3............... 52.34N 1.45E
Yariga-take mtn. Japan 106 C3...... 36.21N 137.39E
Yarlung Zangbo Jiang r. see Brahmaputra r. China 102
Yarm England 15 F3.................. 54.30N 1.21W
Yarmouth Canada 63 L2............. 43.50N 66.08W
Yarmouth England 10 D1............ 50.42N 1.29W
Yaroslavl Russian Fed. 58 F3........ 57.34N 39.52E
Yartsevo Russian Fed. 55 M6........ 55.06N 32.43E
Yasawa Group is. Fiji 111 G4........ 16.47S 171.31E
Yasyel'da r. Belarus 55 J5........... 52.08N 26.20E
Yatagan Turkey 57 I2................ 37.22N 28.08E
Yata Plateau f. Kenya 87 B2......... 2.00S 38.00E
Yate England 10 C2.................. 51.31N 2.24W
Yatton England 10 C2................ 51.24N 2.49W
Yavari r. Peru 76 C4................. 4.30S 70.00W
Yavi, Cerro mtn. Venezuela 71 K2... 5.32N 65.59W
Yây Ninh Vietnam 104 D6............ 11.21N 106.07E
Yazd Iran 95 H5..................... 31.54N 54.22E
Yealmpton England 13 D2........... 50.21N 4.00W
Yefremov Russian Fed. 55 P5....... 53.08N 38.08E
Yegor'yevsk Russian Fed. 55 P6..... 55.21N 39.01E
Yekaterinburg Russian Fed. 58 I3... 56.52N 60.35E
Yelets Russian Fed. 55 P5........... 52.36N 38.30E
Yell i. Scotland 19 Y9................ 60.35N 1.05W
Yellowknife Canada 62 G4.......... 62.30N 114.29W
Yellow Sea Asia 103 M5............. 35.00N 123.00E
Yellowstone r. U.S.A. 64 F6......... 47.55N 103.45W
Yell Sound Scotland 19 Y9.......... 60.35N 1.15W
Yemen Asia 95 G2.................. 15.55N 48.30E
Yenakiyevo Ukraine 55 P3.......... 48.14N 38.15E
Yenisey r. Russian Fed. 59 K4....... 69.00N 86.00E
Yenisey, G. Russian Fed. 58 J3...... 73.00N 79.00E
Yeniseysk Russian Fed. 59 L3....... 58.27N 92.13E
Yeovil England 13 E2................ 50.57N 2.38W
Yerementau Kazakhstan 102 C8..... 51.35N 73.10E
Yerevan Armenia 58 G2............. 40.10N 44.31E
Yeşilırmak r. Turkey 57 M4.......... 41.22N 36.37E
Yes Tor mtn. England 13 C2......... 50.42N 4.00W
Yevpatoriya Ukraine 55 M1.......... 45.12N 33.20E

Yeysk Russian Fed. 53 K6........... 46.43N 38.17E
Yibin China 103 I3................... 28.50N 104.35E
Yichang China 103 K4............... 30.43N 111.22E
Yichun China 103 N7................ 47.41N 129.10E
Yinchuan China 103 J5.............. 38.30N 106.19E
Yingkou China 103 M6.............. 40.40N 122.17E
Yining China 102 E6................. 43.57N 81.23E
Yirga Ch'efē Ethiopia 87 B4......... 6.05N 38.09E
Yli-Kitka l. Finland 43 G4............ 66.10N 28.30E
Ylitornio Finland 43 E4.............. 66.19N 23.40E
Ylöjärvi Finland 43 E3............... 61.35N 23.35E
Yogyakarta Indonesia 104 E2........ 7.48S 110.24E
Yokohama Japan 106 C3............ 35.28N 139.28E
Yokosuka Japan 106 C3............. 35.20N 139.32E
Yonago Japan 106 B3............... 35.27N 133.20E
Yonne r. France 44 E6............... 48.22N 2.57E
York England 15 F2................. 53.58N 1.07W
York d. England 15 F2.............. 53.58N 1.07W
York, C. Australia 110 D4........... 10.58S 142.40E
York, C. Greenland 63 L5........... 75.50N 66.30W
Yorkshire Wolds hills England 15 G3... 54.00N 0.39W
Yorkton Canada 62 H3.............. 51.12N 102.29W
Youghal Rep. of Ire. 20 D1.......... 51.58N 7.51W
Youngstown U.S.A. 65 J5........... 41.05N 80.40W
Yozgat Turkey 57 L3................ 39.50N 34.48E
Ystad Sweden 43 C1................ 55.25N 13.50E
Ystalyfera Wales 12 D3............. 51.47N 3.47W
Ystwyth r. Wales 12 C4............. 52.24N 4.06W
Ythan r. Scotland 19 G2............. 57.20N 2.01W
Yuba City U.S.A. 64 B4............. 39.08N 121.27W
Yubari Japan 106 D4................ 43.04N 141.59E
Yucatán d. Mexico 70 G5............ 20.40N 89.00W
Yucatán pen. Mexico 70 F4......... 19.00N 90.00W
Yucatan Channel Carib. Sea 70 G5... 21.30N 86.00W
Yueyang China 103 K3.............. 29.22N 113.10E
Yugoslavia Europe 56 E5........... 43.00N 21.00E
Yukon r. U.S.A. 62 B4............... 62.35N 164.20W
Yukon Territory d. Canada 62 E4.... 65.00N 135.00W
Yulin China 103 K2.................. 22.38N 110.10E
Yuma U.S.A. 64 D3.................. 32.40N 114.39W
Yumen China 102 H5................ 40.19N 97.12E
Yunak Turkey 57 J3.................. 38.50N 31.42E
Yungas f. Bolivia 76 D3............. 16.20S 65.00W
Yunjinghong China 104 C8.......... 21.59N 100.49E
Yunnan d. China 103 I2............. 24.30N 101.30E
Yushu China 102 H4................ 33.06N 96.48E
Yuxi China 103 I2................... 24.24N 102.29E
Yuzhno-Sakhalinsk Russian Fed. 59 Q2
.... 46.58N 142.45E
Yuzhnoukrayinsk Ukraine 55 L2..... 47.51N 31.09E

Z

Zaandam Neth. 42 D4............... 52.27N 4.49E
Zabīd Yemen 94 F1................. 14.12N 43.19E
Zabol Iran 95 J5.................... 31.00N 61.32E
Zacatecas Mexico 70 D5............ 22.48N 102.33W
Zacatecas d. Mexico 70 D5.......... 24.00N 103.00W
Zadar Croatia 56 B6................ 44.08N 15.14E
Zafra Spain 46 B3.................. 38.25N 6.25W
Zagazig Egypt 94 D5............... 30.36N 31.30E
Zagreb Croatia 56 B6............... 45.49N 15.58E
Zagros Mts. Iran 95 H5............. 32.00N 51.00E
Zahedan Iran 95 J4................. 29.32N 60.54E
Zahle Lebanon 94 E5............... 33.50N 35.55E
Zaire Africa 86 B4.................. 2.00S 22.00E
Zaïre r. Zaïre 84 F1................. 6.00S 12.30E
Zaïre Basin f. Africa 82 E4.......... 1.00S 20.00E
Zaječar Yugo. 56 F5................ 43.55N 22.15E
Zakhō Iraq 94 F6.................. 37.09N 42.40E
Zakynthos i. Greece 56 E2.......... 37.46N 20.46E
Zǎlau Romania 54 H2............... 47.11N 23.03E
Zaliv Petra Veligog b. Russian Fed. 106 B4
.... 43.00N 132.00E
Zambezi r. Mozambique/Zambia 86 C3... 18.15S 35.55E

Zambia Africa 86 B3................. 14.00S 28.00E
Zamboanga Phil. 105 G5............ 6.55N 122.05E
Zamora Ecuador 76 C4.............. 4.05S 79.01W
Zamora Spain 46 C4................ 41.30N 5.45W
Zamość Poland 54 H4.............. 50.43N 23.15E
Zanjan Iran 95 G6.................. 36.40N 48.30E
Zanzibar Tanzania 86 C4............ 6.10S 39.12E
Zanzibar I. Tanzania 86 C4.......... 6.10S 39.12E
Zaozhuang China 103 L4............ 34.40N 117.30E
Zapolyarnyy Russian Fed. 43 G5.... 69.28N 31.04E
Zaporizhzhya Ukraine 55 N2........ 47.50N 35.10E
Zapovednik mtn. Russian Fed. 106 C5... 45.16N 136.15E
Zara Turkey 57 M3................. 39.55N 37.44E
Zaragoza Spain 46 E4............... 41.39N 0.54W
Zarand Iran 95 I5.................. 30.50N 56.35E
Zaraza Venezuela 71 K2............ 9.23N 65.20W
Zaria Nigeria 84 E3................. 11.01N 7.44E
Zarqa Jordan 94 E5................. 32.04N 36.05E
Zarzis Tunisia 52 F3................ 33.34N 11.04E
Zaysan Kazakhstan 102 E7.......... 47.30N 84.57E
Zaysan, L. Kazakhstan 102 E7....... 48.00N 83.30E
Zeebrugge Belgium 42 C3.......... 51.20N 3.13E
Zeeland d. Neth. 42 C3............. 51.30N 3.45E
Zelenograd Russian Fed. 55 O6..... 56.00N 37.16E
Zémio C.A.R. 85 G2................ 5.00N 25.09E
Zengfeng Shan mtn. China 106 A4... 42.36N 128.56E
Zenica Bosnia. 56 C6............... 44.12N 17.55E
Zêzere r. Portugal 46 A3............ 39.28N 8.20W
Zhambyl Kazakhstan 102 C6........ 42.50N 71.25E
Zhangjiakou China 103 K6.......... 41.00N 114.50E
Zhangping China 103 L3............ 25.25N 117.28E
Zhanjiang China 103 K2............ 21.05N 110.12E
Zhaoqing China 103 K2............ 23.02N 112.29E
Zhaotong China 103 I3............. 27.20N 103.39E
Zhashkiv Ukraine 55 L3............. 49.12N 30.05E
Zhejiang d. China 103 M3.......... 29.15N 120.00E
Zheleznogorsk Russian Fed. 55 N5... 52.19N 35.19E
Zhengzhou China 103 K4........... 34.35N 113.38E
Zhezkazgan Kazakhstan 102 B7..... 47.48N 67.24E
Zhlobin Belarus 55 K5.............. 52.50N 30.00E
Zhmerynka Ukraine 55 K3.......... 49.00N 28.02E
Zhob Pakistan 95 K5................ 31.21N 69.31E
Zhob r. Pakistan 95 K5............. 32.04N 69.50E
Zhuzhou China 103 K3............. 27.53N 113.07E
Zhytkavichy Belarus 55 J5.......... 52.12N 27.49E
Zhytomyr Ukraine 55 K4............ 50.18N 28.40E
Zibo China 103 L5.................. 36.50N 118.00E
Ziel, Mt. Australia 110 C3........... 23.24S 132.23E
Zielona Góra Poland 54 D4......... 51.57N 15.30E
Zigong China 103 I3................ 29.20N 104.42E
Žilina Slovakia 54 F3............... 49.14N 18.46E
Zima Russian Fed. 103 I8........... 53.58N 102.02E
Zimbabwe Africa 86 B3............. 18.00S 30.00E
Zimnicea Romania 56 G5............ 43.38N 25.22E
Zinder Niger 84 E3................. 13.46N 8.58E
Zlatoust Russian Fed. 58 H3........ 55.10N 59.38E
Zlín Czech Rep. 54 E3.............. 49.13N 17.41E
Znam'yanka Ukraine 55 M3......... 48.42N 32.40E
Znojmo Czech Rep. 54 E3.......... 48.52N 16.05E
Zolochiv Ukraine 55 I3.............. 49.48N 24.51E
Zolotonosha Ukraine 55 M3........ 49.39N 32.05E
Zonguldak Turkey 57 J4............ 41.26N 31.47E
Zouar Chad 85 F4.................. 20.27N 16.32E
Zouérat Mauritania 84 C4........... 22.44N 12.21W
Zrenjanin Yugo. 56 E6.............. 45.22N 20.23E
Zugspitze mtn. Germany 54 B2...... 47.24N 10.59E
Zuid-Holland d. Neth. 42 D3......... 52.00N 4.30E
Zújar r. Spain 46 C3................ 38.58N 5.40W
Zülpich Germany 42 F2............. 50.41N 6.39E
Zunyi China 103 J3................. 27.41N 106.50E
Zürich Switz. 44 H5................ 47.23N 8.33E
Zutphen Neth. 42 F4................ 52.08N 6.12E
Zūwarah Libya 52 F3.............. 32.56N 12.06E
Zvolen Slovakia 54 F3.............. 48.35N 19.08E
Zwickau Germany 48 F4............ 50.43N 12.30E
Zwolle Neth. 42 F4................. 52.31N 6.06E
Zyryanovsk Kazakhstan 102 E7..... 49.45N 84.16E

References

Social Trends 25 1995 edition HMSO
Regional Trends 30 1995 edition HMSO
FAO Yearbook Production 1994
World Health Statistics Annual 1994
UN Monthly Bulletin of Statistics
UN World Population Chart 1994
World Bank Atlas 1995
World Resources 1994-1995

Photo credits

Satellite images : Science Photo Library

Acknowledgements

General Bathymetric Chart of the Oceans (GEBCO)
International Hydrographic Organisation, Monaco
National Atlas and Thematic Mapping Organisation, Calcutta, India
Ministry of Planning and National Development, Nairobi, Kenya
Instituto Geográfico e Cartográfico, São Paulo, Brazil
Rotterdam Municipal Port Management, Rotterdam, Netherlands